Contents

First published in 1998 by
George Philip Ltd
a division of Octopus Publishing Group Ltd
2-4 Heron Quays
London E14 4JP

www.philips-maps.co.uk

Ninth edition 2001
First impression 2001

To the best of the Publisher's knowledge, the information in this atlas was correct at the time of going to press. No responsibility can be accepted for any errors or their consequences.

The representation in this atlas of any road, drive or track is not evidence of the existence of a right of way. The mapping on page 108 and the town plans of Edinburgh and London are based upon the Ordnance Survey maps with the sanction of the Controller of Her Majesty's Stationery Office, © Crown Copyright. 399817.

The town plan of Dublin is based on Ordnance Survey Ireland maps by permission of the Government Permit number 7153 © Government of Ireland

Ski resorts data compiled by Snow-24 plc 2000

Cartography by Philip's
Copyright © 2001 George Philip Ltd
Printed and bound in Spain by Cayfosa-Quebecor

The scale of the maps on pages 2–16 is 1: 4 250 000 (approximately 67 miles to 1 inch)

The scale of the maps on pages 18–95 is 1: 1 000 000 (approximately 16 miles to 1 inch)

Legend to route

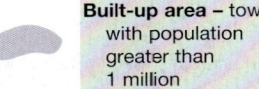

GW01182450

Motorway –
tunnel, under construction

Main through route
under construction

Other major road

Other road

Road numbers
European road number
motorway number, national road number

Distance – in kilometres

International boundary

National boundary

Car ferry and destination   LE HAVRE

Mountain pass

International airport

Hill peak – with height in metres   1089

National park

Town – symbols indicate population size

PARIS ■	greater than 5 million	
BERLIN ◙	2–5 million	
PRAHA ▣	1–2 million	
Oslo ◉	500000–1 million	
Gent ◎	200000–500000	
Amiens ⊙	100000–200000	
Imola ○	50000–100000	
Igualada ○	20000–50000	
Sorrento ○	10000–20000	
Skagen ○	5000–10000	
Lillesand ○	below 5000	

Built-up area – town with population greater than 1 million

Legend to road maps *pages 18–96*

Motorway with junctions – numbered, not numbered
services
tunnel, under construction

Toll Motorway
tunnel

Principal trunk highway – single / dual carriageway
tunnel, under construction

Other main highway – single / dual carriageway
tunnel, under construction

Other important road
under construction

Other road

Road numbers
European road number   E25
motorway number, national road number   A49   135

Mountain pass   Col Bayard 1248

Scenic route, gradient – arrow points uphill

Distances – in kilometres
major   143
minor   28

Principal railway
tunnel

Ferry route with journey time – hours: minutes   Nápoli 15:30

Short ferry route

International boundary

National boundary

✈ **Airport**
⛩ **Ancient monument**
⚒ **Beach**
🏰 **Castle or house**
⌂ **Cave**
National park
Natural park

✦ **Other place of interest**
❀ **Park or garden**
✚ **Religious building**
⛷ **Ski resort**
1754▲ **Spot height**
Verona   Town of tourist interest

Driving regulations

A national vehicle identification plate is always required when taking a vehicle abroad.

It is important for your own safety and that of other drivers to fit headlamp converters or beam deflectors when taking a right-hand drive car to a country where driving is on the right – every country in Europe except the UK and Ireland. When the headlamps are dipped on a right-hand drive car, the lenses of the headlamps cause the beam to shine upwards to the left – and so, when driving on the right, into the eyes of oncoming motorists.

The symbols used are:

- 🚏 Motorway
- ▲ Dual carriageway
- ▲ Single carriageway
- 🏙 Urban area
- ⊙ Speed limit in kilometres per hour (kph)
- 🦺 Seat belts
- 👶 Children
- ♈ Blood alcohol level
- △ Warning triangle
- ⚏ First aid kit
- 💡 Spare bulb kit
- 🔥 Fire extinguisher
- ⛑ Motorcycle helmet
- ⊖ Minimum driving age
- 🪪 Documents required
- ★ Other information

The penalties for infringements of regulations vary considerably from one country to another. In many countries the police have the right to impose on-the-spot fines (you should always request a receipt for any fine paid). Penalties can be severe for serious infringements, particularly for drinking when driving which in some countries can lead to immediate imprisonment. Insurance is important, and you may be forced to take out cover at the frontier if you cannot produce acceptable proof that you are insured.

Please note that driving regulations often change, particularly in the new democracies of eastern Europe. Reliable information for Belarus, Ukraine and Yugoslavia was not available at the time of going to press.

The publishers have made every effort to ensure that the information given here was correct at the time of going to press. No responsibility can be accepted for any errors or their consequences.

Andorra

⊙	🚏	▲	▲	🏙
	n/a	70	70	40

- 🦺 Compulsory in front seats and if fitted in rear seats
- 👶 Over 10 only allowed in front seats if over 150cm
- ♈ 0.08%
- △ Recommended
- ⚏ Recommended
- 💡 Recommended
- 🔥 Recommended
- ⛑ Compulsory for all riders
- ⊖ 18
- 🪪 Driving licence; green card or other proof of insurance; registration document or hire certificate

Austria

⊙	🚏	▲	▲	🏙
	130	100	100	50

If towing trailer under 750kg				
⊙	100	100	100	50

If towing trailer over 750kg				
⊙	100	100	80	50

- 🦺 Compulsory in front seats and if fitted in rear seats
- 👶 Under 12 in front seats only in child safety seat; over 12 must be over 150cm; in rear, under 12 and under 150cm, must have a child safety seat/seat belt; if over 150cm, must wear adult seat belt
- ♈ 0.049%
- △ Compulsory
- ⚏ Compulsory
- 💡 Recommended
- 🔥 Recommended
- ⛑ Compulsory for all riders
- ⊖ 18 (16 for mopeds)
- 🪪 Driving licence; green card; registration document or hire certificate; passport
- ★ If you intend to drive on motorways, a motorway tax disc must be purchased at the border

Belgium

⊙	🚏	▲	▲	🏙
	120*	120	90	50

*Minimum speed of 70kph on motorways

- 🦺 Compulsory in front seats and if fitted in rear seats
- 👶 Under 12 not allowed in front
- ♈ 0.05%
- △ Compulsory
- ⚏ Compulsory
- 🔥 Compulsory
- ⛑ Compulsory for all riders
- ⊖ 18 (16 for mopeds)
- 🪪 Driving licence; green card; registration document or hire certificate; passport

Bulgaria

⊙	🚏	▲	▲	🏙
	120	80	80	50-60

- 🦺 Compulsory in front seats
- 👶 Under 12 not allowed in front seats
- ♈ 0.00%
- △ Compulsory
- ⚏ Compulsory
- 🔥 Compulsory
- ⛑ Compulsory for all riders
- ⊖ 18
- 🪪 Driving licence with translation or international driving permit; green card; registration document or hire certificate

Croatia

⊙	🚏	▲	▲	🏙
	130	80	80	50

If towing				
⊙	110	80	80	50

- 🦺 Compulsory if fitted
- 👶 Under 12 not allowed in front seats
- ♈ 0.05%
- △ Compulsory
- ⚏ Compulsory
- 💡 Compulsory
- ⛑ Compulsory for all riders
- ⊖ 18
- 🪪 Driving licence; green card; registration document or hire certificate; passport

Czech Republic

⊙	🚏	▲	▲	🏙
	130	130	90	50

If towing				
⊙	80	80	80	50

- 🦺 Compulsory in front seats and if fitted in rear seats
- 👶 Under 12 or under 150cm not allowed in front seats
- ♈ 0.00%
- △ Compulsory
- ⚏ Compulsory
- 💡 Compulsory
- ⛑ Compulsory for all riders (unless maximum speed is 40kph or less)
- ⊖ 18 (17 for motorcycles over 50cc, 16 for motorcycles under 125 cc)
- 🪪 Driving licence; international driving permit; green card; registration document or hire certificate; passport; visa

Denmark

⊙	🚏	▲	▲	🏙
	110	80	80	50

If towing				
⊙	70	70	70	50

- 🦺 Compulsory in front seats and if fitted in rear seats
- 👶 Under 3 not allowed in front seat except in a child safety seat; in rear, 3 to 7 years in a child safety seat or on a booster cushion
- ♈ 0.05%
- Compulsory
- ⚏ Recommended
- 🔥 Recommended
- ⛑ Compulsory for all riders
- ⊖ 18
- 🪪 Driving licence; green card or other proof of insurance; registration document or hire certificate
- ★ Dipped headlights must be used day and night

Estonia

⊙	🚏	▲	▲	🏙
	n/a	90	70	50

- 🦺 Compulsory in front seats and if fitted in rear seats
- 👶 Under 12 not allowed in front seats; under 7 must have child safety seat in rear
- ♈ 0.00%
- △ Compulsory
- ⚏ Compulsory
- 💡 Recommended
- 🔥 Compulsory
- ⛑ Compulsory for all riders
- ⊖ 18 (16 for motorcycles)
- 🪪 Driving licence; international driving permit recommended; green card; registration document or hire certificate; passport

Finland

⊙	🚏	▲	▲	🏙
	120	110	90	50

Speed limits are often lowered in winter

- 🦺 Compulsory in front seats and if fitted in rear seats
- 👶 Children must travel with a safety belt in a special child's seat
- ♈ 0.05%
- △ Compulsory
- ⚏ Recommended
- 💡 Recommended
- 🔥 Recommended
- ⛑ Compulsory for all riders
- ⊖ 18
- 🪪 Driving licence; green card recommended; registration document or hire certificate
- ★ Dipped headlights must be used day and night outside built-up areas

France

🛣	🛤	🛤	🏘
130	110	90	50

On wet roads

110	100	80	50

50kph on all roads if fog reduces visibility to less than 50m. Licence will be lost and driver fined for exceeding speed limit by over 40kph

- Compulsory in front seats; compulsory if fitted in rear seats
- Under 10 not allowed in front seats unless in approved safety seat facing backwards; in rear, if 4 or under, must have a child safety seat (rear facing up to 9 months); if 5 to 10 may use a booster seat with suitable seat belt
- 0.05%
- △ Compulsory unless hazard warning lights are fitted; compulsory for vehicles over 3,500kgs or towing a trailer
- Recommended
- Recommended
- Compulsory for all riders
- ⊖ 18 (16 for light motorcycles, 14 for mopeds)
- Driving licence; proof of insurance; registration document or hire certificate

Germany

🛣	🛤	🛤	🏘
no limit*	no limit*	100	50

If towing

no limit*	no limit*	80	50

*130 kph recommended

- Compulsory
- Children under 12 and under 150cm must have a child safety seat, in front and rear
- 0.05%
- △ Compulsory
- Compulsory
- Recommended
- Recommended
- Compulsory for all riders
- ⊖ 18 (motorcycles: 16 if not more than 80cc and limited to 80 kph, 18 if not more than 20kW and not more than 1kW/7kg; 20 if more than 80cc or more than 80kph)
- Driving licence; international driving permit if EU licence (pink) not held; green card or proof of insurance; registration document or hire certificate; passport

Great Britain

🛣	🛤	🛤	🏘
112	112	96	48

If towing

96	96	80	48

- Compulsory in front seats and if fitted in rear seats
- Under 3 not allowed in front seats except with appropriate restraint, and in rear must use child restraint if available; 3-12 and under 150cm must use appropriate restraint or seat belt in front seats, and in rear if available
- 0.08%
- △ Recommended
- Recommended
- Compulsory for all riders
- ⊖ 17 (16 for mopeds)
- Driving licence; green card (recommended) or proof of insurance; registration document or hire certificate
- ★ Driving is on the left

Greece

🛣	🛤	🛤	🏘
120	110	110	50

If towing

90	70	70	40

- Compulsory in front seats and if fitted in rear seats
- Under 12 not allowed in front seats except with suitable safety seat; under 10 not allowed in front seats
- 0.05%
- △ Compulsory
- Compulsory
- Recommended
- Compulsory
- Compulsory for all riders
- ⊖ 18 (16 for low cc motorcycles)
- Driving licence; green card; registration document or hire certificate; passport

Hungary

🛣	🛤	🛤	🏘
120	100	80	50

If towing

80	70	70	50

- Compulsory in front seats and if fitted in rear seats
- Under 12 or under 140cm not allowed in front seats
- 0.00%
- △ Compulsory
- Compulsory
- Compulsory
- Compulsory for all riders
- ⊖ 18
- Driving licence; green card (recommended) or other proof of insurance; registration document or hire certificate; passport
- ★ Dipped headlights must be used night and day

Ireland

🛣	🛤	🛤	🏘
112	112	96	48

If towing

80	80	80	48

- Compulsory in front seats and if fitted in rear seats
- Under 12 not allowed in front seats unless in a child safety seat or other suitable restraint
- 0.08%
- △ Recommended
- Recommended
- Recommended
- Compulsory for all riders
- ⊖ 17
- Driving licence; registration document or hire certificate; green card (recommended) or proof of insurance
- ★ Driving is on the left

Italy

🛣	🛤	🛤	🏘
130	110	90	50

If towing

80	70	70	50

- Compulsory in front seats and if fitted in rear seats
- Under 12 not allowed in front seats except in child safety seat; children under 3 must have special seat in the back
- 0.08%
- △ Compulsory
- Recommended
- Compulsory
- Recommended
- Compulsory for all motorcyclists
- ⊖ 18 (14 for mopeds, 16 for up to 125cc, 20 for up to 350cc)
- Driving licence; green card recommended; registration document or hire certificate; passport

Latvia

🛣	🛤	🛤	🏘
n/a	90	90	50

If towing

n/a	80	80	50

In residential areas limit is 20kph

- Compulsory in front seats and if fitted in rear seats
- If under 150cm must use child restraint in front and rear seats
- 0.05%
- △ Compulsory
- Compulsory
- Recommended
- Compulsory
- Compulsory for all riders
- ⊖ 18 (14 for mopeds, 16 for up to 125cc, 21 for up to 350cc)
- Driving licence; international driving permit if licence is not in accordance with Vienna Convention; green card; registration document or hire certificate; passport
- ★ Cars must use dipped headlights day and night 1Oct–1Apr, all year for motorbikes
- ★ Cars and minibuses under 3.5 tonnes must have winter tyres from 1Dec–1Mar

Lithuania

🛣	🛤	🛤	🏘
130	110	90	60

If towing

70	70	70	60

- Compulsory in front seats and if fitted in rear seats
- Under 12 not allowed in front seats unless in a child safety seat
- 0.04%
- △ Compulsory
- Compulsory
- Recommended
- Compulsory
- Compulsory for all riders
- ⊖ 18 (14 for mopeds)
- Driving licence; green card; registration document or hire certificate; passport; visa
- ★ Dipped head lights must be used day and night from Nov to Mar (all year for motorcyclists) and from 1–7 Sept

Luxembourg

🛣	🛤	🛤	🏘
120	90	90	50

If towing

90	75	75	50

- Compulsory
- Under 12 or 150cm not allowed in front seats unless in a child safety seat; under 12 must have child safety seat or belt in rear seats
- 0.08%
- △ Compulsory
- Recommended
- Recommended
- Recommended
- Compulsory for all riders
- ⊖ 18 (16 for mopeds)
- Driving licence; green card recommended; registration document or hire certificate; passport
- ★ Motorcyclists must use dipped headlights day and night all year

Macedonia

🚗	⚠	▲	⏸
120	100	60	60

If towing

🚗			
80	70	50	50

- 🛇 Compulsory in front seats; compulsory if fitted in rear seats
- 👶 Under 12 not allowed in front seats
- 🍷 0.05%
- △ Compulsory
- 🧰 Compulsory
- 💡 Compulsory
- 🔧 Recommended
- 🪖 Compulsory for all riders
- ⊖ 18 (mopeds 16)
- 🪪 Driving licence; international driving permit; green card; registration document or hire certificate; passport; visa

Netherlands

🚗	⚠	▲	⏸
120	80	80	50

- 🛇 Compulsory if fitted in front and rear seats
- 👶 Under 12 not allowed in front seats except in child restraint; in rear, 0–3 child safety restraint, 4–12 child safety restraint or seat belt
- 🍷 0.5%
- △ Recommended
- 🧰 Recommended
- 💡 Recommended
- 🔧 Recommended
- 🪖 Compulsory for all riders
- ⊖ 18 (16 for mopeds)
- 🪪 Driving licence; green card; registration document and hire certificate; passport

Poland

🚗	⚠	▲	⏸
110*	100	90	60

If towing

🚗			
80*	80	70	60

*40kph minimum
*20kph in residential areas

- 🛇 Compulsory in front seats and if fitted in rear seats
- 👶 Under 10 not allowed in front seats unless in a child safety seat
- 🍷 0.02%
- △ Compulsory
- 🧰 Recommended
- 💡 Recommended
- 🔧 Compulsory
- 🪖 Compulsory for all riders
- ⊖ 17 (mopeds 15, motorbikes 16)
- 🪪 Driving licence and international permit (recommended); registration document or hire certificate; green card; passport
- ★ Between 1 Nov and 1 Mar dipped headlights must be used day and night

Romania

Cars			
120	90	90	50

Vehicles seating eight or more			
90	80	80	50

Motorcycles			
100	80	80	50

Jeep-like vehicles 70kph outside built-up areas, but 60kph in all areas if diesel

- 🛇 Compulsory in front seats; compulsory if fitted in rear seats
- 👶 Under 12 not allowed in front seats
- 🍷 0.0%
- △ Recommended
- 🧰 Compulsory
- 💡 Recommended
- 🔧 Recommended
- 🪖 Compulsory for all riders
- ⊖ 18 (16 for mopeds)
- 🪪 Driving licence; green card; registration document or hire certificate; passport; visa

Slovak Republic

🚗	⚠	▲	⏸
130	90	90	60

- 🛇 Compulsory in front seats; compulsory if fitted in rear seats
- 👶 Under 12 not allowed in front seats unless in a child safety seat
- 🍷 0.0
- △ Compulsory
- 🧰 Compulsory
- 💡 Compulsory
- 🔧 Recommended
- 🪖 Compulsory for motorcyclists
- ⊖ 18 (15 for mopeds)
- 🪪 Driving licence; international driving permit; green card; registration document or hire certificate; passport
- ★ Tow rope recommended
- ★ Passport must be valid for at least eight months after entry

Moldova

🚗	⚠	▲	⏸
90	90	60	60

- 🛇 Compulsory in front seats
- 👶 Under 12 not allowed in front seats
- 🍷 0.00%
- △ Compulsory
- 🧰 Compulsory
- 💡 Compulsory
- 💡 Recommended
- 🪖 Compulsory for all riders
- ⊖ 18 (mopeds 16)
- 🪪 Driving licence; green card; registration document or hire certificate; passport; visa

Norway

🚗	⚠	▲	⏸
80-90	80	80	50

If towing trailer with brakes

🚗			
80	80	80	50

If towing trailer without brakes

🚗			
60	60	60	50

- 🛇 Compulsory in front seats; compulsory if fitted in rear seats
- 👶 Under 4 must have child restraint; over 4 child restraint or seat belt
- 🍷 0.02%
- △ Compulsory
- 🧰 Recommended
- 💡 Recommended
- 🪖 Compulsory for all riders
- ⊖ 18 (16 mopeds, heavy vehicles 18/21)
- 🪪 Driving licence; green card; registration document or hire certificate; passport
- ★ Dipped headlights must be used day and night all year

Portugal

🚗	⚠	▲	⏸
120*	100	90	50

If towing

🚗			
100*	80	70	50

*40kph minumum; 90kph maximum if licence held under 1 year

- 🛇 Compulsory in front seats; compulsory if fitted in rear seats
- 👶 Under 3 not allowed in front seats unless in a child seat; 3–12 not allowed in front seats except in approved restraint system
- 🍷 0.05%
- △ Compulsory
- 🔧 Recommended
- 🪖 Compulsory for all riders
- ⊖ 18 (motorcycles under 50cc 16)
- 🪪 Driving licence; green card; registration document or hire certificate; photographic proof of identity

Russia

🚗	⚠	▲	⏸
130	120	110	60

- 🛇 Compulsory in front seats
- 👶 Under 12 not allowed in front seats
- 🍷 0.00%
- △ Compulsory
- 🧰 Compulsory
- 💡 Recommended
- 🔧 Compulsory
- 🪖 Compulsory
- ⊖ 18
- 🪪 International driving licence with translation; green card or other insurance certificate; registration document or hire certificate

Slovenia

🚗	⚠	▲	⏸
130	100*	90*	50

If towing

🚗			
80	80*	80*	50

*70kph in urban areas

- 🛇 Compulsory in front seats; compulsory if fitted in rear seats
- 👶 Under 12 only allowed in the front seats with special seat; babies must have child safety seats
- 🍷 0.05%
- △ Compulsory
- 🧰 Compulsory
- 💡 Compulsory
- 🔧 Recommended
- 🪖 Compulsory for all riders
- ⊖ 18 (motorbikes up to 125cc - 16, up to 350cc - 18)
- 🪪 Driving licence; registration document or hire certificate; green card; passport

Spain

🚗	🚙	🚐	🏙
120	100	90	50

If towing			
80	80	70	50

- Compulsory in front seats and if fitted in rear seats
- Under 12 not allowed in front seats except in a child safety seat
- 0.05%
- Two compulsory (one for in front, one for behind)
- Compulsory
- Compulsory for all riders
- 18 (18/21 heavy vehicles; 16 for motorcycles up to 125cc; 14 for mopeds up to 75cc)
- Driving licence; green card; registration document or hire certificate; passport

Switzerland

🚗	🚙	🚐	🏙
120	80	80	50

If towing up to 1 ton			
80	80	80	50

If towing over 1 ton			
80	80	60	50

- Compulsory if fitted
- Under 12 not allowed in front seats
- 0.08%
- Compulsory
- Recommended
- Recommended
- Recommended
- Compulsory for all riders
- 18 (mopeds up to 50cc – 14)
- Driving licence; green card; registration document or hire certificate; passport
- ★ If you intend to drive on motorways, however short the journey, a motorway tax disk (vignette) must be purchased at the border

Sweden

🚗	🚙	🚐	🏙
110	90	70	50

If towing trailer with brakes			
80	80	70	50

- Compulsory in front and rear seats
- Under 7 must have safety seat or other suitable restraint
- 0.02%
- Compulsory
- Recommended
- Recommended
- Compulsory for all riders
- 18
- Driving licence; green card; registration document or hire certificate
- ★ Dipped headlights must be used day and night all year

Turkey

🚗	🚙	🚐	🏙
120	90	90	50

If towing			
70	70	70	40

- Compulsory in front seat
- Under 12 not allowed in front seats
- 0.05%
- Two compulsory (one for in front, one for behind)
- Compulsory
- Compulsory
- Compulsory for all riders (except on freight motorcycles)
- 18
- Passport; valid driving licence; international driving permit advised; green card (note that Turkey is in both Europe and Asia); registration document or hire certificate
- ★ Tow rope and tool kit must be carried

Ski resorts

The resorts listed are popular ski centres, therefore road access to most is normally good and supported by road clearing during snow falls. However, mountain driving is never predictable and drivers should make sure they take suitable snow chains as well as emergency provisions and clothing.

Listed for each resort are: the atlas page and grid square; the altitude; the number of lifts; the season start and end dates; the nearest town (with its distance in km) and the telephone number of the local tourist information centre ('00' prefix required for calls from the UK).

Andorra
Pyrenees

Pas de la Casa / Grau Roig 77 A4
2050m, 58 lifts, Dec-May • Andorra La Vella (30km) ☑ +376 801060
🖥 www.pasdelacasa.ad • *Access via Envalira Pass (2407m), highest in Pyrenees, snow chains essential.*

Austria
Alps

A 24-hour driving conditions information line is provided by the Tourist Office of Austria +43 5332 61586.

Bad Gastein 58 A3
1080m, 51 lifts, Dec-Apr • Bad Hofgastein (6km) ☑ +43 6434 25310
🖥 www.badgastein.at
Snow report tel +43 6432 645550.

Bad Hofgastein 58 A3
860m, 51 lifts, Dec-Apr • Salzburg (90km) ☑ +43 6432 7110
🖥 www.badhofgastein.com
Snow report tel +43 64326455.

Bad Kleinkirchheim 58 B3
1100m, 32 lifts, Dec-Apr • Villach (35km) ☑ +43 4240 8212 🖥 www.bkk.co.at
• Snowfone:+43 4240 8222. Near Ebene Reichenau.

Ehrwald 57 A5
1000m, 22 lifts, Dec-Apr • Imst (30km) ☑ +43 5673 2395
🖥 www.tiscover.com/ehrwald
Weather report tel +43 5673 3329.

Innsbruck 57 A6
574m, 4 lifts, Dec-Apr • Innsbruck ☑ +43 5125 9850
🖥 www.tiscover.com/innsbruck
Motorway normally clear. The motorway through to Italy and through the Arlberg Tunnel West to Austria are both toll roads.

Ischgl 57 A5
1400m, 42 lifts, Dec-May • Landeck (25km) ☑ +43 5444 52660
🖥 www.ischgl.com • *Car entry to resort prohibited between 2200hrs and 0600hrs.*

Kaprun 58 A2
800m, 56 lifts, Jan-Dec • Zell am See (10km) ☑ +43 6547 86430
🖥 www.europe-sport-region.com
• Snowfone:+43 6547 8444

Kirchberg in Tyrol 58 A2
860m, 59 lifts, Dec-Apr • Kitzbühel (6km) ☑ +43 5357 2309 🖥 www.kirchberg.at
Easily reached from Munich International Airport (120 km).

Kitzbühel 58 A2
800m, 59 lifts, Dec-Apr • Wörgl (40km) ☑ +43 5356 621550
🖥 www.kitzbuehel.com

Lech/Oberlech 57 A5
1450m, 84 lifts, Dec-Apr • Bludenz (50km) ☑ +43 5583 21610 🖥 www.Lech.at
Roads normally cleared but keep chains accessible because of altitude. Road conditions report tel +43 5583 1515.

Mayrhofen 58 A1
630m, 29 lifts, Dec-Apr • Jenbach (30km) ☑ +43 5285 6760 🖥 www.mayrhofen.com
Chains rarely required.

Obertauern 58 A3
1740m, 27 lifts, Nov-May • Radstadt (20km) ☑ +43 6456 7252
🖥 www.salzburg.com/tourismus/obertauern
Roads normally cleared but chains accessibility recommended. Camper vans and caravans not allowed; park these in Radstadt.

Saalbach Hinterglemm 58 A2
1003m, 52 lifts, Dec-Apr • Zell am See (19km) ☑ +43 6541 6800 68 🖥 www.saalbach.com • *Both village centres are pedestrianised and there is a good ski bus service during the daytime.*

St Anton am Arlberg 57 A5
1304m, 84 lifts, Nov-May • Innsbruck (104km) ☑ +43 5446 22690
w www.stantonamarlberg.com
Snow report tel +43 5446 2565.

Schladming 58 A3
745m, 91 lifts, Nov-Apr • Schladming ☑ +43 3687 22268 🖥 www.schladming.com

Serfaus 57 A5
1427m, 53 lifts, Dec-Apr • Landeck (30km) ☑ +43 5476 6239 🖥 www.nettours.co.at/iba/t/serfaus • *Cars banned from village, use world's only 'hover' powered underground railway.*

Sölden 57 B6
1377m, 32 lifts, all year • Imst (50km) ☑ +43 5254 22120 🖥 www.soelden.com
Roads normally cleared but snow chains recommended because of altitude. The route from Italy and the south over the Timmelsjoch via Obergurgl is closed in the winter and anyone arriving from the south should use the Brenner Pass motorway. Snow information tel +43 5254 2666.

Zell am See 58 A2
758m, 56 lifts, Dec-Mar • Zell am See ☑ +43 6542 770 🖥 www.zellkaprun.at
Snowfone +43 6542 73694 Low altitude, therefore good access and no mountain passes to cross.

Zell im Zillertal (Zell am Ziller) 58 A1
580m, 47 lifts, Dec-Apr • Jenbach (25km) ☑ +43 5282 2281 🖥 www.tiscover.com/zell
Snowfone +43 5282 716526.

Zürs 57 A5
1720m, 84 lifts, Nov-May • Bludenz (30km) ☑ +43 5583 2245 • *Roads normally cleared but keep chains accessible because of altitude. The village has a garage with 24-hour self-service gas/petrol, a breakdown service and wheel chains supply.*

France
Alps

Alpe d'Huez 65 A5
1860m, 85 lifts, Dec-Apr • Grenoble (63km) ☑ +33 4 76 11 44 44
🖥 www.alpedhuez.com • *Snow chains may be required on access road to resort. Road report tel +33 4 76 11 44 50.*

Avoriaz 56 B1
1800m, 217 lifts, Dec-May • Morzine (14km) ☑ +33 4 50 74 02 11
🖥 www.avoriazski.com • *Chains may be required for access road from Morzine. Car-free resort, park on edge of village. Horse-drawn sleigh service available.*

Chamonix-Mont-Blanc 56 C1
1035m, 49 lifts, Nov-May ☑ +33 4 50 53 00 24 🖥 www.chamonix.com

Chamrousse 65 A4
1700m, 26 lifts, Dec-Apr • Grenoble (30km) ☑ +33 4 76 89 92 65
🖥 www.chamrousse.com • *Roads normally cleared, keep chains accessible because of altitude.*

Châtel 56 B1
1200m, 37 lifts, Dec-Apr • Thonon Les Bains (35km) ☑ +33 450 732244
🖥 www.chatel.com

Courchevel 56 C1
1850m, 197 lifts, Dec-Apr • Moûtiers (23km) ☑ +33 47 9 0800 29
🖥 www.courchevel.com • *Roads normally cleared but keep chains accessible. Traffic is 'discouraged' within the four Courchevel resort bases. Traffic information tel +33 4 79 37 73 37.*

Flaine 56 B1
1600m, 74 lifts, Dec-Apr • Cluses (25km) ☑ +33 450 908001 🖥 www.flaine.com
Keep chains accessible for D6 from Cluses to Flaine. Car access for depositing luggage and passengers only. 1500-space car park outside resort. Near Sixt-Fer-á-Cheval.

La Clusaz 55 C6
1100m, 56 lifts, Dec-Apr • Annecy (32km) ☑ +33 4 50 32 65 00 🖥 www.laclusaz.com
Roads normally clear but keep chains accessible for final road from Annecy.

La Plagne 56 C1
2100m, 110 lifts, Dec-Apr Moûtiers (32km) ☑ +33 4 79 09 79 79
🖥 www.laplagne.com • *Ten different centres up to 2100m altitude. Road access via Bozel, Landry or Aime normally cleared.*

Les Arcs 56 C1
1600m, 77 lifts, Dec-Apr • Bourg-St-Maurice (15km) ☏ +33 4 79 07 12 57
🖳 www.lesarcs.com • *Three base areas up to 2000 metres; keep chains accessible. Pay parking at edge of each base resort.*

Les Carroz d'Araches 56 B1
1140m, 74 lifts, Dec-Apr • Cluses (13km) ☏ +33 4 50 90 00 04
🖳 www.lescarroz.com

Les Deux-Alpes 65 B5
1650m, 63 lifts, Nov-May • Grenoble (75km) ☏ +33 4 76 79 22 00
🖳 www.les2alpes.com • *Roads normally cleared, however snow chains recommended for D213 up from valley road (N91).*

Les Gets 56 B1
1172m, 217 lifts, Dec-May • Cluses (18km) ☏ +33 4 50 75 80 80 🖳 www.lesgets.com

Les Ménuires 55 C6
1815m, 197 lifts, Dec-Apr • Moûtiers (27km) ☏ +33 4 79 00 73 00
🖳 www.les-menuires.com • *keep chains accessible for N515A from Moûtiers.*

Les Sept Laux 55 C6
1350m, 29 lifts, Dec-Apr • Grenoble (38km) ☏ +33 4 76 08 17 86 🖳 www.les7laux.com
Roads normally cleared, however keep chains accessible for mountain road up from the A41 motorway. Near St Sorlin d'Arves.

Megève 55 C6
1113m, 121 lifts, Dec-Apr • Sallanches (12km) ☏ +33 4 50 21 27 28
🖳 www.megeve.com • *Horse-drawn sleigh rides available.*

Méribel 55 C6
1400m, 197 lifts, Dec-May • Moûtiers (18km) ☏ +33 4 79 08 60 01
🖳 www.meribel.net • *Keep chains accessible for 18km to resort on D90 from Moûtiers.*

Morzine 56 B2
1000m, 217 lifts, Dec-May • Thonon-Les-Bains (30km) ☏ +33 4 50 74 72 72
🖳 www.morzine.com

Pra Loup 65 B5
1500m, 53 lifts, Dec-Apr • Barcelonnette (10km) ☏ +33 4 92 84 10 04
🖳 www.praloup.com • *Roads normally cleared but chains accessibility recommended.*

Risoul 65 B5
1850m, 58 lifts, Dec-Apr • Briançon (40km) ☏ +33 4 92 46 02 60 🖳 www.risoul.com
Keep chains accessibie. Near Guillestre.

St Gervais 56 C1
850m, 121 lifts, Dec-Apr • Sallanches (10km) ☏ +33 4 50 47 76 08
🖳 www.st-gervais.net

Serre-Chevalier 65 B5
1350m, 79 lifts, Dec-Apr • Briançon (10km) ☏ +33 4 92 24 98 98
🖳 www.serre-chevalier.com • *Made up of 13 small villages along the valley road, which is normally cleared.*

Tignes 56 C1
2100m, 97 lifts, Jan-Dec • Bourg St Maurice (26km) ☏ +33 4 79 40 04 40
🖳 www.tignes.net • *Keep chains accessible because of altitude. Parking information tel +33 4 79 06 39 45.*

Val d'Isère 56 C1
1850m, 97 lifts, Nov-May • Bourg-St-Maurice (30km) ☏ +33 4 79 06 06 60
🖳 www.valdisere.com • *Roads normally cleared but keep chains accessibie .*

Val Thorens 55 C6
2300m, 197 lifts, Nov-May • Moûtiers (37km) ☏ +33 4 79 00 08 08
🖳 www.valthorens.com • *Chains essential – highest ski resort in Europe. Obligatory paid parking on edge of resort.*

Valloire 55 C6
1430m, 36 lifts, Dec-May • Modane (17km) ☏ +33 4 79 59 03 96 🖳 www.skifrance.fr
Road normally clear up to the Col du Galbier, to the south of the resort, which is closed from 1st November to 1st June.

Valmeinier 55 C6
1500m, 36 lifts, Dec-Apr • St Michel de maurienne (20km) ☏ +33 4 79 59 53 69
🖳 www.valmeinier.com • *Access from north on N9 / N902. Col du Galbier, to the south of the resort closed from 1st November to 1st June. Near Valloire.*

Valmorel 55 C6
1400m, 55 lifts, Dec-Apr • Moûtiers (15km) ☏ +33 4 79 09 85 55
🖳 www.valmorel.com
Near St Jean-de-Belleville.

Vars Les Claux 65 B5
1850m, 58 lifts, Dec-May • Briançon (40km) ☏ +33 4 92 46 51 31 🖳 www.vars-ski.com • *Four base resorts up to 1850 metres. Keep chains accessible. Road and weather information tel +33 4 36 68 02 05 and +33 4 91 78 78 78. Snowfone +33 492 46 51 04*

Villard-de-Lans 65 A4
1050m, 29 lifts, Dec-Apr • Grenoble (32km) ☏ +33 476 951038
🖳 www.ot-villard-de-lans.fr

Pyrenees

Font-Romeu 77 A5
1550m, 33 lifts, Dec-Apr • Perpignan (87km) ☏ +33 4 68 30 68 30 🖳 www.font-romeu-station.com • *Roads normally cleared but keep chains accessible .*

St Lary-Soulan 63 D3
830m, 32 lifts, Dec-Apr • Tarbes (75km) ☏ +33 5 62 39 50 81 🖳 www.saintlary.com
• *Access roads constantly cleared of snow.*

Vosges

La Bresse-Hohneck 46 B2
900m, 20 lifts, Dec-Mar • Cornimont (6km) ☏ +33 3 29 25 41 29 🖳 www.skifrance.fr

Germany
Alps

Garmisch-Partenkirchen 57 A6
702m, 38 lifts, Dec-Apr • Munich (95km) ☏ +49 8821 1806
🖳 www.garmisch-partenkirchen.de
Roads usually clear, chains rarely needed.

Oberaudorf 48 C3
483m, 21 lifts, Dec-Apr • Kufstein (15km) ☏ +49 8033 309743
🖳 www.wendelsteinbahn.de/angebot
Motorway normally kept clear. Near Bayrischzell.

Oberstdorf 57 A5
815m, 31 lifts, Dec-Apr • Sonthofen (15km) ☏ +49 8322 7000 🖳 www.oberstdorf.de
Snow information on tel +49 8322 3035 or 1095 or 5757.

Rothaargebirge

Winterberg 37 C1
700m, 55 lifts Dec-Mar • Brilon (30km) ☏ +49 2981 92500 🖳 www.winterberg.de
Roads usually cleared, chains rarely required.

Italy
Alps

Bardonecchia 65 A5
1312m, 21 lifts, Dec-Apr • Bardonecchia ☏ +39 0122 99132
Snowfone +39 0122 99137
🖳 www.commune.bardonecchia.to.it
Resort reached through the 11km Frejus tunnel from France, roads normally cleared.

Bormio 57 B5
1225m, 17 lifts, Dec-Apr • Tirano (40km) ☏ +39 0342 903300
🖳 www.provincia.so.it/ aptvaltellina
Tolls payable in Ponte del Gallo Tunnel, open 0800hrs-2000hrs.

Breuil-Cervinia 56 C2
2050m, 73 lifts, Jan-Dec • Aosta (54km) ☏ +39 0166 949136
🖳 www.vol.it/tts/neve/it/aoste/cervinia
Snow chains strongly recommended.

Courmayeur 56 C1
1224m, 27 lifts, Dec-Apr • Aosta (40km) ☏ +39 0165 842370
🖳 www.cormayeur.com • *Access through the Mont Blanc tunnel from France. Roads constantly cleared.*

Limone Piemonte 66 B1
1009m, 29 lifts, Dec-Apr • Cuneo (27km) ☏ +39 0171 92101 🖳 www.lrcser.it/limone
Roads normally cleared, chains rarely required. Snow report tel +39 171 926254

Livigno 57 B5
1816m, 30 lifts, Dec-Apr • Zernez (CH) (27km) ☏ +39 0342 996379
🖳 www.livigno.net
• *Keep chains accessible. La DrosaTunnel from Zernez, Switzerland is only open from 0800hrs to 2000hrs.*

Sestriere 65 B5
2035m, 91 lifts, Dec-Apr • Oulx (22km) ☏ +39 0122 755444
🖳 www.agora.stm.it/sestriere • *One of Europe's highest resorts, although roads are normally cleared, chains should be accessible.*

Appennines

Roccaraso – Aremogna 90 A1
1285m, 31 lifts, Dec-Apr • Castel di Sangro (7km) ☏ +39 0864 62210
🖳 www.roccaraso.com

Dolomites

Andalo – Pai della Paganella 57 B5
1042m, 22 lifts, Dec-Apr • Trento (40km) ☏ +39 0461 585836

Arabba 58 B1 1612m, 24 lifts, Dec-Apr Brunico (45km) ☏ +39 0436 79130
🖳 www.sunrise.it /dolomiti • *Roads normally cleared but keep chains accessible .*

Cortina d'Ampezzo 58 B2
1224m, 48 lifts, Dec-Apr • Belluno (72km) ☏ +39 0436 3231
🖳 www.sunrise.it/dolomiti • *Access from north on route 51 over the Cimabanche Pass may require chains.*

Corvara (Alta Badia) 58 B1
1568m, 57 lifts, Dec-Apr • Brunico (38km) ☏ +39 0471 836176
🖳 www.dolomitisuperski.com/altabadia
Roads normally clear but keep chains accessible.

Madonna di Campiglio 57 B5
1550m, 60 lifts, Dec-Apr • Trento (60km) ☏ +39 0465 442000
🖳 www.campiglio.net • *Roads normally cleared but keep chains accessible.*

Moena di Fassa (Sorte/Ronchi) 58 B1
1184m, 29 lifts, Dec-Apr • Bolzano (40km) ☏ +39 0462 573122
🖳 www.dolomitisuperski.com/valfassa

Passo del Tonale 57 B5
1883m, 30 lifts, Dec-Aug • Breno (50km) ☏ +39 0364 903838
🖳 www.adamelloski.com/tonalee.html
Located on high mountain pass; keep chains accessible.

Selva di Val Gardena/Wolkenstein Groden 58 B1 1563m, 82 lifts, Dec-Apr • Bolzano (40km) ☏ +39 0471 795122
🖳 www.dolomiti superski.com/selva • *Roads normally cleared but keep chains accessible.*

Norway

Hemsedal 2 F11
650m, 16 lifts, Nov-May Honefoss (150km) ☏ +47 32 060156 🖳 www.hemsedal.com
Be prepared for extreme weather conditions.

Trysil (Trysilfjellet) 2 F13
465m, 24 lifts, Nov-May • Elverum (100km) ☏ +47 62 450911 🖳 www.skiinfo.no/trysil
Be prepared for extreme weather conditions.

Spain
Pyrenees

Baqueira/Beret 76 A3
1500m, 24 lifts, Dec-Apr • Viella (15km) ☏ +34 973 644455 🖳 www.baqueira.es
Roads normally clear but keep chains accessible. Snowfone tel +34 973 645025. Near Salardú

Sistema Penibetico

Sierra Nevada 86 B2
2102m, 19 lifts, Dec–May • Granada (32km) ☏ +34 958 249100
🖳 www.sierranevadaski.com • *Access road designed to be avalanche safe and is snow cleared. Snowfone +34 958 249119 .*

Sweden

Idre Fjäll 2 F13
710m, 30 lifts, Oct–May • Mora (140km) ☏ +46 253 40000 🖳 www.idrefjall.se
Be prepared for extreme weather conditions.

Sälen 2 F13
360m, 101 lifts, Nov-Apr
Malung (70km) ☏ +46 280 20250
🖳 www.salen.nu, www.salenfjallen.se
Be prepared for extreme weather conditions.

Switzerland
Alps

Adelboden 56 B2
1348m, 43 lifts, Dec-Apr • Frutigen (15km) ☏ +41 33 6738080 🖳 www.adelboden.ch
• **Arosa** 57 B4
1800m, 16 lifts, Dec-Apr • Chur (30km) ☏ +41 81 3877020 🖳 www.arosa.ch
Roads cleared but keep chains accessible because of high altitude (1800m).

Crans Montana 56 B2
1500m, 35 lifts, Dec-Apr, Jul-Oct • Sierre (15km) ☏ +41 27 4850404
🖳 www.crans-montana.ch • *Roads normally cleared, however keep chains accessible for ascent from Sierre.*

Davos 57 B4
1560m, 61 lifts, Nov-May • Davos ☏ +41 81 4152121 🖳 www.davos.ch

Engelberg 56 B3
1000m, 26 lifts, Nov-Jun • Luzern (39km) ☏ +41 6397777 🖳 www.engelberg.ch
Straight access road normally cleared.

Flums (Flumserberg) 57 A4
1400m, 17 lifts, Dec-Apr • Buchs (25km) ☏ +41 81 7201818 🖳 www.flumserberg.ch
Roads normally cleared, but 1000 metre vertical ascent; keep chains accessible.

Grindelwald 56 B3
1034m, 30 lifts, Dec-Apr • Interlaken (20km) ☏ +41 36 8541212 🖳 www.grindelwald.ch
Gstaad - Saanenland 56 B2
1000m, 69 lifts, Dec-Apr • Gstaad ☏ +41 33 7488181 🖳 www.gstaad.ch

Klosters 57 B4
1191m, 61 lifts, Dec-Apr • Davos (10km) ☏ +41 81 4102020 🖳 www.klosters.ch

Leysin 56 B2
1398m, 19 lifts, Dec-Apr • Aigle (6km) ☏ +41 24 4942921 🖳 www.leysin.ch

Mürren 56 B2
1650m, 37 lifts, Dec-Apr • Interlaken (18km) ☏ +41 33 8568686 🖳 www.muerren.ch
No road access. Park in Strechelberg (1500 free places) and take the two-stage cable car.

Nendaz 56 B2
1365m, 91 lifts, Nov-Apr • Sion (16km) ☏ +41 27 2895589 🖳 www.nendaz.ch
Roads normally cleared, however keep chains accessible for ascent from Sion. Near Vex.

Saas-Fee 56 B2
1800m, 25 lifts, Jan-Dec • Brig (35km) ☏ +41 27 9581858 🖳 www.saas-fee.ch
Roads normally cleared but keep chains accessible because of altitude.

St Moritz 57 B4
1856m, 58 lifts, Nov-May • Chur (89km) ☏ +41 81 8373333 🖳 www.stmoritz.ch
Roads normally cleared but keep chains accessible because of altitude.

Samnaun 57 B5
1846m, 42 lifts, Dec-May • Scuol (30km) ☏ +41 81 8685858 🖳 www.samnaun.ch
Roads normally cleared but keep chains accessible

Verbier 56 B2
1500m, 91 lifts, Nov-May, Jun-Jul • Martigny (27km) ☏ +41 27 7753888
🖳 www.verbier.ch • *Roads normally cleared.*

Villars 56 B2
1253m, 37 lifts, Nov-Apr, Jun-Jul • Montreux (35km) ☏ +41 24 4953232
🖳 www.villars.ch • *Roads normally cleared but ckeep chains accessible for ascent from N9. Near Bex.*

Wengen 56 B2
1270m, 37 lifts, Dec-Apr • Interlaken (12km) ☏ +41 33 8551414 🖳 www.wengen-muerren.ch • *No road access. Park at Lauterbrunnen and take mountain railway.*

Zermatt 56 B2
1620m, 73 lifts, all year • Brig (42km) ☏ +41 27 9670181 🖳 www.zermatt.ch
Cars not permitted in resort, park in Täsch (3km) and take shuttle train.

Ski resort data compiled by Snow24 plc. www.snow24.com email: info@snow24.com. To the best of the Publisher's knowledge the information in this table was correct at the time of going to press. No responsibility can be accepted for any errors or their consequences.

300 greatest sights of Europe

Belgique *Belgium*

Antwerpen City with many tall gabled Flemish houses on the river. Heart of the city is Great Market with 16–17c guildhouses and Town Hall. 14–16c Gothic cathedral has Rubens paintings. Rubens also at the Rubens House and his burial place in St Jacob's Church. Excellent museums: Mayer van den Berg Museum (applied arts); Koninklijk Museum of Fine Arts (Flemish, Belgian).

Brugge Well-preserved medieval town with narrow streets and canals. Main squares: the Market with 13c Belfort and covered market; the Burg with Basilica of the Holy Blood and Town Hall. The Groeninge Museum and Memling museum in St Jans Hospital show 15c Flemish masters. The Onze Lieve Vrouwekerk has a famous *Madonna and Child* by Michelangelo

Bruxelles Capital of Belgium. The Lower Town is centred on the enormous Grand Place with Hôtel de Ville and rebuilt guildhouses. Symbols of the city include the Manneken Pis and Atomium (giant model of a molecule). The 13c Notre Dame de la Chapelle is the oldest church. The Upper Town contains: Gothic cathedral; Neoclassical Place Royale; 18c King's Palace; Royal Museums of Fine Arts (old and modern masters). Also: much Art Nouveau (Victor Horta Museum, Hôtel Tassel, Hôtel Solvay); Place du Petit Sablon and Place du Grand Sablon; 19c Palais de Justice.

Gent Medieval town built on islands surrounded by canals and rivers. Views from Pont St-Michel. The Graslei and Koornlei quays have Flemish guild houses. The Gothic cathedral has famous Van Eyck altarpiece. Also: Belfort; Cloth Market; Gothic Town Hall; Gravensteen. Museums: Bijloke Museum in beautiful abbey (provincial and applied art); Museum of Fine Arts (old masters).

Namur Reconstructed medieval citadel is the major sight of Namur, which also has a cathedral and provincial museums.

Tournai The Romanesque-Gothic cathedral is Belgium's finest (much excellent art). Fine Arts Museum has a good collection (15–20c).

Bulgariya *Bulgaria*

Black Sea Coast Beautiful unspoiled beaches (Zlatni Pyasŭtsi). The delightful resort Varna is popular. Nesebŭr is famous for Byzantine churches. Also: Danube Delta in Hungary.

Plovdiv City set spectacularly on three hills. The old town has buildings from many periods: 2c Roman stadium and amphitheatre; 14c Dzumaiya Mosque; 19c Koyumdjioglu House and Museum (traditional objects). Nearby: Bačkovo Monastery (frescoes).

Rila Bulgaria's finest monastery, set in the most beautiful scenery of the Rila mountains. The church is richly decorated with frescoes.

Sofiya Capital of Bulgaria. Sights: exceptional neo-Byzantine cathedral; Church of St Sofia; 4c rotunda of St George (frescoes); Byzantine Boyana Church (frescoes) on panoramic Mount Vitoša. Museums: National Historical Museum (particularly for Thracian artefacts); National Art Gallery (icons, Bulgarian art).

Veliko Tŭrnovo Medieval capital with narrow streets. Notable buildings: House of the Little Monkey; Hadji Nicoli Inn; ruins of medieval citadel; Baudouin Tower; churches of the Forty Martyrs and of SS Peter and Paul (frescoes); 14c Monastery of the Transfiguration.

Città del Vaticano
Vatican City

Città del Vaticano Independent state within Rome. On Piazza San Pietro is the 15–16c Renaissance-Baroque Basilica San Pietro (Michelangelo's dome and *Pietà*), the world's most important Roman Catholic church. The Vatican Palace contains the Vatican Museums with many fine art treasures including Michelangelo's frescoes in the Sistine Chapel.

Česka Republica
Czech Republic

Brno Capital of Moravia. Sights: Vegetable Market and Old Town Hall; Capuchin crypt decorated with bones of dead monks; hill of St Peter with Gothic cathedral; Mies van der Rohe's buildings (Bata, Avion Hotel, Togendhat House).

Museums: UPM (modern applied arts); Pražáků Palace (19c Czech art).

České Budějovice Famous for Budvar beer, the medieval town is centred on náměsti Přemysla Otokara II. The Black Tower gives fine views. Nearby: medieval Český Krumlov.

Olomouc Well-preserved medieval university town of squares and fountains. The Upper Square has the Town Hall. Also: 18c Holy Trinity; Baroque Church of St Michael.

Praha Capital of Czech Republic and Bohemia. The Castle Quarter has a complex of buildings behind the walls (Royal Castle; Royal Palace; cathedral). The Basilica of St George has a fine Romanesque interior. The Belvedere is the best example of Renaissance architecture. Hradčani Square has aristocratic palaces and the National Gallery. The Little Quarter has many Renaissance (Wallenstein Palace) and Baroque mansions and the Baroque Church of St Nicholas. The Old Town has its centre at the Old Town Square with the Old Town Hall (astronomical clock), Art Nouveau Jan Hus monument and Gothic Týn church. The Jewish quarter has 14c Staranova Synagogue and Old Jewish Cemetery. The Charles Bridge is famous. The medieval New Town has many Art Nouveau buildings and is centred on Wenceslas Square.

Spas of Bohemia Before World War I, the spa towns of Karlovy Vary (Carls-

bad), Márianske Lázně (Marienbad) and Frartiskovy Lázně (Franzenbad) were the favourite resorts of the Habsburg aristocracy.

Danmark *Denmark*

Hillerød Frederiksborg is a fine red-brick Renaissance castle set among three lakes.

København Capital of Denmark. Old centre has fine early 20c Town Hall. Latin Quarter has 19c cathedral. 18c Kastellet has statue of the Little Mermaid nearby. The 17c Rosenborg Castle was a royal residence, as was the Christianborg (now government offices). Other popular sights: Nyhavn canal; Tivoli Gardens. Excellent art collections: Ny Carlsberg Glyptotek; State Art Museum; National Museum.

Roskilde Ancient capital of Denmark. The marvellous cathedral is a burial place of the Danish monarchy.

Deutschland *Germany*

Aachen Once capital of the Holy Roman Empire. Old town around the Münsterplatz with magnificent cathedral. An exceptionally rich treasure is in the Schatzkammer. The Town Hall is on the medieval Market.

Augsburg Attractive old city. The Town Hall is one of Germany's finest Renaissance buildings. Maximilianstrasse has several Renaissance houses and Rococo Schaezler Palace (good art collection). Churches: Romanesque-

Gothic cathedral; Renaissance St Anne's Church. The Fuggerei, founded 1519 as an estate for the poor, is still in use.

Bamberg Well-preserved medieval town. The island, connected by two bridges, has the Town Hall and views of Klein Venedig. Romanesque-Gothic cathedral (good art) is on an exceptional square of Gothic, Renaissance and Baroque buildings – Alte Hofhalttung; Neue Residenz with State Gallery (German masters); Ratstube.

Berlin Capital of Germany. Sights include: the Kurfürstendamm avenue; Brandenburg Gate, former symbol of the division between East and West Germany; Tiergarten; Unter den Linden; 19c Reichstag. Berlin has many excellent art and history collections. Museum Island includes: Pergamon Museum (classical antiquity, Near and Far East, Islam); Bode Museum (Egyptian, Early Christian, Byzantine and European); Old National Gallery (19–20c German). Dahlem Museums: Picture Gallery (13–18c); Sculpture Collection (13–19c); Prints and Drawings Collection; Die Brücke Museum (German Expressionism). Tiergarten Museums: New National Gallery (19–20c); Decorative Arts Museum; Bauhaus Archive. In the Kreuzberg area: Berlin Museum; Grupius Building with Jewish Museum and Berlin Gallery; remains of Berlin Wall and Checkpoint Charlie House. Schloss Charlottenburg houses a number of collections including the National Gallery's Romantic Gallery; the Egyptian Museum is nearby.

Bodensee Lake Constance, with many pleasant lake resorts. Lindau, on an island, has numerous gabled houses. Birnau has an 18c Rococo church. Konstanz (Swiss side) has the Minster set above the Old Town.

Deutsche Alpenstrasse German Alpine Road in the Bavarian Alps, from Lindau on Bodensee to Berchtesgaden. The setting for 19c fairy-tale follies of Ludwig II of Bavaria (Linderhof, Hohenschwangau, Neuschwanstein), charming old villages (Oberammergau) and Baroque churches (Weiss, Ottobeuren). Garmisch-Partenkirchen has views on Germany's highest peak, the Zugspitze.

Dresden Historic centre with a rich display of Baroque architecture. Major buildings: Castle of the Electors of Saxony; 18c Hofkirche; Zwinger Palace with fountains and pavilions (excellent old masters); Albertinum with excellent Gallery of New Masters; treasury of Grünes Gewölbe. The Baroque-planned New Town contains the Japanese Palace and Schloss Pillnitz.

The facade of Basilica san Pietro, Città del Vaticano

Town Hall, Antwerpen, Belgique

Frankfurt Financial capital of Germany. The historic centre around the Römerberg Square has 13–15c cathedral, 15c Town Hall, Gothic St Nicholas Church, Saalhof (12c chapel). Museums: Museum of Modern Art (post-war); State Art Institute.

Freiburg Old university town with system of streams running through the streets. The Gothic Minster is surrounded by the town's finest buildings. Two towers remain in the medieval walls. The Augustine Museum has a good collection.

Hamburg Port city with many parks, lakes and canals. The Kunsthalle has Old Masters and 19-20c German art. Buildings: 19c Town Hall; Baroque St Michael's Church.

Heidelberg Germany's oldest university town, majestically set on the banks of the river and romantically dominated by the ruined schloss. The Gothic Church of the Holy Spirit is on the Market Place with the Baroque Town Hall. Other sights include the 16c Knight's House and the Baroque Morass Palace with a museum of Gothic art.

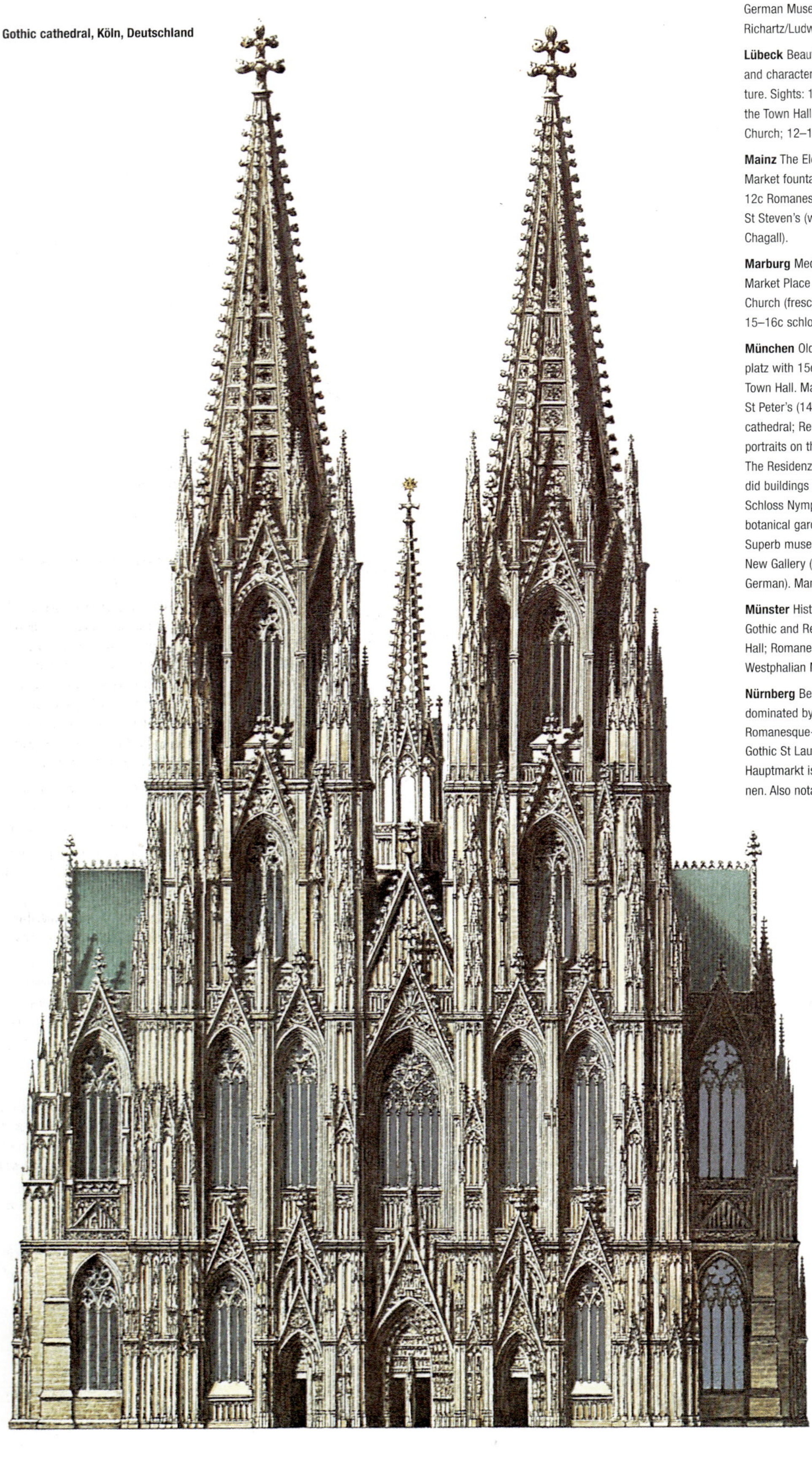

Hildesheim City of Romanesque architecture (much destroyed). Principal sights: St Michael's Church; cathedral (11c interior, sculptured doors, St Anne's Chapel); superb 15c Tempelhaus on the Market Place.

Köln Ancient city with 13–19c cathedral (rich display of art). In the old town are the Town Hall and many Romanesque churches (Gross St Martin, St Maria im Kapitol, St Maria im Lyskirchen, St Ursula, St Georg, St Severin, St Pantaleon, St Apostolen). Museums: Diocesan Museum (religious art); Roman-German Museum (ancient history); Wallraf-Richartz/Ludwig Museum (14–20c art).

Lübeck Beautiful old town built on an island and characterised by Gothic brick architecture. Sights: 15c Holsten Gate; Market with the Town Hall and Gothic brick St Mary's Church; 12–13c cathedral; St Ann Museum.

Mainz The Electoral Palatinate schloss and Market fountain are Renaissance. Churches: 12c Romanesque cathedral; Gothic St Steven's (with stained glass by Marc Chagall).

Marburg Medieval university town with the Market Place and Town Hall, St Elizabeth's Church (frescoes, statues, 13c shrine), 15–16c schloss.

München Old town centred on the Marien-platz with 15c Old Town Hall and 19c New Town Hall. Many richly decorated churches: St Peter's (14c tower); Gothic red-brick cathedral; Renaissance St Michael's (royal portraits on the façade); Rococo St Asam's. The Residenz palace consists of seven splendid buildings holding many art objects. Schloss Nymphenburg has a palace, park, botanical gardens and four beautiful pavilions. Superb museums: Old Gallery (old masters), New Gallery (18–19c), Lenbachhaus (modern German). Many famous beer gardens.

Münster Historic city with well-preserved Gothic and Renaissance buildings: 14c Town Hall; Romanesque-Gothic cathedral. The Westphalian Museum holds regional art.

Nürnberg Beautiful medieval walled city dominated by the 12c Kaiserburg. Romanesque-Gothic St Sebaldus Church and Gothic St Laurence Church are rich in art. On Hauptmarkt is the famous 14c Schöner Brunnen. Also notable is 15c Dürer House. The German National Museum has excellent German medieval and Renaissance art.

Potsdam Beautiful Sanssouci Park contains several 18–19c buildings including: Schloss Sanssouci; Gallery (European masters); Orangery; New Palace; Chinese Teahouse.

Regensburg Medieval city set majestically on the Danube. Views from 12c Steinerne Brücke. Churches: Gothic cathedral; Romanesque St Jacob's; Gothic St Blaisius; Baroque St Emmeram. Other sights: Old Town Hall (museum); Haidplatz; Schloss Thurn und Taxis; State Museum.

Rheintal Beautiful 80km gorge of the Rhein Valley between Mainz and Koblenz with rocks (Loreley), vineyards (Bacharach, Rüdesheim), white medieval towns (Rhens, Oberwesel) and castles. Some castles are medieval (Marksburg, Rheinfels, island fortress Pfalzgrafenstein) others were built or rebuilt in the 19c (Stolzenfels, Rheinstein).

Romantische Strasse Romantic route between Aschaffenburg and Füssen, leading through picturesque towns and villages of medieval Germany. The most popular section is the section between Würzburg and Augsburg, centred on Rothenburg ob der Tauber, an attractive medieval walled town. Also notable are Nördlingen, Harburg Castle, Dinkelsbühl, Creglingen.

Rothenburg ob der Tauber Attractive medieval walled town with tall gabled and half-timbered houses on narrow cobbled streets. The Market Place has Gothic-Renaissance Town Hall, Rattrinke-stubbe and Gothic St Jacob's Church (altarpiece).

Schwarzwald Hilly region between Basel and Karlsruhe, the largest and most picturesque woodland in Germany, with the highest summit, Feldberg, lake resorts (Titisee), health resorts (Baden-Baden) and clock craft (Triberg). Freiburg is regional capital.

Speyer 11c cathedral is one of the largest and best Romanesque buildings in Germany. 12c Jewish Baths are well-preserved.

Stuttgart Largely modern city with old centre around the Old Schloss, Renaissance Alte Kanzlei, 15c Collegiate Church and Baroque New Schloss. Museums: Regional Museum; post-modern State Gallery (old masters, 20c German). The 1930s Weissenhofsiedlung is by several famous architects.

Trier Superb Roman monuments: Porta Nigra; Aula Palatina (now a church); Imperial Baths; amphitheatre. The Regional Museum has Roman artefacts. Also, Gothic Church of Our Lady; Romanesque cathedral.

Ulm Old town with half-timbered gabled houses set on a canal. Gothic 14–19c minster has tallest spire in the world (161m).

Weimar The Neoclassical schloss, once an important seat of government, now houses a good art collection. Church of SS Peter and Paul has a Cranach masterpiece. Houses of famous people: Goethe, Schiller, Liszt. The famous Bauhaus was founded at the School of Architecture and Engineering.

Würzburg Set among vineyard hills, the medieval town is centred on the Market Place with the Rococo House of the Falcon. The 18c episcopal princes' residence (frescoes) is magnificent. The cathedral is rich in art. Work of the great local Gothic sculptor, Riemenschneider, is in Gothic St Mary's Chapel, Baroque New Minster, and the Mainfränkisches Museum.

Eesti *Estonia*

Kuressaare Main town on the island of Saaremaa with the 14c Kuressaare Kindlus.

Pärnu Sea resort with an old town centre. Sights: 15c Red Tower; neoclassical Town Hall; St Catherine's Church.

Tallinn Capital of Estonia. The old town is centred on the Town Hall Square. Sights: 15c Town Hall; Toompea Castle; Three Sisters houses. Churches: Gothic St Nicholas; 14c Church of the Holy Spirit; St Olaf's Church.

Tartu Historic town with 19c university. The Town Hall Square is surrounded by neoclassical buildings. Also: remains of 13c cathedral; Estonian National Museum.

Ellas *Greece*

Athínai Capital of Greece. The Acropolis, with 5c BC sanctuary complex (Parthenon, Propylaia, Erechtheion, Temple of Athena Nike), is the greatest architectural achievement of

Gothic cathedral, Köln, Deutschland

antiquity in Europe. The Agora was a public meeting place in ancient Athens. Pláka has narrow streets and small Byzantine churches (Kapnikaréa). The Olympeum was the largest temple in Greece. Also: Olympic Stadium; excellent collections of ancient artefacts (Museum of Cycladic and Ancient Greek Art; Acropolis Museum; National Archeological Museum; Benáki Museum).

Delphí At the foot of the Mount Parnassós, Delphi was the seat of the Delphic Oracle of Apollo, the most important oracle in Ancient Greece. Delphi was also a political meeting place and the site of the Pythian Games. The Sanctuary of Apollo consists of: Temple of Apollo, led to by the Sacred Way; Theatre; Stadium. The museum has a display of objects from the site (5c BC *Charioteer*).

Epídavros Formerly a spa and religious centre focused on the Sanctuary of Asclepius (ruins). The enormous 4c BC theatre is probably the finest of all ancient theatres.

Greek Islands Popular islands with some of the most beautiful and spectacular beaches in Europe. The many islands are divided into various groups and individual islands: The major groups are the Kikládhes and Dhodhekanisos in the Aegean Sea, the largest islands are Kérkira (Corfu) in the Ionian Sea and Kriti.

Kórinthos Ancient Corinth (ruins), with 5c BC Temple of Apollo, was in 44BC made capital of Roman Greece by Julius Caesar. Set above the city, the Greek-built acropolis hill of Acro-

corinth became the Roman and Byzantine citadel (ruins).

Kriti Largest Greek island, Crete was home to the great Minoan civilization (2800–1100 BC). The main relics are the ruined Palace of Knossós and Mália. Gortys was capital of the Roman province. Picturesque Réthimno has narrow medieval streets, a Venetian fortress and a former Turkish mosque. Mátala has

Abbaye aux Hommes, Caen, France

beautiful beaches and famous caves cut into cliffs. Iráklio (Heraklion), the capital, has a good Archeological Museum.

Metéora The tops of bizarre vertical cylinders of rock and towering cliffs are the setting for 14c Cenobitic monasteries, until recently only accessible by baskets or removable ladders. Méga Metéoron is the grandest and set on the highest point. Roussánou has the most extraordinary site. Varlaám is one of the oldest and most beautiful, with the Ascent Tower and 16c church with frescoes. Áyiou Nikólaou also has good frescoes.

Mistrás Set in a beautiful landscape, Mystra is the site of a Byzantine city, now in ruins, with palaces, frescoed churches, monasteries and houses.

Mykenai The citadel of Mycenae prospered between 1950BC and 1100BC and consists of the royal complex of Agamemnon: Lion Gate, royal burial site, Royal Palace, South House, Great Court.

Óros Ólimpos Mount Olympus, mythical seat of the Greek gods, is the highest, most dramatic peak in Greece.

Olympia In a stunning setting, the Panhellenic Games were held here for a millennium. Ruins of the sanctuary of Olympia consist of the Doric temples of Zeus and Hera and the vast Stadium. There is also a museum (4c BC figure of Hermes).

Ródhos One of the most attractive islands with wonderful sandy beaches. The city of Rhodes has a well-preserved medieval centre with the Palace of the Grand Masters and the Turkish Süleymaniye Mosque

Thessaloníki Largely modern city with Byzantine walls and many fine churches: 8c Ayía Sofia; 11c Panayía Halkéon; 14c Dhódheka Apóstoli; 14c Áyios Nikólaos Orfanós; 5c Áyios Dhimítrios (largest in Greece, 7c Mosaics).

España *Spain*

Ávila Medieval town with 2km-long 11c walls. Pilgrimage site to shrines to St Teresa of Ávila (Convent of Santa Teresa, Convent of the Incarnation).

Barcelona Showcase of Gothic ('Barri Gòtic': cathedral; Santa María de, Mar; mansions on Carrer de Montcada) and *modernista* architecture ('Eixample' area with Manzana de la Discòrdia; Sagrada Família, Güell Park, La Pedrera). Many elegant boulevards (La Rambla, Passeig de Gràcia). Museums: Modern Catalan Art; Picasso Museum, Miró Museum; Tàpies Museum. Nearby: monastery of Montserrat (Madonna); Figueres (Dalí Museum).

Burgos Medieval town with Gothic cathedral, Moorish-Gothic Royal Monastery and Charterhouse of Miraflores.

Cáceres Medieval town surrounded by originally Moorish walls and with several aristocratic palaces with solars.

Córdoba Capital of Moorish Spain with a labyrinth of streets and houses with tile-decorated patios. The 8–10c Mezquita is the finest mosque in Spain. A 16c cathedral was added at the centre of the building and a 17c tower replaced the minaret. The old Jewish quarter has 14c synagogue

El Escorial Immense Renaissance complex of palatial and monastic buildings and mausoleum of the Spanish monarchs..

Granada The Alhambra was hill-top palace-fortress of the rulers of the last Moorish kingdom and is the most splendid example of Moorish art and architecture in Spain. The complex has three principal parts: Alcazaba fortress (11c); Casa Real palace (14c, with later Palace of Carlos V); Generalife gardens. Also: Moorish quarter; gypsy quarter; Royal Chapel with good art in the sacristy.

León Gothic cathedral has notable stained

glass. Royal Pantheon commemorates early kings of Castile and León.

Madrid Capital of Spain, a mainly modern city with 17–19c architecture at its centre around Plaza Mayor. Sights: Royal Palace with lavish apartments; Descalzas Reales Convent (tapestries and other works); Royal Armoury museum. Spain's three leading galleries: Prado (15–18c); Queen Sofia Centre (20c Spanish, Picasso's *Guernica*); Thyssen-Bornemisza Museum (medieval to modern).

Oviedo Gothic cathedral with 12c sanctuary. Three Visigoth (9c) churches: Santullano, Santa María del Naranco, San Miguel de Lillo.

Palma Situated on Mallorca, the largest and most beautiful of the Balearic islands, with an impressive Gothic cathedral.

Picos de Europa Mountain range with river gorges and peaks topped by Visigothic and Romanesque churches.

Pyrenees (Spanish) Unspoiled mountain range with beautiful landscape and villages full of Romanesque architecture (cathedral of Jaca). The Ordesa National Park has many waterfalls and canyons.

Salamanca Delightful old city with some uniquely Spanish architecture: Renaissance Plateresque is famously seen on 16c portal of the university (founded 1215); Baroque Churrigueresque on 18c Plaza Mayo; both styles at the Convent of San Esteban. Also: Romanesque Old Cathedral; Gothic-Plateresque New Cathedral; House of Shells.

Santiago di Compostella Medieval city with many churches and religious institutions. The famous pilgrimage to the shrine of St James the Apostle ends here in the magnificent cathedral, originally Romanesque with many later elements (18c Baroque façade).

Segovia Old town set on a rock with a 1c Roman aqueduct. Also: 16c Gothic cathedral; Alcázar (14–15c, rebuilt 19c); 12-sided 13c

**El Escorial
(cutaway), España**

Templar church of Vera Cruz.

Sevilla City noted for festivals and flamenco. The world's largest Gothic cathedral (15c) retains the Orange Court and minaret of a mosque. The Alcazar is a fine example of Moorish architecture. The massive 18c tobacco factory, now part of the university, was the setting for Bizet's *Carmen*. Barrio de Santa Cruz is the old Jewish quarter with narrow streets and white houses. Casa de Pilatos (15–16c) has a fine domestic patio. Hospital de la Caridad has good Spanish painting. Nearby: Roman Italica with amphitheatre.

Tarragona The city and its surroundings have some of the best-preserved Roman heritage in Spain. Also: Gothic cathedral (cloister); Archaeological Museum.

Toledo Historic city with Moorish, Jewish and Christian past. The small 11c mosque of El Cristo de la Luz is one of the earliest in Spain. Two synagogues have been preserved: Santa María la Blanca; El Tránsito. Churches: San Juan de los Reyes; Gothic cathedral (good artworks). El Greco's *Burial of the Count of Orgaz* is in the Church of Santo Tomé. More of his works are in the El Greco house and, with other art, in Hospital de Santa Cruz.

Valencia The old town has houses and palaces with elaborate façades. Also: Gothic cathedral and Lonja de la Seda church.

Zaragoza Town notable for Moorish architecture (11c Aljafería Palace). The Basilica de Nuestra Señora del Pilar, one of two cathedrals, is highly venerated.

France

Albi Old town with rosy brick architecture. The vast Cathédrale Ste-Cécile (begun 13c) holds some good art. The Berbie Palace houses the Toulouse-Lautrec museum.

Alpes (French) Grenoble, capital of the French Alps, has a good 20c collection in the Museum of Painting and Sculpture. The Vanoise Massif has the greatest number of resorts (Val d'Isère, Courchevel). Chamonix has spectacular views on Mont Blanc, France's and Europe's highest peak.

Amiens France's largest Gothic cathedral has beautiful decoration. The Museum of Picardy has unique 16c panel paintings.

Arles Ancient, picturesque town with Roman relics (1c amphitheatre), 11c cathedral, Archaeological Museum (Roman art).

Avignon Medieval papal capital (1309–77) with 14c walls and many ecclesiastical buildings. Vast Palace of the Popes has stunning frescoes. The Little Palace has fine Italian Renaissance painting. The 12–13c Bridge of St Bénézet is famous.

Bourges The Gothic Cathedral of St Etienne, one of the finest in France, has a superb sculptured choir. Also notable is the House of Jacques Coeur.

Bourgogne Rural wine region with a rich Romanesque, Gothic and Renaissance heritage. The 12c cathedral in Autun and 12c basilica in Vézelay have fine Romanesque sculpture. Monasteries include 11c L'Abbaye de Cluny (ruins) and L'Abbaye de Fontenay. Beaune has beautiful Gothic Hôtel-Dieu and 15c Nicolas Rolin hospices.

Bretagne Brittany is famous for cliffs, sandy beaches and wild landscape. It is also renowned for megalithic monuments (Carnac) and Celtic culture. Its capital, Rennes, has the Palais de Justice and good collections in the Museum of Brittany (history) and Museum of Fine Arts. Also: Nantes; St-Malo.

Caen City with two beautiful Romanesque buildings: Abbaye aux Hommes; Abbaye aux

Dames. The château has two museums (15–20c painting; history). The *Bayeux Tapestry* is displayed in nearby Bayeux.

Carcassonne Unusual double-walled fortified town of narrow streets with an inner fortress. The fine Romanesque Church of St Nazaire has superb stained glass.

Chartres The 12–13c cathedral is an exceptionally fine example of Gothic architecture (Royal Doorway, stained glass, choir screen). The Fine Arts Museum has a good collection.

Châteaux of the Loire The Loire Valley has many 15–16c châteaux built amid beautiful scenery by French monarchs and members of their courts. Among the most splendid are Azay-le-Rideau, Chenonceaux and Loches. Also: Abbaye de Fontévraud.

Clermont-Ferrand The old centre contains the cathedral built out of lava and Romanesque basilica. The Puy de Dôme and Puy de Sancy give spectacular views over some 60 extinct volcanic peaks (*puys*).

Colmar Town characterised by Alsatian half-timbered houses. The Unterlinden Museum has excellent German religious art including the famous Işenheim altarpiece. The Dominican church also has a fine altarpiece.

Corse Corsica has a beautiful rocky coast and mountainous interior. Napoleon's birthplace of Ajaccio has: Fesch Museum with Imperial Chapel and a large collection of Italian art; Maison Bonaparte; cathedral. Bonifacio, a medieval town, is spectacularly set on a rock over the sea.

Côte d'Azur The French Riviera is best known for its coastline and glamorous resorts. There are many relics of artists who worked here: St-Tropez has Musée de l'Annonciade; Antibes has 12c Château Grimaldi with the Picasso Museum; Cagnes has the Renoir House and Mediterranean Museum of Modern Art; St-Paul-de-Vence has the excellent Maeght Foundation and Matisse's Chapelle du Rosaire. Cannes is famous for its film festival. Also: Marseille, Monaco, Nice.

Dijon Great 15c cultural centre. The Palais des Ducs et des Etats is the most notable monument and contains the Museum of Fine Arts. Also: the Charterhouse of Champmol.

Disneyland Paris Europe's largest theme park follows in the footsteps of its famous predecessors in the United States.

Le Puy-en-Velay Medieval town bizarrely set on the peaks of dead volcanoes. It is dominated by the Romanesque cathedral (cloisters). The Romanesque chapel of St-Michel is dramatically situated on the highest rock.

Lyon France's third largest city has an old centre and many museums including the Museum of the History of Textiles and the Museum of Fine Arts (old masters).

Marseille Second lagest city in France. Spectacular views from the 19c Notre-Dame-de-la-Garde. The Old Port has 11–12c Basilique St Victor (crypt, catacombs). Cantini Museum has major collection of 20c French art. Château d'If was the setting for Dumas' *The Count of Monte Cristo*.

Mont-St-Michel Gothic pilgrim abbey (11–12c) set dramatically on a steep rock

island rising from mud flats and connected to the land by a road covered by the tide. The abbey is made up of a complex of buildings.

Nancy A centre of Art Nouveau. The 18c Place Stanislas was constructed by dethroned Polish king Stanislas. Museums: School of Nancy Museum (Art Nouveau furniture); Fine Arts Museum.

Nantes Former capital of Brittany, with the 15c Château des ducs de Bretagne. The cathedral has a striking interior.

Nice Capital of the Côte d'Azur, the old town is centred on the old castle on the hill. The seafront includes the famous 19c Promenade des Anglais. The aristocratic quarter of the Cimiez Hill has the Marc Chagall Museum and the Matisse Museum. Also: Museum of Modern and Contemporary Art (especially neo-Realism and Pop Art).

Paris Capital of France, one of Europe's most interesting cities. The Île de la Cité area, an island in the River Seine has the 12–13c Gothic Notre Dame (wonderful stained glass) and La Sainte-Chapelle (1240–48), one of the jewels of Gothic art. The Left Bank area: Latin Quarter with the famous Sorbonne university; Museum of Cluny housing medieval art; the Panthéon; Luxembourg Palace and Gardens; Montparnasse, interwar artistic and literary centre; Eiffel Tower; Hôtel des Invalides with Napoleon's tomb. Right Bank: the great boulevards (Avenue des Champs-Élysées joining the Arc de Triomphe and Place de la Concorde); 19c Opéra Quarter; Marais, former aristocratic quarter of elegant mansions (Place des Vosges); Bois de Boulogne, the largest park in Paris; Montmartre, centre of 19c bohemianism, with the Basilique Sacré-Coeur. The Church of St Denis is the first gothic church and the mausoleum of the French monarchy. Paris has three of the

world's greatest art collections: The Louvre (to 19c, *Mona Lisa*), Musée d'Orsay (19–20c) and National Modern Art Museum in the Pompidou Centre. Other major museums include: Orangery Museum; Paris Museum of Modern Art; Rodin Museum; Picasso Museum. Notable cemeteries with graves of the famous: Père-Lachaise, Montmartre, Montparnasse. Near Paris are the royal residences of Fontainebleau and Versailles.

Pyrenees (French) Beautiful unspoiled mountain range. Towns include: delightful sea resorts of St-Jean-de-Luz and Biarritz; Pau, with access to the Pyrenees National Park; pilgrimage centre Lourdes.

Reims Together with nearby Epernay, the centre of champagne production. The 13c Gothic cathedral is one of the greatest architectural achievements in France (stained glass by Chagall). Other sights: Palais du Tau (with cathedral sculpture, 11c Basilica of St Rémi; cellars on Place St-Niçaise and Place des Droits-des-Hommes.

Rouen Old centre with many half-timbered houses and 12–13c Gothic cathedral and the Gothic Church of St Maclou with its fascinating remains of a dance macabre on the former cemetery of Aître St-Maclou. The Fine Arts Museum has a good collection.

St-Malo Fortified town (much rebuilt) in a fine coastal setting. There is a magnificent boat trip along the river Rance to Dinan, a splendid well-preserved medieval town.

Strasbourg Town whose historic centre includes a well-preserved quarter of medieval half-timbered Alsatian houses, many of them set on thè canal. The cathedral is one of the best in France. The Palais Rohan contains several museums.

Toulouse Medieval university town charac-

terised by flat pink brick (Hôtel Assézat). The Basilique St Sernin, the largest Romanesque church in France, has many art treasures. Marvellous Church of the Jacobins holds the body of St Thomas Aquinas.

Tours Historic town centred on Place Plumereau. Good collections in the Guilds Museum and Fine Arts Museum.

Versailles Vast royal palace built for Louis XIV, primarily by Mansart, set in large formal gardens with magnificent fountains. The extensive and much-imitated state apartments include the famous Hall of Mirrors and the exceptional Baroque chapel.

Vézère Valley Caves A number of prehistoric sites, most notably the cave paintings of Lascaux (some 17,000 years old), now only seen in a duplicate cave, and the cave of Font de Gaume. The National Museum of Prehistory is in Les Eyzies.

Hrvatska *Croatia*

Dalmacija Exceptionally beautiful coast along the Adriatic. Among its 1185 islands, those of the Kornati Archipelago and Brijuni Islands are perhaps the most spectacular. Along the coast are several attractive medieval and Renaissance towns, most notably Dubrovnik, Split, Šibenik, Trogir, Zadar.

Dubrovnik Surrounded by medieval and Renaissance walls, the city's architecture dates principally from 15–16c. Sights: many churches and monasteries including Church of St Vlah and Dominican monastery (art collection); promenade street of Stradun, Dubrovnik Museums; Renaissance Rector's Palace; Onofrio's fountain; Sponza Palace. The surrounding area has some 80 16c noblemen's summer villas.

Istra (Croatian) Peninsula with a number of

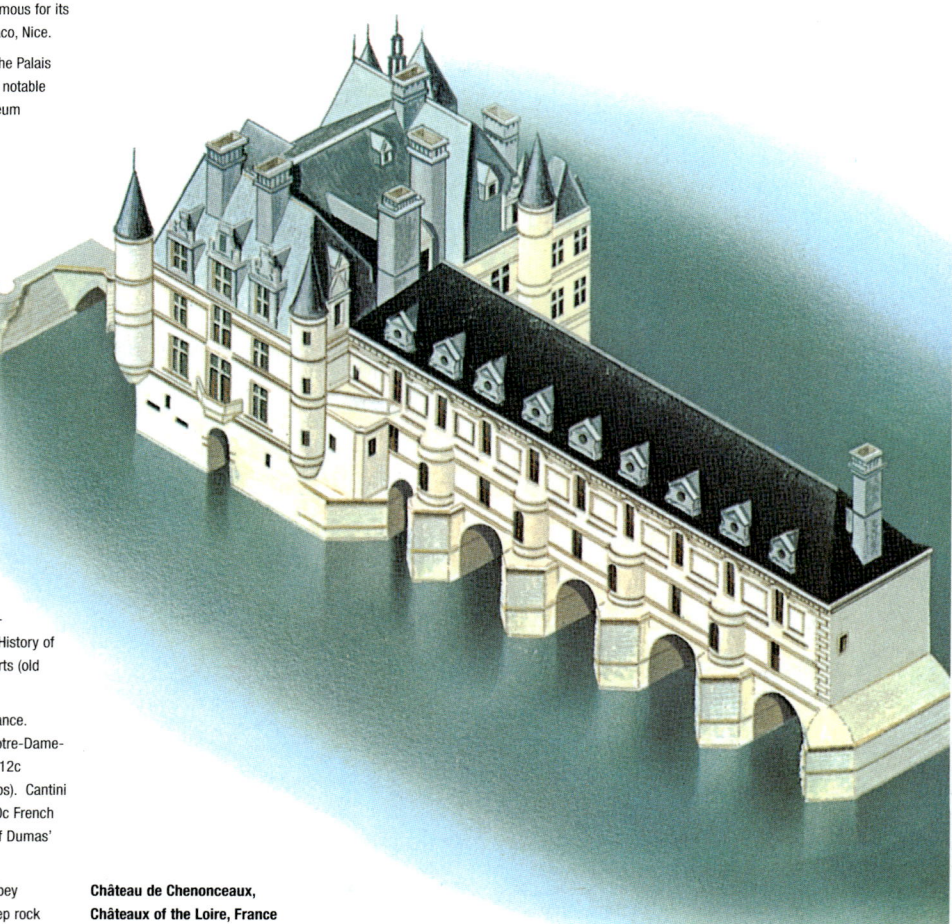

**Château de Chenonceaux,
Châteaux of the Loire, France**

Legend

This guide to sights of Europe has been compiled particularly with the motorist in mind. While many of the places are excellent holiday destinations in themselves, they are all worth a stop or detour on your journey should you be driving that way. With the higher-rated places particularly, it is well worth adapting your travel arrangements to make time for a visit.

Mont-St-Michel ■	**Do not miss**
El Escorial ◆	**Exceptional**
Urbino ●	**First rate**
Wrocław ◆	**Worth visiting**

There are descriptions of the places on this map in the accompanying three pages of text. These point you to the most famous, fascinating or beautiful sights you will find if you visit.

---

ancient coastal towns (Rovinj, Poreč, Pula, Piran in Slovene Istria) and medieval hill-top towns (Motovun). Pula has Roman monuments (exceptional 1c amphitheatre). Poreč has narrow old streets; the mosaics in 6c Byzantine basilica of St Euphrasius are exceptional. See also Slovenia.

Plitvička Jezera Outstandingly beautiful world of water and woodlands with 16 lakes and 92 waterfalls interwoven by canyons.

Split Most notable for the exceptional 4c palace of Roman Emperor Diocletian, elements of which are incorporated into the streets and buildings of the town itself. The town also has a cathedral (11c baptistry) and a Franciscan monastery.

Trogir The 13–15c town centre is surrounded by medieval city walls. Romanesque-Gothic cathedral includes the chapel of Ivan the Blessed. Dominican and Benedictine monasteries house art collections.

Ireland

Aran Islands Islands with spectacular cliffs and notable pre-Christian and Christian sights, especially on Inishmore.

Cashel Town dominated by the Rock of Cashel (61m) topped by ecclesiastical ruins including 13c cathedral; 15c Halls of the Vicars; beautiful Romanesque 12c Cormac's Chapel (fine carvings).

Connemara Beautiful wild landscape of mountains, lakes, peninsulas and beaches. Clifden is the capital.

Cork Pleasant city with its centre along St Patrick's Street and Grand Parade lined with fine 18c buildings. Churches: Georgian St Anne's Shandon (bell tower); 19c cathedral.

County Donegal Rich scenic landscape of mystical lakes and glens and seascape of

cliffs (Slieve League cliffs are the highest in Europe). The town of Donegal has a finely preserved Jacobean castle.

Dublin Capital of Ireland. City of elegant 18c neoclassical and Georgian architecture with gardens and parks (St Stephen's Green, Merrion Square with Leinster House – now seat of Irish parliament). City's main landmark, Trinity College (founded 1591), houses in its Old Library fine Irish manuscripts (7c Book

**Palazzo Publico,
Siena, Italia**

Dolomiti Part of the Alps, this mountain range spreads over the region of Trentino-Alto Adige, with the most picturesque scenery between Bolzano and Cortina d'Ampezzo.

Ferrara Old town centre around Romanesque-Gothic cathedral and Palazzo Communale. Also: Castello Estense; Palazzo Schifanoia (frescoes); Palazzo dei Diamanti housing Pinacoteca Nazionale.

Firenze City with exceptionally rich medieval and Renaissance heritage. Piazza del Duomo has:13–15c cathedral (first dome since antiquity); 14c campanile; 11c baptistry (bronze doors). Piazza della Signoria has: 14c Palazzo Vecchio (frescoes); Loggia della Signoria (sculpture); 16c Uffizi Gallery with one of the world's greatest collections (13–18c). Other great paintings: Museo di San Marco; Palatine Gallery in 15–16c Pitti Palace surrounded by Boboli Gardens. Sculpture: Cathedral Works Museum; Bargello Museum; Academy Gallery (Michelangelo's *David*). Among many other Renaissance palaces: Medici-Riccardi; Rucellai; Strozzi. The 15c church of San Lorenzo has Michelangelo's tombs of the Medici. Many churches have richly frescoed chapels: Santa Maria Novella, Santa Croce, Santa Maria del Carmine. The 13c Ponte Vecchio is one of the most famous sights.

Italian Lakes Beautiful district at the foot of the Alps, most of the lakes with holiday resorts. Many lakes are surrounded by aristocratic villas (Maggiore, Como, Garda).

Mántova Attractive city surrounded by three lakes. Two exceptional palaces: Palazzo Ducale (Sala del Pisanello; Camera degli Sposi, Castello San Giorgio); luxurious Palazzo Tè (brilliant frescoes). Also: 15c Church of Sant'Andrea; 13c law courts.

Milano Modern city, Italy's fashion and design capital (Corso and Galleria Vittoro Emmanuelle II). Churches include: Gothic cathedral (1386–1813), the world's largest (4c baptistry); Romanesque St Ambrose; 15c San Satiro; Santa Maria delle Grazie with Leonardo da Vinci's *Last Supper* in the convent refectory. Great art collections, Brera Gallery, Ambrosian Library, Museum of Contemporary Art. Castello Sforzesco (15c, 19c) also has a gallery. The famous La Scala theatre opened in 1778. Nearby: monastery at Pavia.

Napoli Historical centre around Gothic cathedral (crypt). Spaccanapoli area has numerous churches (bizarre Cappella Sansevero, Gesù Nuovo, Gothic Santa Chiara with fabulous tombs). Buildings: 13c Castello Nuovo; 13c Castel dell'Ovo; 15c Palazzo Cuomo. Museums: National Archeological Museum (artefacts from Pompeii and Herculaneum); National Museum of Capodimonte (Renaissance painting). Nearby: spectacular coast around Amalfi; Pompeii; Herculaneum.

Orvieto Medieval hill-top town with a number of monuments including the Romanesque-Gothic cathedral (façade, frescoes).

Pádova Pleasant old town with arcaded streets. Basilica del Santo is a place of pilgrimage to the tomb of St Anthony. Giotto's frescoes in the Scrovegni chapel are exceptional. Also: Piazza dei Signori with Palazzo del Capitano; vast Palazzo della Ragione; church of the Eremitani (frescoes).

Palermo City with Moorish, Norman and Baroque architecture, especially around the main squares (Quattro Canti, Piazza Pretoria, Piazza Bellini). Sights: remains of Norman palace (12c Palatine Chapel); Norman cathedral; Regional Gallery (medieval); some 8000 preserved bodies in the catacombs of the Cappuchin Convent. Nearby: 12c Norman Duomo di Monreale.

of Durrow, 8c Book of Kells). Two Norman cathedrals: Christ Church; St Patrick's. Other buildings: originally medieval Dublin Castle with State Apartments; James Gandon's masterpieces: Custom House; Four Courts. Museums: National Museum (Irish history); National Gallery (old masters, Impressionists, Irish painting); Guinness Brewery Museum; Dublin Writers' Museum (Joyce, Wilde, Yeats and others).

Glendalough Impressive ruins of an important early Celtic (6c) monastery with 9c cathedral, 12c St Kevin's Cross, oratory of St Kevin's Church.

Kilkenny Charming medieval town, with narrow streets dominated by 12c castle (restored 19c). The 13c Gothic cathedral has notable tomb monuments.

Newgrange One of the best passage graves in Europe, the massive 4500-year-old tomb has stones richly decorated with patterns.

Ring of Kerry Route around the Iveragh peninsula with beautiful lakes (Lough Leane), peaks overlooking the coastline and islands (Valencia Island, Skelling). Also: Killarney; ruins of 15c Muckross Abbey.

Italia *Italy*

Alpi (Italian) Wonderful stretch of the Alps running from the Swiss and French borders to Austria. The region of Valle d'Aosta is one of the most popular ski regions, bordered by the highest peaks of the Alps.

Agrigento Set on a hill above the sea and famed for the Valley of the Temples. The nine originally 5c Doric temples are Sicily's best-preserved Greek remains.

Arezzo Beautiful old town set on a hill dominated by 13c cathedral. Piazza Grande is surrounded by medieval and Renaissance palaces. Main sight: Piero della Francesca's frescoes in the choir of San Francesco.

Assisi Hill-top town that attracts crowds of pilgrims to the shrine of St Francis of Assisi at the Basilica di San Francesco, consisting of two churches, Lower and Upper, with superb frescoes (particularly Giotto's in the Upper).

Bologna Elegant city with oldest university in Italy. Historical centre around Piazza Maggiore and Piazza del Nettuno with the Town Hall, Palazzo del Podestà, Basilica di San Petronio. Other churches: San Domenico; San Giacomo Maggiore. The two towers (one incomplete) are symbols of the city. Good collection in the National Gallery (Bolognese).

Romanesque cathedral, Pisa, Italia

Parma Attractive city centre, famous for Corregio's frescoes in the Romanesque cathedral and church of St John the Evangelist, and Parmigianino's frescoes in the church of Madonna della Steccata. Their works are also in the National Gallery.

Perúgia Hill-top town centred around Piazza Quattro Novembre with the cathedral, Fontana Maggiore and Palazzo dei Priori. Also: Collegio di Cambio (frescoes); National Gallery of Umbria; many churches.

Pisa Medieval town centred on the Piazza dei Miracoli. Sights: famous Romanesque Leaning Tower, Romanesque cathedral (excellent façade, Gothic pulpit); 12–13c Baptistry; 13c Camposanto cloistered cemetery (fascinating 14c frescoes).

Ravenna Ancient town with exceptionally well-preserved Byzantine mosaics. The finest are in 5c Mausoleo di Galla Placidia and 6c Basilica of San Vitale. Good mosaics also in the basilicas of Sant'Apollinare in Classe and Sant'Apollinare Nuovo.

Roma Capital of Italy, exceptionally rich in sights from many eras. Ancient sights: Colosseum; Arch of Constantine; Trajan's Column; Roman and Imperial fora; hills of Palatino and Campidoglio (Capitoline Museum shows antiquities); Pantheon; Castel Sant' Angelo; Baths of Caracalla. Early Christian sights: catacombs (San Calisto, San Sebastiano, Domitilla); basilicas (San Giovanni in Laterano, Santa Maria Maggiore, San Paolo Fuori le Mura). Rome is known for richly decorated Baroque churches: il Gesù, Sant'Ignazio, Santa Maria della Vittoria, Chiesa Nuova. Other churches, often with art treasures: Romanesque Santa Maria in Cosmadin, Gothic Santa Maria Sopra Minevra, Renaissance Santa Maria del Popolo, San Pietro in Vincoli. Several Renaissance and Baroque palaces and villas house superb art collec-

tions (Palazzo Barberini, Palazzo Doria Pamphilj, Palazzo Spada, Palazzo Corsini, Villa Giulia, Galleria Borghese) and are beautifully frescoed (Villa Farnesina). Fine Baroque public spaces with fountains: Piazza Navona; Piazza di Spagna with the Spanish Steps, Trevi Fountain. Nearby: Tivoli; Villa Adriana. Rome also contains the Vatican City (Città del Vaticano).

Sardegna Sardinia has some of the most beautiful beaches in Italy (Alghero). Unique are the nuraghi, some 7000 stone constructions (Su Nuraxi, Serra Orios), the remains of an old civilization (1500–400 BC). Old towns include Cagliari and Sássari.

Sicilia Surrounded by beautiful beaches and full of monuments of many periods, Sicily is the largest island in the Mediterranean. Taormina with its Greek theatre has one of the most spectacular beaches, lying under the mildly active volcano Mount Etna. Also: Agrigento; Palermo, Siracusa.

Siena Outstanding 13–14c medieval town centred on beautiful Piazza del Campo with Gothic Palazzo Publico (frescoes of secular life). Delightful Romanesque-Gothic Duomo (Libreria Piccolomini, baptistry, art works). Many other richly decorated churches. Fine Sienese painting in Pinacoteca Nazionale and Museo dell'Opera del Duomo.

Siracusa Built on an island connected to the mainland by a bridge, the old town has a 7c cathedral, ruins of the Temple of Apollo; Fountain of Arethusa; archaeological museum. On the mainland: 5c BC Greek theatre with seats cut out of rock; Greek fortress of Euralus; 2c Roman amphitheatre; 5–6c Catacombs of St John.

Torino City centre has 17-18c Baroque layout dominated by twin Baroque churches. Also: 15c cathedral (holds Turin Shroud);Palazzo Reale; 18c Superga Basilica; Academy of Science with two museums (Egyptian antiquities; European painting).

Urbino Set in beautiful hilly landscape, Urbino's heritage is mainly due to the 15c court of Federico da Montefeltro at the magnificent Ducal Palace (notable Studiolo), now also a gallery.

Venezia Stunning old city built on islands in a lagoon, with some 150 canals. The Grand Canal is crossed by the famous 16c Rialto Bridge and is lined with elegant palaces (Gothic Ca'd'Oro and Ca'Foscari, Renaissance Palazzo Grimani, Baroque Rezzonico). The district of San Marco has the core of the best known sights and is centred on Piazza San Marco with 11c Basilica di San Marco (bronze horses, 13c mosaics) and Ducal Palace (connected with the prison by the famous Bridge of Sighs). Many churches (Santa Maria Gloriosa dei Frari, Santa Maria della Salute, Redentore, San Giorgio Maggiore, San Giovanni e Paolo) and scuole (Scuola di San Rocco, Scuola di San Giorgio degli Schiavoni) have excellent works of art. The Gallery of the Academy houses superb 14–18c Venetian art. The Guggenheim Museum holds 20c art.

Verona Old town with remains of 1c Roman Arena and medieval sights including the Palazzo degli Scaligeri; Arche Scaligere; Romanesque Santa Maria Antica; Castelvecchio; Ponte Scaliger. The famous 14c House of Juliet has associations with *Romeo and Juliet*. Many churches with fine art works (cathedral; Sant'Anastasia; basilica di San Zeno Maggiore).

Vicenza Beautiful town, famous for the architecture of Palladio, including the Olympic Theatre (extraordinary stage), Corso Palladio with many of his palaces, and Palazzo Chiericati. Nearby: Villa Rotonda, the most influential of all Palladian buildings.

Volcanic Region Region from Naples to Sicily. Mount Etna is one of the most famous European volcanoes.

Vesuvius dominates the Bay of Naples and has at its foot two of Italy's finest Roman sites, Pompeii and Herculaneum, both destroyed by its eruption in 79AD. Stromboli is one of the beautiful Aeolian Islands.

Jugoslavia *Yugoslavia*

Beograd Capital of Yugoslavia. The largely modern city is set between the Danube and Sava rivers. The National Museum holds European art. To the south there are numerous fascinating medieval monasteries, richly embellished with frescoes.

Latvija *Latvia*

Riga Well-preserved medieval town centre around the cathedral. Sights: Riga Castle; medieval Hanseatic houses; Great Guild Hal ; Gothic Church of St Peter; Art Nouveau buildings in the New Town. Nearby: Baroque Rundale Castle.

Lietuva *Lithuania*

Vilnius Baroque old town with fine architecture including: cathedral; Gediminas Tower; university complex; Archbishop's Palace; Church of St Anne. Also: remains of Jewish life; Vilnius Picture Gallery (16–19c regional); Lithuanian National Museum.

Luxembourg

Luxembourg Capital of Luxembourg, built on a rock with fine views. Old town is around the Place d'Armes. Buildings: Grand Ducal Palace; fortifications of Rocher du Bock; cathedral. Museum of History and Art holds an excellent regional collection.

Magyarorszàg *Hungary*

Balaton The 'Hungarian sea', famous for its holiday resorts: Balatonfüred, Tihany, Badasconytomaj, Keszthely.

Budapest Capital of Hungary on River Danube, with historic area centring on the Castle Hill of Buda district. Sights include: Matthias church; Pest district with late 19c architecture, centred on Ferenciek tere; neo-Gothic Parliament Building on river; Millennium Monument. The Royal Castle houses a number of museums: Hungarian National Gallery, Budapest History Museum; Ludwig Collection. Other museums: National Museum of Fine Arts (excellent Old and Modern masters); Hungarian National Museum (Hungarian history). Famous for public thermal baths: Király and Rudas baths, both made under Turkish rule; Gellért baths, the most visited.

Esztergom Medieval capital of Hungary set in scenic landscape. Sights: Hungary's largest basilica (completed 1856); royal palace ruins.

Pécs Attractive old town with Europe's fifth oldest university (founded 1367). Famous for Turkish architecture (Mosque of Gazi Kasim Pasha, Jakovali Hassan Mosque).

Sopron Beautiful walled town with many Gothic and Renaissance houses. Nearby: Fertöd with the marvellous Eszergázy Palace.

Makedonija *Macedonia*

Skopje Historic town with Turkish citadel, fine 15c mosques, oriental bazaar, ancient bridge. Superb Byzantine churches nearby.

Ohrid Old town, beautifully set by a lake, with houses of wood and brick, remains of a Turkish citadel, many churches (two cathedrals; St Naum south of the lake).

Malta

Valletta Capital of Malta. Historic walled city, founded in 16c by the Maltese Knights, with 16c Grand Master's Palace and a richly decorated cathedral.

Monaco

Monaco Major resort area in a beautiful location. Sights include: Monte Carlo casino, Prince's Palace at Monaco-Ville; 19c cathedral; oceanographic museum.

Nederland *The Netherlands*

Amsterdam Capital of the Netherlands. Old centre has picturesque canals lined with distinctive elegant 17–18c merchants' houses. Dam Square has 15c New Church and Royal Palace. Other churches include Westerkerk. The Museumplein has three world-famous museums: Rijksmuseum (several art collections including 15–17c painting); Van Gogh Museum; Municipal Museum (art from 1850 on). Other museums: Anne Frank House; Jewish Historical Museum; Rembrandt House.

Delft Well-preserved old Dutch town with gabled red-roofed houses along canals. Gothic churches: New Church; Old Church. Famous for Delftware (two museums).

Den Haag Seat of Government and of the royal house of the Netherlands. The 17c Mauritshuis houses the Royal Picture Gallery (excellent 15–18c Flemish and Dutch). Other good collections: Prince William V Gallery; Hesdag Museum; Municipal Museum

Redentore (cutaway),
Venezia, Italia

Westerkerk, Amsterdam, Nederland

Haarlem Many medieval gabled houses centred on the Great Market with 14c Town Hall and 15c Church of St Bavon. Museums: Frans Hals Museum; Teylers Museum.

Het Loo Former royal palace and gardens set in a vast landscape (commissioned by future Queen of England, Mary Stuart).

Keukenhof Landscaped gardens, planted with bulbs of many varieties, are the largest flower gardens in the world.

Leiden University town of beautiful gabled houses set along canals. The Rijksmuseum Van Oudheden is Holland's most important home to archaeological artefacts from the Antiquity. The 16c Hortus Botanicus is one of the oldest botanical gardens in Europe. The Cloth Hall with van Leyden's *Last Judgement*.

Rotterdam The largest port in the world. The Boymans-van Beuningen Museum has a huge and excellent decorative and fine art collection (old and modern). Nearby: 18c Kinderdijk with 19 windmills.

Utrecht Delightful old town centre along canals with the Netherlands' oldest university and Gothic cathedral. Good art collections: Central Museum; National Museum.

Norge *Norway*

Bergen Norway's second city in a scenic setting. The Quay has many painted wooden medieval buildings. Sights: 12c Romanesque St Mary's Church; Bergenhus fortress with 13c Haakon's Hall; Rosenkrantztårnet; Grieghallen; Rasmus Meyer Collection (Norwegian art); Bryggens Museum.

Lappland (Norwegian) Vast land of Finnmark is home to the Sámi. Nordkapp is the northern point of Europe. Also Finland, Sweden.

Norwegian Fjords Beautiful and majestic landscape of deep glacial valleys filled by the sea. The most thrilling fjords are between Bergen and Ålesund.

Oslo Capital of Norway with a modern centre. Buildings: 17c cathedral; 19c city hall; 19c royal palace; 19c Stortinget (housing parliament); 19c University; 13c Akershus (castle); 12c Akerskirke (church). Museums: National Gallery; Munch Museum; Viking Ship Museum; Folk Museum (reconstructed buildings).

Stavkirker Wooden medieval stave churches of bizarre pyramidal structure, carved with images from Nordic mythology. Best preserved in southern Norway.

Tromsø Main arctic city of Norway with a university and two cathedrals.

Trondheim Set on the edge of a fjord, a modern city with the superb Nidaros cathedral (rebuilt 19c). Also: Stiftsgaard (royal residence); Applied Arts Museum.

Österreich *Austria*

Graz University town, seat of imperial court to 1619. Historic centre around Hauptplatz. Imperial monuments: Burg; mausoleum of Ferdinand II; towers of 16c schloss; 17c Schloss Eggenburg. Also: 16c Town Hall; Zeughaus; 15c cathedral. Museums: Old Gallery (Gothic, Flemish); New Gallery (good 19–20c).

Innsbruck Old town is reached by Maria-Theresien-Strasse with famous views. Buildings: Goldenes Dachl (1490s); 18c cathedral; remains of Hofburg imperial residence; 16c Hofkirche (tomb of Maximilian I).

Krems On a hill above the Danube, medieval quarter has Renaissance mansions. Also: Gothic Piaristenkirche; Wienstadt Museum.

Linz Port on the Danube. Historic buildings are concentrated on Hauptplatz below the imperial 15c schloss. Notable: Baroque Old Cathedral; 16c Town Hall; New Gallery.

Melk Set on a rocky hill above the Danube, the fortified abbey is the greatest Baroque achievement in Austria – particularly the Grand Library and abbey church.

Salzburg Set in subalpine scenery, the town was associated with powerful 16-17c prince-archbishops. The 17c cathedral has a complex of archiepiscopal buildings: the Residence and its gallery (excellent 16–19c); the 13c Franciscan Church (notable altar). Other sights: Mozart's birthplace; the Hohensalzburg fortress; the Collegiate Church of St Peter (cemetery, catacombs); scenic views from Mönchsberg and Hettwer Bastei. The Grosse Festspielhaus runs the Salzburg festival.

Salzkammergut Natural beauty with 76 lakes (Wolfgangersee, Altersee, Gosausee, Traunsee, Grundlsee) in mountain scenery. Attractive villages (St Wolfgang) and towns (Bad Ischl, Gmunden) include Hallstatt, famous for Celtic remains.

Wien Capital of Austria. The historic centre lies within the Ring. Churches: Gothic St Stephen's Cathedral; 17c Imperial Vault; 14c Augustine Church; 14c Church of the Teutonic Order (treasure); 18c Baroque churches (Jesuit Church, Franciscan Church, St Peter, St Charles). Imperial residences: Hofburg; Schönbrunn. Architecture of Historicism on Ringstrasse (from 1857). Art Nouveau: Station Pavilions, Postsparkasse, Looshaus, Majolicahaus. Exceptional museums: Art History Museum (antiquities, old masters); Cathedral and Diocesan Museum (15c); Academy of Fine Arts (Flemish); Belvedere (Gothic, Baroque, 19–20c).

Polska *Poland*

Częstochowa Centre of Polish Catholicism, with the 14c monastery of Jasna Góra a pilgrimage site to the icon of the Black Madonna for six centuries.

Gdańsk Medieval centre with: 14c Town Hall (state rooms); Gothic brick St Mary's Church, Poland's largest; Long Market has fine buildings (Artus Court); National Art Museum.

Kraków Old university city, rich in architecture, centred on superb 16c Marketplace with Gothic-Renaissance Cloth Hall containing the Art Gallery (19c Polish), Clock Tower, Gothic red-brick St Mary's Church (altarpiece). Czartoryski Palace has city's finest art collection. Wawel Hill has the Gothic cathedral and splendid Renaissance Royal Palace. The former Jewish ghetto in Kazimierz district has 16c Old Synagogue, now a museum.

Poznań Town centred on the Old Square with Renaissance Town Hall and Baroque mansions. Also: medieval castle; Gothic cathedral; National Museum (European masters).

Tatry One of Europe's most delightful mountain ranges with many beautiful ski resorts (Zakopane). Also in Slovakia.

Warszawa Capital of Poland, with many historic monuments in the Old Town with the Royal Castle (museum) and Old Town Square surrounded by reconstructed 17–18c merchants' houses. Several churches including: Gothic cathedral; Baroque Church of the Nuns of Visitation. Richly decorated royal palaces and gardens: Neoclassical Łazienki Palace; Baroque palace in Wilanów. The National Museum has Polish and European art.

Wrocław Historic town centred on the Market Square with 15c Town Hall and mansions. Churches: Baroque cathedral; St Elizabeth; St Adalbert. National Museum displays fine art. Vast painting of Battle of Racławice is specially housed.

Portugal

Alcobaça Monastery of Santa Maria, one of the best examples of a Cistercian abbey, founded in 1147 (exterior 17–18c). The church is Portugal's largest (14c tombs).

Algarve Modern seaside resorts among picturesque sandy beaches and rocky coves (Praia da Rocha). Old towns: Lagos; Faro.

Batalha Abbey is one of the masterpieces of French Gothic and Manueline architecture (tombs, English Perpendicular chapel, unfinished pantheon).

Braga Historic town with cathedral and large Archbishop's Palace.

Coimbra Old town with narrow streets set on a hill. The Romanesque cathedral is particularly fine (portal). The university (founded 1290) has a fascinating Baroque library. Also: Museum of Machado de Castro; many monasteries and convents.

Évora Centre of the town, surrounded by walls, has narrow streets of Moorish character and medieval and Renaissance architecture. Churches: 12–13c Gothic cathedral; São Francisco with a chapel decorated with bones of some 5000 monks; 15c Convent of Dos Lóis. The Jesuit university was founded in 1559. Museum of Évora holds fine art (particularly Flemish and Portugese).

Guimarães Old town with a castle with seven towers on a vast keep. Churches: Romanesque chapel of São Miguel; São Francisco. Alberto Sampaio Museum and Martins Sarmento Museum are excellent.

Lisboa Capital of Portugal. Baixa is the Neoclassical heart of Lisbon with the Praça do Comércio and Rossio squares. São Jorge castle (Visigothic, Moorish, Romanesque) is surrounded by the medieval quarters. Bairro Alto is famous for *fado* (songs). Monastery of Jerónimos is exceptional. Churches: 12c cathedral; São Vicente de Fora; São Roque (tiled chapels); Torre de Belém; Convento da Madre de Deus. Museums: Gulbenkian Museum (ancient, oriental, European), National Museum of Antique Art (old masters), Modern Art Centre; Azulejo Museum (decorative tiles). Nearby: palatial monastic complex Mafra; royal resort Sintra.

Porto Historic centre with narrow streets. Views from Clérigos Tower. Churches: São Francisco; cathedral. Soares dos Reis Museum holds fine and decorative arts (18–19c). The suburb of Vila Nova de Gaia is the centre for port wine.

Tomar Attractive town with the Convento de Cristo, founded in 1162 as the headquarters of the Knights Templar (Charola temple, chapter house, Renaissance cloisters).

Romania

Bucovina Beautiful region in northern Romanian Moldova renowned for a number of 15–16c monasteries and their fresco cycles. Of particularly note are Moldovita, Voroneţ and Suceviţa.

Bucureşti Capital of Romania with the majority of sites along the Calea Victoriei and centring on Piaţa Revoluţei with 19c Romanian Athenaeum and 1930s Royal Palace housing the National Art Gallery. The infamous 1980s Civic Centre with People's Palace is a symbol of dictatorial aggrandisement.

Carpaţii The beautiful Carpathian Mountains have several ski resorts (Sinaia) and peaks noted for first-rate mountaineering (Făgăraşuiui, Rodnei).

Danube Delta Europe's largest marshland, a spectacular nature reserve. Travel in the area is by boat, with Tulcea the starting point for visitors. The Romanian Black Sea Coast has a stretch of resorts (Mamaia, Eforie) between Constantaţ and the border, and well-preserved Roman remains in Histria.

Transilvania Beautiful and fascinating scenic region of medieval citadels (Timişoara, Sibiu) provides a setting for the haunting image of the legendary Dracula (Sighişoara, Braşov, Bran Castle). Cluj-Napoca is the main town.

Rossiya *Russia*

Moskva Capital of Russia, with many monuments. Within the Kremlin's red walls are: 15c Cathedral of the Dormition; 16c Cathedral of the Archangel; Cathedral of the Annunciation (icons), Armour Palace. Outside the walls, Red Square has the Lenin Mausoleum and 16c St Basil's Cathedral. There are a number of monasteries (16c Novodevichi). Two superb museums: Tretiakov Art Gallery (Russian); Pushkin Museum of Fine Art (European). Kolomenskoe, once a royal summer retreat, has the Church of the Ascension. The VDNKh is a symbol of the Stalinist era.

Novgorod One of Russia's oldest towns, centred on 15c Kremlin with St Sophia Cathedral (iconostasis, west door). Two other cathedrals: St Nicholas; St George. Museum of History, Architecture and Art has notable icons and other artefacts.

Petrodvorets Grand palace with numerous pavilions (Monplaisir) set in beautiful parkland interwoven by a system of fountains,

Melk, Österreich

cascades and waterways connected to the sea.

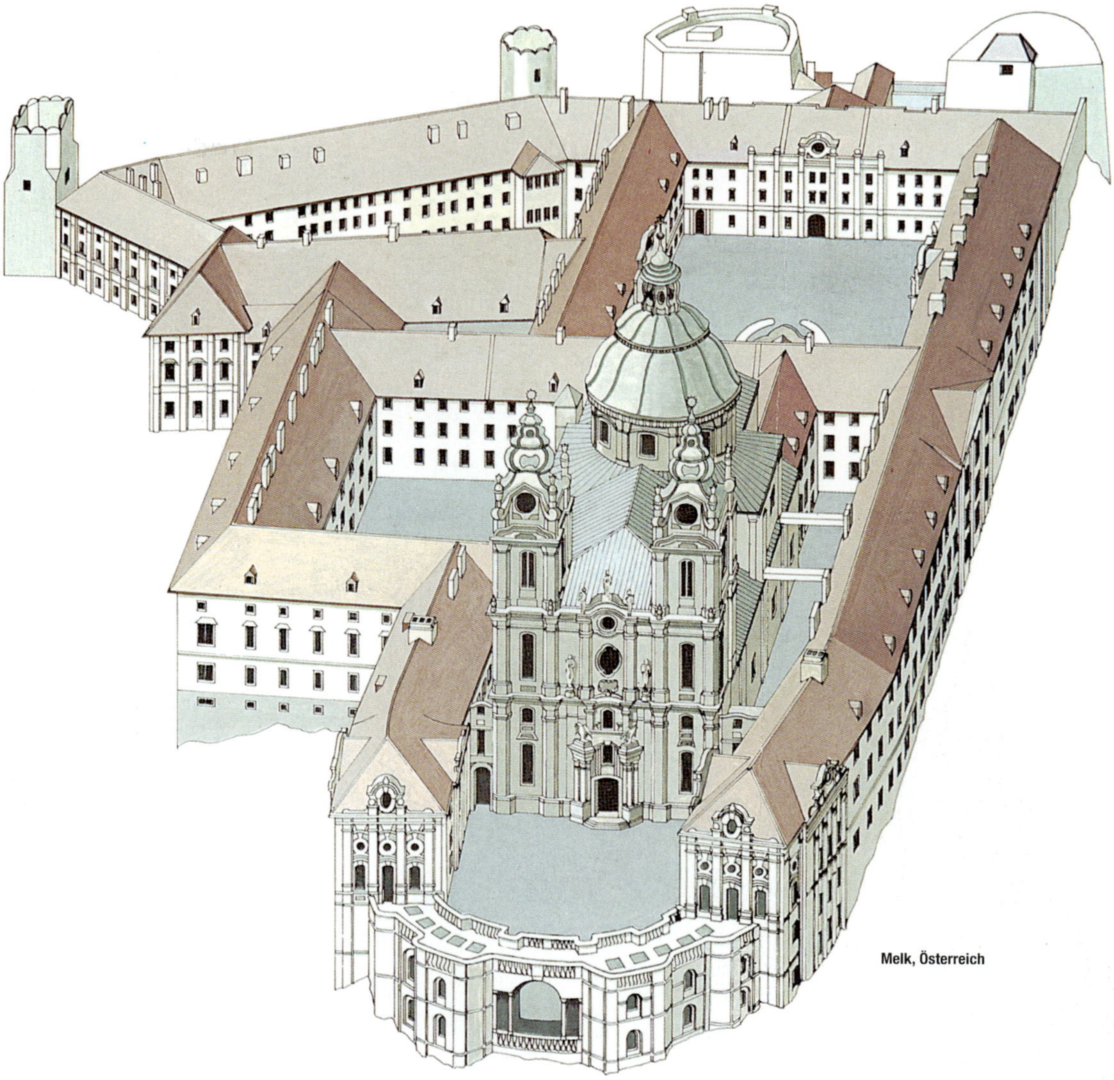

Pushkin (Tsarskoye Selo) Birthplace of Alexander Pushkin, with the vast Baroque Catherine Palace – splendid state apartments, beautiful gardens and lakes.

Sankt Peterburg Founded in 1703 with the SS Peter and Paul Fortress and its cathedral by Peter the Great, and functioning as seat of court and government until 1918. Many of the most famous sights are around elegant Nevski Prospekt. The Hermitage, one of the world's largest and finest art collections is housed in five buildings including the Baroque Winter and Summer palaces. The Mikhailovsky Palace houses the Russian Museum (Russian art). Other sights: neoclassical Admiralty; 19c St Isaac's Cathedral and St Kazan Cathedral; Vasilievsky Island with 18c Menshikov Palace; Alexander Nevsky Monastery; 18c Smolny Convent.

Sergiev Posad (Zagorsk) Trinity St Sergius monastery with 15c cathedral.

Schweiz *Switzerland*

Alpen (Swiss) The most popular Alpine region is the Berner Oberland with the town of Interlaken a starting point for exploring the large number of picturesque peaks (Jungfrau). The valleys of the Graubünden have famous ski resorts (Davos, St Moritz). Zermatt lies below the highest and most recognizable Swiss peak, the Matterhorn.

Basel Medieval university town with

Majolicahaus, Wien, Österreich

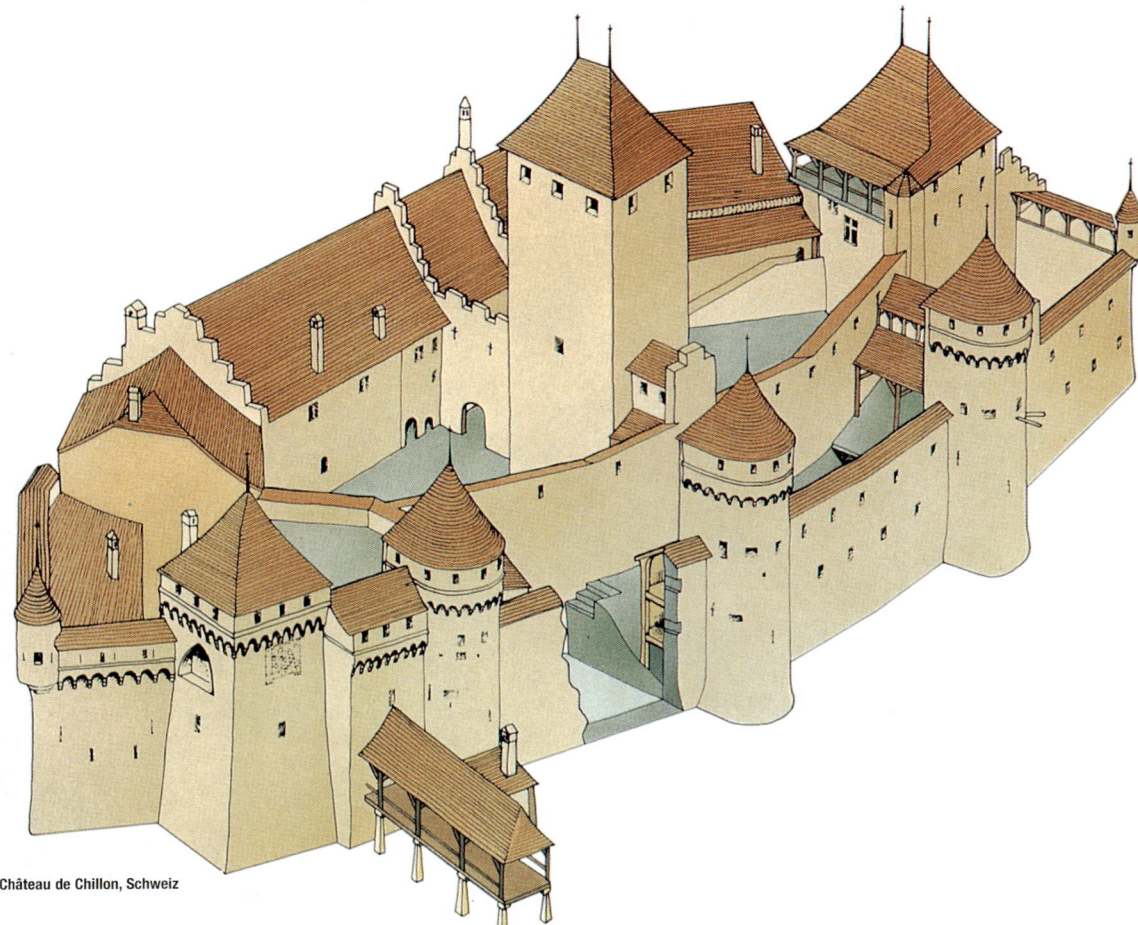

Château de Chillon, Schweiz

Romanesque-Gothic cathedral (tomb of Erasmus). Superb collections: Art Museum; Museum of Contemporary Art.

Bern Capital of Switzerland. Medieval centre has fountains, characteristic streets (Spital-gasse) and tower-gates. The Bärengraben is famed for its bears. Also: Gothic cathedral; good Fine Arts Museum.

Genève Wonderfully situated on the lake with the world's highest fountain. The historic area is centred on the Romanesque cathedral and Place du Bourg du Four. Excellent collections: Art and History Museum; Museum of Modern Art in 19c Petit Palais. On the lake shore: splendid medieval Château de Chillon.

Interlaken Starting point for excursions to the most delightful part of the Swiss Alps, the Bernese Oberland, with Grindelwald and Lauterbrunnen – one of the most thrilling valleys leading up to the ski resort of Wengen with views on the Jungfrau.

Luzern On the beautiful shores of Vierwald-stättersee, a charming medieval town of white houses on narrow streets and of wooden bridges (Kapellbrücke, Spreuer-brücke). It is centred on the Kornmarkt with the Renaissance Old Town Hall and Am Rhyn-Haus (Picasso collection).

Zürich Set on Zürichsee, the old quarter is around Niederdorf with 15c cathedral. Gothic Fraumünster has stained glass by Chagall. Museums: Swiss National Museum (history); Art Museum (old and modern masters); Bührle Foundation (Impressionists, Post-impressionists).

Shquipëria *Albania*

Berat Fascinating old town with picturesque Ottoman Empire buildings and traditional Balkan domestic architecture.

Tiranë Capital of Albania. Skanderbeg Square has main historic buildings. Also: 18c Haxhi Ethem Bey Mosque; Art Gallery (Albanian); National Museum of History. Nearby: medieval Krujë; Roman monuments.

Slovenija *Slovenia*

Istra (Slovene) Two town centres, Koper and Piran, with medieval and Renaissance squares and Baroque palaces. See also Croatia.

Julijske Alpe Wonderfully scenic section of the Alps with lakes (Bled, Bohinj), deep valleys (Planica, Vrata) and ski resorts (Kranjska Gora, Bohinjska Bistrica).

Karst Caves Numerous caves with huge galleries, extraordinary stalactites and stalagmites, and underground rivers. The most spectacular are Postojna (the most famous, with Predjamski Castle nearby) and Škocjan.

Ljubljana Capital of Slovenia. The old town, dominated by the castle (good views), is principally between Prešeren Square and Town Hall (15c, 18c), with the Three Bridges and colonnaded market. Many Baroque churches (cathedral, St Jacob, St Francis, Ursuline) and palaces (Bishop's Palace, Seminary, Gruber Palace). Also: 17c Križanke church and monastery complex; National Gallery and Modern Gallery show Slovene art.

Slovenska Republika *Slovakia*

Bratislava Capital of Slovakia, dominated by the castle (Slovak National Museum, good views). Old Town centred on the Main Square with Old Town Hall and Jesuit Church. Many 18–19c palaces (Mirbach Palace, Pálffy Palace, Primate's Palace), churches (Gothic cathedral, Corpus Christi Chapel) and muse-

ums (Slovak National Gallery).

Košice Charming old town with many Baroque and neoclassical buildings and Gothic cathedral.

Spišské Podhradie Region, east of the Tatry, full of picturesque medieval towns (Levoča, Kežmarok, Prešov) and architectural monuments (Spišský Castle).

Tatry Beautiful mountain region. Poprad is an old town with 19c villas. Starý Smokovec is a popular ski resort. See also Poland.

Suomi *Finland*

Finnish Lakes Area of outstanding natural beauty covering about one third of the country with thousands of lakes, of which Päi-jänne and Saimaa are the most important. Tampere, industrial centre of the region, has numerous museums, including the Sara Hildén Art Museum (modern). Savonlinna has the medieval Olavinlinna Castle. Kuopio has the Orthodox and Regional Museums.

Helsinki Capital of Finland. The 19c neoclassical town planning between the Esplanade and Senate Square includes the Lutheran cathedral. There is also a Russian Orthodox cathedral. The Constructivist Stockmann Department Store is the largest in Europe. The Main Train Station is Art Nouveau. Gracious 20c buildings in Mannerheimintie avenue include Finlandiatalo by Alvar Aalto. Many good museums: Art Museum of the Ateneum (19–20c); National Museum; Museum of Applied Arts; Helsinki City Art Museum (modern Finnish); Open Air Museum (vernacular architecture); 18c fortress of Suomenlinna has several museums.

Lappland (Finnish) Vast unspoiled rural area. Lappland is home to thousands of nomadic Sámi living in a traditional way. The capital, Rovaniemi, was rebuilt after WWII in

the form of reindeer antlers; museums show Sámi history and culture. Nearby is the Artic Circle with the famous Santa Claus Village. Inarim
is a centre of Sámi culture. See also Norway and Sweden.

Sverige *Sweden*

Abisko Popular resort in the Swedish part of Lapland set in an inspiring landscape of lakes and mountains.

Göteborg Largest port in Sweden, the historic centre has 17–18c Dutch architectural character (Kronhuset). The Art Museum has interesting Swedish works.

Gotland Island with Sweden's most popular beach resorts (Ljugarn) and unspoiled countryside with churches in Baltic Gothic style (Dahlem, Bunge). Visby is an pleasant walled medieval town.

Lappland (Swedish) Swedish part of Lapland with 18c Arvidsjaur the oldest preserved Sámi village. Jokkmokk is a Sámi cultural centre, Abisko a popular resort in fine scenery. Also Finland, Norway.

Lund Charming university city with medieval centre and a fine 12c Romanesque cathedral (14c astronomical clock, carved tombs).

Malmö Old town centre set among canals and parks dominated by a red-brick castle (museums) and a vast market square with Town Hall and Gothic Church of St Peter.

Mora Delightful village on the shores of Siljan Lake in the heart of the Dalarna region, home to folklore and traditional crafts.

Stockholm Capital of Sweden built on a number of islands. The Old Town is largely on three islands with 17–18c houses, Baroque Royal Castle (apartments and museums), Gothic cathedral, parliament. Riddarholms

church has tombs of the monarchy. Museums include: Modern Gallery (one of world's best modern collections); Nordiska Museet (cultural history); open-air Skansen (Swedish houses). Baroque Drottningholm Castle is the residence of the monarchy.

Swedish Lakes Beautiful region around the Vättern and Vänern Lakes. Siljan Lake is in the Dalarna region where folklore and crafts are preserved (Leksand, Mora, Rättvik).

Uppsala Appealing university town with a medieval centre around the massive Gothic cathedral.

Türkiye *Turkey*

Istanbul Divided by the spectcular Bosphorus, the stretch of water that separates Europe from Asia, the historic district is surrounded by the Golden Horn, Sea of Marmara and the 5c wall of Theodosius. Major sights: 6c Byzantine church of St Sophia (converted first to a mosque in 1453 and then a museum in 1934); 15c Topkapi Palace; treasury and Archaeological Museum; 17c Blue Mosque; 19c Bazaar; 16c Süleymaniye Mosque; 12c Kariye Camii; European district with Galata Tower and 19c Dolmabahçe Palace.

Ukraina *Ukraine*

Kyïv Capital of Ukraine, known for its cathedral (11c, 17c) with Byzantine frescoes and mosaics. The Monastery of the Caves has churches, monastic buildings and catacombs.

United Kingdom

Antrim Coast Spectacular coast with diverse scenery of glens (Glenarm, Glenariff), cliffs (Murlough Bay) and the famous Giant's Causeway, consisting of some 40,000 basalt columns. Carrickefergus Castle is the largest and best-preserved Norman castle in Ireland.

Bath Elegant spa town with notable 18c architecture: Circus, Royal Crescent, Pulteney Bridge, Assembly Rooms; Pump Room. Also: well-preserved Roman baths; superb Perpendicular Gothic Bath Abbey. Nearby: Elizabethan Longleat House; exceptional 18c landscaped gardens at Stourhead.

Belfast Capital of Northern Ireland. Sights: Donegall Square with 18c Town Hall; neo-Romanesque Protestant cathedral; University Square; Ulster Museum (European painting).

Brighton Resort with a sea-front of Georgian, Regency and Victorian buildings with the Palace Pier, and an old town of narrow lanes. The main sight is the 19c Royal Pavilion in Oriental styles.

Bristol Old port city with the fascinating Floating Harbour. Major sights include Gothic 13–14c Church of St Mary Redcliffe and 19c Clifton Suspension Bridge.

Caernarfon Town dominated by a magnificent 13c castle, one of a series built by Edward I in Wales (others include Harlech, Conwy, Beaumaris, Caerphilly).

Cambridge City with university founded in the early 13c. Peterhouse (1284) is the oldest college. Most famous colleges were founded in 14–16c: Queen's, King's (with the superb Perpendicular Gothic 15–16c King's College Chapel), St John's (with famous 19c Bridge of Sighs), Trinity, Clare, Gonville and Caius, Magdalene. Museums: excellent Fitzwilliam Museum (classical, medieval, old masters). Kettle's Yard (20c British).

Canterbury Medieval city and old centre of Christianity. The Norman-Gothic cathedral has many sights and was a major medieval pilgrimage site (as related in Chaucer's *Canterbury Tales*). St Augustine, sent to convert the English in 597, founded St Augustine's Abbey, now in ruins.

Cardiff Capital of Wales, most famous for its medieval castle, restored 19c in Greek, Gothic and Oriental styles. Also: National Museum and Gallery.

Chatsworth One of the richest aristocratic country houses in England (largely 17c) set in a large landscaped park. The palatial interior has some 175 richly furnished rooms and a major art collection.

Chester Charming medieval city with complete walls. The Norman-Gothic cathedral has several abbey buildings.

Cornish Coast Scenic landscape of cliffs and sandy beaches with picturesque villages (Fowey, Mevagissey). St Ives has the Tate Gallery with work of the St Ives Group. The island of St Michael's Mount holds a priory.

Durham Historic city with England's finest Norman cathedral and a castle, both placed majestically on a rock above the river.

Edinburgh Capital of Scotland, built on volcanic hills. The medieval Old Town is dominated by the castle set high on a volcanic rock (Norman St Margaret's Chapel, state apartments, Crown Room). Holyrood House (15c and 17c) has lavishly decorated state apartments and the ruins of Holyrood Abbey (remains of Scottish monarchs). The 15c cathedral has the Crown Spire and Thistle Chapel. The New Town has good Georgian architecture (Charlotte Square, Georgian House). Excellent museums: Scottish National Portrait Gallery, National Gallery of Scotland; Scottish National Gallery of Modern Art.

Glamis Castle In beautiful, almost flat landscaped grounds, 14c fortress, rebuilt 17c, gives a fairy-tale impression.

Glasgow Scotland's largest city, with centre around George Square and 13–15c Gothic cathedral. The Glasgow School of Art is the masterpiece of Charles Rennie Mackintosh.

Fine art collections: Glasgow Museum and Art Gallery; Hunterian Gallery; Burrell Collection.

Hadrian's Wall Built to protect the northernmost border of the Roman Empire in the 2c AD, the walls originally extended some 120km with castles every mile and 16 forts. Best-preserved walls around Hexam; forts at Housesteads and Chesters.

Lake District Beautiful landscape of lakes (Windermere, Coniston) and England's high peaks (Scafell Pike, Skiddaw, Old Man), famous for its poets, particularly Wordsworth.

Leeds Castle One of the oldest and most romantic English castles, standing in the middle of a lake. Most of the present appearance dates from 19c.

Lincoln Old city perched on a hill with narrow streets, majestically dominated by the Norman-Gothic cathedral and castle.

Loch Ness In the heart of the Highlands, the lake forms part of the scenic Great Glen running from Inverness to Fort William. Famous as home of the fabled Loch Ness Monster (exhibition at Drumnadrochit). Nearby: ruins of 14–16c Urquhart Castle.

London Capital of UK and Europe's largest city. To the east of the medieval heart of the city – now the largely modern financial district and known as the City of London – is the Tower of London (11c White Tower, Crown Jewels) and 1880s Tower Bridge. The popular heart of the city and its entertainment is the West End, around Piccadilly Circus, Leicester Square and Trafalgar Square (Nelson's Column). Many sights of political and royal power: Whitehall (Banqueting House, 10 Downing Street, Horse Guards); Neo-Gothic Palace of Westminster (Houses of Parliament) with Big Ben; The Mall leading to Buckingham Palace (royal residence, famous ceremony of the Changing of the Guard). Numerous churches include: 13–16c Gothic Westminster Abbey (many tombs, Henry VII's Chapel); Wren's Baroque St Paul's Cathedral,

St Mary-le-Bow, spire of St Bride's, St Stephen Walbrook. Museums of world fame: British Museum (prehistory, oriental and classical antiquity, medieval); Victoria and Albert Museum (decorative arts); National Gallery (old masters to 19c); National Portrait Gallery (historic and current British portraiture); Tate – Britain and Modern; Science Museum; Natural History Museum. Madame Tussaud's waxworks museum is hugely popular. Other sights include: Kensington Palace; Greenwich with Old Royal Observatory (Greenwich meridian), Baroque Royal Naval College, Palladian Queen's House; Tudor Hampton Court Palace; Syon House. Nearby: Windsor Castle (art collection, St George's Chapel).

Longleat One of the earliest and finest Elizabethan palaces in England. The palace is richly decorated. Some of the grounds have been turned into a pleasure park, with the Safari Park, the first of its kind outside Africa.

Norwich Medieval quarter has half-timbered houses. 15c castle keep houses a museum and gallery. Many medieval churches include the Norman-Gothic cathedral..

Oxford Old university city. Earliest colleges date from 13c: University College; Balliol; Merton. 14–16c colleges include: New College; Magdalen; Christ Church (perhaps the finest). Other buildings: Bodleian Library; Radcliffe Camera; Sheldonian Theatre; cathedral. Good museums: Ashmolean Museum (antiquity to 20c); Museum of Modern Art; Christ Church Picture Gallery (14–17c). Nearby: outstanding 18c Blenheim Palace.

Radcliffe Camera (cutaway), Oxford, United Kingdom

Petworth House (17c) with one of the finest country-house art collections (old masters), set in a huge landscaped park.

Salisbury Pleasant old city with a magnificent 13c cathedral built in an unusually unified Gothic style. Nearby: Wilton House.

Stonehenge Some 4000 years old, one of the most famous and haunting Neolithic monuments in Europe. Many other Neolithic sites are nearby.

Stourhead Early 18c palace famous for its grounds, one of the finest examples of neoclassical landscaped gardening, consisting of a lake surrounded by numerous temples.

Stratford-upon-Avon Old town of Tudor and Jacobean half-timbered houses, famed as the birth and burial place of William Shakespeare. Nearby: Warwick Castle.

Wells Charming city with beautiful 12–16c cathedral (west facade, scissor arches, chapter house, medieval clock). Also Bishop's Palace; Vicar's Close.

Winchester Historic city with 11–16c cathedral (tombs of early English kings). Also: 13c Great Hall; Winchester College; St Cross almshouses.

York Attractive medieval city surrounded by well-preserved walls with magnificent Gothic 13–15c Minster. Museums: York City Art Gallery (14–19c); Jorvik Viking Centre. Nearby: Castle Howard.

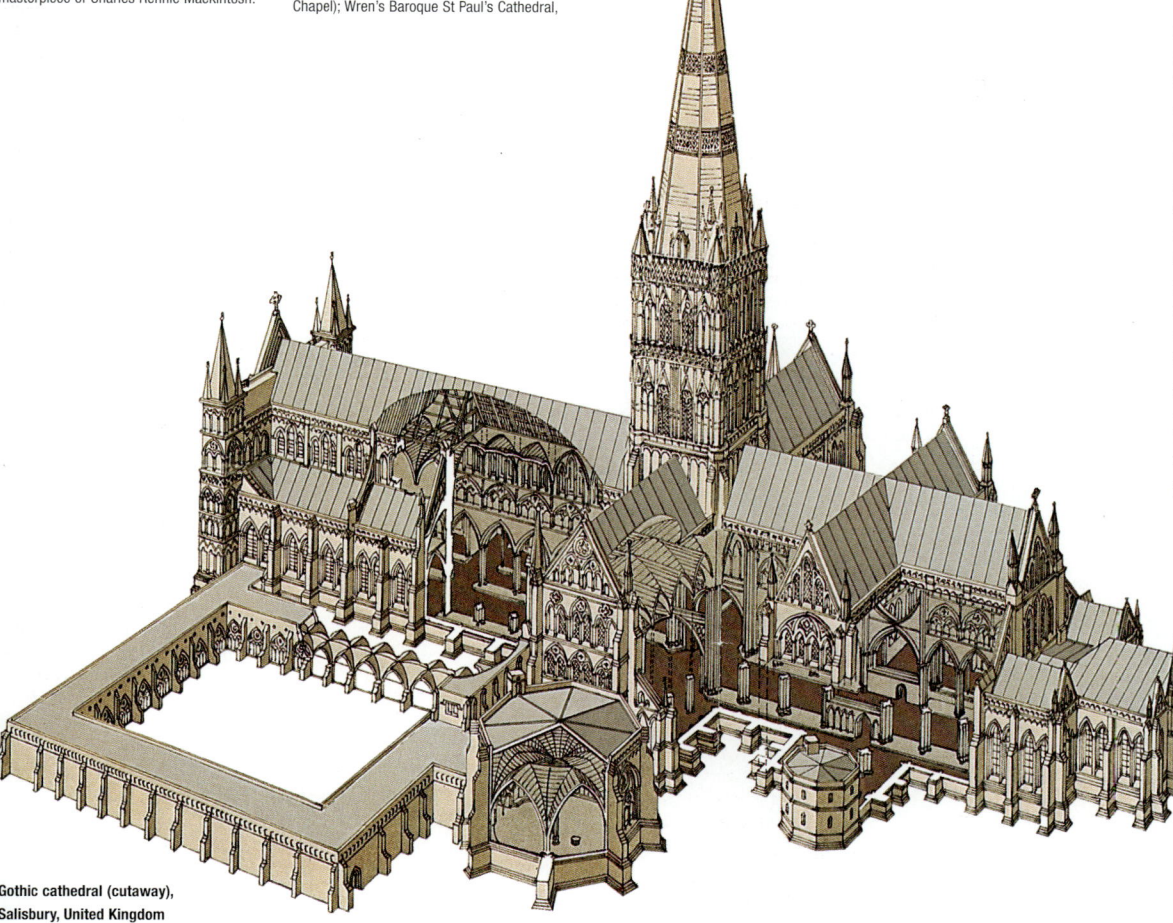

Gothic cathedral (cutaway), Salisbury, United Kingdom

History and culture of Europe

The following definitions describe some of the key terms in the timeline below.

Aegean civilization Bronze Age cultures, chiefly Minoan (on Crete, at its height c.1700BC–c.1100BC) and Mycenaean (at its height c.1580BC–c.1120BC).

art deco Style characterized by the non-functional use of streamlined industrial designs. Flat, bright colours were often employed in geometric decoration.

art nouveau Style most influential in the dec-orative arts. It was richly ornamental and asymmetrical, with plant and animal motifs and whirling patterns of sinuous lines.

baroque Style of art and architecture which at its best was a blend of light, colour, and movement calculated to overwhelm through emotional appeal. Buildings were heavily decorated with ornament and free-standing sculpture. Baroque became increasingly complex and florid. The term is often used to describe the period as well as the style.

Byzantine Empire Christian, Greek-speaking, Eastern Roman Empire that outlasted the Western Empire by nearly 1000 years. The area of the Byzantine Empire varied greatly, and its history from c.600 was marked by continual military crisis and recovery.

Carolingian period Cultural revival in France and Italy beginning under the encouragement of Charlemagne, who gathered notable educators and artists to his court at Aachen.

Counter-Reformation Revival of the Roman Catholic Church in Europe, beginning as a reaction to the Reformation. The reforms were largely conservative, trying to remove many of the abuses of the late medieval church and win new prestige for the papacy. The Council of Trent (1545-63) generated many of the key decisions and doctrines.

Dark Ages Term that at one time was used to imply cultural and economic backward-ness, but now is used to indicate ignorance of the period due to lack of historical evidence.

Enlightenment (Age of Reason) Philosophical movement that influenced many aspects of 18th-century society. It was inspired by the scientific and philosophical revolutions of the late 17th century and stressed the use of reason and the rational side of human nature.

Franks Germanic people who settled in the region of the Rhine in the 3rd century. Under Clovis I they built the Merovingian Empire in Gaul. This became divided, but was reunited by the Carolingians. The partition of this empire is the origin of Germany and France.

Gothic Architecture and painting character-ized by the pointed arch and ribbed vault. Religious in inspiration, its greatest expres-sion was the cathedral. Gothic sculpture was elegant and more realistic than Romanesque. The Gothic style was also well expressed in manuscript illumination.

Greece, ancient The early period is known as Archaic. Classical Greece, from the defeat of the second Persian invasion in 479BC to

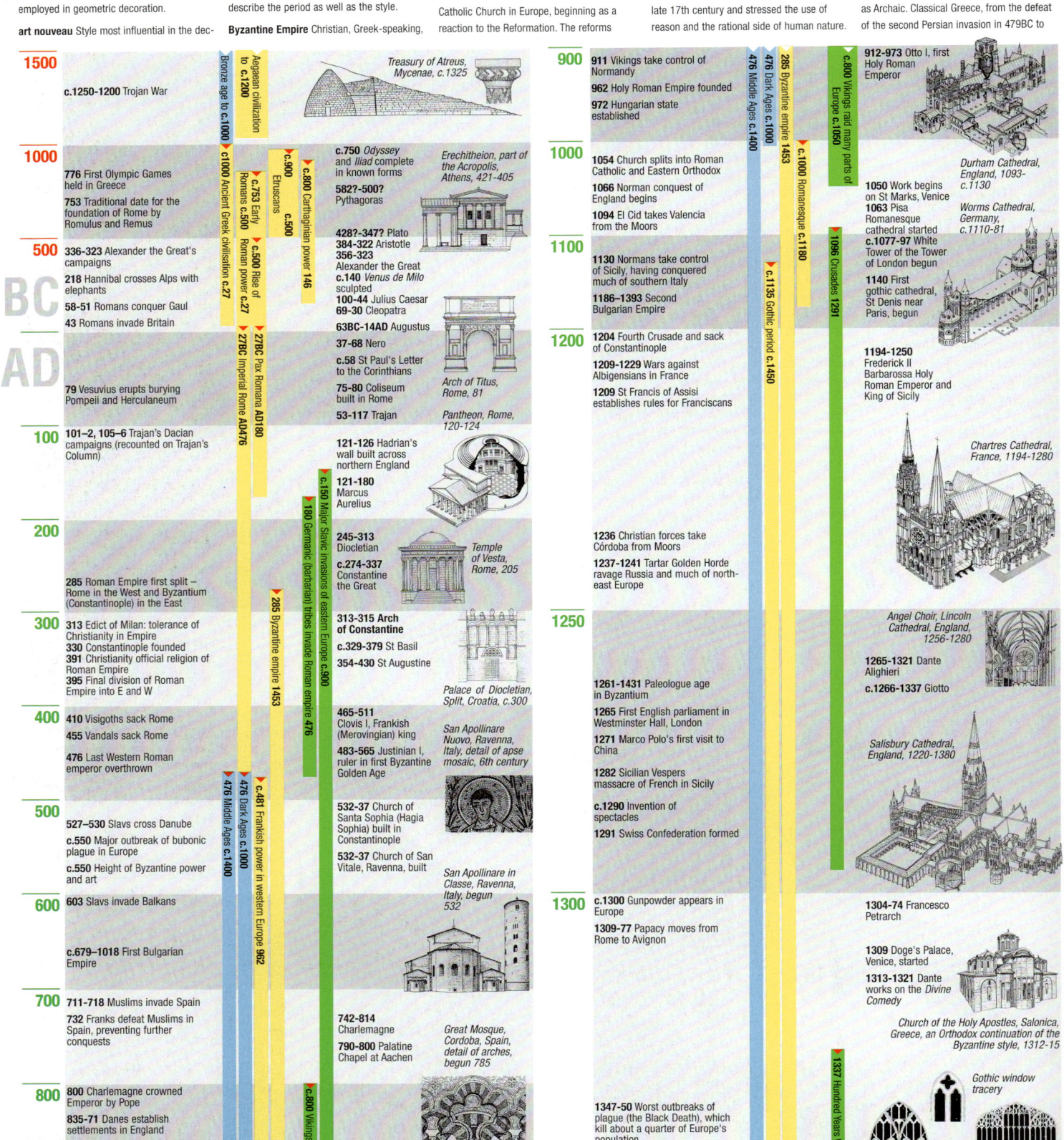

1500

c.1250-1200 Trojan War

Bronze age to c.1000

Aegean civilization to c.1200

Treasury of Atreus, Mycenae, c.1325

1000

776 First Olympic Games held in Greece

753 Traditional date for the foundation of Rome by Romulus and Remus

c1000 Ancient Greek civilization c.27

c.900 Etruscans

c.753 Early Romans c.500

c.800 Carthaginian power 146

c.750 *Odyssey* and *Iliad* complete in known forms

582?-500? Pythagoras

Erechtheion, part of the Acropolis, Athens, 421-405

500

336-323 Alexander the Great's campaigns

218 Hannibal crosses Alps with elephants

58-51 Romans conquer Gaul

43 Romans invade Britain

c.500 Rise of Roman power c.27

428?-347? Plato
384-322 Aristotle
356-323 Alexander the Great
c.140 *Venus de Milo* sculpted
100-44 Julius Caesar
69-30 Cleopatra
63BC-14AD Augustus
37-68 Nero
c.58 St Paul's Letter to the Corinthians
75-80 Coliseum built in Rome
53-117 Trajan

BC
AD

79 Vesuvius erupts burying Pompeii and Herculaneum

27BC Pax Romana AD180

27BC Imperial Rome AD476

Arch of Titus, Rome, 81

Pantheon, Rome, 120-124

100

101–2, 105–6 Trajan's Dacian campaigns (recounted on Trajan's Column)

121-126 Hadrian's wall built across northern England

121-180 Marcus Aurelius

c.150 Major Slavic invasions of eastern Europe c.900

180 Germanic (barbarian) tribes invade Roman empire 476

200

285 Byzantine empire 1453

245-313 Diocletian

c.274-337 Constantine the Great

Temple of Vesta, Rome, 205

300

285 Roman Empire first split – Rome in the West and Byzantium (Constantinople) in the East

313 Edict of Milan: tolerance of Christianity in Empire
330 Constantinople founded
391 Christianity official religion of Roman Empire
395 Final division of Roman Empire into E and W

313-315 Arch of Constantine

c.329-379 St Basil
354-430 St Augustine

Palace of Diocletian, Split, Croatia, c.300

400

410 Visigoths sack Rome
455 Vandals sack Rome
476 Last Western Roman emperor overthrown

476 Middle Ages c.1400

476 Dark Ages c.1000

c.481 Frankish power in western Europe 962

465-511 Clovis I, Frankish (Merovingian) king

483-565 Justinian I, ruler in first Byzantine Golden Age

San Apollinare Nuovo, Ravenna, Italy, detail of apse mosaic, 6th century

500

527–530 Slavs cross Danube
c.550 Major outbreak of bubonic plague in Europe
c.550 Height of Byzantine power and art

532-37 Church of Santa Sophia (Hagia Sophia) built in Constantinople

532-37 Church of San Vitale, Ravenna, built

600

603 Slavs invade Balkans

c.679–1018 First Bulgarian Empire

San Apollinare in Classe, Ravenna, Italy, begun 532

700

711-718 Muslims invade Spain
732 Franks defeat Muslims in Spain, preventing further conquests

742-814 Charlemagne
790-800 Palatine Chapel at Aachen

Great Mosque, Cordoba, Spain, detail of arches, begun 785

800

800 Charlemagne crowned Emperor by Pope
835-71 Danes establish settlements in England
c.860 Vikings raiders reach Mediterranean

c.800 Vikings raid...

900

911 Vikings take control of Normandy
962 Holy Roman Empire founded
972 Hungarian state established

476 Middle Ages c.1400

476 Dark Ages c.1000

285 Byzantine empire 1453

c.800 Vikings raid many parts of Europe c.1050

1000

1054 Church splits into Roman Catholic and Eastern Orthodox
1066 Norman conquest of England begins
1094 El Cid takes Valencia from the Moors

c.1000 Romanesque c.1180

c912-973 Otto I, first Holy Roman Emperor

Durham Cathedral, England, 1093-c.1130

1100

1130 Normans take control of Sicily, having conquered much of southern Italy
1186–1393 Second Bulgarian Empire

c.1135 Gothic period c.1450

1096 Crusades 1291

1050 Work begins on St Marks, Venice
1063 Pisa Romanesque cathedral started

Worms Cathedral, Germany, c.1110-81

c.1077-97 White Tower of the Tower of London begun
1140 First gothic cathedral, St Denis near Paris, begun

1200

1204 Fourth Crusade and sack of Constantinople
1209-1229 Wars against Albigensians in France
1209 St Francis of Assisi establishes rules for Franciscans

1194-1250 Frederick II Barbarossa Holy Roman Emperor and King of Sicily

Chartres Cathedral, France, 1194-1280

1236 Christian forces take Córdoba from Moors
1237-1241 Tartar Golden Horde ravage Russia and much of north-east Europe

1250

1261-1431 Paleologue age in Byzantium
1265 First English parliament in Westminster Hall, London
1271 Marco Polo's first visit to China
1282 Sicilian Vespers massacre of French in Sicily
c.1290 Invention of spectacles
1291 Swiss Confederation formed

Angel Choir, Lincoln Cathedral, England, 1256-1280

1265-1321 Dante Alighieri
c.1266-1337 Giotto

Salisbury Cathedral, England, 1220-1380

1300

c.1300 Gunpowder appears in Europe
1309-77 Papacy moves from Rome to Avignon

1304-74 Francesco Petrarch

1309 Doge's Palace, Venice, started
1313-1321 Dante works on the *Divine Comedy*

Church of the Holy Apostles, Salonica, Greece, an Orthodox continuation of the Byzantine style, 1312-15

1337 Hundred Years War...

1347-50 Worst outbreaks of plague (the Black Death), which kill about a quarter of Europe's population

Gothic window tracery

the death of Alexander the Great in 323BC, is traditionally regarded as the birthplace of Western civilization. Many ideas in art, literature, philosophy and science emerged. Hellenistic Greece is the period between classical Greece and Imperial Rome, distinguished by scientific advances and by more elaborate and naturalistic styles in the visual arts.

High Renaissance Brief period regarded as the height of Italian (particularly Roman) Renaissance art, brought to an end by the sack of Rome by the troops of Charles V.

Historicism, 19th-century Revival of past architectural styles. Ancient Greek and Gothic forms predominated, though buildings were constructed in a wide range of styles, including Renaissance, Romanesque and baroque.

Holy Roman Empire Empire centred on Germany, which aimed to echo ancient Rome. It was founded when Otto I was crowned in Rome (some date it from the coronation of Charlemagne). The Emperor claimed to be the worldly sovereign of Christendom ruling in co-operation with the Pope. After 1648 the Empire became a loose confederation, containing hundreds of virtually independent states. It was abolished by Napoleon I.

Imperial Rome Period of Roman history starting when Augustus declared himself emperor, ending the Roman republic. Most of the empire had already been conquered.

impressionism French art movement with the aim of producing more spontaneous, less calculated work. Impressionists explored the possibilities of painting outdoors and the effects of light. Impressionism became widely influential from the late 1880s.

international gothic Style of painting characterized by naturalistic detail, elegant elongated figures and jewel-like colour.

mannerism Loose term applied to the art and architecture of Italy between the High Renaissance and the Baroque. A self-conscious style, it aimed to exceed earlier work in emotional impact. Painting is characterized by elongated figures in distorted poses, often using lurid colours.

Middle Ages Period between the disintegration of the Roman Empire and the Renaissance. The Middle Ages were, above all, the age of the Christian church and of the social structure known as the feudal system.

modern art Loose term that describes painting and sculpture that breaks from traditions going back to the Renaissance. There have been many movements, including fauvism, cubism, surrealism and expressionism.

neoclassicism Movement in art and architecture that grew out of the Enlightenment. Exponents admired and imitated the order and clarity of ancient Greek and Roman art.

Pax Romana Period when ancient Rome was so powerful that its authority could not be challenged by outside forces and peace was maintained in the empire.

Reformation Sixteenth-century movement that sought reform of the Catholic Church and resulted in the development of Protestantism. The starting date is often given as 1517, when Martin Luther nailed his 95 theses to the door of the Schlosskirche in Wittenburg, Germany, protesting against abuses of the clergy. In Zurich, the Reformation was led by Ulrich Zwingli and then by John Calvin.

Renaissance Period of rapid cultural and economic development. An important element in this was humanism, which involved a

---

1350

1353 First Ottoman (Turkish) invasion of Europe

1378-81 War of Chioggia – Venice takes control of Mediterranean

1378-1417 Great Schism in the Papacy between Rome and Avignon

1389 Battle of Kosovo - Turks gain firm foothold in the Balkans

476 Middle Ages c.1400 · c.1135 Gothic period c.1450 · 285 Byzantine empire 1453 · c.1370 International Gothic style c.1450 · 1337 Hundred Years War between England and France 1453

1353 Giovanni Boccaccio writes the *Decameron*

1377-1446 Filippo Brunelleschi
1378-1455 Lorenzo Ghiberti
1386-1466 Donatello
1387/1400-55 Fra Angelico
c.1390-1441 Jan van Eyck
1386-1400 Geoffrey Chaucer's *Canterbury Tales*

Church of the Holy Cross, Schwabish-Gemund, Germany, begun c.1350

1400

c.1400 onward Full plate armour begins to be used instead of chain main

1414 Discovery of Vitruvius' ancient treatise on architecture

1415 Introduction of oil paints by Jan and Hubert van Eyck in the Netherlands

1434-94 Medici family gain power in Florence

1431 Joan of Arc executed at Rouen

c.1440 Gutenberg invents moveable type allowing large-scale printing

c.1400 Renaissance c.1600

c.1400-1464 Roger van der Weyden
1401-c1428 Masaccio
1404-72 Leon Battista Alberti
1415-92 Piero della Francesca
c.1420 Work begins on dome of Florence Cathedral
1434 Van Eyck paints the *Arnolfini Marriage*
c.1445-1510 Sandro Botticelli

Foundling Hospital, Florence, Italy, from 1429

Town Hall, Louvain, Belgium, 1448-63

1450

1453 Turks capture Constantinople

1479 Aragon and Castile unite to become Spain

1479 Start of Spanish Inquisition

1492 Christopher Columbus reaches the Americas; Spanish and Portuguese colonization begins

1494 Spanish take Granada, the last Moorish stronghold

1499 Portuguese discover sea route to India

c.1450 Late Gothic period c.1550 · 1495 High Renaissance 1527 · c.1480 Great age of European discovery c.1580

c.1450-1516 Hieronymus Bosch
1452-1519 Leonardo da Vinci
1466?-1536 Erasmus of Rotterdam
1471-1528 Albrecht Dürer
1475-1564 Michelangelo Buonarotti
1473-1543 Nicolaus Copernicus
1483-1512 Raphael Sanzio
c.1487-1576 Titian
1492/9-1546 Giuliano Romano
1497/8-1543 Hans Holbein the Younger
c.1480 Botticelli paints *The Birth of Venus*

St Georges Chapel, Windsor Castle, England, 1481-1528

St Maria Novella, Florence, Italy, from 1458

1500

1506 Antique statue of the Laocoon discovered near Rome, sparking increased interest in the forms of Hellenistic sculpture

1517 Martin Luther publishes his 95 Theses in Wittenberg

1522 Magellan's expedition completes circumnavigation of the globe

1527 Sack of Rome by Imperial troops

1541 John Calvin founds church in Geneva

1543 Copernicus publishes idea that Earth revolves around the Sun

1517 Reformation c.1600 · c.1520 Mannerism c.1610

1500 Bosch paints *The Garden of Earthly Delights*
1503 Leonardo da Vinci paints *Mona Lisa*
1504 Michelangelo sculpts *David*
1506 St Peter's, Rome, begun on Boromini's plan
1508-1512 Michelangelo paints Sistine Chapel
1508-80 Andrea Palladio
1513 Machiavelli's *The Prince*
1541-1614 El Greco
1547 Ivan IV (the Terrible) Tsar of Russia

Palazzo Strozzi, Florence, Italy, from 1490

Bibliotecha Laurenziana, door to library, Florence, Italy, from 1524

1550

1545-63 Council of Trent
1562 Netherlands revolt against Spanish rule
1562-98 Wars of Religion in France; end with religious tolerance under Edict of Nantes
1557-82 Livonia War between Sweden and its Baltic neighbours
1571 Ottoman Turk navy defeated by Holy League at Battle of Lepanto
1572 St Bartholomew's Day Massacre in Paris
1572-1648 Dutch revolt against Spanish rule
1581 Independence of United Provinces (Netherlands)
1588 English fleet defeats Spanish Armada

c.1400 Renaissance c.1600 · 1545 Counter Reformation 1648 · c.1520 Mannerism c.1610 · c.1480 Great age of European discovery c.1580

1558-1603 Elizabeth I Queen of England
1564-1616 William Shakespeare
1571-1610 Michelangelo Merisi da Caravaggio
1573-1652 Inigo Jones
1577-1640 Peter Paul Rubens
1581/5-1666 Frans Hals
1594-1665 Nicolas Poussin
1598-1680 Gianlorenzo Bernini
1599-1660 Diego Velazquez
1599-1641 Sir Anthony Van Dyck
1598-1668 François Mansart

Palace of Charles V, Granada, Spain, detail, begun 1526

S. Georgio Maggiore, Venice, Italy

1600

1607 First English colony in North America at Jamestown
1618 Defenestration of Prague starts Thirty Year's War
1630 Sweden enters Thirty Year's War
1635 Peace of Prague ends German involvement in Thirty Years' War
1635 France enters Thirty Years' War
1642-5 English Civil War
1648 Treaty of Westphalia ends Thirty Years' War
1649 Execution of Charles I of England

c.1600 Baroque c.1750 · 1618 Thirty Years' War 1648

1600-92 Claude Lorraine
1603 *Hamlet* written by Shakespeare
1606-69 Rembrandt van Rijn
1624 Frans Hals paints *The Laughing Cavalier*
1624 Palace of Versailles started
1627-1725 Peter I, the Great, of Russia
1632-75 Jan Vermeer
1632-1723 Sir Christopher Wren
1633 Galileo tried for heresy
1642 Rembrandt paints *The Night Watch*

Mauritzhuis, The Hague, Netherlands, c.1633

1650

1652-3, 1665-7, 1672-4 1st, 2nd and 3rd Anglo-Dutch wars
1660 Restoration of English monarchy
1666 Great Fire of London
1671 Spain and United Provinces ally against France
1671 Hungarian Revolt and Reign of Terror
1682 Spain and Holy Roman Empire ally against France
1683 Turks besiege Vienna
1685 Edict of Nantes revoked and Huguenots leave France
1689 English Parliament passes Bill of Rights
1699 Habsburgs recover Hungary from Turks

1661 Louis XIV takes power in France
1667 John Milton, *Paradise Lost*
1667-70 Main façade of Louvre
1687 Isaac Newton publishes *Principia Mathematica*
1696 Peter I, the Great, becomes Tsar of Russia
1696-1770 Giovanni Battista Tiepolo

S. Carlo alle Quatro Fontane, Rome, Italy, detail, begun 1633

Troja Palace, Prague, Czech Republic, 1679-96

1700

1700-21 Great Northern War between Sweden and Russia and its allies
1702-1713 War of Spanish Succession (ends with Peace of Utrecht)
1703 St Petersburg founded
1704 "Grand Alliance" of Holland, England and Austria defeat France at Blenheim
1707 Act of Union between England and Scotland
1730 Methodism founded by John and Charles Wesley
1740-86 Prussia under Frederick the Great
1740-8 War of Austrian Succession

c.1700 Rococo c.1750 · c.1700 Age of Enlightenment 1789 · c.1730 Gothic Revival c.1780

1719 Daniel Defoe, *Robinson Crusoe*
1720 J.S.Bach *Brandenburg Concertos*
1726 Jonathan Swift, *Gulliver's Travels*
1728-92 Robert Adam
1742 Handel's *Messiah*
1746-1828 Goya
1748-1825 Jacques-Louis David
1749-1832 Johann Wolfgang von Goethe

Baroque interior, St John Nepomuk, Munich, Germany, 1732-46

Amalienburg Palace, near Munich, Rococo detail and decoration, 1734

1750

1755 Earthquake destroys Lisbon

1756-63 Britain defeats France in Seven Years' War (ends with Treaty of Paris)

1772 Partition of Poland between Austria and Russia

1776 Britain's North American colonies declare indepence (gained 1783)

1783 Montgolfier brothers ascend in hot-air balloon

1789-99 French Revolution

1797 Fall of Venetian Republic to forces of Napoleon

1799 Napoleon Bonaparte seizes power in France

1800

1803-1815 Napoleonic Wars

1805 Battle of Trafalgar

1806 End of Holy Roman Empire

1812 Napoleon invades Russia

1815 Battle of Waterloo

1820-28 War of Greek Independence

c.1825 Joseph Niépce produces first known photograph

1830 July Revolution in France

1830 Independence of Belgium from Netherlands

1845 Irish potato famine

1848 Revolutions all round Europe, particularly France, Germany, Hungary, Italy

1850

1853-6 Crimean War

1860 Garibaldi's Expedition of the Thousand leads to founding of Kingdom of Italy (1861)

1870-1 Franco-Prussian War

1871-1940 Third Republic in France

1885 Karl Benz in Germany builds first car with internal combustion engine

1893 Lumiére brothers invent cinematograph

1897-9 Marconi demonstrates radio communication

1900

1903 Wright brothers make first powered flight

1914-1918 World War I

1917 Russian Revolution

1919 Treaty of Versailles

1922 USSR established

1922 Mussolini in power in Italy

1923 Hitler leads Munich Putsch

1929 Wall Street Crash heralds Great Depression of the 1930s

1933 Hitler becomes Chancellor of Germany

1936-39 Spanish Civil War

1939 Germany invades Poland, provoking World War II

Vertical timeline bars:
c.1730 Gothic Revival c.1780
c.1750 Neoclassicism c.1810
c.1760 Greek Revival c.1830
c.1700 Age of Enlightenment 1789
c.1760 Industrial Revolution c.1900
c.1730 Romanticism c.1850
c.1800 Historicism in architecture c.1900
from 1863 Modern art
c.1870 Impressionism c.1890
1867 Austro-Hungarian Empire 1918
c.1880 Height of European Imperialism 1914
c.1890 Art Nouveau 1914
from c.1905 Modernism in architecture
from c.1910 Abstract art
c.1925 Art Deco 1939

1762-96 Catherine the Great Empress of Russia

1769-1821 Napoleon Bonaparte

1775-1851 JMW Turner

1780-1867 Jean Auguste Dominique Ingres

1781 Kant *Critique of Pure Reason*

1798 Wordsworth and Coleridge *Lyrical Ballads*

1799 Beethoven's First Symphony

Kedleston Hall, England, 1757-70

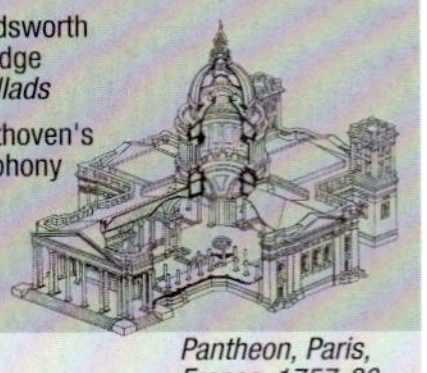

1821 Constable *The Hay Wain*

1830-40 Helsinki Cathedral

1832-83 Edouard Manet

1834-96 William Morris

1834-1917 Edgar Degas

1839 Dickens *Oliver Twist*

1839-1906 Paul Cezanne

1840-1917 Auguste Rodin

1840-1926 Claude Monet

1841-1919 Pierre Auguste Renoir

1848 Marx and Engels *Communist Manifesto*

1848-55 Pre-Raphaelites (style continues later)

Pantheon, Paris, France, 1757-80

Crystal Palace, London England, 1851

1848-1903 Paul Gauguin

1853 Verdi *La Traviata*

1853-90 Vincent van Gogh

1859 Charles Darwin *The Origin of Species*

1859-91 Georges Seurat

1863 Manet paints *Dejeuner sur l'Herbe*, often regarded as the first modern painting

1863-1944 Edvard Munch

1865-69 Tolstoy *War and Peace*

1867 Marx *Das Kapital*

1869-1954 Henri Matisse

1874 First Impressionist exhibition in Paris

1878-1953 Stalin

1875 Bizet *Carmen*

1898-1976 Alvar Aalto

Votivkirche, Vienna 1856-79

1900 Sigmund Freud *The Interpretation of Dreams*

1902 Edvard Munch *The Scream* exhibited

1904-89 Salvador Dali

1905 Einstein publishes special theory of relativity

1907 First cubist exhibition

1913 Stravinsky *The Rite of Spring*

1916 Einstein publishes general theory of relativity

1919 Bauhaus movement founded

1932 Aldous Huxley *Brave New World*

1937 Pablo Picasso *Guernica*

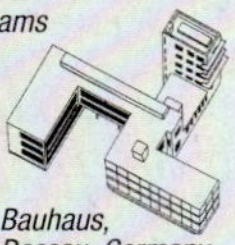

Bauhaus, Dessau, Germany, 1925

Gruntvig Church, Copenhagen, Denmark, 1920-40

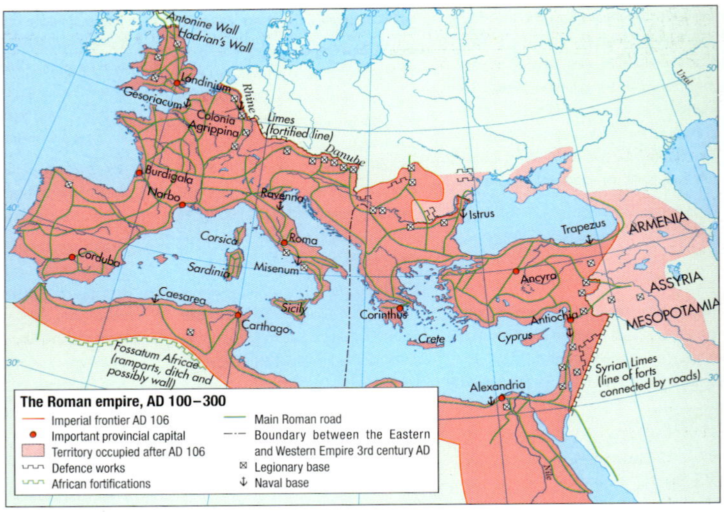

---

revival of interest in classical learning and emphasis on the philosophical and moral importance of the human individual. There was a great flowering of all the arts. Architectural and artistic style emerged in Italy and was heavily influenced by Greek and Roman models and by humanism. There was development of perspective, increasing use of secular and pagan subjects, a rise of portraiture, constant experimentation, and growing concern for the expression of the individual artist. The ideas spread and were emulated with national variations.

rococo Playful, light style of art, architecture and decoration that developed from baroque.

Rococo brought to interior decoration swirls, scrolls, shells and arabesques. It was also applied to furniture, porcelain and silverware.

Romanesque Architectural style characterized by heavy round arches and massive walls, often decorated with carving or, originally, painted scenes.

romanticism Movement that valued individual experience and intuition, rather than the orderly, structured universe of neoclassicism. An emphasis on nature was also a characteristic. In music, the term refers to the rather later period from c.1800 to 1910.

The Roman empire, AD 100-300

— Imperial frontier AD 106
● Important provincial capital
▨ Territory occupied after AD 106
⌇⌇ Defence works
⌇⌇ African fortifications
— Main Roman road
--- Boundary between the Eastern and Western Empire 3rd century AD
⌖ Legionary base
↓ Naval base

Europe c.1400

— Boundary of the Holy Roman Empire
▨ Habsburg territories
▨ Luxembourg territories
▨ Crown of Aragon
▨ Burgundian territories
▨ Angevin territories
▨ Union of Kalmar 1397
▨ Union of Krewo 1385/6
▨ Ottoman Empire
▨ Ottoman advance

European alliances 1914

▨ Triple Alliance
▨ Triple Entente
▨ Ally of Central Powers 1914
▨ Future ally of Central Powers
▨ Ally of Entente Powers 1914
▨ Future ally of Entente Powers

European politics and economics

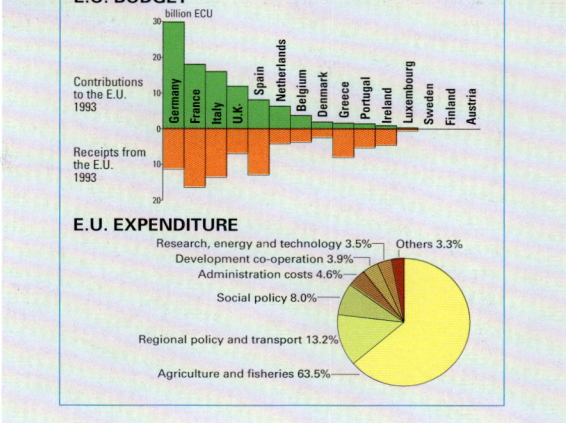

E.U. BUDGET

billion ECU

Contributions to the E.U. 1993

Receipts from the E.U. 1993

Germany, France, Italy, U.K., Spain, Netherlands, Belgium, Denmark, Greece, Portugal, Ireland, Luxembourg, Sweden, Finland, Austria

E.U. EXPENDITURE

Research, energy and technology 3.5% — Others 3.3%
Development co-operation 3.9%
Administration costs 4.6%
Social policy 8.0%
Regional policy and transport 13.2%
Agriculture and fisheries 63.5%

Principat d'Andorra
Andorra

Area 453 sq km (175 sq miles)
Population 75,000
Capital (population) Andorra la Vella
Languages Catalan (official), French, Spanish
GDP per capita 1992 US$ 18,000
Currency French francs and Spanish pesetas; euro
Government independent state and co-principality
Head of state co-princes: Juan Alanis, Bishop of Urgel, 1971 and Jacques Chirac (see France), 1995
Head of government Chief Executive Marc Forné Molné, 1994

Recent events

In 1993 a new democratic constitution was adopted that reduced the roles of the President of France and the Bishop of Urgel to purely constitutional figureheads.

Economy

The main sources of income include agriculture; the sale of water and hydroelectricity to Catalonia; tourism, particularly skiing. Andorra's links with France have led to the adoption of the euro.

Belarus *Belorussia*

Area 297,600 sq km (80,154 sq miles)
Population 10,409,000
Capital (population) Minsk (1,700,000)
Languages Belarussian, Russian (both official)
GDP per capita 1995 US$4,220
Currency Belarussian rouble = 100 kopek
Head of state Alexander Lukashenko, 1994
Head of government Sergey Ling, 1996

Recent events

Belarus was a founder member of the CIS. The administrative centre of the CIS is in Minsk. In 1997, despite opposition from nationalists, Belarus signed a Union Treaty with Russia, committing it to integration with Russia.

Economy

Belarus has faced problems in the transition to a free-market economy. In 1995 an agreement with Russia enabled Belarus to receive subsidised fuel. Agriculture, especially meat and dairy farming, is important.

Belgique *Belgium*

Area 30,510 sq km (11,780 sq miles)
Population 10,175,000
Capital (population) Brussels/Bruxelles (952,000)
Languages Dutch, French, German (all official)
GDP per capita 1995 US$24,541
Currency Belgian franc = 100 centimes; euro
Government federal constitutional monarchy
Head of state King Albert II, 1993
Head of government Guy Verhofstadt, Flemish Liberal Democrats (VLD), 1999

Recent events

A central domestic issue has been the tension between Dutch-speaking Flemings and French-speaking Walloons. In 1993 Belgium adopted a federal system of government, and each of the regions has its own parliament. In 1996-97, Belgium was shocked by large-scale child-abuse scandals.

Economy

Belgium is a major trading nation. The leading activity is manufacturing and products include steel and chemicals. Agriculture employs only 3% of the workforce, but the country is mostly self-sufficient. Barley and wheat are the chief crops, but the most valuable activities are dairy farming and livestock rearing.

Bosna-Herzegovina
Bosnia-Herzegovina

Area 51,129 sq km (19,745 sq miles)
Population 3,366,000
Capital (population) Sarajevo (526,000)
Language Serbian/Croatian
GDP per capita 1991 US$3,200
Currency Convertible Mark = 100 paras
Government federal republic
Head of state Ante Jelavic, Croatian Democratic Union (HDZ), 1999
Heads of government co-prime ministers Haris Silajdzic, Party for Bosnia and Herzegovina (SBIH), 1997, and Svetozar Mihajlovic, Coalition 'Sloga' (KS), 1999

Recent events

In 1992 a referendum approved independence from the Yugoslav federation. The Bosnian Serb population was against independence and in the resulting war occupied over two-thirds of the land. Croat forces seized other parts of the country. After many attempts at a settlement, the Dayton Peace Accord affirmed that Bosnia-Herzegovina was a single state but partitioned it into a Muslim-Croat federation and a Serbian republic. A tripartite presidency was set up. NATO troops remain as a peace-keeping force.

Economy

Excluding Macedonia, Bosnia was the least developed of the former republics of Yugoslavia. Its economy has been shattered by the war.

Bulgariya *Bulgaria*

Area 110,910 sq km (42,822 sq miles)
Population 8,240,000
Capital (population) Sofia (1,117,000)
Languages Bulgarian (official), Turkish
GDP per capita 1995 US$4,480
Currency Lev = 100 stotinki
Government multiparty republic
Head of state President Peter Stoyanov, Union of Democratic Forces (SDS), 1997
Head of government Ivan Kostov, Union of Democratic Forces (SDS), 1997

Recent events

In 1990 the first non-communist president for 40 years, Zhelyu Zhelev, was elected. A new constitution (1991) saw the adoption of free-market reforms. Elections in 1997, prompted by the resignation of the previous government, were won by a centre-right coalition.

Economy

Bulgaria is a lower-middle-income developing country, faced with a difficult transition to a market economy. Manufacturing is the leading economic activity but has outdated technology. The main products are chemicals, metals, machinery and textiles. Mineral reserves include molybdenum. Wheat and maize are the main crops. The valleys of the Maritsa are ideal for winemaking, plums and tobacco. Tourism is increasing rapidly.

Česka Republica
Czech Republic

Area 78,864 sq km (30,449 sq miles)
Population 10,286,000
Capital (population) Prague/Praha (1,213,000)
Languages Czech (official), Moravian
GDP per capita 1995 US$5,479
Currency Czech Koruna = 100 haler
Government multiparty republic
Head of state President Václav Havel, 1993
Head of government Milos Zeman, Chairman of the Chamber of Deputies, Czech Social Democratic Party (CSSD), 1998

Recent events

Free elections were held in 1990, resulting in the re-election of Vaclav Havel. In 1992 the government agreed to the secession of the Slovak Republic, and on 1 January 1993 the Czech Republic was created.

Economy

The country has deposits of coal, uranium, iron ore, magnesite, tin and zinc. Industries include chemicals, beer, iron and steel, and machinery. Private ownership of land is gradually being restored. Agriculture employs 12% of the workforce. Livestock raising is important. Crops include grains, fruit, and hops for brewing.

Danmark *Denmark*

Area 43,070 sq km (16,629 sq miles)
Population 5,334,000
Capital (population) Copenhagen/København (1,353,000)
Language Danish (official)
GDP per capita US$32,752
Currency Krone = 100 øre
Government parliamentary monarchy
Head of state Queen Margrethe II, 1972
Head of government Poul Nyrop Rasmussen, Social Democrats (SD), 1993

Recent events

In 1992 Denmark rejected the Maastricht Treaty, but reversed the decision in a second referendum (1993). In 1998 the Amsterdam Treaty was ratified by a further referendum.

Economy

Danes enjoy a high standard of living. Denmark is self-sufficient in oil and natural gas. Products include furniture, electrical goods and textiles. Services, including tourism, form the largest sector (63% of GDP). Farming employs only 4% of the workforce but is highly productive. Fishing is also important.

Deutschland *Germany*

Area 356,910 sq km (137,803 sq miles)
Population 82,079,000
Capital (population) Berlin (3,472,000)
Language German (official)
GDP per capita 1998 US$26,217
Currency Deutschmark = 100 pfennig; euro
Government federal multiparty republic
Head of state Johannes Rau, Social Democratic Party (SPD), 1999
Head of government Chancellor Gerhard Schröder, Social Democratic Party in coalition with the Green Party (SPD/Grüne), 1998

Recent events

Germany is a major supporter of the European Union, and former chancellor Helmut Köhl was the driving force behind the creation of the euro. During 1999 state elections in the former German Democratic Republic saw massive losses for the Social Democrats.

Economy

Germany is one of the world's greatest economic powers. Services form the largest economic sector. Machinery and transport equipment account for 50% of exports. It is the world's third-largest car producer. Other major products: ships, iron, steel, petroleum, tyres. It has the world's second-largest lignite mining industry. Other minerals: copper, potash, lead, salt, zinc, aluminium. Germany is the world's second-largest producer of hops and beer, and fifth-largest of wine. Other products: cheese and milk, barley, rye, pork.

Eesti *Estonia*

Area 44,700 sq km (17,300 sq miles)
Population 1,421,000
Capital (population) Tallinn (435,000)
Languages Estonian (official), Russian
GDP per capita 1992 US$2,750
Currency Kroon = 100 sents
Government multiparty republic
Head of state President Lennart Meri, National Coalition Party Pro Patria (RK Isamaa), 1992
Head of government Mart Laar, Estonian National Independence Party (ERSP), 1999

Recent events

In 1992 Estonia adopted a new constitution and multiparty elections were held. Since independence Estonia has been ruled by a succession of coalition or minority governments.

Economy

Privatisation and free-trade reforms have increased foreign investment and trade with the European Union. Chief natural resources are oil shale and forests. Manufactures include petrochemicals, fertilisers and textiles. Agriculture and fishing are important. Barley, potatoes and oats are major crops.

Ellas *Greece*

Area 131,990 sq km (50,691 sq miles)
Population 10,662,000
Capital (population) Athens/Athinai (3,097,000)
Language Greek (official)
GDP per capita 1995 US$11,555
Currency Drachma = 100 lepta
Head of government Kostas Simitis, Panhellenic Socialist Party (PASOK), 1996
Government multiparty republic
Head of state President Konstantinos Stephanopoulos, Political Spring Party (PA), 1995

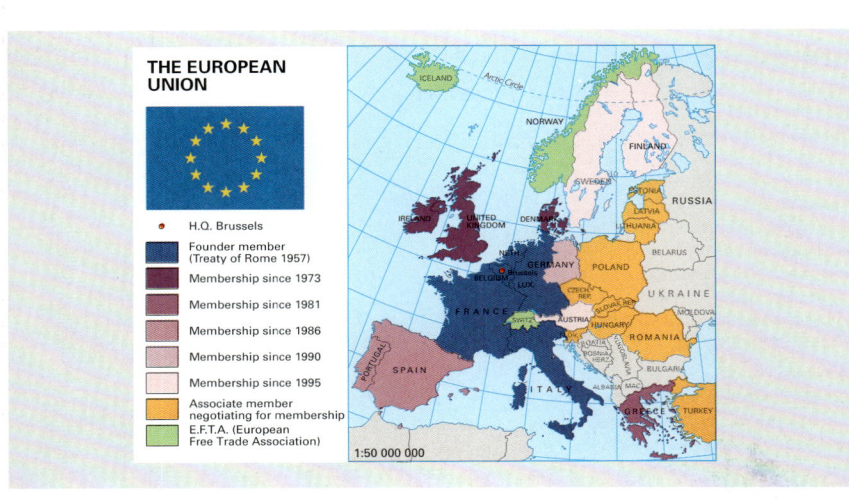

THE EUROPEAN UNION

- H.Q. Brussels
- Founder member (Treaty of Rome 1957)
- Membership since 1973
- Membership since 1981
- Membership since 1986
- Membership since 1990
- Membership since 1995
- Associate member negotiating for membership
- E.F.T.A. (European Free Trade Association)

1:50 000 000

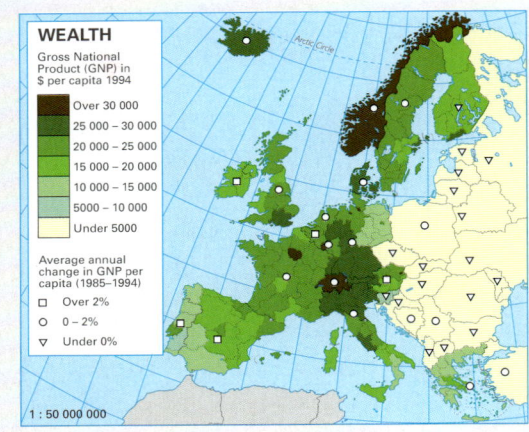

WEALTH

Gross National Product (GNP) in $ per capita 1994

- Over 30 000
- 25 000 – 30 000
- 20 000 – 25 000
- 15 000 – 20 000
- 10 000 – 15 000
- 5000 – 10 000
- Under 5000

Average annual change in GNP per capita (1985–1994)

- □ Over 2%
- ○ 0 – 2%
- ▽ Under 0%

1 : 50 000 000

Recent events

In 1981 Greece joined the European Community and Andreas Papandreou became Greece's first socialist prime minister (1981-89, 1993-96). Konstantinos Stephanopoulos became president in 1995. In 1998 forest fires raged over one million hectares of Attica.

Economy

Greece is one of the poorest members of the European Union. Manufacturing is important. Products: textiles, cement, chemicals, metallurgy. Minerals: lignite, bauxite, chromite. Farmland covers 33% of Greece, grazing land 40%. Major crops: tobacco, olives, grapes, cotton, wheat. Livestock are raised. Shipping and tourism are also major sectors.

España *Spain*

Area 504,780 sq km (194,896 sq miles)
Population 39,134,000
Capital (population) Madrid (3,041,000)
Languages Castilian Spanish (official), Catalan, Galician, Basque
GDP per capita 1995 US$14,786
Currency Peseta = 100 céntimos; euro
Government constitutional monarchy
Head of state King Juan Carlos, 1975
Head of government José María Aznar, People's Party (PP), 1996

Recent events

Spain joined NATO in 1982 and the European Community in 1986. There is an historic tension between central government and the regions. From 1959 the militant Basque organization ETA waged a campaign of terror but announced a ceasefire in 1998. In 1996 the government was forced to call early elections after allegations of complicity in an illegal anti-terrorist campaign. After 13 years in office, the Spanish Socialist Workers' Party (PSOE) was defeated. José María Aznar formed a minority administration.

Economy

Spain has rapidly transformed from a largely poor, agrarian society into a prosperous industrial nation. Agriculture now employs only 10% of the workforce. Spain is the world's third-largest wine producer. Other crops include citrus fruits, tomatoes and olives. Industries: cars, ships, chemicals, electronics, metal goods, steel, textiles.

France

Area 551,500 sq km (212,934 sq miles)
Population 58,805,000
Capital (population) Paris (9,469,000)
Languages French (official), Breton, Occitan
GDP per capita 1995 US$23,954
Currency Franc = 100 centimes; euro
Government multiparty republic
Head of state President Jacques Chirac, Assembly for the Republic (RPR), 1995

Head of government Lionel Jospin, 1997 (Socialist Party)

Recent events

Jacques Chirac's welfare economic reforms in order to meet the criteria for European Monetary Union (EMU) brought strikes and unemployment and led to the election in 1997 of a socialist prime minister, Lionel Jospin.

Economy

France is a leading industrial nation. It is the world's fourth-largest manufacturer of cars. Industries include chemicals and steel. It is the leading producer of farm products in western Europe. Livestock and dairy farming are vital sectors. It is the world's second-largest producer of cheese and wine. Tourism is a major industry.

Hrvatska *Croatia*

Area 56,538 sq km (21,824 sq miles)
Population 4,672,000
Capital (population) Zagreb (931,000)
Language Croatian
GDP per capita 1991 US$ 5,600
Currency Kuna = 100 lipas
Government multiparty republic
Head of state President Stjepan Mesic, 2000
Head of government Ivica Racan, Croatian National Party (HNS). Coalition with Social Democratic Party of Croatia (SDP), 2000.

Recent events

A 1991 referendum voted overwhelmingly in favour of independence. Serb-dominated areas took up arms to remain in the federation. Serbia armed Croatian Serbs, war broke out between Serbia and Croatia, and Croatia lost much territory. In 1992 United Nations peacekeeping troops were deployed. In 1995 Croatian government forces occupied Krajina and 150,000 Serbs fled. Following the Dayton Peace Accord (1995), Croatia and Yugoslavia established diplomatic relations (1996). An agreement between the Croatian government and Croatian Serbs provided for the eventual reintegration of Krajina into Croatia (1998). Elections called after the death of President Tudjman in December 1999. Stjepan Mesic elected president in 2000.

Economy

The wars have badly disrupted Croatia's relatively prosperous economy. Croatia has a wide range of manufacturing industries, such as steel, chemicals, oil refining, and wood products. Agriculture is the principal employer. Crops include maize, soya beans, sugar beet and wheat.

Ireland, Republic of

Area 70,280 sq km (27,135 sq miles)
Population 3,619,000
Capital (population) Dublin (1,024,000)

Languages Irish, English (both official)
GDP per capita 1995 US$23,284
Currency Irish punt = 100 new pence; euro
Government multiparty republic
Head of state President Mary McAleese, 1997
Head of government Taoiseach Bertie Ahern, 1997 (Fianna Fáil)

Recent events

The Anglo-Irish Agreement (1985) gave Ireland a consultative role in the affairs of Northern Ireland. Following a 1995 referendum, divorce was legalised. Abortion remains a contentious political issue. In 1997 elections Bertie Ahern became taoiseach and Mary McAleese became president. In the Good Friday Agreement (1998) the Irish Republic gave up its constitutional claim to Northern Ireland and a North-South Ministerial Council was established.

Economy

Ireland has benefited greatly from its membership of the European Union. Grants have enabled the modernisation of farming, which employs 14% of the workforce. Major products include cereals, cattle and dairy products, sheep, sugar beet and potatoes. Fishing is important. Traditional sectors, such as brewing, distilling and textiles, have been supplemented by high-tech industries, such as electronics. Tourism is the most important component of the service industry.

Italia *Italy*

Area 301,270 sq km (116,320 sq miles)
Population 56,783,000
Capital (population) Rome/Roma (92,688,000)
Language Italian (official)
GDP per capita 1995 US$20,680
Currency Lira = 100 centesimi; euro
Government multiparty republic
Head of state President Carlo Ciampi, 1997
Head of government Massimo D'Alema (DS), Olive Alliance and Party of the Democratic Left (PDS), 1998

Recent events

Elections in 1996 were won by the left-wing Olive Tree alliance and Romano Prodi became prime minister (1996-98). In 1998 the Communist Refoundation (RC) withdrew its support for Prodi's government and Massimo D'Alema, leader of the Party of the Democratic Left (PDS), became prime minister.

Economy

Italy's main industrial region is the north-western triangle of Milan, Turin and Genoa. It is the world's eighth-largest car and steel producer. Machinery and transport equipment account for 37% of exports. Agricultural production is important. Italy is the world's largest producer of wine. Tourism is a vital economic sector.

Jugoslavija *Yugoslavia*

Area 102,170 sq km (39,449 sq miles)
Population 10,500,000
Capital (population) Belgrade/Beograd (1,137,000)
Languages Serbian (official), Albanian
GDP per capita 1992 US$4,000
Currency Yugoslav new dinar = 100 paras
Government federal republic
Head of state Vojislav Kostunica, 2000 Democratic Party of Serbia
Head of government Momir Bulatovic, Serb Socialist Party (SPS), 1998,

Recent events

In 1989 Slobodan Milosevic´ became president of Serbia and called for the creation of a "Greater Serbia". Serbian attempts to dominate the Yugoslav federation led to the secession of Slovenia and Croatia (with

which Serbia fought a brief war) in 1991 and to Bosnia-Herzegovina's declaration of independence in March 1992. In April 1992 Serbia and Montenegro announced the formation of a new Yugoslav federation and invited Serbs in Croatia and Bosnia-Herzegovina to join. Serbian aid to the Bosnian Serb campaign of "ethnic cleansing" in the civil war that had broken out in Bosnia led the United Nations to impose sanctions on Serbia, which prompted Milosevic´ to sever support for the Bosnian Serbs. In 1995 Milosevic´ signed the Dayton Peace Accord, which ended the Bosnian war. In 1997 Milosevic´ became president of Yugoslavia. In 1998 fighting erupted in Kosovo between Albanian nationalists and Serbian security forces. In 1999, following the forced expulsion of Albanians from Kosovo, NATO bombed Yugoslavia, forcing withdrawal of Serbian forces from Kosovo. In September 2000 elections were held with Kostunica the victor. However Milosevic´ refused to hand over power. After a week of civil unrest and increased support for Kostunica, Milosevic´ was finally ousted

Economy

Yugoslavia's lower-middle income economy has been devastated by war and economic sanctions. Hyperinflation is one of the greatest problems. Industrial production has collapsed. Natural resources include bauxite, coal and copper. There is some oil and natural gas. Manufacturing includes aluminium, cars, machinery, plastics, steel and textiles. Agriculture is important.

Latvija *Latvia*

Area 64,589 sq km (24,938 sq miles)
Population 2,385,000
Capital (population) Riga (840,000)
Languages Latvian (official), Russian
GDP per capita 1995 US$3,370
Currency Lats = 100 santimi
Government multiparty republic
Head of state President Vaira Vike-Freiberga, 1999
Head of government Andris Skele, People's Party (TP), 1999

Recent events

In 1993 Latvia held its first multiparty elections. In 1994 it adopted a law restricting the naturalisation of non-Latvians, including many Russian settlers. In 1995 Latvia joined the Council of Europe and formally applied to join the EU. In 1998 elections the People's Party emerged as the largest single party, but a coalition government was formed by Vilis Kristopans of Latvia's Way who then resigned on the election of Vaira Vike-Freiberga as president and Andris Skele was then elected prime minister.

Economy

Latvia is a lower-middle-income country. The

country has to import many of the materials needed for manufacturing. Latvia produces only 10% of the electricity it needs, and the rest has to be imported from Belarus, Russia and Ukraine. Manufactures include electronic goods, farm machinery and fertiliser. Farm exports include beef, dairy products and pork.

Liechtenstein

Area 157 sq km (61 sq miles)
Population 32,000
Capital Vaduz
Language German (official)
GDP per capita 1991 US$34,000
Currency Swiss franc = 100 centimes
Government independent principality
Head of state Prince Hans Adam II, 1989
Head of government Mario Frick, Patriotic Union (VU), 1993

Recent events

Independent principality in western central Europe in a currency and customs union with Switzerland. In 1990 the principality joined the UN. Liechtenstein has a constitutional and hereditary monarchy; the ruling family is the Austrian house of Liechtenstein. Women finally received the vote in 1984.

Economy

Liechtenstein is the fourth-smallest country in the world and one of the richest per capita. Since 1945 it has rapidly developed a specialised manufacturing base. The major part of state revenue is derived from international companies attracted by low taxation rates. Tourism is increasingly important.

Lietuva *Lithuania*

Area 65,200 sq km (25,200 sq miles)
Population 3,600,000
Capital (population) Vilnius (576,000)
Languages Lithuanian (official), Russian, Polish
GDP per capita 1995 US$4,120
Currency Litas = 100 centai
Government multiparty republic
Head of state President Valdas Adamkus, 1998
Head of government Andrius Kubilius, conservative alliance (TS-LK), 1999

Recent events

The Soviet Union recognised Lithuania as an independent republic in September 1991. In 1993 Soviet troops completed their withdrawal. In 1996 Lithuania signed a treaty of association with the EU. In 1998 an independent candidate, Valdas Adamkus, was elected president.

Economy

Lithuania is a developing country. It is dependent on Russian raw materials. Manufacturing is the most valuable export sector: major

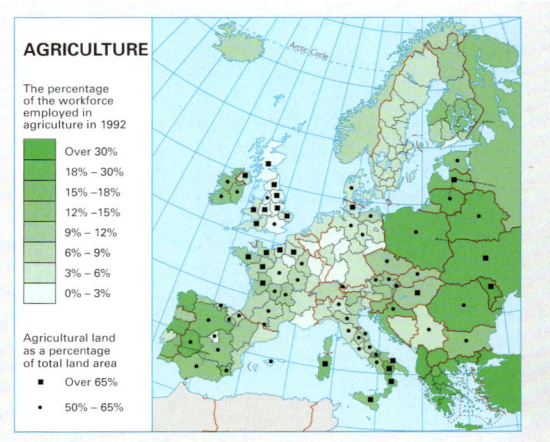

AGRICULTURE

The percentage of the workforce employed in agriculture in 1992

- Over 30%
- 18% – 30%
- 15% – 18%
- 12% – 15%
- 9% – 12%
- 6% – 9%
- 3% – 6%
- 0% – 3%

Agricultural land as a percentage of total land area

- ■ Over 65%
- • 50% – 65%

products include chemicals, electronic goods and machine tools. Dairy and meat farming and fishing are also important activities.

Luxembourg

Area 2,590 sq km (1,000 sq miles)
Population 425,000
Capital (population) Luxembourg (76,000)
Languages Luxembourgian/Letzeburgish (official), French, German
GDP per capita 1995 US$42,732
Currency Luxembourg Franc = 100 centimes; euro
Government constitutional monarchy (or grand duchy)
Head of state Grand Duke Henri, 2000
Head of government Jean-Claude Juncker, coalition between Christian Social People's Party (PCS) and the Conservative Democratic Party (PDL), 1999

Recent events
Following 1994 elections, the Christian Social People's Party (CD) and the Luxembourg Socialist Workers' Party (SOC) formed a coalition government. Jean-Claude Juncker (CD) became prime minister. In 1998 Grand Duke Jean conferred many constitutional powers upon his son and heir, Prince Henri and abdicated in his favour in October 2000.

Economy
There are rich deposits of iron ore, and Luxembourg is a major producer of iron and steel. Other industries include chemicals, textiles, tourism, banking and electronics. Farmers raise cattle and pigs. Major crops include cereals, fruits and grapes for winemaking. The city of Luxembourg is a major centre of European administration and finance.

Magyarorszàg *Hungary*

Area 93,030 sq km (35,919 sq miles)
Population 10,208,000
Capital (population) Budapest (1,909,000)
Language Hungarian (official)
GDP per capita 1995 US$4,652
Currency Forint = 100 filler
Government multiparty republic
Head of state President Ferenc Madl, 2000
Head of government Viktor Orbán, Federation of Young Democrats - Hungarian Civic Party (FiDeSz-MPP), 1998

Recent events
In 1990 multiparty elections were won by the conservative Democratic Forum. In 1998 elections the Federation of Young Democrats-Hungarian Civic Party (Fidesz-MPP) emerged as the largest party and Viktor Orban became prime minister.

Economy
Since the early 1990s, Hungary has adopted market reforms and privatisation programmes. The economy has suffered from the collapse in exports to the former Soviet Union and Yugoslavia. The manufacture of machinery and transport is the most valuable sector. Hungary's resources include bauxite, coal and natural gas. Major crops include grapes for wine-making, maize, potatoes, sugar beet and wheat. Tourism is a growing sector.

Makedonija *Macedonia*

Area 25,710 sq km (9,927 sq miles)
Population 2,009,000
Capital (population) Skopje (541,000)
Languages Macedonian (official), Albanian
GDP per capita 1995 US$1,550
Currency Dinar = 100 paras
Government multiparty republic
Head of state Boris Trajkovski, Internal Macedonian Revolutionary Organisation-Democratic Party for Macedonian National Unity (VMRO/DPMNE), 1999
Head of government Prime Minister Ljubco Georgievski, (VMRO/DPMNE), 1998

Recent events
In 1993 the UN accepted the new republic as a member. In 1994 Greece banned Macedonian trade through Greece. The ban was lifted in 1995, when Macedonia agreed to redesign its flag and remove any claims to Greek Macedonia from its constitution. Internal tensions exist between Macedonians and the Albanian minority. In 1998 elections a right-wing coalition formed a new government.

Economy
Macedonia is a developing country. The poorest of the six former republics of Yugoslavia, its economy was devastated by UN trade damaged by sanctions against Yugoslavia and by the Greek embargo. The size of national debt is a major obstacle. Manufactures, especially metals, dominate exports. Agriculture employs 17% of the workforce. Major crops include cotton, fruits, maize, tobacco and wheat.

Malta

Area 316 sq km (122 sq miles)
Population 379,000
Capital (population) Valetta (102,000)
Languages Maltese, English (both official)
GDP per capita 1992 US$8,281
Currency Maltese lira = 100 cents
Government multiparty republic
Head of state President Guido de Marco, Nationalist Party (PN), 1999
Head of government Edward Fenech Adami, Nationalist Party (PN), 1998

Recent events
In 1990 Malta applied to join the European Community. In 1997 the newly elected Malta Labour Party pledged to rescind the application. The Nationalist Party, led by the pro-European Edward Fenech Adami, regained power in 1998 elections.

Economy
Malta is an upper-middle-income developing country. Machinery and transport equipment account for more than 50% of exports. Malta's historic naval dockyards are now used for commercial shipbuilding and repair. The state-owned Malta Drydocks is Malta's leading industry. Manufactures include chemicals, electronic equipment and textiles. The largest sector is services, especially tourism. The main crops are barley, fruits, vegetables and wheat.

Moldova

Area 33,700 sq km (13,010 sq miles)
Population 4,458,000
Capital (population) Chisinau (700,000)
Language Moldovan/Romanian (official)
GDP per capita 1992 US$3,670
Currency Leu = 100 bani
Government multiparty republic
Head of state President Petru Lucinschi, 1996
Head of government Dumitru Braghis, 1999

Recent events
In 1994 multiparty elections were won by the former communists of the Agrarian Democratic Party. A referendum rejected reunification with Romania. Parliament voted to join the CIS. A new constitution (1994) established a presidential parliamentary republic. In 1996 Petru Lucinschi was elected president.

Economy
Moldova is a lower-middle-income developing economy. Agriculture is important and major products include fruits and grapes for wine-making. Farmers also raise livestock, including dairy cattle and pigs. Moldova has to import materials and fuels for its industries. Major manufactures include agricultural machinery and consumer goods. Exports include food, wine, tobacco, textiles and footwear.

Monaco

Area 1.5 sq km (0.6 sq miles)
Population 32,000
Capital (population) Monaco-Ville
Languages French (official), Italian, Monegasque
GDP per capita 1991 US$16,000
Currency French francs; euro
Government principality
Head of state Prince Rainier III, 1949
Minister of State Michel Lévêque, National Democratic Union (UND), 1997

Recent events
Monaco has been ruled by the Grimaldi family since the end of the 13th century. Monaco's links with France, under whose protection it has been since 1860, led to the adoption of the euro.

Economy
The chief source of income is tourism, attracted by the casinos of Monte Carlo. There is some light industry, including printing, textiles and postage stamps.

Nederland
The Netherlands

Area 41,526 sq km (16,033 sq miles)
Population 15,731,000
Capital (population) Amsterdam (1,100,000); administrative capital 's-Gravenhage (The Hague)
Languages Dutch (official), Frisian
GDP per capita 1995 US$ 24,921
Currency Guilder = 100 cents; euro
Government constitutional monarchy
Head of state Queen Beatrix, 1980
Head of government Wim Kok, Labour Party (PvdA), 1994

Recent events
In 1994 Wim Kok was elected prime minister. In 1998 he was re-elected as head of a centre-left coalition.

Economy
The Netherlands has prospered through its close European ties. Private enterprise has successfully combined with progressive social policies. It is highly industrialised. Products include aircraft, chemicals, electronics and machinery. Natural resources include natural gas. Agriculture is intensive and mechanised, employing only 5% of the workforce. Dairy farming is the leading agricultural activity. Major products are cheese, barley, flowers and bulbs.

Norge *Norway*

Area 323,900 sq km (125,000 sq miles)
Population 4,420,000
Capital (population) Oslo (714,000)
Languages Norwegian (official), Lappish, Finnish
GDP per capita 1995 US$33,174. Member of NATO.
Currency Krone = 100 ore
Government constitutional monarchy
Head of state King Harald V, 1991
Head of government Jens Stoltenberg, Labour Party, 2000

Recent events
In 1991 Olav V was succeeded by his son, Harald V. In 1997 elections prime minister Thorbjoern Jagland was defeated by a centrist coalition led by Kjell Magne Bondevik.

Economy
Norway has one of the world's highest standards of living. Its chief exports are oil and natural gas. Norway is the world's eighth-largest producer of crude oil. Per capita, Norway is the world's largest producer of hydro-electricity. Major manufactures include petroleum products, chemicals, aluminium, wood pulp and paper. The chief farming activities are dairy and meat production, but Norway has to import food. Norway has the largest fish catch in Europe after Russia.

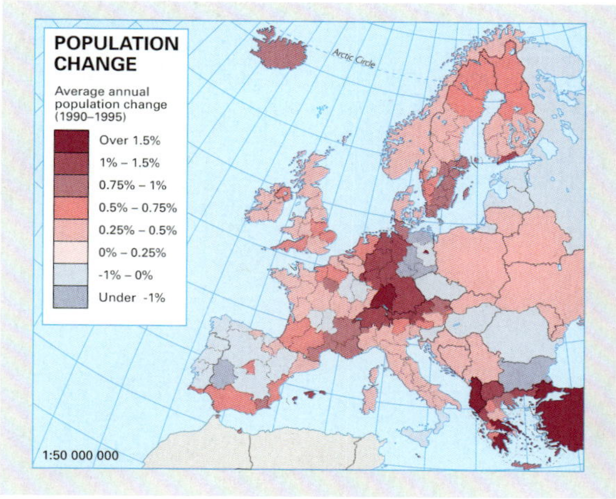
POPULATION CHANGE
Average annual population change (1990–1995)
Over 1.5%
1% – 1.5%
0.75% – 1%
0.5% – 0.75%
0.25% – 0.5%
0% – 0.25%
-1% – 0%
Under -1%
Arctic Circle
1:50 000 000

Österreich *Austria*

Area 83,850 sq km (32,374 sq miles)
Population 8,134,000
Capital (population) Vienna/Wien (1,560,000)
Languages German (official)
GDP per capita US$26,108
Currency Schilling = 100 groschen; euro
Government federal republic
Head of state President Thomas Klestil, People's Party (OVP), 1992
Federal Chancellor Viktor Klima, Social Democrats (SPO), 1997

Recent events
Austria became a member of the European Union in 1995. In general elections in 1999, the extreme right Freedom Party, under Jörg Haider, made gains at the expense of the Social Democrats.

Economy
Austria is a wealthy nation which, despite plenty of hydroelectric power, is dependent on the import of fossil fuels. Austria's leading economic activity is the manufacture of metals. Dairy and livestock farming are the principal agricultural activities. Tourism is an important industry.

Polska *Poland*

Area 312,680 sq km (120,726 sq miles)
Population 38,607,000
Capital (population) Warsaw/Warszawa (1,638,000)
Language Polish (official)
GDP per capita 1995 US$4,089
Currency Zloty = 100 groszy
Government multiparty republic
Head of state Aleksander Kwasniewski, Alliance of the Democratic Left (SdRP/SLD), 1995
Head of government Jerzy Buzek, Solidarity Electoral Action (AWS), 1997

Recent events
In 1996 Poland joined the Organisation for Economic Cooperation and Development (OECD). In 1997 it was invited to join NATO. Elections in 1997 were won by the Solidarity Electoral Alliance (AWS), a centre-right coalition.

Economy
Of the workforce, 27% is employed in agriculture and 37% in industry. Poland is the world's fifth-largest producer of lignite and seventh-largest producer of bituminous coal. Copper ore is also a vital resource. Manufacturing accounts for 24% of exports. Poland is the world's fifth-largest producer of ships. Agriculture remains important. Major crops include barley, potatoes and wheat. The transition to a free-market economy has caused many problems, but economic growth is slowly returning.

Portugal

Area 92,390 sq km (35,670 sq miles)
Population 9,928,000
Capital (population) Lisbon/Lisboa (2,561,000)
Language Portuguese (official)
GDP per capita 1995 US$11,122
Currency Escudo = 100 centavos; euro
Government multiparty republic
Head of state Jorge Sampaio, 1996, PS
Head of government Antonio Guterres, Socialist Party (PS), 1995

Recent events
In 1986 Portugal joined the European Community. In 1996 Jorge Sampaio became president. In 1999 the Socialist Party failed by three seats to gain an absolute majority.

Economy
In 1999 Portugal adopted the euro. Its commitment to the European Union (EU) has seen the economy emerge from recession. Manufacturing accounts for 33% of exports. Textiles, footwear and clothing are major exports. Portugal is the world's fifth-largest producer of tungsten and the world's eighth-largest producer of wine. Olives, potatoes and wheat are also grown. Tourism is a rapidly growing sector.

Romania

Area 237,500 sq km (91,699 sq miles)
Population 22,396,000
Capital (population) Bucharest/Bucuresti (2,061,000)
Languages Romanian (official), Hungarian
GDP per capita 1995 U$4,360
Currency Romanian leu = 100 bani
Government multiparty republic
Head of state President Emil Constantinescu, National Farmers' Party Christian and Democratic/Christian Democrats (PNTCD/CDR), 1996
Head of government Radu Vasile, National Farmers' Party Christian and Democratic/Christian Democrats (PNTCD/CDR), 1998

Recent events
A new constitution was introduced in 1991. 1995 saw Romania applying to join the European Union. In the 1996 elections

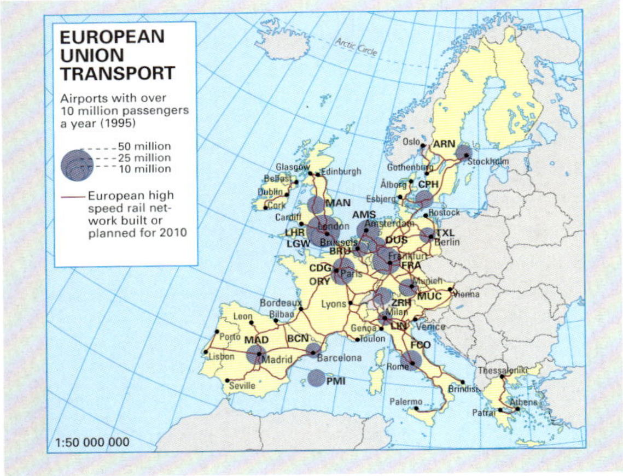
EUROPEAN UNION TRANSPORT
Airports with over 10 million passengers a year (1995)
50 million
25 million
10 million
European high speed rail network built or planned for 2010
Arctic Circle
Oslo
ARN
Stockholm
Glasgow
Edinburgh
Gothenburg
Belfast
Ålborg
CPH
Dublin
Cork
Esbjerg
MAN
Rostock
Cardiff
AMS
Amsterdam
London
LHR
LGW
Brussels
BRU
DUS
TXL
Berlin
Frankfurt
FRA
CDG
ORY
Paris
Munich
MUC
Vienna
Bordeaux
Lyons
ZRH
Milan
LIN
Venice
Leon
Bilbao
Genoa
Toulon
Porto
MAD
BCN
FCO
Lisbon
Madrid
Barcelona
Rome
Thessaloniki
Seville
PMI
Brindisi
Palermo
Athens
Patrai
1:50 000 000

Ion Iliescu, a former communist official, was defeated by Emil Constantinescu and his centre-right coalition. In 1998 disputes within the coalition led to the resignation of the prime minister.

Economy
Industry accounts for 40% of GDP. Oil, natural gas and antimony are the main mineral resources. Agriculture employs 29% of the workforce. Romania is the world's second-largest producer of plums (after China). It is the world's ninth-largest producer of wine. Other major crops include maize and cabbages. Economic reform is slow. Unemployment and foreign debt remain high.

Rossiya *Russia*

Area 17,075,000 sq km (6,592,800 sq miles)
Population 146,861,000
Capital (population) Moscow/Moskva (9,233,000)
Languages Russian (official), and many others
GDP per capita 1995 US$4,480
Currency Russian rouble = 100 kopeks
Government federal multiparty republic
Head of state Vladimir Putin. 2000
Head of government Prime Minister Yevgeny Primakov, 2000

Recent events
In 1991 Boris Yeltsin was elected President of the Russian Republic. In 1992 the Russian Federation became a co-founder of the CIS, composed of former Soviet Republics. Also in 1992 a new Federal Treaty was signed between the central government and the autonomous republics within the Russian Federation. Chechnya refused to sign, and declared independence. In December 1993 a new democratic constitution was adopted. From 1994 to 1996, Russia was embroiled in a costly civil war in Chechnya. In 998 the stock market collapsed and the rouble was devalued by 50%. In 1999 war flared up again in Chechnya. Boris Yeltsin resigned on 31st December 1999, handing over authority to his preferred successor Vladimir Putin, who was then officially elected president in spring 2000. Russia continues to suffer considerable political and economic instability

Economy
In 1993 mass privatisation began. By 1996, 80% of the Russian economy was in private hands. A major problem remains the size of Russia's foreign debt. Industry employs 46% of the workforce and contributes 48% of GDP. Mining is the most valuable activity. Russia is the world's leading producer of natural gas and nickel, the second largest producer of aluminium and phosphates. and the third-largest of crude oil, lignite and brown coal. Light industries are growing in importance. Most farmland is still government-owned or run as collectives, with important products barley, oats, rye, potatoes, beef and veal.

San Marino

Area 61 sq km (24 sq miles)
Population 25,000
Capital (population) San Marino (4,335)
GDP per capita 1991 US$17,000
Currency Italianlira/San Marino lira = 100 centesimi; euro
Language Italian (official)
Government multiparty republic
Heads of state co-Captains Regent: Mario Bollini, San Marino Socialist Party (PSS), and Giuseppe Arzilli, Christian Democrats (PCDS),, 1999

Recent events
World's smallest republic and perhaps Europe's oldest state, San Marino's links with Italy led to the adoption of the euro.

Economy
The economy is largely agricultural. Tourism is vital to the state's income.

Schweiz *Switzerland*

Area 41,290 sq km (15,942 sq miles)
Population 7,260,000
Capital (population) Bern (324,000)
Languages French, German, Italian, Romansch (all official)
GDP per capita 1995 US$36,762
Currency Swiss Franc = 100 centimes
Government federal republic
Head of state President Adolph Olgi 2000
Head of government Federal Chancellor Francois Couchepin, Free Democratic Party (FDP), 1991

Recent events
A referendum (1986) rejected Swiss membership of the UN to avoid compromising its neutrality. European Community membership was similarly rejected (1992). In 1995 the ruling coalition, led by the Christian Democrats, was re-elected. The President of the Confederation is elected annually.

Economy
Switzerland is wealthy and industrialised. Manufactures include chemicals, electrical equipment, machinery, precision instruments, watches and textiles. Livestock raising, notably dairy farming, is the chief agricultural activity. Tourism is important, and Swiss banks attract worldwide investment.

Shquipëria *Albania*

Area 28,750 sq km (11,100 sq miles)
Population 3,331,000
Capital (population) Tirana/Tiranë (251,000)
Languages Albanian (official), Greek
GDP per capita 1992 US$3,500
Currency Lek = 100 Quindars
Government multiparty republic
Head of state President Rexhep Medjani, 1997
Ruling party Pandeli Majko, 1998, Socialist Party of Albania (PS), 1997

Recent events
In 1997 the collapse of nationwide pyramid finance schemes sparked a large-scale rebellion in southern Albania. A government of national reconciliation was formed new elections agreed. Unrest continued through 1998 and 1999.

Economy
Albania is Europe's poorest country, and 56% of the workforce are engaged in agriculture. Private ownership of land has been encouraged since 1991. Crops include fruits, maize, olives, potatoes, sugar beet, vegetables, and wheat. Livestock farming is also important. Chromite, copper, and nickel are exported. Other resources include oil, brown coal, and hydroelectricity.

Slovenija *Slovenia*

Area 20,251 sq km (7,817 sq miles)
Population 1,972,000
Capital (population) Ljubljana (280,000)
Languages Slovene
GDP per capita 1992 US$6,330
Currency Tolar = 100 stotin
Government multiparty republic
Head of state Milan Kučan, 1990
Head of government Janez Drnosek, Liberal Democrats of Slovenia (LDS), 1997

Recent events
In 1990 Slovenia declared itself independent, which led to brief fighting between Slovenes and the federal army. In 1992 the European Community recognised Slovenia's independence. In 1996 a coalition government, led by the Liberal Democrats, was set up. In 1996 Slovenia applied to join the European Union.

Economy
The transformation of a centrally planned economy and the fighting in other parts of former Yugoslavia have caused problems for Slovenia. Manufacturing is the leading activity. Major manufactures include chemicals, machinery, transport equipment, metal goods and textiles. Major crops include maize, fruit, potatoes and wheat.

Slovenska Republika *Slovakia*

Area 49,035 sq km (18,932 sq miles)
Population 5,393,000
Capital (population) Bratislava (451,000)
Languages Slovak (official), Hungarian
GDP per capita 1995 US$3,610
Currency Koruna = 100 halierov
Government multiparty republic
Head of state President Rudolf Schuster, Party of Civic Understanding (SOP), 1999
Head of government Mikulás Dzurinda, coalition government led by Slovak Democratic Coalition (SDK), 1998

Recent events
In 1993 the Slovak Republic became a sovereign state, breaking peaceably from the Czech Republic, with which it maintains close relations. In 1996 the Slovak Republic and Hungary ratified a treaty confirming their borders and stipulating basic rights for the 560,000 Hungarians in Slovakia. Following elections in 1998, a coalition government was formed, led by Mikulás Dzurinda of the Slovak Democratic Coalition.

Economy
The transition from communism to private ownership has been painful with industrial output falling, unemployment and inflation rising. In 1995 the privatisation programme was suspended. Manufacturing employs 33% of the workforce. Bratislava and Košice are the chief industrial cities. Major products include ceramics, machinery and steel. Farming employs 12% of the workforce. Crops include barley and grapes. Tourism is growing.

Suomi *Finland*

Area 338,130 sq km (130,552 sq miles)
Population 5,149,000
Capital (population) Helsinki (525,000)
Languages Finnish, Swedish (both official)
GDP per capita 1992 US$25,099
Currency Markka = 100 penniä; euro
Government multiparty republic
Head of state President Tarja Kaarina Halonen, 2000
Head of government Paavo Lipponen, Social Democratic Party (SDP), 1995

Recent events
In 1986 Finland became a member of EFTA, and in 1995 it joined the European Union. A new constitution was established in March 2000.

Economy
Forests are Finland's most valuable resource, with wood and paper products accounting for 35% of exports. Engineering, shipbuilding and textile industries have grown. Farming employs 9% of the workforce. Livestock and dairy farming are the chief activities.

Sverige *Sweden*

Area 449,960 sq km (173,730 sq miles)
Population 8,887,000
Capital (population) Stockholm (1,553,000)
Languages Swedish (official), Finnish
GDP per capita 1995 US$26,863
Currency Swedish krona = 100 ore
Government constitutional monarchy
Head of state King Carl XVI Gustaf, 1973
Head of government Göran Persson, Social Democratic Workers' Party (SSA), 1996

Recent events
In 1995 Sweden joined the European Union. The Social Democrats have been in government almost continuously since 1932. Göran Persson was re-elected in 1998. The cost of maintaining Sweden's extensive welfare services has become a major political issue.

Economy
Sweden is a highly developed industrial country. It has rich iron ore deposits, but other industrial materials are imported. Steel is a major product, used to manufacture aircraft, cars, machinery and ships. Forestry and fishing are important. Livestock and dairy farming are valuable activities; crops include barley and oats.

Türkiye *Turkey*

Area 779,450 sq km (300,946 sq miles)
Population 69,568,000
Capital (population) Ankara (3,028,000)
Languages Turkish (official), Kurdish
GDP per capita 1995 US$5,580
Currency Turkish lira = 100 kurus
Government multiparty republic
Head of state President Süleyman Demirel, True Path Party (DYP), 1993
Head of government Bülent Ecevit, Democratic Left Party (DSP), 1999

Recent events
Since 1984 Turkey has been fighting the Kurdish Workers Party (PKK) in south-eastern Turkey, Syria and northern Iraq. Turkey has often been accused of violating the human rights of Kurds. In 1999 Turkey captured the PKK leader, Abdullah ...calan. Süleyman Demirel was elected president in 1993.

Economy
Turkey is a lower-middle income developing country. Agriculture employs 47% of the workforce. Turkey is a leading producer of citrus fruits, barley, cotton, wheat, tobacco and tea. It is a major producer of chromium and phosphate fertilisers. Tourism is a vital source of foreign exchange.

Ukraina *Ukraine*

Area 603,700 sq km (233,100 sq miles)
Population 50,125,000
Capital (population) Kiev/Kyviv (2,630,000)
Languages Ukrainian (official), Russian
GDP per capita 1995 US$2,400
Currency Hryvna = 100 kopeks
Government multiparty republic
Head of state President Leonid Kuchma, 1994
Head of government Prime Minister Victor Yuschenko, 2000

Recent events
The Chernobyl disaster of 1986 contaminated large areas of Ukraine. Tensions with Russia over the Crimea, the Black Sea fleet, the control of nuclear weapons and oil and gas reserves were eased by a 1992 treaty. Leonid Kuchma was elected president in 1994. He continued the policy of establishing closer ties with the West and sped up the pace of privatisation. Kuchma was re-elected in 1999. There are continuing disputes over the the powers of the Crimean legislature.

Economy
Ukraine is a lower-middle-income economy. Agriculture is important. It is the world's leading producer of sugar beet, the second-largest producer of barley, and a major producer of wheat. Ukraine has extensive raw materials, including coal (though many mines are exhausted), iron ore and manganese ore. Ukraine is reliant on oil and natural gas imports. Ukraine's debt to Russia has been partly offset by allowing Russian firms majority shares in many Ukrainian industries.

United Kingdom

Area 243,368 sq km (94,202 sq miles)
Population 58,970,000
Capital (population) London (8,089,000)
Languages English (official), Welsh (also official in Wales), Gaelic
GDP per capita 1995 US$19,260
Currency Sterling (pound) = 100 pence
Government constitutional monarchy
Head of state Queen Elizabeth II, 1952
Head of government Tony Blair, Labour Party, 1997

Recent events
The United Kingdom of Great Britain and Northern Ireland is a union of four countries. Great Britain is composed of England, Scotland and Wales. In 1997 referenda on devolution saw Scotland and Wales gain their own legislative assemblies. The Scottish assembly was given tax-varying power. The Good Friday Agreement (1998) offered the best chance of peace in Northern Ireland for a generation.

Economy
The UK is a major industrial and trading nation. Cars remain a significant product, but the economy has become more service-centred and high-technology industries have grown in importance. The UK is a producer of oil, petroleum products, natural gas, potash, salt and lead. Agriculture employs only 2% of the workforce. Major crops include hops for beer, potatoes, carrots, sugar beet and strawberries. Sheep are the leading livestock, with poultry, beef and dairy cattle important. Fishing is a major activity. Financial services and tourism are the leading service industries.

1 : 4 250 000

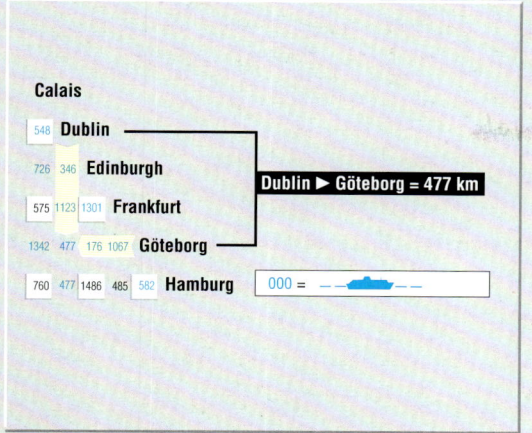

Calais
548	**Dublin**
726	346	**Edinburgh**
575	1123	1301	**Frankfurt**
1342	477	176	1067	**Göteborg**
760	477	1486	485	582	**Hamburg**

Dublin ► Göteborg = 477 km

000 = ⛴

Amsterdam
2945 **Athínai**
1505 3192 **Barcelona**
1484 3742 2803 **Bergen**
650 2412 1863 1309 **Berlin**
197 2895 1308 1586 764 **Bruxelles**
2245 1219 2644 3037 1707 2181 **Bucuresti**
1420 1530 1999 2212 882 1358 852 **Budapest**
367 3100 1269 1783 956 215 2398 1573 **Calais**
533 3630 1817 270 1504 763 3021 2196 548 **Dublin**
1093 3826 1995 176 1696 941 3124 2299 726 346 **Edinburgh**
441 2499 1313 1508 550 383 1804 979 575 1123 1301 **Frankfurt**
1029 3080 2362 819 668 1145 1734 1550 1342 477 176 1067 **Göteborg**
447 2719 1780 1023 286 563 2014 1189 760 477 1486 485 582 **Hamburg**
1560 2539 2338 1063 475 1239 1834 1009 1431 1318 1236 1598 505 1113 **Helsinki**
2756 1145 2990 3653 2223 2706 690 1341 2911 3537 3657 2314 2891 2530 2350 **Istanbul**
965 2782 2090 1103 370 1081 2077 1252 1278 752 479 795 284 518 803 2593 **København**
256 2684 1376 1427 566 198 1983 1158 390 938 1116 180 986 404 1517 2499 714 **Köln**
2331 4460 1268 3723 2869 3141 3917 3222 2069 2617 2795 2400 3282 2700 3817 4342 3014 2339 **Lisboa**
480 3200 1387 458 1074 333 2591 1766 118 430 608 693 122 878 1991 3107 1188 508 2187 **London**
406 2661 1190 1613 749 209 2052 1227 424 972 1150 240 1172 590 1703 2472 900 186 2160 542 **Luxembourg**
1790 3809 617 3183 2364 1600 3262 2622 1528 1634 2254 1930 2742 2160 3276 3589 2473 1798 651 1646 1628 **Madrid**
1210 2683 509 2435 1541 1030 2154 1505 1063 1588 1789 1023 1994 1412 2525 2479 1722 1006 1777 1182 822 1126 **Marseille**
1085 2182 1038 2141 1060 890 1668 992 1072 1620 1798 683 1700 1118 1535 1993 1428 868 2315 1190 679 1655 538 **Milano**
2457 2930 3655 2223 1821 2585 1761 2099 2800 3348 3526 2312 1665 2115 1160 2605 2325 2387 4875 2918 2852 4224 3270 3027 **Moskva**
839 2106 1340 1788 594 789 1497 672 994 1524 1720 398 1347 765 1069 1907 969 580 2545 1094 525 2010 1011 473 2305 **München**
1347 3372 2680 503 960 1463 2667 1842 1660 773 729 1385 316 900 697 3089 590 1304 3604 1778 1490 3063 2312 2018 1823 1559 **Oslo**
510 2917 988 1922 1051 320 2307 1482 281 829 1007 591 1481 899 2012 2727 1209 495 1821 399 351 1280 782 857 2903 810 1799 **Paris**
950 2067 1750 1675 345 888 1362 537 1097 1635 1816 512 1013 652 770 1878 715 690 2870 1205 753 2329 1399 853 1853 388 1305 1061 **Praha**
1691 1140 1385 2706 1502 1520 1904 1263 1678 2226 2404 1289 2265 1683 1977 2237 1993 1474 2653 1796 1285 2002 876 606 3362 918 2583 1389 1309 **Roma**
2347 4223 1031 3736 2894 2150 3709 3010 2078 2626 2804 2344 3295 2713 3826 4034 3023 2318 401 2196 2178 550 1540 2078 4774 2371 3613 1830 2781 2446 **Sevilla**
2206 828 2453 3103 1673 2156 391 790 2361 2891 3087 1764 2341 1980 1800 550 2043 1949 3706 2461 1922 3037 1929 1443 2252 1367 2632 2177 1328 1687 3484 **Sofiya**
1393 3418 2726 1063 1006 1509 2713 1888 1673 2254 1069 1431 505 946 167 3185 590 1350 3650 1824 1536 3109 2358 2064 1228 1600 530 1845 1351 2629 3659 2679 **Stockholm**
1256 2128 2366 1909 606 1350 1473 648 1542 2110 2268 1136 1274 886 361 1989 956 1152 3480 1345 2960 2015 1469 1245 996 1506 1677 616 1853 3397 1439 1612 **Warszawa**
1168 1772 1856 1970 640 1114 1067 242 1308 1954 2034 731 1308 947 1088 1583 1010 916 3100 1524 993 2473 1353 818 2137 430 1600 1240 295 1126 2876 1033 1646 727 **Wien**
816 2426 1030 1938 863 619 1810 985 804 1352 1530 464 1497 915 2164 2323 1433 589 2296 922 410 1647 699 292 2552 303 1815 592 691 898 2061 1173 1861 1307 743 **Zürich**

km

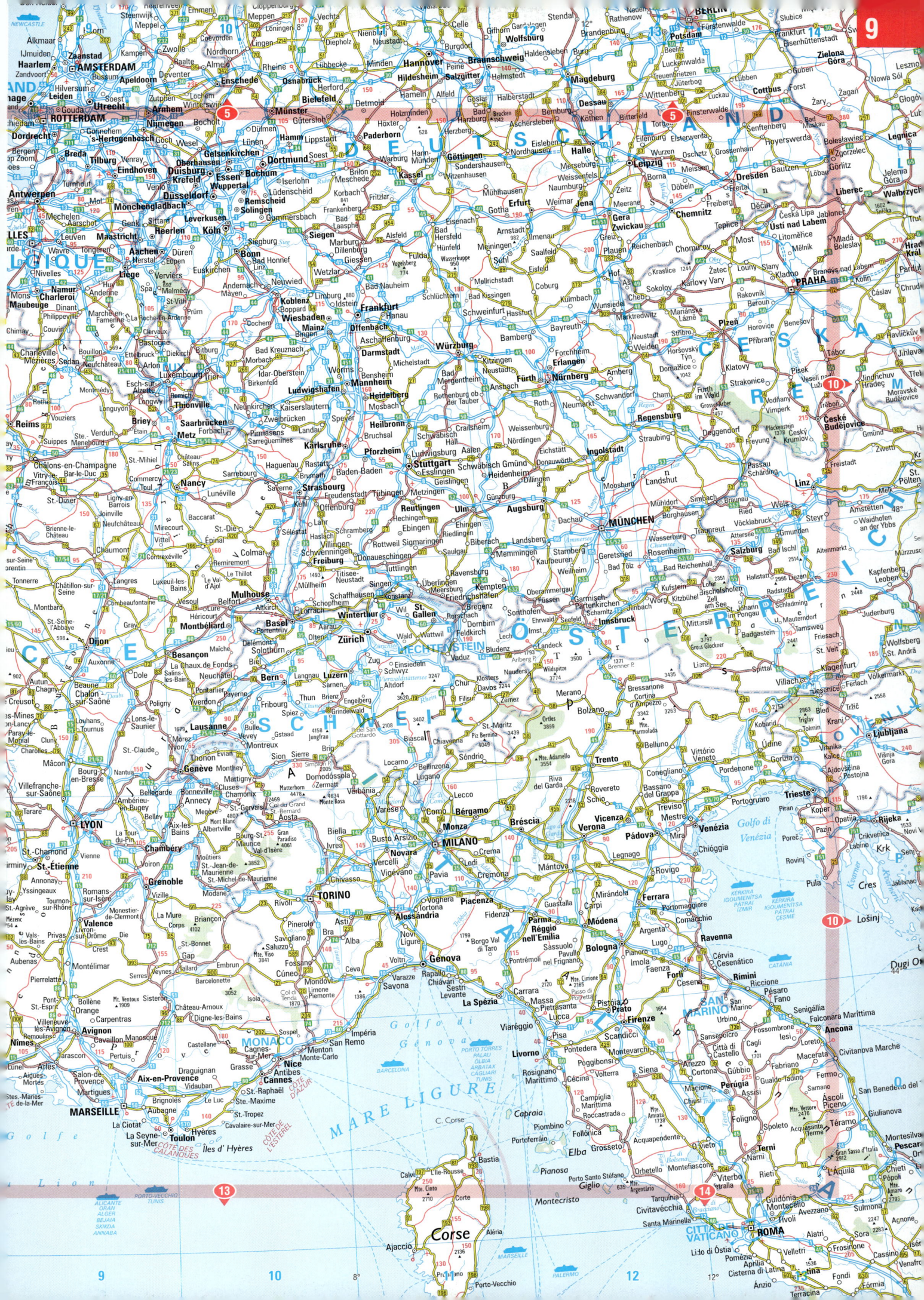

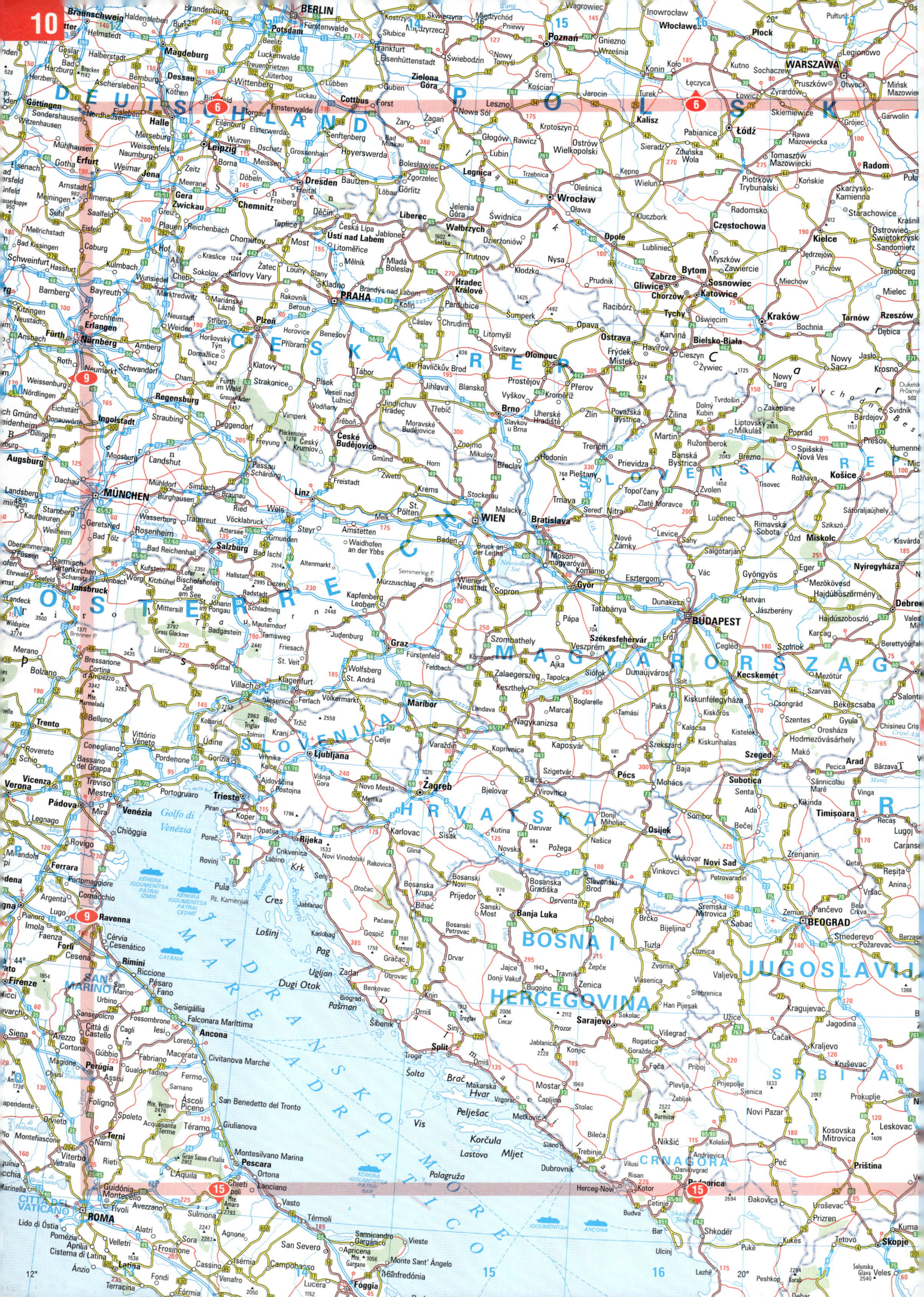

1 : 1 000 000

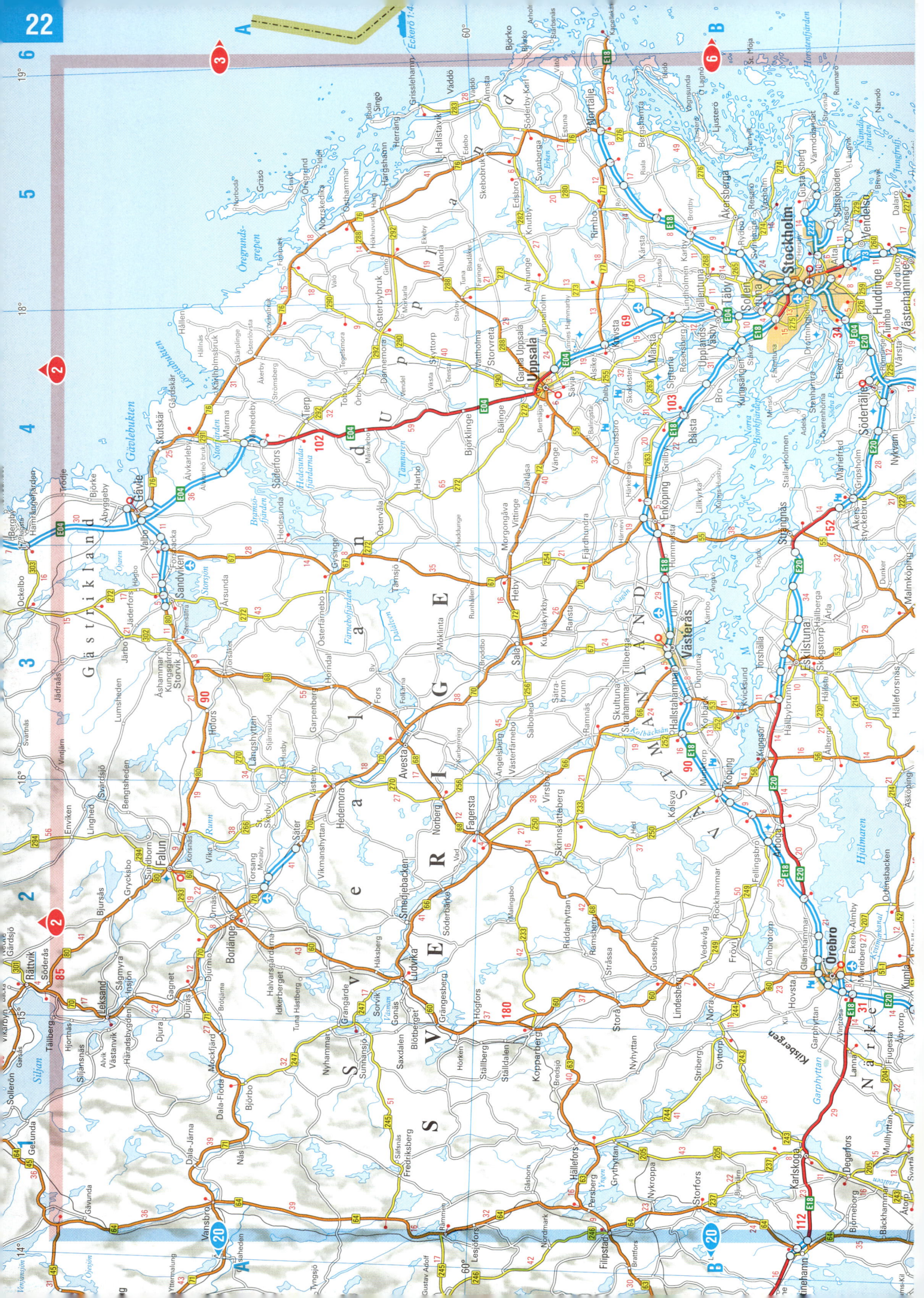

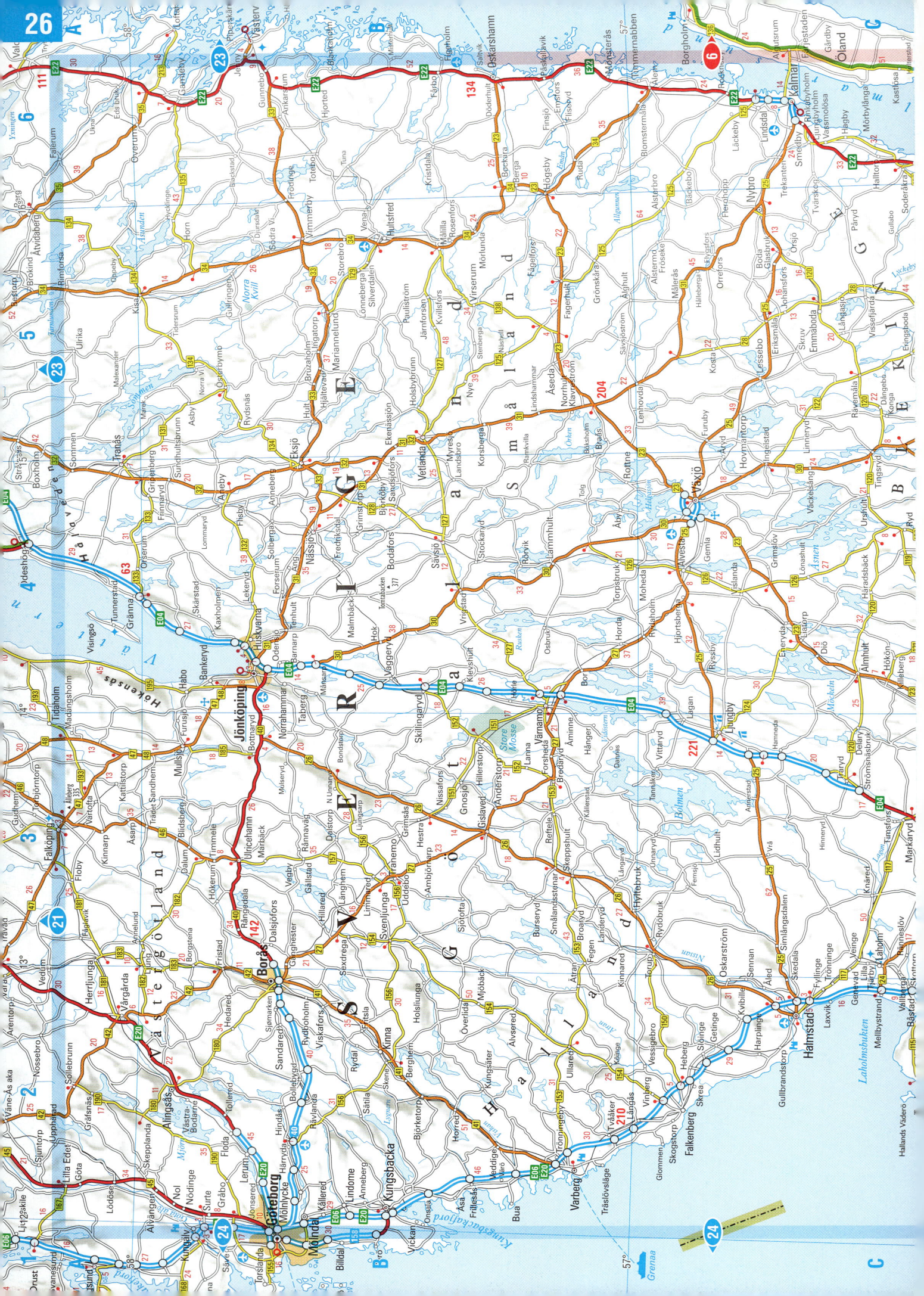

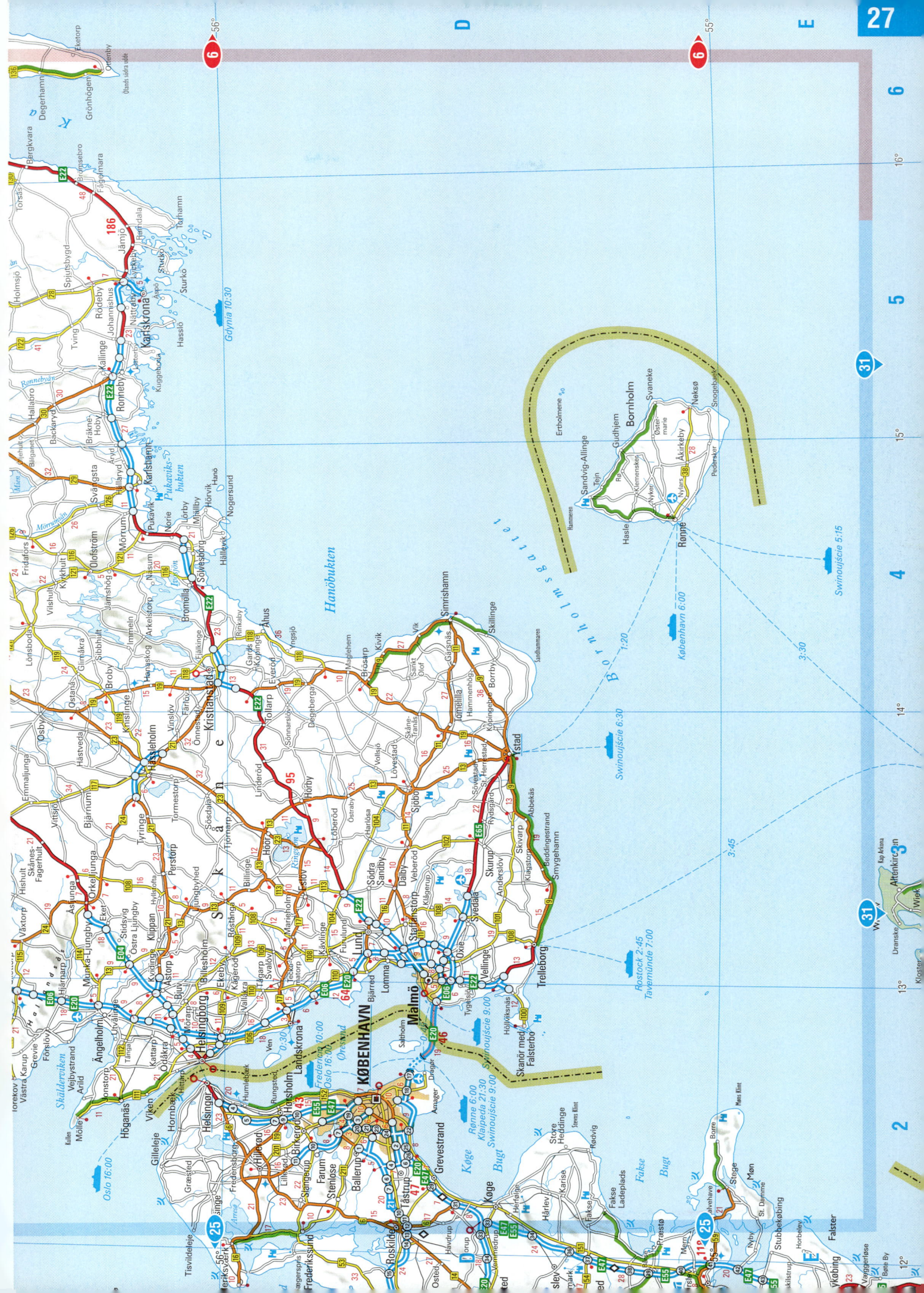

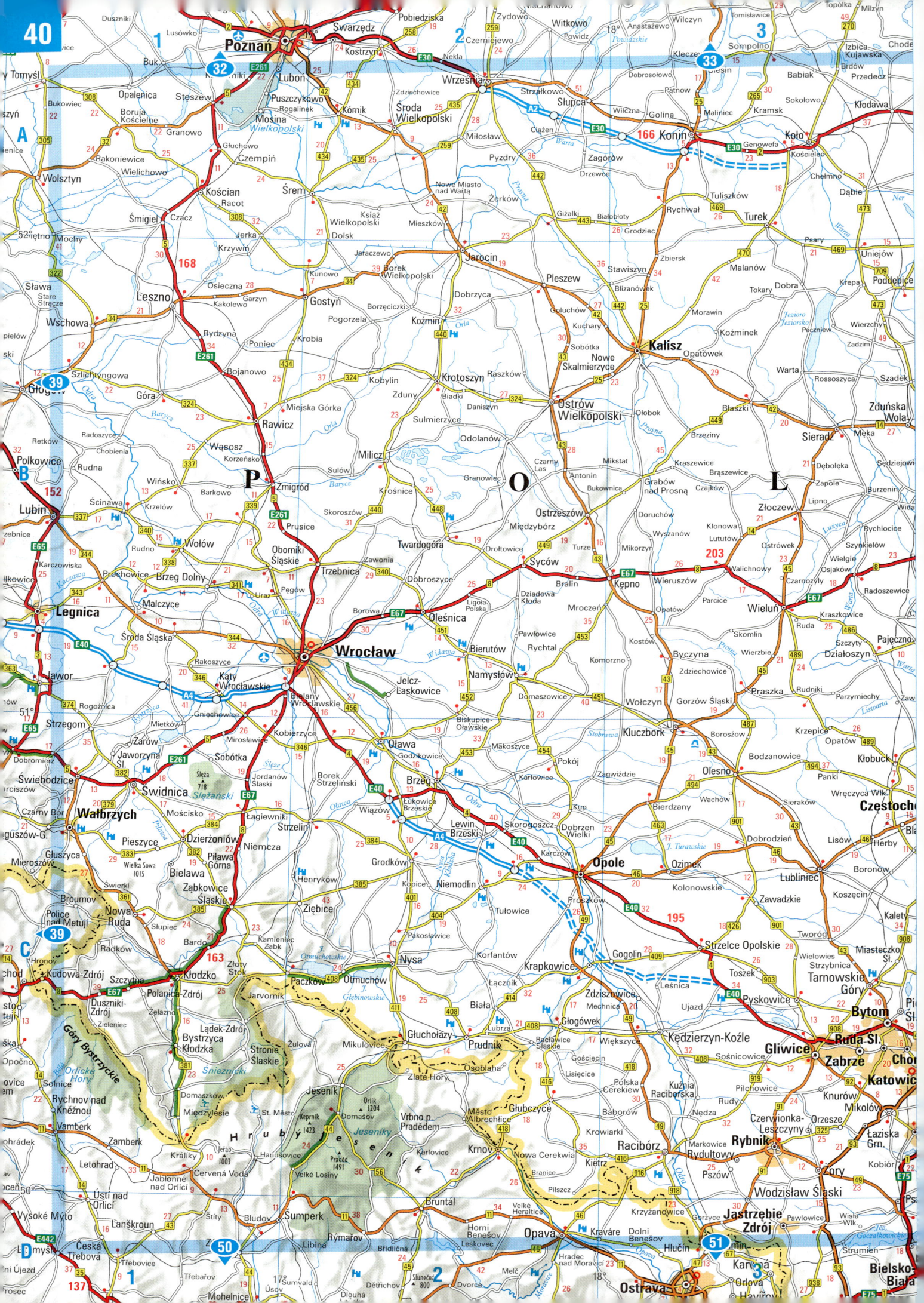

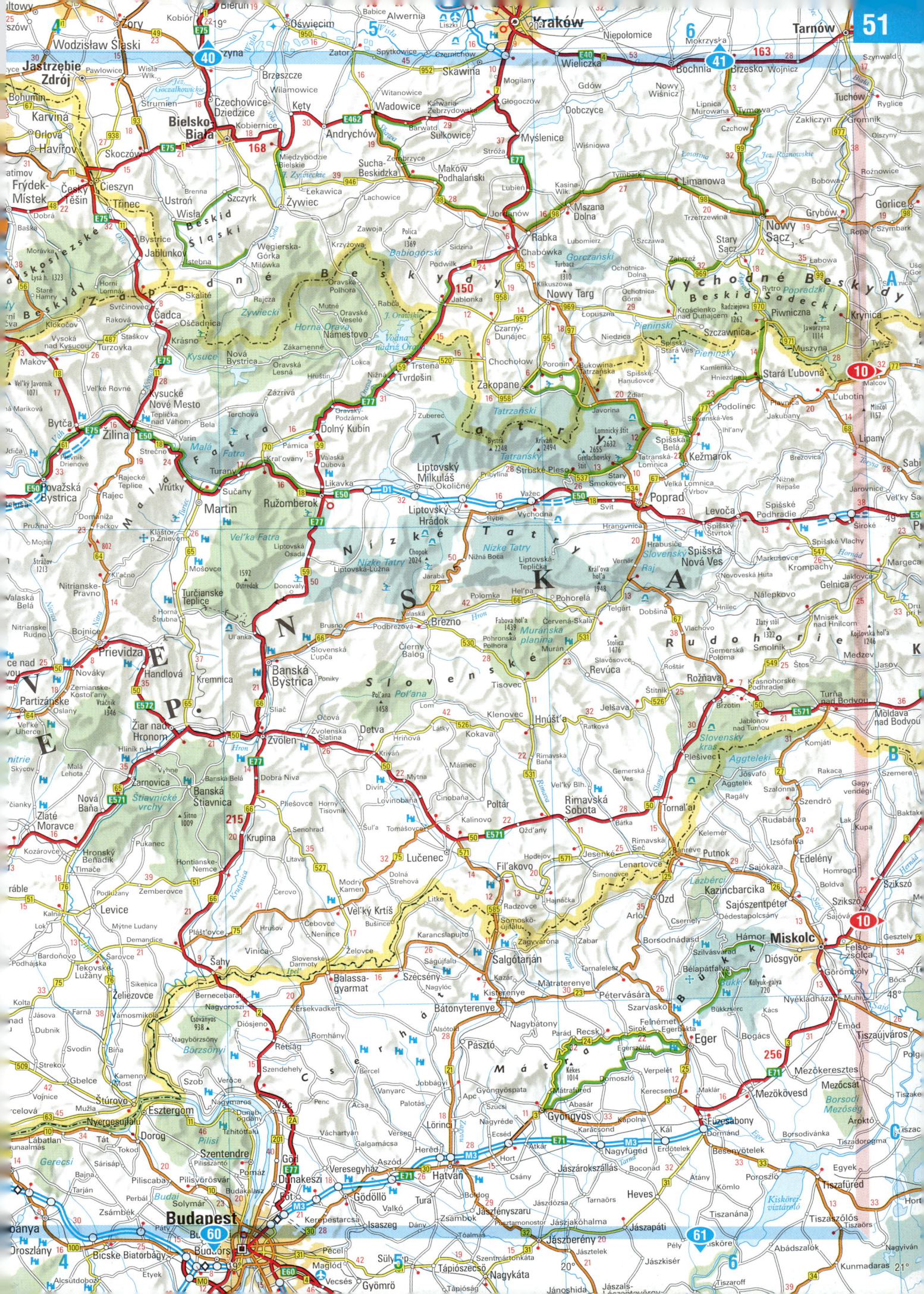

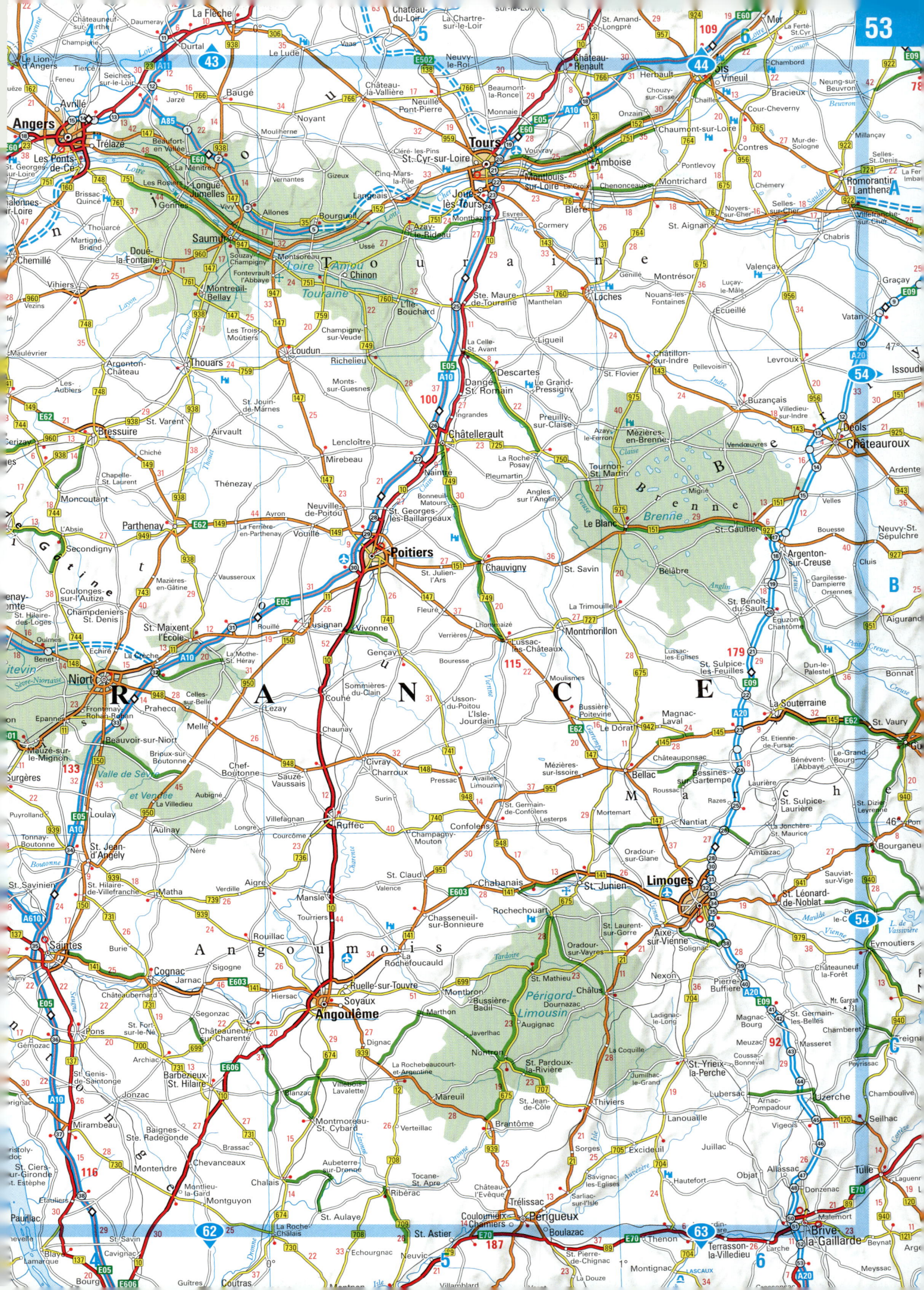

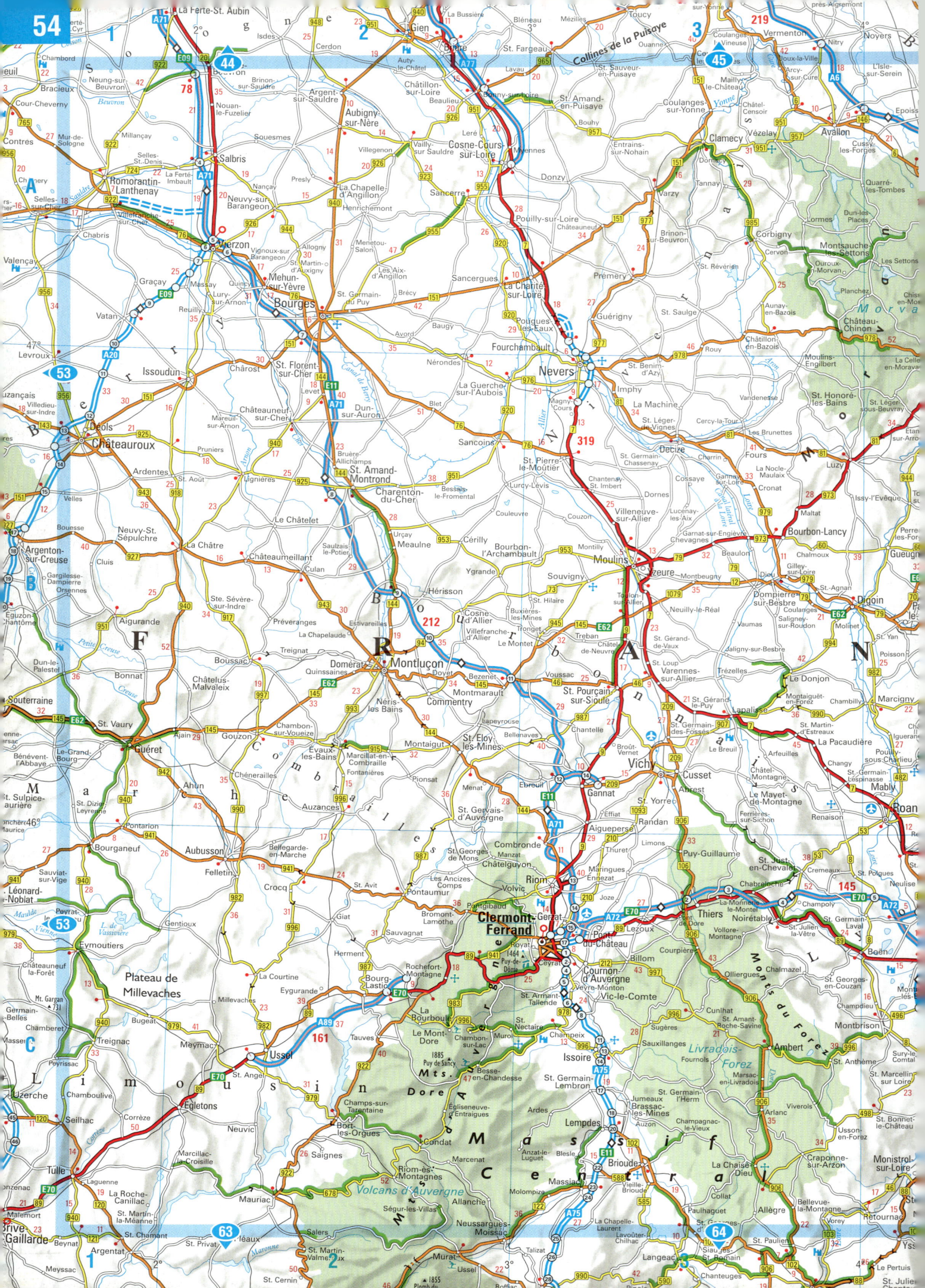

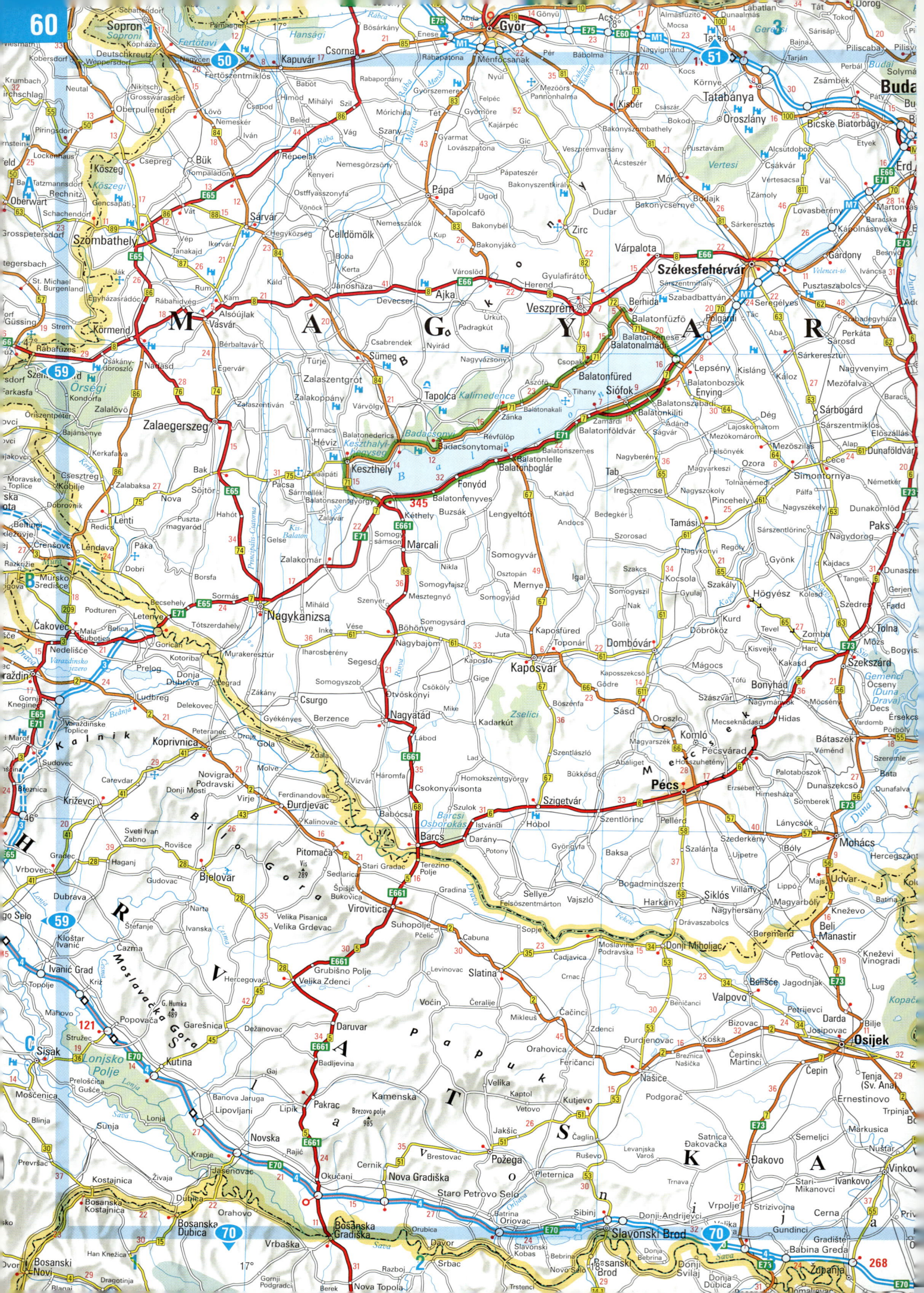

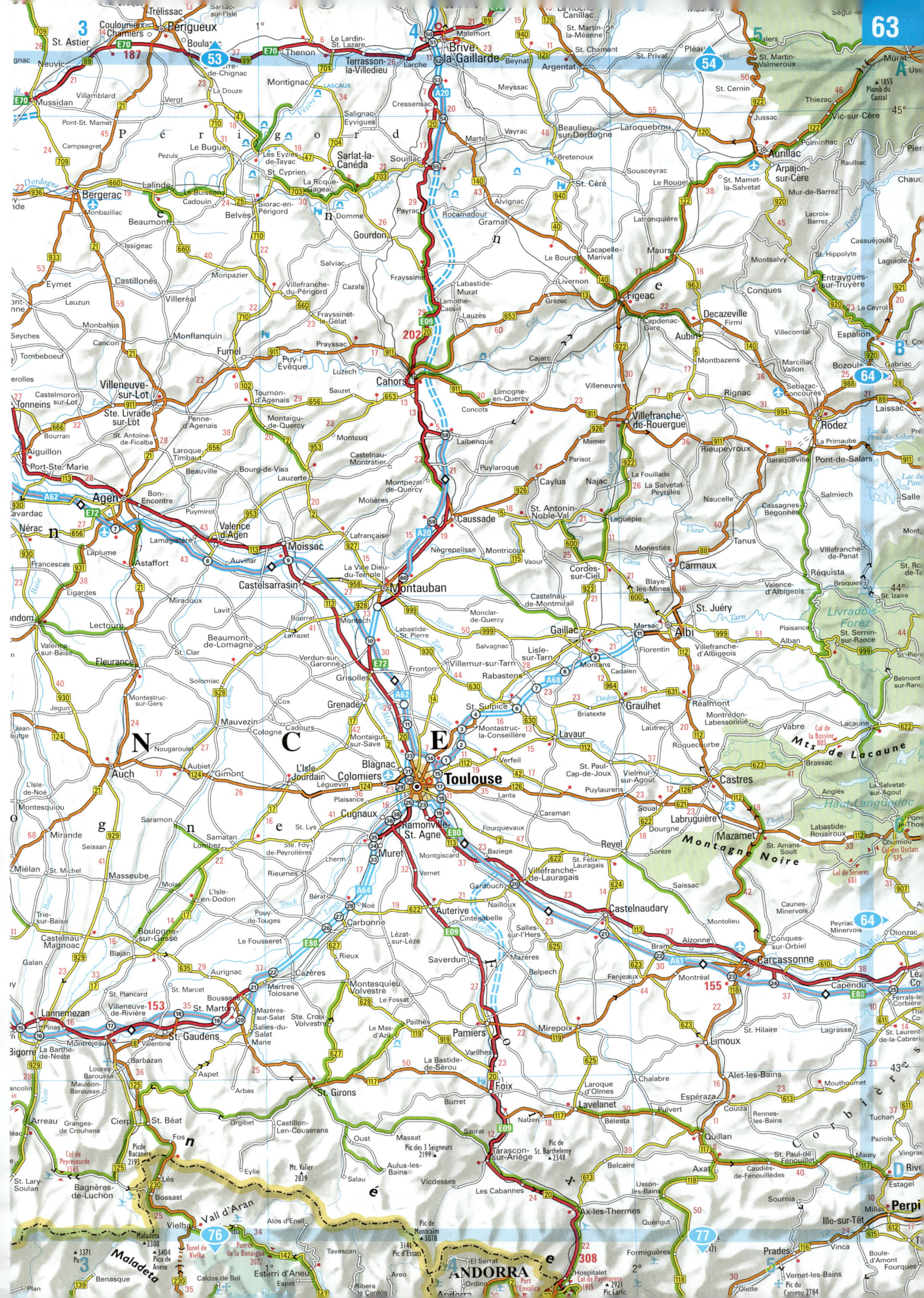

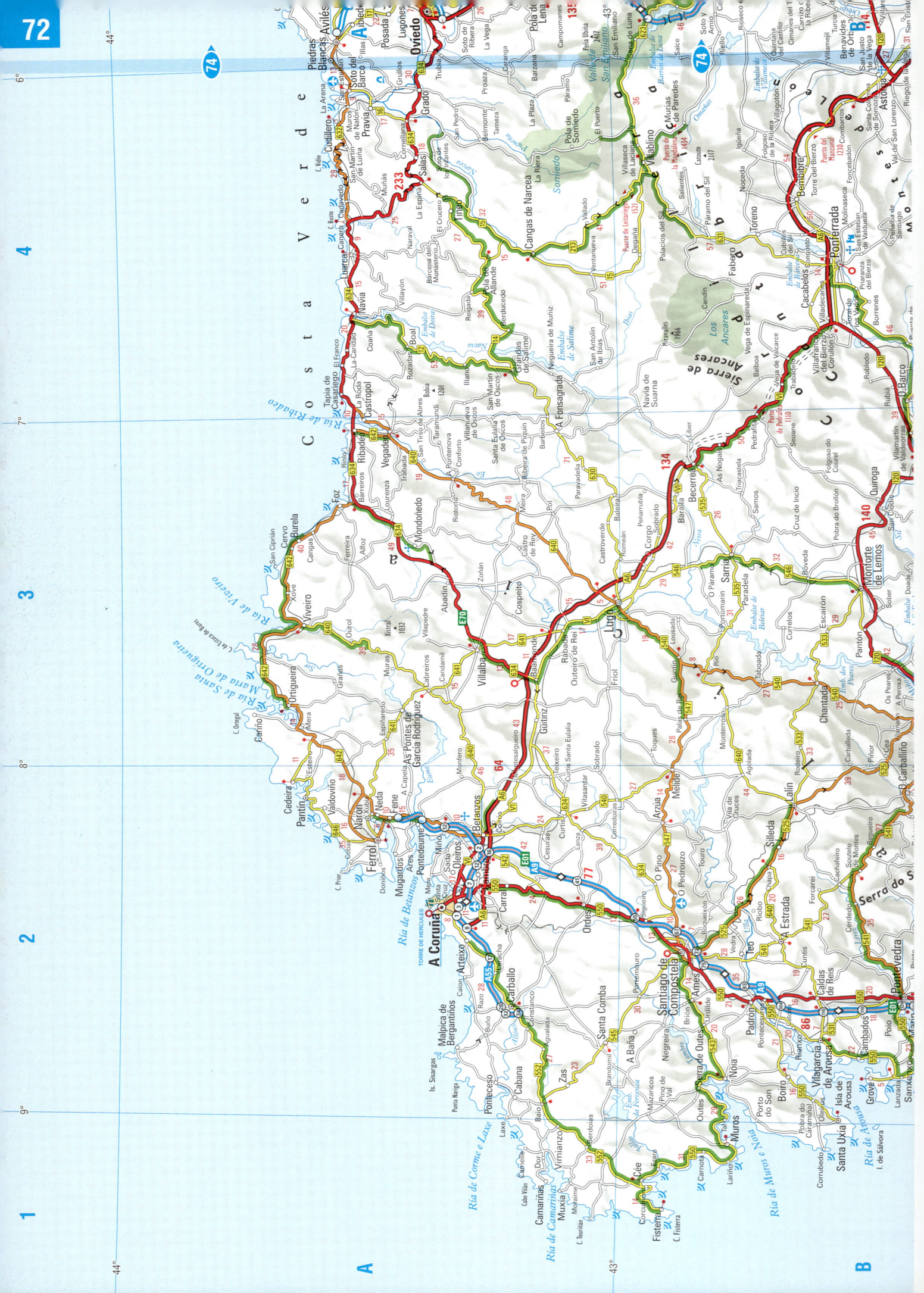

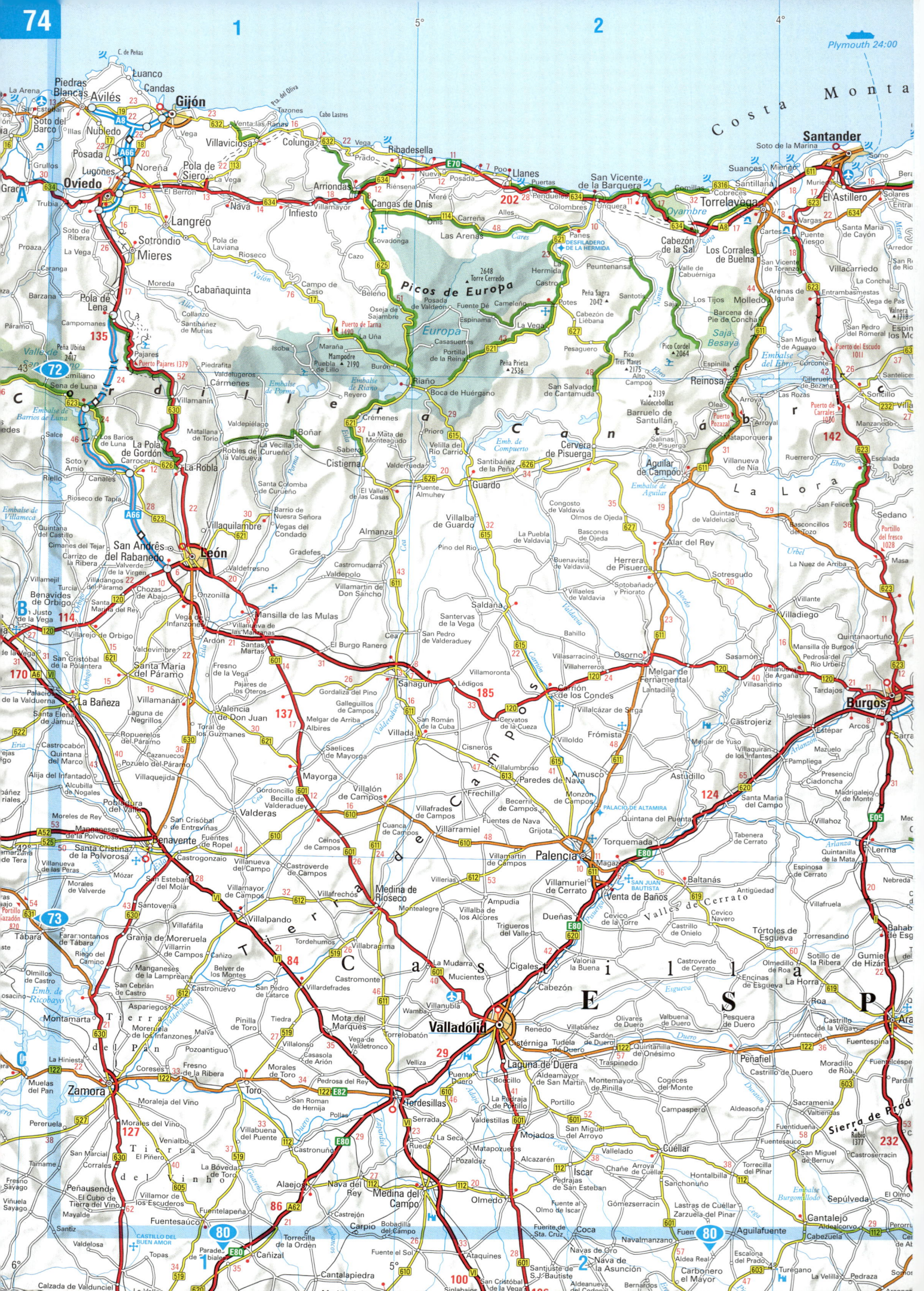

Map — Catalunya / Roussillon / Andorra

Countries/Regions: ANDORRA, Pyrénées, Pirineos Orientales, Roussillon, Costa Brava, Costa Dorada, Cerdaña

Major cities: BARCELONA, L'Hospitalet de Llobregat, Perpignan, Tarragona, Girona, Figueres, Reus, Manresa, Terrassa, Sabadell, Badalona, Santa Coloma de Gramenet, Mataró, Granollers, Andorra la Vella

Ferry routes:
- Génova 17:00
- Maó 9:00
- Palma de Mallorca 3:00
- Eivissa 9:30

Selected place names: Tarascon-sur-Ariège, Ax-les-Thermes, Puigcerdà, Bourg-Madame, Mont-Louis, Prades, Céret, Le Boulou, La Jonquera, Portbou, Roses, Cadaqués, L'Escala, Palamós, Palafrugell, Sant Feliu de Guíxols, Lloret de Mar, Blanes, Calella, Arenys de Mar, Premià de Mar, El Masnou, Vic, Ripoll, Olot, Banyoles, Berga, Cardona, Solsona, La Seu d'Urgell, Organyà, Ponts, Agramunt, Tàrrega, Cervera, Igualada, Montblanc, Valls, El Vendrell, Vilanova i la Geltrú, Sitges, Castelldefels, El Prat de Llobregat, Gavà, Vilafranca del Penedès, Martorell, Molins de Rei, Rubí, Cambrils, Salou

Grid references: A, B, C (right margin); 4, 5, 6 (bottom)

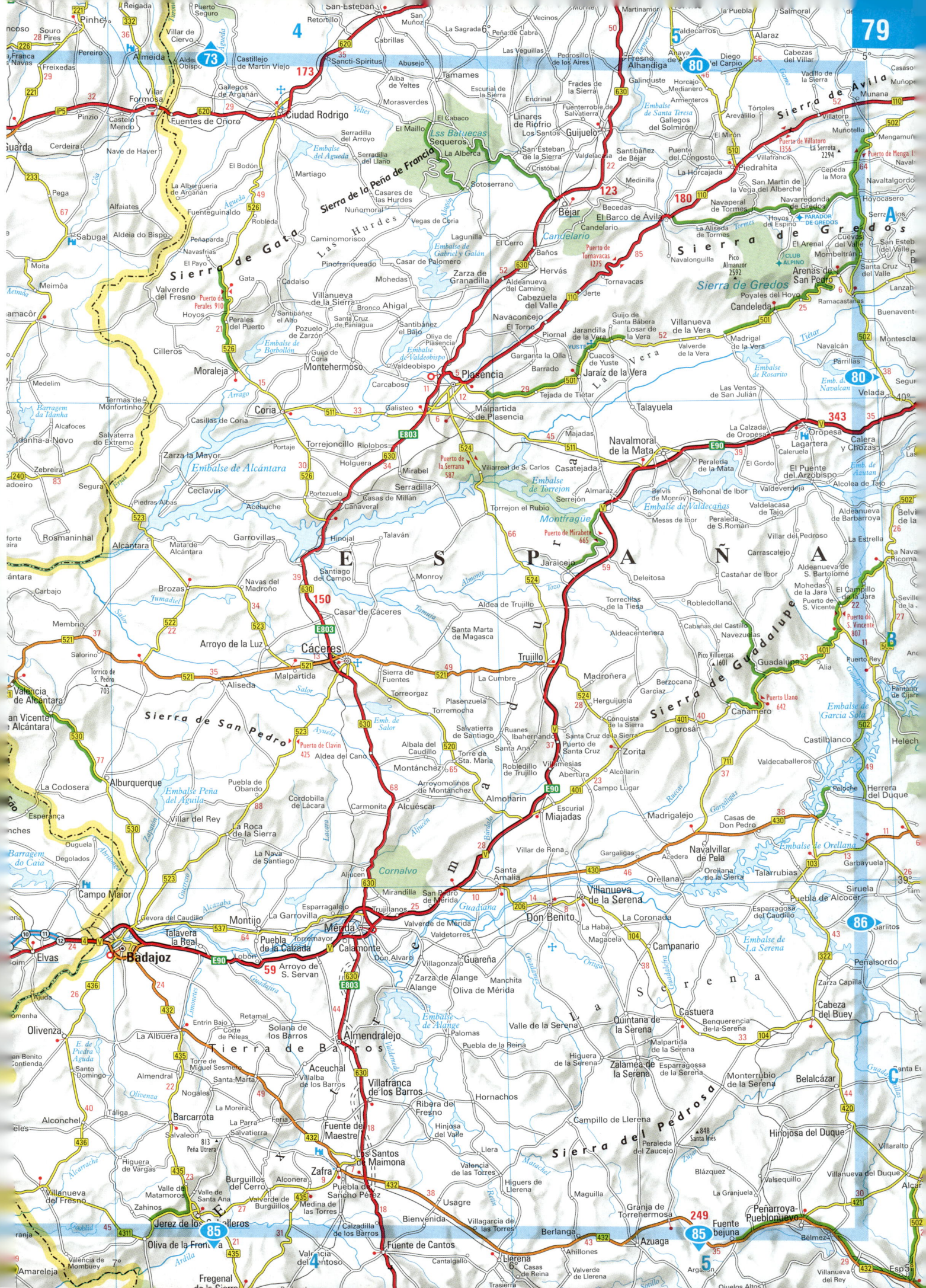

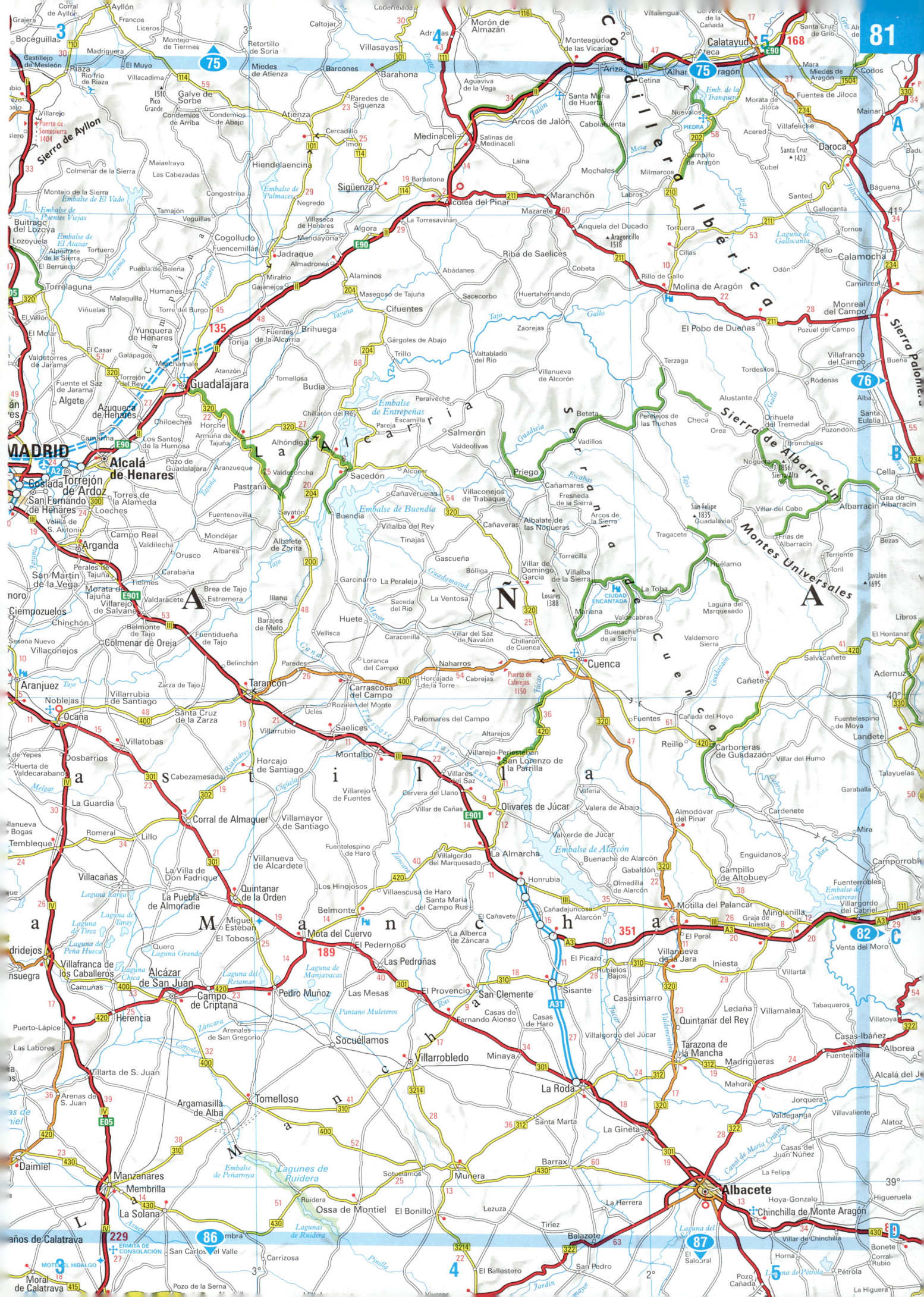

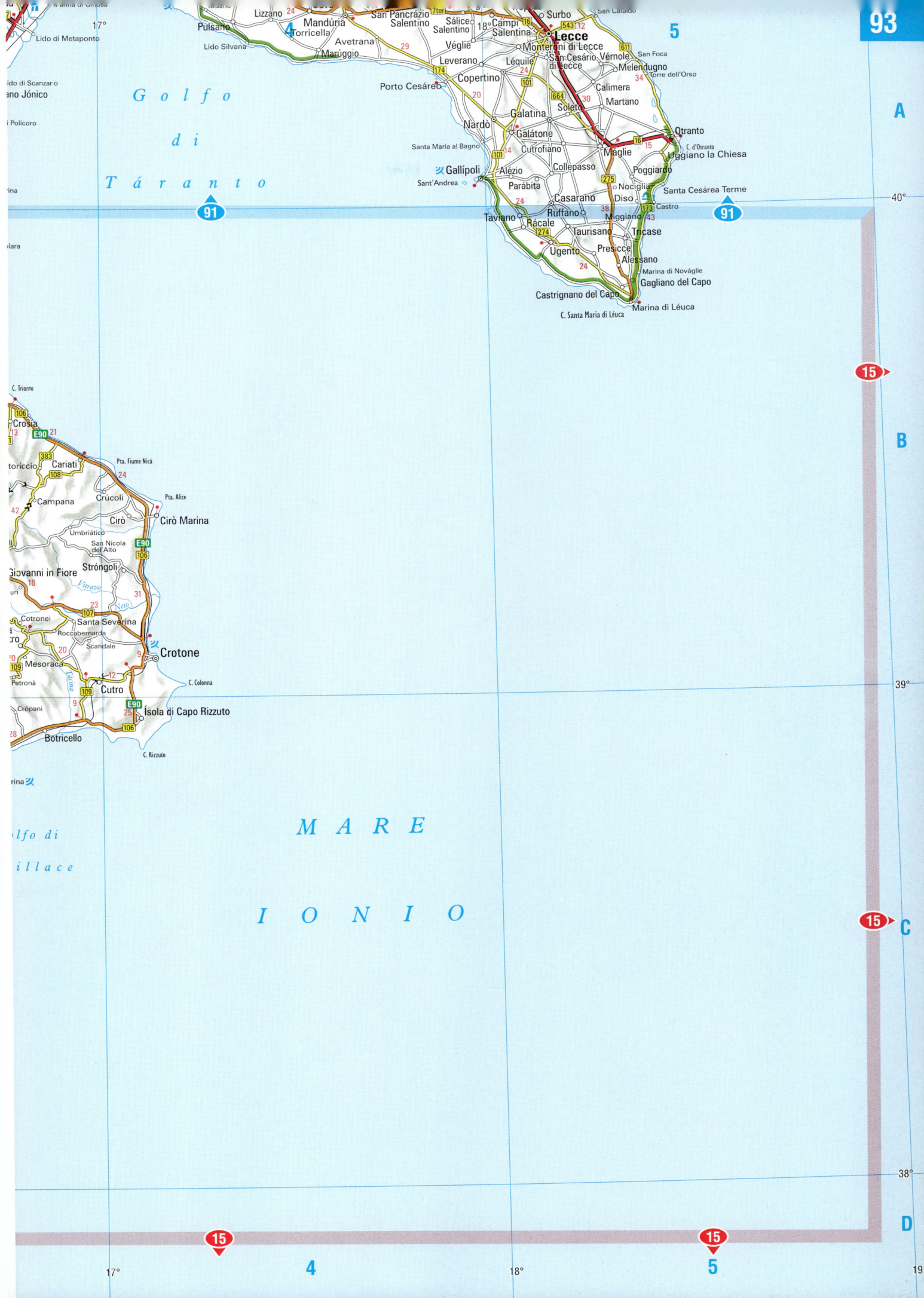

Lizzano 24
Pulsano
Lido Silvana
Torricella
Avetrana
Marúggio
Manduria
San Pancrázio Salentino
Sálice Salentino
Véglie
Leverano
Copertino
Porto Cesáreo
Nardò
Santa Maria al Bagno
Galátone
Gallípoli
Sant'Andrea
Cutrofiano
Alézio
Parábita
Casarano
Taviano
Rácale
Ugento
Campi Salentina
Monteróni di Lecce
San Cesário di Lecce
Léquile
Soleto
Galatina
Collepasso
Ruffano
Taurisano
Presicce
Alessano
Castrignano del Capo
C. Santa Maria di Léuca
Surbo
San Cataldo
Lecce
Vérnole
Calimera
Martano
Maglie
Collepasso
Poggiardo
Nociglia
Diso
Miggiano
Tricase
Marina di Nováglie
Gagliano del Capo
Marina di Léuca
San Foca
Melendugno
Torre dell'Orso
Otranto
C. d'Otranto
Uggiano la Chiesa
Santa Cesárea Terme
Castro

Golfo di Táranto

MARE

IONIO

C. Trionto
Crosia
Cariati
Campana
Crúcoli
Cirò
Umbriático
San Nicola dell'Alto
Stróngoli
Giovanni in Fiore
Cotronei
Santa Severina
Roccabernarda
Scandale
Mesoraca
Petronà
Crópani
Botricello
Cutro
Ísola di Capo Rizzuto
Crotone
Pta. Fiume Nicá
Pta. Alice
Cirò Marina
C. Colonna
C. Rizzuto

Golfo di
illace

Lido di Metaponto
ano Jónico
di Policoro
olara
ina
rina

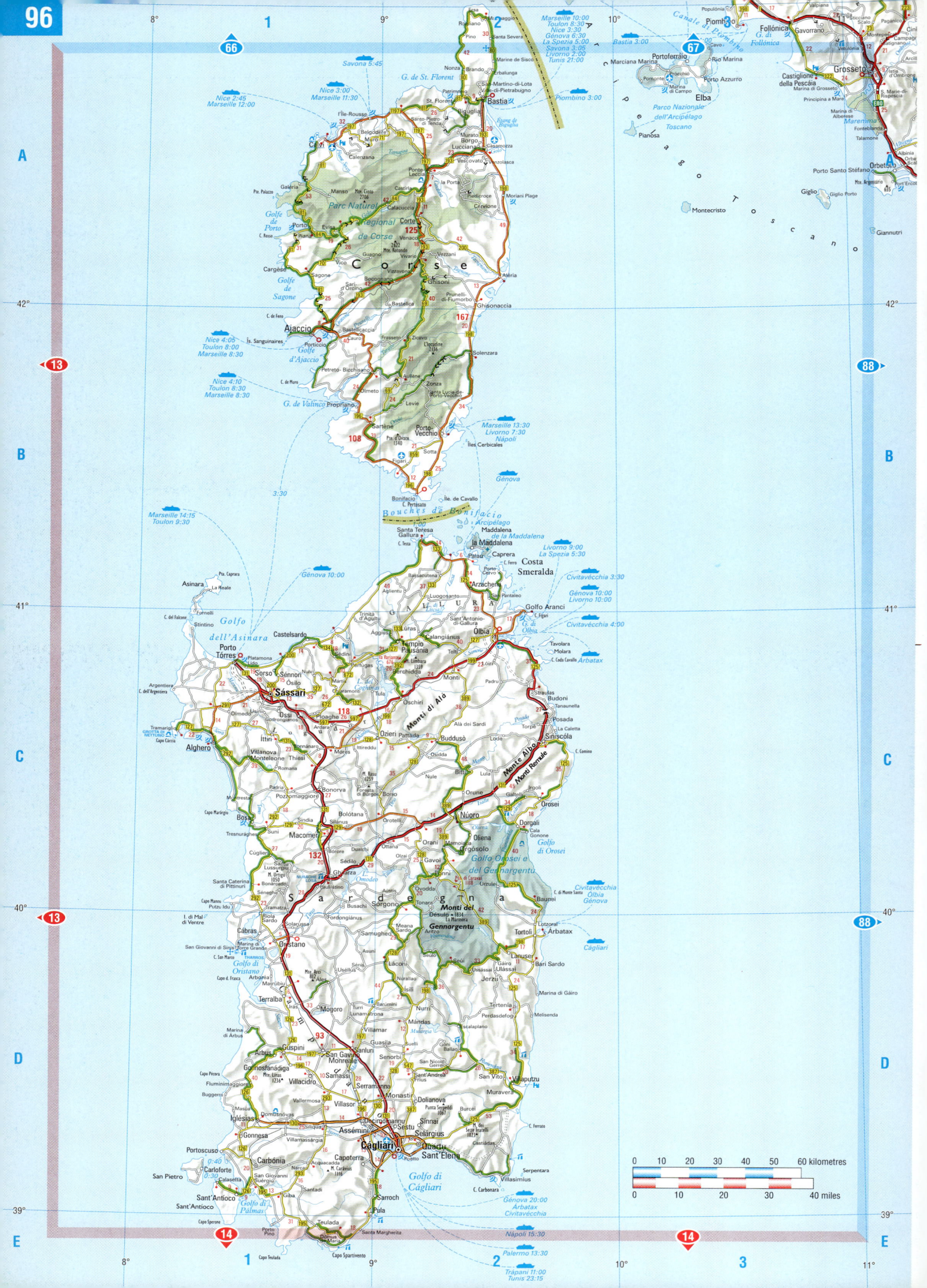

City plans • Plans de villes
Stadtpläne • Piante di città

Motorway	Autoroute		Autobahn		Autostrada
Through route	Route principale		Schnellstrasse		Strada d'importanza regionale
Secondary road	Route secondaire		Nebenstrasse		Strada d'interesse locale
Dual carriageway	Chaussées séparées		Zweispurig Schnellstrasse		Strada a carreggiate doppie
Other road	Autre route		Nebenstrecke		Altra strada
Tunnel	Tunnel		Tunnel		Galleria stradale
Limited access / pedestrian road	Rue réglementée / rue piétonne		Beschränkter Zugang / Fussgängerzone		Strada pedonale / a accesso limitato
One-way street	Sens unique		Einbahnstrasse		Senso unico
Parking	Parc de stationnement		Parkplatz		Parcheggio
Motorway number	Numéro d'autoroute		Autobahnnummer		Numero di autostrada
National road number	Numéro de route nationale		Nationalstrassennummer		Numero di strada nazionale
European road number	Numéro de route européenne		Europäische Strassennummer		Numero di strada europea
Destination	Destination		Ziel		Destinazione
Car ferry	Bac passant les autos		Autofähre		Traghetto automobili
Railway	Chemin de fer		Eisenbahn		Ferrovia
Rail/bus station	Gare / gare routière		Bahnhof / Busstation		Stazione ferrovia / pullman
Underground, metro station	Station de métro		U-Bahnstation		Metropolitano
Cable car	Téléférique		Drahtseilbahn		Funivia
Abbey, cathedral	Abbaye, cathédrale		Abtei, Kloster, Kathedrale		Abbazia, duomo
Church of interest	Église intéressante		Interessante Kirche		Chiesa da vedere
Synagogue	Synagogue		Synagoge		Sinagoga
Hospital	Hôpital		Krankenhaus		Ospedale
Police station	Police		Polizeiwache		Polizia
Post office	Bureau de poste		Postamt		Ufficio postale
Tourist information	Office de tourisme		Informationsbüro		Ufficio informazioni turistiche
Place of interest	Autre curiosité		Sonstige Sehenswürdigkeit		Luogo da vedere

Approach maps • Agglomérations
Carte régionale • Regionalkarte

Toll motorway – with motorway number	**A10**	Autoroute – avec numéro d'autoroute	Gebührenpflichtige Autobahn – mit Autobahnnummer	**A10**	Autostrada a pedaggio – con numero
Toll-free motorway with European road number	**E51**	Autoroute avec numéro de route européenne	Gebührenfreie Autobahn – Europäische Strassennummer	**E51**	Autostrada – con numero di strada europea
Motorway services		Aire de service	Autobahnservice		Area di servizio autostradale
Motorway junction	**24**	Échangeur d'autoroute	Autobahnkreuz	**24**	Raccordi autostradali
Under construction	= = = =	En construction	Im Bau	= = = =	In construzione
Tunnel	)======(	Tunnel	Tunnel	)======(	Galleria stradale
Major route dual carriageway	**14**	Route principale chausées séparées	Hauptstrecke		Strada di grande comunicazione
single carriageway	**14**	chausée sans séparation	zweispurige	**14**	carreggiata doppia
Secondary route dual carriageway	**96**	Route secondaire chausées séparées	Schnellstrasse	**14**	carreggiata unica
single carriageway	**96**	chausées sans séparation	Nebenstrasse		Strada d'interesse locale
Other road		Autre route	zweispurige	**96**	carreggiata doppia
Car ferry		Bac passant les autos	Schnellstrasse	**96**	carreggiata unica
Destination	**GIRONA**	Destination	Nebenstrecke		Altra strada
Railway		Chemin de fer	Autofähre		Traghetto automobili
Railway station	Estación Central	Gare	Ziel	**GIRONA**	Destinazione
Height above sea level – in metres	▲ 234	Altitude – en mètres	Eisenbahn		Ferrovia
Airport		Aéroport principal	Hauptbahnhof	Estación Central	Stazione ferrovia
Airfield		Autre aéroport	Höhe über dem Meeresspiegel	▲ 234	Altezza in metri
City plan coverage area		Région de plan de ville	Flughafen		Aeroporto
			Flugplatz		Aerodromo/campo d'aviazione
			Vom Stadtplan abgedecktes Gebiet		Area della pianta della città

Alicante

0   km   0.5

Antwerpen

0   km   1

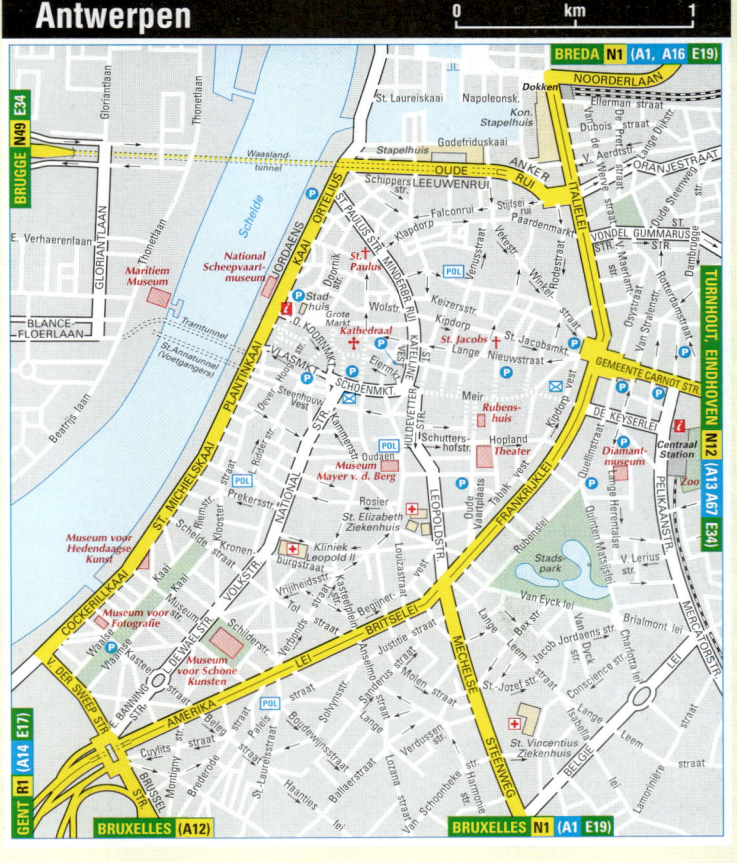

Amsterdam

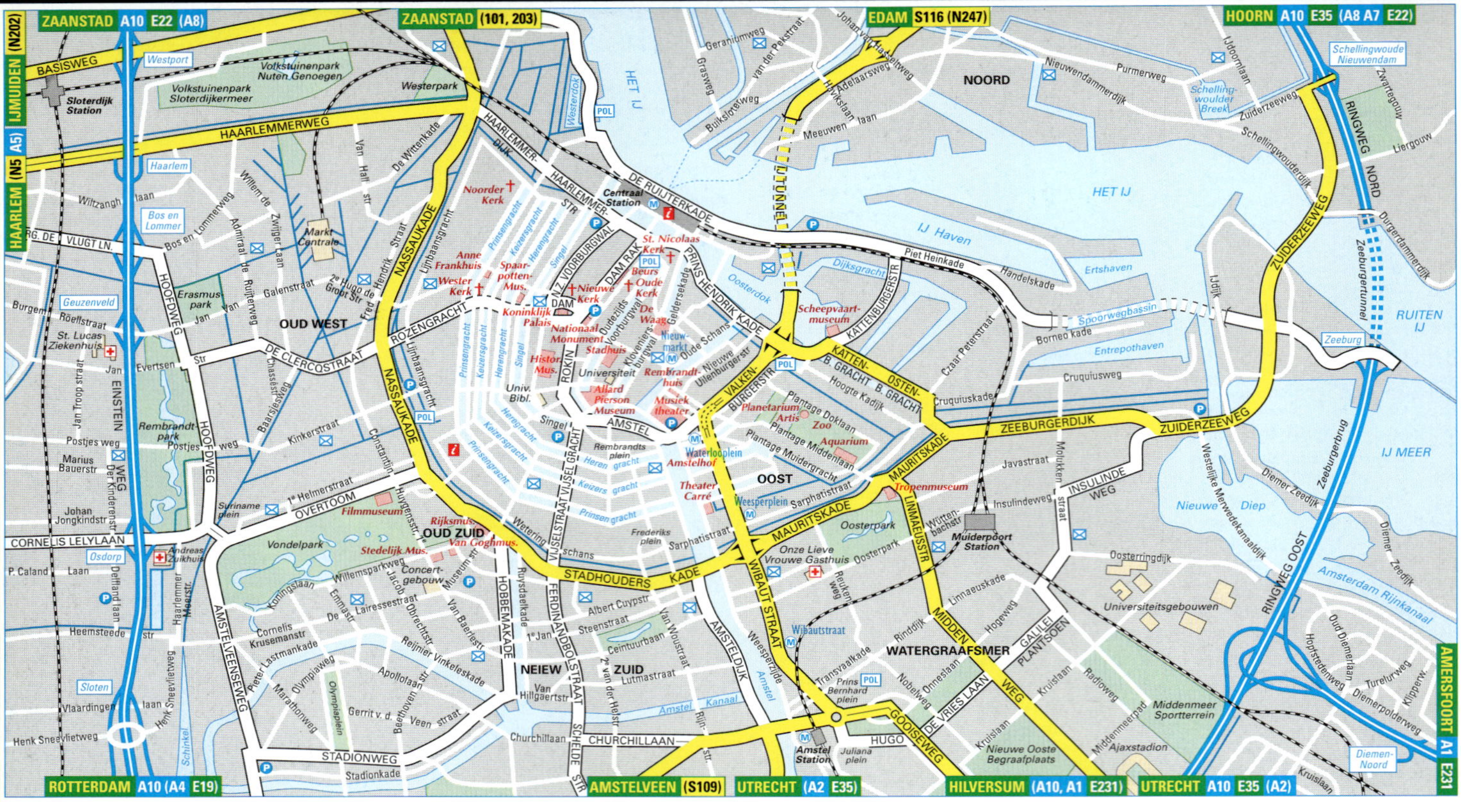

Athínai

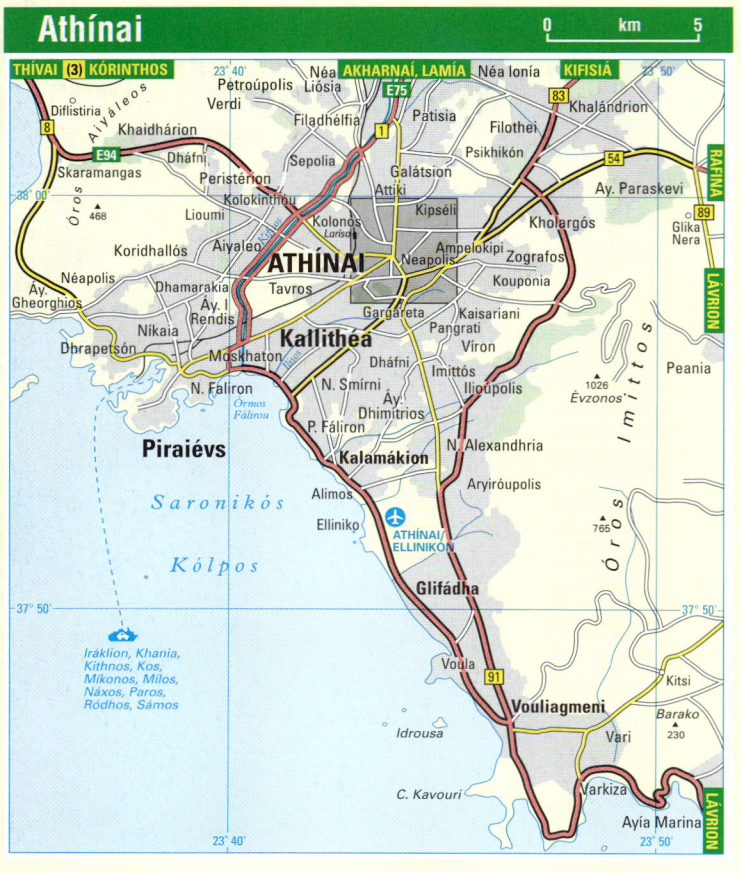

Athínai

Berlin

0 km 5

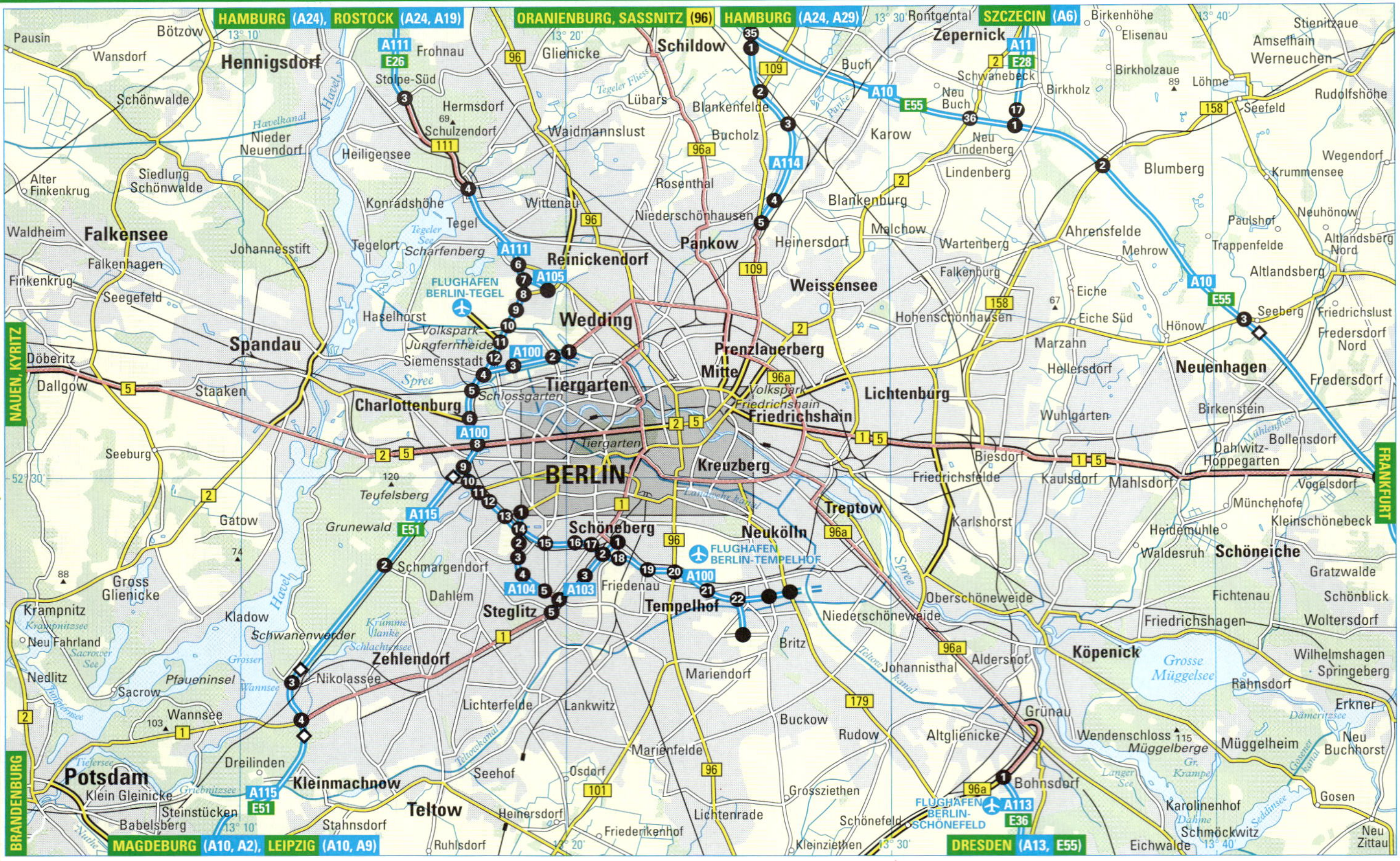

HAMBURG (A24), ROSTOCK (A24, A19) — ORANIENBURG, SASSNITZ (96) — HAMBURG (A24, A29) — SZCZECIN (A6)

NAUEN, KYRITZ

BRANDENBURG

FRANKFURT

MAGDEBURG (A10, A2), LEIPZIG (A10, A9) — DRESDEN (A13, E55)

BERLIN

Hennigsdorf, Falkensee, Spandau, Charlottenburg, Tiergarten, Wedding, Reinickendorf, Pankow, Weissensee, Prenzlauerberg, Mitte, Friedrichshain, Lichtenburg, Kreuzberg, Schöneberg, Neukölln, Treptow, Steglitz, Tempelhof, Zehlendorf, Köpenick, Potsdam, Teltow

FLUGHAFEN BERLIN-TEGEL
FLUGHAFEN BERLIN-TEMPELHOF
FLUGHAFEN BERLIN-SCHÖNEFELD

Berlin

0 km 1

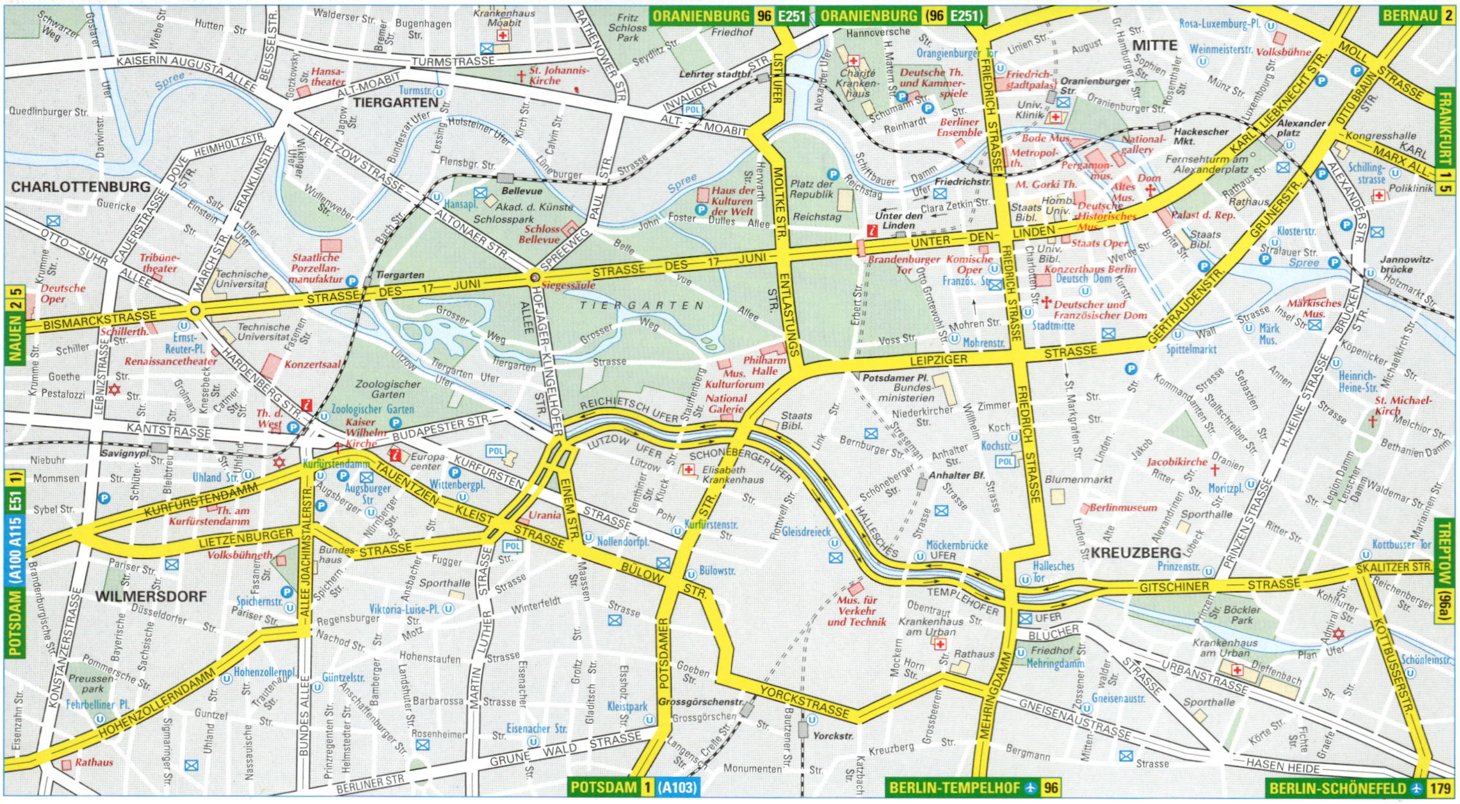

ORANIENBURG 96 E251 — ORANIENBURG (96 E251) — BERNAU 2

NAUEN 2 5 — FRANKFURT 1 5

POTSDAM (A100 A115 E51 1)

POTSDAM 1 (A103) — BERLIN-TEMPELHOF 96 — BERLIN-SCHÖNEFELD 179

TREPTOW (96a)

CHARLOTTENBURG, TIERGARTEN, MITTE, WILMERSDORF, KREUZBERG

Deutsche Oper, Staatliche Porzellanmanufaktur, Schloss Bellevue, Haus der Kulturen der Welt, Reichstag, Brandenburger Tor, Unter den Linden, Staatsoper, Berliner Ensemble, Pergamon, Nationalgalerie, Dom, Rathaus, Alexanderplatz, Fernsehturm am Alexanderplatz, Philharmonie, Kulturforum, Zoologischer Garten, Kaiser Wilhelm Kirche, Europa-Center, Technische Universität, Mus. für Verkehr und Technik, Berlinmuseum, Jacobikirche

Bordeaux

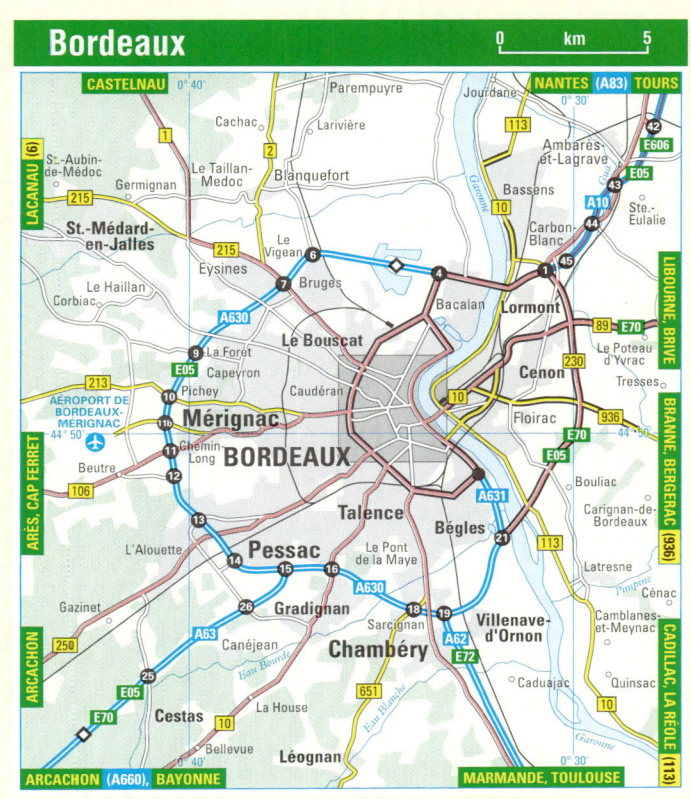

Bordeaux

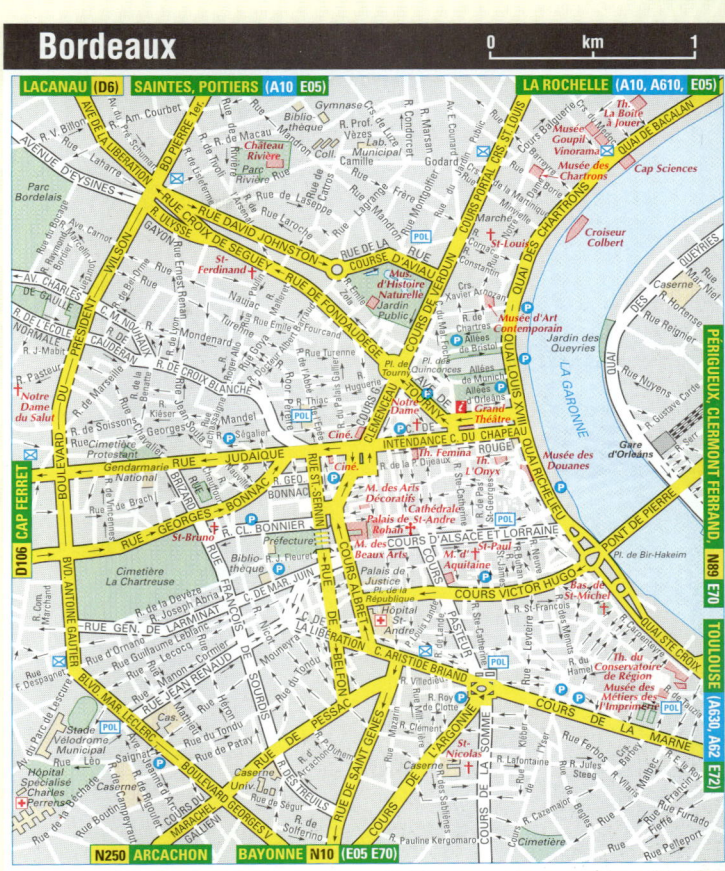

Budapest

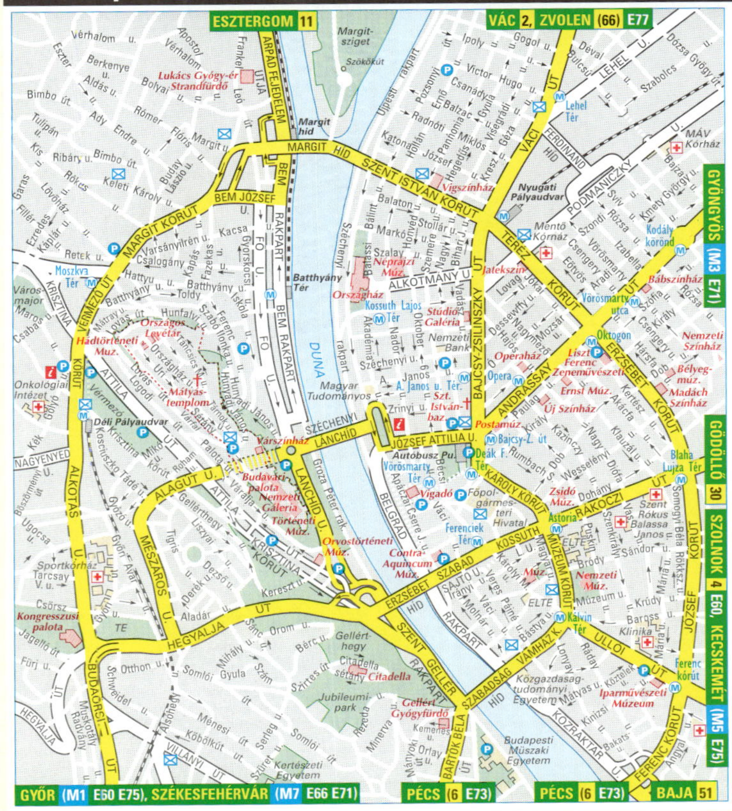

Dublin

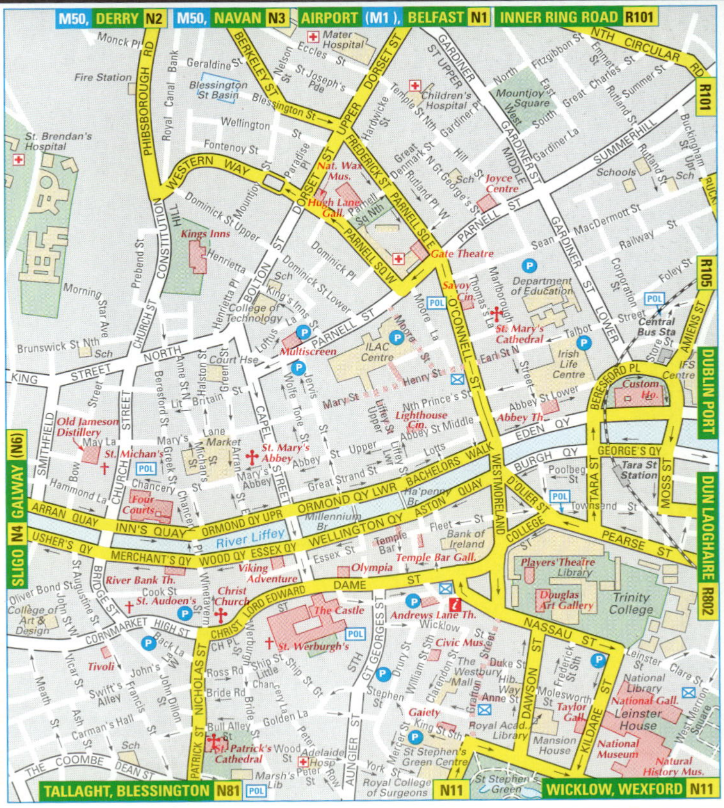

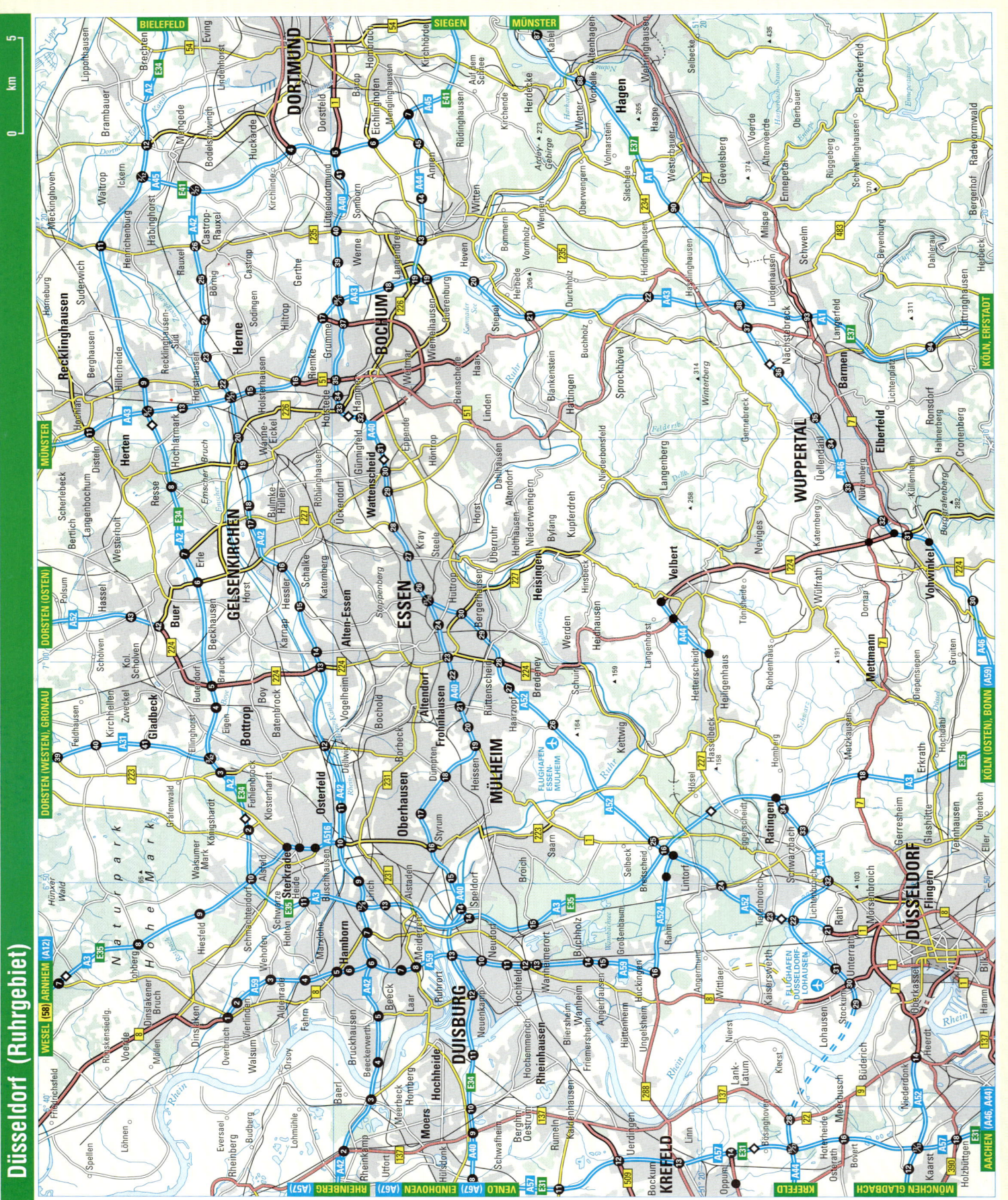

Düsseldorf

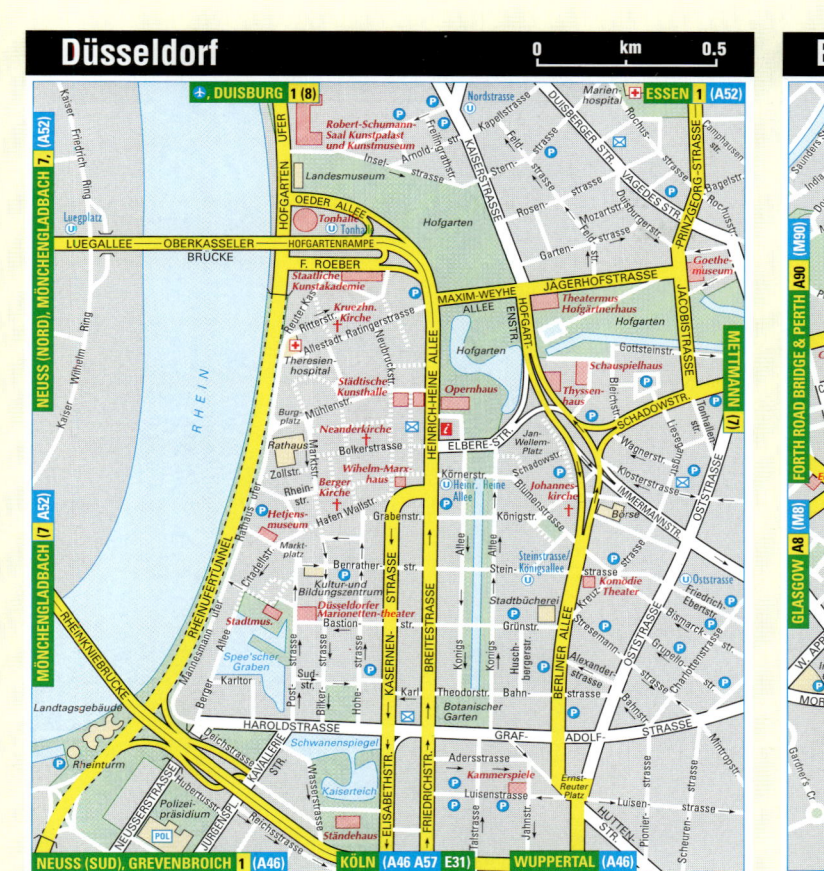

Edinburgh

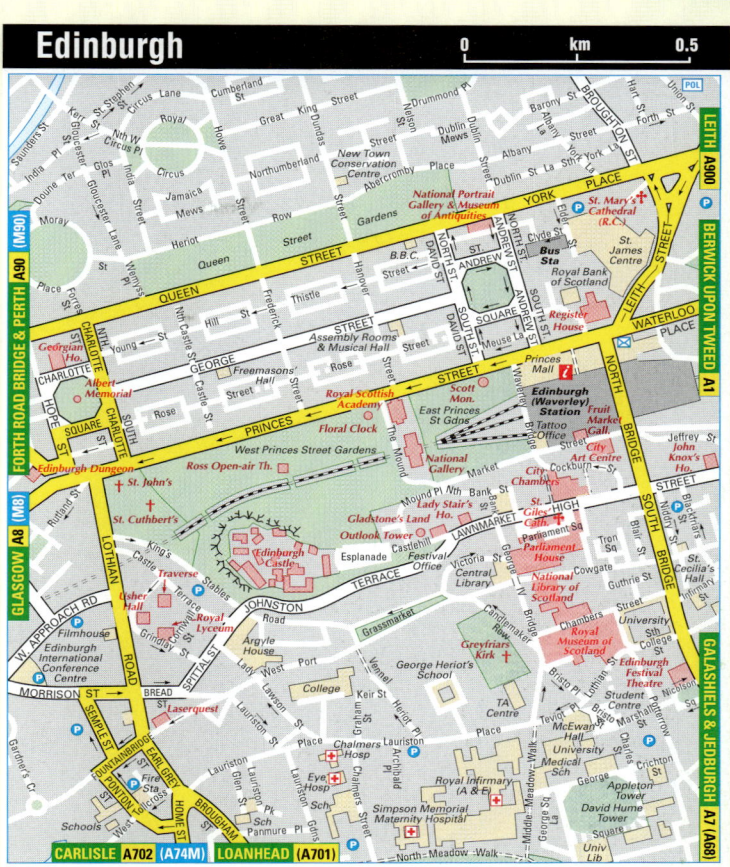

Firenze

Frankfurt

Genève

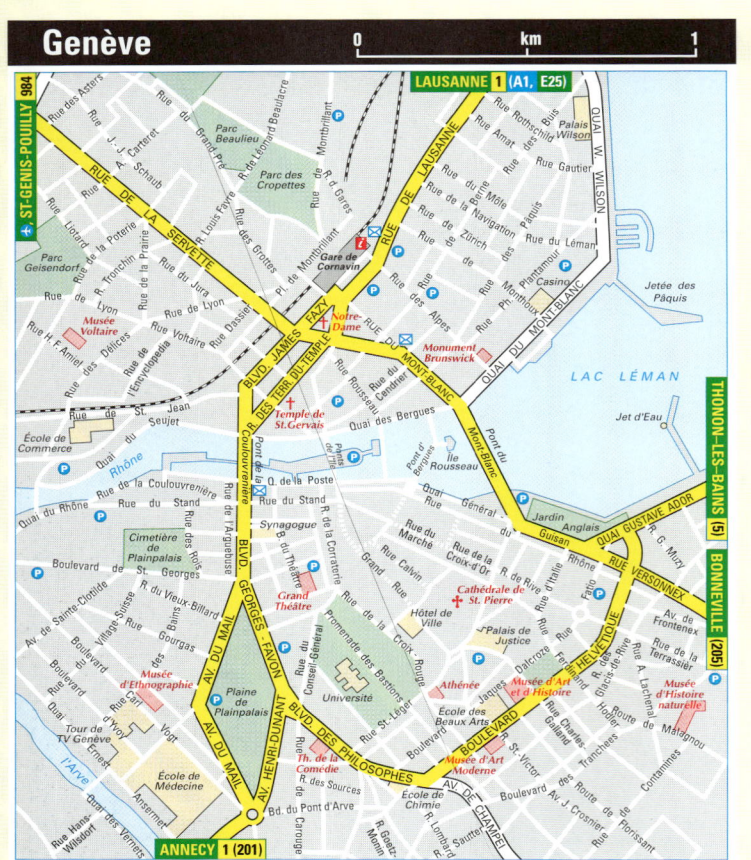

Göteborg

Hamburg

Hamburg

Helsinki

0 km 10

HYVINKÄÄ, HÄMEENLINNA, TAMPERE (3) — TUUSULA, JÄRVENPÄÄ (145) — LAHTI

SALO, TURKU/ÅBO (1) — HANKO/HANGÖ (25) — PORVOO/BORGÅ, KOTKA (7)

HELSINKI

Järventausta, Skogby, Ruotsinkylä, Myllykylä, Korso, Maantiekylä, Nikinmäki, Hindsby, Gesterby
Ollila, Ketunkorpi, Kongo, Linna, Seutula, Mäkiniitty, Hanala, Rekola, Myras, Viirila, Littjofs, Massby, Immersby
Takkula, Lahnus, Vestra, Kivistö, Koivupää, HELSINKI-VANTAAN LENTOASEMA, Harjusuo, Kunikaanmäki, Degermossa
Heinässuo, Veikkola, Siikajärvi, Röylä, Perusmäki, Odilampi, Petas, Vantaanpuisto, Vantaa, Hiekkaharju, Itä Hakkila, Nybygget, Sotunki
Nuuksio, Gobbacka, Martinkylä, Vantaankoski, Ylästö, Simonkylä, Tikkurila, Kaskela, Östersundom
Kolmiranta, Brobacka, Rastaala, Hämeenkylä, Friherrs, Haltiavuori, Haltiala, Tapanila, Puistola, Hakunila, Västerskog
Nupuri, Oittaa, Laaksolahti, Kaivoksela, Paloheinä, Pakila, Pukinmäki, Malmi, Rajakylä
Västerkulla, Bemböle, Kauniainen, Konala, Haaga, Pirkkola, Oulunkylä, Käpylä, Viikki, Mellunkylä, Mellunmäki, Vartiokylä
Espoo Esbo, Kilo, Leppävaara, Munkkiniemi, Pasila, Herttoniemi, Myllypuro, Puotila, Vuosaari, Kallvik
Kauklahti, Nuijala, Tuomarila, Puolarmetsä, Henttaa, Otaniemi, Laajaranta, **HELSINKI**, Roihuvuori, Tammisalo, Vartiosaari
Bobäck, Olari, Mankkaa, Lehtisaari, Hietaniemi, Kulosaari, Jollas, Granlandet
Vehkalahti, Nöykkiö, Tapiola, Laajasalo, Villinki, Trutlandet, Hanskinen
Gästerby, Masala, Jorvas, Espoonlahti, Westend, Lauttasaari, Santahamina, Estlotan, Eestiluoto
Gunnarsby, Kirkkonummi Kyrkslätt, Nokkala, Soukka, Miessaari, Svinö, Melkki, Pihlajasaari, Vallisaari, Musta Hevonen, Isosaari
Estby, Medvastö, Pentala, Lehtisaaret, Rysäkari, Harmaja, Kuivasaari

Stockholm, Lübeck, Travemünd, Tallinn, Rostock

Sibbo fjärden / Sipoon selkä

Helsinki

0 km 1

HÄMEENLINNA 3 E12 (3) — HELSINGIN LENTOASEMA (137, 45) — LAHTI 4 E75 (4) — PORVOO 170 (7, E18)

KIRKKONUMMI

HELSINKI (detailed city map with street names)

KULOSAARI BRÄNDO, SÖRNÄINEN SÖRNÄS, KLUUVI GLOET, TAKA TÖÖLÖ, BORTRE TÖLÖ, ALPPIHARJU ÅSHÖJDEN
LAUTTASAARI DRUMSÖ, LÄNSISATAMA VÄSTRA HAMNEN, LAAJASALO DEGERÖ
Seurasaari Fölisön, Mäntyniemi, Korkeasaari Högholmen, Katajanokka Skatudden
Kruunuvuorenselkä Kronbergsfjärden, Seurasaarenselkä Fölisöfjärden

København

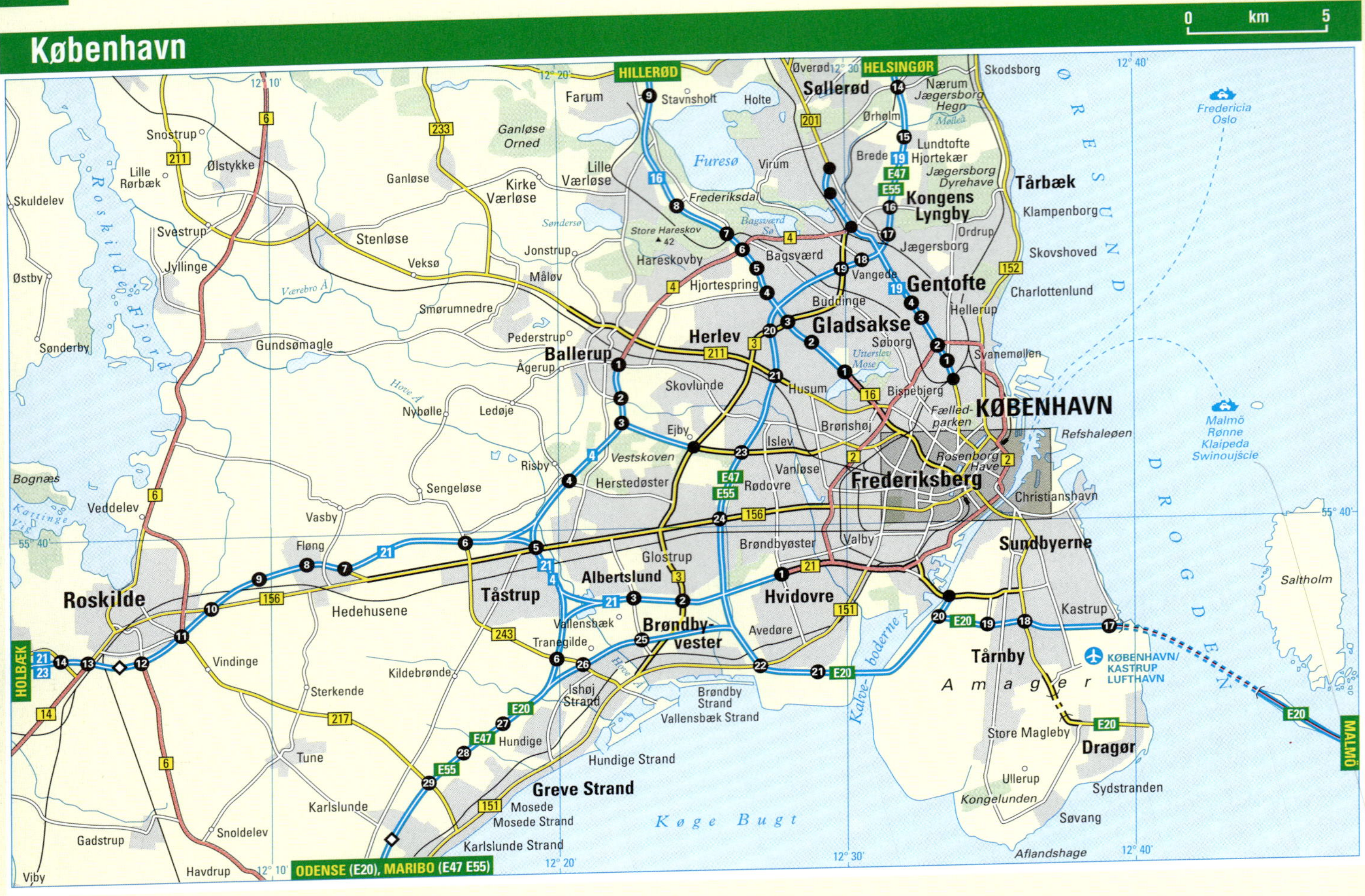

0 km 5

HILLERØD · HELSINGØR

Øverød · Søllerød · Nærum · Jægersborg Hegn · Skodsborg · Fredericia Oslo

Farum · Stavnsholt · Holte · Ørholm · Brede · Lundtofte · Jægersborg · Hjortekær · Jægersborg Dyrehave · Tårbæk · Klampenborg

Snostrup · Ganløse Orned · Lille Værløse · Furesø · Virum · Kongens Lyngby · Ordrup · Skovshoved

Ølstykke · Ganløse · Kirke Værløse · Frederiksdal · Vangede · Gentofte · Charlottenlund

Lille Rørbæk · Stenløse · Jonstrup · Store Hareskov · Bagsværd · Buddinge · Hellerup · Ø R E S U N D

Svestrup · Jylling · Veksø · Måløv · Hareskovby · Hjortespring · Søborg · Svanemøllen

Østby · Smørumnedre · Herlev · Gladsakse · Husum · Utterslev Mose · Malmö Rønne Klaipeda Swinoujscie

Sønderby · Pederstrup · Ballerup · Ågerup · Skovlunde · Bispebjerg · Fælled-parken · KØBENHAVN · Refshaleøen

Gundsømagle · Ledøje · Ejby · Islev · Brønshøj · Rosenborg Have

Bognæs · Nybølle · Vestskoven · Herstedøster · Vanløse · Rødovre · Frederiksberg · Christianshavn · D R O G D E N

Veddelev · Risby · Glostrup · Brøndbyøster · Valby · Sundbyerne · Saltholm

Roskilde · Hedehusene · Sengeløse · Albertslund · Hvidovre · Kastrup

Vindinge · Vallensbæk · Brøndby-vester · Avedøre · Tårnby · KØBENHAVN/KASTRUP LUFTHAVN · A m a g e r

Vasby · Tranegilde · Ishøj Strand · Brøndby Strand · Vallensbæk Strand · Store Magleby · Dragør

Tune · Hundige · Hundige Strand · Køge Bugt · Ullerup · Sydstranden · MALMÖ

Gadstrup · Snoldelev · Karlslunde · Greve Strand · Mosede · Mosede Strand · Kongelunden · Søvang

Viby · Havdrup · Karlslunde Strand · Aflandshage

ODENSE (E20), MARIBO (E47 E55)

København

0 km 1

HILLERØD · HELSINGØR (E47 E55) · ØSTERBRO · HELLERUP · HELSINGØR (E47 E55)

Hvidkildevej · Fuglebakken Sta. · Nørrebro · Nørrebro · Rigshospitalet · Den lille Havfrue

Godthåbsvej Sta. · Frederiksberg Hospital · Assistens Kirkegård · Østre Anlæg · Kastellet · Trinitatismuseet · Kunstindustrimuseet

Frederiksberg Sta. · Forum · Botanisk Have · Rosenborg Have · Amalienborg · Holmen

FREDERIKSBERG · Frederiksberg Have · Radhus · Planetarium · Det Ny Teater · Tivoli · Christiansborg · CHRISTIANSHAVN

Zoologisk Have · Frederiksberg Slot · Hovedbane Gaard · Carlsberg Glyptotek Museum · Christians Kirke · Stadsgraven

ROSKILDE · ROSKILDE VEJ · VESTERBROGADE · VESTERBRO · KØGE (E20 E47 E55) · KØBENHAVN (KASTRUP)

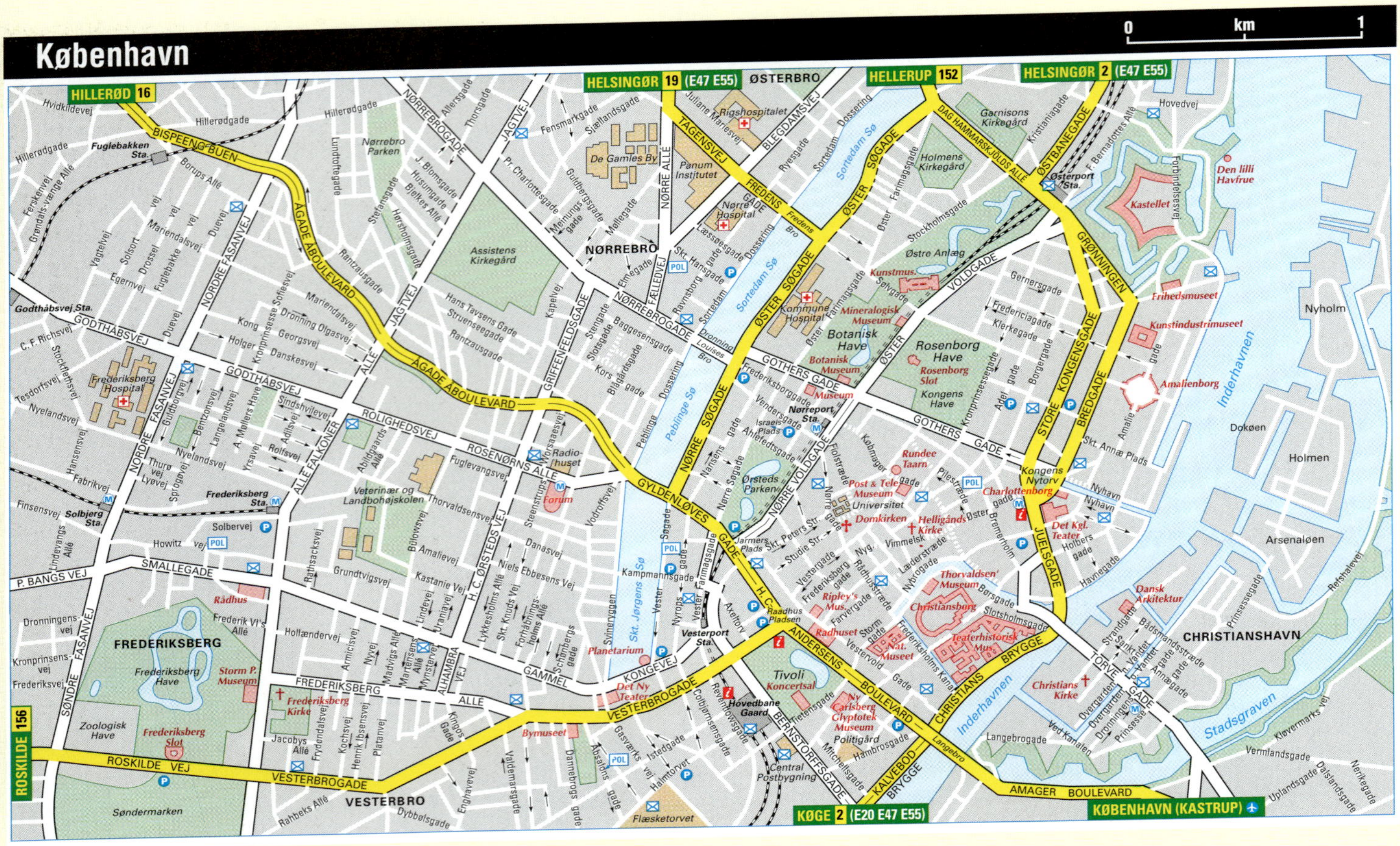

Köln

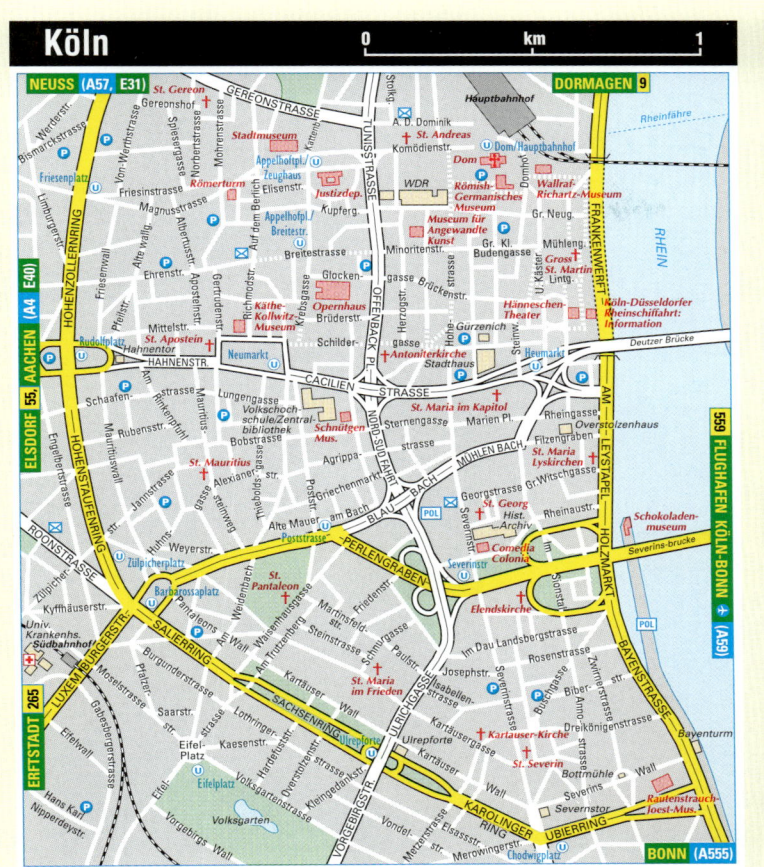

Luxembourg

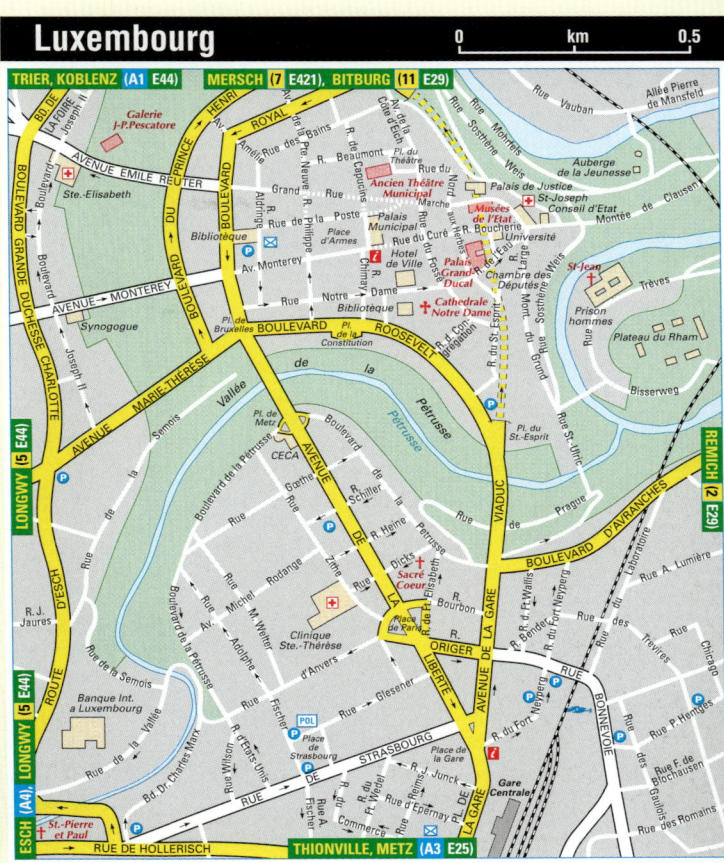

Lisboa

Lisboa

London

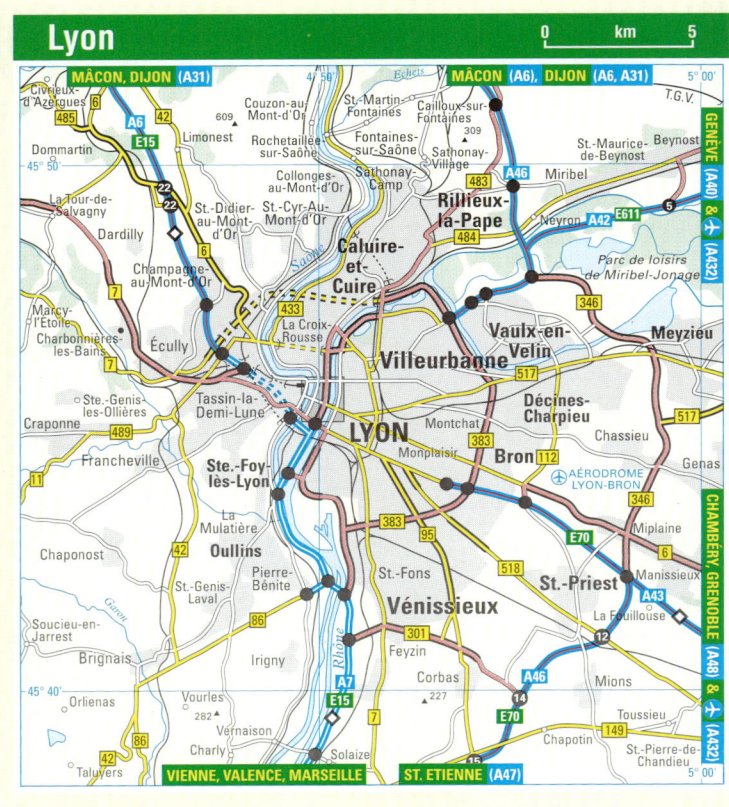

Lyon

Lyon

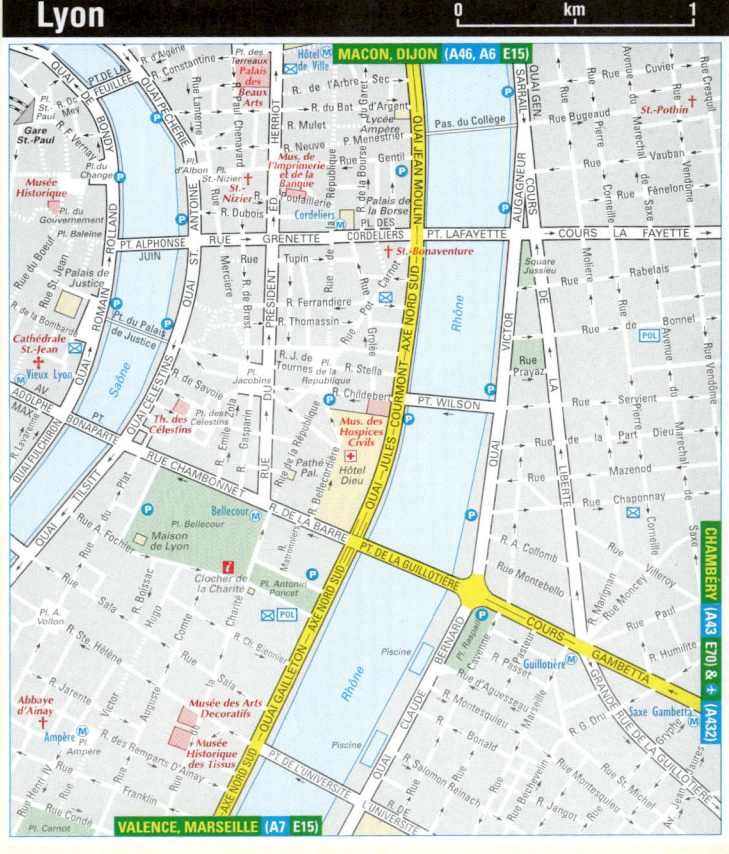

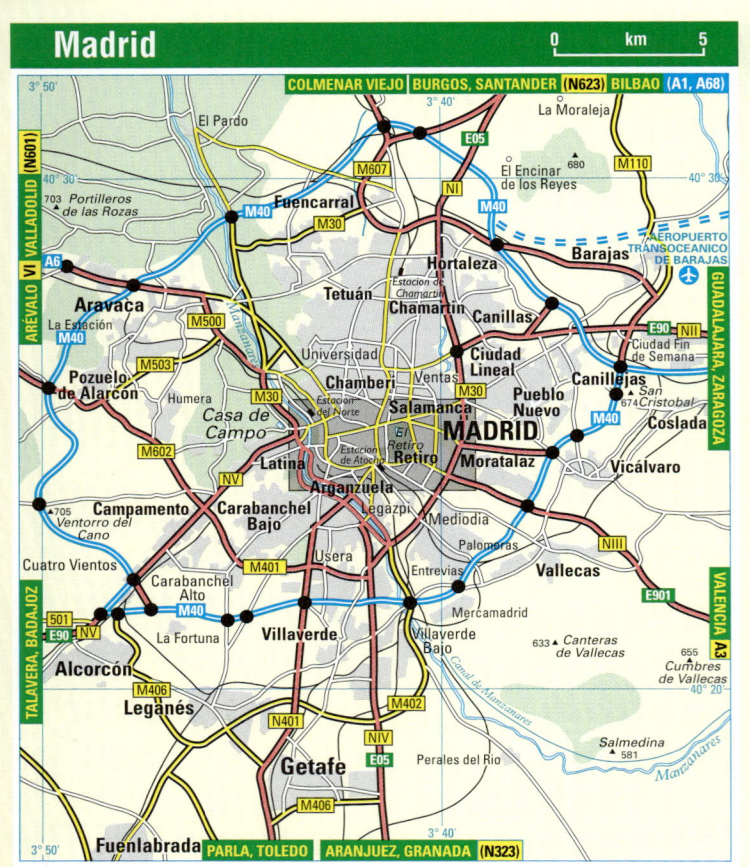

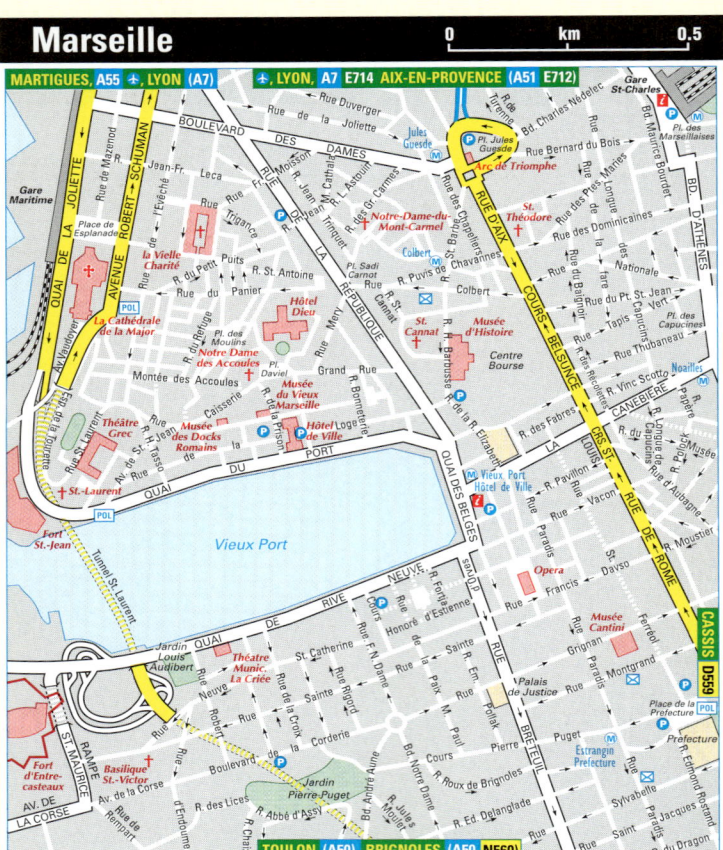

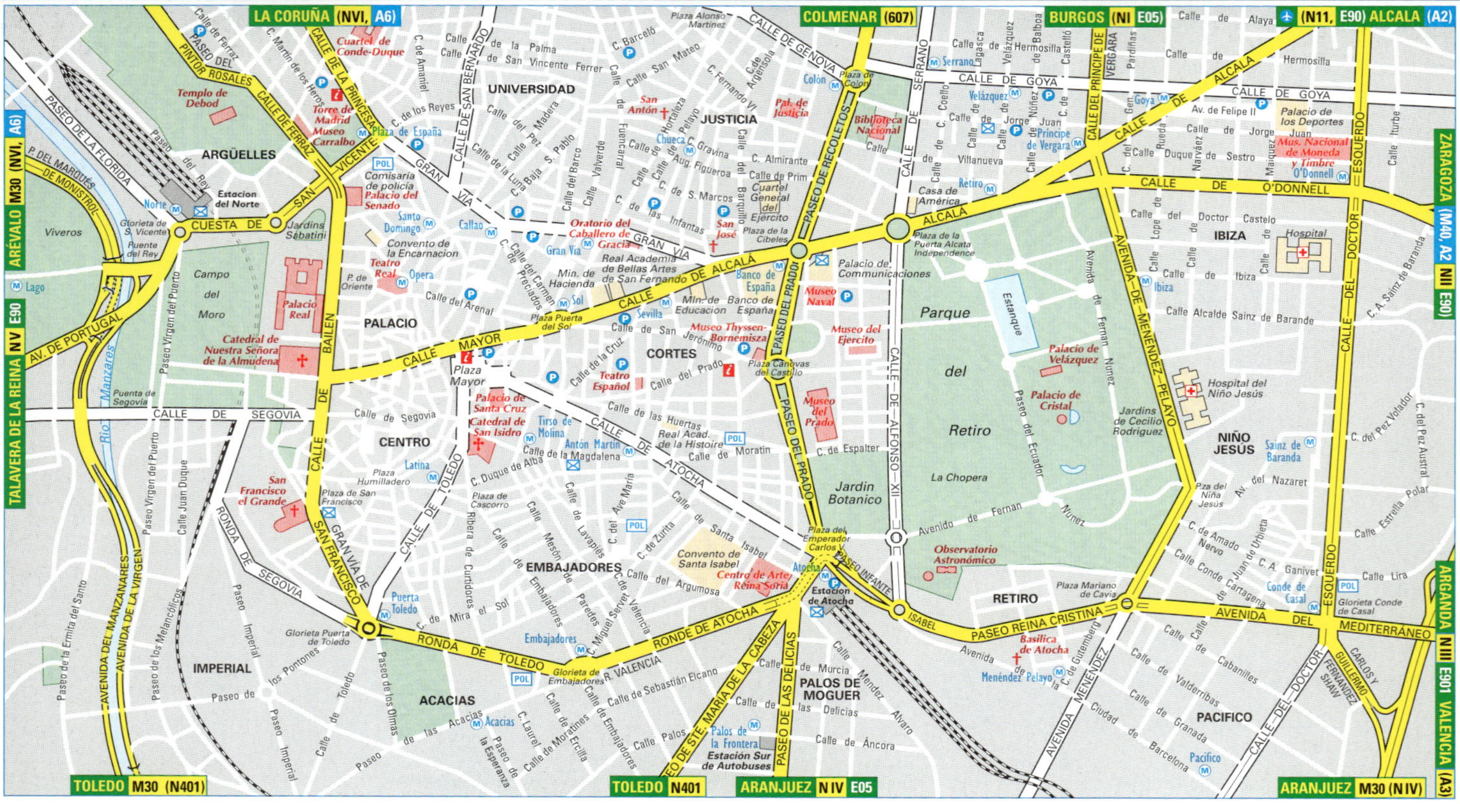

Milano

0 km 5

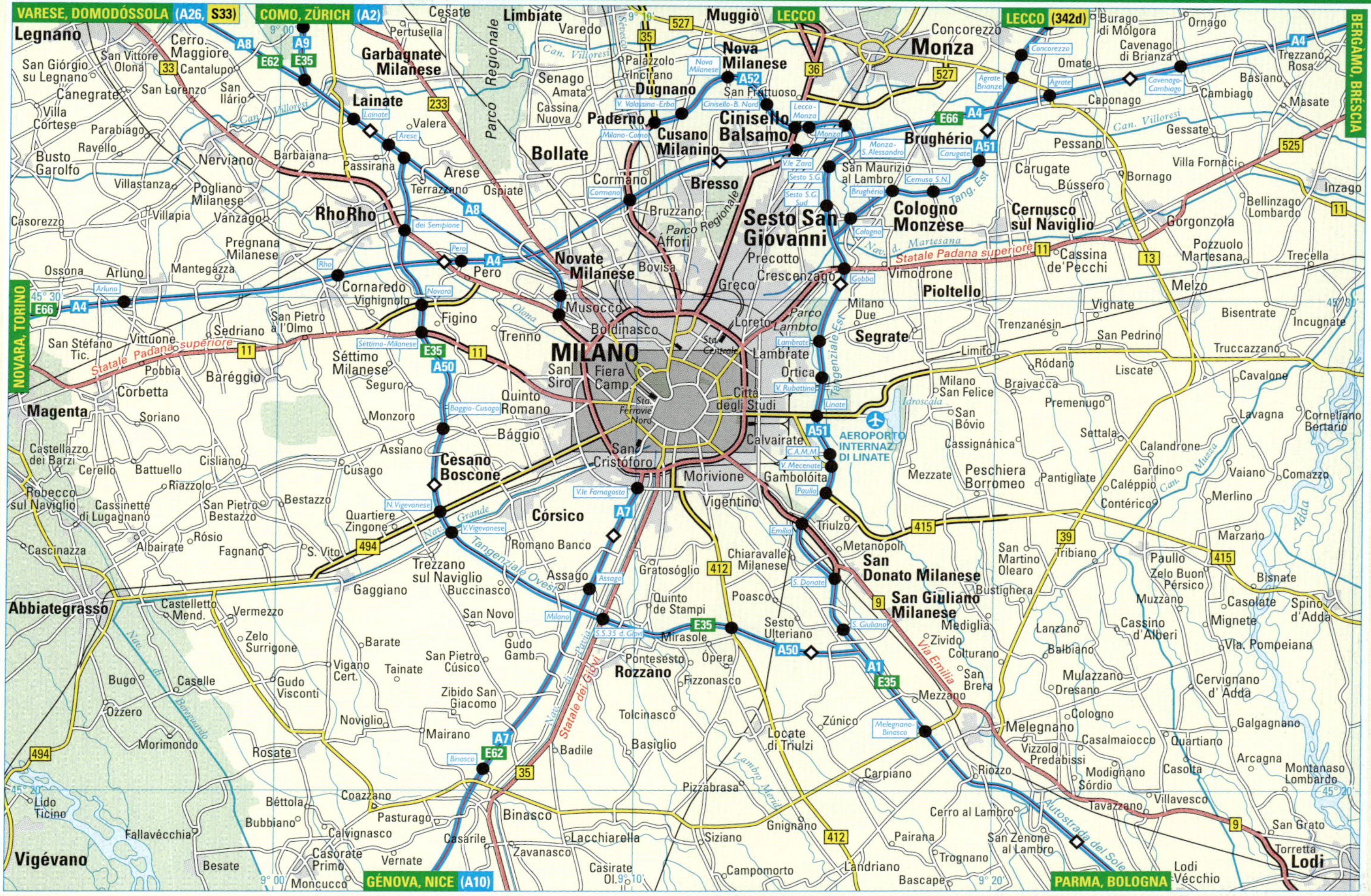

VARESE, DOMODÓSSOLA (A26) S33 COMO, ZÜRICH (A2) LECCO LECCO (342d) BERGAMO BRESCIA

Legnano
Cesate
Limbiate
Varedo
Muggió
Concorezzo
Burago di Mólgora
Ornago

Garbagnate Milanese
Nova Milanese
Monza
Cavenago di Brianza
Omate

Lainate
Dugnano
Paderno
Cusano Milanino
Ciniseló Balsamo
Brughério
Pessano
Carúgate

Bollate
Bresso
Cologno Monzese
Cernusco sul Naviglio
Cassina de' Pecchi
Gorgonzola

RhoRho
Novate Milanese
Sesto San Giovanni
Vimodrone
Pioltello

Arese
Pero
Segrate
Melzo

NOVARA, TORINO

MILANO

Sèttimo Milanese
Fiera Campo

AEROPORTO INTERNAZ. DI LINATE

Magenta
Cesano Boscone
Córsico

Abbiategrasso

Chiaravalle Milanese
San Donato Milanese
San Giuliano Milanese

Rozzano

Melegnano
Lodi

Vigévano

GÈNOVA, NICE (A10) PARMA, BOLOGNA

Milano

0 km 1

DOMODÓSSOLA (A8) VARESE 233 COMO 35 MONZA (36) BERGAMO 11 (525)

Stazione Porta Garibaldi
Stazione Centrale

Fiera
Arco della Pace
Parco Sempione
Castello Sforzesco
Giardini Pubblici

Duomo
Teatro alla Scala

Università Cattolica

S. SIRO, MAGENTA 11

LINATE + BRESCIA (11)

ABBIATEGRASSO 494 GENOVA (A7 E62) PAVIA 35 LODI 9 PARMA (A51, A1)

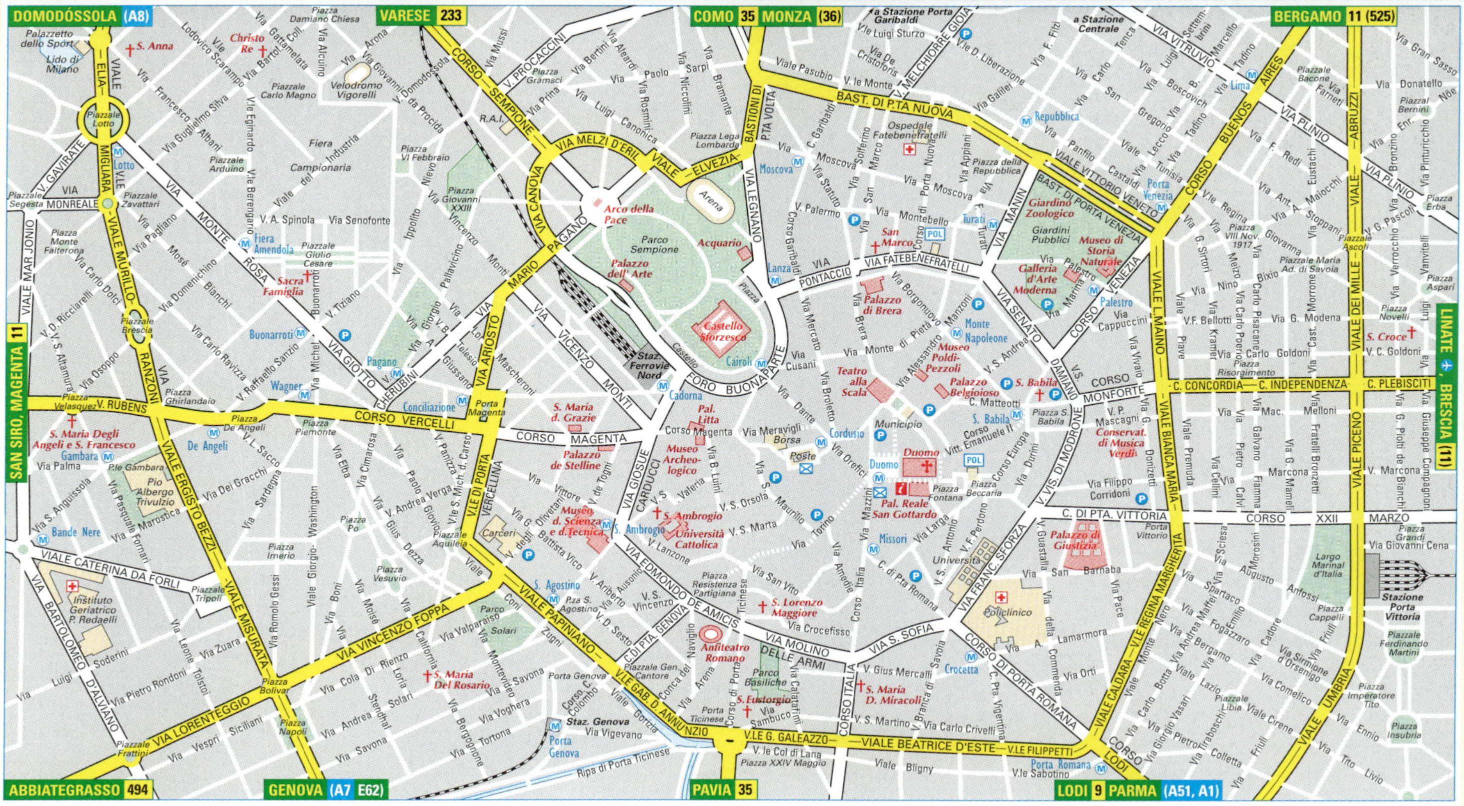

München

München

Nápoli

Nápoli

Oslo

0 km 5

BERGEN · E16 · Utvika · Brulokka

GJOVIK, LILLEHAMMER · JESSHEIM, HAMAR

N o r d m a r k a

Heggelelva · Slakteren · Sorkedalen · Turter · Sandermosen · 451 · Slattum · Nittedal · Glosli · 4

60° 00' · Homledal · By · Tryvannshogda ▲531 · Maridalen · Skytta · Skedsmo-Korset · 60° 00'

Solihogda · Ila · Holmenkollen · Maridalsvatnet · 22 · Romas · Vestli · Stovner · 407 · E06 · Hvam · Kjeller · 120

Bogstadvatn · Burundvatn · Sognsvatn · 418 · Kjelsas · RING 3 · Rodtvet · Gorud · 4 · 163 · Hoybraten · Strommen · 159 · Skjetten · Lillestrom · 120

Holtsfjorden · 285 · 284 · Rustad · Smestad · Skui · 379 · Bærums Verk · Lijordet · Roa · Ris · OSLO · RING 2 · Ullevål · Sinsen · 4 · E06 · Alna · Lorenskog · Rud

Sylling · 160 · 164 · Stabekk · Haslum · Ullern · Skoyen · Toyen · E6 · Bryn · Oppsal · Boler · Losby · Ramstadsjoen · Rælingen

Tanum · Bærum · Hovik · 166 · Lysaker · Vestbane sto. · Sentralst. · Ryen · 363 · Nokkelvann · Nordre Elvaga

E16 · E18 · FORNEBU · Bygdoy · Hovedoya · Bekkelaget · Lambertseter · Ostmark-kapellet

Kolsås · Sandvika · Snaroya · Forneby · Lindoya · E6 · Nordstrand · Sondre Elvaga

Hvalstad · Neseya · Ostoya · Ormoya · Malmoya · Ljabru · Skullerud

Slependen · Nesbru · Bronnoya · Nesoddtangen · Oksval · Flaskebekk · Skoklefall · Hauketo · 155 · Klemetsrud · Sandbakken · 368 · Tonekollen

Sorsdal · Asker · 165 · E18 · Konglungen · Bunnefjorden · 157 · 215 · Torvvik · Ingierstrand · Kolbotn · Krokhol

59° 50' · Lierskogen · Blakstad · Voien · Oslofjorden · Nesodden · Fjellstrand · E6 · Siggerud · 155 · 59° 50'

Tranby · Skogen · Dikemark · 167 · Svestad · Hasle · 156 · Oppegård · Bru · Binningsvatna

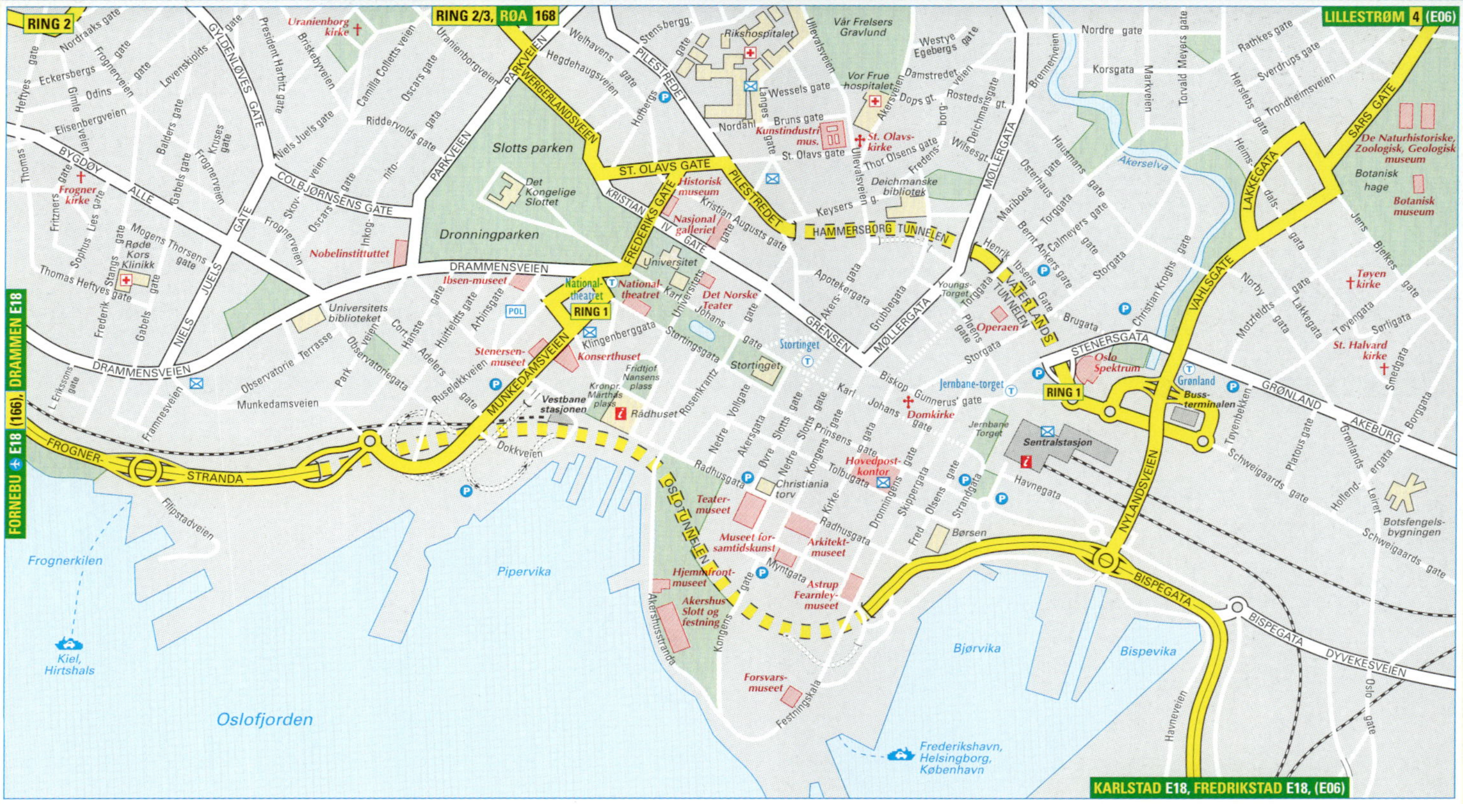

Lier · 289 · E18 · Frogner · Reistad · Slemmestad · Nærsnes · Garder · Blylaget · 152 · 134 · E18 · Oppegård · Myrvoll

DRAMMEN, KRISTIANSAND · ASKIM, KARLSTAD · MOSS, FREDRIKSTAD

Oslo

0 km 0.5

RING 2 · RING 2/3 · ROA 168 · LILLESTROM 4 (E06)

Uranienborg kirke · Rikshospitalet · Vår Frelsers Gravlund · De Naturhistoriske, Zoologisk, Geologisk museum

Vor Frue Hospitaset · St. Olavs kirke · Botanisk hage · Botanisk museum

St. Olavs Gate · Kunstindustri mus. · Deichmanske bibliotek

Slotts parken · Det Kongelige Slottet · Historisk museum · Nasjonal galleriet

Dronningparken · Nobelinstituttet · Universitet · Toyen kirke

FORNEBU · E18 (166), DRAMMEN E18 · Ibsen-museet · National-theatret · Det Norske Teater · Operaen · St. Halvard kirke · Oslo Spektrum

Universitets biblioteket · RING 1 · Stortinget · Jernbane-torget · Bussterminalen · RING 1 · GRONLAND

Stenersen-museet · Konserthuset · Vestbane stasjonen · Rådhuset · Domkirke · Sentralstasjon

FROGNER · STRANDA · Christiania torv · Hovedpost-kontor · Jernbane Torget

Dokkveien · Teater-museet · Museet for samtidskunst · Arkitekt-museet · Astrup Fearnley-museet

Frognerkilen · Pipervika · Hjemmefront-museet · Akershus Slott og festning · Bjorvika · Bispevika

Kiel, Hirtshals · Forsvars-museet · Frederikshavn, Helsingborg, Kobenhavn

Oslofjorden · Oslofjorden

KARLSTAD E18, FREDRIKSTAD E18, (E06)

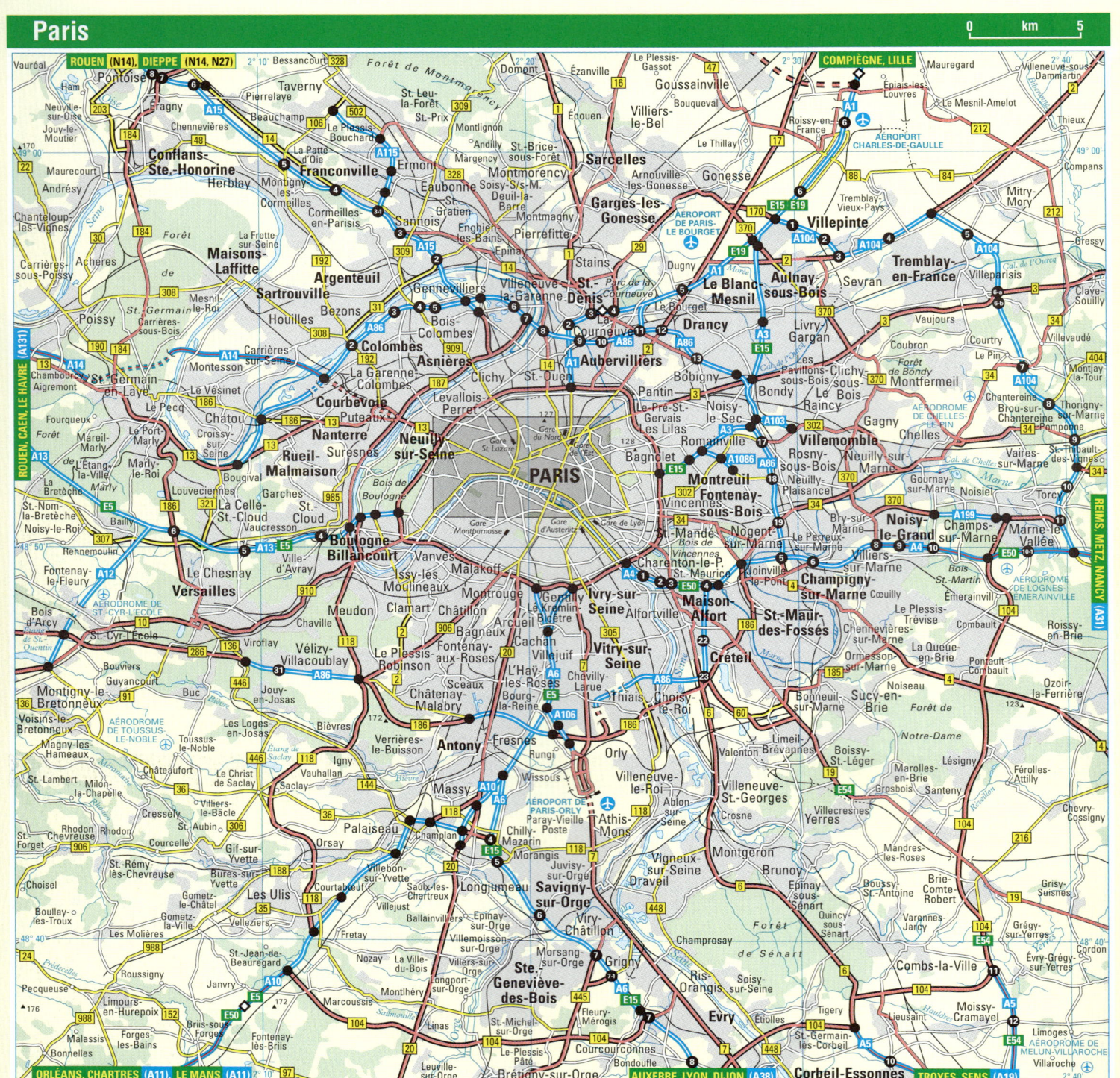

Paris

0 — km — 1

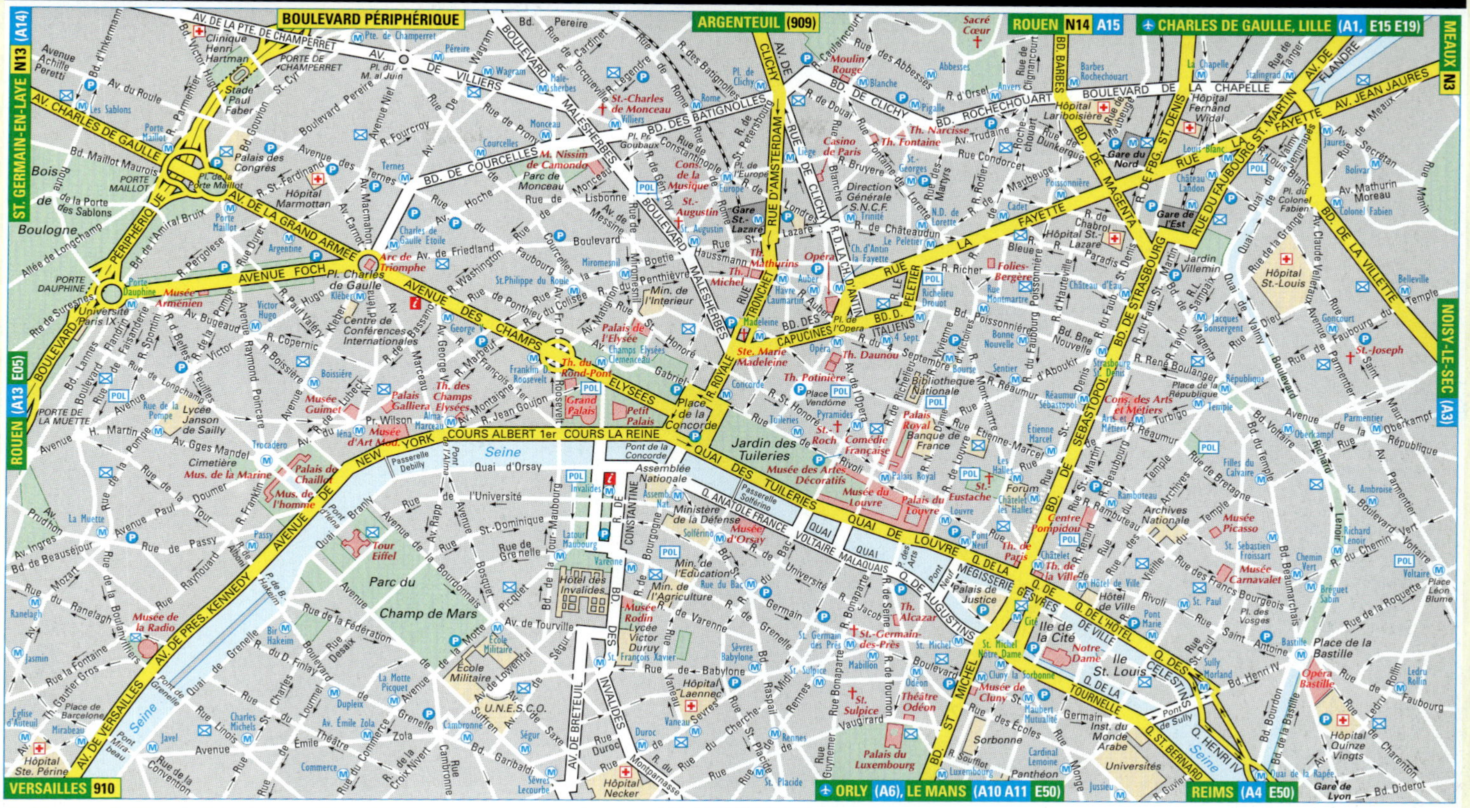

Praha

0 — km — 5

Praha

0 — km — 1

Roma

0 km 5

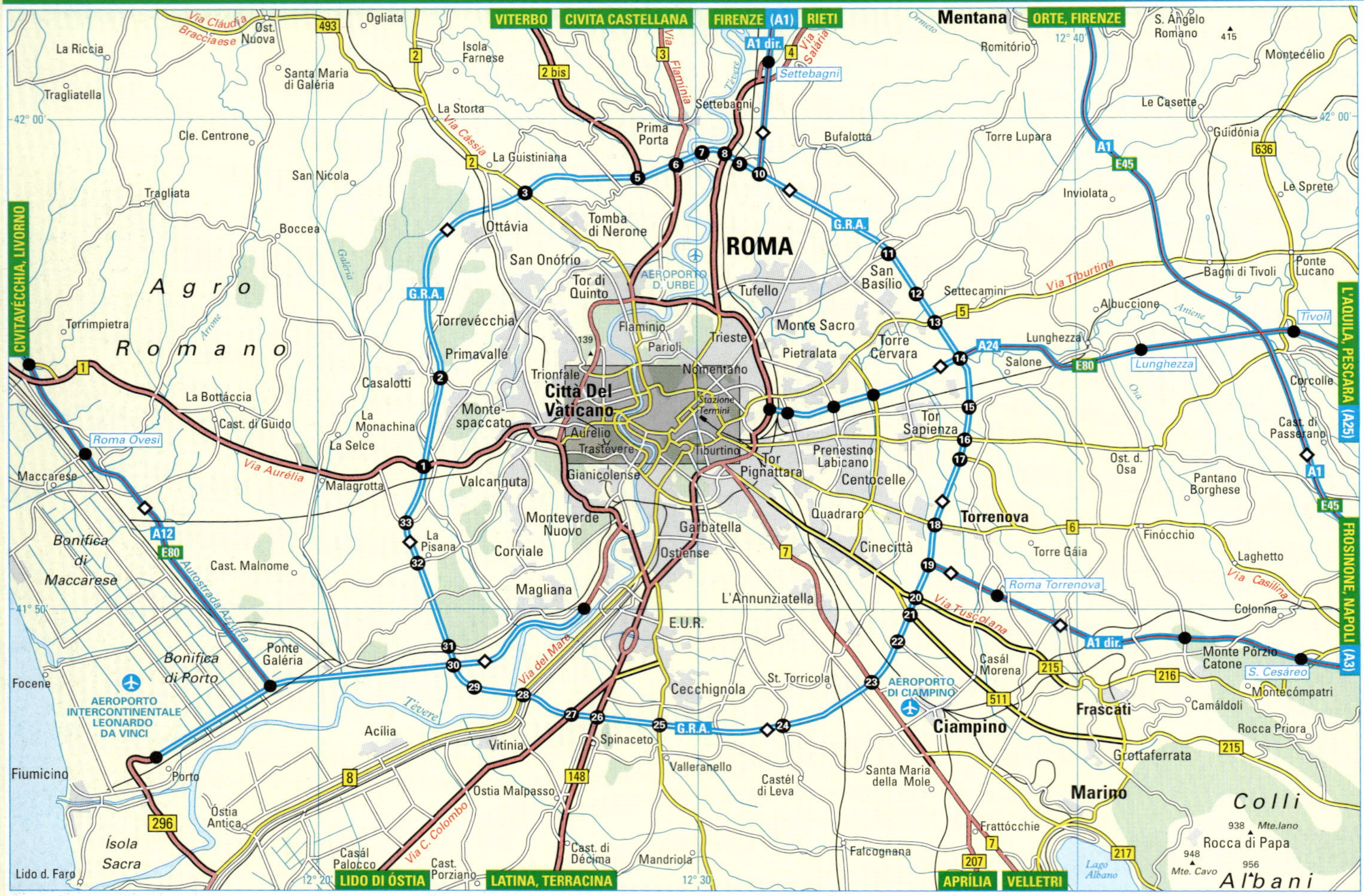

VITERBO | CIVITA CASTELLANA | FIRENZE (A1) | RIETI | Mentana | ORTE, FIRENZE

ROMA

Citta Del Vaticano

G.R.A.

Agro Romano

CIVITAVÉCCHIA, LIVORNO

AEROPORTO INTERCONTINENTALE LEONARDO DA VINCI

Fiumicino

Bonifica di Maccarese

Bonifica di Porto

Ísola Sacra

Lido d. Faro

LIDO DI ÓSTIA | LATINA, TERRACINA | APRÍLIA | VELLETRI

L'AQUILA, PESCARA (A25)

FROSINONE, NAPOLI (A3)

Tivoli

Frascati

Marino

Ciampino

AEROPORTO DI CIAMPINO

Colli Albani

Rocca di Papa

Roma

0 km 1

TERNI (3) | VITERBO (2) | FIRENZE 4 (A1 dir, A1 E35)

CITTÀ DEL VATICANO

Museo Vaticani

S. Pietro in Vaticano

Villa Borghese

CORSO D'ITALIA

Termini

Centrale Roma Termini

CIVITAVÉCCHIA 1 (A12 E80)

Villa Doria Pamphili

'LEONARDO DA VINCI' (A12) | LATINA 148 | FROSINONE 6 (A1 E45)

Colosseo

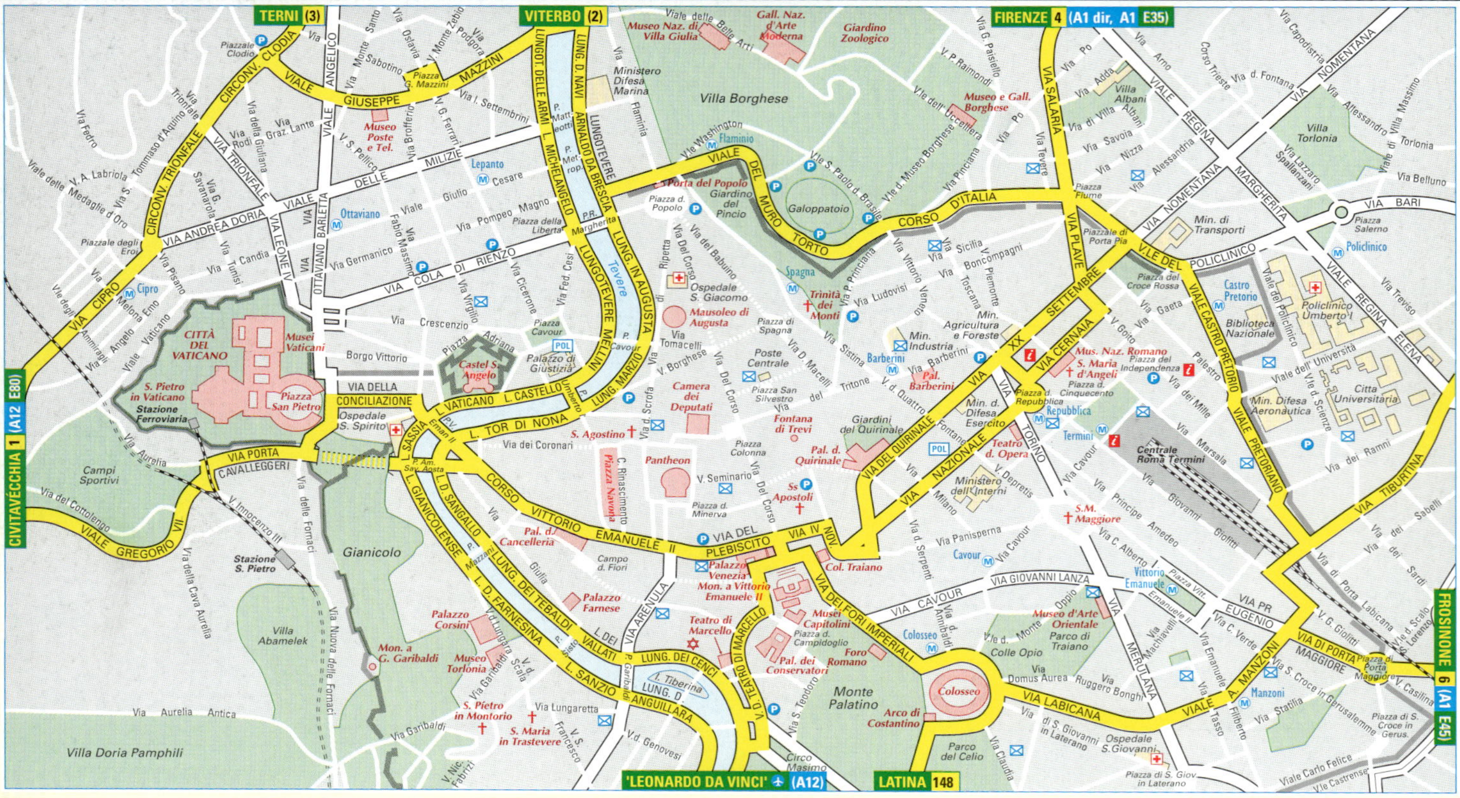

Stockholm

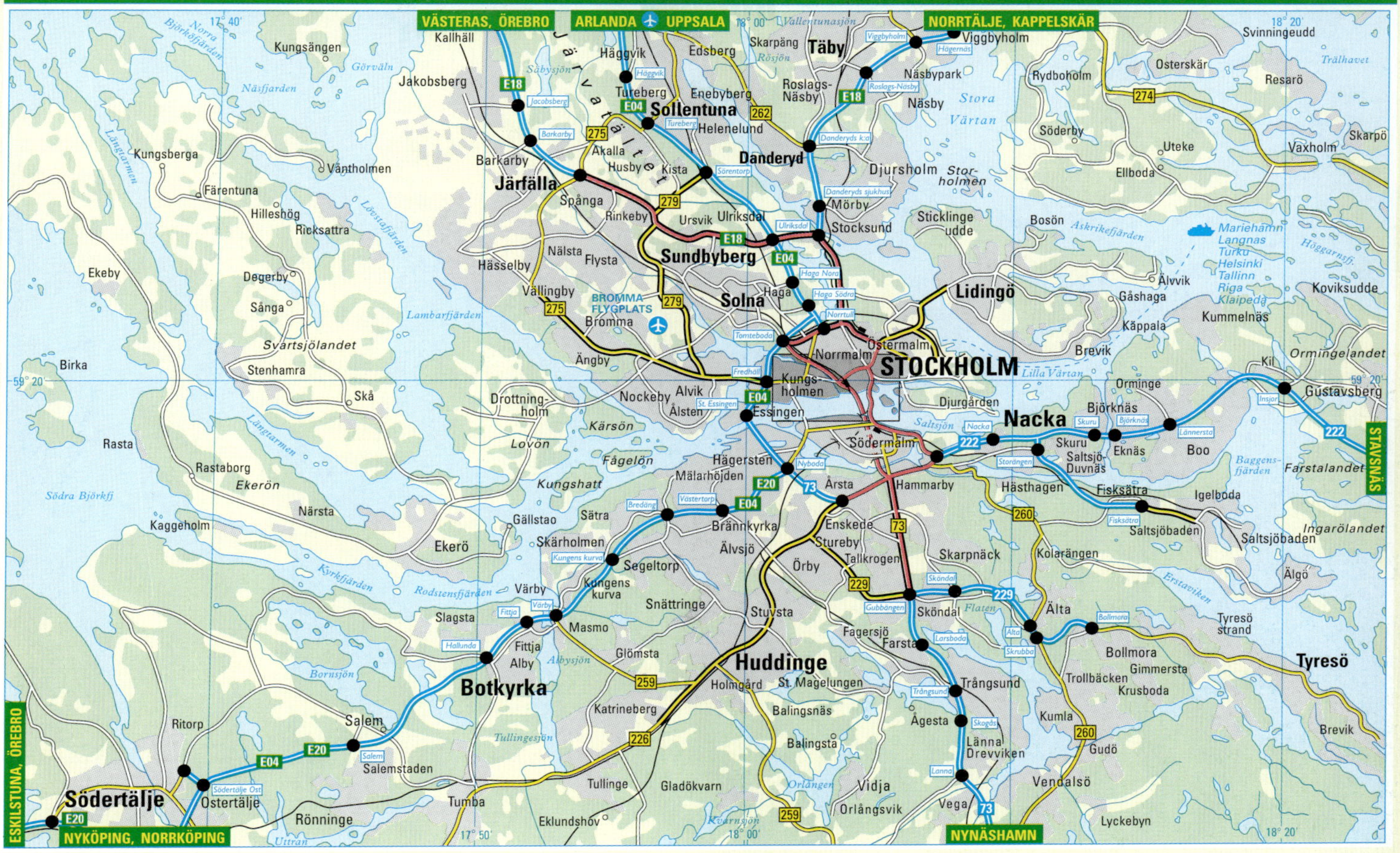

0 km 5

VÄSTERÅS, ÖREBRO · ARLANDA ✈ UPPSALA · NORRTÄLJE, KAPPELSKÄR

Kallhäll · Edsberg · Skarpnäck · Viggbyholm · Svinningeudd
Kungsängen · Häggvik · Täby · Hagernäs · Österskär · Resarö
Jakobsberg · E18 · Sollentuna · Roslags-Näsby · Näsbypark · Rydboholm
Barkarby · Akalla · Husby · Kista · Danderyd · Djursholm · Storholmen · Ellboda · Vaxholm · Skarpö
Järfälla · Spånga · Rinkeby · Ursvik · Ulriksdal · Mörby · Stocksund · Sticklinge udde · Bosön · Koviksudde
Hässelby · Nälsta · Flysta · Sundbyberg · Solna · Haga · Lidingö · Brevik · Kummelnäs
Vällingby · BROMMA FLYGPLATS · Ängby · Bromma · Norrmalm · **STOCKHOLM** · Djurgården · Orminge · Gustavsberg
Drottningholm · Nockeby · Alvik · Älvsten · Essingen · Kungsholmen · Södermalm · Nacka · Skuru · Eknäs · Boo
Lovön · Kärsön · Fågelön · Hägersten · Mälarhöjden · Årsta · Hammarby · Hästhagen · Fisksätra · Saltsjöbaden
Kungshatt · Sätra · Segeltorp · Bränkyrka · Enskede · Stureby · Skarpnäck · Kolarängen
Ekerö · Skärholmen · Kungens kurva · Snättringe · Älvsjö · Örby · Tallkrogen · Sköndal · Älta
Värby · Masmo · Glömsta · Stuvsta · Fagersjö · Farsta · Trollbäcken · Bollmora · Tyresö
Slagsta · Fittja · Alby · Huddinge · St Mägelungen · Holmgård · Trångsund · Krusboda
Botkyrka · Katrineberg · Balingsnäs · Ågesta · Kumla · Gudö · Vendelsö
Salem · Salemstaden · Tullinge · Balingsta · Länna · Drevviken
Ritorp · Tumba · Gladökvarn · Vidja · Örlångsvik · Lyckebyn
Södertälje · Östertälje · Rönninge · Eklundshöv · Vega
NYKÖPING, NORRKÖPING · NYNÄSHAMN

Stockholm

0 km 1

VÄSTERÅS (E04, E18) · UPPSALA (E04), NORRTÄLJE E04, (E18) · LIDINGÖ E20 227

STADSHAGEN · NORRMALM · ÖSTERMALM
Karlberg · Vasaparken · Observatorielunden · Johanneskyrkan · Strindbergsmuseet · Kungliga Biblioteket
KUNGSHOLMEN · Sabbatsbergs sjukhus · Stora teatern · Hötorget · Humlegården
Sankt Görans sjukhus · Fridhemsplan · DROTTNINGHOLMSVÄGEN · Kronobergs parken · Rådhuset
MARIEBERG · Polishuset · T-Centralen · Konserthuset · Dramatiska teatern · Historiska museet
Rålambshovs sjukhus · FLEMINGGATAN · Stadshuset · Klara kyrka · Kulturhuset · Kungsträdgården · Nordiska museet
Friluftsteater · RIDDARHOLMEN · Riksdagshuset · Medelhavsmuseet · Operan · Junibacken · Vasamuseet
LÅNGHOLMEN · Riddarholmskyrkan · GAMLA STAN · Storkyrkan · Tyska kyrkan · SKEPPSHOLMEN · Moderna museet
Mälaren · Riddarfjärden · SÖDERMALM · Slussen · Saltsjön · Kastellholmen
Leksaksmuseet · NYNÄSHAMN 73 (73) · GUSTAVSBERG 222 (222)

Strasbourg

Strasbourg

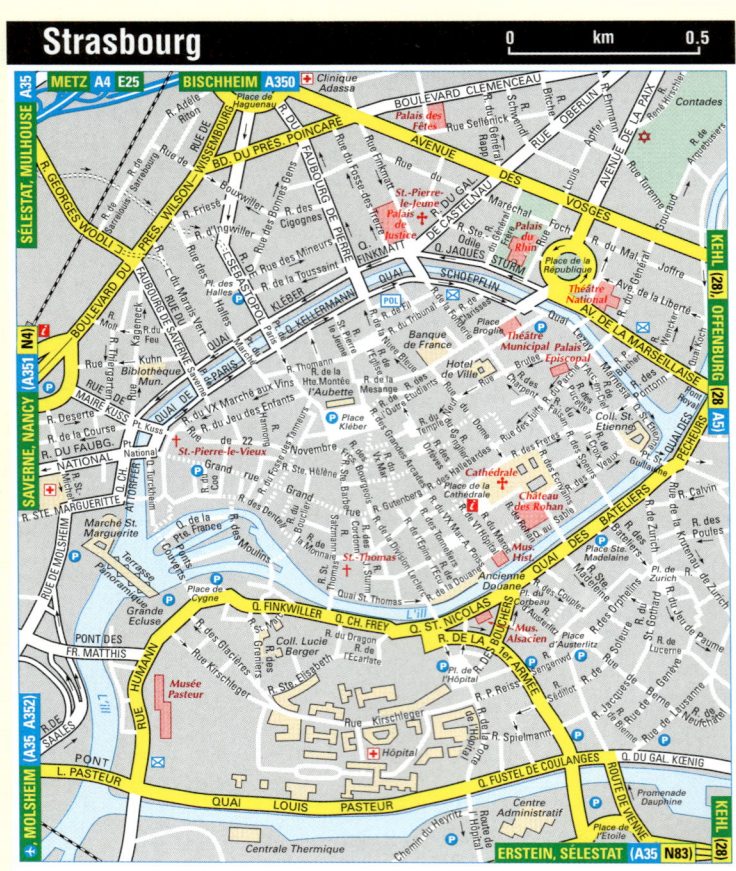

Sevilla

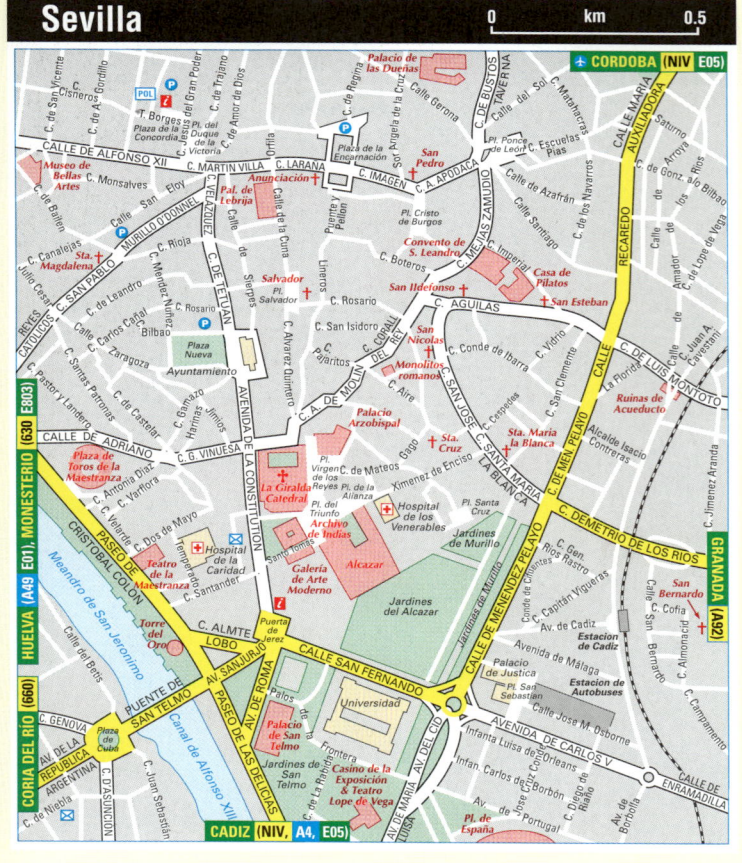

Stuttgart

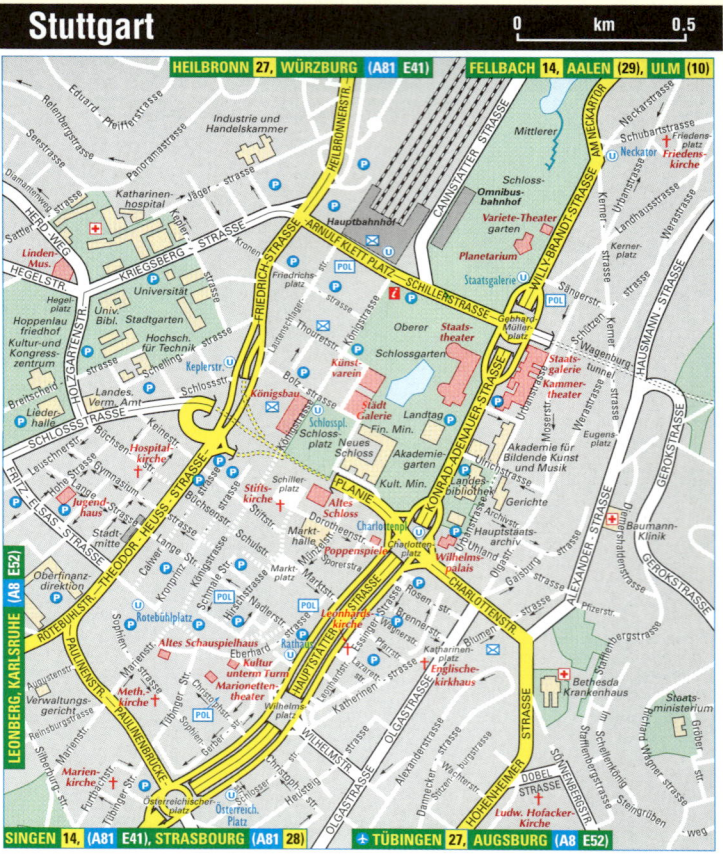

Torino

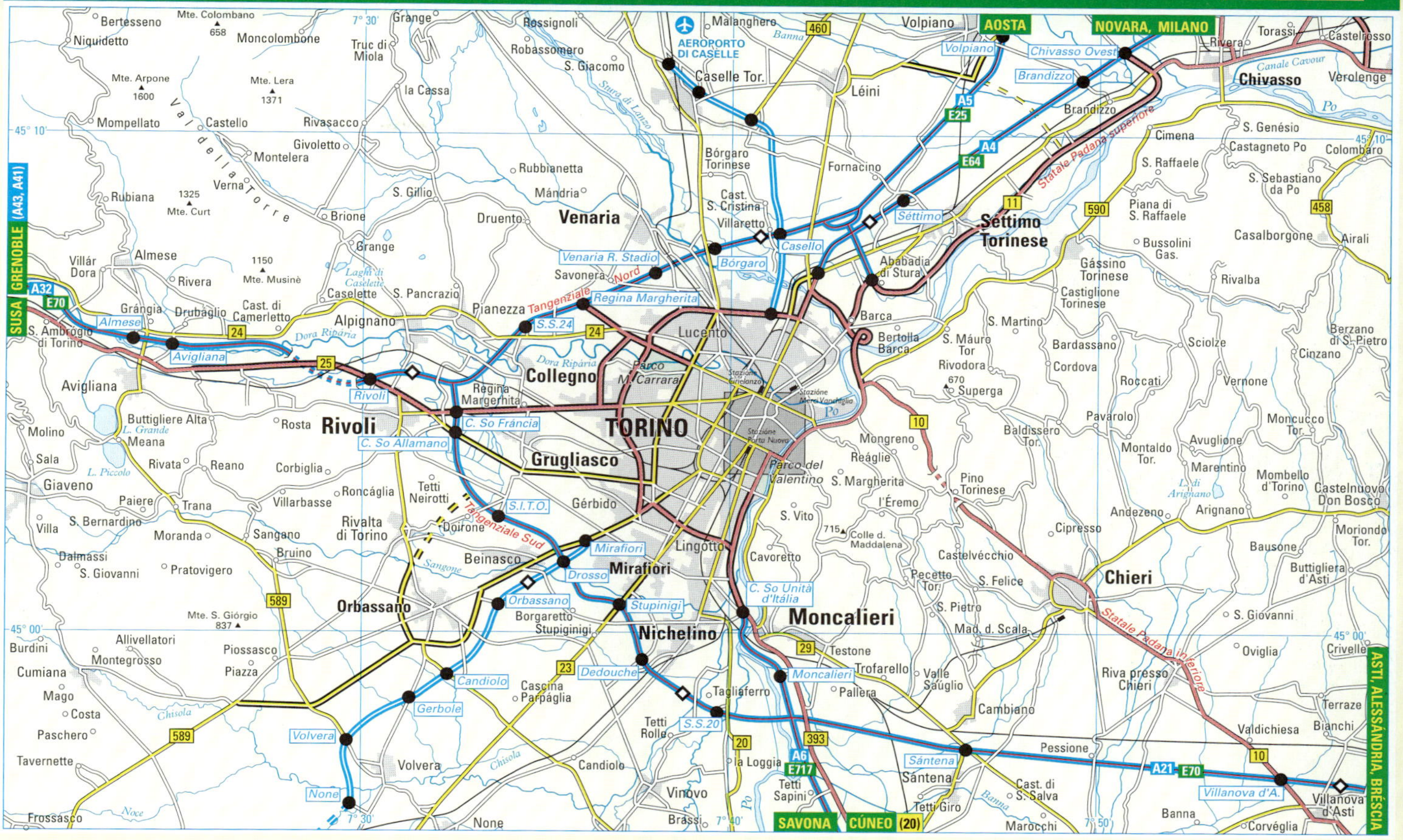

0 km 5

Torino

0 km 1

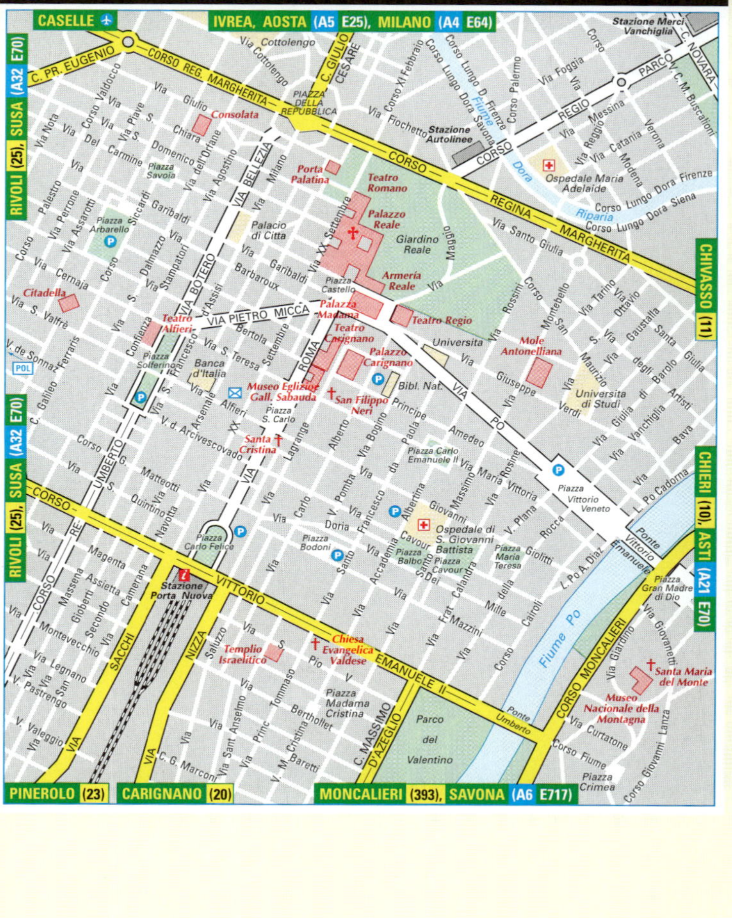

Warszawa

0 km 1

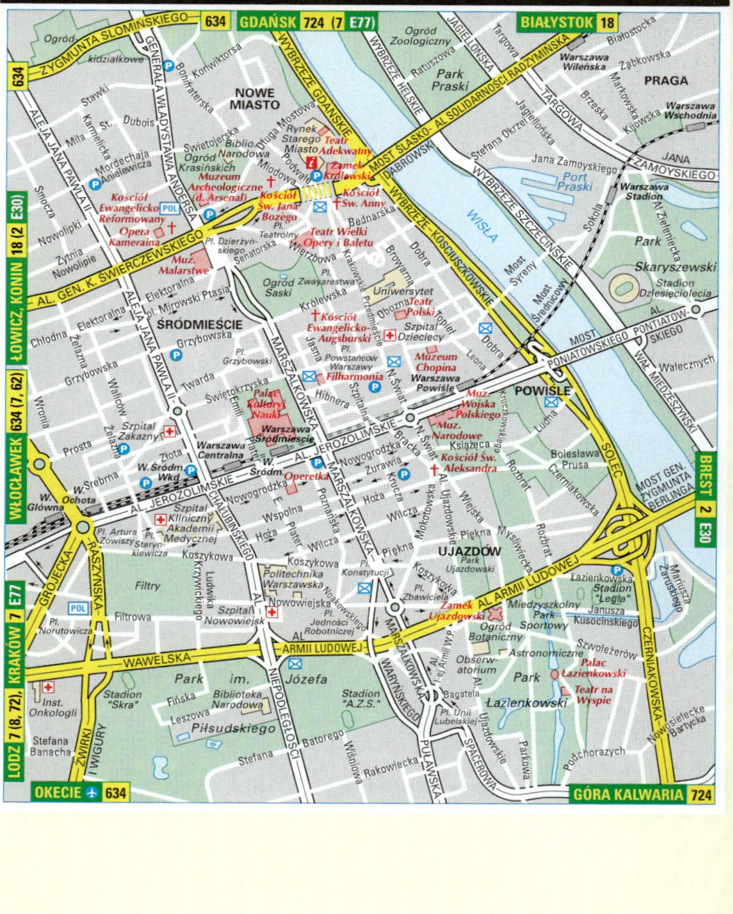

Wien

Wien

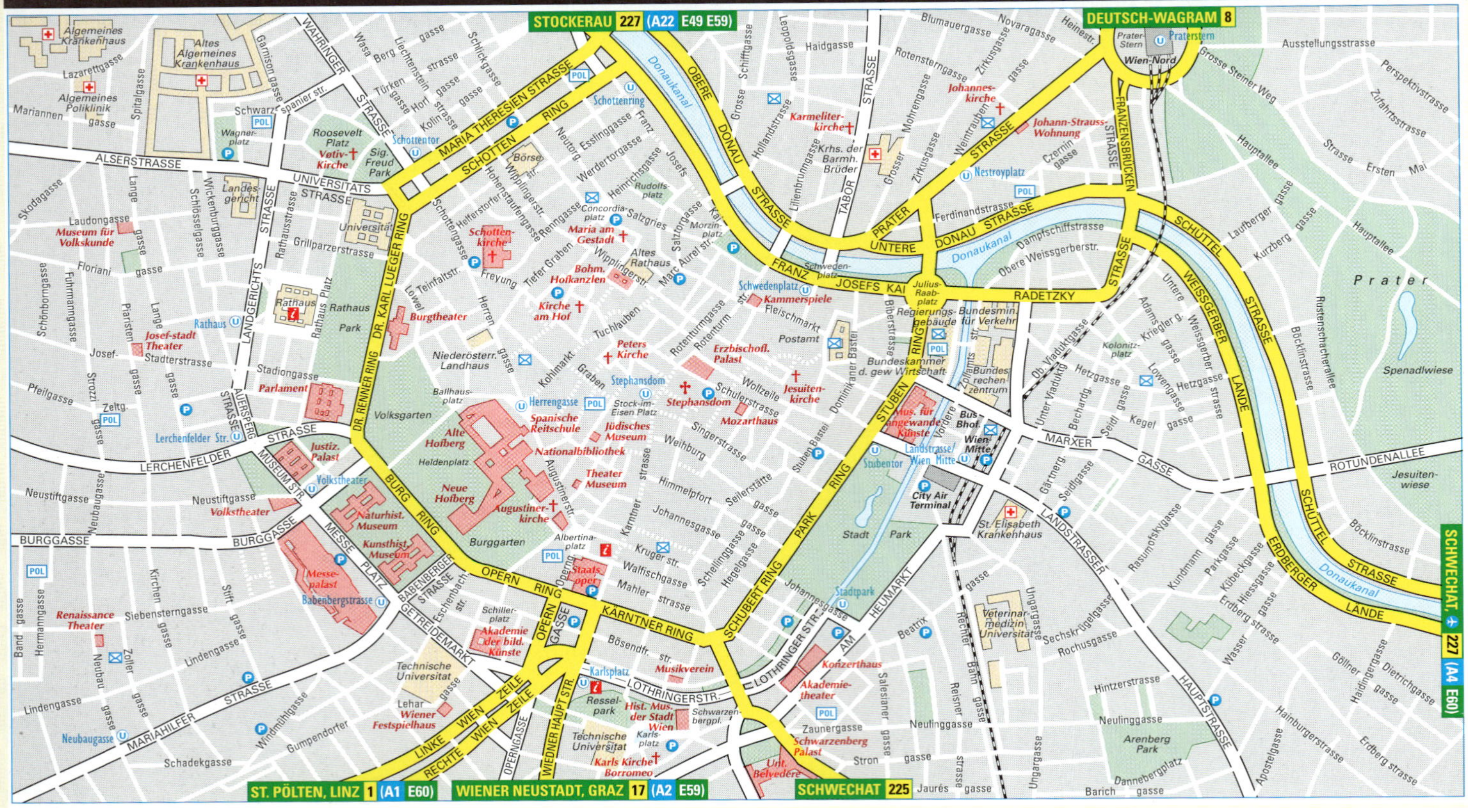

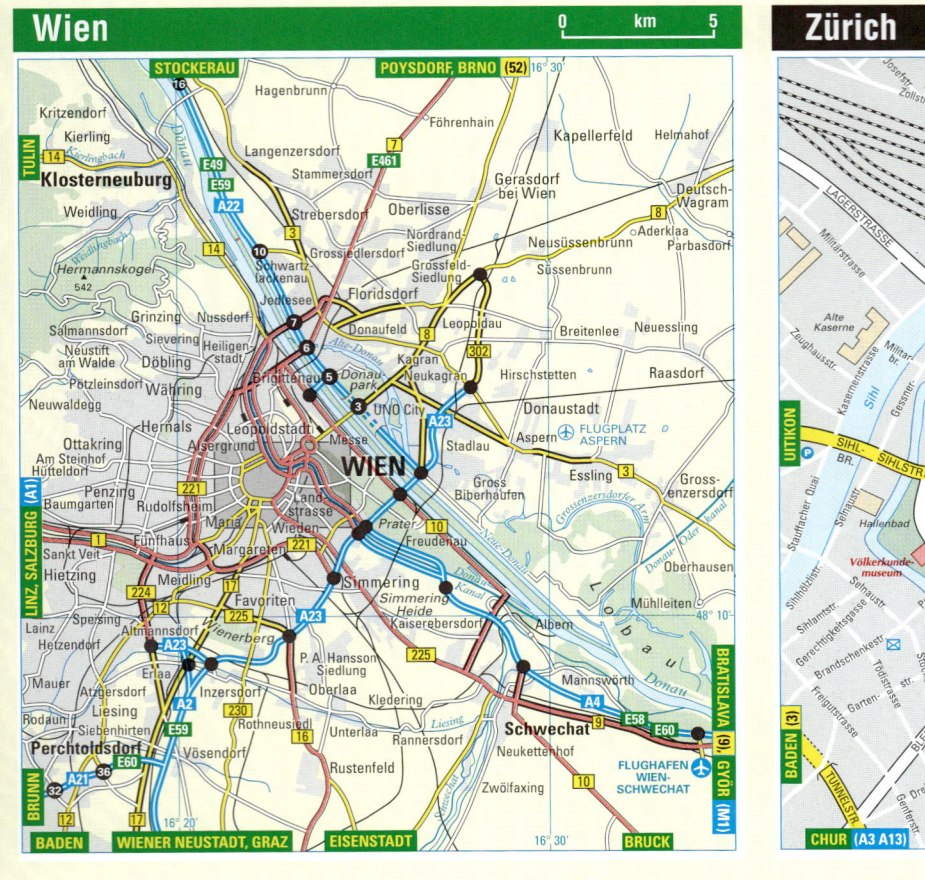

Zürich

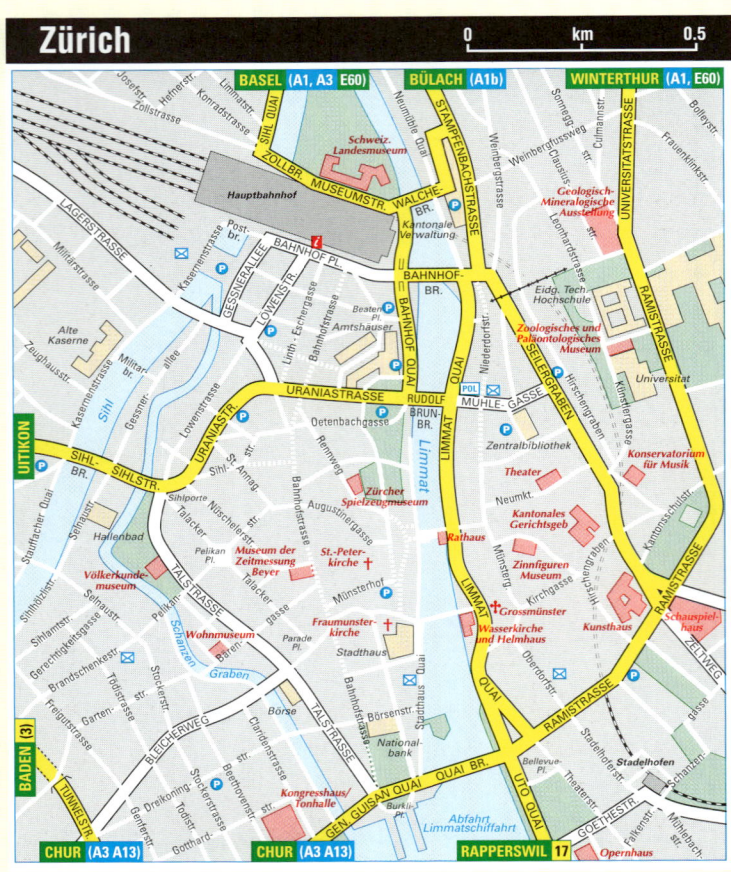

GB	F		D	I
Austria	Autriche	A	Österreich	Austria
Albania	Albanie	AL	Albanien	Albania
Andorra	Andorre	AND	Andorra	Andorra
Belgium	Belgique	B	Belgien	Belgio
Bulgaria	Bulgarie	BG	Bulgarien	Bulgaria
Bosnia-Hercegovina	Bosnia-Herzegovine	BIH	Bosnien-Herzegowina	Bosnia-Herzogovina
Belarus	Belarus	BY	Weissrussland	Bielorussia
Switzerland	Suisse	CH	Schweiz	Svizzera
Czech Republic	République Tchèque	CZ	Tschechische Republik	Repubblica Ceca
Germany	Allemagne	D	Deutschland	Germania
Denmark	Danemark	DK	Dänemark	Danimarca
Spain	Espagne	E	Spanien	Spagna
Estonia	Estonie	EST	Estland	Estonia
France	France	F	Frankreich	Francia
Finland	Finlande	FIN	Finnland	Finlandia
Liechtenstein	Liechtenstein	FL	Liechtenstein	Liechtenstein
United Kingdom	Royaume Uni	GB	Grossbritannien und Nordirland	Regno Unito
Gibraltar	Gibraltar	GBZ	Gibraltar	Gibilterra
Greece	Grèce	GR	Greichenland	Grecia
Hungary	Hongrie	H	Ungarn	Ungheria
Croatia	Croatie	HR	Kroatien	Croazia
Italy	Italie	I	Italien	Italia
Ireland	Irlande	IRL	Irland	Irlanda
Luxembourg	Luxembourg	L	Luxemburg	Lussemburgo
Lithuania	Lituanie	LT	Litauen	Lituania
Latvia	Lettonie	LV	Lettland	Lettonia
Malta	Malte	M	Malta	Malta
Monaco	Monaco	MC	Monaco	Monaco
Moldavia	Moldavie	MD	Moldawien	Moldavia
Macedonia	Macédoine	MK	Makedonien	Macedonia
Norway	Norvège	N	Norwegen	Norvegia
Netherlands	Pays-Bas	NL	Niederlande	Paesi Bassi
Portugal	Portugal	P	Portugal	Portogallo
Poland	Pologne	PL	Polen	Polonia
Romania	Roumanie	RO	Rumanien	Romania
San Marino	Saint-Marin	RSM	San Marino	San Marino
Russia	Russie	RUS	Russland	Russia
Sweden	Suède	S	Schweden	Svezia
Slovak Republic	République Slovaque	SK	Slowak Republik	Repubblica Slovacca
Slovenia	Slovénie	SLO	Slowenien	Slovenia
Turkey	Turquie	TR	Türkei	Turchia
Ukraine	Ukraine	UA	Ukraine	Ucraina
Yugoslavia	Yougoslavie	YU	Jugoslawien	Jugoslavia

A

A Baña E 72 B2
A Bola E 73 B3
A Cañiza E 73 B2
A Capela E 72 A2
A Coruña E 72 A2
A Estrada E 72 B2
A Fonsagrada E 72 A3
A Guarda E 73 C2
A Gudiña E 73 B3
A Merca E 73 B3
A Peroxa E 72 B3
A Pontenova E 72 A3
A Rúa E 73 B3
A Teixeira E 73 B3
A Veiga E 73 B3
A-Ver-o-Mar P 73 C2
Aabybro DK 24 B2
Aach D 57 A4
Aachen D 36 C2
Aalen D 47 B6
Aalsmeer NL 35 A5
Aalst B 35 C5
Aalten NL 36 B2
Aalter B 35 B4
Äänekoski FIN 3 E19
Aarau CH 56 A3
Aarberg CH 56 A2
Aarburg CH 56 A2
Aardenburg NL 35 B4
Aarschot B 35 C5
Aba H 60 A3
Abádanes E 81 B4
Abades E 80 B2
Abadin E 72 A3
Abádszalók H 61 A5
Abaliget H 60 B3
Abanilla E 82 C1
Abano Terme I 58 C1
Abarán E 87 A4
Abasár H 51 C6
Abbadia San Salvatore I 67 D5
Abbehausen D 29 B5
Abbekäs S 27 D3
Abbeville F 34 C2
Abbiategrasso I 56 C3
Abda H 50 C3
Abejar E 75 C4
Abela P 84 B2
Abenberg D 48 A1
Abenójar E 86 A1
Åbenrå DK 25 D2
Abensberg D 48 B2
Aberaeron GB 4 K4
Aberdeen GB 4 H5
Aberdyfi GB 4 K4
Aberfeldy GB 4 H5
Abergavenny GB 4 L5
Abertura E 79 B5
Aberystwyth GB 4 K4
Abetone I 67 B4
Abfaltersbach A 58 B2
Abiego E 76 A2
Abild DK 25 E1
Abingdon GB 4 L6
Abiul P 78 B2
Abla E 87 B3
Ablis F 44 B2
Abondance F 56 B1
Abony H 61 A5
Abrantes P 78 B2
Abrest F 54 B3
Abriès F 65 B5
Abrud RO 11 N18
Absdorf A 50 B1
Abtenau A 58 A3
Abtsgmünd D 47 B5
Abusejo E 79 A4
Åby, *Kronoberg* S 26 B4
Åby, *Östergötland* S 23 C3
Åbytorp S 22 B2
Acate I 90 A2
Accadía I 90 A2
Accéglio I 65 B5
Accettura I 90 B3
Acciaroli I 90 B2
Accous F 62 C2
Accúmoli I 68 D2
Acedera E 79 B5
Acehuche E 79 B4
Acered E 81 A5
Acerenza I 90 B2
Acerno I 90 B2
Acerra I 89 C4
Aceuchal E 79 C4
Achene B 35 C6
Achenkirch A 58 A1
Achensee A 58 A1
Achenthal A 58 A1
Achern D 47 B4
Acheux-en-Amienois F 34 C3
Achim D 29 B6
Aci Castello I 95 B4
Aci Catena I 95 B4
Acilia I 88 B2
Acireale I 95 B4
Acquacadda I 96 D1
Acquanegra sul Chiese I 57 C5
Acquapendente I 67 D5
Acquasanta Terme I 68 D2
Acquasparta I 88 A2
Acquaviva I 67 C5
Acquaviva delle Fonti I 91 B3
Acquaviva Picena I 68 D2
Acqui Terme I 66 B2
Acquigny F 44 A2
Acri I 92 B3
Acs H 50 C4
Acsa H 51 C5
Acsteszér H 60 A2
Acy-en-Multien F 45 A3
Ada YU 61 C5
Adamuz E 86 A1
Ádánd H 60 B3
Adanero E 80 B2
Adapazarı TR 16 R22
Adaševci YU 71 A4
Adeanueva de Ebro E 75 B5
Adelboden CH 56 B2
Adelebsen D 37 B5
Adélfia I 91 A3
Adelmannsfelden D 47 B6
Adelsheim D 47 A5
Adelsö S 22 B4
Ademuz E 82 A1
Adenau D 36 C2
Adendorf D 30 B2
Adinkerke B 34 B3
Adjud RO 11 N20
Adliswil CH 56 A3
Admont A 59 A4
Ådneram N 18 B3
Adony H 60 A3
Adorf, *Hessen* D 37 B4
Adorf, *Sachsen* D 38 C2
Adra E 86 C2
Adradas E 75 C4
Adrall E 77 A4
Adrano I 95 B3
Ádria I 67 A6
Adzaneta E 82 A2
Ærøskøbing DK 25 E3
Aesch CH 56 A2
Affing D 48 B1
Affoltern CH 56 A3
Åfjord N 2 E12
Aflenz Kurort A 59 A5
Afragóla I 89 C4
Afritz A 58 B3
Afyonkarahisar TR 16 S22
Ágasegyháza H 61 B4
Agay F 65 C5
Agazzano I 66 B3
Agde F 64 C2
Agen F 63 B3
Ager E 76 B3
Agerbæk DK 25 D1
Agerskov DK 25 D2
Ageyevo RUS 7 J25
Agger DK 24 C1
Aggersund DK 24 B2
Ággius I 96 C2
Aggsbach Dorf A 49 B6
Aggsbach Markt A 49 B6
Aggtelek H 51 B6
Agiči BIH 69 B5
Agira I 95 B3
Ağlasun TR 16 T22
Aglientu I 96 B2
Agnières F 65 B4
Agno CH 56 C3
Agnone I 89 B4
Agolada E 72 B2
Agon Coutainville F 43 A4
Ágordo I 58 B2
Agost E 82 C2
Agramón E 87 A4
Agramunt E 77 B4
Agreda E 75 C5
Agrigento I 94 B2
Agrinion GR 15 S17
Agrón E 86 B2
Agrópoli I 90 B1
Agua Longa P 73 C2
Aguadulce, *Almería* E 87 C3
Aguadulce, *Sevilla* E 86 B1
Agualada E 72 A2
Aguarón E 76 B1
Aguas E 76 A2
Aguas Belas P 78 B2
Aguas de Busot E 82 C2
Aguas de Moura P 78 C2
Águas Frias P 73 C3
Aguas Santas P 73 C2
Aguaviva E 76 C2
Aguaviva de la Vega E 81 A4
Agudo E 80 D2
Águeda P 78 A2
Aguessac F 64 B2
Agugliano I 68 C2
Aguiar P 78 C3
Aguiàr da Beira P 73 D3
Aguilafuente E 80 A2
Aguilar de Campóo E 74 B2
Aguilar de la Frontera E 86 B1
Aguilas E 87 B4
Ahaus D 36 A2
Ahigal E 79 A4
Ahigal de Villarino E 73 C4
Ahillones E 85 A5
Ahlbeck, *Mecklenburg-Vorpommern* D 31 B6
Ahlbeck, *Mecklenburg-Vorpommern* D 31 B6
Ahlen D 36 B3
Ahlhorn D 29 C5
Ahrensbök D 30 A2
Ahrensburg D 30 B2
Ahrenshoop D 30 A4
Ahun F 54 B2
Åhus S 27 D4
Aibar E 75 B5
Aich D 48 B3
Aicha D 49 B4
Aichach D 48 B2
Aidone I 95 B3
Aiello Cálabro I 92 B3
Aigen im Mühlkreis A 49 B4
Aigle CH 56 B1
Aignan F 62 C3
Aignay-le-Duc F 45 C5
Aigre F 53 C5
Aigrefeuille-d'Aunis F 52 B4
Aigrefeuille-sur-Maine F 52 A3
Aiguablava E 77 B6
Aiguebelle F 55 C6
Aigueperse F 54 B3
Aigues-Mortes F 64 C3
Aigues-Vives F 64 C1
Aiguilles F 65 B5
Aiguillon F 63 B3
Aigurande F 54 B1
Ailefroide F 65 B5
Aillant-sur-Tholon F 45 C4
Ailly-sur-Noye F 44 A3
Ailly-sur-Somme F 44 A3
Aimargues F 64 C3
Aime F 55 C6
Ainaži LV 6 H19
Ainet A 58 B2
Ainhoa F 62 C1
Ainsa E 76 A3
Airaines F 34 D2
Aire-sur-la-Lys F 34 C3
Aire-sur-l'Adour F 62 C2
Airole I 66 C1
Airolo CH 56 B3
Airvault F 53 B4
Aisey-sur-Seine F 45 C5
Aïssey F 55 A6
Aisy-sur-Armançon F 45 C5
Aiterhofen D 48 B3
Aitona E 76 B3
Aitrach D 47 C6
Aiud RO 11 N18
Aix-en-Othe F 45 B4
Aix-en-Provence F 65 C4
Aix-les-Bains F 55 C5
Aixe-sur-Vienne F 53 C6
Aiyion GR 15 S18
Aizenay F 52 B3
Aizkraukle LV 7 H19
Aizpute LV 6 H17
Ajaccio F 96 B1
Ajain F 54 B1
Ajdovščina SLO 58 C3
Ajka H 60 A2
Ajo E 75 A3
Ajofrín E 80 C3
Ajuda P 79 C3
Akasztó H 61 B4
Akçakoca TR 16 R22
Aken D 38 B2
Åkerby S 22 A4
Åkernes N 19 C4
Åkers styckebruk S 22 B4
Åkersberga S 22 B5
Akharnaí GR 15 S18
Akhisar TR 16 S20
Åkirkeby DK 27 D4
Akkarfjord N 2 A18
Akkrum NL 28 B2
Åkra N 18 B3
Åkrehamn N 18 B2
Akşehir TR 16 S22
Aktsyabrski BY 7 K21
Åkvåg N 19 C6
Akyazı TR 16 R22
Ala I 57 C6
Ala dei Sardi I 96 C2
Alà di Stura I 56 C2
Alaejos E 74 C1
Alagna Valsésia I 56 C2
Alagón E 76 B1
Alaior, *Menorca* E 83
Alájar E 85 B4
Alakurtti RUS 3 C22
Alameda E 86 B1
Alameda de la Sagra E 80 B3
Alamedilla E 86 B2
Alamillo E 86 A1
Alaminos E 81 B4
Alandroal P 78 C3
Alange E 79 C4
Alanís E 85 A5
Alanno I 89 A3
Alap H 60 B3
Alaquáso E 82 B2
Alar del Rey E 74 B2
Alaraz E 80 B1
Alarcón E 81 C4
Alaró, *Mallorca* E 83
Alaşehir TR 16 S21
Alássio I 66 B2
Alatoz E 82 B1
Alatri I 89 B3
Alavus FIN 3 E18
Alba E 81 B5
Alba I 66 B2
Alba Adriática I 68 D2
Alba de Tormes E 80 B1
Alba de Yeltes E 79 A4
Alba-Iulia RO 11 N18
Albacete E 81 D5
Albæk DK 24 B3
Albaida E 82 C2
Albala del Caudillo E 79 B4
Albaladejo E 87 A3
Albalat E 82 B2
Albalate de Cinca E 76 B3
Albalate de las Nogueras E 81 B4
Albalate del Arzobispo E 76 B2
Albalete de Zorita E 81 B4
Alban F 63 C5
Albánchez E 87 B3
Albanchez de Ubeda E 86 B2
Albano Laziale I 88 B2
Albanyà E 77 A5
Albaredo d'Adige I 57 C6
Albares E 81 B3
Albarracín E 81 B5
Albatana E 87 A4
Albatarrec E 76 B3
Albatera E 82 C2
Albbruck D 47 C4
Albedin E 86 B1
Albelda de Iregua E 75 B4
Albenga I 66 B2
Albens F 55 C5
Ålberga, *Södermanland* S 22 B3
Ålberga, *Södermanland* S 23 C3
Albergaria-a-Nova P 73 D2
Albergaria-a-Velha P 78 A2
Albergaria dos Doze P 78 B2
Alberge P 78 C2
Alberic E 82 B2
Albernoa P 84 B3
Alberobello I 91 B4
Alberoni I 58 C2
Albersdorf D 29 A6
Albersloh D 36 B3
Albert F 34 C3
Albertirsa H 61 A4
Albertville F 55 C6
Alberuela de Tubo E 76 B2
Albi F 63 C5
Albidona I 92 B3
Albínia I 88 A1
Albino I 57 C4
Albires E 74 B1
Albisola Marina I 66 B2
Albocácer E 76 C3
Albolote E 86 B2
Albondón E 86 C2
Alborea E 82 B1
Ålborg DK 24 B2
Albox E 87 B3
Albrechtice nad Vitavou CZ 49 A5
Albstadt D 47 B5
Albufeira P 84 B2
Albuñol E 86 C2
Albuñuelas E 86 C2
Alburquerque E 79 B3
Alcácer do Sal P 78 C2
Alcáçovas P 78 C2
Alcadozo E 87 A4
Alcafoces P 79 B3
Alcains P 78 B3
Alcalá de Guadaira E 85 B5
Alcalá de Gurrea E 76 A2
Alcalá de Henares E 81 B3
Alcalá de la Selva E 76 C2
Alcalá de los Gazules E 85 C5
Alcalá de Xivert E 82 A3
Alcalá del Júcar E 82 B1
Alcalá del Río E 85 B5
Alcalá del Valle E 85 C5
Alcalá la Real E 86 B2
Álcamo I 94 B1
Alcampell E 76 B3
Alcanadre E 75 B4
Alcanar E 76 C3
Alcanede P 78 B2
Alcanena P 78 B2
Alcañices E 73 C4
Alcántara E 79 B4
Alcantarilha P 84 B2
Alcantarilla E 87 B4
Alcañiz E 76 B2
Alcara il Fusi I 95 A3
Alcaracejos E 86 A1
Alcaraz E 87 A3
Alcaria Ruiva P 84 B3
Alcarraz E 76 B3
Alcaudete E 86 B1
Alcaudete de la Jara E 80 C2
Alcázar de San Juan E 81 C3
Alcazarén E 74 C2
Alcoba E 80 C2
Alcobaça P 78 B1
Alcobendas E 81 B3
Alcocer E 81 B4
Alcochete P 78 C2
Alcoentre P 78 B2
Alcolea, *Almería* E 86 C3
Alcolea, *Córdoba* E 86 B1
Alcolea de Calatrava E 80 D2
Alcolea de Cinca E 76 B3
Alcolea de Tajo E 80 C1
Alcolea del Pinar E 81 A4
Alcolea del Río E 85 B5
Alcollarin E 79 B5
Alconchel E 79 C3
Alconera E 79 C4
Alcontar E 87 B3
Alcora E 82 A2
Alcorcón E 80 B3
Alcorisa E 76 C2
Alcossebre E 82 A3
Alcoutim P 84 B3
Alcover E 77 B4
Alcoy E 82 C2
Alcsútdoboz H 60 A3
Alcubierre E 76 B2
Alcubilla de Avellaneda E 75 C3
Alcubilla de Nogales E 74 B1
Alcubillas E 86 A2
Alcublas E 82 B2
Alcúdia, *Mallorca* E 83
Alcudia de Guadix E 86 B2
Alcuéscar E 79 B4
Aldea de Trujillo E 79 B5
Aldea del Cano E 79 B4
Aldea del Fresno E 80 B2
Aldea del Obispo E 79 A4
Aldea del Rey E 86 A2
Aldea Real E 80 A2
Aldeacentenera E 79 B5
Aldeadávila de la Ribera E 73 C4
Aldealcorvo E 80 A3
Aldealuenga de Santa Maria E 75 C3
Aldeamayor de San Martin E 74 C2
Aldeanueva de Barbarroya E 80 C1
Aldeanueva de San Bartolomé E 80 C1
Aldeanueva del Camino E 79 A5
Aldeanueva del Codonal E 80 A2
Aldeapozo E 75 C4
Aldeaquemada E 86 A2
Aldearrubia E 80 A1
Aldeaseca de la Frontera E 80 B1
Aldeasoña E 74 C2
Aldeatejada E 80 B1
Aldeavieja E 80 B2
Aldehuela E 82 A1
Aldehuela de Calatañazor E 75 C4
Aldeia da Serra P 78 C3
Aldeia do Bispo P 79 A4
Aldeia do Mato P 78 B2
Aldeia Gavinha P 78 B1
Aldeire E 86 B2
Aldenhoven D 36 C2
Aldersbach D 48 B4
Aldudes F 62 C1
Åled S 26 C2
Aledo E 87 B4
Alegria E 75 B4
Aleksa Šantić YU 61 C4
Aleksandrovac YU 71 B6
Aleksandrovac YU 71 C6
Aleksandrów Kujawski PL 33 C4
Aleksandrów Łódżki PL 41 B4
Aleksin RUS 7 J25
Ålem S 26 C6
Alençon F 43 B6
Alenquer P 78 B1
Alenya F 77 A5
Aléria F 96 A2
Alès F 64 B3
Áles I 96 D1
Alessándria I 66 B2
Alessándria della Rocca I 94 B2
Alessano I 93 B5
Ålestrup DK 24 C2
Ålesund N 2 E10
Alet-les-Bains F 63 D5
Alexandria RO 16 Q19
Alexandroúpolis GR 16 R19
Alézio I 91 B5
Alfacar E 86 B2
Alfaiates P 79 A4
Alfajarin E 76 B2
Alfambra E 76 C1
Alfambra P 84 B2
Alfândega da Fé P 73 C4
Alfarela de Jafes P 73 C3
Alfarelos P 78 A2
Alfarim P 78 C1
Alfarnate E 86 C1
Alfaro E 75 B5
Alfarrás E 76 B3
Alfaz del Pi E 82 C2
Alfedena I 89 B4
Alfeizarão P 78 B1
Alfeld, *Bayern* D 48 A2
Alfeld, *Niedersachsen* D 37 B5
Alfena P 73 C2
Alferce P 84 B2
Alfhausen D 29 C4
Alfonsine I 67 B6
Alforja E 76 B3
Alfoz E 72 A3
Alfundão P 84 A2
Algaida, *Mallorca* E 83
Algar E 85 C5
Älgarås S 21 C6
Ålgård N 18 C2
Algarinejo E 86 B1
Algarrobo E 86 C1
Algatocin E 85 C5
Algeciras E 85 C5
Algemesí E 82 B2
Algés P 78 C1
Algete E 81 B3
Alghero I 96 C1
Älghult S 26 B5
Alginet E 82 B2
Algodonales E 85 C5
Algodor E 80 C3
Algodor P 84 B3
Algora E 81 B4
Algoz P 84 B2
Alguaire E 76 B3
Alguazas E 87 A4
Algutsrum S 26 C6
Algyő H 61 B5
Alhama de Almería E 87 C3
Alhama de Aragón E 75 C5
Alhama de Granada E 86 C2
Alhama de Murcia E 87 B4
Alhambra E 86 A2
Alhandra P 78 C1
Alhaurin de la Torre E 86 C1
Alhaurín el Grande E 86 C1
Alhendin E 86 B2
Alhóndiga E 81 B4
Ali Terme I 95 B4
Alia E 80 C1
Ália I 94 B2
Aliaga E 76 C2
Aliağa TR 16 S20
Alibunar YU 71 A5
Alicante E 82 C2
Alicún de Ortega E 86 B2
Alife I 89 B4
Alija del Infantado E 74 B1
Alijó P 73 C3
Alimena I 95 B3
Alingsås S 21 D4
Alinyà E 77 A4
Aliseda E 79 B4
Alixan F 65 B4
Aljaraque E 85 B3
Aljezur P 84 B2
Aljorra E 87 B4
Aljubarrota P 78 B2
Aljucen E 79 B4
Aljustrel P 84 B2
Alken B 35 C6
Alkmaar NL 28 C1
Alkoven A 49 B5
Allaines F 44 B2
Allaire F 43 C3
Allanche F 54 C2
Alland A 50 B2
Allariz E 73 B3
Allassac F 53 C6
Allauch F 65 C4
Alleen N 19 C4
Allègre F 54 C3
Allemont F 55 C6
Allendorf D 37 C4
Allentsteig A 49 B6
Allepuz E 76 C2
Allersberg D 48 A2
Allershausen D 48 B2
Alles E 74 A2
Allevard F 55 C6
Allingåbro DK 24 C3
Allmannsdorf D 47 C5
Allo E 75 B4
Allogny F 54 A2
Allones, *Eure et Loire* F 44 B2
Allones, *Maine-et-Loire* F 53 A5
Allonnes F 43 C6
Allons F 62 B2
Allos F 65 B5
Allstedt D 38 B1
Allumiere I 88 A1
Almaceda P 78 B3
Almacelles E 76 B3
Almachar E 86 C1
Almada P 78 C1
Almadén E 86 A1
Almadén de la Plata E 85 B4
Almadenejos E 86 A1
Almadrones E 81 B4
Almagro E 86 A2
Almajano E 75 C4
Almansa E 82 C1
Almansil P 84 B2
Almanza E 74 B1
Almaraz E 79 B5
Almargen E 85 C5
Almarza E 75 C4
Almásfüzitő H 50 C4
Almassora E 82 B2
Almazán E 75 C4
Almazul E 75 C4
Alme D 37 B4
Almedina E 86 A3
Almedinilla E 86 B1
Almeida E 73 C4
Almeida P 73 D4
Almeirim P 78 B2
Almelo NL 28 C3
Almenar E 76 B3
Almenar de Soria E 75 C4
Almenara E 82 B2
Almendra P 73 D3
Almendral E 79 C4
Almendral de la Cañada E 80 B2
Almendralejo E 79 C4
Almenno San Bartolomeo I 57 C4
Almere NL 28 C2
Almería E 87 C3
Almerimar E 87 C3
Almese I 66 A1
Almexial P 84 B3
Älmhult S 26 C4
Almodôvar P 84 B2
Almodóvar del Campo E 86 A1
Almodóvar del Pinar E 81 C5
Almodóvar del Río E 85 B5
Almofala P 73 D3
Almogia E 86 C1
Almoharin E 79 B4
Almonacid de la Sierra E 75 C5
Almonacid de Toledo E 80 C3
Almonaster la Real E 85 B4
Almonte E 85 B4
Almoradí E 82 C2
Almoraima E 85 C5
Almorox E 80 B2
Almoster P 78 B2
Almsta S 22 B5
Almudena E 87 A4
Almudévar E 76 A2
Almuñécar E 86 C2
Almunge S 22 B5
Almuradiel E 86 A2
Almussafes E 82 B2

Alnwick GB 4 J6
Álora E 86 C1
Alos d'Ensil E 77 A4
Alosno E 85 B3
Alozaina E 86 C1
Alpbach A 58 A1
Alpedrete de la Sierra E 81 B3
Alpedrinha P 78 A3
Alpen D 36 B2
Alpera E 82 C1
Alphen aan de Rijn NL 35 A5
Alpiarça P 78 B2
Alpignano I 66 A1
Alpirsbach D 47 B4
Alpu TR 16 S22
Alpuente E 82 B1
Alqueva P 84 A3
Alquézar E 76 A3
Als DK 24 C3
Alsasua E 75 B4
Alsdorf D 36 C2
Alselv DK 25 D1
Alsfeld D 37 C5
Alsike S 22 B4
Alsleben D 38 B1
Alsónémedi H 61 A4
Alsótold H 51 C5
Alsóújlak H 60 A1
Alstätte D 36 A2
Alsterbro S 26 C5
Alstermo S 26 C5
Alt Ruppin D 31 C4
Alta N 3 B18
Älta S 22 B5
Altamura I 91 B3
Altarejos E 81 C4
Altaussee A 49 C4
Altavilla Irpina I 89 B4
Altavilla Silentina I 90 B2
Altdöbern D 39 B4
Altdorf CH 56 B3
Altdorf D 48 B3
Altdorf bei Nürnberg D 48 A2
Alte P 84 B2
Altea E 82 C2
Altedo I 67 B5
Altenweddingen D 38 A1
Altena D 36 B3
Altenau D 37 B6
Altenberg D 39 C3
Altenberge D 36 A3
Altenbruch D 29 B5
Altenburg D 38 C2
Altenfelden A 49 B4
Altengronau D 37 C5
Altenheim D 46 B3
Altenhundem D 36 B4
Altenkirchen, *Mecklenburg-Vorpommern* D 31 A5
Altenkirchen, *Radom* D 36 C3
Altenkunstadt D 38 C1
Altenmarkt A 49 C5
Altenmarkt D 48 B3
Altenmarkt im Pongall A 58 A3
Altensteig D 47 B4
Altentreptow D 31 B5
Altenwalde D 29 B5
Alter do Chão P 78 B3
Altfraunhofen D 48 B3
Altheim A 49 B4
Altheim D 47 A5
Althofen A 59 B4
Altıntaş TR 16 S22
Altkirch F 46 C3
Altlandsberg D 31 C5
Altlewin D 31 C6
Altmannstein D 48 B2
Altmorschen D 37 B5
Altmunster A 49 C4
Alto Campoó E 74 A2
Altofonte I 94 A2
Altomonte I 92 B3
Altopáscio I 67 C4
Altötting D 48 B3
Altreichenau D 49 B4
Altshausen D 47 C5
Altstätten CH 57 A4
Altura E 82 B2
Altusried D 47 C6
Alūksne LV 7 H20
Alunda S 22 A5
Alustante E 81 B5
Alvaiázere P 78 B2
Alvalade P 84 B2
Älvängen S 21 D4
Alvarenga P 73 D2
Alvares P 78 A2
Alvdal N 2 E12
Älvdalen S 2 F14
Alverca P 78 C1
Alvesta S 26 C4
Alvignac F 63 B4
Alvignano I 89 B4
Alvimare F 44 A1
Alviobeira P 78 B2
Alvito P 84 A3
Älvkarleby S 22 A4
Älvkarleö bruk S 22 A4
Alvor P 84 B2
Alvorge P 78 B2
Alvøy N 18 A2
Alvsbacka S 20 B5
Älvsbyn S 3 D17
Älvsered S 26 B2
Alwernia PL 41 C4
Alytus LT 6 J19
Alzénau D 37 C5
Alzey D 47 A4
Alzira E 82 B2
Alzonne F 63 C5
Amadora P 78 C1
Åmål S 21 B4
Amalfi I 89 C4
Amaliás GR 15 T17
Amance F 46 C2
Amancey F 55 A6
Amándola I 68 D2
Amantea I 92 B3
Amarante P 73 C2
Amareleja P 84 A3
Amares P 73 C2
Amaseno I 89 B3
Amatrice I 89 A3
Amay B 35 C6
Ambarnyy RUS 3 D23
Ambazac F 53 C6
Amberg D 48 A2
Ambérieu-en-Bugey F 55 C5
Ambérieux-en-Dombes F 55 B4
Ambert F 54 C3
Ambés F 62 A2
Ambjörby S 20 A5
Ambjörnarp S 26 B3
Ambleteuse F 34 C2
Amboise F 53 A5
Ambrières-les-Vallées F 43 B5
Amden CH 57 A4
Amel B 36 C2
Amélia I 88 A2
Amélie-les-Bains-Palalda F 77 A5
Amelinghausen D 30 B2
Amendoa P 78 B2
Amendoeira P 84 B3
Amendolara I 91 C3
Amer E 77 A5
Amerongen NL 35 A6
Amersfoort NL 35 A6
Ames E 72 B2
Amfilokhía GR 15 S17
Amfípolis GR 15 R18
Amieira, *Évora* P 84 A3
Amieira, *Portalegre* P 78 B3
Amieiro P 78 A2
Amiens F 44 A3
Åminne S 26 B3
Åmli N 19 C5
Åmmeberg S 23 C1
Amorbach D 47 A5
Amorebieta E 75 A4
Amorosa P 73 C2
Amorosi I 89 B4
Åmot, *Buskerud* N 19 B6
Åmot, *Telemark* N 19 B4
Åmotfors S 20 B4
Åmotsdal N 19 B5
Amou F 62 C2
Ampezzo I 58 B2
Ampfing D 48 B3
Ampflwang A 49 B4
Amplepuis F 55 C4
Amposta E 76 C3
Ampudia E 74 C2
Ampuero E 75 A3
Amriswil CH 57 A4
Amstelveen NL 35 A5
Amsterdam NL 28 C1
Amstetten A 49 B5
Amtzell D 47 C5
Amurrio E 75 A4
Amusco E 74 B2
An Uaimh IRL 4 K3
Åna-Sira N 18 C3
Anacapri I 89 C4
Anadia P 78 A2
Anadon E 76 C1
Anagni I 88 B3
Ananyiv UA 11 N21
Ånäset S 3 D17
Anastażewo PL 33 C4
Anaya de Alba E 80 B1
Ança P 78 A2
Ancede P 73 C2
Ancenis F 52 A3
Ancerville F 45 B6
Anchuras E 80 C2
Ancona I 68 C2
Ancora P 73 C2
Ancy-le-Franc F 45 C5
Andalo I 57 B5
Åndalsnes N 2 E10
Andance F 55 C4
Andau A 50 C3
Andebu N 20 B2
Andeer CH 57 B4
Andelfingen CH 47 C4
Andelot F 45 B6
Andelot-en-Montagne F 55 B5
Andenes N 2 B15
Andenne B 35 C6
Anderlues B 35 C5
Andermatt CH 56 B3
Andernach D 36 C3
Andernos-les-Bains F 62 B1
Anderslöv S 27 D3
Anderstorp S 26 B3
Andijk NL 28 C2
Andoain E 75 A4
Andocs H 60 B2
Andolsheim F 46 B3
Andorra E 76 C2
Andorra La Vella AND 77 A4
Andosilla E 75 B5
Andover GB 4 L6
Andratx, *Mallorca* E 83
Andreapol RUS 7 H23
Andréspol PL 41 B4
Andrest F 62 C3
Andretta I 90 B2
Andrezieux-Bouthéon F 55 C4
Ándria I 90 A3
Andrijevica YU 71 D4
Andritsaina GR 16 T19
Andrychów PL 51 A5
Andselv N 3 B16
Andújar E 86 A1
Anduze F 64 B2
Åneby N 20 A2
Aneby S 26 B4
Añes E 75 A3
Anet F 44 B2
Anfo I 57 C5
Ang S 26 B4
Anga S 23 D5
Angaïs F 62 C2
Ånge S 2 E14
Angeja P 78 A2
Ängelholm S 27 C2
Ängelsberg S 22 B3
Anger A 59 A5
Angera I 56 C3
Angermünde D 31 B6
Angern A 50 B2
Angers F 53 A4
Angerville F 44 B3
Anghiari I 68 C1
Anglès E 77 B5
Anglés, *Tarn* F 63 C5
Angles, *Vendée* F 52 B3
Angles sur l'Anglin F 53 B5
Anglesola E 77 B4
Anglet F 62 C1
Anglure F 45 B4
Angoulême F 53 C5
Angoulins F 52 B3
Angsö S 22 B3
Angües E 76 A2
Anguiano E 75 B4
Anguillara Sabazia I 88 A2
Anguillara Véneta I 58 C1
Anhée B 35 C5
Anholt DK 24 C4
Aniane F 64 C2
Aniche F 35 C4
Ånimskog S 21 C4
Anina RO 10 P17
Anizy-le-Château F 45 A4
Anjalankoski FIN 3 F20
Ankaran SLO 58 C3
Ankarsrum S 23 D3
Anklam D 31 B5
Ankum D 29 C4
Anlauftal A 58 A3
Annaberg A 49 C6
Annaberg-Buchholz D 38 C3
Annaberg im Lammertal A 58 A3
Annaburg D 38 B3
Annahütte D 39 B3
Annan GB 4 J5
Anneberg, *Halland* S 21 D4
Anneberg, *Jönköping* S 26 B4
Annecy F 55 C6
Annelund S 21 D5
Annemasse F 55 B6
Annerstad S 26 C3
Annevoie-Rouillon B 35 C5
Annonay F 55 C4
Annot F 65 C5
Annweiler D 46 A3
Añora E 86 A1
Anould F 46 B2
Anquela del Ducado E 81 B4
Anröchte D 36 B4
Ans DK 25 C2
Ansager DK 25 D1
Ansbach D 47 A6
Anse F 55 C4
Anserœul B 35 C4
Ansfelden A 49 B5
Ansião P 78 B2
Ansó E 62 D2
Ansoain E 75 B5
Antalya TR 16 T22
Antas E 87 B4
Antegnate I 57 C4
Antequera E 86 B1
Anterselva di Mezzo I 58 B2
Antibes F 65 C6
Antigüedad E 74 C2
Antillo I 95 B4
Antoing B 35 C4
Antonin PL 40 B2
Antrain F 43 B4
Antrim GB 4 J3
Antrodoco I 88 A3
Antronapiana I 56 B3
Antuzede P 78 A2
Antwerpen B 35 B5
Anversa d'Abruzzi I 89 B3
Anvin F 34 C3
Anzat-le-Luguet F 54 C3
Anzi I 90 B2
Ánzio I 88 B2
Anzola d'Emilia I 67 B5
Anzón E 75 C5
Aoiz E 62 D1
Aosta I 56 C2
Apalhão P 78 B3
Apátfalva H 61 B5
Apatin YU 61 C4
Apatity RUS 3 C23
Apc H 51 C5
Apécchio I 68 C1
Apeldoorn NL 36 A1
Apen D 29 B4
Apenburg D 30 C3
Apensen D 29 B6
Apiro I 68 C2
Apolda D 38 B1
Apostag H 61 B3
Äppelbo S 20 A6
Appennino I 68 D2
Appenzell CH 57 A4
Appiano I 57 B6
Appingedam NL 28 B3
Appoigny F 45 C4
Apremont-la-Forêt F 46 B1
Aprica I 57 B5
Apricena I 90 A2
Aprigliano I 92 B3
Aprília I 88 B2
Apt F 65 C4
Apúlia P 73 C2
Aquiléia I 58 C3
Aquilónia I 90 B2
Aquino I 89 B3
Arabayona E 80 A1
Arabba I 58 B1
Aracena E 85 B4
Arad RO 61 B6
Aradac YU 61 C5
Aragona I 94 B2
Aramits F 62 C2
Aramon F 64 C3
Aranda de Duero E 74 C3
Aranda de Moncayo E 75 C5
Arandjelovac YU 71 B5
Aranjuez E 81 B3
Arantzazu E 75 B4
Aranzueque E 81 B3
Aras de Alpuente E 82 B1
Arauzo de Miel E 75 C3
Arazede P 78 A2
Arbas F 63 D3
Árbatax I 96 D2
Arbeca E 76 B3
Arberg D 48 A1
Arbesbach A 49 B5
Arboga S 22 B2
Arbois F 55 B5
Arbon CH 57 A4
Arboréa I 96 D1
Arbório I 56 C3
Arbroath GB 4 H5
Arbùcies E 77 B5
Arbuniel E 86 B2
Arbus I 96 D1
Arc-en-Barrois F 45 C5
Arc-et-Senans F 55 A5
Arc-lès-Gray F 55 A5
Arc-sur-Tille F 55 A5
Arcachon F 62 B1
Arce I 89 B3
Arcen NL 36 B2
Arces-Dilo F 45 B4
Arcévia I 68 C1
Archena E 87 A4
Archez E 86 C2
Archiac F 53 C4
Archidona E 86 B1
Archivel E 87 A4
Arcidosso I 67 D5
Arcille I 67 D5
Arcis-sur-Aube F 45 B5
Arco I 57 C5
Arcones E 80 B3
Arcos E 74 B3
Arcos de Jalón E 81 A4
Arcos de la Frontera E 85 C5
Arcos de la Sierra E 81 B4
Arcos de las Salinas E 82 B1
Arcos de Valdevez P 73 C2
Arcozelo P 78 A3
Arcusa E 76 A3
Arcy-sur-Cure F 45 C4
Årdal N 18 B3
Ardala S 21 C5
Ardales E 86 C1
Ardara I 96 C1
Ardee IRL 4 K3
Arden DK 24 C2
Ardentes F 54 B1
Ardenza I 67 C4
Ardes F 54 C3
Ardez CH 57 B5
Ardisa E 76 A2
Ardón E 74 B1
Ardooie B 35 C4
Ardore I 92 C3
Ardres F 34 C2
Ardrossan GB 4 J4
Are N 18 B2
Åre S 2 E13
Areia Branca P 78 B1
Aremark N 20 B3
Arenales de San Gregorio E 81 C3
Arenas E 86 C1
Arenas de Iguña E 74 A2
Arenas de San Juan E 81 C3
Arenas de San Pedro E 80 B1
Arenas del Rey E 86 C2
Arendal N 19 C5
Arendonk B 35 B6
Arengosse F 62 B2
Arentorp S 21 C4
Arenys de Mar E 77 B5
Arenys de Munt E 77 B5
Arenzano I 66 B2
Areo E 77 A4
Ares E 72 A2
Arès F 62 B1
Ares del Maestrat E 76 C2
Areu E 77 A4
Arette F 62 C2
Aretxabaleta E 75 A4
Arevalillo E 80 B1
Arévalo E 80 A2
Arez P 78 B3
Arezzo I 67 C5
Arfeuilles F 54 B3
Argallón E 85 A5
Argamasilla de Alba E 81 C3
Argamasilla de Calatrava E 86 A1
Arganda E 81 B3
Arganil P 78 A2
Argegno I 57 C4
Argelès-Gazost F 62 C2
Argelès-sur-Mer F 77 A6
Argent-sur-Sauldre F 54 A2
Argenta I 67 B5
Argentan F 43 B5
Argentat F 63 A4
Argentera I 65 B5
Argenteuil F 44 B3
Argenthal D 36 D3
Argentiera I 96 C1
Argenton-Château F 53 B4
Argenton-sur-Creuse F 53 B6
Argentona E 77 B5
Argentré F 43 B5
Argentré-du-Plessis F 43 B4
Árgos GR 15 T18
Argostólion GR 15 S17
Argote E 75 B4
Arguedas E 75 B5
Argueil F 44 A2
Arholma S 22 B6
Århus DK 25 C3
Ariano Irpino I 90 A2
Ariano nel Polésine I 68 B1
Aribe E 62 D1
Arienzo I 89 B4
Arild S 27 C2
Arilje YU 71 C5
Ariño E 76 B2
Arinthod F 55 B5
Arisgotas E 80 C3
Aritzo I 96 D2
Ariza E 75 C4
Årjäng S 20 B4
Arjeplog S 3 C16
Arjona E 86 B1
Arjonilla E 86 B1
Arkelstorp S 27 C4
Arklow IRL 4 K3
Arkösund S 23 C3
Ärla S 22 B3
Arlanc F 54 C3
Arlanzón E 75 B3
Arlebosc F 64 A3
Arlena di Castro I 88 A1
Arles F 64 C3
Arles-sur-Tech F 77 A5
Arló H 51 B6
Arlon B 46 A1
Armação de Pera P 84 B2
Armadale GB 4 H4
Armagh GB 4 J3
Armamar P 73 C3
Armeno I 56 C3
Armenteros E 80 B1
Armentières F 34 C3
Armilla E 86 B2
Armiñón E 75 B4
Armuña de Tajuña E 81 B3
Arnac-Pompadour F 53 C6
Arnage F 43 C6
Arnas F 55 B4
Årnäs S 21 C5
Arnay-le-Duc F 55 A4
Arnborg DK 25 C2
Arnbruck D 48 A3
Arneburg D 30 C4
Arnedillo E 75 B4
Arnedo E 75 B4
Arneguy F 62 C1
Arnés E 76 C3
Årnes N 20 A3
Arnfels A 59 B5
Arnhem NL 36 B1
Arnö S 23 C4
Arnoldstein A 58 B3
Arnsberg D 36 B4
Arnschwang D 48 A3
Arnsdorf D 39 B3
Arnstadt D 37 C6
Arnstein D 37 D5
Arnstorf D 48 B3
Arnum DK 25 D1
Aroche E 85 B4
Ároktő H 51 C6
Arolla CH 56 B2
Arolsen D 37 B5
Arona I 56 C3
Åros N 20 B2
Arosa CH 57 B4
Arosa P 73 C2
Årøsund DK 25 D2
Arouca P 73 D2
Årøysund N 20 B2
Arpajon F 44 B3
Arpajon-sur-Cère F 63 B5
Arpino I 89 B3
Arquata del Tronto I 68 D2
Arques F 34 C3
Arques-la-Bataille F 44 A2
Arquillos E 86 A2
Arraia-Maeztu E 75 B4
Arraiolos P 78 C2
Arrancourt F 46 B2
Arras F 34 C3
Arrasate E 75 A4
Arreau F 63 D3
Arredondo E 75 A3
Arrens-Marsous F 62 D2
Arriate E 85 C5
Arrifana P 84 B2
Arrigorriaga E 75 A4
Arriondas E 74 A1
Arroba de los Montes E 80 C2
Arromanches-les-Bains F 43 A5
Arronches P 78 B3
Arroniz E 75 B4
Arrou F 44 B2
Arroya E 74 B2
Arroya de Cuéllar E 74 C2
Arroyal E 74 B2
Arroyo de la Luz E 79 B4
Arroyo de San Servan E 79 C4
Arroyo del Ojanco E 86 A3
Arroyomolinos de León E 85 A4
Arroyomolinos de Montánchez E 79 B4
Arruda dos Vinhos P 78 C1
Års DK 24 C2
Ars-en-Ré F 52 B3
Ars-sur-Moselle F 46 A2
Arsac F 62 B2
Arsiè I 58 C1
Arsiero I 57 C6
Årslev DK 25 D3
Ársoli I 88 A3
Arsunda S 22 A3
Artà, *Mallorca* E 83
Árta GR 15 S17
Artajona E 75 B5
Artegna I 58 B3
Arteixo E 72 A2
Artemare F 55 C5
Arten I 58 B1
Artena I 88 B2
Artenay F 44 B2
Artern D 38 B1
Artés E 77 B4
Artesa de Segre E 77 B4
Arth CH 56 A3
Arthez-de-Béarn F 62 C2
Arthon-en-Retz F 52 A3
Artieda E 76 A2
Artix F 62 C2
Artsyz UA 11 N21
Artziniega E 75 A3
Arudy F 62 C2
Årup DK 25 D3
Arveyres F 62 B2
Arvidsjaur S 3 D16
Arvieux F 65 B5
Arvika S 20 B4
Åryd, *Blekinge* S 27 C5
Åryd, *Kronoberg* S 26 C4
Arzachena I 96 B2
Arzacq-Arraziguet F 62 C2
Arzano F 42 C2
Aržano HR 70 C1
Arzberg D 38 C2
Arzignano I 57 C6
Arzila P 78 A2
Arzl im Pitztal A 57 A5
Arzúa E 72 B2
As B 35 B6
Aš CZ 38 C2
Ås N 20 B2
As Neves E 73 B2
As Nogaís E 72 B3
As Pontes de García Rodríguez E 72 A3
Aså DK 24 B3
Åsa S 24 B5
Ašanja YU 71 B5
Åsarna S 2 E14
Åsarp S 21 C5
Asasp F 62 C2
Åsbro S 23 B2
Asby S 23 D2
Ascain F 62 C1
Ascea I 90 B2
Ascha D 48 A3
Aschach an der Donau A 49 B5
Aschaffenburg D 37 D5
Aschbach Markt A 49 B5
Ascheberg, *Nordrhein-Westfalen* D 36 B3
Ascheberg, *Schleswig-Holstein* D 30 A2
Aschendorf D 29 B4
Aschersleben D 38 B1
Asciano I 67 C5
Ascó E 76 B3
Áscoli Piceno I 68 D2
Áscoli Satriano I 90 A2
Ascona CH 56 B3
Ascoux F 44 B3
Åseda S 26 B5
Asendorf D 29 C6
Asenovgrad BG 16 Q19
Åsensbruk S 21 C4
Åseral N 19 C4
Asfeld F 45 A5
Åsgårdstrand N 20 B2
Åshammar S 22 A3
Ashbourne GB 4 K6
Ashford GB 4 L7
Ashington GB 4 J6
Ashmyany BY 7 J19
Asiago I 57 C6
Asipovichy BY 7 K21
Asker N 20 B2
Askersund S 23 C1
Askim N 20 B3
Askland N 19 C5
Asköping S 22 B3
Askøy N 2 F9
Asljunga S 27 C3
Asnæs DK 25 D4
Ásola I 57 C5
Asolo I 58 C1
Asotthalom H 61 B4
Aspach A 49 B4
Aspang Markt A 59 A6
Aspariegos E 74 C1
Asparn an der Zaya A 50 B2
Aspberg S 20 B5
Aspe E 82 C2
Aspet F 63 C3
Äspö S 27 C5
Aspres-sur-Buëch F 65 B4
Assafora P 78 C1
Asse B 35 C5
Assel D 29 B6
Asselborn L 36 C1
Assémini I 96 D1
Assen NL 28 C3
Assenede B 35 B4
Assens, *Aarhus Amt.* DK 24 C3
Assens, *Fyns Amt.* DK 25 D2
Assesse B 35 C6
Assisi I 68 C1
Assling D 48 C3
Asso I 57 C4
Ássoro I 95 B3
Assumar P 78 B3
Astaffort F 63 B3
Asten NL 36 B1
Asti I 66 B2
Astorga E 72 B4
Åstorp S 27 C2
Astudillo E 74 B2
Asuni I 96 D1
Asványráró H 50 C3
Aszód H 51 C5
Aszófő H 60 B2
Atalaia P 78 B3
Atalho P 78 C2
Átány H 51 C6
Atanzón E 81 B3
Ataquines E 80 A2
Atarfe E 86 B2
Ateca E 75 C5
Atella I 90 B2
Atessa I 89 A4
Ath B 35 C4
Athies F 45 A3
Athies-sous-Laon F 45 A4
Athínai GR 15 T18
Athlone IRL 4 K3
Athy IRL 4 K3
Atienza E 81 A4
Atina I 89 B3
Atkár H 51 C5
Åtorp S 22 B1
Ätrå N 19 B5
Ätran S 26 B2
Atri I 89 A3
Atripalda I 89 C4
Attendorn D 36 B3
Attichy F 45 A4
Attigliano I 88 A2
Attigny F 45 A5
Åtvidaberg S 23 C2
Atzendorf D 38 B1
Au, *Steiermark* A 49 C6
Au, *Vorarlberg* A 57 A4
Au, *Bayern* D 48 B2
Au, *Bayern* D 48 C2
Aub D 47 A6
Aubagne F 65 C4
Aubange B 46 A1
Aubel B 36 C1
Aubenas F 64 B3
Aubenton F 45 A5
Auberive F 45 C6
Aubeterre-sur-Dronne F 53 C5
Aubiet F 63 C3
Aubigné F 53 B4
Aubigny F 52 B3
Aubigny-au-Bac F 35 C4
Aubigny-en-Artois F 34 C3
Aubigny-sur-Nère F 54 A2
Aubin F 63 B5
Aubonne CH 55 B6
Aubrac F 64 B1
Aubusson F 54 C2
Auch F 63 C3
Audenge F 62 B1
Auderville F 43 A4
Audierne F 42 B1
Audincourt F 56 A1
Audruicq F 34 C3
Audun-le-Roman F 46 A1
Audun-le-Tiche F 46 A1
Aue, *Nordrhein-Westfalen* D 36 B4
Aue, *Sachsen* D 38 C2
Auerbach, *Bayern* D 48 A2
Auerbach, *Sachsen* D 38 C2
Auffach A 58 A2
Augignac F 53 C5
Augsburg D 48 B1
Augusta I 95 B4
Augusten-borg DK 25 E2
Augustfehn D 29 B4
Augustów PL 6 K18
Aukrug D 30 A1
Aulendorf D 47 C5
Aulla I 67 B3
Aullène F 96 B2
Aulnay F 53 B4
Aulnoye-Aymeries F 35 C4
Ault F 34 C2
Aulum DK 25 C1
Aulus-les-Bains F 63 D4
Auma D 38 C1
Aumale F 44 A2
Aumetz F 46 A1
Aumont-Aubrac F 64 B2
Aunay-en-Bazois F 54 A3
Aunay-sur-Odon F 43 A5
Auneau F 44 B2
Auneuil F 44 A2
Auning DK 25 C3
Aups F 65 C5
Aura D 37 C5
Auray F 42 C3
Aurich D 29 B4
Aurignac F 63 C3
Aurillac F 63 B5
Auriol F 65 C4
Auritz-Burguette E 62 D1
Auronzo di Cadore I 58 B2
Auros F 62 B2
Auroux F 64 B2
Aurskog N 20 B3
Aursmoen N 20 B3
Ausónia I 89 B3
Ausservillgraton A 58 B2
Austad N 19 C4
Austbygda N 19 A5
Aústis I 96 C2
Austmarka N 20 A4
Austre Moland N 19 C5
Austre Vikebygd N 18 B2
Auterive F 63 C4
Autheuil-Authouillet F 44 A2
Authon F 65 B5
Authon-du-Perche F 44 B1
Autol E 75 B5
Autreville F 46 B1
Autrey-lès-Gray F 55 A5
Autun F 55 B4
Auty-le-Châtel F 44 C3
Auvelais B 35 C5
Auvillar F 63 B3
Auxerre F 45 C4
Auxi-le-Château F 34 C3
Auxon F 45 B4
Auxonne F 55 A5
Auxy F 55 B4
Auzances F 54 B2
Auzon F 54 C3
Availles-Limouzine F 53 B5
Avaldsnes N 18 B2
Avallon F 54 A3
Aveiras de Cima P 78 B2
Aveiro P 78 A2
Avelgem B 35 C4
Avellino I 89 C4
Avenches CH 56 B2
Aversa I 89 C4
Avesnes-le-Comte F 34 C3
Avesnes-sur-Helpe F 35 C4
Avesta S 22 A3
Avetrana I 91 B4
Avezzano I 89 A3
Avià E 77 A4
Aviano I 58 B2
Aviemore GB 4 H5
Avigliana I 66 A1
Avigliano I 90 B2
Avignon F 64 C3
Ávila E 80 B2
Avilés E 74 A1
Avintes P 73 C2
Avinyo E 77 B4
Ávio I 57 C5
Avioth F 45 A6
Avis P 78 B3
Avize F 45 B5
Ávola I 95 C4
Avon F 44 B3
Avord F 54 A2
Avranches F 43 B4
Avril F 46 A1
Avrillé F 53 A4
Avtovac BIH 70 C3
Awans B 35 C6
Ax-les-Thermes F 77 A4
Axams A 57 A6
Axat F 63 D5
Axel NL 35 B4
Axvall S 21 C5
Ay F 45 A5
Aya E 75 A4
Ayamonte E 84 B3
Aydın TR 16 T20
Ayelo de Malferit E 82 C2
Ayer CH 56 B2
Ayerbe E 76 A2
Ayette F 34 C3
Ayiá GR 15 S18
Aylesbury GB 4 L6
Ayllón E 75 C3
Ayna E 87 A3
Ayódar E 82 B2
Ayora E 82 B1
Ayr GB 4 J4
Ayron F 53 B5
Aytos BG 16 Q20
Ayvacık TR 16 S20
Ayvalık TR 16 S20
Aywaille B 35 C6
Azaila E 76 B2
Azambuja P 78 B2
Azambujeira P 78 B2
Azanja YU 71 B5
Azannes-et-Soumazannes F 46 A1
Azanúy-Alins E 76 B3
Azaruja P 78 C3
Azay-le-Ferron F 53 B6
Azay-le-Rideau F 53 A5
Azcoitia E 75 A4
Azé F 55 B4
Azeiteiros P 78 B3
Azenhas do Mar P 78 C1
Azinhaga P 78 B2
Azinhal P 84 B3
Azinheira dos Bairros P 84 A2
Aznalcázar E 85 B4
Aznalcóllar E 85 B4
Azóia P 78 B2
Azpeitia E 75 A4
Azuaga E 85 A5
Azuara E 76 B2
Azuqueca de Henares E 81 B3
Azur F 62 C1
Azzano Décimo I 58 C2

B

Bénévent-l'Abbaye F 53 B6
Benevento I 89 B4
Benfeld F 46 B3
Benfica P 78 B2
Bengtsfors S 21 B4
Beničanci HR 60 C3
Benicarló E 76 C3
Benicássim E 82 A3
Benidorm E 82 C2
Benifaió E 82 B2
Beniganim E 82 C2
Benisa E 82 C3
Benkovac HR 69 B4
Benneckenstein D 37 B6
Bénodet F 42 C1
Benquerencia de la Serena E 79 C5
Bensafrim P 84 B2
Bensdorf D 30 C4
Benshausen D 37 C6
Bensheim D 47 A4
Bentwisch D 30 A4
Beočin YU 61 C4
Beograd YU 71 B5
Berane YU 71 D4
Beranga E 75 A3
Berat AL 15 R16
Bérat F 63 C4
Beratzhausen D 48 A2
Bérbaltavár H 60 A1
Berbegal E 76 B2
Berbenno di Valtellina I 57 B4
Berberana E 75 B3
Bercedo E 75 A3
Bercel H 51 C5
Bercenay-le-Hayer F 45 B4
Berceto I 67 B4
Berchem B 35 C4
Berchidda I 96 C2
Berching D 48 A2
Berchtesgaden D 48 C4
Bérchules E 86 C2
Bercianos de Aliste E 73 C4
Berck F 34 C2
Berclaire d'Urgell E 76 B3
Berdoias E 72 A1
Berducedo E 72 A3
Berdún E 76 A2
Berdychiv UA 11 M21
Bereguardo I 56 C4
Berehove UA 11 M18
Berek BIH 70 A2
Beremend H 60 C3
Berestechko UA 11 L19
Berettyóújfalu H 10 N17
Berezhany UA 11 M19
Berezivka UA 11 N22
Berezna UA 11 L22
Berg D 48 A2
Berg S 23 C3
Berg im Gau D 48 B2
Berga, Sachsen-Anhalt D 37 B7
Berga, Thüringen D 38 C2
Berga E 77 A4
Berga S 26 B6
Bergama TR 16 S20
Bérgamo I 57 C4
Bergara E 75 A4
Berge, Brandenburg D 31 C4
Berge, Niedersachsen D 29 C4
Berge, Telemark N 19 B5
Berge, Telemark N 19 B5
Bergen, Mecklenburg-Vorpommern D 31 A5
Bergen, Niedersachsen D 30 C1
Bergen, Niedersachsen D 30 C2
Bergen N 18 A2
Bergen NL 28 C1
Bergen op Zoom NL 35 B5
Bergerac F 63 B3
Bergères-lés-Vertus F 45 B5
Bergeyk NL 35 B6
Berghausen D 47 B4
Bergheim D 36 C2
Berghem S 26 B2
Bergisch Gladbach D 36 C3
Bergkamen D 36 B3
Bergkvara S 27 C6
Berglern D 48 B2
Bergneustadt D 36 B3
Bergs slussar S 23 C2
Bergshamra S 22 B5
Bergtheim D 47 A6
Bergues F 34 C3
Bergum NL 28 B2
Bergün Bravuogn CH 57 B4
Bergwitz D 38 B2
Berhida H 60 A3
Beringel P 84 A3
Beringen B 35 B6
Berja E 86 C3
Berkenthin D 30 B2
Berkheim D 47 B6
Berkhof D 29 C6
Berkovići BIH 70 C3
Berkovitsa BG 15 Q18
Berlanga E 85 A5
Berlanga de Duero E 75 C4
Berlevag N 2 A21
Berlikum NL 28 B2
Berlin D 31 C5
Berlstedt D 38 B1
Bermeo E 75 A4
Bermillo de Sayago E 73 C4
Bern CH 56 B2
Bernalda I 91 B3
Bernardos E 80 A2
Bernartice, Jihočeský CZ 49 A5
Bernartice, Vychodočeský CZ 39 C5
Bernau, Baden-Württemberg D 47 C4
Bernau, Bayern D 48 C3
Bernau, Brandenburg D 31 C5
Bernaville F 34 C3
Bernay F 44 A1
Bernburg D 38 B1
Berndorf A 50 C2
Berne D 29 B5
Bernecebarati H 51 B4
Bernhardsthal A 50 B2
Bernkastel-Kues D 46 A3
Bernolakovo SK 50 B3
Bernsdorf D 39 B4
Bernstadt D 39 B4
Bernstein A 59 A6
Bernués E 76 A2
Beromünster CH 56 A3
Beroun CZ 39 D4
Berre-l'Etang F 65 C4
Berrocal E 85 B4
Bersenbrück D 29 C4
Bershad' UA 11 M21
Berthåga S 22 B4
Berthelming F 46 B2
Bertincourt F 34 C3
Bertinoro I 68 B1
Bertogne B 35 C6
Bertrix B 45 A6
Berville-sur-Mer F 44 A1
Berwick-upon-Tweed GB 4 J5
Berzasca RO 10 P17
Berzence H 60 B2
Berzocana E 79 B5
Besalú E 77 A5
Besançon F 55 A6
Besenfeld D 47 B4
Besenyőtelek H 51 C6
Besenyszög H 61 A5
Beshenkovichi BY 7 J21
Besigheim D 47 B5
Běšiny CZ 49 A4
Beška YU 71 A5
Besle F 43 C4
Besnyö H 60 A3
Bessais-le-Fromental F 54 B2
Bessan F 64 C2
Besse-en-Chandesse F 54 C2
Bessé-sur-Braye F 44 C1
Bessèges F 64 B3
Bessines-sur-Gartempe F 53 B6
Best NL 35 B6
Bestorp S 23 C2
Betanzos E 72 A2
Betelu E 75 A5
Bétera E 82 B2
Beteta E 81 B4
Béthenville F 45 A5
Béthune F 34 C3
Beton-Bazoches F 45 B4
Bettembourg L 46 A2
Betterdorf L 46 A2
Bettna S 23 C3
Béttola I 66 B3
Bettona I 68 C1
Betxi E 82 B2
Betz F 45 A3
Betzdorf D 36 C3
Beuil F 65 B5
Beuzeville F 44 A1
Bevagna I 68 D1
Bevens-bruk S 23 B2
Beveren B 35 B5
Beverley GB 4 K6
Bevern D 37 B5
Beverstedt D 29 B5
Beverungen D 37 B4
Beverwijk NL 28 C1
Bex CH 56 B2
Bexhill GB 4 L7
Beychevelle F 62 A2
Beykoz TR 16 R21
Beynat F 63 A4
Bezas E 82 A1
Bezau A 57 A4
Bezdan YU 61 C3
Bèze F 55 A5
Bezenet F 54 B2
Bezhetsk RUS 7 H25
Béziers F 64 C2
Bezzecca I 57 C5
Biadki PL 40 B2
Biała PL 40 C2
Biała PL 41 B4
Biała Podlaska PL 6 K18
Biała Rawska PL 41 B5
Białaczów PL 41 B5
Biale Błota PL 32 B3
Białobłoty PL 40 A2
Białobrzegi PL 41 B5
Białogard PL 32 B1
Białośliwie PL 32 B3
Biały Bór PL 32 B2
Białystok PL 6 K18
Biancavilla I 95 B3
Bianco I 92 C3
Biandrate I 56 C3
Biar E 82 C2
Biarritz F 62 C1
Bias F 62 B1
Biasca CH 56 B3
Biatorbágy H 60 A3
Bibbiena I 67 C5
Bibbona I 67 C4
Biberach, Baden-Württemberg D 47 B4
Biberach, Baden-Württemberg D 47 B5
Bibinje HR 69 B4
Bibione I 58 C3
Biblis D 47 A4
Bíccari I 90 A2
Bichl D 48 C2
Bichlbach A 57 A5
Bicorp E 82 B2
Bicske H 51 C4
Bidache F 62 C1
Bidart F 62 C1
Biddinghuizen NL 28 C2
Bideford GB 4 L4
Bie S 23 B3
Bieber D 37 C5
Biebersdorf D 39 B3
Biedenkopf D 37 C4
Biel CH 56 A2
Biel E 76 A2
Bielany Wroclawskie PL 40 B1
Bielawa PL 40 C1
Bielawy PL 41 A4
Bielefeld D 37 A4
Biella I 56 C3
Bielsa E 76 A3
Bielsk PL 33 C5
Bielsk Podlaski PL 6 K18
Bielsko-Biała PL 51 A5
Bienenbuttel D 30 B2
Bieniow PL 39 B5
Bienservida E 87 A3
Bienvenida E 85 A4
Bierdzany PL 40 C3
Bierné F 43 C5
Biersted DK 24 B2
Bierun PL 41 C4
Bierutów PL 40 B2
Bierwart B 35 C6
Bierzwina PL 32 B1
Bierzwnik PL 32 B1
Biescas E 76 A2
Biesenthal D 31 C5
Biesiekierz PL 32 A2
Bietigheim-Bissingen D 47 B5
Bièvre B 45 A6
Bieżuń PL 33 C5
Biga TR 16 R20
Bigadiç TR 16 S21
Biganos F 62 B2
Bigas P 73 D3
Bigastro E 82 C2
Bignasco CH 56 B3
Biguglia F 96 A2
Bihać BIH 69 B4
Biharnagybajom H 61 A6
Bijeljani BIH 70 C3
Bijeljina BIH 71 B4
Bijelo Polje YU 71 C4
Bijuesca E 75 C5
Bila Tserkva UA 11 M22
Bilaj HR 69 B4
Bilbao E 75 A4
Bilcza PL 41 C5
Bileća BIH 70 D3
Bilecik TR 16 R22
Biled RO 61 C5
Biłgoraj PL 11 L18
Bilhorod-Dnistrovskyy UA 11 N22
Bílina CZ 39 C3
Bilje HR 60 C3
Billdal S 24 B4
Billerbeck D 36 B3
Billesholm S 27 C2
Billinge S 27 D3
Billingsfors S 21 C4
Billom F 54 C3
Billund DK 25 D2
Bilopillya UA 7 L24
Bílovec CZ 50 A4
Bilstein D 36 B4
Bilthoven NL 35 A6
Bilzen B 35 C6
Bíňa SK 51 C4
Binaced E 76 B3
Binasco I 57 C4
Binche B 35 C5
Bindlach D 38 D1
Bindslev DK 24 B3
Binefar E 76 B3
Bingen D 36 D3
Binic F 42 B3
Binz D 31 A5
Biograd na Moru HR 69 C4
Bionaz I 56 C2
Bioska YU 71 C4
Birda RO 61 C6
Birkeland N 19 C5
Birkenfeld, Baden-Württemberg D 47 B4
Birkenfeld, Rheinland-Pfalz D 46 A3
Birkenhead GB 4 K5
Birkerød DK 27 D2
Birkfeld A 59 A5
Birmingham GB 4 K6
Birr IRL 4 K3
Birresborn D 36 C2
Birstein D 37 C5
Biržai LT 6 H19
Bisáccia I 90 A2
Bisacquino I 94 B2
Bisbal de Falset E 76 B3
Biscarosse F 62 B1
Biscarosse Plage F 62 B1
Biscarrués E 76 A2
Biscéglie I 91 A3
Bischheim F 46 B3
Bischofsheim D 37 C5
Bischofshofen A 58 A3
Bischofswerda D 39 B4
Bischofswiesen D 48 C3
Bischofszell CH 57 A4
Bischwiller F 46 B3
Bisenti I 89 A3
Bishop Auckland GB 4 J6
Bisignano I 92 B3
Bisingen D 47 B4
Biskupice-Oławskie PL 40 B2
Biskupiec PL 33 B5
Bismark D 30 C3
Bispingen D 30 B1
Bissen L 46 A2
Bissendorf D 36 A4
Bisserup DK 25 D4
Bistango I 66 B2
Bistarac Donje BIH 70 B3
Bistrica BIH 70 B2
Bistrica YU 71 C4
Bistrica YU 71 D4
Bistrica ob Sotli SLO 59 B5
Bistrița RO 11 N19
Bisztynek PL 33 A6
Bitburg D 36 D2
Bitche F 46 A3
Bitetto I 91 A3
Bitola MK 15 R17
Bitonto I 91 A3
Bitschwiller F 46 C3
Bitterfeld D 38 B2
Bitti I 96 C2
Biville-sur-Mer F 34 D2
Bivona I 94 B2
Biwer L 46 A2
Bizeljsko SLO 59 B5
Bizovac HR 60 C3
Bjåen N 19 B4
Bjärnum S 27 C3
Bjärred S 27 D3
Bjelland, Vest-Agder N 18 C3
Bjelland, Vest-Agder N 19 C4
Bjelovar HR 60 C1
Bjerkreim N 18 C3
Bjerreby DK 25 E3
Bjerringbro DK 25 C2
Björbo S 22 A1
Björkelangen N 20 B3
Björketorp S 26 B2
Björklinge S 22 A4
Björko, Stockholm S 22 B6
Björkö, Västra Götaland S 24 B4
Björköby S 26 B4
Björkvik S 23 C3
Björneborg S 20 B6
Björnerod S 21 B3
Bjørnevatn N 3 B21
Björnlunda S 23 B4
Björsäter S 23 C3
Bjurtjärn S 20 B6
Bjuv S 27 C2
Blace YU 71 C6
Blachownia PL 40 C3
Blackburn GB 4 K5
Blackpool GB 4 K5
Blackstad S 23 D3
Blacy F 45 B5
Bladåker S 22 A5
Blagaj BIH 69 A5
Blagaj BIH 70 C2
Blagnac F 63 C4
Blagoevgrad BG 15 Q18
Blaichach D 57 A5
Blain F 52 A3
Blainville-sur-l'Eau F 46 B2
Blairgowrie GB 4 H5
Blajan F 63 C3
Blakstad N 19 C5
Blâmont F 46 B2
Blanca E 87 A4
Blancos E 73 C3
Blanes E 77 B5
Blangy-sur-Bresle F 44 A2
Blankaholm S 23 D3
Blankenberge B 35 B4
Blankenburg D 37 B6
Blankenfelde D 38 A3
Blankenhain D 38 C1
Blankenheim D 36 C2
Blanquefort F 62 B2
Blansko CZ 50 A2
Blanzac F 53 C5
Blanzy F 55 B4
Blaricum NL 35 A6
Blascomillán E 80 B1
Blascosancho E 80 B2
Błaszki PL 40 B3
Blatná CZ 49 A4
Blatné SK 50 B3
Blatnice CZ 50 B3
Blatnika BIH 70 B2
Blato HR 70 D1
Blato na Cetini HR 70 C1
Blatten CH 56 B2
Blatzheim D 36 C2
Blaubeuren D 47 B5
Blaufelden D 47 A5
Blaustein D 47 B5
Blaye F 62 A2
Blaye-les-Mines F 63 B5
Blázquez E 79 C5
Bleckede D 30 B2
Blecua E 76 A2
Bled SLO 59 B4
Bleiburg A 59 B4
Bleichenbach D 37 C5
Bleicherode D 37 B6
Bléneau F 45 C3
Blera I 88 A2
Blérancourt F 45 A4
Bléré F 53 A5
Blesle F 54 C3
Blet F 54 B2
Bletterans F 55 B5
Blidö S 22 B5
Blidsberg S 21 D5
Blieskastel D 46 A3
Bligny-sur-Ouche F 55 A4
Blikstorp S 21 C6
Blinja HR 59 C6
Blizanówek PL 40 B3
Bliżyn PL 41 B5
Blois F 44 C2
Blokhus DK 24 B2
Blokzijl NL 28 C2
Blombacka S 20 B5
Blomberg D 37 B5
Blomskog S 20 B4
Blomstermåla S 26 C6
Błonie PL 41 A5
Blonville-sur-Mer F 43 A6
Blötberget S 22 A2
Blovice CZ 49 A4
Blšany CZ 38 C3
Bludenz A 57 A4
Bludov CZ 50 A2
Blumberg D 47 C4
Bø N 19 B6
Boa Vista P 78 B2
Boal E 72 A4
Boan YU 71 D4
Boario Terme I 57 C5
Boba H 60 A2
Bobadilla, Logroño E 75 B4
Bobadilla, Málaga E 86 B1
Bobadilla del Campo E 80 A1
Bobadilla del Monte E 80 B3
Bóbbio I 66 B3
Bóbbio Pellice I 65 B6
Bobigny F 44 B3
Bobingen D 48 B1
Böblingen D 47 B5
Bobolice PL 32 B2
Boboras E 72 B2
Bobowa PL 51 A6
Bobrinets UA 11 M23
Bobrova CZ 50 A1
Bobrovitsa UA 11 L22
Bobrowice PL 39 B5
Bobrówko PL 32 C1
Boca de Huérgano E 74 B2
Bocairent E 82 C2
Bočar YU 61 C5
Bocchigliero I 92 B3
Boceguillas E 75 C3
Bochnia PL 51 A6
Bocholt B 35 B6
Bocholt D 36 B2
Bochov CZ 38 C3
Bochum D 36 B3
Bockara S 26 B6
Bockenem D 37 A6
Bockfliess A 50 B2
Bockhorn D 29 B5
Bočna SLO 59 B4
Bocognano F 96 A2
Boconád H 51 C6
Bőcs H 51 B6
Boczów PL 39 A4
Boda, Stockholm S 22 A5
Boda, Värmland S 20 B5
Boda Glasbruk S 26 C5
Bodafors S 26 B4
Bodajk H 60 A3
Boddin D 30 B3
Bödefeld-Freiheit D 37 B4
Boden S 3 D17
Bodenmais D 48 A4
Bodenteich D 30 C2
Bodenwerder D 37 B5
Bodio CH 56 B3
Bodjani YU 61 C4
Bodmin GB 4 L4
Bodø N 2 C14
Bodonal de la Sierra E 85 A4
Bodrum TR 16 T20
Bodzanów PL 33 C6
Bodzanowice PL 40 C3
Bodzechów PL 41 C6
Bodzentyn PL 41 C5
Boecillo E 74 C2
Boëge F 55 B6
Boën F 54 C3
Bogács H 51 C6
Bogadmindszent H 60 C3
Bogajo E 73 D4
Bogarra E 87 A3
Bogarre E 86 B2
Bogatić YU 71 B4
Bogatynia PL 39 C4
Bogdaniec PL 31 C7
Boge S 23 D5
Bogen D 48 B3
Bogen S 20 A4
Bogense DK 25 D3
Bognanco Fonti I 56 B3
Bognes N 2 B15
Bogno CH 56 B4
Bogoria PL 41 C6
Boguchwaly PL 33 B6
Bogumiłowice PL 41 B4
Boguslav UA 11 M22
Boguszów-Gorce PL 39 C6
Bogutovac YU 71 C5
Bogyiszló H 60 B3
Bohain-en-Vermandois F 35 D4
Böheim-kirchen A 50 B1
Bohinjska Bistrica SLO 58 B3
Böhlen D 38 B2
Böhmenkirch D 47 B5
Bohmte D 29 C5
Bohodukhiv UA 7 L24
Bohonal de Ibor E 79 B5
Böhönye H 60 B2
Bohumin CZ 51 A4
Boiro E 72 B2
Bois-d'Amont F 55 B6
Boisseron F 64 C3
Boitzenburg D 31 B5
Boixols E 77 A4
Boizenburg D 30 B2
Bojadła PL 39 B5
Bojano I 89 B4
Bojanowo PL 40 B1
Bøjden DK 25 D3
Bojkovice CZ 50 A3
Bojná SK 50 B4
Bojnice SK 51 B4
Boka YU 61 C5
Böklund D 29 A6
Bokod H 60 A3
Böksholm S 26 B4
Boksitogorsk RUS 7 G23
Bol HR 69 C5
Bolaños de Calatrava E 86 A2
Bolbec F 44 A1
Bölcske H 61 B3
Bolderslev DK 25 E2
Boldog H 51 C5
Boldva H 51 B6
Bolea E 76 A2
Bolekhiv UA 11 M18
Bolesławiec PL 39 B5
Boleszkowice PL 31 C6
Bolewice PL 32 C2
Bólgheri I 67 C4
Bolhrad UA 11 P21
Boliden S 3 D17
Bolimów PL 41 A5
Boliqueime P 84 B2
Boljevci YU 71 B5
Boljkovci YU 71 B5
Bolkhov RUS 7 K25
Bolków PL 39 C6
Bollebygd S 26 B2
Bollène F 64 B3
Bólliga E 81 B4
Bollnäs S 2 F15
Bollullos E 85 B4
Bollullos par del Condado E 85 B4
Bologna I 67 B5
Bologne F 45 B6
Bolognetta I 94 B2
Bolognola I 68 D2
Bologoye RUS 7 H24
Bolótana I 96 C1
Bolsena I 88 A1
Bolshaya Vradiyevka UA 11 N22
Bolstad S 21 C4
Bolsward NL 28 B2
Boltaña E 76 A3
Boltenhagen D 30 B3
Boltigen CH 56 B2
Bolton GB 4 K5
Bolu TR 16 R22
Bolvadin TR 16 S22
Bóly H 60 C3
Bolzaneto I 66 B2
Bolzano I 57 B6
Bomba I 89 A4
Bombarral P 78 B1
Bömenzien D 30 C3
Bomlitz D 29 C6
Bømlo N 18 B2
Bøn N 20 A3
Bon-Encontre F 63 B3
Bonaduz CH 57 B4
Bonanza E 85 C4
Boñar E 74 B1
Bonárcado I 96 C1
Bonares E 85 B4
Bonassola I 66 B3
Bondal N 19 B5
Bondeno I 67 B5
Bondorf D 47 B4
Bondstorp S 26 B3
Bonete E 82 C1
Bonifacio F 96 B2
Bonigen CH 56 B2
Bonin PL 32 A2
Bonn D 36 C3
Bonnánaro I 96 C1
Bonnat F 54 B1
Bonndorf D 47 C4
Bonnétable F 44 B1
Bonnétage F 56 A1
Bonneuil-les-Eaux F 44 A3
Bonneuil-Matours F 53 B5
Bonneval F 44 B2
Bonneval-sur-Arc F 56 C2
Bonneville F 55 B6
Bonnières-sur-Seine F 44 A2
Bonnieux F 65 C4
Bönningheim D 47 A5
Bonny-sur-Loire F 54 A2
Bono E 76 A3
Bono I 96 C2
Bonorva I 96 C1
Bønsnes N 20 A2
Bonyhád H 60 B3
Boom B 35 B5
Boos F 44 A2
Boostedt D 30 A2
Bopfingen D 47 B6
Boppard D 36 C3
Boqueixón E 72 B2
Bor CZ 48 A3
Bor S 26 B4
Bor YU 11 P18
Boran-sur-Oise F 44 A3
Borås S 26 B2
Borba P 78 C3
Borbona I 88 A3
Borča YU 71 B5
Borci BIH 70 C3
Borculo NL 36 A2
Bordány H 61 B4
Bordeaux F 62 B2
Bordeira P 84 B2
Bordesholm D 30 A2
Bordighera I 66 C1
Bording DK 25 C2
Bordón E 76 C2
Bore I 67 B3
Borek Strzeliński PL 40 C2
Borek Wielkopolski PL 40 B2
Borello I 68 B1
Borensberg S 23 C2
Borgentreich D 37 B5
Börger D 29 C4
Borger NL 28 C3
Borggård S 23 C2
Borghamn S 23 C1
Borghetta di Vara I 67 B3
Borghetto d'Arróscia I 66 B1
Borghetto Santo Spirito I 66 B2
Borgholm S 26 C6
Borghorst D 36 A3
Bórgia I 92 C3
Borgloon B 35 C6
Børglum DK 24 B2
Borgo F 96 A2
Borgo a Mozzano I 67 C4
Borgo alla Collina I 67 C5
Borgo Pace I 68 C1
Borgo San Dalmazzo I 66 B1
Borgo San Lorenzo I 67 C5
Borgo Val di Taro I 67 B3
Borgo Valsugana I 57 B6
Borgo Vercelli I 56 C3
Borgoforte I 67 A4
Borgofranco d'Ivrea I 56 C2
Borgomanero I 56 C3
Borgomasino I 56 C2
Borgonovo Val Tidone I 66 A3
Borgorose I 88 A3
Borgosésia I 56 C3
Borgstena S 21 D5
Borgvik S 20 B4
Borisovka RUS 7 L25
Borja E 75 C5
Bork D 36 B3
Borken D 36 B2
Borkop DK 25 D2
Borkowice PL 41 B5
Borkowo PL 33 C6
Borkum D 28 B3
Borlänge S 22 A2
Bormes-les-Mimosas F 65 C5
Bórmio I 57 B5
Bormujos E 85 B4
Borna D 38 B2
Borne NL 36 A2
Borne Sulinowo PL 32 B2
Bornes P 73 C4
Bornheim D 36 C2
Bornhöved D 30 A2
Börnicke D 31 C4
Bornos E 85 C5
Borobia E 75 C5
Borodino RUS 7 J24
Borohrádek CZ 39 C6
Boronów PL 40 C3
Bórore I 96 C1
Borosźów PL 40 C3
Borota H 61 B4
Borovany CZ 49 B5
Borovichi RUS 7 G23
Borovnica SLO 59 C4
Borovo HR 61 C3
Borovsk RUS 7 J25
Borovy CZ 49 A4
Borowa PL 40 B2
Borowie PL 41 B6
Borox E 80 B3
Borrby S 27 D4
Borre DK 27 E2
Borre N 20 B2
Borredá E 77 A4
Borrenes E 72 B4
Borriol E 82 A2
Borris DK 25 D1
Borşa RO 11 N19
Borsdorf D 38 B2
Borsfa H 60 B1
Borský Mikuláš SK 50 B3
Borsodivánka H 51 C6
Borsodnádasd H 51 B6
Bort-les-Orgues F 54 C2
Börte N 19 B4
Boruja Kościelne PL 39 A6
Borup DK 25 D4
Boryslav UA 11 M18
Boryspil UA 11 L22
Boryszyn PL 32 C1
Borzęciczki PL 40 B2
Borzęcin PL 41 A5
Borzna UA 7 L23
Borzonasca I 66 B3
Borzyszkowy PL 32 A3
Borzytuchom PL 32 A3
Bosa I 96 C1
Bošáca SK 50 B3
Bosanci HR 59 C5
Bosanska Dubica BIH 60 C1
Bosanska Gradiška BIH 60 C2
Bosanska Kostajnica BIH 60 C1
Bosanska Krupa BIH 69 B5
Bosanski Brod BIH 70 A2
Bosanski Novi BIH 69 A5
Bosanski Petrovac BIH 69 B5
Bosanski Šamac BIH 70 A3
Bosansko Grahovo BIH 69 B5
Bošany SK 50 B4
Bösárkány H 50 C3
Bosau D 30 A2
Bósca H 61 B4
Bosco Chiesanuova I 57 C6
Bösdorf D 30 A2
Bösel D 29 B4
Bösingfeld D 37 A5
Boskoop NL 35 A5
Boskovice CZ 50 A2
Bošnjaci HR 70 A3
Bossast E 63 D3
Bossolasco I 66 B2
Boštanj SLO 59 B5
Boston GB 4 K6
Bostrak N 19 B5
Böszénfa H 60 B2
Bot E 76 B3
Botajica BIH 70 B3
Bøte By DK 30 A3
Boticas P 73 C3
Botilsäter S 21 B5
Botoš YU 61 C5
Botoşani RO 11 N20
Botricello I 93 C3
Bottendorf D 37 B4
Bottnaryd S 26 B3
Bottrop D 36 B2
Botunje YU 71 B6
Boturić YU 71 C5
Bötzingen D 46 B3
Bouaye F 52 A3
Bouça P 73 C3
Boucau F 62 C1
Bouchain F 35 C4
Bouchoir F 44 A3
Boudreville F 45 C5
Boudry CH 56 B1
Bouesse F 53 B6
Bouguenais F 52 A3
Bouhy F 54 A3
Bouillargues F 64 C3
Bouillon B 45 A6
Bouilly F 45 B4
Bouin F 52 B3
Boulay-Moselle F 46 A2
Boulazac F 53 C5
Boule-d'Amont F 77 A5
Bouligny F 46 A1
Boulogne-sur-Gesse F 63 C3
Boulogne-sur-Mer F 34 C2
Bouloire F 44 C1
Bouquemaison F 34 C3
Bourbon-Lancy F 54 B3
Bourbon-l'Archambault F 54 B3
Bourbonne-les-Bains F 46 C1
Bourbourg F 34 C3
Bourbriac F 42 B2
Bourcefranc-le-Chapus F 52 C3
Bourdeaux F 65 B4
Bouresse F 53 B5
Bourg F 62 A2
Bourg-Achard F 44 A1
Bourg-Argental F 55 C4
Bourg-de-Péage F 65 A4
Bourg-de-Thizy F 55 B4
Bourg-de-Visa F 63 B3
Bourg-en-Bresse F 55 B5
Bourg-et-Comin F 45 A4
Bourg-Lastic F 54 C2
Bourg-Madame F 77 A4
Bourg-St. Andéol F 64 B3
Bourg-St. Maurice F 56 C1
Bourganeuf F 54 C1
Bourges F 54 A2
Bourgneuf-en-Retz F 52 A3
Bourgogne F 45 A5
Bourgoin-Jallieu F 55 C5
Bourgtheroulde F 44 A1
Bourgueil F 53 A5
Bourmont F 46 B1
Bournemouth GB 4 L6
Bourneville F 44 A1
Bournezeau F 52 B3
Bourran F 63 B3
Bourret F 63 C4
Bourron-Marlotte F 44 B3
Boussac F 54 B2
Boussens F 63 C3
Boutersem B 35 C5
Bouttencourt F 34 D2
Bouvières F 65 B4
Bouvron F 52 A3
Bouxwiller F 46 B3
Bouzas E 73 B2
Bouzonville F 46 A2
Bova I 95 B4
Bova Marina I 95 B4
Bovalino Marina I 92 C3
Bovallstrand S 21 C3
Bovec SLO 58 B3
Bóveda E 72 B3
Bóvegno I 57 C5
Bovenau D 30 A1
Bovenden D 37 B5
Bóves I 66 B1
Bovino I 90 A2
Bovlingbjerg DK 24 C1
Bovolenta I 58 C1
Bovolone I 57 C6
Boxberg, Baden-Württemberg D 47 A5
Boxberg, Sachsen D 39 B4
Boxholm S 23 C2
Boxmeer NL 36 B1
Boxtel NL 35 B6
Božava HR 69 B3

Bozburun TR 16 T21
Bozdoğan TR 16 T21
Bożepole Wielkie PL 32 A3
Boževac YU 71 B6
Boží Dar CZ 38 C2
Božice CZ 50 B2
Bozouls F 64 B1
Bozüyük TR 16 S22
Bózzolo I 67 A4
Bra I 66 B1
Braås S 26 B5
Brabrand DK 25 C3
Bracciano I 88 A2
Bracieux F 53 A6
Bräcke S 2 E14
Brackenheim D 47 A5
Brackwede D 37 B4
Brad RO 11 N18
Bradford GB 4 K6
Bradina BIH 70 C3
Brådland N 18 C3
Brædstrup DK 25 D2
Braemar GB 4 H5
Braga P 73 C2
Bragança P 73 C4
Brăila RO 11 P20
Braine F 45 A4
Braine-le-Comte B 35 C5
Braives B 35 C6
Brake D 29 B5
Brakel B 35 C4
Brakel D 37 B5
Bräkne-Hoby S 27 C5
Brålanda S 21 C4
Bralin PL 40 B2
Brallo di Pregola I 66 B3
Bram F 63 C5
Bramafan F 65 C5
Bramberg am Wildkogel A 58 A2
Bramdrupdam DK 25 D2
Bramming DK 25 D1
Bramsche D 29 C4
Branca I 68 C1
Brancaleone Marina I 92 D3
Brand, *Nieder Östereich* A 49 B6
Brand, *Vorarlberg* A 57 A4
Brand-Erbisdorf D 38 C3
Brandbu N 20 A2
Brande DK 25 D2
Brande-Hornerkirchen D 29 B6
Brandenberg A 58 A1
Brandenburg D 31 C4
Brandis D 38 B2
Brando F 96 A2
Brandomil E 72 A2
Brandshagen D 31 A5
Brandval N 20 A4
Brandýs nad Labem CZ 39 C4
Branice PL 40 C2
Braniewo PL 33 A5
Branik SLO 58 C3
Brankovina YU 71 B4
Branky CZ 50 A3
Branne F 62 B2
Brannenburg-Degerndorf D 48 C3
Brantôme F 53 C5
Branzi I 57 B4
Bras d'Asse F 65 C5
Braslaw BY 7 J20
Braşov RO 11 P19
Brasparts F 42 B2
Brassac, *Charente* F 53 C4
Brassac, *Tarn* F 63 C5
Brassac-les-Mines F 54 C3
Brasschaat B 35 B5
Brastad S 21 C3
Břasy CZ 49 A4
Brąszewice PL 40 B3
Bratislava SK 50 B3
Brattfors S 20 B6
Bratunac BIH 71 B4
Braubach D 36 C3
Braunau A 48 B4
Braunfels D 37 C4
Braunlage D 37 B6
Braunsbedra D 38 B1
Braunschweig D 37 A6
Bray IRL 4 K3
Bray Dunes F 34 B3
Bray-sur-Seine F 45 B4
Bray-sur-Somme F 44 A3
Brazatortas E 86 A1
Brazey-en-Plaine F 55 A5
Brbinj HR 69 B4
Brčko BIH 70 B3
Brdani YU 71 C5
Brdów PL 33 C4
Brea de Tajo E 81 B3
Brécey F 43 B4
Brechen D 36 C4
Brechin GB 4 H5
Brecht B 35 B5
Brecketfeld D 36 B3
Břeclav CZ 50 B2
Brecon GB 4 L5
Brécy F 54 A2
Breda E 77 B5
Breda NL 35 B5
Bredaryd S 26 B3
Breddin D 30 C4
Bredebro DK 25 D1
Bredelar D 37 B4
Bredenfelde D 31 B5
Bredsjö S 22 B1
Bredstedt D 29 A5
Bredsten DK 25 D2
Bree B 35 B6
Bregana HR 59 C5
Breganze I 58 C1
Bregenz A 57 A4
Bréhal F 43 B4
Brehna D 38 B2
Breidenbach F 46 A3
Breil-sur-Roya F 66 C1
Breisach D 46 B3
Breitenbach CH 56 A2
Breitenbach D 37 C5
Breitenberg D 49 B4
Breitenfelde D 30 B2
Breitengussbach D 37 D6
Breivikbotn N 2 A18
Brejning DK 25 D2
Brekken N 2 E12
Brekkestø N 19 C5
Brekstad N 2 E11
Brem-sur-Mer F 52 B3
Bremen D 29 B5
Bremerhaven D 29 B5
Bremervörde D 29 B6
Bremgarten CH 56 A3
Brenderup DK 25 D2
Brenes E 85 B5
Brengova SLO 59 B5
Brenna PL 51 A4
Breno I 57 C5
Brénod F 55 B5
Brensbach D 47 A4
Brescello I 67 B4
Bréscia I 57 C5
Breskens NL 35 B4
Bresles F 44 A3
Bresnica YU 71 C5
Bressana I 66 A3
Bressanone I 58 B1
Bressuire F 53 B4
Brest BY 6 K18
Brest F 42 B1
Brest HR 58 C3
Brestač YU 71 B4
Brestanica SLO 59 C5
Brestova HR 68 A3
Brestovac HR 60 C2
Bretenoux F 63 B4
Breteuil, *Eure* F 44 B1
Breteuil, *Oise* F 44 A3
Brétigny-sur-Orge F 44 B3
Bretten D 47 A4
Bretteville-sur-Laize F 43 A5
Brettheim D 47 A6
Breuil-Cervínia I 56 C2
Breukelen NL 35 A6
Brevik N 19 B6
Brevik S 22 B5
Breza BIH 70 B3
Brežice SLO 59 C5
Bréziers F 65 B5
Brezna YU 71 C5
Breznica HR 59 B6
Breznica Našička HR 60 C3
Březnice CZ 49 A4
Brezno SK 51 B5
Brezolles F 44 B2
Březová nad Svitavou CZ 50 A2
Brezovica SK 50 B3
Brezovica SK 51 A6
Brezovica SLO 59 B4
Brezovo Polje Selo BIH 70 B3
Briançon F 65 B5
Brianconnet F 65 C5
Briare F 44 C3
Briatexte F 63 C4
Briático I 92 C3
Briaucourt F 45 B6
Bribir HR 59 C4
Bricquebec F 43 A4
Bridgend GB 4 L5
Bridgwater GB 4 L5
Břidličná CZ 50 A3
Bridport GB 4 L5
Brie-Comte-Robert F 44 B3
Briec F 42 B1
Brienne-le-Château F 45 B5
Brienon-sur-Armançon F 45 C4
Brienz CH 56 B3
Brienza I 90 B2
Brieskow Finkenheerd D 39 A4
Brietlingen D 30 B2
Brieva de Cameros E 75 B4
Briey F 46 A1
Brig CH 56 B3
Brighton GB 4 L6
Brignogan-Plage F 42 B1
Brignoles F 65 C5
Brihuega E 81 B4
Brijuni HR 68 B2
Brillon-en-Barrois F 45 B6
Brilon D 37 B4
Brinches P 84 A3
Bríndisi I 91 B4
Brinje HR 69 A4
Brinon-sur-Beuvron F 54 A3
Brinon-sur-Sauldre F 54 A2
Brión E 72 B2
Briones E 75 B4
Brionne F 44 A1
Brioude F 54 C3
Brioux-sur-Boutonne F 53 B4
Briouze F 43 B5
Briscous F 62 C1
Brisighella I 67 B5
Brissac-Quincé F 53 A4
Brissago CH 56 B3
Bristol GB 4 L5
Brive-la-Gaillarde F 53 C6
Briviesca E 75 B3
Brixlegg A 58 A1
Brka BIH 70 B3
Brnaze HR 69 C5
Brněnec CZ 50 A2
Brno CZ 50 A2
Bro S 22 B4
Broager DK 25 E2
Broaryd S 26 B3
Broby S 27 C4
Brobyværk DK 25 D3
Bročanac BIH 70 C2
Broćanac YU 70 D3
Brocas F 62 B2
Brock D 36 A3
Brockel D 29 B6
Broczyno PL 32 B2
Brod na Kupi HR 59 C4
Brodalen S 21 C3
Brodarevo YU 71 C4
Broddbo S 22 B3
Brodek u Přerova CZ 50 A3
Broden-bach D 36 C3
Brodick GB 4 J4
Brodnica PL 33 B5
Brodnica Graniczna PL 33 A4
Brody PL 33 C6
Brody, *Zielona Góra* PL 39 A5
Brody, *Zielona Góra* PL 39 B4
Brody UA 11 L19
Broglie F 44 B1
Brójce PL 39 A5
Brokind S 23 C2
Brolo I 95 A3
Brome D 30 C2
Bromölla S 27 C4
Bromont-Lamothe F 54 C2
Brömsebro S 27 C5
Bronchales E 81 B5
Bronco E 79 A4
Brønderslev DK 24 B2
Broni I 66 A3
Brønnøysund N 2 D13
Brøns DK 25 D1
Bronte I 95 B3
Bronzani Mejdan BIH 70 B1
Bronzolo I 57 B6
Broons F 43 B3
Broquies F 64 B1
Brørup DK 25 D2
Brösarp S 27 D4
Brostrud N 19 A5
Brotas P 78 C2
Brötjärna S 22 A2
Broto E 76 A2
Brottby S 22 B5
Brou F 44 B2
Brouage F 52 C3
Broumov CZ 40 C1
Broût-Vernet F 54 B3
Brouvelieures F 46 B2
Brouwershaven NL 35 B4
Brovary UA 11 L22
Brovst DK 24 B2
Brozas E 79 B4
Brozzo I 57 C5
Brtnice CZ 49 A6
Brtonigla HR 58 C3
Bruay-la-Buissière F 34 C3
Bruchhausen-Vilsen D 29 C6
Bruchsal D 47 A4
Bruck, *Bayern* D 48 A3
Brück, *Brandenburg* D 38 A2
Bruck an der Grossglocknerstrasse A 58 A2
Bruck an der Leitha A 50 B2
Bruck an der Mur A 59 A5
Brückl A 59 B4
Bruckmühl D 48 C2
Brue-Auriac F 65 C4
Brüel D 30 B3
Bruen CH 56 B3
Bruère-Allichamps F 54 B2
Brugg CH 56 A3
Brugge B 35 B4
Brüggen D 36 B2
Brühl D 36 C2
Bruinisse NL 35 B5
Brûlon F 43 C5
Brumano I 57 C4
Brumath F 46 B3
Brummen NL 36 A2
Brumov-Bylnice CZ 50 A4
Brumunddal N 2 F12
Brunau D 30 C3
Brunehamel F 45 A5
Brünen D 36 B2
Brunete E 80 B2
Brunflo S 2 E14
Brunico I 58 B1
Brunkeberg N 19 B5
Brunn D 31 B5
Brunnen CH 56 B3
Brunsbüttel D 29 B6
Brunssum NL 36 C1
Bruntál CZ 50 A3
Brus YU 71 C6
Brušane HR 69 B4
Brusasco I 56 C3
Brusio CH 57 B5
Brusno SK 51 B5
Brusque F 64 C1
Brusson I 56 C2
Brüssow D 31 B6
Brusy PL 32 B3
Bruvno HR 69 B4
Bruvoll N 20 A3
Bruxelles B 35 C5
Bruyères F 46 B2
Bruz F 43 B4
Bruzaholm S 26 B5
Brwinów PL 41 A5
Bryansk RUS 7 K24
Bryne N 18 C2
Brzeće YU 71 C5
Brzeg PL 40 C2
Brzeg Dolny PL 40 B1
Brześć Kujawski PL 33 C4
Brzesko PL 51 A6
Brzeszcze PL 51 A5
Brzezie PL 32 B2
Brzeziny PL 40 B3
Brzeziny PL 41 B4
Brzeźnica Nowa PL 41 B4
Brzeżno PL 32 B1
Brzotin SK 51 B6
Brzozie Lubawskie PL 33 B5
Bua S 24 B5
Buarcos P 78 A2
Buaveg N 18 B2
Bubbio I 66 B2
Bubry F 42 C2
Bucak TR 16 T22
Bučany SK 50 B3
Buccheri I 95 B3
Buccino I 90 B2
Bucelas P 78 C1
Buch D 48 B3
Buch, *Bayern* D 47 B6
Buchach UA 11 M19
Buchbach D 48 B3
Buchboden A 57 A4
Buchen, *Baden-Württemberg* D 47 A5
Büchen, *Schleswig-Holstein* D 30 B2
Buchenberg D 47 C6
Buchères F 45 B5
Buchholz D 29 B6
Buchloe D 48 B1
Buchlovice CZ 50 A3
Bucholz D 30 B4
Buchs CH 57 A4
Buchy F 44 A2
Bückeburg D 37 A5
Buckie GB 4 H5
Bückwitz D 30 C4
Bučovice CZ 50 A3
Bucsa H 61 A6
Bucureşti RO 11 P20
Bucy-lés-Pierreport F 45 A4
Buczek PL 41 B4
Budakalasz H 51 C5
Budakeszi H 61 A3
Budaörs H 61 A4
Budapest H 61 A4
Buddusò I 96 C2
Bude GB 4 L4
Budeč CZ 49 A6
Büdelsdorf D 29 A6
Budens P 84 B2
Budia E 81 B4
Budimlić-Japra BIH 69 B5
Büdingen D 37 C5
Budinšćina HR 59 B6
Budišov CZ 50 A3
Budmerice SK 50 B3
Budoni I 96 C2
Búdrio I 67 B5
Budva YU 15 Q16
Budyně nad Ohří CZ 39 C4
Budziszewice PL 41 B4
Budzyń PL 32 C2
Bue N 18 C2
Bueña E 76 C1
Buenache de Alarcón E 81 C4
Buenache de la Sierra E 81 B5
Buenaventura E 80 B2
Buenavista de Valdavia E 74 B2
Buendia E 81 B4
Bueu E 72 B2
Buezo E 75 B3
Bugac H 61 B4
Bugarra E 82 B2
Bugeat F 54 C1
Buggerru I 96 D1
Bugojno BIH 70 B2
Bugyi H 61 A4
Bühl D 47 B4
Bühl, *Bayern* D 57 A5
Bühlertal D 47 B4
Bühlertann D 47 A5
Buia I 58 B3
Builth Wells GB 4 K5
Buis-les-Baronnies F 65 B4
Buitenpost NL 28 B3
Buitrago del Lozoya E 81 B3
Bujalance E 86 B1
Bujaraloz E 76 B2
Buje HR 58 C3
Bujedo E 75 B3
Bük H 60 A1
Buk PL 32 C2
Bükkösd H 60 B2
Bükkzsérc H 51 C6
Bukovci SLO 59 B5
Bukowiec PL 39 A6
Bukowina Tatrzańska PL 51 A6
Bukownica PL 40 B3
Bukowno PL 41 C4
Bülach CH 56 A3
Buldan TR 16 S21
Bulgnéville F 46 B1
Bülkau D 29 B5
Bulkowo PL 33 C6
Bullas E 87 A4
Bulle CH 56 B2
Büllingen B 36 C2
Buna BIH 70 C2
Bunclody IRL 4 K3
Buncrana IRL 4 J3
Bunde, *Niedersachsen* D 29 B4
Bünde, *Nordrhein-Westfalen* D 37 A4
Bundoran IRL 4 J2
Bunić HR 69 B4
Buño E 72 A2
Buñol E 82 B2
Bunsbeek B 35 C5
Buñuel E 75 C5
Bunyola, *Mallorca* E 83
Buonabitácolo I 90 B2
Buonalbergo I 90 A1
Buonconvento I 67 C5
Buonvicino I 92 B2
Burano I 58 C2
Burbach D 36 C4
Burcei I 96 D2
Burdur TR 16 T22
Bureå S 3 D17
Burela E 72 A3
Büren D 37 B4
Büren an der Aare CH 56 A2
Burg, *Cottbus* D 39 B4
Burg, *Magdeburg* D 38 A1
Burg, *Schleswig-Holstein* D 29 B6
Burg auf Fehmarn D 30 A3
Burg Stargard D 31 B5
Burgas BG 16 Q20
Burgau A 59 A6
Burgau D 47 B6
Burgau P 84 B2
Burgbernheim D 47 A6
Burgdorf CH 56 A2
Burgdorf D 30 C2
Burgebrach D 48 A1
Bürgel D 38 C1
Burghaslach D 47 A6
Burghausen D 48 B3
Burgheim D 48 B2
Búrgio I 94 B2
Burgkirchen D 48 B3
Burgkunstadt D 38 C1
Burglengenfeld D 48 A3
Burgo P 73 D2
Burgoberbach D 47 A6
Burgohondo E 80 B2
Burgos E 74 B3
Burgsinn D 37 C5
Burgstädt D 38 C2
Burgstall D 30 C3
Burgsvik S 6 H16
Burgui E 62 D2
Burguillos E 85 B5
Burguillos de Toledo E 80 C3
Burguillos del Cerro E 79 C4
Burhaniye TR 16 S20
Burhave D 29 B5
Burie F 53 C4
Burjassot E 82 B2
Burk D 47 A6
Burkhardtsdorf D 38 C2
Burlada E 75 B5
Burladingen D 47 B5
Burlage D 29 B4
Burnley GB 4 K5
Burón E 74 A1
Buronzo I 56 C3
Burovac YU 71 B6
Burow D 31 B5
Burret F 63 D4
Burriana E 82 B2
Bürs A 57 A4
Bursa TR 16 R21
Burseryd S 26 B3
Bürstadt D 47 A4
Burujón E 80 C2
Bury GB 4 K5
Bury St. Edmunds GB 4 K7
Buryn UA 7 L23
Burzenin PL 40 B3
Busachi I 96 C1
Busalla I 66 B2
Busana I 67 B4
Busano I 56 C2
Busca I 66 B1
Busch D 30 C3
Buševec HR 59 C6
Bušince SK 51 B5
Buskhyttan S 23 C3
Busko-Zdrój PL 41 C5
Busot E 82 C2
Busovača BIH 70 B2
Busquistar E 86 C2
Bussang F 46 C2
Busseto I 67 B4
Bussière-Badil F 53 C5
Bussière-Poitevine F 53 B5
Bussolengo I 57 C5
Bussoleno I 56 C2
Bussum NL 35 A6
Busto Arsizio I 56 C3
Büsum D 29 A5
Butera I 95 B3
Butgenbach B 36 C2
Butryny PL 33 B6
Bütschwil CH 56 A4
Buttstädt D 38 B1
Butzbach D 37 C4
Bützfleth D 29 B6
Bützow D 30 B3
Buxières-les-Mines F 54 B2
Buxtehude D 29 B6
Buxton GB 4 K6
Buxy F 55 B4
Büyükçekmece TR 16 R21
Buzançais F 53 B6
Buzancy F 45 A5
Buzău RO 11 P20
Buzet HR 58 C3
Buzsák H 60 B2
Buzy F 62 C2
By S 22 A3
Byala BG 16 Q19
Byaroza BY 6 K19
Byczyna PL 40 B3
Bydgoszcz PL 33 B4
Bygland N 19 C4
Byglandsfjord N 19 C4
Bykhaw BY 7 K22
Bykle N 19 B4
Bylderup-Bov DK 25 E2
Byrum DK 24 B3
Byšice CZ 39 C4
Byske S 3 D17
Býškovice CZ 50 A3
Bysław PL 32 B3
Bystré CZ 50 A2
Bystřice, *Středočeský* CZ 51 A4
Bystřice, *Středočeský* CZ 49 A5
Bystřice n Pernštejnem CZ 50 A2
Bystřice pod Hostýnem CZ 50 A3
Bystrzyca Kłodzka PL 40 C1
Bytča SK 51 A4
Bytom PL 40 C3
Bytom Odrzański PL 39 B5
Bytów PL 32 A3
Bzenec CZ 50 B3
Bzince SK 50 B3

C

Cabacos P 78 B2
Cabaj-Čápor SK 50 B4
Cabana E 72 A2
Cabanac-et-Villagrains F 62 B2
Cabañaquinta E 74 A1
Cabanas P 84 B3
Cabañas de Yepes E 81 C3
Cabañas del Castillo E 79 B5
Cabanelles E 77 A5
Cabanes E 82 A3
Cabanillas E 75 B5
Čabar HR 59 C4
Cabasse F 65 C5
Cabdella E 77 A4
Cabeceiras de Basto P 73 C2
Cabeço de Vide P 78 B3
Cabella Ligure I 66 B3
Cabeza del Buey E 79 C5
Cabeza la Vaca E 85 A4
Cabezamesada E 81 C3
Cabezarados E 86 A1
Cabezarrubias del Puerto E 86 A1
Cabezas del Villar E 80 B1
Cabezas Rubias E 85 B3
Cabezón E 74 C2
Cabezón de la Sal E 74 A2
Cabezón de Liébana E 74 A2
Cabezuela E 80 A3
Cabezuela del Valle E 79 A5
Cabo de Gata E 87 C3
Cabo de Palos E 87 B5
Cabolafuenta E 81 A4
Cabourg F 43 A5
Cabra E 86 B1
Cabra P 78 A3
Cabra del Santo Cristo E 86 B2
Cábras I 96 D1
Cabreiro P 73 C2
Cabreiros E 72 A3
Cabrejas E 81 B4
Cabrela P 78 C2
Cabrillas E 73 D4
Cabuna HR 60 C2
Cacabelos E 72 B4
Čačak YU 71 C5
Cáccamo I 94 B2
Caccuri I 93 B3
Cacela P 84 B3
Cacém P 78 C1
Cáceres E 79 B4
Cachafeiro E 72 B2
Cachopo P 84 B3
Čachtice SK 50 B3
Cacin E 86 B2
Čačinci HR 60 C2
Cadafais P 78 C1
Cadalen F 63 C5
Cadalso E 79 A4
Cadaqués E 77 A6
Cadaval P 78 B1
Cadavedo E 72 A4
Čadavica BIH 70 B1
Čadca SK 51 A4
Cadéac F 63 D3
Cadelbosco di Sopra I 67 B4
Cadenazzo CH 56 B3
Cadenberge D 29 B6
Cadenet F 65 C4
Cadeuil F 52 C4
Cádiar E 86 C2
Cadillac F 62 B2
Cádiz E 85 C4
Čadjavica HR 60 C2
Cadouin F 63 B3
Cadours F 63 C4
Cadrete E 76 B2
Caen F 43 A5
Caernarfon GB 4 K4
Cafede P 78 B3
Caggiano I 90 B2
Cagli I 68 C1
Cágliari I 96 D2
Čaglin HR 60 C2
Cagnano Varano I 90 A2
Cagnes-sur-Mer F 65 C6
Caher IRL 4 K3
Caherciveen IRL 4 L1
Cahors F 63 B4
Cahul MD 11 P21
Caiazzo I 89 B4
Caion E 72 A2
Cairnryan GB 4 J4
Cairo Montenotte I 66 B2
Caivano I 89 C4
Cajarc F 63 B4
Čajetina YU 71 C4
Čajniče BIH 70 C4
Čakovec HR 59 B6
Çal TR 16 S21
Cala E 85 B4
Cala d'Or, *Mallorca* E 83
Cala Galdana, *Menorca* E 83
Cala Gonone I 96 C2
Cala Llonga E 83 C4
Cala Millor, *Mallorca* E 83
Cala Ratjada, *Mallorca* E 83
Calabritto I 90 B2
Calaceite E 76 C3
Calacuccia F 96 A2
Calaf E 77 B4
Calafat RO 11 P18
Calafell E 77 B4
Calahonda E 86 C2
Calahorra E 75 B5
Calais F 34 C2
Calalzo di Cadore I 58 B2
Calamocha E 76 C1
Calamonte E 79 C4
Calañas E 85 B4
Calanda E 76 C2
Calangiánus I 96 C2
Călăraşi RO 11 P20
Calascibetta I 95 B3
Calasetta I 96 D1
Calasparra E 87 A4
Calatafimi I 94 B1
Calatayud E 75 C5
Calatorao E 75 C5
Calau D 39 B3
Calbe D 38 B1
Calcena E 75 C5
Calcinelli I 68 C1
Calco I 57 C4
Caldaro sulla strada del vino I 57 B6
Caldarola I 68 C2
Caldas da Rainha P 78 B1
Caldas de Boì E 76 A3
Caldas de Malavella E 77 B5
Caldas de Reis E 72 B2
Caldas de San Jorge P 73 D2
Caldas de Vizela P 73 C2
Caldaso de los Vidrios E 80 B2
Caldearenas E 76 A2
Caldelas P 73 C2
Calders E 77 B4
Caldes de Montbui E 77 B5
Caldirola I 66 B3
Calella, *Barcelona* E 77 B5
Calella, *Girona* E 77 B6
Calenzana F 96 A1
Calera de León E 85 A4
Calera y Chozas E 80 C2
Caleruega E 75 C3
Caleruela E 80 C1
Cales de Mallorca, *Mallorca* E 83
Calestano I 67 B4
Calimera I 91 B5
Calitri I 90 B2
Calizzano I 66 B2
Callac F 42 B2
Callas F 65 C5
Calliano, *Piemonte* I 66 A2
Calliano, *Trentino Alto Adige* I 57 C6
Callosa de Ensarriá E 82 C2
Callosa de Segura E 82 C2
Callús E 77 B4
Čalma YU 71 A4
Calmbach D 47 B4
Calolziocorte I 57 C4
Calonge E 77 B6
Čalovec SK 50 C3
Calpe E 82 C3
Caltabellotta I 94 B2
Caltagirone I 95 B3
Caltanissetta I 95 B3
Caltavuturo I 94 B2
Caltojar E 75 C4
Caluire-et-Cuire F 55 C4
Caluso I 56 C2
Calvello I 90 B2
Calvi F 96 A1
Calviá, *Mallorca* E 83
Calvisson F 64 C3
Calvörde D 30 C3
Calw D 47 B4
Calzada de Calatrava E 86 A2
Calzada de Valdunciel E 80 A1
Calzadilla de los Barros E 85 A4
Camaiore I 67 C4
Camarasa E 76 B3
Camarena E 80 B2
Camarès F 64 C1
Camaret-sur-Aigues F 64 B3
Camaret-sur-Mer F 42 B1
Camarillas E 76 C2
Camariñas E 72 A1
Camarma E 81 B3
Camarzana de Tera E 73 B4
Camas E 85 B4
Camastra I 94 B2
Cambados E 72 B2
Cambarinho P 78 A2
Cambil E 86 B2
Cambo-les-Bains F 62 C1
Cambrai F 35 C4
Cambre E 72 A2
Cambridge GB 4 K7
Cambrils E 77 B4
Cambs D 30 B3
Camburg D 38 B1
Cameleño E 74 A2
Çameli TR 16 T21
Camelle E 72 A1
Camerano I 68 C2
Camerino I 68 C2
Camerota I 90 B2
Camigliatello Silano I 92 B3
Caminha P 73 C2
Caminomorisco E 79 A4
Caminreal E 76 C1
Camisano Vicentino I 58 C1
Cammarata I 94 B2
Camogli I 66 B3
Camors F 42 C3
Campagna I 90 B2
Campagnano di Roma I 88 A2
Campagnático I 67 D5
Campan F 62 C3
Campana I 93 B3
Campanario E 79 C5
Campanillas E 86 C1
Campano E 85 C4
Campaspero E 74 C2
Campbeltown GB 4 J4
Campello E 82 C2
Campelos P 78 B1
Campi Bisénzio I 67 C5
Campi Salentina I 91 B5
Campico López E 87 B4
Campíglia Maríttima I 67 C4
Campillo de Altobuey E 81 C5
Campillo de Aragón E 81 A5
Campillo de Arenas E 86 B2
Campillo de Llerena E 79 C5
Campillos E 86 B1
Câmpina RO 11 P19
Campli I 68 D2
Campo E 76 A3
Campo de Bacerros E 73 B3
Campo de Caso E 74 A1
Campo de Criptana E 81 C3
Campo Ligure I 66 B2
Campo Lugar E 79 B5
Campo Maior P 79 B3
Campo Molino I 65 B6
Campo Real E 81 B3
Campo Túres I 58 B1
Campobasso I 89 B4
Campobello di Licata I 94 B2
Campobello di Mazara I 94 B1
Campodársego I 58 C1
Campodolcino I 57 B4
Campofelice di Roccella I 94 B2
Campofiorito I 94 B2
Campofórmido I 58 B3
Campofranco I 94 B2
Campofrio E 85 B4
Campogalliano I 67 B4
Campolongo I 58 B2
Campomanes E 74 A1
Campomarino I 89 B5
Camporeale I 94 B2
Camporeggiano I 68 C1
Camporrells E 76 B3
Camporrobles E 82 B1
Campos P 73 C3
Campos del Port, *Mallorca* E 83
Camposa P 73 C2
Camposampiero I 58 C1
Camposanto I 67 B5
Campotéjar E 86 B2
Campotosto I 89 A3
Camprodón E 77 A5
Campsegret F 63 B3
Camuñas E 81 C3
Çan TR 16 R20
Can Pastilla, *Mallorca* E 83
C'an Picafort, *Mallorca* E 83
Cana I 67 D5
Cañada del Hoyo E 81 C5
Cañada Rosal E 85 B5
Cañadajuncosa E 81 C4
Čanak HR 69 B4
Çanakkale TR 16 R20
Canal San Bovo I 58 B1
Canale I 66 B1
Canales, *Asturias* E 74 B1
Canales, *Castellón de la Plana* E 82 B2
Canals E 82 C2
Cañamares E 81 B4

Champdeniers-St. Denis F 53 B4
Champdieu F 54 C4
Champdôtre F 55 A5
Champeix F 54 C3
Champéry CH 56 B1
Champigne F 43 C5
Champignelles F 45 C4
Champigny-sur-Veude F 53 A5
Champlitte-et-le-Prelot F 46 C1
Champoluc I 56 C2
Champoly F 54 C3
Champorcher I 56 C2
Champrond-en-Gâtine F 44 B2
Champs-sur-Tarentaine F 54 C2
Champs-sur-Yonne F 45 C4
Champtoceaux F 52 A3
Chamrousse F 65 A4
Chamusca P 78 B2
Chanac F 64 B2
Chanaleilles F 64 B2
Chandrexa de Queixa E 73 B3
Chañe E 74 C2
Changy F 54 B3
Chantada E 72 B3
Chantelle F 54 B3
Chantenay-St. Imbert F 54 B3
Chanteuges F 64 A2
Chantilly F 44 A3
Chantonnay F 52 B3
Chão de Codes P 78 B2
Chaource F 45 B4
Chapa E 72 B2
Chapareillan F 55 C5
Chapelle Royale F 44 B2
Chapelle-St. Laurent F 53 B4
Charenton-du-Cher F 54 B2
Charleroi B 35 C5
Charleville-Mézières F 45 A5
Charlieu F 54 B4
Charlottenberg S 20 B4
Charly F 45 B4
Charmes F 46 B2
Charmes-sur-Rhône F 64 B3
Charmey CH 56 B2
Charny F 45 C4
Charolles F 55 B4
Chârost F 54 B2
Charquemont F 56 A1
Charrin F 54 B3
Charroux F 53 B5
Chartres F 44 B2
Charzykow PL 32 B3
Chasseneuil-sur-Bonnieure F 53 C5
Chassigny F 45 C6
Château-Arnoux F 65 B5
Château-Chinon F 54 A3
Château-d'Oex CH 56 B2
Château-d'Olonne F 52 B3
Château-du-Loir F 44 C1
Château-Gontier F 43 C5
Château-la-Vallière F 53 A5
Château-Landon F 44 B3
Château-l'Evêque F 53 C5
Château-Porcien F 45 A5
Château-Renault F 44 C1
Château-Salins F 46 B2
Château-Thierry F 45 A4
Châteaubernard F 53 C4
Châteaubourg F 43 B4
Châteaubriant F 43 C4
Châteaudun F 44 B2
Châteaugiron F 43 B4
Châteaulin F 42 B1
Châteaumeillant F 54 B2
Châteauneuf, *Nièvre* F 54 A3
Châteauneuf, *Saône-et-Loire* F 55 B4
Châteauneuf-de-Randon F 64 B2
Châteauneuf-d'Ille-et-Vilaine F 43 B4
Châteauneuf-du-Faou F 42 B2
Châteauneuf-du-Pape F 64 B3
Châteauneuf-en-Thymerais F 44 B2
Châteauneuf la-Forêt F 53 C6
Châteauneuf-le-Rouge F 65 C4
Châteauneuf-sur-Charente F 53 C4
Châteauneuf-sur-Cher F 54 B2
Châteauneuf-sur-Loire F 44 C3
Châteauneuf-sur-Sarthe F 43 C5
Châteauponsac F 53 B6
Châteauredon F 65 B5
Châteaurenard, *Bouches du Rhône* F 64 C3
Châteaurenard, *Loiret* F 45 C3
Châteauroux F 53 B6
Châteauroux-les-Alpes F 65 B5
Châteauvillain F 45 B5
Châtel F 56 B1
Châtel-Censoir F 54 A3
Châtel-de-Neuvre F 54 B3
Châtel-Montagne F 54 B3
Châtel-St. Denis CH 56 B1
Châtel-sur-Moselle F 46 B2
Châtelaillon-Plage F 52 B3
Châtelaudren F 42 B3
Châtelet B 35 C5
Châtelguyon F 54 C3
Châtellerault F 53 B5
Châtelus-Malvaleix F 54 B2
Châtenois F 46 B1
Châtenois-les-Forges F 56 A1
Chatham GB 4 L7
Châtillon I 56 C2
Châtillon-Coligny F 45 C3
Châtillon-en-Bazois F 54 A3
Châtillon-en-Diois F 65 B4
Châtillon-sur Chalaronne F 55 B4
Châtillon-sur-Indre F 53 B6
Châtillon-sur-Loire F 54 A2
Châtillon-sur-Marne F 45 A4
Châtillon-sur-Seine F 45 C5
Châtres F 45 B4
Chauchina E 86 B2
Chaudes-Aigues F 64 B2
Chaudrey F 45 B5
Chauffailles F 55 B4
Chaulnes F 44 A3
Chaumont Gistoux B 35 C5
Chaumergy F 55 B5
Chaumont F 45 B6
Chaumont-en-Vexin F 44 A2
Chaumont-Porcien F 45 A5
Chaumont-sur-Aire F 45 B6
Chaumont-sur-Loire F 53 A6
Chaunay F 53 B5
Chauny F 45 A4
Chaussin F 55 B5
Chauvigny F 53 B5
Chavagnes-en-Paillers F 52 B3
Chavanges F 45 B5
Chaves P 73 C3
Chavignon F 45 A4
Chazelles-sur-Lyon F 55 C4
Chazey-Bons F 55 C5
Cheb CZ 38 C2
Chebsara RUS 7 G26
Checa E 81 B5
Chęciny PL 41 C5
Chef-Boutonne F 53 B4
Chekalin RUS 7 J25
Chekhovo RUS 33 A6
Cheles E 78 C3
Chella E 82 B2
Chelles F 44 B3
Chełm PL 11 L18
Chełmno PL 33 B4
Chełmno PL 40 A3
Chelmsford GB 4 L7
Chełmża PL 33 B4
Cheltenham GB 4 L5
Chelva E 82 B2
Chémery F 53 A6
Chemery-sur-Bar F 45 A5
Chemillé F 53 A4
Chemin F 55 B5
Chemnitz D 38 C2
Chénerailles F 54 B2
Cheniménil F 46 B2
Chenonceaux F 53 A6
Chenôve F 55 A4
Chera E 82 B2
Cherasco I 66 B1
Cherbourg F 43 A4
Cherchiara di Calábria I 92 B3
Cherepovets RUS 7 G25
Cherkasy UA 11 M23
Chernihiv UA 11 L22
Chernivtsi UA 11 M19
Chernyakhovsk RUS 6 J17
Chéroy F 45 B3
Cherven BY 7 K21
Chervonohrad UA 11 L19
Cherykaw BY 7 K22
Chessy-lès-Pres F 45 B4
Cheste E 82 B2
Chester GB 4 K5
Chesterfield GB 4 K6
Chevagnes F 54 B3
Chevanceaux F 53 C4
Chevillon F 45 B6
Chevilly F 44 B2
Chézery-Forens F 55 B5
Chialamberto I 56 C2
Chiampo I 57 C6
Chianale I 65 B6
Chianciano Terme I 67 C5
Chiaramonte Gulfi I 95 B3
Chiaramonti I 96 C1
Chiaravalle I 68 C2
Chiaravalle Centrale I 92 C3
Chiaréggio I 57 B4
Chiari I 57 C4
Chiaromonte I 90 B3
Chiasso CH 56 C4
Chiávari I 66 B3
Chiavenna I 57 B4
Chiché F 53 B4
Chiclana de la Frontera E 85 C4
Chiclana de Segura E 86 A2
Chieri I 66 A1
Chiesa in Valmalenco I 57 B4
Chieti I 89 A4
Chieti Scalo I 89 A4
Chiéuti I 89 B5
Chigirin UA 11 M23
Chillarón de Cuenca E 81 B4
Chillarón del Rey E 81 B4
Chilleurs-aux-Bois F 44 B3
Chillón E 86 A1
Chilluevar E 86 B2
Chiloeches E 81 B3
Chimay B 35 C5
Chimeneas E 86 B2
Chinchilla de Monte Aragón E 82 C1
Chinchón E 81 B3
Chinon F 53 A5
Chióggia I 58 C2
Chiomonte I 65 A5
Chipiona E 85 C4
Chirac F 64 B2
Chirens F 55 C5
Chirivel E 87 B3
Chişinău MD 11 N21
Chisineu Criş RO 10 N17
Chissey-en-Morvan F 55 A4
Chiusa I 57 B6
Chiusa di Pésio I 66 B1
Chiusa Scláfani I 94 B2
Chiusaforte I 58 B3
Chiusi I 67 C5
Chiva E 82 B2
Chivasso I 56 C2
Chlewiska PL 41 B5
Chludowo PL 32 C2
Chlum u Třeboně CZ 49 B5
Chlumec nad Cidlinou CZ 39 C5
Chmielnik PL 41 C5
Chobienice PL 39 A5
Choceň CZ 39 C6
Choceń PL 33 C5
Chochołow PL 51 A5
Chocianów PL 39 B5
Chociw PL 41 B4
Chociwel PL 31 B7
Choczewo PL 32 A3
Chodaków PL 41 A5
Chodecz PL 33 C5
Chodov CZ 38 C2
Chodzież PL 32 C2
Chojna PL 31 C6
Chojnice PL 32 B3
Chojno PL 32 C2
Chojnów PL 39 B5
Cholet F 52 A4
Chomérac F 64 B3
Chomutov CZ 38 C3
Chop UA 11 M18
Chorges F 65 B5
Chornobyl UA 11 L22
Chortkiv UA 11 M19
Chorzew PL 40 B3
Chorzów PL 40 C3
Choszczno PL 32 B1
Chotcza-Józefów PL 41 B6
Chotěboř CZ 49 A6
Chouilly F 45 A5
Chouto P 78 B2
Chouzy-sur-Cisse F 53 A6
Chozas de Abajo E 74 B1
Chrast, *Vychodočeský* CZ 50 A1
Chrást, *Západočeský* CZ 49 A4
Chrastava CZ 39 C5
Chřibská CZ 39 C4
Christiansfeld DK 25 D2
Chroberz PL 41 C5
Chropyně CZ 50 A3
Chrudim CZ 39 D5
Chrzanów PL 41 C4
Chtelnica SK 50 B3
Chudovo RUS 7 G22
Chueca E 80 C3
Chur CH 57 B4
Churriana E 86 C2
Churwalden CH 57 B4
Chvalšiny CZ 49 B5
Chwaszczyno PL 33 A4
Chynava CZ 39 C4
Chýnov CZ 49 B5
Ciacova RO 61 C6
Ciadîr-Lunga MD 11 N21
Ciadoncha E 74 B3
Cianciana I 94 B2
Ciano d'Enza I 67 B4
Ciążen PL 40 A2
Cibakhaza H 61 B5
Ciborro P 78 C2
Cicagna I 66 B3
Cicciano I 89 C4
Cičevac YU 71 C6
Ciciliano I 88 B2
Cicognolo I 57 C5
Cidadelhe P 73 D3
Cidones E 75 C4
Ciechanów PL 33 C6
Ciechocinek PL 33 C4
Cielądz PL 41 B5
Ciemnik PL 32 B1
Ciempozuelos E 81 B3
Ciepielów PL 41 B6
Čierny Balog SK 51 B5
Cierp F 63 D3
Cierpice PL 33 C4
Ciervana E 75 A3
Cierznie PL 32 B3
Cieslé PL 33 C6
Cieszyn PL 51 A4
Cieutat F 62 C3
Cieza E 87 A4
Cifer SK 50 B3
Çifteler TR 16 S22
Cifuentes E 81 B4
Cigales E 74 C2
Cigliano I 56 C3
Cillas E 81 B5
Cilleros E 79 A4
Cilleruelo de Arriba E 75 C3
Cilleruelo de Bezana E 74 B3
Cimalmotto CH 56 B3
Cimanes del Tejar E 74 B1
Ciminna I 94 B2
Cimişlia MD 11 N21
Cimoláis I 58 B2
Cîmpulung RO 11 P19
Cinctorres E 76 C2
Çine TR 16 T21
Činěves CZ 39 C5
Ciney B 35 C6
Cinfães P 73 C2
Cingia de Botti I 67 A4
Cingoli I 68 C2
Cinigiano I 67 D5
Cinobaňa SK 51 B5
Cinq-Mars-la-Pile F 53 A5
Cinquefrondí I 92 C3
Cintegabelle F 63 C4
Cintruénigo E 75 B5
Ciółkowo PL 33 C5
Ciperez E 73 D4
Cirat E 82 B2
Cirella I 92 B2
Cirencester GB 4 L5
Cirey-sur-Vezouze F 46 B2
Ciria E 75 C5
Ciriè I 56 C2
Cirigliano I 90 B3
Cirò I 93 B4
Cirò Marina I 93 B4
Ciry-le-Noble F 55 B4
Cislău RO 11 P20
Cismon del Grappa I 58 C1
Cisneros E 74 B2
Cissac-Médoc F 52 C4
Čista CZ 38 C3
Cisterna di Latina I 88 B2
Cistérniga E 74 C2
Cisternino I 91 B4
Cistierna E 74 B1
Čitluk BIH 70 C2
Citov CZ 39 C4
Città della Pieve I 67 D6
Città di Castello I 68 C1
Città Sant'Angelo I 89 A4
Cittadella I 58 C1
Cittaducale I 88 A2
Cittanova I 92 C3
Ciudad Real E 80 D3
Ciudad Rodrigo E 79 A4
Ciudadela de Menorca, *Menorca* E 83
Cividale del Friuli I 58 B3
Cívita I 88 A3
Cívita Castellana I 88 A2
Civitanova Alta I 68 C2
Civitanova Marche I 68 C2
Civitavécchia I 88 A1
Civitella di Romagna I 67 B5
Civitella di Tronto I 68 D2
Civitella Roveto I 89 B3
Civray F 53 B5
Çivril TR 16 S21
Cizur Mayor E 75 B5
Cjutadilla E 77 B4
Clacton-on-Sea GB 4 L7
Clairvaux-les-Lacs F 55 B5
Clamecy F 54 A3
Claremorris IRL 4 K2
Clausthal-Zellerfeld D 37 B6
Cláut I 58 B2
Claye-Souilly F 44 B3
Cléder F 42 B1
Clefmont F 46 B1
Cléguérec F 42 B2
Clelles F 65 B4
Clenze D 30 C2
Cléon-d'Andran F 64 B3
Cléré-les-Pins F 53 A5
Clères F 44 A2
Clermont F 44 A3
Clermont-en-Argonne F 45 A6
Clermont-Ferrand F 54 C3
Clermont-l'Hérault F 64 C2
Clerval F 55 A6
Clervaux L 36 C2
Clèry-St. André F 44 C2
Cles I 57 B6
Clisson F 52 A3
Clohars-Carnoët F 42 C2
Clones IRL 4 J3
Clonmel IRL 4 K3
Cloppenburg D 29 C5
Cloyes-sur-le-Loir F 44 C2
Cluis F 54 B1
Cluj-Napoca RO 11 N18
Cluny F 55 B4
Cluses F 55 B6
Clusone I 57 C4
Coaña E 72 A4
Cobas E 72 A2
Cobertelade E 75 C4
Cobeta E 81 B4
Cóbh IRL 4 L2
Cobreces E 74 A2
Coburg D 37 C6
Coca E 80 A2
Cocentaina E 82 C2
Cochem D 36 C3
Codigoro I 68 B1
Codogno I 57 C4
Codos E 75 C5
Codróipo I 58 C2
Codrongianos I 96 C1
Coelhoso P 73 C4
Coesfeld D 36 B3
Coevorden NL 28 C3
Cofrentes E 82 B1
Cogeces del Monte E 74 C2
Cognac F 53 C4
Cogne I 56 C2
Cognin F 55 C5
Cogolin F 65 C5
Cogollos de Guadix E 86 B2
Cogollos-Vega E 86 B2
Cogolludo E 81 B3
Coimbra P 78 A2
Coín E 86 C1
Coirós E 72 A2
Čoka YU 61 C5
Col SLO 59 C4
Colares P 78 C1
Cölbe D 37 C4
Colbitz D 38 A1
Colchester GB 4 L7
Colditz D 38 B2
Coldstream GB 4 J5
Colera E 77 A6
Coleraine GB 4 J3
Colfiorito I 68 C1
Cólico I 57 B4
Coligny F 55 B5
Colindres E 75 A3
Coll de Nargó E 77 A4
Collado-Mediano E 80 B2
Collado Villalba E 80 B3
Collagna I 67 B4
Collanzo E 74 A1
Collat F 54 C3
Colle di Val d'Elsa I 67 C5
Colle Isarco I 57 B6
Colle Sannita I 89 B4
Collécchio I 67 B4
Colledimezzo I 89 B4
Colleferro I 88 B3
Collelongo I 89 B3
Collepasso I 91 B5
Collepepe I 68 D1
Collesalvetti I 67 C4
Collesano I 94 B2
Colli a Volturno I 89 B4
Collinée F 42 B3
Collinghorst D 29 B4
Cóllio I 57 C5
Collobrières F 65 C5
Colmar F 46 B3
Colmars F 65 B5
Colmenar E 86 C1
Colmenar de la Sierra E 81 A3
Colmenar de Oreja E 81 B3
Colmenar Viejo E 80 B3
Colobraro I 90 B3
Cologna Véneta I 57 C6
Cologne F 63 C3
Cologne al Serio I 57 C4
Colombey-les-Belles F 46 B1
Colombey-les-deux-Églises F 45 B5
Colombres E 74 A2
Colomera E 86 B2
Colomers E 77 A5
Colomiers F 63 C4
Colònia de Sant Jordi, *Mallorca* E 83
Colorno I 67 B4
Colos P 84 B2
Cölpin D 31 B5
Colunga E 74 A1
Coma-ruga E 77 B4
Comácchio I 68 B1
Combarros E 72 B4
Combeaufontaine F 46 C1
Comblain-au-Pont B 35 C6
Combloux F 56 C1
Combourg F 43 B4
Combronde F 54 C3
Comeglians I 58 B2
Comillas E 74 A2
Comines F 35 C4
Cómiso I 95 C3
Comloşu Mare RO 61 C5
Commensacq F 62 B2
Commentry F 54 B2
Commerau D 39 B4
Commercy F 46 B1
Como I 57 C4
Cómpeta E 86 C2
Compiègne F 44 A3
Comporta P 78 C2
Comps-sur-Artuby F 65 C5
Comrat MD 11 N21
Comunanza I 68 D2
Cona, *Emilia Romagna* I 67 B5
Cona, *Veneto* I 58 C2
Concarneau F 42 C2
Conceição P 84 B2
Conches-en-Ouche F 44 B1
Concordia Sagittária I 58 C2
Concordia sulla Sécchia I 67 B4
Concots F 63 B4
Condat F 54 C2
Condé-en-Brie F 45 B4
Condé-sur-l'Escaut F 35 C4
Conde-sur-Marne F 45 A5
Condé-sur-Noireau F 43 B5
Condeixa P 78 A2
Condemios de Abajo E 81 A3
Condemios de Arriba E 81 A3
Condino I 57 C5
Condom F 63 C3
Condove I 66 A1
Condrieu F 55 C4
Conegliano I 58 C2
Conflans-sur-Lanterne F 46 C2
Confolens F 53 B5
Conforto E 72 A3
Congosto E 72 B4
Congosto de Valdavia E 74 B2
Congostrina E 81 A3
Conil de la Frontera E 85 C4
Conlie F 43 B5
Conliège F 55 B5
Connantre F 45 B4
Connaux F 64 B3
Connerré F 44 B1
Čonoplja YU 61 C4
Conques F 63 B5
Conques-sur-Orbiel F 63 C5
Conquista E 86 A1
Conquista de la Sierra E 79 B5
Consándolo I 67 B5
Consélice I 67 B5
Conselve I 58 C1
Consolacão P 78 B1
Constancia P 78 B2
Constanco E 72 A2
Constanța RO 11 P21
Constanti E 77 B4
Constantina E 85 B5
Consuegra E 81 C3
Consuma I 67 C5
Contarina I 68 A1
Conthey CH 56 B2
Contigliano I 88 A2
Contis-Plage F 62 B1
Contrada I 89 C4
Contres F 53 A6
Contrexéville F 46 B1
Controne I 90 B2
Contursi Termi I 90 B2
Conty F 44 A3
Conversano I 91 B4
Conwy GB 4 K5
Coole F 45 B5
Cope E 87 B4
Copertino I 91 B5
Copparo I 67 B5
Coppenbrugge D 37 A5
Corabia RO 16 Q19
Córaci I 92 B3
Coralići BIH 69 B4
Corato I 90 A3
Coray F 42 B2
Corbeil-Essonnes F 44 B3
Corbeny F 45 A4
Corbera E 82 B2
Corbie F 44 A3
Corbigny F 54 A3
Corbion B 45 A5
Corby GB 4 K6
Corconte E 74 A3
Corcubión E 72 B1
Corcumello I 89 A3
Cordenòns I 58 C2
Cordes-sur-Ciel F 63 B4
Córdoba E 86 B1
Cordobilla de Lácara E 79 B4
Cordovado I 58 C2
Corella E 75 B5
Coreses E 74 C1
Corga de Lobão P 73 D2
Cori I 88 B2
Coria E 79 B4
Coria del Río E 85 B4
Corigliano Cálabro I 92 B3
Corinaldo I 68 C1
Cório I 56 C2
Coripe E 85 C5
Cork IRL 4 L2
Corlay F 42 B2
Corleone I 94 B2
Corleto Monforte I 90 B2
Corleto Perticara I 90 B3
Çorlu TR 16 R20
Cormainville F 44 B2
Cormatin F 55 B4
Cormeilles F 44 A1
Cormery F 53 A5
Cormòns I 58 C3
Cormoz F 55 B5
Cornago E 75 B4
Cornberg D 37 B5
Cornellana E 72 A4
Corneşti MD 11 N21
Corníglio I 67 B4
Cornimont F 46 C2
Corniolo I 67 C5
Cornuda I 58 C2
Cornudella de Montsant E 76 B3
Cornudilla E 75 B3
Cornus F 64 C2
Corps F 65 B4
Corps Nuds F 43 C4
Corral de Almaguer E 81 C3
Corral de Ayllon E 75 C3
Corral de Calatrava E 86 A1
Corral-Rubio E 82 C1
Corrales E 74 C1
Corredoiras E 72 A2
Corréggio I 67 B4
Corrèze F 54 C1
Corridónia I 68 C2
Corrubedo E 72 B1
Córsico I 57 C4
Corte F 96 A2
Corte de Peleas E 79 C4
Corte Pinto P 84 B3
Corteconcepción E 85 B4
Cortegaca P 73 D2
Cortegada E 73 B2
Cortegana E 85 B4
Cortemaggiore I 67 B3
Cortemilia I 66 B2
Cortes E 75 C5
Cortes de Aragón E 76 C2
Cortes de Arenoso E 82 A2
Cortes de Baza E 87 B3
Cortes de la Frontera E 85 C5
Cortes de Pallás E 82 B2
Cortiçadas P 78 C2
Cortico P 73 C3
Cortijo de Arriba E 80 C2
Cortijos Nuevos E 87 A3
Cortina d'Ampezzo I 58 B2
Cortona I 67 C5
Coruche P 78 C2
Corullón E 72 B4
Corvara in Badia I 58 B1
Corvera E 87 B4
Cosenza I 92 B3
Coslada E 81 B3
Cosne-Cours-sur-Loire F 54 A2
Cosne d'Allier F 54 B2
Cospeito E 72 A3
Cossato I 56 C3
Cossaye F 54 B3
Cossé-le-Vivien F 43 C5
Cossonay CH 55 B6
Costa da Caparica P 78 C1
Costa de Santo André P 84 A2
Costa Nova P 78 A2
Costalpino I 67 C5
Costaros F 64 B2
Costeşti RO 11 P19
Costigliole d'Asti I 66 B2
Costigliole Saluzzo I 66 B1
Coswig, *Sachsen-Anhalt* D 38 B2
Coswig, *Sachsen* D 38 B3
Cotronei I 93 B3
Cottbus D 39 B4
Coublanc F 46 C1
Couches F 55 B4
Couço P 78 C2
Coucouron F 64 B2
Coucy-le-Château-Auffrique F 45 A4
Couëron F 52 A3
Couhé F 53 B5
Couiza F 63 D5
Coulanges F 54 B3
Coulanges-la-Vineuse F 45 C4
Coulanges-sur-Yonne F 54 A3
Couleuvre F 54 B2
Coulmier-le-Sec F 45 C5
Coulommiers F 45 B4
Coulonges-sur-l'Autize F 53 B4
Coulounieix-Chamiers F 53 C5
Coupéville F 45 B5
Couptrain F 43 B5
Cour-Cheverny F 53 A6
Coura P 73 C2
Courcelles B 35 C5
Courcelles-Chaussy F 46 A2
Courchevel F 56 C1
Courcôme F 53 C5
Courçon F 52 B4
Courgenay CH 56 A2
Courmayeur I 56 C1
Courniou F 64 C1
Cournon-d'Auvergne F 54 C3
Cournonterral F 64 C2
Courpière F 54 C3
Cours-la-Ville F 55 B4
Coursan F 64 C2
Courseulles-sur-Mer F 43 A5
Courson-les-Carrières F 45 C4
Courtalain F 44 B2
Courtenay F 45 B4
Courtomer F 44 B1
Courville F 44 B2
Coussac-Bonneval F 53 C6
Coutances F 43 A4
Couterne F 43 B5
Coutras F 62 A2
Couvet CH 56 B1
Couvin B 35 C5
Couzon F 54 B3
Covadonga E 74 A1
Covaleda E 75 C4
Covarrubias E 75 B3
Covas P 73 C2
Coventry GB 4 K6
Coviglião I 67 B5
Covilhã P 78 A3
Cox F 63 C4
Cózar E 86 A2
Cozes F 52 C4
Craco I 91 B3
Crailsheim D 47 A6
Craiova RO 11 P18
Craon F 43 C5
Craonne F 45 A4
Craponne F 55 C4
Craponne-sur-Arzon F 54 C3
Crato P 78 B3
Crawinkel D 37 C6
Crawley GB 4 L6
Crecente E 73 B2
Crèches-sur-Saône F 55 B4
Crécy-en-Ponthieu F 34 C2
Crécy-la-Chapelle F 45 B3
Crécy-sur-Serre F 45 A4
Creglingen D 47 A6
Creil F 44 A3
Creissels F 64 B2
Crema I 57 C4
Cremeaux F 54 C3
Crémenes E 74 B1
Crémieu F 55 C5
Cremlingen D 37 A6
Cremona I 67 A4
Creney F 45 B5
Črenšovci SLO 59 B6
Créon F 62 B2
Crepaja YU 71 A5
Crépy F 45 A4
Crépy-en-Valois F 45 A3
Cres HR 69 B3
Crescentino I 56 C3
Crespino I 67 B5
Crespos E 80 B2
Cressensac F 63 A4
Crest F 65 B4
Cresta CH 57 B4
Créteil F 44 B3
Creully F 43 A5
Creussen D 48 A2
Creutzwald F 46 A2
Creuzburg D 37 B6
Crevalcore I 67 B5
Crèvecœur-le-Grand F 44 A3
Crevillente E 82 C2
Crévola d'Ossola I 56 B3
Crewe GB 4 K5
Criales E 75 B3
Criel-sur-Mer F 34 C2
Crikvenica HR 59 C4
Crillon F 44 A2
Crimmitschau D 38 C2
Crinitz D 39 B3
Cripán E 75 B4
Criquetot-l'Esneval F 43 A6
Crispiano I 91 B4
Crissolo I 65 B6
Cristóbal E 79 A5
Crivitz D 30 B3
Črna SLO 59 B4
Crna Bara YU 61 C5
Crna Bara YU 71 B4
Crnac HR 60 C2
Crnča YU 71 B4
Crni Lug BIH 69 B5
Crni Lug HR 59 C4
Črni Vrh SLO 59 C4
Crnjelovo Donje BIH 71 B4
Črnomelj SLO 59 C5
Crocq F 54 C2
Crodo I 56 B3
Cromer GB 4 K7
Cronat F 54 B3
Cropalati I 92 B3
Crópani I 93 C3
Crosía I 93 B3
Crotone I 93 B4
Crottendorf D 38 C2
Crouy F 45 A5
Crozon F 42 B1
Cruas F 64 B3
Cruceni RO 61 B6
Crúcoli I 93 B4
Cruis F 65 B4
Cruseilles F 55 B6
Cruz de Incio E 72 B3
Crvenka YU 61 C4
Črveny Kamen SK 50 A4
Csabacsüd H 61 B5
Csabrendek H 60 A2
Csákány-doroszló H 59 B6
Csákvár H 60 A3
Csanádapáca H 61 B5
Csanádpalota H 61 B5
Csány H 51 C5
Csanytelek H 61 B5
Csapod H 60 A1
Császár H 60 A3

Császártöltés H 61 B4
Csávoly H 61 B4
Csemö H 61 A4
Csengöd H 61 B4
Csépa H 61 B5
Csepreg H 60 A1
Cserkeszölö H 61 B5
Csernely H 51 B6
Csökmö H 61 A6
Csököly H 60 B2
Csokonyavisonta H 60 B2
Csólyospálos H 61 B4
Csongrád H 61 B5
Csopak H 60 B2
Csorna H 50 C3
Csorvás H 61 B5
Csurgo H 60 B2
Cuacos de Yuste E 79 A5
Cualedro E 73 C3
Cuanca de Campos E 74 B1
Cuba P 84 A3
Cubel E 81 A5
Cubelles E 77 B4
Cubillos E 75 C4
Cubillos del Sil E 72 B4
Cubo de la Solana E 75 C4
Cucuron F 65 C4
Cudillero E 72 A4
Cuéllar E 74 C2
Cuenca E 81 B4
Cuers F 65 C5
Cuerva E 80 C2
Cueva de Agreda E 75 C5
Cuevas Bajas E 86 B1
Cuevas de San Clemente E 75 B3
Cuevas de San Marcos E 86 B1
Cuevas del Almanzora E 87 B4
Cuevas del Becerro E 85 C5
Cuevas del Campo E 86 B3
Cuevas del Valle E 80 B1
Cuges-les-Pins F 65 C4
Cúglieri I 96 C1
Cugnaux F 63 C4
Cuijk NL 36 B1
Cuinzier F 55 B4
Cuiseaux F 55 B5
Cuisery F 55 B5
Culan F 54 B2
Culemborg NL 35 B6
Cúllar E 87 B3
Cullera E 82 B2
Cully CH 56 B1
Culoz F 55 C5
Cumbres de San Bartolomé E 85 A4
Cumbres Mayores E 85 A4
Cumiana I 66 B1
Čumić YU 71 B5
Cumnock GB 4 J4
Cúneo I 66 B1
Cunlhat F 54 C3
Čunski HR 68 B3
Cuntis E 72 B2
Cuorgnè I 56 C2
Cupello I 89 A4
Cupra Maríttima I 68 C2
Cupramontana I 68 C2
Čuprija YU 71 C6
Curinga I 92 C3
Currelos E 72 B3
Curtea de Argeș RO 11 P19
Curtici RO 61 B6
Curtis E 72 A2
Curtis Santa Eulalia E 72 A2
Čurug YU 61 C5
Cusano Mutri I 89 B4
Cusset F 54 B3
Cussy-les-Forges F 54 A4
Cutanda E 76 C1
Cutro I 93 B3
Cutrofiano I 91 B5
Cuts F 45 A4
Cuvilly F 44 A3
Cuxhaven D 29 B5
Cvikov CZ 39 C4
Cwmbran GB 4 L5
Cybinka PL 39 A4
Czacz PL 40 A1
Czajków PL 40 B3
Czaplinek PL 32 B2
Czarlin PL 33 A4
Czarna-Dąbrówka PL 32 A3
Czarna Woda PL 33 B4
Czarnca PL 41 C4
Czarne PL 32 B2
Czarnków PL 32 C2
Czarnowo PL 33 B4
Czarnozyly PL 40 B3
Czarny Bór PL 39 C6
Czarny-Dunajec PL 51 A5
Czarny Las PL 40 B2
Czchow PL 51 A6
Czechowice-Dziedzice PL 51 A4
Czempiń PL 40 A1
Czermno PL 41 B5
Czernichow PL 51 A5
Czerniejewo PL 32 C3
Czernikowo PL 33 C4
Czersk PL 32 B3
Czerwieńsk PL 39 A5
Czerwionka-Leszczyny PL 40 C3
Czerwonka PL 33 B6
Częstochowa PL 41 C4
Czeszewo PL 32 C3
Człopa PL 32 B2
Człuchów PL 32 B3

D

Daaden D 36 C3
Dabas H 61 A4
Dąbie PL 40 A3
Dąbki PL 32 A2
Dabo F 46 B3
Dabrowa PL 32 C3
Dąbrowa Górnicza PL 41 C4
Dąbrowa Tarnowska PL 41 C5
Dąbrowice PL 33 C5
Dabrowno PL 33 B6
Dachau D 48 B2
Dačice CZ 49 A6
Dägebüll D 29 A5
Dagmersellen CH 56 A2
Dahlen D 38 B2
Dahlenburg D 30 B2
Dahme D 38 B3
Dahn D 46 A3
Dähre D 30 C2
Daimiel E 81 C3
Đakovica YU 15 Q17
Đakovo HR 60 C3
Dal, *Akershus* N 20 A3
Dal, *Telemark* N 19 B5
Dala-Floda S 22 A1
Dala-Husby S 22 A2
Dala-Järna S 22 A1
Dalaas A 57 A5
Dalaman TR 16 T21
Dalarö S 22 B5
Dalby DK 25 D3
Dalby, *Skåne* S 27 D3
Dalby, *Uppsala* S 22 B4
Dalen, *Akershus* N 20 B3
Dalen, *Telemark* N 19 B5
Daleszyce PL 41 C5
Dalheim L 46 A2
Dalhem S 23 D5
Dalias E 87 C3
Dalj HR 61 C3
Dals Långed S 21 C4
Dals Rostock S 21 C4
Dalsjöfors S 26 B3
Dalskog S 21 C4
Dalstorp S 26 B3
Daluis F 65 B5
Dalum D 29 C4
Dalum S 21 D5
Damasławek PL 32 C3
Damazan F 62 B3
Dammarie-les-Lys F 44 B3
Dammartin-en-Goële F 44 A3
Damme D 29 C5
Damnica PL 32 A3
Dampierre F 55 A5
Dampierre-sur-Salon F 55 A5
Damüls A 57 A4
Damville F 44 B2
Damvillers F 45 A6
Damwoude NL 28 B2
Dangé-St. Romain F 53 B5
Dångebo S 26 C5
Dangers F 44 B2
Dangeul F 44 B1
Danilovgrad YU 15 Q16
Danischenhagen D 30 A2
Daniszyn PL 40 B2
Danjoutin F 46 C2
Dannas S 26 B3
Dannemarie F 46 C3
Dannemora S 22 A4
Dannenberg D 30 B3
Dánszentmiklós H 61 A4
Dány H 61 A4
Daoulas F 42 B1
Darabani RO 11 M20
Darány H 60 C2
Darda HR 60 C3
Dardesheim D 37 B6
Darfeld D 36 A3
Darfo I 57 C5
Dargiń PL 32 A2
Dargun D 31 B4
Darlington GB 4 J6
Darłowo PL 32 A2
Darmstadt D 47 A4
Darney F 46 B2
Daroca E 81 A5
Darque P 73 C2
Dartmouth GB 4 L5
Daruvar HR 60 C2
Darvas H 61 A6
Dassel D 37 B5
Dassow D 30 B2
Datça TR 16 T20
Datteln D 36 B3
Dattenfeld D 36 C3
Daugard DK 25 D2
Daugavpils LV 7 J20
Daumeray F 43 C5
Daun D 36 C2
Davle CZ 49 A5
Davor HR 60 C2
Davos CH 57 B4
Davyd Haradok BY 7 K20
Dax F 62 C1
De Haan B 35 B4
De Koog NL 28 B1
De Panne B 34 B3
De Wijk NL 28 C3
Deauville F 43 A6
Deba E 75 A4
Debar MK 15 R17
Debe Wielkie PL 41 A6
Dębica PL 41 C6
Dębnica Kaszubska PL 32 A3
Dębno PL 31 C6
Dębolęka PL 40 B3
Dębowa Łaka PL 33 B5
Debrc YU 71 B4
Debrecen H 10 N17
Debrznica PL 39 A5
Debrzno PL 32 B3
Debstedt D 29 B5
Decazeville F 63 B5
Dechtice SK 50 B3
Decima I 88 B2
Decimomannu I 96 D1
Děčín CZ 39 C4
Decize F 54 B3
Decollatura I 92 B3
Decs H 60 B3
Dedelow D 31 B5
Dedemsvaart NL 28 C3
Dédestapolcsány H 51 B6
Dedovichi RUS 7 H21
Dég H 60 B3
Degaña E 72 B4
Degeberga S 27 D4
Degerfors S 22 B1
Degerhamn S 27 C6
Degernes N 20 B3
Deggendorf D 48 B3
Deggingen D 47 B5
Dego I 66 B2
Degolados P 79 B3
Dehesas de Guadix E 86 B2
Dehesas Viejas E 86 B2
Deia, *Mallorca* E 83
Deining D 48 A2
Deinze B 35 C4
Déiva Marina I 66 B3
Dej RO 11 N18
Deje S 20 B5
Delary S 26 C3
Delbrück D 37 B4
Delden NL 36 A2
Deleitosa E 79 B5
Delekovec HR 60 B1
Delémont CH 56 A2
Delft NL 35 A5
Delfzijl NL 28 B3
Délia I 94 B2
Delianuova I 92 C2
Deliblato YU 71 B6
Deliceto I 90 A2
Delitzsch D 38 B2
Dellach A 58 B3
Delle F 56 A2
Delme F 46 B2
Delmen-horst D 29 B5
Delnice HR 59 C4
Delvinë AL 15 S17
Demandice SK 51 B4
Demidov RUS 7 J22
Demigny F 55 B4
Demirci TR 16 S21
Demirköy TR 16 R20
Demmin D 31 B5
Demonte I 65 B6
Demyansk RUS 7 H23
Den Burg NL 28 B1
Den Ham NL 28 C3
Den Helder NL 28 C1
Den Oever NL 28 C2
Denain F 35 C4
Denbigh GB 4 K5
Dender-monde B 35 B5
Denekamp NL 28 C3
Denia E 82 C3
Denizli TR 16 T21
Denkendorf D 48 B2
Denklingen D 36 C3
Denta RO 61 C6
Déols F 53 B6
Derby GB 4 K6
Dereköy TR 16 R20
Derenberg D 37 B6
Derhaci UA 7 L25
Dermbach D 37 C6
Dermulo I 57 B6
Deronje YU 61 C4
Deruta I 68 D1
Derval F 43 C4
Derventa BIH 70 B2
Desana I 56 C3
Descartes F 53 B5
Desenzano del Garda I 57 C5
Deševa BIH 70 C3
Desimirovac YU 71 B5
Désio I 57 C4
Deskle SLO 58 B3
Desná CZ 39 C5
Dešov CZ 49 B6
Despotovac YU 71 B6
Despotovo YU 61 C4
Dessau D 38 B2
Deštná CZ 49 A5
Destriana E 73 B4
Désulo I 96 C2
Desvres F 34 C2
Deszk H 61 B5
Deta RO 61 C6
Detmold D 37 B4
Dětřichov CZ 50 A3
Dettelbach D 47 A6
Dettingen D 47 B5
Dettwiller F 46 B3
Detva SK 51 B5
Deurne NL 36 B1
Deutsch Wagram A 50 B2
Deutschkreutz A 50 C2
Deutschlandsberg A 59 B5
Deva RO 11 P18
Dévaványa H 61 A5
Devecser H 60 A2
Deventer NL 36 A2
Devinska Nova Ves SK 50 B2
Devrek TR 16 R22
Đevrske HR 69 C4
Deza E 75 C4
Dežanovac HR 60 C2
Dezzo I 57 C5
Dhidhimótikhon GR 16 R20
Dhomokós GR 15 S18
Diamante I 92 B2
Dianalund DK 25 D4
Diano d'Alba I 66 B2
Diano Marina I 66 C2
Dicomano I 67 C5
Die F 65 B4
Diebling F 46 A2
Dieburg D 47 A4
Diego del Carpio E 80 B1
Diekirch L 46 A2
Diélette F 43 A4
Diémoz F 55 C5
Dienten am Hochkönig A 58 A2
Diepenbeck B 35 C6
Diepholz D 29 C5
Dieppe F 44 A2
Dierberg D 31 B4
Dierdorf D 36 C3
Dieren NL 36 A2
Dierhagen D 30 A4
Diesdorf D 30 C2
Diessen D 48 C2
Diest B 35 C6
Dietenheim D 47 B6
Dietfurt D 48 A2
Dietikon CH 56 A3
Dietzenbach D 37 C4
Dieue-sur-Meuse F 45 A6
Dieulefit F 65 B4
Dieulouard F 46 B2
Dieuze F 46 B2
Diever NL 28 C3
Diez D 36 C4
Diezma E 86 B2
Differdange L 46 A1
Dignac F 53 C5
Dignano I 58 B2
Digne-les-Bains F 65 B5
Digny F 44 B2
Digoin F 54 B3
Dijon F 55 A5
Diksmuide B 34 B3
Dilar E 86 B2
Dillenburg D 36 C4
Dillingen, *Bayern* D 47 B6
Dillingen, *Saarland* D 46 A2
Dilsen B 36 B1
Dimaro I 57 B5
Dimitrovgrad BG 16 Q19
Dinami I 92 C3
Dinan F 43 B3
Dinant B 35 C5
Dinar TR 16 S22
Dinard F 43 B3
Dingden D 36 B2
Dingelstädt D 37 B6
Dingle IRL 4 K1
Dingle S 21 C3
Dingolfing D 48 B3
Dingtuna S 22 B3
Dingwall GB 4 H4
Dinkelsbühl D 47 A6
Dinkelscherben D 47 B6
Dinklage D 29 C5
Dinslaken D 36 B2
Dinxperlo NL 36 B2
Diö S 26 C4
Diósgyör H 51 B6
Diósjeno H 51 C5
Diou F 54 B3
Dipperz D 37 C5
Dippoldiswalde D 39 C3
Dirdal N 18 C3
Dirksland NL 35 B5
Dirlewang D 47 C6
Dischingen D 47 B6
Disentis CH 56 B3
Diso I 93 A5
Dissen D 36 A4
Ditzingen D 47 B5
Ditzum D 29 B4
Divača SLO 58 C3
Dives-sur-Mer F 43 A5
Divín SK 51 B5
Divion F 34 C3
Divišov CZ 49 A5
Divonne les Bains F 55 B6
Dixmont F 45 B4
Dizy-le-Gros F 45 A5
Djura S 22 A1
Djurås S 22 A2
Djurmo S 22 A2
Djursdala S 26 B5
Dlouhá Loucka CZ 50 A3
Długowola PL 41 B6
Dmitriyev Lgovskiy RUS 7 K24
Dmitrov RUS 7 H25
Dmitrovsk-Orlovskiy RUS 7 K24
Dno RUS 7 H21
Doade E 72 B3
Dobanovci YU 71 B5
Dobbertin D 30 B4
Dobbiaco I 58 B2
Dobczyce PL 51 A6
Dobele LV 6 H18
Döbeln D 38 B3
Doberlug-Kirchhain D 38 B3
Dobern D 39 B4
Dobersberg A 49 B6
Dobiegniew PL 32 C1
Dobieszyn PL 41 B6
Doboj BIH 70 B3
Dobošnica BIH 70 B3
Doboz H 61 B6
Dobrá CZ 51 A4
Dobra PL 40 B3
Dobra, *Szczecin* PL 31 B6
Dobra, *Szczecin* PL 31 B7
Dobrá Niva SK 51 B5
Dobřany CZ 49 A4
Dobre PL 33 C4
Dobre Miasto PL 33 B6
Dobreta-Turnu-Severin RO 11 P18
Dobri H 60 B1
Dobri Do YU 71 D6
Dobrica YU 61 C5
Dobrich BG 16 Q20
Dobříš CZ 49 A5
Dobro E 75 B3
Dobrodzień PL 40 C3
Döbrököz H 60 B3
Dobromierz PL 39 C6
Dobrosołowo PL 33 C4
Dobroszyce PL 40 B2
Dobrovnik SLO 59 B6
Dobrush BY 7 K22
Dobruška CZ 39 C6
Dobrzany PL 32 B1
Dobrzen Wielki PL 40 C2
Dobrzyca PL 32 A1
Dobrzyca PL 32 B2
Dobrzyca PL 40 B2
Dobrzyń nad Wisłą PL 33 C5
Dobšiná SK 51 B6
Dochamps B 35 C6
Döderhult S 26 B6
Doesburg NL 36 A2
Doetinchem NL 36 B2
Dogliani I 66 B1
Dogueno P 84 B3
Dois Portos P 78 B1
Doische B 35 C5
Dojč SK 50 B3
Dokkedal DK 24 C3
Dokkum NL 28 B2
Dokležovje SLO 59 B6
Doksy CZ 39 C4
Dol-de-Bretagne F 43 B4
Dolancourt F 45 B5
Dolceácqua I 66 C1
Dole F 55 A5
Dølemo N 19 C5
Dolenja vas SLO 59 C4
Dolenjske Toplice SLO 59 C5
Dolgellau GB 4 K5
Dolianova I 96 D2
Dolice PL 31 B7
Doljani HR 69 B5
Döllach im Mölltal A 58 B2
Dolle D 30 C3
Dollnstein D 48 B2
Dollot F 45 B4
Döllstadt D 37 B6
Dolná Strehová SK 51 B5
Dolné Saliby SK 50 B3
Dolni Benešov CZ 50 A4
Dolni Bousov CZ 39 C5
Dolni Kounice CZ 50 A2
Dolni Kralovice CZ 49 A6
Dolni Újezd CZ 50 A2
Dolni Žandov CZ 38 C2
Dolný Kubín SK 51 A5
Dolo I 58 C2
Dolores E 82 C2
Dolovo YU 71 B5
Dölsach A 58 B2
Dolsk PL 40 A2
Dolynska UA 11 M23
Domaljevac BIH 70 A3
Domaniç TR 16 S21
Domaniža SK 51 A4
Domanovići BIH 70 C2
Domašov CZ 40 C2
Domaszék H 61 B4
Domaszków PL 40 C1
Domaszowice PL 40 B2
Domat-Ems CH 57 B4
Domažlice CZ 48 A3
Dombås N 2 E11
Dombasle-sur-Meurthe F 46 B2
Dombegyház H 61 B6
Dombóvár H 60 B3
Domène F 55 C5
Domérat F 54 B2
Domfessel F 46 B3
Domfront F 43 B5
Domfront-en-Champagne F 43 B6
Domingão P 78 B2
Domingo Pérez, *Granada* E 86 B2
Domingo Pérez, *Toledo* E 80 C2
Dömitz D 30 B3
Dommartin F 45 B5
Dommartin-le-Franc F 45 B5
Domme F 63 B4
Dommitzsch D 38 B2
Domodóssola I 56 B3
Domoszló H 51 C6
Dompaire F 46 B2
Dompierre-du-Chemin F 43 B4
Dompierre-sur-Besbre F 54 B3
Dompierre-sur-Mer F 52 B3
Domrémy-la-Pucelle F 46 B1
Dömsöd H 61 A4
Domsure F 55 B5
Dómus de Maria I 96 E1
Domusnóvas I 96 D1
Domžale SLO 59 B4
Don Alvaro E 79 C4
Don Benito E 79 C5
Doña Mencía E 86 B1
Donado E 73 B4
Donaueschingen D 47 C4
Donauwörth D 48 B1
Doncaster GB 4 K6
Donegal IRL 4 J2
Donestebe-Santesteban E 62 C1
Donges F 52 A2
Dongo I 57 B4
Doniños E 72 A2
Donja Bebrina HR 70 A3
Donja Brela HR 70 C1
Donja Dubica BIH 70 A3
Donja Dubrava HR 60 B1
Donja Kupčina HR 59 C5
Donja Šatornja YU 71 B5
Donja Stubica HR 59 C5
Donje Brišnik BIH 70 C2
Donje Ljupče YU 71 D6
Donje Stative HR 59 C5
Donji-Andrijevci HR 60 C3
Donji Kazanci BIH 69 C5
Donji Koričáni BIH 70 B2
Donji Lapac HR 69 B4
Donji Malovan BIH 70 C2
Donji Miholjac HR 60 C3
Donji Mosti HR 60 B1
Donji Poloj HR 59 C5
Donji-Rujani BIH 69 C5
Donji Srb HR 69 B5
Donji Svilaj BIH 70 A3
Donji Tovarnik YU 71 B4
Donji Vakuf BIH 70 B2
Donnalucata I 95 C3
Donnemarie-Dontilly F 45 B4
Donnersbach A 59 A4
Donnersbachwald A 59 A4
Donnerskirchen A 50 C2
Donorático I 67 C4
Donostia-San Sebastián E 75 A5
Donovaly SK 51 B5
Donzenac F 53 C6
Donzère F 64 B3
Donzy F 54 A3
Doorn NL 35 A6
Dor E 72 A1
Dorchester GB 4 L5
Dørdal N 19 C6
Dordrecht NL 35 B5
Dörenthe D 36 A3
Dorf Mecklenburg D 30 B3
Dorfen D 48 B3
Dorfgastein A 58 A3
Dorfmark D 29 C6
Dorgali I 96 C2
Dorking GB 4 L6
Dormagen D 36 B2
Dormánd H 51 C6
Dormans F 45 A4
Dornava SLO 59 B5
Dornbirn A 57 A4
Dornburg D 38 B1
Dorndorf D 37 C6
Dornecy F 54 A3
Dornes F 54 B3
Dornhan D 47 B4
Dornum D 29 B4
Dorog H 51 C4
Dorogobuzh RUS 7 J23
Dorohoi RO 11 N20
Dorotowo PL 33 B6
Dörpen D 29 C4
Dorsten D 36 B2
Dortan F 55 B5
Dortmund D 36 B3
Doruchów PL 40 B3
Dorum D 29 B5
Dörverden D 29 C6
Dörzbach D 47 A5
Dos Aguas E 82 B2
Dos Hermanas E 85 B5
Dos-Torres E 86 A1
Dosbarrios E 81 C3
Dötlingen D 29 C5
Dottignies B 35 C4
Döttingen CH 56 A3
Douai F 35 C4
Douarnenez F 42 B1
Douchy F 45 C4
Douchy-les-Mines F 35 C4
Doucier F 55 B5
Doudeville F 44 A1
Doué-la-Fontaine F 53 A4
Douglas GB 4 J4
Doulaincourt F 45 B6
Doulevant-le-Château F 45 B5
Doullens F 34 C3
Dour B 35 C4
Dourdan F 44 B3
Dourgne F 63 C5
Dournazac F 53 C5
Douro Calvo P 73 D3
Douvaine F 55 B6
Douvres-la-Délivrande F 43 A5
Douzy F 45 A6
Dover GB 4 L7
Dovje SLO 58 B3
Dovre N 2 F11
Downpatrick GB 4 J4
Doyet F 54 B2
Dozule F 43 A5
Drača YU 71 B5
Dračevo BIH 70 D3
Drachten NL 28 B3
Draga SLO 59 C4
Drăgăşani RO 11 P19
Dragatuš SLO 59 C5
Dragichyn BY 7 K19
Draginja YU 71 B4
Dragocvet YU 71 C6
Dragolovci BIH 70 B2
Dragoni I 89 B4
Dragør DK 27 D2
Dragotina HR 59 C6
Dragotinja BIH 70 A1
Dragozetići HR 68 A3
Draguignan F 65 C5
Drahnsdorf D 38 B3
Drahonice CZ 49 A5
Drahovce SK 50 B3
Dráma GR 16 R19
Drammen N 20 B2
Drangedal N 19 B6
Dransfeld D 37 B5
Dranske D 31 A5
Drassburg A 50 C2
Drávaszabolcs H 60 C3
Dravograd SLO 59 B5
Drawno PL 32 B1
Drawsko Pomorskie PL 32 B1
Draženov CZ 48 A3
Draževac YU 71 B5
Dražice HR 59 C4
Drebkau D 39 B4
Dreieich D 37 C4
Dreisen D 47 A4
Dren YU 71 C5
Drenovac YU 71 C6
Drenovci HR 70 B3
Drensteinfurt D 36 B3
Dresden D 39 B3
Dretyń PL 32 A2
Dreux F 44 B2
Dřevohostice CZ 50 A3
Drewitz D 38 A2
Drezdenko PL 32 C1
Drežnica HR 69 A4
Drežnik-Grad HR 69 B4
Drietona SK 50 B3
Driffield GB 4 J6
Dringenberg D 37 B5
Drinić BIH 69 B5
Drinjača BIH 71 B4
Drinovci BIH 70 C2
Drlače YU 71 B4
Drnholec CZ 50 B2
Drniš HR 69 C5
Drnje HR 60 B1
Drnovice CZ 50 A2
Dro I 57 C5
Drøbak N 20 B2
Drobin PL 33 C5
Drochia MD 11 M20
Drochtersen D 29 B6
Drogheda IRL 4 K3
Drohobych UA 11 M18
Drołtowice PL 40 B2
Dronero I 66 B1
Dronninglund DK 24 B3
Dronrijp NL 28 B2
Dronten NL 28 C2
Drosendorf A 49 B6
Drösing A 50 B2
Drottningholm S 22 B4
Droué F 44 B2
Drulingen F 46 B3
Drummore GB 4 J4
Drunen NL 35 B6
Druskininkai LT 6 J18
Druten NL 35 B6
Druya BY 7 J20
Družetići YU 71 B5
Drvar BIH 69 B5
Drvenik HR 70 C2
Drwalew PL 41 B6
Drzewce PL 40 A2
Drzewiany PL 32 B2
Drzewica PL 41 B5
Dualchi I 96 C1
Duas Igrejas P 73 C4
Dub YU 71 C4
Dubá CZ 39 C4
Dubăsari MD 11 N21
Duben D 39 B3
Dübendorf CH 56 A3
Dubi CZ 39 C3
Dubica HR 60 C1
Dublin IRL 4 K3
Dubna RUS 7 H25
Dubňany CZ 50 B3
Dubnica nad Váhom SK 50 B4
Dubnik SK 51 C4
Dubno UA 11 L19
Dubodiel SK 50 B4
Dubona YU 71 B5
Dubovac YU 71 B6
Dubovic BIH 69 B5
Dubranec HR 59 C5
Dubrava HR 60 C1
Dubrave BIH 70 B3
Dubravica HR 59 C5
Dubravica YU 71 B6
Dubrovnik HR 70 D3
Dubrovytsya UA 11 L20
Ducey F 43 B4
Duchcov CZ 39 C3
Ducherow D 31 B5
Dučina YU 71 B5
Duclair F 44 A1
Dudar H 60 A2
Duderstadt D 37 B6
Dudeştii Vechi RO 61 B5
Dueñas E 74 C2
Dueville I 58 C1
Duffel B 35 B5
Duga Poljana YU 71 C5
Duga Resa HR 59 C5
Dugi Rat HR 69 C5
Dugny-sur-Meuse F 45 A6
Dugo Selo HR 59 C6
Dugopolje HR 69 C5
Duino I 58 C3
Duisburg D 36 B2
Dukhovshchina RUS 7 J23
Dukovany CZ 50 A2
Dülken D 36 B2
Dülmen D 36 B3
Dulovo BG 16 Q20
Dumbarton GB 4 J4
Dumfries GB 4 J5
Dun Laoghaire IRL 4 K3
Dun-le-Palestel F 53 B6
Dun-les-Places F 54 A4
Dun-sur-Auron F 54 B2
Dun-sur-Meuse F 45 A6
Dunaalmás H 51 C4
Dunab-ogdány H 51 C5
Dunafalva H 60 B3
Dunaföldvár H 60 B3
Dunaharaszti H 61 A4
Dunajská Streda SK 50 C3
Dunakeszi H 51 C5
Dunakiliti H 50 C3
Dunakömlöd H 60 B3
Dunapataj H 61 B3
Dunaszekcsö H 60 B3
Dunaszentgyorgy H 60 B3
Dunatetétlen H 61 B4
Dunaújváros H 61 B3
Dunavecse H 61 B3
Dunbar GB 4 J5
Dundee GB 4 H5
Dunfermline GB 4 H5
Dungannon GB 4 J3
Dungarvan IRL 4 K3
Duninowo PL 32 A2
Dunker S 22 B3
Dunkerque F 34 B3
Dunleer IRL 4 K3
Dunningen D 47 B4
Dunoon GB 4 J4
Duplek SLO 59 B5
Dupnitsa BG 15 Q18
Durach D 47 C6
Đurakovac YU 71 D5
Durana E 75 B4
Durance F 62 B3
Durango E 75 A4
Durankulak BG 16 Q21
Duras F 62 B3
Durban-Corbières F 64 D1
Dürbheim D 47 B4
Durbuy B 35 C6
Dúrcal E 86 C2
Đurdjenovac HR 60 C3
Đurdjevac HR 60 B2
Đurdjevik BIH 70 B3
Düren D 36 C2
Durham GB 4 J6
Đurinci YU 71 B5
Durlach D 47 B4
Đurmanec HR 59 B5
Dürnkrut A 50 B2
Dürrboden CH 57 B4
Dürrenboden CH 56 B3
Durrës AL 15 R16
Dursunbey TR 16 S21
Durtal F 43 C5
Durup DK 24 C1
Dusina BIH 70 C2
Dusnok H 61 B3
Dusocin PL 33 B4
Düsseldorf D 36 B2
Dusslingen D 47 B5
Duszniki PL 32 C2
Duszniki-Zdrój PL 40 C1
Dutovlje SLO 58 C3
Duved S 2 E13
Düzce TR 16 R22
Dvor HR 69 A5
Dvorce CZ 50 A3
Dvorníky SK 50 B3
Dvory nad Žitavou SK 50 C4
Dvůr Králové nad Labem CZ 39 C5
Dyatkovo RUS 7 K24
Dybvad DK 24 B3
Dygowo PL 32 A1
Dymer UA 11 L22
Dywity PL 33 B6
Džanići BIH 70 C2
Dziadowa Kłoda PL 40 B2
Działdowo PL 33 B6
Działoszyce PL 41 C5
Działoszyn PL 40 B3
Dziemiany PL 32 A3
Dzierząźnia PL 33 C6
Dzierzgoń PL 33 B5
Dzierzgowo PL 33 B6
Dzierżoniów PL 40 C1
Dzisna BY 7 J21
Dziwnów PL 31 A6
Dzyarzhynsk BY 7 K20
Dzyatlava BY 7 K19

E

Ea E 75 A4
East Kilbride GB 4 J4
Eastbourne GB 4 L7
Eaux-Bonnes F 62 D2
Eauze F 62 C3
Ebberup DK 25 D2
Ebbs A 48 C3
Ebeleben D 37 B6
Ebeltoft DK 25 C3
Eben im Pongau A 58 A3
Ebene Reichenau A 58 B3
Ebensee A 49 C4
Ebensfeld D 37 C6
Eberbach D 47 A4
Ebergötzen D 37 B6
Ebermann-Stadt D 48 A2
Ebern D 37 C6
Eberndorf A 59 B4
Ebersbach D 39 B4
Ebersberg D 48 B2
Ebersdorf, *Bayern* D 38 C1
Ebersdorf, *Niedersachsen* D 29 B6
Eberstein A 59 B4
Eberswalde D 31 C5
Ebnat-Kappel CH 57 A4
Éboli I 90 B2
Ebrach D 47 A6
Ebreichsdorf A 50 C2
Ebreuil F 54 B3
Ebstorf D 30 B2
Eceabat TR 16 R20
Echallens CH 55 B6
Echauri E 75 B5
Echiré F 53 B4
Échirolles F 65 A4
Echourgnac F 62 A3
Echt NL 36 B1
Echte D 37 B6
Echternach L 46 A2
Ecija E 85 B5
Ečka YU 61 C5
Eckartsberga D 38 B1
Eckelshausen D 37 C4
Eckental D 48 A2
Eckernförde D 30 A1
Eckerö FIN 3 F16
Éclaron F 45 B5
Écommoy F 44 C1
Écouché F 43 B5
Ecouis F 44 A2
Ecséd H 51 C5

Ecsegfalva H 61 A5
Écueillé F 53 A6
Ed S 21 C3
Eda S 20 B4
Eda glasbruk S 20 B4
Edam NL 28 C2
Edane S 20 B4
Ede NL 35 A6
Edebäck S 20 A5
Edebo S 22 A5
Edelény H 51 B6
Edelschrott A 59 A5
Edemissen D 30 C2
Edenkoben D 47 A4
Edesheim D 47 A4
Edewecht D 29 B4
Édhessa GR 15 R18
Edinburgh GB 4 J5
Edineţ MD 11 M20
Edirne TR 16 R20
Edland N 19 B4
Edolo I 57 B5
Edremit TR 16 S20
Eds bruk S 23 C3
Edsbro S 22 B5
Edsleskog S 21 B4
Edsvalla S 20 B5
Eekloo B 35 B4
Eemshaven NL 28 B3
Eerbeek NL 36 A2
Eersel NL 35 B6
Eferding A 49 B5
Effiat F 54 B3
Efteløt N 19 B6
Egeln D 38 B1
Eger H 51 C6
Egerbakta H 51 C6
Egernsund DK 25 E2
Egersund N 18 C3
Egerszólát H 51 C6
Egervár H 60 B1
Egg A 57 A4
Egg D 47 B6
Eggedal N 19 A6
Eggenburg A 50 B1
Eggenfelden D 48 B3
Eggesin D 31 B6
Eghezée B 35 C5
Egiertowo PL 33 A4
Égletons F 54 C2
Egling D 48 C2
Eglisau CH 47 C4
Égliseneuve-d'Entraigues F 54 C2
Eglofs D 47 C5
Egmond aan Zee NL 28 C1
Egna I 57 B6
Eğridir TR 16 T22
Egtved DK 25 D2
Eguilles F 65 C4
Eguilly-sous-Bois F 45 B5
Éguzon-Chantôme F 53 B6
Egyek H 51 C6
Egyházasrádóc H 60 A1
Ehekirchen D 48 B2
Ehingen D 47 B5
Ehra-Lessien D 30 C2
Ehrang D 46 A2
Ehrenfriedersdorf D 38 C2
Ehrenhain D 38 C2
Ehrenhausen A 59 B5
Ehringshausen D 37 C4
Ehrwald A 57 A5
Eibar E 75 A4
Eibelstadt D 47 A6
Eibenstock D 38 C2
Eibergen NL 36 A2
Eibiswald A 59 B5
Eichenbarleben D 38 A1
Eichendorf D 48 B3
Eichstätt D 48 B2
Eickelborn D 36 B4
Eidsberg N 20 B3
Eidsfoss N 19 B7
Eidskog N 20 A4
Eidsvoll N 20 A3
Eikefjord N 2 F9
Eikelandsosen N 18 A2
Eiken N 19 C4
Eikstrand N 19 B6
Eilenburg D 38 B2
Eilsleben D 38 A1
Einbeck D 37 B5
Eindhoven NL 35 B6
Einsiedeln CH 56 A3
Einville-au-Jard F 46 B2
Eisenach D 37 C6
Eisenberg, *Rheinland-Pfalz* D 47 A4
Eisenberg, *Thüringen* D 38 C1
Eisenerz A 59 A4
Eisenhüttenstadt D 39 A4
Eisenkappel A 59 B4
Eisenstadt A 50 C2
Eisentratten A 58 B3
Eisfeld D 37 C6
Eisleben D 38 B1
Eislingen D 47 B5
Eitensheim D 48 B2
Eiterfeld D 37 C5
Eitorf D 36 C3
Eivissa E 83 C4
Eixo P 78 A2
Ejby DK 25 D2
Ejea de los Caballeros E 76 A1
Ejstrupholm DK 25 D2
Ejulve E 76 C2
Eke B 35 C4
Ekeby, *Gotland* S 23 D5
Ekeby, *Skåne* S 27 D2
Ekeby, *Uppsala* S 22 A5
Ekeby-Almby S 22 B2
Ekenäs S 21 C5
Ekenässjön S 26 B5
Ekerö S 22 B4
Eket S 27 C3
Eketorp S 27 C6
Ekshärad S 20 A5
Eksjö S 26 B4
El Alamo, *Madrid* E 80 B3
El Alamo, *Sevilla* E 85 B4
El Algar E 87 B5
El Almendro E 84 B3
El Alquián E 87 C3
El Arahal E 85 B5
El Arenal E 80 B1
El Arguellite E 87 A3
El Astillero E 74 A3
El Ballestero E 87 A3
El Barco de Ávila E 79 A5
El Berrón E 74 A1
El Berrueco E 81 B3
El Bodón E 79 A4
El Bonillo E 87 A3
El Bosque E 85 C5
El Bullaque E 80 C2
El Burgo E 86 C1
El Burgo de Ebro E 76 B2
El Burgo de Osma E 75 C3
El Burgo Ranero E 74 B1
El Buste E 75 C5
El Cabaco E 79 A4
El Callejo E 75 A3
El Campillo E 85 B4
El Campillo de la Jara E 80 C1
El Cañavete E 81 C4
El Carpio E 86 B1
El Carpio de Tajo E 80 C2
El Casar E 81 B3
El Casar de Escalona E 80 B2
El Castillo de las Guardas E 85 B4
El Centenillo E 86 A2
El Cerro E 79 A5
El Cerro de Andévalo E 85 B4
El Comenar E 85 C5
El Coronil E 85 B5
El Crucero E 72 A4
El Cubo de Tierra del Vino E 80 A1
El Cuervo E 85 C4
El Ejido E 87 C3
El Escorial E 80 B2
El Espinar E 80 B2
El Frago E 76 A2
El Franco E 72 A4
El Frasno E 75 C5
El Garrobo E 85 B4
El Gastor E 85 C5
El Gordo E 80 C1
El Grado E 76 A3
El Granado E 84 B3
El Grao de Castelló E 82 B3
El Grau E 82 C2
El Higuera E 86 B1
El Hijate E 87 B3
El Hontanar E 82 A1
El Hoyo E 86 A2
El Madroño E 85 B4
El Maillo E 79 A4
El Masnou E 77 B5
El Mirón E 80 B1
El Molar E 81 B3
El Molinillo E 80 C2
El Morell E 77 B4
El Muyo E 75 C3
El Olmo E 74 C3
El Palo E 86 C1
El Pardo E 80 B3
El Payo E 79 A4
El Pedernoso E 81 C4
El Pedroso E 85 B5
El Peral E 81 C5
El Perelló, *Tarragona* E 76 C3
El Perelló, *Valencia* E 82 B2
El Picazo E 81 C4
El Pinell de Bray E 76 B3
El Piñero E 74 C1
El Pla de Santa Maria E 77 B4
El Pobo E 76 C2
El Pobo de Dueñas E 81 B5
El Pont d'Armentera E 77 B4
El Port de la Selva E 77 A6
El Port de Llançà E 77 A6
El Port de Sagunt E 82 B2
El Prat de Llobregat E 77 B5
El Provencio E 81 C4
El Puente E 75 A3
El Puente del Arzobispo E 80 C1
El Puerto E 72 A4
El Puerto de Santa María E 85 C4
El Real de la Jara E 85 B4
El Real de San Vincente E 80 B2
El Robledo E 80 C2
El Rocio E 85 B4
El Rompido E 85 B3
El Ronquillo E 85 B4
El Royo E 75 C4
El Rubio E 86 B1
El Sabinar E 87 A3
El Saler E 82 B2
El Salobral E 87 A4
El Saucejo E 85 B5
El Serrat AND 77 A4
El Temple E 76 B2
El Tiemblo E 80 B2
El Toboso E 81 C4
El Tormillo E 76 B2
El Torno E 79 A5
El Valle de las Casas E 74 B1
El Vellón E 81 B3
El Vendrell E 77 B4
El Villar de Arnedo E 75 B4
El Viso E 86 A1
El Viso del Alcor E 85 B5
Élancourt F 44 B2
Elbasan AL 15 R17
Elbeuf F 44 A1
Elbingerode D 37 B6
Elbląg PL 33 A5
Elburg NL 28 C2
Elche E 82 C2
Elche de la Sierra E 87 A3
Elchingen D 47 B6
Elda E 82 C2
Eldena D 30 B3
Eldingen D 30 C2
Elek H 61 B6
Elemir YU 61 C5
Elgin GB 4 H5
Elgoibar E 75 A4
Elizondo E 62 C1
Ełk PL 6 K18
Elkhovo BG 16 Q20
Ellenberg D 47 A6
Ellezelles B 35 C4
Ellingen D 48 A1
Ellmau A 58 A2
Ellös S 21 C3
Ellrich D 37 B6
Ellwangen D 47 B6
Elm CH 57 B4
Elm D 29 B6
Elmalı TR 16 T21
Elmshorn D 29 B6
Elmstein D 46 A3
Elne F 77 A5
Elorrio E 75 A4
Előszállás H 60 B3
Éloyes F 46 B2
Els Castells E 77 A4
Elsdorf D 36 C2
Elsenfeld D 47 A5
Elsfleth D 29 B5
Elspeet NL 35 A6
Elst NL 36 B1
Elster D 38 B2
Elsterberg D 38 C2
Elsterwerda D 38 B3
Elstra D 39 B4
Eltmann D 37 D6
Eltville D 36 C4
Elvas P 79 C3
Elven F 42 C3
Elverum N 2 F12
Elxleben D 37 B6
Ely GB 4 K7
Elzach D 47 B4
Elze D 37 A5
Embrun F 65 B5
Embún E 76 A2
Emden D 29 B4
Emet TR 16 S21
Emirdağ TR 16 S22
Emlichheim D 28 C3
Emmaboda S 26 C5
Emmaljunga S 27 C3
Emmeloord NL 28 C2
Emmen CH 56 A3
Emmen NL 28 C3
Emmendingen D 46 B3
Emmer-Compascuum NL 29 C4
Emmerich D 36 B2
Emmern D 37 A5
Emőd H 51 C6
Émpoli I 67 C4
Emsbüren D 29 C4
Emsdetten D 36 A3
Emsfors S 26 B6
Emskirchen D 48 A1
Emstek D 29 C5
Encamp AND 77 A4
Encarnaçao P 78 C1
Encinas de Abajo E 80 B1
Encinas de Esgueva E 74 C2
Encinas Reales E 86 B1
Encinasola E 85 A4
Encio E 75 B3
Enciso E 75 B4
Endingen D 46 B3
Endrinal E 79 A5
Endrőd H 61 B5
Enebakk N 20 B3
Eneryda S 26 C4
Enese H 50 C3
Enez TR 16 R20
Eng A 58 A1
Enge-sande D 25 E1
Engelberg CH 56 B3
Engelhartszell A 49 B4
Engelskirchen D 36 C3
Engen D 47 C4
Engerdal N 2 F12
Engesvang DK 25 C2
Enghien B 35 C5
Engstingen D 47 B5
Engter D 29 C5
Enguera E 82 C2
Enguidanos E 82 B1
Enkenbach D 46 A3
Enkhuizen NL 28 C2
Enköping S 22 B4
Enna I 95 B3
Ennezat F 54 C3
Ennigerloh D 36 B4
Enningdal N 21 C3
Ennis IRL 4 K2
Enniscorthy IRL 4 K3
Enniskillen GB 4 J3
Enns A 49 B5
Eno FIN 3 E22
Enontekiö FIN 3 B18
Ens NL 28 C2
Enschede NL 36 A2
Ensdorf D 48 A2
Ensisheim F 46 C3
Enstaberga S 23 C3
Entlebuch CH 56 A3
Entrácque I 66 B1
Entradas P 84 B2
Entrains-sur-Nohain F 54 A3
Entrambasaguas E 74 A3
Entrambasmestas E 74 A3
Entraygues-sur-Truyère F 63 B5
Entre-os-Rios P 73 C2
Entrevaux F 65 C5
Entrin Bajo E 79 C4
Entroncamento P 78 B2
Entzheim F 46 B3
Envermeu F 44 A2
Enying H 60 B3
Enzingerboden A 58 A2
Enzklösterle D 47 B4
Épagny F 45 A4
Epalinges CH 56 B1
Epannes F 53 B4
Epe D 36 A3
Epe NL 28 C2
Épernay F 45 A4
Épernon F 44 B2
Epfig F 46 B3
Epierre F 55 C6
Épila E 76 B1
Épinac F 55 B4
Épinal F 46 B2
Episcopia I 90 B3
Epoisses F 55 A4
Eppenbrunn D 46 A3
Eppendorf D 38 C3
Eppingen D 47 A4
Eraclea I 58 C2
Eraclea Mare I 58 C2
Erba I 57 C4
Erbach, *Baden-Württemberg* D 47 B5
Erbach, *Hessen* D 47 A4
Erbalunga F 96 A2
Erbendorf D 48 A3
Érchie I 91 B4
Ercolano I 89 C4
Ercsi H 60 A3
Érd H 60 A3
Erdek TR 16 R20
Erdevik YU 71 A4
Erding D 48 B2
Erdőtelek H 51 C6
Erdut HR 61 C4
Erdweg D 48 B2
Ereğli TR 16 R22
Erfde D 29 A6
Erfjord N 18 B3
Erfstadt D 36 C2
Erfurt D 38 C1
Ergli LV 7 H19
Érice I 94 A1
Ericeira P 78 C1
Eriksmåla S 26 C5
Eringsboda S 26 C5
Eriswil CH 56 A2
Erkelenz D 36 B2
Erkner D 31 C5
Erkrath D 36 B2
Erla E 76 A2
Erlangen D 48 A2
Erli I 66 B2
Erlsbach A 58 B2
Ermelo NL 35 A6
Ermenonville F 44 A3
Ermezinde P 73 C2
Ermidas P 84 A2
Ermsleben D 38 B1
Erndtebrück D 36 C4
Ernée F 43 B5
Ernestinovo HR 60 C3
Ernstbrunn A 50 B2
Erolzheim D 47 B6
Erquelinnes B 35 C5
Erquy F 42 B3
Erra P 78 C2
Erratzu E 62 C1
Errindlev DK 30 A3
Erro E 62 D1
Ersa F 66 D3
Érsekcsanád H 61 B3
Érsekvadkert H 51 C5
Erstein F 46 B3
Erstfeld CH 56 B3
Ertebølle DK 24 C2
Ertingen D 47 B5
Ervedal, *Coimbra* P 78 A2
Ervedal, *Portalegre* P 78 B3
Ervenik HR 69 B4
Ervidel P 84 B2
Ervy-le-Châtel F 45 B4
Erwitte D 37 B4
Erxleben D 38 A1
Erzsébet H 60 B3
Es Caná E 83 B4
Es Castell, *Menorca* E 83
Es Mercadal, *Menorca* E 83
Es Migjorn Gran, *Menorca* E 83
Es Port d'Alcúdia, *Mallorca* E 83
Es Pujols E 83 C4
Es Soleràs E 76 B3
Esbjerg DK 25 D1
Esbly F 44 B3
Escacena del Campo E 85 B4
Escairón E 72 B3
Escalada E 74 B3
Escalante E 75 A3
Escalaplano I 96 D2
Escalona E 80 B2
Escalona del Prado E 80 A2
Escalonilla E 80 C2
Escalos de Baixo P 78 B3
Escalos de Cima P 78 B3
Escamilla E 81 B4
Escañuela E 86 B1
Escatrón E 76 B2
Esch-sur-Alzette L 46 A1
Eschach D 47 C5
Eschau D 47 A5
Eschede D 30 C2
Eschenau D 48 A2
Eschenbach D 48 A2
Eschenz CH 47 C4
Eschershausen D 37 B5
Eschwege D 37 B6
Eschweiler D 36 C2
Escobasa de Almazán E 75 C4
Escoeuilles F 34 C2
Escombreras E 87 B5
Escos F 62 C1
Escource F 62 B1
Escragnolles F 65 C5
Escurial E 79 B5
Escurial de la Sierra E 79 A5
Esens D 29 B4
Esgos E 73 B3
Eskilhem S 23 D5
Eskilsäter S 21 C5
Eskilstrup DK 25 E4
Eskilstuna S 22 B3
Eskişehir TR 16 S22
Eslarn D 48 A3
Eslava E 75 B5
Eslida E 82 B2
Eslohe D 36 B4
Eslöv S 27 D3
Eşme TR 16 S21
Espalion F 64 B1
Esparragalejo E 79 C4
Esparragosa del Caudillo E 79 C5
Esparragossa de la Serena E 79 C5
Esparreguera E 77 B4
Esparron F 65 C4
Espe N 18 A3
Espedal N 18 C3
Espejo, *Alava* E 75 B3
Espejo, *Córdoba* E 86 B1
Espeland N 18 A2
Espelkamp D 29 C5
Espeluche F 64 B3
Espeluy E 86 A2
Espera E 85 C5
Esperança P 79 B3
Espéraza F 63 D5
Espéria I 89 B3
Espevær N 18 B2
Espiel E 85 A5
Espinama E 74 A2
Espiñaredo E 72 A3
Espinasses F 65 B5
Espinelves E 77 B5
Espinhal P 78 A2
Espinho P 73 C2
Espinilla E 74 A2
Espinosa de Cerrato E 74 C3
Espinosa de los Monteros E 75 A3
Espinoso del Rey E 80 C2
Espirito Santo P 84 B3
Espluga de Francolí E 77 B4
Esplús E 76 B3
Espolla E 77 A5
Espoo FIN 3 F19
Esporles, *Mallorca* E 83
Esposende P 73 C2
Espot E 77 A4
Esquedas E 76 A2
Esquivias E 80 B3
Essen B 35 B5
Essen, *Niedersachsen* D 29 C4
Essen, *Nordrhein-Westfalen* D 36 B3
Essenbach D 48 B3
Essertaux F 44 A3
Essingen D 47 B6
Esslingen D 47 B5
Essoyes F 45 B5
Estacas E 73 B2
Estadilla E 76 A3
Estagel F 64 D1
Estaires F 34 C3
Estang F 62 C2
Estarreja P 73 D2
Estartit E 77 A6
Estavayer-le-Lac CH 56 B1
Este I 58 C1
Esteiro E 72 A2
Estela P 73 C2
Estella E 75 B4
Estellencs, *Mallorca* E 83
Estepa E 86 B1
Estépar E 74 B3
Estepona E 85 C5
Esternay F 45 B4
Esterri d'Aneu E 77 A4
Esterwegen D 29 C4
Estissac F 45 B4
Estivadas E 73 B3
Estivareilles F 54 B2
Estivella E 82 B2
Estói P 84 B3
Estopiñán E 76 B3
Estoril P 78 C1
Estoublon F 65 C5
Estrée-Blanche F 34 C3
Estrées-St. Denis F 44 A3
Estrela P 84 A3
Estremera E 81 B3
Estremoz P 78 C3
Estuna S 22 B5
Esyres F 53 A5
Esztergom H 51 C4
Etables-sur-Mer F 42 B3
Étain F 46 A1
Étalans F 55 A6
Etalle B 46 A1
Étampes F 44 B3
Etang-sur-Arroux F 55 B4
Étaples F 34 C2
Etauliers F 53 C4
Etne N 18 B2
Etoges F 45 B4
Etréaupont F 45 A4
Étréchy F 44 B3
Étrépagny F 44 A2
Étretat F 43 A6
Étrœungt F 35 C4
Étroubles I 56 C2
Ettal D 48 C2
Ettelbruck L 46 A2
Etten NL 35 B5
Ettenheim D 46 B3
Ettlingen D 47 B4
Ettringen D 48 B1
Etxarri-Aranatz E 75 B4
Etyek H 60 A3
Eu F 34 C2
Euerdorf D 37 C6
Eulate E 75 B4
Eupen B 36 C2
Europoort NL 35 B5
Euskirchen D 36 C2
Eutin D 30 A2
Évaux-les-Bains F 54 B2
Evergem B 35 B4
Everöd S 27 D4
Eversberg D 37 B4
Everswinkel D 36 B3
Évian-les-Bains F 55 B6
Evisa F 96 A1
Evje N 19 C4
Evolène CH 56 B2
Évora P 78 C3
Evoramonte P 78 C3
Evran F 43 B4
Evrecy F 43 A5
Évreux F 44 A2
Évron F 43 B5
Évry F 44 B3
Ewersbach D 36 C4
Excideuil F 53 C6
Exeter GB 4 L5
Exmes F 43 B6
Exmouth GB 4 L5
Eydehamn N 19 C5
Eyguians F 65 B4
Eyguières F 65 C4
Eygurande F 54 C2
Eylie F 63 D3
Eymet F 63 B3
Eymoutiers F 54 C1
Eystrup D 29 C6
Ezaro E 72 B1
Ezcaray E 75 B4
Ezcároz E 62 D1
Ezine TR 16 S20
Ezmoriz P 73 D2

F

Fabara E 76 B3
Fábbrico I 67 B4
Fabero E 72 B4
Fábiánsebestyén H 61 B5
Fåborg DK 25 D3
Fabrègues F 64 C2
Fabriano I 68 C1
Fabrizia I 92 C3
Facha P 73 C2
Facinas E 85 C5
Fačkov SK 51 A4
Fadagosa P 78 B3
Fadd H 60 B3
Faédis I 58 B3
Faenza I 67 B5
Fafe P 73 C2
Fagagna I 58 B3
Făgăras RO 11 P19
Fågelfors S 26 B5
Fågelmara S 27 C5
Fågelsta S 23 C2
Fagerhult S 26 B5
Fagernes N 2 F11
Fagersanna S 21 C6
Fagersta S 22 A2
Fåglavik S 21 C5
Fagnano Castello I 92 B3
Fagnières F 45 B5
Faido CH 56 B3
Fains F 45 B6
Fajsz H 60 B3
Fakse DK 25 D5
Fakse Ladeplads DK 27 D2
Falaise F 43 B5
Falcade I 58 B1
Falces E 75 B5
Fălciu RO 11 N21
Falconara I 95 B3
Falconara Maríttima I 68 C2
Falcone I 95 A4
Falerum S 23 C3
Făleşti MD 11 N20
Falkenberg, *Bayern* D 48 A3
Falkenberg, *Brandenburg* D 38 B3
Falkenberg S 26 C2
Falkensee D 31 C5
Falkenstein, *Bayern* D 48 A3
Falkenstein, *Sachsen* D 38 C2
Falkenthal D 31 C5
Falköping S 21 C5
Fall D 58 A1
Falla S 23 C2
Fallingbostel D 29 C6
Falmouth GB 4 L4
Falset E 76 B3
Fălticeni RO 11 N20
Falun S 22 A2
Fana N 18 A2
Fanano I 67 B4
Fanjeaux F 63 C5
Fano I 68 C2
Făntânele RO 61 B6
Fara in Sabina I 88 A2
Fara Novarese I 56 C3
Faramontanos de Tábara E 74 C1
Farasdues E 76 A1
Fårbo S 26 B6
Fårentuna S 22 B4
Färgelanda S 21 C3
Faringe S 22 B5
Farini I 66 B3
Fariza E 73 C4
Färjestaden S 26 C6
Farkasfa H 59 B6
Farlete E 76 B2
Färlöv S 27 C4
Farmos H 61 A4
Farnă SK 51 C4
Farnese I 88 A1
Farnroda D 37 C6
Faro P 84 B3
Farra d'Alpago I 58 B2
Fårsala GR 15 S18
Farsø DK 24 C2
Farsund N 18 C3
Farum DK 27 D2
Fårup DK 24 C2
Fasana I 90 B2
Fasano I 91 B4
Fassberg D 30 C2
Fastiv UA 11 L21
Fatesh RUS 7 K24
Fátima P 78 B2
Faucogney-et-la-Mer F 46 C2
Fauguerolles F 62 B3
Faulenrost D 31 B4
Faulquemont F 46 A2
Fauquembergues F 34 C3
Fauske N 2 C14
Fauville-en-Caux F 44 A1
Fauvillers B 46 A1
Favara I 94 B2
Faverges F 55 C6
Faverney F 46 C2
Favignana I 94 B1
Fay-aux-Loges F 44 C3
Fayence F 65 C5
Fayet F 64 C1
Fayl-Billot F 46 C1
Fayón E 76 B3
Fécamp F 44 A1
Feda N 18 C3
Fegen S 26 B3
Fegyvernek H 61 A5
Fehrbellin D 31 C4
Fehring A 59 B6
Feichten A 57 A5
Feiring N 20 A3
Feistritz im Rosental A 59 B4
Feketić YU 61 C4
Felanitx, *Mallorca* E 83
Feld am See A 58 B3
Feldbach A 59 B5
Feldberg D 31 B5
Feldkirch A 57 A4
Feldkirchen in Kärnten A 59 B4
Feldkirchen-Westerham D 48 C2
Felgueiras P 73 C2
Felitto I 90 B2
Félix E 87 C3
Felixstowe GB 4 L7
Felizzano I 66 B2
Felletin F 54 C2
Fellingsbro S 22 B2
Felnac RO 61 B6
Felnémet H 51 C6
Felpéc H 60 A2
Fels am Wagram A 50 B1
Felsberg D 37 B5
Felső-zsolca H 51 B6
Felsőnyék H 60 B3
Felsőszentiván H 61 B4
Felsőszentmárton H 60 C2
Felsted DK 25 E2
Feltre I 58 B1
Femsjö S 26 C3
Fene E 72 A2
Fenestrelle I 65 A6
Fénétrange F 46 B3
Feneu F 43 C5
Fengersfors S 21 C4
Fensmark DK 25 D4
Ferdinandovac HR 60 B2
Ferdinandshof D 31 B5
Fère-Champenoise F 45 B4
Fère-en-Tardenois F 45 A4
Ferentillo I 88 A2
Ferentino I 88 B3
Feria E 79 C4
Feričanci HR 60 C2
Ferla I 95 B3
Ferlach A 59 B4
Ferleiten A 58 A2
Fermil P 73 C3
Fermo I 68 C2
Fermoselle E 73 C4
Fermoy IRL 4 K2
Fernán Nuñez E 86 B1
Fernán Peréz E 87 C3
Fernancabellero E 80 C3
Fernão Ferro P 78 C1
Fernay-Voltaire F 55 B6
Ferpécle CH 56 B2
Ferrals-les-Corbières F 64 C1
Ferrandina I 91 B3
Ferrara I 67 B5
Ferrara di Monte Baldo I 57 C5
Ferreira E 72 A3
Ferreira do Alentejo P 84 A2
Ferreira do Zêzere P 78 B2
Ferreras de Abajo E 73 C4
Ferreras de Arriba E 73 C4
Ferreries, *Menorca* E 83
Ferreruela E 76 B1
Ferreruela de Tabara E 73 C4
Ferret CH 56 C2
Ferrette F 56 A2
Ferriere I 66 B3
Ferrière-la-Grande F 35 C4
Ferrières, *Loiret* F 44 B3
Ferrières, *Oise* F 44 A3
Ferrières-sur-Sichon F 54 B3
Ferrol E 72 A2
Fertörakos H 50 C2
Fertöszentmiklós H 50 C2
Ferwerd NL 28 B2
Festieux F 45 A4
Feteşti RO 11 P20
Fethiye TR 16 T21
Fetsund N 20 B3
Feucht D 48 A2
Feuchtwangen D 47 A6
Feudingen D 36 C4
Feuges F 45 B5
Feuquières F 44 A2
Feurs F 55 C4
Fevik N 19 C5
Fiamignano I 88 A3
Fiano I 56 C2
Ficarazzi I 94 A2
Ficarolo I 67 B5
Fichtelberg D 38 C1
Ficulle I 68 D1
Fidenza I 67 B4
Fidjeland N 18 C3
Fieberbrunn A 58 A2
Fier AL 15 R16
Fiera di Primiero I 58 B1
Fiesch CH 56 B3
Fiésole I 67 C5
Fiesso Umbertiano I 67 B5
Figari F 96 B2
Figeac F 63 B5
Figeholm S 26 B6
Figgjo N 18 C2
Figline Valdarno I 67 C5
Figols E 76 A3
Figueira da Foz P 78 A2
Figueira de Castelo Rodrigo P 73 D4
Figueira dos Caveleiros P 84 A2
Figueiredo P 78 B3
Figueiredo de Alva P 73 D3
Figueiró dos Vinhos P 78 B2
Figueres E 77 A5
Figueroles E 82 A2
Figueruela de Arriba E 73 C4
Filadélfia I 92 C3
Fil'akovo SK 51 B5
Filderstadt D 47 B5
Filiaşi RO 11 P18
Filiatrá GR 15 T17
Filipstad S 20 B6
Filisur CH 57 B4
Filottrano I 68 C2
Filskov DK 25 D2
Filtvet N 20 B2
Filzmoos A 58 A3
Finale Emilia I 67 B5
Finale Lígure I 66 B2
Fiñana E 87 B3
Finike TR 16 T22
Finkenberg A 58 A1
Finnerödja S 23 C1
Finnsnes N 3 B16
Finócchio I 88 B2
Finsjö S 26 B6
Finsland N 19 C4
Finspång S 23 C2
Finsterwalde D 39 B3
Finsterwolde NL 29 B4
Fiorenzuola d'Arda I 67 B3
Firenze I 67 C5
Firenzuola I 67 B5
Firmi F 63 B5
Firminy F 55 C4
Firmo I 92 B3
Fischamend Markt A 50 B2
Fischbach A 59 A5
Fischbach D 46 A3
Fischbeck D 30 C4
Fischen D 57 A5
Fishguard GB 4 L4
Fiskebäckskil S 21 C3
Fismes F 45 A4
Fisterra E 72 B1
Fitero E 75 B5
Fitjar N 18 B2
Fiuggi I 88 B3
Fiumata I 88 A3
Fiumefreddo Brúzio I 92 B3
Fiumefreddo di Sicilia I 95 B4
Fiumicino I 88 B2
Fivizzano I 67 B4
Fjæra N 18 B3
Fjälkinge S 27 C4
Fjällbacka S 21 C3
Fjärdhundra S 22 B3

Gislaved S 26 B3
Gislev DK 25 D3
Gisors F 44 A2
Gissi I 89 A4
Gistad S 23 C2
Gistel B 34 B3
Gistrup DK 24 C3
Giswil CH 56 B3
Giugliano in Campania I 89 C4
Giulianova I 68 D2
Giulvăz RO 61 C5
Giurgiu RO 16 Q19
Give DK 25 D2
Givet F 35 C5
Givors F 55 C4
Givry B 35 C5
Givry F 55 B4
Givry-en-Argonne F 45 B5
Givskud DK 25 D2
Giżalki PL 40 A2
Gizeux F 53 A5
Giżycko PL 6 J17
Gizzeria I 92 C3
Gizzeria Lido I 92 C3
Gjedved DK 25 D2
Gjerlev DK 24 C3
Gjermundshamn N 18 A2
Gjerrild DK 24 C3
Gjerstad N 19 C6
Gjirokastër AL 15 R17
Gjøl DK 24 B2
Gjøvik N 2 F12
Gladbeck D 36 B2
Gladenbach D 37 C4
Glamoč BIH 70 B1
Glamsbjerg DK 25 D3
Gland CH 55 B6
Glandorf D 36 A3
Glanegg A 59 B4
Glanshammar S 22 B2
Glarus CH 56 A4
Glasgow GB 4 J4
Glashütte, *Bayern* D 48 C2
Glashütte, *Sachsen* D 39 C3
Glastonbury GB 4 L5
Glatzau A 59 B5
Glauchau D 38 C2
Glava S 20 B4
Glavatičevo BIH 70 C3
Glavičice BIH 71 B4
Glavnik YU 71 D6
Gledica YU 71 C5
Glein A 59 A4
Gleinstätten A 59 B5
Gleisdorf A 59 A5
Glenrothes GB 4 H5
Glesien D 38 B2
Gletsch CH 56 B3
Glimåkra S 27 C4
Glina HR 59 C6
Glinde D 30 B2
Glinojeck PL 33 C6
Gliwice PL 40 C3
Glödnitz A 59 B4
Gloggnitz A 50 C1
Głogoczów PL 51 A5
Glogonj YU 71 B5
Glogovac YU 71 B6
Głogów PL 39 B6
Głogówek PL 40 C2
Glomel F 42 B2
Glommen S 26 C2
Glommersträsk S 3 D16
Glonn D 48 C2
Glorenza I 57 B5
Gloria P 78 B2
Gloucester GB 4 L5
Głowaczów PL 41 B6
Główczyce PL 32 A3
Glöwen D 30 C4
Głowno PL 41 B4
Gložan YU 61 C4
Głubczyce PL 40 C2
Głuchołazy PL 40 C2
Głuchów PL 41 B5
Głuchowo PL 40 A1
Glücksburg D 25 E2
Glückstadt D 29 B6
Glumina BIH 70 B4
Glumsø DK 25 D4
Glušci YU 71 B4
Glusk BY 7 K21
Głuszyca PL 40 C1
Glyngøre DK 24 C1
Gmünd, *Karnten* A 58 B3
Gmünd, *Nieder Östereich* A 49 B5
Gmund D 48 C2
Gmunden A 49 C4
Gnarrenburg D 29 B6
Gnesau A 58 B3
Gnesta S 23 B4
Gniechowice PL 40 B1
Gniew PL 33 B4
Gniewkowo PL 33 C4
Gniezno PL 32 C3
Gnoien D 31 B4
Gnojnice BIH 70 C2
Gnojno PL 41 C5
Gnosjö S 26 B3
Goch D 36 B2
Gochsheim D 37 C6
Göd H 51 C5
Goddelsheim D 37 B4
Gódega di Sant'Urbano I 58 C2
Godegård S 23 C2
Godelheim D 37 B5
Goderville F 44 A1
Godiasco I 66 B3
Godič SLO 59 B4
Godkowo PL 33 A5
Gödöllő H 51 C5
Gödre H 60 B2
Godzikowice PL 40 C2
Godziszewo PL 33 A4
Goes NL 35 B4
Goetzenbrück F 46 B3
Góglio I 56 B3
Gogolin PL 40 C3
Göhren D 31 A5
Goirle NL 35 B6
Góis P 78 A2
Góito I 57 C5
Goizueta E 75 A5
Gojna Gora YU 71 C5
Gójsk PL 33 C5
Gol N 2 F11
Gola HR 60 B2
Gołańcz PL 32 C3
Gölcük TR 16 R21
Golčův Jenikov CZ 49 A6
Gołczewo PL 31 B6
Goldach CH 57 A4
Goldbach D 37 C5
Goldbeck D 30 C3
Goldberg D 30 B4
Goldenstedt D 29 C5
Gołębiewo PL 33 A4
Golegã P 78 B2
Goleniów PL 31 B6
Golfo Aranci I 96 C2
Golina PL 40 A3
Gölle H 60 B3
Göllersdorf A 50 B2
Golling an der Salzach A 49 C4
Golnice PL 39 B5
Golnik SLO 59 B4
Gölpazarı TR 16 R22
Gols A 50 C2
Golspie GB 4 H5
Golssen D 38 B3
Golub-Dobrzyń PL 33 B5
Golubinci YU 71 B5
Goluchów PL 40 B2
Golzow D 38 A2
Gomagoi I 57 B5
Gómara E 75 C4
Gomaringen D 47 B5
Gomes Aires P 84 B2
Gómezserracin E 74 C2
Gommern D 38 A1
Gomulin PL 41 B4
Gonäs S 22 A2
Goncelin F 55 C5
Gończyce PL 41 B6
Gondomar E 73 B2
Gondomar P 73 C2
Gondrecourt-le-Château F 46 B1
Gondrin F 62 C3
Gönen TR 16 R20
Gonfaron F 65 C5
Goñi E 75 B5
Goni I 96 D2
Gonnesa I 96 D1
Gonnosfanádiga I 96 D1
Gönyü H 50 C3
Gonzaga I 67 B4
Gooik B 35 C5
Goole GB 4 K6
Goor NL 36 A2
Göpfritz an der Wild A 49 B6
Goppenstein CH 56 B2
Göppingen D 47 B5
Gor E 86 B3
Góra PL 33 C6
Góra PL 40 B1
Góra Kalwaria PL 41 B6
Gorafe E 86 B2
Gorawino PL 32 B1
Goražde BIH 70 C3
Gordaliza del Pino E 74 B1
Gørding DK 25 D1
Górdola CH 56 B3
Gordoncillo E 74 B1
Gorenja Vas SLO 59 B4
Gorenje Jelenje HR 59 C4
Gorey GB 43 A3
Gorey IRL 4 K3
Gorgonzola I 57 C4
Gorica HR 69 B4
Gorican HR 60 B1
Gorinchem NL 35 B5
Goritsy RUS 7 H25
Göritz D 31 B5
Gorízia I 58 C3
Górki PL 33 C5
Gorleben D 30 B3
Gørlev DK 25 D4
Görlitz D 39 B4
Górliz E 75 A4
Görmin D 31 B5
Górna Grupa PL 33 B4
Gorna Oryakhovitsa BG 16 Q19
Gornja Gorevnica YU 71 C5
Gornja Klina YU 71 D5
Gornja Ploča HR 69 B4
Gornja Radgona SLO 59 B5
Gornja Sabanta YU 71 C6
Gornja Trešnjevica YU 71 B5
Gornja Tuzla BIH 70 B3
Gornje Polje YU 70 D3
Gornje Ratkovo BIH 70 B1
Gornji Grad SLO 59 B4
Gornji Humac HR 69 C5
Gornji Jasenjani BIH 70 C2
Gornji Kamengrad BIH 69 B5
Gornji Kneginec HR 59 B6
Gornji Kosinj HR 69 B4
Gornji Milanovac YU 71 B5
Gornji Podgradci BIH 70 A2
Gornji Ravno BIH 70 C2
Gornji Sjenicak HR 59 C5
Gornji Vakuf BIH 70 C2
Górno PL 41 C5
Görömböly H 51 B6
Górowo Iławeckie PL 33 A6
Gorredijk NL 28 B3
Gorron F 43 B5
Görzke D 38 A2
Gorzkowice PL 41 B4
Górzno PL 33 B5
Gorzów Śląski PL 40 B3
Gorzów Wielkopolski PL 31 C7
Górzyca PL 31 C6
Gorzyce PL 51 A4
Gorzyń PL 32 C1
Górzyn PL 39 B4
Gorzyno PL 32 A3
Gosaldo I 58 B1
Gosau A 49 C4
Gościcino PL 33 A4
Gościęcin PL 40 C3
Gościm PL 32 C1
Gościno PL 32 A1
Gosdorf A 59 B5
Goslar D 37 B6
Goslice PL 33 C5
Gospič HR 69 B4
Gosport GB 4 L6
Goss Ilsede D 37 A6
Gössäter S 21 C5
Gossau CH 57 A4
Gössnitz D 38 C2
Gössweinstein D 48 A2
Gostkow PL 41 B4
Göstling an der Ybbs A 49 C5
Gostomia PL 32 B2
Gostycyn PL 32 B3
Gostyń PL 40 B2
Gostynin PL 33 C5
Goszczyn PL 41 B5
Göta S 21 C4
Göteborg S 21 D3
Götene S 21 C5
Gotha D 37 C6
Gothem S 23 D5
Gotse Delchev BG 15 R18
Gottersdorf D 48 B3
Göttingen D 37 B5
Götzis A 57 A4
Gouarec F 42 B2
Gouda NL 35 A5
Gourdon F 63 B4
Gourgançon F 45 B5
Gourin F 42 B2
Gournay-en-Bray F 44 A2
Gouveia P 78 A3
Gouvy B 36 C1
Gouzeacourt F 35 C4
Gouzon F 54 B2
Govedari HR 70 D2
Govérnolo I 67 A4
Gowarczów PL 41 B5
Gowidlino PL 32 A3
Goyatz D 39 A4
Göynük TR 16 R22
Gozdnica PL 39 B5
Gozdowo PL 33 C5
Gozee B 35 C5
Graal-Müritz D 30 A4
Grabenstätt D 48 C3
Gråbo S 21 D4
Grabovac HR 70 C1
Grabovac YU 71 B5
Grabovci YU 71 B4
Grabow D 30 B3
Grabów PL 41 A4
Grabow nad Pilicą PL 41 B6
Grabów nad Prosną PL 40 B3
Grabowno PL 32 B3
Grabs CH 57 A4
Gračac HR 69 B4
Gračanica BIH 70 B3
Graçay F 54 A1
Grad SLO 59 B6
Gradac HR 70 C2
Gradac YU 71 C4
Gradac YU 71 C5
Gradačac BIH 70 B3
Gradec HR 59 C6
Gradefes E 74 B1
Grades A 59 B4
Gradil P 78 C1
Gradina HR 60 C2
Gradina YU 71 C4
Gradisca d'Isonzo I 58 C3
Gradište HR 70 A3
Grado E 72 A4
Grado I 58 C3
Grærup Strand DK 25 D1
Græsted DK 27 C2
Grafenau D 49 B4
Gräfenberg D 48 A2
Gräfenhainichen D 38 B2
Grafenschlag A 49 B6
Grafenstein A 59 B4
Gräfenthal D 38 C1
Grafentonna D 37 B6
Grafenwöhr D 48 A2
Grafing D 48 B2
Grafling D 48 B3
Gräfsnäs S 21 C4
Gragnano I 89 C4
Grahovo SLO 58 B3
Grainau D 57 A6
Graja de Iniesta E 81 C5
Grajera E 75 C3
Gram DK 25 D2
Gramais A 57 A5
Gramat F 63 B4
Gramatneusiedl A 50 B2
Grambow D 31 B6
Grammichele I 95 B3
Gramzow D 31 B6
Gran N 20 A2
Granada E 86 B2
Grañas E 72 A3
Granátula de Calatrava E 86 A2
Grancey-le-Château F 45 C6
Grand-Champ F 42 C3
Grand Couronne F 44 A2
Grand-Fougeray F 43 C4
Grandas de Salime E 72 A4
Grandcamp-Maisy F 43 A4
Grândola P 84 A2
Grandpré F 45 A5
Grandrieu B 35 C5
Grandrieu F 64 B2
Grandson CH 56 B1
Grandvillars F 56 A1
Grandvilliers F 44 A2
Grañén E 76 B2
Grangärde S 22 A1
Granges-de Crouhens F 63 D3
Granges-sur-Vologne F 46 B2
Grängesberg S 22 A1
Gräningen D 30 C4
Granitola-Torretta I 94 B1
Granja, *Évora* P 84 A3
Granja, *Porto* P 73 C2
Granja de Moreruela E 74 C1
Granja de Torrehermosa E 85 A5
Gränna S 26 A4
Granollers E 77 B5
Granön S 3 D16
Granowiec PL 40 B2
Granowo PL 40 A1
Gransee D 31 B5
Gransherad N 19 B6
Grantham GB 4 K6
Granville F 43 B4
Grasberg D 29 B6
Grasö S 22 A5
Grassano I 90 B3
Grassau D 48 C3
Grasse F 65 C5
Gråsten DK 25 E2
Grästorp S 21 C4
Gratkorn A 59 A5
Gratwein A 59 A5
Graulhet F 63 C4
Graus E 76 A3
Grávalos E 75 B5
Grave NL 36 B1
Gravedona I 57 B4
Gravelines F 34 B3
Gravellona Toce I 56 C3
's Gravendeel NL 35 B5
's-Gravenhage NL 35 A5
Gravens DK 25 D2
's Gravenzande NL 35 A5
Graveson F 64 C3
Gravina in Púglia I 91 B3
Gray F 55 A5
Grayvoron RUS 7 L24
Graz A 59 A5
Grazalema E 85 C5
Grążawy PL 33 B5
Grazzano Visconti I 66 B3
Greåker N 20 B3
Great Yarmouth GB 4 K7
Grebbestad S 21 C3
Grebenstein D 37 B5
Grębocin PL 33 B4
Greding D 48 A2
Gredstedbro DK 25 D1
Greenock GB 4 J4
Grefrath D 36 B2
Greifenburg A 58 B3
Greiffenberg D 31 B5
Greifswald D 31 A5
Grein A 49 B5
Greipstad N 19 C4
Greiz D 38 C2
Grenaa DK 25 C3
Grenade F 63 C4
Grenade-sur-l'Adour F 62 C2
Grenchen CH 56 A2
Grendi N 19 C4
Grenoble F 55 C5
Gréoux-les-Bains F 65 C4
Gresenhorst D 30 A4
Gressoney-la-Trinité I 56 C2
Gressoney-St.-Jean I 56 C2
Gressthal D 37 C6
Gressvik N 20 B2
Gresten A 49 C6
Gretna Green GB 4 J5
Greussen D 37 B6
Greve in Chianti I 67 C5
Greven, *Mecklenburg-Vorpommern* D 30 B2
Greven, *Nordrhein-Westfalen* D 36 A3
Grevená GR 15 R17
Grevenbroich D 36 B2
Grevenbrück D 36 B3
Grevenmacher L 46 A2
Grevesmühlen D 30 B3
Grevestrand DK 27 D2
Grevie S 27 C2
Grez-Doiceau B 35 C5
Grez-en-Bouère F 43 C5
Grèzec F 63 B4
Grezzana I 57 C6
Grgar SLO 58 C3
Grgurevci YJ 71 A4
Gries A 57 A6
Gries in Sellrain A 57 A6
Griesbach D 49 B4
Griesheim D 47 A4
Grieskirchen A 49 B4
Griffen A 59 B4
Grignan F 64 B3
Grignano I 58 C3
Grigno I 58 B1
Grignols F 62 B2
Grignon F 55 C6
Grijota E 74 B2
Grijpskerk NL 28 B3
Grillby S 22 B4
Grimaud F 65 C5
Grimbergen B 35 C5
Grimma D 38 B2
Grimmen D 31 A5
Grimmialp CH 56 B2
Grimsås S 26 B3
Grimsby GB 4 K6
Grimslöv S 26 C4
Grimstad N 19 C5
Grimstorp S 26 B4
Grindelwald CH 56 B3
Grindheim N 19 C4
Grindsted DK 25 D1
Griñón E 80 B3
Gripenberg S 23 D1
Gripsholm S 22 B4
Grisolles F 63 C4
Grisslehamn S 22 A5
Grndina BIH 70 B1
Gröbming A 58 A3
Gröbzig D 38 B1
Grocka YU 71 B5
Gröditz D 38 B3
Gródki PL 33 B6
Grodków PL 40 C2
Grodziec PL 40 A3
Grodzisk Mazowiecki PL 41 A5
Groenlo NL 36 A2
Groesbeek NL 36 B1
Grohote HR 69 C5
Groitzsch D 38 B2
Groix F 42 C2
Grójec PL 41 B5
Grom PL 33 B6
Gromiljca BIH 70 C3
Grömitz D 30 A2
Gromnik PL 51 A6
Gromo I 57 C4
Gronau, *Niedersachsen* D 37 A5
Gronau, *Nordrhein-Westfalen* D 36 A3
Grönenbach D 47 C6
Grong N 2 D13
Grönhögen S 27 C6
Groningen D 38 B1
Groningen NL 28 B3
Grono CH 57 B4
Grönskåra S 26 B5
Grootegast NL 28 B3
Gropello Cairoli I 56 C3
Grorud N 20 B2
Grósio I 57 B5
Grošnica YU 71 C5
Gross Beeren D 31 C5
Gross Berkel D 37 A5
Gross-botwar D 47 B5
Gross-Dölln D 31 B5
Gross-Gerau D 47 A4
Gross-hartmannsdorf D 38 C3
Gross Kreutz D 31 C4
Gross Lafferde D 37 A6
Gross Leutheb D 39 A4
Gross Oesingen D 30 C2
Gross Reken D 36 B3
Gross Sarau D 30 B2
Gross Särchen D 39 B4
Gross Schönebeck D 31 C5
Gross-schweinbarth A 50 B2
Gross Umstadt D 47 A4
Gross Warnow D 30 B3
Gross-Weikersdorf A 50 B1
Gross-Welle D 30 B4
Gross Wokern D 30 B4
Grossalmerode D 37 B5
Grossarl A 58 A3
Grossbodungen D 37 B6
Grossburgwedel D 30 C1
Grosschönau D 39 C4
Grossenbrode D 30 A3
Grossengottern D 37 B6
Grossenhain D 38 B3
Grossenkneten D 29 C5
Grossenlüder D 37 C5
Grossensee D 30 B2
Grossenzersdorf A 50 B2
Grosseto I 67 D5
Grossgerungs A 49 B5
Grossglobnitz A 49 B6
Grosshabersdorf D 48 A1
Grossharras A 50 B2
Grosshöchstetten CH 56 B2
Grosskrut A 50 B2
Grosslohra D 37 B6
Grossmehring D 48 B2
Grossostheim D 47 A5
Grosspertholz A 49 B5
Grosspetersdorf A 59 A6
Grosspostwitz D 39 B4
Grossraming A 49 C5
Grossräschen D 39 B4
Grossrinderfeld D 47 A5
Grossröhrsdorf D 39 B4
Grossschirma D 38 C3
Grosssiegharts A 49 B6
Grosssölk A 58 A3
Grosswarasdorf A 59 A6
Grosswilfersdorf A 59 A5
Grostenquin F 46 B2
Grosuplje SLO 59 C4
Grotli N 2 E10
Grottáglie I 91 B4
Grottaminarda I 90 A2
Grottammare I 68 D2
Grotte di Castro I 88 A1
Grotteria I 92 C3
Gróttole I 90 B3
Grouw NL 28 B2
Grove E 72 B2
Grožnjan HR 58 C3
Grua N 20 A2
Grube D 30 A3
Grubišno Polje HR 60 C2
Grude BIH 70 C2
Grudovo BG 16 Q20
Grudusk PL 33 B6
Grudziądz PL 33 B4
Grue N 20 A4
Gruissan F 64 C2
Grullos E 72 A4
Grumo Áppula I 91 A3
Grums S 20 B5
Grünau im Almtal A 49 C4
Grünberg D 37 C4
Grünburg A 49 C5
Gründau D 37 C5
Gründelhardt D 47 A5
Grundlsee A 49 C4
Grundsund S 21 C3
Grunewald D 39 B3
Grungedal N 19 B4
Grunow D 39 A4
Grünstadt D 47 A4
Gruyères CH 56 B2
Gruža YU 71 C5
Grybów PL 51 A6
Grycksbo S 22 A1
Gryfice PL 31 B7
Gryfino PL 31 B6
Gryfów Śląski PL 39 B5
Grymyr N 20 A2
Gryt S 23 C3
Grytgöl S 23 C2
Grythyttan S 22 B1
Grytnäs S 23 C4
Grzmiąca PL 32 B2
Grzybno PL 31 B6
Grzywna PL 33 B4
Gschnitz A 57 A6
Gschwend D 47 B5
Gstaad CH 56 B2
Gsteig CH 56 B2
Guadahortuna E 86 B2
Guadalajara E 81 B3
Guadalaviar E 81 B5
Guadalcanal E 85 A5
Guadalcázar E 86 B1
Guadalix de la Sierra E 80 B3
Guadálmez E 86 A1
Guadalupe E 80 C1
Guadamur E 80 C2
Guadarrama E 80 B2
Guadiaro E 85 C5
Guadix E 86 B2
Guagnano I 91 B4
Guagno F 96 A1
Guajar-Faragüit E 86 C2
Gualchos E 86 C2
Gualdo Tadino I 68 C1
Gualtieri I 67 B4
Guarcino I 89 B3
Guarda P 78 A3
Guardamar del Segura E 82 C2
Guardão P 78 A2
Guardavalle I 92 C3
Guardea I 88 A2
Guárdia I 90 B2
Guárdia Sanframondi I 89 B4
Guardiagrele I 89 A4
Guardiarégia I 89 B4
Guardias Viejas E 87 C3
Guardiola de Bergueda E 77 A4
Guardo E 74 B2
Guareña E 79 C4
Guaro E 86 C1
Guarromán E 86 A2
Guasila I 96 D2
Guastalla I 67 B4
Gúbbio I 68 C1
Guben D 39 B4
Gubin PL 39 B4
Guča YU 71 C5
Gudavac BIH 69 B5
Guderup DK 25 E2
Gudhem S 21 C5
Gudhjem DK 27 D4
Gudovac HR 60 C1
Gudow D 30 B2
Gudvangen N 2 F10
Guebwiller F 46 C3
Guéjar-Sierra E 86 B2
Guéméné-Penfao F 43 C4
Guéméné-sur-Scorff F 42 B2
Güeñes E 75 A3
Guer F 43 C3
Guérande F 52 A2
Guéret F 54 B1
Guérigny F 54 A3
Guesa E 62 D1
Gueugnon F 54 B4
Guglionesi I 89 B4
Gühlen Glienicke D 31 B4
Guia P 78 B2
Guichen F 43 C4
Guidizzolo I 57 C5
Guidónia-Montecélio I 88 B2
Guiglia I 67 B4
Guignes F 44 B3
Guijo E 86 A1
Guijo de Coria E 79 A4
Guijo de Santa Bábera E 79 A5
Guijuelo E 79 A5
Guildford GB 4 L6
Guillaumes F 65 B5
Guillena E 85 B4
Guillestre F 65 B5
Guilvinec F 42 C1
Guimarães P 73 C2
Guincho P 78 C1
Guînes F 34 C2
Guingamp F 42 B2
Guipavas F 42 B1
Guiscard F 45 A4
Guiscriff F 42 B2
Guise F 45 A4
Guisona E 77 B4
Guitiriz E 72 A3
Guîtres F 62 A2
Gujan-Mestras F 62 B1
Gulbene LV 7 H20
Guldborg DK 25 E4
Gullabo S 26 C5
Gullbrandstorp S 26 C2
Gullhaug N 20 B2
Gullringen S 23 D2
Gullspång S 21 C6
Güllük TR 16 T20
Gumiel de Hizán E 74 C3
Gummersbach D 36 B3
Gumünden D 46 A3
Gundel-fingen D 46 B3
Gundelfingen D 47 B6
Gundelsheim D 47 A5
Gunderschoffen F 46 B3
Gunderts-hausen A 48 B3
Gundinci HR 60 C3
Gunja HR 70 B3
Gunnarn S 2 D15
Gunnarskog S 20 B4
Gunnebo S 23 D3
Günselsdorf A 50 C2
Guntersblum D 47 A4
Guntersdorf A 50 B2
Guntín E 72 B3
Günzburg D 47 B6
Gunzenhausen D 48 A1
Gurk A 59 B4
Gurrea de Gállego E 76 A2
Gušće HR 60 C1
Gusev RUS 6 J18
Gúspini I 96 D1
Gusselby S 22 B2
Güssing A 59 A6
Gusswerk A 49 C6
Gustav Adolf S 20 A5
Gustavsberg S 22 B5
Gustavsfors S 20 B4
Güstrow D 30 B4
Gusum S 23 C3
Gutenstein A 50 C1
Gütersloh D 37 B4
Guttannen CH 56 B3
Guttaring A 59 B4
Guttau D 39 B4
Güttingen CH 47 C5
Gützkow D 31 B5
Guzów PL 41 A5
Gvardeysk RUS 6 J17
Gvarv N 19 B6
Gvozd YU 70 D4
Gvozdansko HR 59 C6
Gwda Wielka PL 32 B2
Gy F 55 A5
Gyál H 61 A4
Gyarmat H 60 A2
Gyé-sur-Seine F 45 B5
Gyékényes H 60 B2
Gylling DK 25 D3
Gyoma H 61 B5
Gyömöre H 60 A2
Gyömrö H 61 A4
Gyón H 61 A4
Gyöngyfa H 60 C2
Gyöngyös H 51 C5
Gyöngyöspata H 51 C5
Gyönk H 60 B3
Györ H 50 C3
Györszemere H 60 A2
Gypsera CH 56 B2
Gysinge S 22 A3
Gyttorp S 22 B1
Gyula H 61 B6
Gyulafirátót H 60 A2
Gyulaj H 60 B3

H

Haacht B 35 C5
Haag, *Nieder Östereich* A 49 B5
Haag, *Ober Östereich* A 49 B4
Haag D 48 B3
Haaksbergen NL 36 A2
Haamstede NL 35 B4
Haan D 36 B3
Haapajärvi FIN 3 E19
Haapsalu EST 6 G18
Haarlem NL 28 C1
Habas F 62 C2
Habay B 46 A1
Habo S 26 B4
Habry CZ 49 A6
Habsheim F 46 C3
Hachenburg D 36 C3
Hacinas E 75 C3
Hadamar D 36 C4
Hadersdorf am Kamp A 49 B6
Haderslev DK 25 D2
Hadmersleben D 38 B1
Hadsten DK 25 C3
Hadsund DK 24 C3
Hadyach UA 7 L24
Hadžići BIH 70 C3
Hægebostad N 19 C4
Hægeland N 19 C4
Haganj HR 60 C1
Hagby S 26 C6
Hage D 29 B4
Hagen, *Niedersachsen* D 29 B5
Hagen, *Nordrhein-Westfalen* D 36 B3
Hagenbach D 47 A4
Hagenow D 30 B3
Hagetmau F 62 C2
Hagfors S 20 A5
Hagondange F 46 A2
Haguenau F 46 B3
Hahnbach D 48 A2
Hahnslätten D 36 C4
Hahót H 60 B1
Haiger D 36 C4
Haigerloch D 47 B4
Hainburg A 50 B2
Hainfeld A 50 B1
Hainichen D 38 C3
Hajdúböszörmény H 10 N17
Hajdučica YU 61 C5
Hajdúszoboszló H 61 A6
Hajnáčka SK 51 B5
Hajnówka PL 6 K18
Hajós H 61 B4
Hakkas S 3 C17
Håksberg S 22 A2
Halaszi H 50 C3
Halberstadt D 38 B1
Hald Ege DK 25 C2
Haldem D 29 C5
Halden N 20 B3
Haldensleben D 38 A1
Halenbeck D 30 B4
Halfing D 48 C3
Halhjem N 18 A2
Halifax GB 4 K6
Hall S 23 D5
Hall in Tirol A 57 A6
Hallabro S 27 C5
Hällabrottet S 23 B2
Hällaryd S 27 C4
Hällberga S 22 B3
Hällbybrunn S 22 B3
Halle B 35 C5
Halle, *Nordrhein-Westfalen* D 37 A4
Halle, *Sachsen-Anhalt* D 38 B1
Hälleberga S 26 C5
Hällefors S 22 B1
Hälleforsnäs S 22 B3
Hallein A 48 C4
Hällekis S 21 C5
Hällen S 22 A4
Hallenberg D 37 B4
Hällestad S 23 C2
Hällevadsholm S 21 C3
Hällevik S 27 C4
Hälleviksstrand S 21 C3
Hallingby N 20 A2
Hällnäs S 22 A4
Hallsberg S 23 B2
Hållsta S 22 B3
Hallstahammar S 22 B3
Hallstatt A 58 A3
Hallstavik S 22 A5
Halltorp S 26 C6
Halluin F 35 C4
Halmstad S 26 C2
Hals DK 24 B3
Haltdalen N 2 E12
Haltern D 36 B3
Halvarsgårdarna S 22 A2
Halver D 36 B3
Halvrimmen DK 24 B2
Ham F 45 A4
Hamar N 2 F12
Hamarhaug N 18 A2
Hambach F 46 A3
Hambergen D 29 B5
Hambergsund S 21 C3
Hambuhren D 30 C1
Hamburg D 30 B2
Hamdorf D 29 A6
Hämeenlinna FIN 3 F19
Hameln D 37 A5
Hamersleben D 38 A1
Hamilton GB 4 J4
Hamina FIN 3 F20
Hamm D 36 B3
Hammar S 23 C1
Hammarö S 20 B5
Hamme B 35 B5
Hammel DK 25 C2
Hammelburg D 37 C5
Hammelspring D 31 B5
Hammenhög S 27 D4
Hammerfest N 2 A18
Hammershøj DK 24 C2
Hammerum DK 25 C2
Hamminkeln D 36 B2
Hamneda S 26 C3
Hamont B 35 B6
Hámor H 51 B6
Han Knežica BIH 60 C1
Han Pijesak BIH 70 B3
Hanaskog S 27 C4
Hanau D 37 C4
Händelöp S 23 D3
Handlová SK 51 B4
Hanerau-Hademarschen D 29 A6
Hånger S 26 B3
Hanken S 23 C1
Hankensbüttel D 30 C2
Hanko FIN 3 G18
Hannover D 30 C1
Hannut B 35 C6
Hanstedt D 30 B2
Hanstholm DK 24 B1
Hantsavichy BY 7 K20
Hanušovice CZ 40 C1
Haparanda S 3 D19
Haradok BY 7 J21
Harads S 3 C17
Häradsbäck S 26 C4
Harbo S 22 A4
Harboør DK 24 C1
Harburg, *Bayern* D 48 B1
Harburg, *Hamburg* D 30 B1
Hårby DK 25 D3
Harc H 60 B3
Hardegarijp NL 28 B2
Hardegsen D 37 B5

Hardelot Plage F 34 C2
Hardenbeck D 31 B5
Hardenberg NL 28 C3
Harderwijk NL 28 C2
Hardheim D 47 A5
Hardt D 47 B4
Hareid N 2 E10
Haren D 29 C4
Haren NL 28 B3
Harestua N 20 A2
Harfleur F 43 A6
Harg S 22 A5
Hargicourt F 35 D4
Hargnies F 35 C5
Hargshamn S 22 A5
Harkány H 60 C3
Härkeberga S 22 B4
Harkebrügge D 29 B4
Harlech GB 4 K4
Hårlev DK 27 D2
Harlingen NL 28 B2
Harlösa S 27 D3
Harlow GB 4 L7
Härnevi S 22 B4
Härnösand S 2 E15
Haro E 75 B4
Háromfa H 60 B2
Haroué F 46 B2
Harplinge S 26 C2
Harpstedt D 29 C5
Harrogate GB 4 K6
Härryda S 21 D4
Harsefeld D 29 B6
Harsewinkel D 36 B4
Hârşova RO 11 P20
Harstad N 2 B15
Harsum D 37 A5
Harta H 61 B4
Hartberg A 59 A5
Hartennes F 45 A4
Hartha D 38 B2
Hartlepool GB 4 J6
Hartmanice CZ 49 A4
Hartmannsdorf A 59 A5
Harwich GB 4 L7
Harzgerode D 38 B1
Häselgehr A 57 A5
Haselünne D 29 C4
Haslach D 47 B4
Haslach an der Mühl A 49 B5
Hasle DK 27 D4
Haslev DK 25 D4
Hasloch D 47 A5
Hasparren F 62 C1
Hasselfelde D 37 B6
Hasselfors S 23 B1
Hasselt B 35 C6
Hasselt NL 28 C3
Hassfurt D 37 C6
Hassleben D 31 B5
Hässleholm S 27 C3
Hasslö S 27 C5
Hassloch D 47 A4
Hästholmen S 23 C1
Hastière-Lavaux B 35 C5
Hastings GB 4 L7
Hästveda S 27 C3
Hatlestrand N 18 A2
Hattem NL 28 C3
Hatten D 29 B5
Hatten F 46 B3
Hatting DK 25 D2
Hattingen D 36 B3
Hattstadt F 46 B3
Hattstedt D 29 A6
Hatvan H 51 C5
Hatvik N 18 A2
Hau D 36 B2
Haudainville F 45 A6
Hauge N 18 C3
Haugesund N 18 B2
Haughom N 18 C3
Haugsdorf A 50 B2
Haukeland N 18 A2
Haukeligrend N 19 B4
Haukipudas FIN 3 D19
Haulerwijk NL 28 B3
Haunersdorf D 48 B3
Hausach D 47 B4
Hausham D 48 C2
Hausmannstätten A 59 B5
Hausvik N 18 C3
Haut-Fays B 35 C6
Hautefort F 53 C6
Hauterives F 55 C5
Hauteville-Lompnès F 55 C5
Hautmont F 35 C4
Hautrage B 35 C4
Hauzenberg D 49 B4
Havant GB 4 L6
Havdrup DK 25 D5
Havelange B 35 C6
Havelberg D 30 C4
Havelte NL 28 C3
Haverfordwest GB 4 L4
Håverud S 21 C4
Havířov CZ 51 A4
Havixbeck D 36 B3
Havlíčkův Brod CZ 49 A6
Havndal DK 24 C3
Havneby DK 25 D1
Havnsø DK 25 D4
Havøysund N 2 A19
Havrebjerg DK 25 D4
Havstenssund S 21 C3
Hawick GB 4 J5
Hayange F 46 A2
Hayrabolu TR 16 R20
Haysyn UA 11 M21
Hayvoron UA 11 M21
Hazebrouck F 34 C3
Hazlov CZ 38 C2
Héas F 62 D3
Heberg S 26 C2
Heby S 22 B3
Hechingen D 47 B4
Hechlingen D 48 B1
Hecho E 62 D2
Hechtel B 35 B6
Hechthausen D 29 B6
Heckelberg D 31 C5
Hecklingen D 38 B1
Hed S 22 B2
Hedared S 21 D4
Heddal N 19 B6
Hédé F 43 B4
Hede S 2 E13
Hedekas S 21 C3
Hedemora S 22 A2
Hedensted DK 25 D2
Hedersleben D 38 B1
Hedesunda S 22 A4
Heede D 29 C4
Heek D 36 A3
Heemstede NL 28 C1
Heerde NL 28 C3
's Heerenberg NL 36 B2
Heerenveen NL 28 C2
Heerhugowaard NL 28 C1
Heerlen NL 36 C1
Heeze NL 35 B6
Hegyeshalom H 50 C3
Hegyközség H 60 A1
Heide D 29 A6
Heidelberg D 47 A4
Heiden D 36 B2
Heidenau D 39 C3
Heidenheim D 47 B6
Heidenreichstein A 49 B6
Heikendorf D 30 A2
Heilbad Heiligenstadt D 37 B6
Heilbronn D 47 A5
Heiligenblut A 58 A2
Heiligendamn D 30 A3
Heiligendorf D 30 C2
Heiligengrabe D 30 B4
Heiligenhafen D 30 A2
Heiligenhaus D 36 B2
Heiligenkreuz A 59 B6
Heiligenstadt D 48 A2
Heiloo NL 28 C1
Heilsbronn D 48 A1
Heimburg D 37 B6
Heimdal N 2 E12
Heinerscheid L 36 C2
Heinersdorf D 31 C6
Heining D 49 B4
Heiningen D 47 B5
Heinola FIN 3 F20
Heinsberg D 36 B2
Heist-op-den-Berg B 35 B5
Hejdeby S 23 D5
Hejls DK 25 D2
Hejnice CZ 39 C5
Hel PL 33 A4
Helchteren B 35 B6
Heldburg D 37 C6
Heldrungen D 38 B1
Helechosa E 80 C2
Helfenberg A 49 B5
Helgen N 19 B6
Helgeroa N 19 C6
Hellas S 21 C4
Helle N 18 C3
Helleland N 18 C3
Hellendoorn NL 28 C3
Hellenthal D 36 C2
Hellesylt N 2 E10
Hellevoetsluis NL 35 B5
Hellín E 87 A4
Hellvi S 23 D5
Hellvik N 18 C2
Helm-brechts D 38 C1
Helmond NL 35 B6
Helmsdale GB 4 G5
Helmstedt D 37 A6
Hel'pa SK 51 B5
Helsa D 37 B5
Helsingborg S 27 C2
Helsinge DK 27 C2
Helsingør DK 27 C2
Helsinki FIN 3 F19
Hemau D 48 A2
Hemer D 36 B3
Héming F 46 B2
Hemmet DK 25 D1
Hemmingstedt D 29 A6
Hemmoor D 29 B6
Hemnes N 20 B3
Hemnesberget N 2 C13
Hemse S 6 H16
Hemsedal N 2 F11
Hemslingen D 29 B6
Hen N 20 A2
Henån S 21 C3
Hendaye F 75 A5
Hendek TR 16 R22
Hendungen D 37 C6
Hengelo, *Gelderland* NL 36 A2
Hengelo, *Overijssel* NL 36 A2
Hengersberg D 48 B4
Hénin-Beaumont F 34 C3
Henne Strand DK 25 D1
Henneberg D 37 C6
Hennebont F 42 C2
Hennigsdorf D 31 C5
Hennstedt D 29 A6
Henrichemont F 54 A2
Henryków PL 40 C2
Henrykowo PL 33 A6
Henstedt-Ulzburg D 30 B1
Heppenheim D 47 A4
Herad N 18 C3
Herálec CZ 50 A2
Herand N 18 A3
Herbault F 44 C2
Herbern D 36 B3
Herbeumont B 45 A6
Herbignac F 52 A2
Herbisse F 45 B5
Herbitzheim F 46 A3
Herbolzheim D 46 B3
Herborn D 36 C4
Herbrechtingen D 47 B6
Herby PL 40 C5
Herceg-Novi YU 15 Q16
Hercegovać HR 60 C2
Hercegovacka Goleša YU 71 C4
Hercegszántó H 61 B4
Herchen D 36 C3
Heréd H 51 C5
Hereford GB 4 K5
Herefoss N 19 C5
Herencia E 81 C3
Herend H 60 B2
Herent B 35 C5
Herentals B 35 B5
Hérépian F 64 C2
Herfølge DK 25 D5
Herford D 37 A4
Herguijuela E 79 B5
Héric F 52 A3
Héricourt F 56 A1
Héricourt-en-Caux F 44 A1
Hérimoncourt F 56 A1
Heringsdorf D 30 A3
Herisau CH 57 A4
Hérisson F 54 B2
Herk-de-Stad B 35 C6
Herlufmagle DK 25 D4
Hermagor A 58 B3
Hermannsburg D 30 C2
Heřmanův Městec CZ 39 D5
Herment F 54 C2
Hermeskeil D 46 A2
Hermisende E 73 C4
Hermonville F 45 A4
Hermsdorf D 38 C1
Hernani E 75 A5
Hernansancho E 80 B2
Herne D 36 B3
Herning DK 25 C1
Herøya N 19 B6
Herramelluri E 75 B3
Herräng S 22 A5
Herre N 19 B6
Herrenberg D 47 B4
Herrera E 86 B1
Herrera de Alcántara E 78 B3
Herrera de los Navarros E 76 B1
Herrera de Pisuerga E 74 B2
Herrera del Duque E 80 C1
Herrerias E 84 B3
Herreros del Suso E 80 B1
Herrestad S 21 C3
Herrhamra S 23 C4
Herrlisheim F 46 B3
Herrljunga S 21 C5
Herrnhut D 39 B4
Herrsching D 48 B2
Hersbruck D 48 A2
Hersby S 22 B5
Herscheid D 36 B3
Herselt B 35 B5
Herstal B 35 C6
Herten D 36 B3
's-Hertogenbosch NL 35 B6
Hervás E 79 A5
Hervik N 18 B2
Herxheim D 47 A4
Herzberg, *Brandenburg* D 31 C4
Herzberg, *Brandenburg* D 38 B3
Herzberg, *Niedersachsen* D 37 B6
Herzebrock D 36 B4
Herzfelde D 31 C5
Herzlake D 29 C4
Herzogen-aurach D 48 A1
Herzogenbuchsee CH 56 A2
Herzogenburg A 49 B6
Herzsprung D 30 B4
Hesby N 18 B2
Hesdin F 34 C3
Hesel D 29 B4
Heskestad N 18 C3
Hesselager DK 25 D3
Hessisch Lichtenau D 37 B5
Hessisch-Oldendorf D 37 A5
Hestra S 26 B3
Hettange-Grande F 46 A2
Hettstedt D 38 B1
Heuchin F 34 C3
Heudicourt-sous-les-Côtes F 46 B1
Heunezel F 46 B2
Heuqueville F 43 A6
Heves H 51 C6
Héviz H 60 B2
Hexham GB 4 J5
Hidas H 60 B3
Hieflau A 49 C5
Hiendelaencina E 81 A4
Hiersac F 53 C5
High Wycombe GB 4 L6
Higuera de Arjona E 86 B2
Higuera de Calatrava E 86 B1
Higuera de la Serena E 79 C5
Higuera de la Sierra E 85 B4
Higuera de Vargas E 79 C4
Higuera la Real E 85 A4
Higuers de Llerena E 79 C4
Higueruela E 82 C1
Híjar E 76 B2
Hilchenbach D 36 B4
Hildburghausen D 37 C6
Hilden D 36 B2
Hilders D 37 C5
Hildesheim D 37 A5
Hillared S 26 B3
Hille D 37 A4
Hillegom NL 35 A5
Hillerød DK 27 D2
Hillerstorp S 26 B3
Hillesheim D 36 C2
Hillestad N 20 B2
Hillmersdorf D 38 B3
Hilpoltstein D 48 A2
Hiltpoltstein D 48 A2
Hilvarenbeek NL 35 B6
Hilversum NL 35 A6
Himarë AL 15 R16
Himesháza H 60 B3
Himmelberg A 59 B4
Himmelpforten D 29 B6
Himód H 60 A2
Hindås S 21 D4
Hindelang D 57 A5
Hindelbank CH 56 A2
Hinderavåg N 18 B2
Hinjosa del Valle E 79 C4
Hinnerup DK 25 C3
Hinneryd S 26 C3
Hinojal E 79 B4
Hinojales E 85 B4
Hinojos E 85 B4
Hinojosa del Duque E 79 C5
Hinojosas de Calatrava E 86 A1
Hinterhornbach A 57 A5
Hinterriss A 57 A6
Hintersee A 49 C4
Hintersee D 31 B6
Hinterstoder A 49 C5
Hintertux A 58 A1
Hinterweidenthal D 46 A3
Hinwil CH 56 A3
Hippolytushoef NL 28 C1
Hirschaid D 48 A1
Hirschau D 48 A2
Hirschfeld D 38 B3
Hirschhorn D 47 A4
Hirsingue F 46 C3
Hirson F 45 A5
Hirtshals DK 24 B2
Hirzenhain D 37 C5
Hishult S 27 C3
Hittarp S 27 C2
Hittisau A 57 A4
Hitzacker D 30 B3
Hjallerup DK 24 B3
Hjältevad S 26 B5
Hjärnarp S 27 C2
Hjartdal N 19 B5
Hjellestad N 18 A2
Hjelmeland N 18 B3
Hjerkinn N 2 E11
Hjerm DK 24 C1
Hjerpsted DK 25 D1
Hjerting DK 25 D1
Hjo S 21 C6
Hjordkær DK 25 D2
Hjørring DK 24 B2
Hjorted S 23 D3
Hjortkvarn S 23 C2
Hjortsberga S 26 C4
Hjukse N 19 B6
Hjuksebø N 19 B6
Hliník nad Hronom. SK 51 B4
Hlinsko CZ 50 A1
Hlohovec SK 50 B3
Hluboká nad Vltavou CZ 49 A5
Hlučín CZ 50 A4
Hlukhiv UA 7 L23
Hlyboka UA 11 M19
Hlybokaye BY 7 J20
Hniezdne SK 51 A6
Hnilec SK 51 B6
Hnúšťa SK 51 B5
Hobol H 60 B2
Hobro DK 24 C2
Hobscheid L 46 A1
Hochdonn D 29 A6
Hochdorf CH 56 A3
Hochfelden F 46 B3
Hochspeyer D 46 A3
Höchst im Odenwald D 47 A5
Höchstadt, *Bayern* D 48 A1
Höchstädt, *Bayern* D 47 B6
Hochstenbach D 36 C3
Hockenheim D 47 A4
Hodejov SK 51 B5
Hodenhagen D 29 C6
Hodkovice CZ 39 C5
Hódmezövásárhely H 61 B5
Hodonín CZ 50 B3
Hodslavice CZ 50 A4
Hoedekenskerke NL 35 B4
Hoegaarden B 35 C5
Hoek van Holland NL 35 B5
Hoenderlo NL 36 A1
Hof D 38 C1
Hof N 20 B2
Hofbieber D 37 C5
Hofgeismar D 37 B5
Hofheim, *Bayern* D 37 C6
Hofheim, *Hessen* D 37 C4
Hofkirchen im Mühlkreis A 49 B4
Hofors S 22 A3
Höganäs S 27 C2
Hogdal S 21 B3
Högfors S 22 B2
Högklint S 23 D5
Högsäter S 21 C4
Högsby S 26 B6
Högsjö S 23 B2
Hogstad S 23 C2
Högyész H 60 B3
Hohen Neuendorf D 31 C5
Hohenau A 50 B2
Hohenberg A 49 C6
Hohenbucko D 38 B3
Hohenburg D 48 A2
Hohenems A 57 A4
Hohenhameln D 37 A6
Hohenhausen D 37 A4
Hohenlinden D 48 B2
Hohenlockstedt D 29 B6
Hohenmölsen D 38 B2
Hohennauen D 30 C4
Hohenseeden D 38 A2
Hohentauern A 59 A4
Hohentengen D 47 C4
Hohenwepel D 37 B5
Hohenwestedt D 29 A6
Hohenwutzen D 31 C6
Hohenzieritz D 31 B5
Hohn D 29 A6
Hohne D 30 C2
Hohnstorf D 30 B2
Højer DK 25 E1
Højslev Stby DK 24 C2
Hok S 26 B4
Hokenkirchen D 29 B4
Hökerum S 21 D5
Hökhuvud S 22 A5
Hokksund N 19 B6
Hökön S 26 C4
Hola Pristan UA 11 N23
Holbæk, *Aarhus Amt.* DK 24 C3
Holbæk, *Vestsjællands Amt.* DK 25 D4
Holdenstedt D 30 C2
Holdhus N 18 A2
Holdorf D 29 C5
Holeby DK 30 A3
Hølen N 20 B2
Holešov CZ 50 A3
Holguera E 79 B4
Holíč SK 50 B3
Holice CZ 39 C5
Holice SK 50 C3
Hollabrunn A 50 B2
Høllen N 19 C4
Hollfeld D 38 D1
Hollstadt D 37 C6
Hollum NL 28 B2
Höllviksnäs S 27 D2
Holmedal S 20 B3
Holmegil N 20 B3
Holmestrand N 20 B2
Holmsbu N 20 B2
Holmsjö S 27 C5
Holmsund S 3 E17
Hölö S 23 B4
Holsbybrunn S 26 B5
Holsljunga S 26 B2
Holstebro DK 25 C1
Holsted DK 25 D1
Holt N 19 C5
Holten NL 36 A2
Holtwick D 36 A3
Holum N 19 C4
Holwerd NL 28 B2
Holyhead GB 4 K4
Holýšov CZ 48 A4
Holzdorf D 38 B3
Holzhausen D 37 A4
Holzheim D 47 B6
Holzkirchen D 48 C2
Holzminden D 37 B5
Holzthaleben D 37 B6
Homberg, *Hessen* D 37 B5
Homberg, *Hessen* D 37 C5
Homburg D 46 A3
Hommelvik N 2 E12
Hommersåk N 18 C2
Homokmegy H 61 B4
Homokszentgyörgy H 60 B2
Homrogd H 51 B6
Homyel BY 7 K22
Hondarribia E 75 A5
Hondón de los Frailes E 82 C2
Hondschoote F 34 C3
Hönebach D 37 C5
Hønefoss N 20 A2
Honfleur F 43 A6
Høng DK 25 D4
Hönningen D 36 C2
Honningsvåg N 2 A20
Hönö S 24 B4
Honrubia E 81 C4
Hontalbilla E 74 C2
Hontianske-Nemce SK 51 B4
Hontoria de la Cantera E 75 B3
Hontoria de Valdearados E 75 C3
Hontoria del Pinar E 75 C3
Hoofddorp NL 35 A5
Hoogerheide NL 35 B5
Hoogeveen NL 28 C3
Hoogezand-Sappemeer NL 28 B3
Hoogkarspel NL 28 C2
Hoogkerk NL 28 B3
Hoogstede D 28 C3
Hoogstraten B 35 B5
Hooksiel D 29 B5
Höör S 27 D3
Hoorn NL 28 C2
Hopfgarten A 58 A2
Hopfgarten in Defereggen A 58 B2
Hopsten D 29 C4
Hoptrup DK 25 D2
Hora Svatého Sebestiána CZ 38 C3
Horaždóvice CZ 49 A4
Horb am Neckar D 47 B4
Horbelev DK 25 E5
Hørby DK 24 B3
Hörby S 27 D3
Horcajada de la Torre E 81 B4
Horcajo de los Montes E 80 C2
Horcajo de Santiago E 81 C3
Horcajo-Medianero E 80 B1
Horche E 81 B3
Horda S 26 B4
Hořesedly CZ 38 C3
Horezu RO 11 P19
Horgen CH 56 A3
Horgoš YU 61 B4
Hořice CZ 39 C5
Horjul SLO 59 B4
Horka D 39 B4
Hörken S 22 A1
Horki BY 7 J22
Hörle S 26 B4
Horn A 49 B6
Horn D 37 B4
Horn S 23 D2
Horna E 82 C1
Horná Mariková SK 50 A4
Horná Streda SK 50 B3
Horná Štrubna SK 51 B4
Horná Súča SK 50 B3
Hornachos E 79 C4
Hornachuelos E 85 B5
Hornanes N 18 B2
Hornbæk, *Aarhus Amt.* DK 24 C2
Hornbæk, *Frederiksværk* DK 27 C2
Hornberg D 47 B4
Hornburg D 37 A6
Horndal S 22 A3
Horne, *Fyns Amt.* DK 25 D3
Horne, *Ribe Amt.* DK 25 D1
Hörnebo S 21 C6
Horneburg D 29 B6
Horní Bečva CZ 50 A4
Horni Benešov CZ 50 A3
Horni Cerekev CZ 49 A6
Horní Jiřetín CZ 38 C3
Horní Lomná CZ 51 A4
Horni Maršov CZ 39 C5
Horní Planá CZ 49 B5
Horni Slavkov CZ 38 C2
Horni Vltavice CZ 49 B4
Hørning DK 25 C3
Hörningsholm S 23 B4
Hornnes N 19 C4
Horno D 39 B4
Hornos E 87 A3
Hornoy-le-Bourg F 44 A2
Hornslet DK 25 C3
Hornstein A 50 C2
Hörnum D 25 E1
Hornum DK 24 C2
Horný Tisovnik SK 51 B5
Horodenka UA 11 M19
Horodnya UA 11 L22
Horodok, *Khmelnytskyy* UA 11 M20
Horodok, *Lviv* UA 11 M18
Horodyshche UA 11 M22
Horokhiv UA 11 L19
Horovice CZ 49 A4
Horred S 26 B2
Hörsching A 49 B5
Horsens DK 25 D2
Horsham GB 4 L6
Hørsholm DK 27 D2
Horslunde DK 25 E4
Horšovský Týn CZ 48 A3
Horst NL 36 B2
Horstel D 36 A3
Horsten D 29 B4
Horstmar D 36 A3
Hort H 51 C5
Horta P 73 C3
Horten N 20 B2
Hortezuela E 75 C4
Hortiguela E 75 B3
Hortobágy H 61 A6
Hørve DK 25 D4
Hörvik S 27 C4
Hösbach D 37 C5
Hosena D 39 B4
Hosenfeld D 37 C5
Hosingen L 36 C2
Hospental CH 56 B3
Hossegor F 62 C1
Hosszuhetény H 60 B3
Hostal de Ipiés E 76 A2
Hoštálkova CZ 50 A3
Hostalric E 77 B5
Hostens F 62 B2
Hostěradice CZ 50 B2
Hostinné CZ 39 C5
Hostomice CZ 49 A5
Hostouň CZ 48 A3
Hoting S 2 D15
Hotton B 35 C6
Houdain F 34 C3
Houdan F 44 B2
Houdelaincourt F 46 B1
Houeillès F 62 B3
Houffalize B 36 C1
Houlgate F 43 A5
Hourtin F 52 C3
Hourtin-Plage F 52 C3
Houthalen B 35 B6
Houyet B 35 C5
Hov DK 25 D3
Hova S 21 C6
Høvåg N 19 C5
Hovden N 19 B4
Hovedgård DK 25 D2
Hovelhof D 37 B4
Hoven DK 25 D1
Hovmantorp S 26 C5
Hovsta S 22 B2
Höxter D 37 B5
Hoya D 29 C6
Hoya de Santa Maria E 85 B4
Hoya-Gonzalo E 82 C1
Høyanger N 2 F10
Hoyerswerda D 39 B4
Høyjord N 20 B2
Hoym D 38 B1
Hoyo de Manzanares E 80 B3
Hoyo de Pinares E 80 B2
Hoyocasero E 80 B2
Hoyos E 79 A4
Hoyos del Espino E 80 B1
Hrabusiče SK 51 B6
Hradec Králové CZ 39 C5
Hradec nad Moravicí CZ 50 A3
Hrádek CZ 50 B2
Hrádek nad Nisou CZ 39 C4
Hradište SK 51 B4
Hranice, *Severomoravsky* CZ 50 A3
Hranice, *Západočeský* CZ 38 C2
Hranovnica SK 51 B6
Hrasnica BIH 70 C3
Hrastnik SLO 59 B5
Hrebenka UA 7 L23
Hřensko CZ 39 C4
Hriňová SK 51 B5
Hrochov CZ 50 A2
Hrochův Tynec CZ 39 D5
Hrodna BY 6 K18
Hrodzyanka BY 7 K21
Hronov CZ 39 C6
Hronský Beňadik SK 51 B4
Hrotovice CZ 50 A2
Hrtkovci YU 71 B4
Hrušov SK 51 B5
Hrušovany nad Jevišovkou CZ 50 B2
Hřuštin SK 51 A5
Hrvaćani BIH 70 B2
Hrvace HR 69 C5
Hrymayliv UA 11 M20
Huben A 58 B2
Hückel-hoven D 36 B2
Hückeswagen D 36 B3
Hucqueliers F 34 C2
Huddersfield GB 4 K6
Huddinge S 22 B4
Huddunge S 22 A3
Hude D 29 B5
Hudiksvall S 2 F15
Huélago E 86 B2
Huélamo E 81 B5
Huelgoat F 42 B2
Huelma E 86 B2
Huelva E 85 B4
Huéneja E 86 B3
Huércal de Almeria E 87 C3
Huércal-Overa E 87 B4
Huerta de Abajo E 75 B3
Huerta de Valdecarabanos E 81 C3
Huerta del Rey E 75 C3
Huertahernando E 81 B4
Huesa E 86 B2
Huesca E 76 A2
Huéscar E 87 B3
Huete E 81 B4
Huétor Tájar E 86 B1
Hüfingen D 47 C4
Hufthamar N 18 A2
Huglfing D 48 C2
Huissen NL 36 B1
Huittinen FIN 3 F18
Huizen NL 35 A6
Hulín CZ 50 A3
Hüls D 36 B2
Hulsig DK 24 B3
Hulst NL 35 B5
Hult S 26 B5
Hulterstad S 26 C6
Hultsfred S 26 B5
Humanes E 81 B3
Humble DK 25 E3
Humenné SK 10 M17
Humilladero E 86 B1
Humlebæk DK 27 D2
Humlum DK 24 C1
Hummelsta S 22 B3
Humpolec CZ 49 A6
Hundested DK 25 D4
Hundvåg N 18 B2
Hunedoara RO 11 P18
Hünfeld D 37 C5
Hungen D 37 C4
Hunnebostrand S 21 C3
Hunstanton GB 4 K7
Huntly GB 4 H5
Hünxe D 36 B2
Hurbanovo SK 50 C4
Hürbel D 47 B5
Hurdal N 20 A3
Hurezani RO 11 P18
Hürth D 36 C2
Hurup DK 24 C1
Husby D 25 E2
Husby DK 25 C1
Huşi RO 11 N21
Husina BIH 70 B3
Husínec CZ 49 A4
Huskvarna S 26 B4
Husnes N 18 B2
Hüsten D 36 B3
Hustopeče CZ 50 B2
Hustopeče nad Bečvou CZ 50 A3
Husum D 29 A6
Huta PL 32 C2
Hutovo BIH 70 D2
Hüttenberg A 59 B4
Hüttlingen D 47 B6
Hüttschlag A 58 A3
Huttwil CH 56 A2
Huy B 35 C6
Hval N 20 A2
Hvåle N 19 A6
Hvaler N 21 B3
Hvalpsund DK 24 C2
Hvar HR 69 C5
Hvarnes N 19 B6
Hvidbjerg DK 24 C1
Hvide Sande DK 25 D1
Hvittingfoss N 19 B7
Hybe SK 51 A5
Hycklinge S 23 D2
Hyères F 65 C5
Hyéres Plage F 65 C5
Hylestad N 19 B4
Hylke DK 25 D2
Hyllstofta S 27 C3
Hyltebruk S 26 B3
Hynnekleiv N 19 C5
Hyvinkää FIN 3 F19

I

Iam RO 71 A6
Iaşi RO 11 N20
Ibahernando E 79 B5
Ibarranguelua E 75 A4
Ibbenbüren D 36 A3
Ibeas de Juarros E 75 B3
Ibi E 82 C2
Ibros E 86 A2
Ichenhausen D 47 B6
Ichnya UA 7 L23
Ichtegem B 35 B4
Ichtershausen D 37 C6
Idanha-a-Novo P 79 B3
Idar-Oberstein D 46 A3
Idd N 21 B3
Idiazábal E 75 B4
Idkerberget S 22 A2
Idön S 22 A5
Idre S 2 F13
Idrija SLO 59 C4
Idritsa RUS 7 H21
Idstein D 36 C4
Idvor YU 61 C5
Iecca Mare RO 61 C5
Ielsi I 89 B4
Ieper B 34 C3
Ierápetra GR 16 U19
Ierissós GR 15 R18
Iesi I 68 C2
Ig SLO 59 C4
Igal H 60 B2
Igea E 75 B4
Igea Marina I 68 B1
Igelfors S 23 C2
Igersheim D 47 A5
Iggesund S 2 F15
Iglesias E 74 B3
Iglésias I 96 D1
Igls A 57 A6
Iğneada TR 16 R21
Igny-Comblizy F 45 A4
Igorre E 75 A4
Igoumenítsa GR 15 S17
Igries E 76 A2
Igualada E 77 B4
Igüeña E 72 B4
Iguerande F 54 B4
Iharosberény H 60 B2
Ihl'any SK 51 A6
Ihlienworth D 29 B5
Ihringen D 46 B3
Ihrlerstein D 48 B2
Ii FIN 3 D19
Iisalmi FIN 3 E20
IJmuiden NL 28 C1
IJsselmuiden NL 28 C2
IJzendijke NL 35 B4
Ikast DK 25 C2
Ikervár H 60 A1
il Castagno I 67 C4
Ilandža YU 61 C5
Ilanz CH 57 B4
Ilava SK 50 B4
Iława PL 33 B5
Ilche E 76 B3
Ilfracombe GB 4 L4
Ílhavo P 78 A2
Ilidža BIH 70 C3
Ilijaš BIH 70 C3
Ilirska Bistrica SLO 59 C4
Ilkley GB 4 K6
Illana E 81 B4
Illano E 72 A4
Illar E 87 C3
Illas E 74 A1
Illats F 62 B2
Ille-sur-Têt F 77 A5
Illertissen D 47 B6
Illescas E 80 B3
Illfurth F 46 C3
Illichivsk UA 11 N22
Illiers-Combray F 44 B2
Illkirch-Graffenstaden F 46 B3
Illmersdorf D 38 B3
Illmitz A 50 C2
Íllora E 86 B2
Illueca E 75 C5
Ilmajoki FIN 3 E18
Ilmenau D 37 C6
Ilok HR 61 C4
Ilomantsi FIN 3 E22
Iłow PL 33 C6
Iłowa PL 39 B5
Iłowo-Osada PL 33 B6
Ilsenburg D 37 B6
Ilshofen D 47 A5
Ilz A 59 A5
Iłża PL 41 B6
Imatra FIN 3 F21
Imielin PL 41 C4
Imingen N 19 A5
Immeln S 27 C4
Immenhausen D 37 B5
Immenstadt D 57 A5
Ímola I 67 B5
Imon E 81 A4
Imotski HR 70 C2
Impéria I 66 C2
Imphy F 54 B3
Imsland N 18 B2
Imst A 57 A5
Inari FIN 3 B20
Inca, *Mallorca* E 83
Incinillas E 75 B3
Indjija YU 71 A5
İnegöl TR 16 R21
Inerthal CH 56 A3

Infiesto E 74 A1
Ingatorp S 26 B5
Ingedal N 20 B3
Ingelheim D 36 D4
Ingelmunster B 35 C4
Ingelstad S 26 C4
Ingolfsland N 19 B5
Ingolstadt D 48 B2
Ingrandes, *Maine-et-Loire* F 52 A4
Ingrandes, *Vienne* F 53 B5
Ingwiller F 46 B3
Inhulec UA 11 N23
Iniesta E 81 C5
Inke H 60 B2
Innertkirchen CH 56 B3
Innervillgraten A 58 B2
Innsbruck A 57 A6
Inowłódz PL 41 B5
Inowrocław PL 33 C4
Ins CH 56 A2
Ińsko PL 32 B1
Interlaken CH 56 B2
Intragna CH 56 B3
Introbio I 57 C4
Invergordon GB 4 H4
Inverness GB 4 H4
Inveruno I 56 C3
Inverurie GB 4 H5
Ioánnina GR 15 S17
Iolanda di Savoia I 67 B5
Ion Corvin RO 11 P20
Ióppolo I 92 C2
İpsala TR 16 R20
Ipswich GB 4 K7
Iráklion GR 16 U19
Irdning A 59 A4
Iregszemcse H 60 B3
Irgoli I 96 C2
Irig YU 71 A4
Ironbridge GB 4 K5
Irpin UA 11 L22
Irrel D 46 A2
Irsina I 90 B3
Iruela E 73 B4
Irún E 75 A5
Irurita E 62 C1
Irurzun E 75 B5
Irvine GB 4 J4
Is-sur-Tille F 55 A5
Isaba E 62 D2
Isabela E 86 A2
Isaszeg H 61 A4
Íscar E 74 C2
Ischgl A 57 A5
Íschia I 89 C3
Ischia di Castro I 88 A1
Ischitella I 90 A2
Isdes F 44 C3
Ise N 20 B3
Iselle I 56 B3
Iseltwald CH 56 B2
Isen D 48 B3
Isenbüttel D 30 C2
Iseo I 57 C5
Iserlohn D 36 B3
Isérnia I 89 B4
Isigny-sur-Mer F 43 A4
Ísili I 96 D2
Isla Canela E 84 B3
Isla Cristina E 84 B3
Islares E 75 A3
Ismaning D 48 B2
Isna P 78 B3
Isny D 47 C6
Isoba E 74 A1
Isola F 65 B6
Isola del Gran Sasso d'Itália I 89 A3
Ísola del Liri I 89 B3
Ísola della Scala I 57 C6
Isola delle Fémmine I 94 A2
Ísola di Capo Rizzuto I 93 C4
Isona E 77 A4
Ispagnac F 64 B2
Isparta TR 16 T22
Isperikh BG 16 Q20
Íspica I 95 C3
Isselburg D 36 B2
Issigeac F 63 B3
Issogne I 56 C2
Issoire F 54 C3
Issoncourt F 45 B6
Issoudun F 54 B2
Issum D 36 B2
Issy-l'Evêque F 54 B3
Istán E 86 C1
İstanbul TR 16 R21
Istebna PL 51 A4
Ístia d'Ombrone I 67 D5
Istiaia GR 15 S18
Istok YU 71 D5
Istres, *Bouches du Rhône* F 64 C3
Istvándi H 60 B2
Itoiz E 62 D1
Ítrabo E 86 C2
Itri I 89 B3
Ittireddu I 96 C1
Íttiri I 96 C1
Itzehoe D 29 B6
Ivalo FIN 3 B20
Iván H 60 A1
Ivanava BY 7 K19
Ivančice CZ 50 B4
Ivančna Gorica SLO 59 C4
Iváncsa H 61 A3
Ivanec HR 59 B6
Ivanić Grad HR 59 C6
Ivanjica YU 71 C5
Ivanjska BIH 70 B2
Ivanka SK 50 B4
Ivankovo HR 60 C3
Ivano-Frankivsk UA 11 M19
Ivanovice na Hané CZ 50 A3
Ivanska HR 60 C1
Ivatsevichy BY 7 K19
Ivoz Ramet B 35 C6
Ivrea I 56 C2
Ivry-en-Montagne F 55 A4
Ivry-la-Bataille F 44 B2
Iwaniska PL 41 C6
Iwiny PL 39 B5
Iwuy F 35 C4
Izarra E 75 B4
Izbica Kujawska PL 33 C4
Izbište YU 71 A6
Izeda P 73 C4
Izegem B 35 C4
Izernore F 55 B5
Izmayil UA 11 P21
İzmir TR 16 S20
Iznájar E 86 B1
Iznalloz E 86 B2
Iznatoraf E 86 A2
İznik TR 16 R21
Izola SLO 58 C3
Izsák H 61 B4
Izsófalva H 51 B6
Izyaslav UA 11 L20

J

Jabalquinto E 86 A2
Jablanac HR 69 B3
Jablanica BIH 70 C2
Jablonec nad Jizerou CZ 39 C5
Jablonec nad Nisou CZ 39 C5
Jablonica SK 50 B3
Jablonka PL 51 A5
Jabłonna PL 41 A5
Jablonné nad Orlicí CZ 40 C1
Jablonne Podještědí CZ 39 C4
Jablonov nad Turňou SK 51 B6
Jabłonowo Pomorskie PL 33 B5
Jablúnka CZ 50 A3
Jablunkov CZ 51 A4
Jabučje YU 71 B5
Jabugo E 85 B4
Jabuka YU 71 B5
Jabuka YU 71 C4
Jabukovac HR 59 C6
Jaca E 76 A2
Jáchymov CZ 38 C2
Jacobidrebber D 29 C5
Jade D 29 B5
Jadraque E 81 B4
Jægerspris DK 25 D4
Jaén E 86 B2
Jagare BIH 70 B2
Jagel D 29 A6
Jagenbach A 49 B6
Jagodina YU 71 C6
Jagodnjak HR 60 C3
Jagodzin PL 39 B5
Jagstheim D 47 A6
Jagstzell D 47 A6
Jahodna SK 50 B3
Jajce BIH 70 B2
Ják H 60 A1
Jakabszállás H 61 B4
Jaklovce SK 51 B6
Jakovlje HR 59 C5
Jakšic HR 60 C2
Jakubany SK 51 A6
Jalance E 82 B1
Jalasjärvi FIN 3 E18
Jalhay B 36 C1
Jaligny-sur-Besbre F 54 B3
Jallais F 52 A4
Jalón E 82 C2
Jâlons F 45 B5
Jamena YU 70 B4
Jamilena E 86 B2
Jämjö S 27 C5
Jamnička Kiselica HR 59 C5
Jamno PL 32 A2
Jamoigne B 45 A6
Jämsä FIN 3 F19
Jämshög S 27 C4
Janakkala FIN 3 F19
Jandelsbrunn D 49 B4
Jänickendorf D 38 A3
Janikowo PL 33 C4
Janja BIH 71 B4
Janjina HR 70 D2
Janki PL 41 A5
Janki PL 41 B4
Jankov CZ 49 A5
Jankowo Dolne PL 32 C3
Jánoshalma H 61 B4
Jánosháza H 60 A2
Jánoshida H 61 A5
Jánossomorja H 50 C3
Janovice nad Uhlavou CZ 49 A4
Janów PL 41 C4
Janowiec Wielkopolski PL 32 C3
Janowo PL 33 B6
Janville F 44 B2
Janzé F 43 C4
Jarabá SK 51 B5
Jaraczewo PL 40 B2
Jarafuel E 82 B1
Jaraicejo E 79 B5
Jaraíz de la Vera E 79 A5
Jarak YU 71 B4
Jarandilla de la Vera E 79 A5
Jaray E 75 C4
Jard-sur-Mer F 52 B3
Jaren N 20 A2
Jargeau F 44 C3
Jarkovac YU 61 C5
Järlåsa S 22 B4
Jarmen D 31 B5
Järna S 23 B4
Jarnac F 53 C4
Järnforsen S 26 B5
Jarny F 46 A1
Jarocin PL 40 B2
Jaroměř CZ 39 C5
Jaroměřice nad Rokytnou CZ 50 A1
Jaroslav CZ 39 C6
Jaroslavice CZ 50 B2
Jarosław PL 11 L18
Jaroslawiec PL 32 A2
Jarošov nad Nežarkou CZ 49 A6
Järpås S 21 C4
Järpen S 2 E13
Järvenpää FIN 3 F19
Jarvorník CZ 40 C1
Jarzé F 53 A4
Jaša Tomic YU 61 C5
Jasenak HR 59 C5
Jasenica BIH 69 B5
Jasenice HR 69 B4
Jasenovac HR 60 C1
Jasenovo YU 71 B6
Jasenovo YU 71 C4
Jasień PL 39 B5
Jasienica PL 39 B4
Jasika YU 71 C6
Jasło PL 10 M17
Jasov SK 51 B6
Jásova SK 51 C4
Jasseron F 55 B5
Jastarnia PL 33 A4
Jastrebarsko HR 59 C5
Jastrowie PL 32 B2
Jastrzębia-Góra PL 33 A4
Jastrzębie Zdrój PL 51 A4
Jászals-Lószentgyörgy H 61 A5
Jászapáti H 61 A5
Jászárokszállás H 51 C5
Jászberény H 61 A4
Jászdózsa H 51 C6
Jászfényszaru H 51 C5
Jászjakóhalma H 61 A5
Jászkarajenö H 61 A5
Jászkisér H 61 A5
Jászladány H 61 A5
Jászszentlászló H 61 B4
Jásztelek H 61 A5
Játar E 86 C2
Jatznick D 31 B5
Jaun CH 56 B2
Jausiers F 65 B5
Jávea E 82 C3
Jävenitz D 30 C3
Javerlhac F 53 C5
Javier E 76 A1
Javorani BIH 70 B2
Javorina SK 51 A6
Javron F 43 B5
Jawor PL 39 B6
Jaworzno PL 41 C4
Jaworzyna Śl. PL 40 C1
Jayena E 86 C2
Jażow PL 39 B4
Jebel RO 61 C6
Jebjerg DK 24 C2
Jedburgh GB 4 J5
Jedlinsk PL 41 B6
Jedlnia PL 41 B6
Jedlnia Letnisko PL 41 B6
Jedovnice CZ 50 A2
Jędrychow PL 33 B5
Jędrzejów PL 41 C5
Jedwabno PL 33 B6
Jegłownik PL 33 A5
Jegun F 63 C3
Jēkabpils LV 7 H19
Jektevik N 18 B2
Jelakci YU 71 C5
Jelcz-Laskowice PL 40 B2
Jelenec SK 50 B4
Jelenia Góra PL 39 C5
Jelgava LV 6 H18
Jelka SK 50 B3
Jelling DK 25 D2
Jels DK 25 D2
Jelsa HR 69 C5
Jelsa N 18 B3
Jelšava SK 51 B6
Jemgum D 29 B4
Jemnice CZ 49 A6
Jena D 38 C1
Jenaz CH 57 B4
Jenbach A 58 A1
Jenikow PL 31 B7
Jennersdorf A 59 B6
Jenny S 23 D3
Jerchel D 30 C3
Jeres del Marquesado E 86 B2
Jerez de la Frontera E 85 C4
Jerez de los Caballeros E 85 A4
Jerica E 82 B2
Jerichow D 30 C4
Jerka PL 40 A1
Jermenovci YU 61 C4
Jerslev DK 24 B3
Jerte E 79 A5
Jerup DK 24 B3
Jerxheim D 37 A6
Jerzmanowice PL 41 C4
Jerzu I 96 D2
Jerzwałd PL 33 B5
Jesberg D 37 C5
Jesenice, *Středočeský* CZ 38 C3
Jesenice, *Středočeský* CZ 39 D4
Jesenice SLO 59 B4
Jeseník CZ 40 C2
Jesenké SK 51 B6
Jésolo I 58 C2
Jessen D 38 B2
Jessheim N 20 A3
Jessnitz D 38 B2
Jesteburg D 30 B1
Jeumont F 35 C5
Jeven-stedt D 29 A6
Jever D 29 B4
Jevíčko CZ 50 A2
Jevišovice CZ 50 B1
Jevnaker N 20 A2
Jezerane HR 69 A4
Jezero BIH 70 B2
Jezero HR 69 A4
Jeziorany PL 33 B6
Jezów PL 41 B4
Jičín CZ 39 C5
Jičíněves CZ 39 C5
Jihlava CZ 49 A6
Jijona E 82 C2
Jilemnice CZ 39 C5
Jilové CZ 39 C4
Jilové u Prahy CZ 49 A5
Jimbolia RO 61 C5
Jimena E 86 B2
Jimena de la Frontera E 85 C5
Jimera de Libar E 85 C5
Jimramov CZ 50 A2
Jince CZ 49 A4
Jindřichovice CZ 38 C2
Jindřichův Hradec CZ 49 A6
Jirkov CZ 38 C3
Jistebnice CZ 49 A5
Joachimsthal D 31 C5
João da Loura P 84 A2
Jobbágyi H 51 C5
Jochberg A 58 A2
Jódar E 86 B2
Jodoigne B 35 C5
Joensuu FIN 3 E21
Jœuf F 46 A1
Jõgeva EST 7 G20
Johann-georgen-stadt D 38 C2
Johannishus S 27 C5
Johanniskirchen D 48 B3
Johansfors S 26 C5
John o'Groats GB 4 G5
Jõhvi EST 7 G20
Joigny F 45 C4
Joinville F 45 B6
Jokkmokk S 3 C16
Jöllenbeck D 37 A4
Jönåker S 23 C3
Jonava LT 6 J19
Jonchery-sur-Vesle F 45 A4
Jondal N 18 A3
Jondalen N 19 B6
Joniškis LT 6 H18
Jönköping S 26 B4
Jønnbu N 19 B6
Jonsered S 21 D4
Jonstorp S 27 C2
Jonzac F 53 C4
Jorba E 77 B4
Jordanów PL 51 A5
Jordanów Ślaski PL 40 C1
Jordanowo PL 39 A5
Jordbro S 23 C4
Jördenstorf D 31 B4
Jordøse DK 25 D3
Jork D 29 B6
Jörn S 3 D17
Jørpeland N 18 B3
Jorquera E 82 B1
Jošan HR 69 B4
Jošanička Banja YU 71 C5
Jošavka BIH 70 B2
Josipdol HR 59 C5
Josipovac HR 60 C3
Jössefors S 20 B4
Josselin F 42 C3
Jósvafö H 51 B6
Jouarre F 45 B4
Joué-lès-Tours F 53 A5
Joué-sur-Erdre F 52 A3
Joure NL 28 C2
Joutseno FIN 3 F21
Joux-la-Ville F 45 C4
Jouy F 44 B2
Jouy-le-Châtel F 45 B4
Jouy-le-Potier F 44 C2
Joyeuse F 64 B3
Joze F 54 C3
Józefów PL 41 A6
Juan-les-Pins F 65 C6
Juankoski FIN 3 E21
Jübek D 29 A6
Jubera E 75 B4
Jubrique E 85 C5
Jüchsen D 37 C6
Judaberg N 18 B2
Judenburg A 59 A4
Juelsminde DK 25 D3
Jugon-les-Lacs F 43 B3
Juillac F 53 C6
Juillan F 62 C3
Juist D 29 B4
Julianadorp NL 28 C1
Jülich D 36 C2
Jullouville F 43 B4
Jumeaux F 54 C3
Jumièges F 44 A1
Jumilhac-le-Grand F 53 C6
Jumilla E 87 A4
Juncosa E 76 B3
Juneda E 76 B3
Jung S 21 C5
Jungingen D 47 B5
Junglingster L 46 A2
Juniville F 45 A5
Junosuando S 3 C18
Junqueira P 73 C3
Juprelle B 35 C6
Jurata PL 33 A4
Jurbarkas LT 6 J18
Jurjevo HR 69 B3
Jūrmala LV 6 H18
Juromenha P 78 C3
Jursla S 23 C3
Jussac F 63 B5
Jussey F 46 C1
Jussy F 45 A4
Juta H 60 B2
Jüterbog D 38 B3
Juuka FIN 3 E21
Juvigny-le-Terte F 43 B4
Juvigny-sous-Andaine F 43 B5
Juzennecourt F 45 B5
Jyderup DK 25 D4
Jyväskylä FIN 3 E19

K

Kaamanen FIN 3 B20
Kaarssen D 30 B3
Kaatscheuvel NL 35 B6
Kaba H 61 A6
Kåbdalis S 3 C16
Kačarevo YU 71 B5
Kačikol YU 71 D6
Kács H 51 C6
Kadan CZ 38 C3
Kadarkút H 60 B2
Kaduy RUS 7 G25
Kågeröd S 27 D3
Kahl D 37 C5
Kahla D 38 C1
Kainach bei Voitsberg A 59 A5
Kaindorf A 59 A5
Kaisersesch D 36 C3
Kaiserslautern D 46 A3
Kaisheim D 48 B1
Kajaani FIN 3 D20
Kajárpéc H 60 A2
Kajdacs H 60 B3
Kakanj BIH 70 B3
Kakasd H 60 B3
Kakolewo PL 40 B1
Kál H 51 C6
Kalabáka GR 15 S17
Kalače YU 71 D5
Kalajoki FIN 3 D18
Kalámai GR 15 T18
Kalbe D 30 C3
Kalce SLO 59 C4
Káld H 60 A2
Kale TR 16 T21
Kalefeld D 37 B6
Kalenić YU 71 C5
Kalesija BIH 70 B3
Kalety PL 40 C3
Kalevala RUS 3 D22
Kalhovd N 19 A5
Kali HR 69 B4
Kaliningrad RUS 33 A6
Kalinkavichy BY 7 K21
Kalinovac HR 60 B2
Kalinovik BIH 70 C3
Kalinovo SK 51 B5
Kaliska PL 33 A4
Kaliska PL 33 B4
Kalisko PL 41 B4
Kalisz PL 40 B3
Kalisz Pomorski PL 32 B1
Kalix S 3 D18
Kalkan TR 16 T21
Kalkar D 36 B2
Kall D 36 C2
Källby S 21 C5
Kållered S 21 D4
Kållerstad S 26 B3
Kallinge S 27 C5
Kallmünz D 48 A2
Kållvik S 23 C4
Kalmar S 26 C6
Kalmthout B 35 B5
Kalná SK 51 B4
Kalocsa H 61 B3
Káloz H 60 B3
Kals A 58 B2
Kalsdorf A 59 B5
Kaltbrunn CH 56 A4
Kaltenbach A 58 A1
Kaltenkirchen D 30 B1
Kaltennordheim D 37 C6
Kaluga RUS 7 J25
Kalundborg DK 25 D4
Kalush UA 11 M19
Kałuszyn PL 41 A6
Kalvehave DK 25 D5
Kalwang A 59 A4
Kalwaria-Zebrzydowska PL 51 A5
Kalyazin RUS 7 H25
Kam H 60 A1
Kamen D 36 B3
Kamenice CZ 50 A1
Kamenice nad Lipou CZ 49 A6
Kameničná SK 50 C4
Kamenný Most SK 51 C4
Kamenny Ujezd CZ 49 B5
Kamenska HR 60 C2
Kamensko HR 70 C1
Kamenz D 39 B4
Kamičak BIH 69 B5
Kamień PL 41 B5
Kamień Krajeński PL 32 B3
Kamień Pomorski PL 31 B6
Kamieniec Zabk PL 40 C1
Kamienka SK 51 A6
Kamienna Góra PL 39 C6
Kamieńsk PL 41 B4
Kaminka UA 11 M23
Kamnik SLO 59 B4
Kamp-Lintfort D 36 B2
Kampen NL 28 C2
Kampinos PL 41 A5
Kampor HR 69 B3
Kamyanets-Podil's'kyy UA 11 M20
Kamyanka-Buz'ka UA 11 L19
Kamýk n Vltavou CZ 49 A5
Kanal SLO 58 B3
Kandalaksha RUS 3 C23
Kandel D 47 A4
Kandern D 46 C3
Kandersteg CH 56 B2
Kandıra TR 16 R22
Kandyty PL 33 A6
Kanfanar HR 68 A2
Kangasala FIN 3 F19
Kaniów PL 39 B4
Kanjiža YU 61 B5
Kankaanpää FIN 3 F18
Kannus FIN 3 E18
Kapellen A 49 C6
Kapellen B 35 B5
Kapellskär S 22 B6
Kapfenberg A 59 A5
Kapfenstein A 59 B5
Kaplice CZ 49 B5
Kapljuh BIH 69 B5
Kápolna H 51 C6
Kápolnásnyék H 60 A3
Kaposfö H 60 B2
Kaposfüred H 60 B2
Kaposszekcsö H 60 B3
Kaposvár H 60 B2
Kappel D 46 B3
Kappeln D 30 A1
Kappelshamn S 23 D5
Kappl A 57 A5
Kaprun A 58 A2
Kaptol HR 60 C2
Kapuvár H 50 C3
Karabiğa TR 16 R20
Karaburun TR 16 S20
Karacabey TR 16 R21
Karacasu TR 16 T21
Karachev RUS 7 K24
Karácsond H 51 C6
Karád H 60 B2
Karan YU 71 C4
Karancslapujto H 51 B5
Karasjok N 3 B19
Karasu TR 16 R22
Karbenning S 22 A3
Kårberg S 23 C1
Karby D 30 A1
Karby DK 24 C1
Karby S 22 B5
Karcag H 61 A5
Karczew PL 41 A6
Karczów PL 40 C2
Karczowiska PL 39 B6
Kardašova Řečice CZ 49 A5
Kardhítsa GR 15 S17
Kärdla EST 6 G18
Kardoskút H 61 B5
Kargowa PL 39 A5
Karise DK 27 D2
Káristos GR 16 S19
Karkal TR 16 R21
Karkkila FIN 3 F19
Karl Liebknecht RUS 7 L24
Karlholmsbruk S 22 A4
Karlino PL 32 A1
Karlobag HR 69 B4
Karlovac HR 59 C5
Karlovčic YU 71 B5
Karlovice CZ 40 C2
Karlovo BG 16 Q19
Karlovy Vary CZ 38 C2
Karłowice PL 40 C2
Karlsborg S 23 C1
Karlshamn S 27 C4
Karlshöfen D 29 B6
Karlshus N 20 B2
Karlskoga S 22 B1
Karlskrona S 27 C5
Karlsrud N 19 A5
Karlsruhe D 47 A4
Karlstad S 20 B5
Karlstadt D 37 D5
Karlstetten A 49 B6
Karlstift A 49 B5
Karmacs H 60 B2
Kärna S 21 D3
Karnobat BG 16 Q20
Karojba HR 58 C3
Karow D 30 B4
Karpacz PL 39 C5
Kärrbo S 22 B3
Karrebaeksminde DK 25 D4
Karsin PL 32 B3
Kårsta S 22 B5
Karstädt D 30 B3
Kartitsch A 58 B2
Kartuzy PL 33 A4
Karup DK 25 C2
Karviná CZ 51 A4
Kås DK 24 B2
Kaş TR 16 T21
Kašava CZ 50 A3
Kasejovice CZ 49 A4
Kashin RUS 7 H25
Kašina HR 59 C6
Kasina-Wielka PL 51 A6
Kaskinen FIN 3 E17
Kašperské Hory CZ 49 A4
Kassel D 37 B5
Kastav HR 59 C4
Kaštel-Stari HR 69 C5
Kaštel Zegarski HR 69 B4
Kastellaun D 36 C3
Kastélli GR 16 U18
Kasterlee B 35 B5
Kastl D 48 A2
Kastlösa S 26 C6
Kastorf D 30 B2
Kastoría GR 15 R17
Kastsyukovichy BY 7 K23
Kaszaper H 61 B5
Katerbow D 31 C4
Kateríni GR 15 R18
Katlenburg-Lindau D 37 B6
Katovice CZ 49 A4
Katowice PL 41 C4
Katrineholm S 23 C3
Kattarp S 27 C2
Kattilstorp S 21 C5
Katwijk NL 35 A5
Kąty Wrocławskie PL 40 B1
Katymár H 61 B4
Katzenelnbogen D 36 C3
Katzhütte D 38 C1
Kaub D 36 C3
Kaufbeuren D 48 C1
Kauhajoki FIN 3 E18
Kauhava FIN 3 E18
Kaulsdorf D 38 C1
Kaunas LT 6 J18
Kaupanger N 2 F10
Kautokeino N 3 B18
Kautzen A 49 B6
Kavajë AL 15 R16
Kavála GR 16 R19
Kavarna BG 16 Q21
Kävlinge S 27 D3
Kawcze PL 32 A2
Kaxholmen S 26 B4
Kaysersberg F 46 B3
Kazanlŭk BG 16 Q19
Kazár H 51 B5
Kazimierza Wielka PL 41 C5
Kazincbarcika H 51 B6
Kaźmierz PL 32 C2
Kcynia PL 32 B3
Kdyně CZ 48 A4
Kecel H 61 B4
Kecskemét H 61 B4
Kėdainiai LT 6 J18
Kędzierzyn-Koźle PL 40 C3
Keerbergen B 35 B5
Kehl D 46 B3
Kehrigk D 39 A3
Keighley GB 4 K6
Keila EST 6 G19
Kelberg D 36 C2
Kelbra D 38 B1
Kelč CZ 50 A3
Kelchsau A 58 A2
Kelebia H 61 B4
Kelemér H 51 B6
Kelheim D 48 B2
Kell D 46 A2
Kellinghusen D 29 B6
Kelmis B 36 C2
Kelsterbach D 37 C4
Kematen A 57 A6
Kemberg D 38 B2
Kemer TR 16 T22
Kemeten A 59 A6
Kemi FIN 3 D19
Kemijärvi FIN 3 C20
Kemnath D 48 A2
Kemnitz, *Brandenburg* D 38 A2
Kemnitz, *Mecklenburg-Vorpommern* D 31 A5
Kempen D 36 B2
Kempten D 47 C6
Kemptthal CH 56 A3
Kendal GB 4 J5
Kenderes H 61 A5
Kengyel H 61 A5
Kenyeri H 60 A2
Kenzingen D 46 B3
Kępice PL 32 A2
Kępno PL 40 B3
Kerava FIN 3 F19
Kerecsend H 51 C6
Kerekegyhaza H 61 B4
Kerepestarcsa H 61 A4
Kérien F 42 B2
Kerkafalva H 59 B6
Kerken D 36 B2
Kerkira GR 15 S16
Kerkrade NL 36 C2
Kerlouan F 42 B1
Kernascléden F 42 B2
Kernhof A 49 C6
Kerns CH 56 B3
Kerpen D 36 C2
Kerta H 60 A2
Kerteminde DK 25 D3
Kerzers CH 56 B2
Keşan TR 16 R20
Kesselfall A 58 A2
Kestenga RUS 3 D22
Keszthely H 60 B2
Kétegyháza H 61 B6
Kéthely H 60 B2
Kętrzyn PL 6 J17
Kettering GB 4 K6
Kęty PL 51 A5
Ketzin D 31 C4
Keuruu FIN 3 E19
Kevelaer D 36 B2
Kevermes H 61 B6
Kevi YU 61 C4
Kežmarok SK 51 A6
Khalkís GR 15 S18
Khaniá GR 16 U19
Kharkiv UA 7 L25
Kharmanli BG 16 R19
Khaskovo BG 16 R19
Kherson UA 11 N23
Khimki RUS 7 J25
Khíos GR 16 S20
Khmelnik UA 11 M20
Khmelnytskyy UA 11 M20
Khodoriv UA 11 M19
Kholm RUS 7 H22
Khóra Sfakion GR 16 U19
Khorol UA 11 M23
Khotyn UA 11 M20
Khoyniki BY 11 L21
Khust UA 11 M18
Khvoynaya RUS 7 G24
Kınık TR 16 S20
Kırka TR 16 S22
Kırklareli TR 16 R20
Kızılhisar TR 16 T21
Kiáton GR 15 T18
Kibæk DK 25 C1
Kiefersfelden D 48 C3
Kiel D 30 A1
Kielce PL 41 C5
Kiełczygłów PL 41 B4
Kiełpino PL 33 A4
Kielpiny PL 33 B5
Kiernozia PL 41 A4
Kierspe D 36 B3
Kietrz PL 40 C3
Kietz D 31 C6
Kiezmark PL 33 A4
Kifino Selo BIH 70 C3
Kije PL 41 C5
Kijevo HR 69 C5
Kikinda YU 61 C5
Kil N 19 C6
Kil, *Örebro* S 22 B2
Kil, *Värmland* S 20 B5
Kila S 20 B4
Kilb Rabenstein A 49 B6
Kildare IRL 4 K3
Kildinstroy RUS 3 B23
Kilegrend N 19 B5
Kilen N 19 B5
Kilimli TR 16 R22
Kiliya UA 11 P21
Kilkee IRL 4 K2
Kilkenny IRL 4 K3
Kilkís GR 15 R18
Killarney IRL 4 K2
Killeberg S 26 C4
Kilmarnock GB 4 J4
Kilrush IRL 4 K2
Kilsmo S 23 B2
Kimasozero RUS 3 D22
Kimi GR 16 S19
Kimovsk RUS 7 J25
Kimratshofen D 47 C6
Kimry RUS 7 H25
Kimstad S 23 C2
Kindberg A 59 A5
Kindelbruck D 38 B1
Kingisepp RUS 7 G21
King's Lynn GB 4 K7
Kingston upon Hull GB 4 K6
Kinna S 26 B2
Kinnared S 26 B3
Kinnarp S 21 C5
Kinne-Kleva S 21 C5
Kinrooi B 36 B1
Kinsale IRL 4 L2
Kiparissía GR 15 T17
Kipfenburg D 48 B2
Kirberg D 36 C4
Kirchbach in Steiermark A 59 B5
Kirchberg CH 56 A2
Kirchberg, *Baden-Württemberg* D 47 A5
Kirchberg, *Rheinland-Pfalz* D 46 A3
Kirchberg am Wechsel A 50 C1
Kirchberg an der Pielach A 49 B6
Kirchberg im Tirol A 58 A2
Kirchbichl A 58 A2
Kirchdorf, *Bayern* D 49 B4
Kirchdorf, *Mecklenburg-Vorpommern* D 30 B3
Kirchdorf, *Niedersachsen* D 29 C5
Kirchdorf an der Krems A 49 C5
Kirchdorf in Tirol A 58 A2
Kirchenlamitz D 38 C1
Kirchenthumbach D 48 A2
Kirchhain D 37 C4
Kirchheim, *Baden-Württemberg* D 47 B5
Kirchheim, *Bayern* D 47 B6
Kirchheim, *Hessen* D 37 C5
Kirchheim-bolanden D 47 A4
Kirchhundem D 36 B4
Kirchlintein D 29 C6
Kirchschlag A 59 A6
Kirchweidach D 48 B3
Kirchzarten D 46 C3
Kirillov RUS 7 G26
Kirishi RUS 7 G23
Kirkcaldy GB 4 H5
Kirkcudbright GB 4 J4
Kirkehamn N 18 C3
Kirkenær N 20 A4
Kirkenes N 3 B22
Kirkkonummi FIN 3 F19
Kirkwall GB 4 G5
Kirn D 46 A3
Kirov RUS 7 J24
Kirovohrad UA 11 M23
Kirovsk RUS 3 C23
Kirtorf D 37 C5
Kiruna S 3 C17
Kisa S 23 D2
Kisač YU 61 C4
Kisbér H 60 A3
Kiseljak BIH 70 C3
Kisielice PL 33 B5
Kisköre H 61 A5
Kiskörös H 61 B4
Kiskunfélegyháza H 61 B4
Kiskunhalas H 61 B4
Kiskunlacháza H 61 A3
Kiskunmajsa H 61 B4
Kislang H 60 B3
Kisslegg D 47 C5
Kissolt H 61 B4
Kist D 47 A5
Kistanje HR 69 C4
Kistelek H 61 B4
Kisterenye H 51 B5
Kisújszállás H 61 A5
Kisvárda H 11 M18
Kisvejke H 60 B3
Kiszkowo PL 32 C3
Kiszombor H 61 B5

Kitee FIN 3 E22
Kíthira GR 15 T18
Kittendorf D 31 B4
Kittilä FIN 3 C19
Kittsee A 50 B3
Kitzbühel A 58 A2
Kitzingen D 47 A6
Kiuruvesi FIN 3 E20
Kivertsi UA 11 L19
Kivik S 27 D4
Kiwity PL 33 A6
Kjellerup DK 25 C2
Kjøllefjord N 2 A20
Kjopmannskjaer N 20 B2
Kľačno SK 51 B4
Kladanj BIH 70 B3
Kläden D 30 C3
Klädesholmen S 21 D3
Kladnica YU 71 C5
Kladnice HR 69 C5
Kladno CZ 39 C4
Kladruby CZ 48 A3
Klagenfurt A 59 B4
Klågerup S 27 D3
Klagstorp S 27 D3
Klaipėda LT 6 J17
Klaistow D 38 A2
Klana HR 59 C4
Klanac HR 69 B4
Klanjec HR 59 B5
Klardorf D 48 A3
Klarup DK 24 B3
Klašnice BIH 70 B2
Klässbol S 20 B4
Klášterec nad Ohří CZ 38 C3
Kláštor pod Znievom SK 51 B4
Klatovy CZ 49 A4
Klaus an der Pyhrnbahn A 49 C5
Klazienaveen NL 28 C3
Klecko PL 32 C3
Kleczew PL 33 C4
Klein Plasten D 31 B4
Klein Sankt Paul A 59 B4
Kleinsölk A 58 A3
Kleinzell A 50 C1
Klejtrup DK 24 C2
Klek YU 61 C5
Klemensker DK 27 D4
Klenak YU 71 B4
Klenci pod Cerchovem CZ 48 A3
Klenica PL 39 B5
Klenje YU 71 B4
Klenovec SK 51 B5
Klenovica HR 69 A3
Klenovnik HR 59 B6
Kleppe N 18 C2
Kleptow D 31 B5
Kletnya RUS 7 K23
Kleve D 36 B2
Klevshult S 26 B4
Klewki PL 33 B6
Kličevac YU 71 B6
Kliening A 59 B4
Klietz D 30 C4
Klikuszowa PL 51 A5
Klimkovice CZ 50 A4
Klimontów PL 41 C6
Klimovichi BY 7 K22
Klin RUS 7 H25
Klinča Sela HR 59 C5
Klingenbach A 50 C2
Klingenberg D 47 A5
Klingenmunster D 47 A4
Klingenthal D 38 C2
Klintehamn S 6 H16
Klintsy RUS 7 K23
Kliny PL 41 B5
Klipley DK 25 E2
Klippan S 27 C3
Klis HR 69 C5
Klitmøller DK 24 B1
Klixbüll D 25 E1
Kljajićevo YU 61 C4
Ključ BIH 69 B5
Klobouky CZ 50 B2
Kłobuck PL 40 C3
Kłodawa PL 31 C7
Kłodawa PL 40 A3
Kłodzko PL 40 C1
Kløfta N 20 A3
Klokkarvik N 18 A2
Klokkerholm DK 24 B3
Klokočov SK 51 A4
Kłomnice PL 41 C4
Klonowa PL 40 B3
Kloosterzande NL 35 B4
Kłopot PL 39 A4
Kloštar Ivanić HR 59 C6
Kloster D 31 A5
Kloster DK 25 C1
Klösterle A 57 A5
Klostermansfeld D 38 B1
Klosterneuburg A 50 B2
Klosters CH 57 B4
Kloten CH 56 A3
Klötze D 30 C3
Kluczbork PL 40 C3
Kluczewo PL 32 B2
Kluisbergen B 35 C4
Klundert NL 35 B5
Klutz D 30 B3
Klwów PL 41 B5
Klyetsk BY 7 K20
Knaben N 18 C3
Knapstad N 20 B3
Knäred S 26 C3
Knesebeck D 30 C2
Knesselare B 35 B4
Knežak SLO 59 C4
Kneževi Vinogradi HR 60 C3
Kneževo HR 60 C3
Knić YU 71 C5
Knin HR 69 B5
Knislinge S 27 C4
Knittelfeld A 59 A4
Knivsta S 22 B4
Knokke-Heist B 35 B4
Knurów PL 40 C3
Knutby S 22 B5
Kobarid SLO 58 B3
København DK 27 D2
Kobenz A 59 A4
Kobersdorf A 50 C2
Kobiernice PL 51 A5
Kobierzyce PL 40 C1
Kobilje SLO 59 B6
Kobiór PL 40 C3
Koblenz CH 47 C4
Koblenz D 36 C3
Kobryn BY 6 K19
Kobylanka PL 31 B6
Kobylin PL 40 B2
Kobyłka PL 41 A6
Kobylniki PL 33 C6
Kocaeli (İzmit) TR 16 R21
Kočani MK 15 R18
Koceljevo YU 71 B4
Kočerin BIH 70 C2
Kočevje SLO 59 C4
Kočevska Reka SLO 59 C4
Kochel am see D 48 C2
Kocs H 50 C4
Kocsér H 61 A4
Kocsola H 60 B3
Koczala PL 32 B3
Kodal N 20 B2
Kodersdorf D 39 B4
Kodrab PL 41 B4
Koekelare B 34 B3
Köflach A 59 A5
Køge DK 27 D2
Kohlberg D 48 A3
Kohtla-Järve EST 7 G20
Köinge S 26 B2
Kojetín CZ 50 A3
Kokava SK 51 B5
Kokkola FIN 3 E18
Kokori BIH 70 B2
Kokoski PL 33 A4
Koksijde B 34 B3
Kola BIH 70 B2
Kola RUS 3 B23
Köla S 20 B4
Kołacin PL 41 B4
Kolari FIN 3 C18
Kolárovo SK 50 C3
Kolašin YU 71 D4
Kolbäck S 22 B3
Kolbacz PL 31 B6
Kolbermoor D 48 C3
Kołbiel PL 41 A6
Kolbnitz A 58 B3
Kolbotn N 20 B2
Kolby Kås DK 25 D3
Kolczewo PL 31 B6
Kolczyglowy PL 32 A3
Kolding DK 25 D2
Kölesd H 60 B3
Kolín CZ 39 C5
Kolind DK 25 C3
Kolinec CZ 49 A4
Koljane HR 69 C5
Kølkær DK 25 C2
Kölleda D 38 B1
Kollum NL 28 B3
Köln D 36 C2
Koło PL 40 A3
Kołobrzeg PL 32 A1
Kolochau D 38 B3
Kolomyya UA 11 M19
Kolonowskie PL 40 C3
Koloveč CZ 48 A4
Kolpino RUS 7 G22
Kolpny RUS 7 K25
Kolrep D 30 B4
Kolsko PL 39 B5
Kolsva S 22 B2
Kolta SK 51 B4
Kolunič BIH 69 B5
Koluszki PL 41 B4
Kolut YU 61 C3
Kølvrå DK 25 C2
Komarica BIH 70 B2
Komárno SK 50 C4
Komárom H 50 C4
Komen SLO 58 C3
Komin HR 70 C2
Komiža HR 69 C5
Komjáti H 51 B6
Komjatice SK 50 B4
Komletinci HR 70 A3
Komló H 60 B3
Kömlo H 51 C6
Komoča SK 50 C4
Komorniki PL 40 A1
Komorzno PL 40 B3
Komotini GR 16 R19
Konak YU 61 C5
Konakovo RUS 7 H25
Konary PL 41 B6
Konarzyny PL 32 B3
Kondorfa H 59 B6
Kondoros H 61 B5
Kondrovo RUS 7 J24
Køng DK 25 D4
Konga S 26 C5
Kongerslev DK 24 C3
Kongsberg N 19 B6
Kongshamn N 19 C5
Kongsmark DK 25 D1
Kongsvinger N 20 A4
Konice CZ 50 A2
Konie PL 41 B5
Koniecpol PL 41 C4
Königs Wusterhausen D 38 A3
Königsberg D 37 C6
Königsbronn D 47 B6
Königsbrück D 39 B3
Königsbrunn D 48 B1
Königsdorf D 48 C2
Königsee D 38 C1
Königshorst D 31 C4
Königslutter D 37 A6
Königssee D 48 C3
Königstein, *Hessen* D 37 C4
Königstein, *Sachsen* D 39 C4
Königstetten A 50 B2
Königswartha D 39 B4
Königswiesen A 49 B5
Königswinter D 36 C3
Konin PL 40 A3
Köniz CH 56 B2
Konjevići BIH 71 B4
Konjevrate HR 69 C5
Konjic BIH 70 C2
Konjščina HR 59 B6
Könnern D 38 B1
Konnerud N 20 B2
Konopiska PL 40 C3
Konotop PL 39 B5
Konotop UA 7 L23
Końskie PL 41 B5
Konsmo N 19 C4
Konstancin-Jeziorna PL 41 A6
Konstantynów Łódźki PL 41 B4
Konstanz D 47 C5
Kontich B 35 B5
Kontiolahti FIN 3 E21
Konz D 46 A2
Kopčany SK 50 B3
Koper SLO 58 C3
Kopervik N 18 B2
Kópháza H 50 C2
Kopice PL 40 C2
Kopidlno CZ 39 C5
Köping S 22 B2
Köpingebro S 27 D3
Koppang N 2 F12
Kopparberg S 22 B1
Koppom S 20 B4
Koprivna BIH 70 B3
Koprivnica HR 60 B1
Kopřivnice CZ 50 A4
Koprzywnica PL 41 C6
Kopstal L 46 A2
Kopychyntsi UA 11 M19
Kopytkowo PL 33 B4
Korbach D 37 B4
Körbecke D 36 B4
Korçë AL 15 R17
Korčula HR 70 D2
Korczyców PL 39 A4
Korenevo RUS 7 L24
Korenita YU 71 B4
Korets UA 11 L20
Korfantów PL 40 C2
Korgen N 2 C13
Korinth DK 25 D3
Kórinthos GR 15 T18
Korita BIH 69 B5
Korita HR 70 D2
Korkuteli TR 16 T22
Körmend H 60 A1
Korne PL 32 A3
Korneuburg A 50 B2
Kornevo RUS 33 A6
Kórnik PL 40 A2
Kornsjø N 21 C3
Környe H 60 A3
Koromačno HR 68 B3
Koronowo PL 32 B3
Körösladány H 61 B6
Köröstarcsa H 61 B6
Korosten UA 11 L21
Korostyshev UA 11 L21
Korsberga, *Jönköping* S 26 B5
Korsberga, *Skaraborg* S 21 C6
Korshavn N 21 B2
Korsnäs S 22 A2
Korsør DK 25 D4
Korsun Shevchenkovskiy UA 11 M22
Kortrijk B 35 C4
Koryčany CZ 50 A3
Koryukovka UA 7 L23
Korzeńsko PL 40 B1
Korzybie PL 32 A2
Kosanica YU 71 C4
Kosaya Gora RUS 7 J25
Kösching D 48 B2
Kościan PL 40 A1
Kościelec PL 40 A3
Kościerzyna PL 32 A3
Koserow D 31 A5
Košetice CZ 49 A6
Košice SK 10 M17
Kosjerić YU 71 C4
Koška HR 60 C3
Kosovska Mitrovica YU 71 D5
Kosta S 26 C5
Kostajnica HR 60 C1
Kostajnik YU 71 B4
Kostanjevica SLO 59 C5
Kostelec na Hané CZ 50 A3
Kostelec nad Černými Lesy CZ 39 C4
Kostice CZ 39 C3
Kostkowo PL 33 A4
Kostojevići YU 71 B4
Kostolac YU 71 B6
Kostopil UA 11 L20
Kostów PL 40 B3
Kostrzyn PL 31 C6
Kostrzyn PL 32 C3
Koszalin PL 32 A2
Koszęcin PL 40 C3
Kőszeg H 59 A6
Koszwaly PL 33 A4
Koszyce PL 41 C5
Kot SLO 59 C5
Kötelek H 61 A5
Köthen D 38 B1
Kotka FIN 3 F20
Kotomierz PL 33 B4
Kotor YU 15 Q16
Kotor Varoš BIH 70 B2
Kotoriba HR 60 B1
Kotorsko BIH 70 B3
Kotovsk UA 11 N21
Kotraža YU 71 C5
Kötschach A 58 B2
Kötzting D 48 A3
Koudum NL 28 C2
Kouřim CZ 39 C4
Kout na Šumave CZ 48 A4
Kouvola FIN 3 F20
Kovačevac YU 71 B5
Kovačica YU 71 A5
Kovdor RUS 3 C22
Kovel' UA 11 L19
Kovilj YU 61 C5
Kovin YU 71 B5
Kovren YU 71 C4
Kowal PL 33 C5
Kowalewo Pomorskie PL 33 B4
Kowalów PL 31 C6
Kowary PL 39 C5
Köyceğiz TR 16 T21
Kozáni GR 15 R17
Kozarac BIH 70 B1
Kozarac HR 59 C5
Kozárovce SK 51 B4
Kozelets UA 11 L22
Kozelsk RUS 7 J24
Kozica HR 70 C2
Koziegłowy PL 41 C4
Kozienice PL 41 B6
Kozina SLO 58 C3
Kozje SLO 59 B5
Kozlu TR 16 R22
Kozluk BIH 71 B4
Koźmin PL 40 B2
Koźminek PL 40 B3
Kozolupy CZ 49 A4
Kożuchów PL 39 B5
Kožuhe BIH 70 B3
Kozyatyn UA 11 M21
Krackow D 31 B6
Krag PL 32 A2
Kragenæs DK 25 E4
Kragerø N 19 C6
Kragi PL 32 B2
Kragujevac YU 71 B5
Kraiburg D 48 B3
Krajenka PL 32 B2
Krajišnik YU 61 C5
Krajková CZ 38 C2
Krajné SK 50 B3
Krajnik Dolny PL 31 B6
Krakača BIH 69 A4
Kraków PL 41 C4
Krakow am See D 30 B4
Králíky CZ 40 C1
Kraljevica HR 59 C4
Kraljevo YU 71 C5
Kráľov Brod SK 50 B3
Kraľovany SK 51 A5
Kralovice CZ 38 D3
Kralupy nad Vltavou CZ 39 C4
Králův Dvůr CZ 49 A5
Kramfors S 2 E15
Kramsach A 58 A1
Kramsk PL 40 A3
Kråmvik N 19 B5
Kranenburg D 36 B2
Kranichfeld D 38 C1
Kranídhion GR 15 T18
Kranj SLO 59 B4
Kranjska Gora SLO 58 B3
Krapanj HR 69 C4
Krapina HR 59 B5
Krapje HR 60 C1
Krapkowice PL 40 C2
Kraselov CZ 49 A4
Krašić HR 59 C5
Krāslava LV 7 J20
Kraslice CZ 38 C2
Krasna PL 41 B5
Krasna Lipa CZ 39 C4
Kraśnik PL 11 L18
Krašnja SLO 59 B4
Krásno SK 51 A4
Krasno Polje HR 69 B4
Krásnohorské Podhradie SK 51 B6
Krasnokutsk UA 7 L24
Krasnozavodsk RUS 7 H26
Krasnystaw PL 11 L18
Krasnyy RUS 7 J22
Krasnyy Kholm RUS 7 G25
Krasocin PL 41 C5
Kraszewice PL 40 B3
Kraszkowice PL 40 B3
Kraubath A 59 A4
Krausnick D 39 A3
Krautheim D 47 A5
Kravaře, *Severočeský* CZ 39 C4
Kravaře, *Severomoravský* CZ 50 A4
Kravarsko HR 59 C6
Kraznějov CZ 49 A4
Krčedin YU 71 A5
Krefeld D 36 B2
Krembz D 30 B3
Kremenchuk UA 11 M23
Kremenets UA 11 L19
Kremmen D 31 C5
Kremna YU 71 C4
Kremnica SK 51 B4
Krempe D 29 B6
Krems A 49 B6
Kremsbrücke A 58 B3
Kremsmünster A 49 B5
Křemže CZ 49 B5
Křenov CZ 50 A2
Krepa PL 40 B3
Krepsko PL 32 B2
Kreševo BIH 70 C3
Kressbronn D 47 C5
Kretinga LT 6 J17
Krettsy RUS 7 G23
Kreuth D 48 C2
Kreuzau D 36 C2
Kreuzlingen CH 47 C5
Kreuztal D 36 C3
Krewelin D 31 C5
Krezluk BIH 70 B2
Krieglach A 59 A5
Kriegsfeld D 46 A3
Kriens CH 56 A3
Krimml A 58 A2
Krimpen aan de IJssel NL 35 B5
Křinec CZ 39 C5
Kristdala S 26 B6
Kristiansand N 19 C5
Kristianstad S 27 C4
Kristiansund N 2 E10
Kristiinankaupunki FIN 3 E17
Kristinehamn S 20 B6
Krivaň SK 51 B5
Križ HR 60 C1
Křižanov CZ 50 A2
Križevci HR 60 B1
Krk HR 69 A3
Krka SLO 59 C4
Krnjača YU 71 B5
Krnjak HR 59 C5
Krnjeuša BIH 69 B5
Krnjevo YU 71 B6
Krnov CZ 40 C2
Krobia PL 40 B1
Kroczyce PL 41 C4
Krøderen N 19 A6
Krokek S 23 C3
Krokom S 2 E14
Krokowa PL 33 A4
Krokstad-elva N 19 B6
Kroksund N 20 B3
Krolevets UA 7 L23
Kroměříž CZ 50 A3
Krommenie NL 28 C1
Krompachy SK 51 B6
Kromy RUS 7 K24
Kronach D 38 C1
Kronshagen D 30 A2
Kronshtadt RUS 7 G21
Kröpelin D 30 A3
Kropp D 29 A6
Kroppenstedt D 38 B1
Kropstädt D 38 B2
Krościenko nad Dunajcem PL 51 A6
Kröslin D 31 A5
Krośnice PL 40 B2
Krośniewice PL 41 A4
Krosno PL 10 M17
Krosno Odrzańskie PL 39 A5
Krostitz D 38 B2
Krotoszyn PL 40 B2
Krottendorf A 59 A5
Krouna CZ 50 A2
Krowiarki PL 40 C3
Kršan HR 59 C4
Krško SLO 59 C5
Krstac YU 70 C3
Krstur YU 61 B5
Křtiny CZ 50 A2
Kruft D 36 C3
Kruishoutem B 35 C4
Krulyewshchyna BY 7 J20
Krumbach A 59 A6
Krumbach D 47 B6
Krün D 57 A6
Krupá CZ 39 C3
Krupa na Vrbasu BIH 70 B2
Krupanj YU 71 B4
Krupina SK 51 B5
Krupka CZ 39 C3
Krupki BY 7 J21
Kruså DK 25 E2
Krušćica BIH 70 B2
Kruševac YU 71 C6
Kruszwica PL 33 C4
Kruszyn PL 33 C5
Krychaw BY 7 K22
Krynica PL 51 A6
Krynica Morska PL 33 A5
Krzęcin PL 32 B1
Krzelów PL 40 B1
Krzepice PL 40 C3
Krzepielów PL 39 B6
Krzeszowice PL 41 C4
Krzeszyce PL 31 C7
Krzynowłaga Mała PL 33 B6
Krzywiń PL 40 B1
Krzyż Wielkopolski PL 32 C2
Krzyżanowice PL 50 A4
Krzyżowa PL 51 A5
Ksiaz Wielkopolski PL 41 C5
Książ Wielkopolski PL 40 A2
Kłębowiec PL 32 B2
Kübekháza H 61 B5
Küblis CH 57 B4
Kuchary PL 40 B2
Kuchl A 48 C4
Kucice PL 33 C6
Kuciste HR 70 D2
Kućište YU 71 D5
Kucura YU 61 C4
Kuczbork-Osada PL 33 B6
Kudowa-Zdrój PL 39 C6
Kufstein A 48 C3
Kuggeboda S 27 C5
Kühbach D 48 B2
Kuhmo FIN 3 D21
Kuhmoinen FIN 3 F19
Kuhnsdorf A 59 B4
Kuhstedt D 29 B5
Kuinre NL 28 C2
Kuivastu EST 6 G18
Kukës AL 15 Q17
Kuklin PL 33 B6
Kukljica HR 69 B4
Kukujevci YU 71 A4
Kula TR 16 S21
Kula YU 61 C4
Kula YU 71 B6
Kuldīga LV 6 H17
Kulen Vakuf BIH 69 B5
Kulina BIH 70 B3
Kulmain D 48 A2
Kulmbach D 38 C1
Kumane YU 61 C5
Kumanovo MK 15 Q17
Kumla S 22 B2
Kumlakyrkby S 22 B3
Kumluca TR 16 T22
Kumrovec HR 59 B5
Kunadacs H 61 B4
Kunágota H 61 B6
Kunbaja H 61 B4
Kunda EST 7 G20
Kundl A 58 A1
Kunfehértó H 61 B4
Kungälv S 21 D3
Kungs-Husby S 22 B4
Kungsängen S 22 B4
Kungsäter S 26 B2
Kungsbacka S 24 B5
Kungsgården S 22 A3
Kungshamn S 21 C3
Kungsör S 22 B3
Kunhegyes H 61 A5
Kunmadaras H 61 A5
Kunovice CZ 50 A3
Kunów PL 41 C6
Kunowo PL 40 B2
Kunštát CZ 50 A2
Kunszállás H 61 B4
Kunszentmárton H 61 B5
Kunszentmiklós H 61 A4
Kunžak CZ 49 A6
Künzelsau D 47 A5
Kuolajärvi RUS 3 C21
Kuopio FIN 3 E20
Kup H 60 A2
Kup PL 40 C2
Kupa H 51 B6
Kupci YU 71 C6
Kupferzell D 47 A5
Kupinec HR 59 C5
Kupinečki Kraljevac HR 59 C5
Kupinovo YU 71 B5
Kupirovo HR 69 B5
Kupjak HR 59 C4
Kuppenheim D 47 B4
Kupres BIH 70 C2
Küps D 38 C1
Kurd H 60 B3
Kŭrdzhali BG 16 R19
Kuressaare EST 6 G18
Kurikka FIN 3 E18
Kuřim CZ 50 A2
Kurki PL 33 B6
Kurort Oberwiesenthal D 38 C2
Kurort Schmalkalden D 37 C6
Kurort Stolberg D 37 B6
Kurort Wippra D 38 B1
Kurów PL 11 L18
Kurowice PL 41 B4
Kursk RUS 7 L25
Kuršumlija YU 71 C6
Kuršumlijska Banja YU 71 C6
Kürten D 36 B3
Kurzelów PL 41 C4
Kusadak YU 71 B5
Kuşadası TR 16 T20
Kusel D 46 A3
Kusey D 30 C3
Küsnacht CH 56 A3
Kütahya TR 16 S22
Kutenholz D 29 B6
Kutina HR 60 C1
Kutjevo HR 60 C2
Kutná Hora CZ 39 D5
Kutno PL 41 A4
Küttingen CH 56 A3
Kúty SK 50 B3
Kuusamo FIN 3 D21
Kuusankoski FIN 3 F20
Kuvshinovo RUS 7 H24
Kuzmin YU 71 A4
Kuźnia Raciborska PL 40 C3
Kuźnica Czarnkowska PL 32 C2
Kuźnica Żelichowska PL 32 C2
Kværndrup DK 25 D3
Kvänum S 21 C5
Kvås N 19 C4
Kvasice CZ 50 A3
Kvernaland N 18 C2
Kvibille S 26 C2
Kvicksund S 22 B3
Kvidinge S 27 C3
Kvikne N 2 E12
Kvilda CZ 49 A4
Kville S 21 C3
Kvillsfors S 26 B5
Kvinesdal N 18 C3
Kvinlog N 18 C3
Kvinnherad N 18 B3
Kvissel DK 24 B3
Kviteseid N 19 B5
Kvitsøy N 18 B2
Kwakowo PL 32 A3
Kwidzyn PL 33 B4
Kwilcz PL 32 C2
Kyjov CZ 50 B3
Kyle of Lochalsh GB 4 H4
Kyllburg D 36 C2
Kynšperk nad Ohří CZ 38 C2
Kyritz D 30 C4
Kyrkesund S 21 C3
Kyrkhult S 27 C4
Kysucké Nové Mesto SK 51 A4
Kyustendil BG 15 Q18
Kyyiv UA 11 L22
Kyyjärvi FIN 3 E19

L

La Adrada E 80 B2
La Alameda E 86 A2
La Alberca E 79 A4
La Alberca de Záncara E 81 C4
La Albergueria de Argañán E 79 A4
La Albuera E 79 C4
La Aldea del Portillo del Busto E 75 B3
La Algaba E 85 B4
La Aliseda de Tormes E 80 B1
La Almarcha E 81 C4
La Almolda E 76 B2
La Almunia de Doña Godina E 75 C5
La Antillas E 84 B3
La Arena E 72 A4
La Aulaga E 85 B4
La Balme-de-Sillingy F 55 C6
La Bañeza E 74 B1
La Barca de la Florida E 85 C5
La Barre-de-Monts F 52 B2
La Barre-en-Ouche F 44 B1
La Barrosa E 85 C4
La Barthe-de-Neste F 63 C3
La Bassée F 34 C3
La Bastide-de-Sèrou F 63 C4
La Bastide-des-Jourdans F 65 C4
La Bastide-Puylaurent F 64 B2
La Bathie F 55 C6
La Baule-Escoublac F 52 A2
La Bazoche-Gouet F 44 B1
La Bégude-de-Mazenc F 64 B3
La Bernerie-en-Retz F 52 A2
La Bisbal d'Empordà E 77 B6
La Boissière F 43 A6
La Bourboule F 54 C2
La Bóveda de Toro E 74 C1
La Brède F 62 B2
La Bresse F 46 B2
La Bridoire F 55 C5
La Brillanne F 65 C4
La Bruffière F 52 A3
La Bussière F 44 C3
La Caillère F 52 B4
La Caletta I 96 C2
La Calmette F 64 C3
La Calzada de Oropesa E 80 C1
La Campana E 85 B5
La Cañada E 80 B2
La Canourgue F 64 B2
La Capelle F 35 D4
La Cardanchosa E 85 A5
La Caridad E 72 A4
La Carlota E 86 B1
La Carolina E 86 A2
La Cava E 76 C3
La Cavalerie F 64 B2
La Celle-en-Moravan F 55 A4
La Celle-St. Avant F 53 A5
La Cerca E 75 B3
La Chaise-Dieu F 54 C3
La Chaize-le-Vicomte F 52 B3
La Chambre F 55 C6
La Chapelaude F 54 B2
La Chapelle-d'Angillon F 54 A2
La Chapelle-en-Aalgaudémar F 65 B5
La Chapelle-en-Vercors F 65 B4
La Chapelle-Glain F 43 C4
La Chapelle-la-Reine F 44 B3
La Chapelle-Laurent F 54 C3
La Chapelle-St. Luc F 45 B5
La Chapelle-sur-Erdre F 52 A3
La Chapelle-Vicomtesse F 44 C2
La Charce F 65 B4
La Charité-sur-Loire F 54 A3
La Chartre-sur-le-Loir F 44 C1
La Châtaigneraie F 53 B4
La Châtre F 54 B1
La Chaussée-sur-Marne F 45 B5
La Chaux-de-Fonds CH 56 A1
La Cheppe F 45 A5
La Chèze F 42 B3
La Ciotat F 65 C4
La Clayette F 55 B4
La Clusaz F 55 C6
La Codosera E 79 B3
La Concha E 74 A3
La Condamine-Châtelard F 65 B5
La Contienda E 85 A4
La Coquille F 53 C5
La Coronada E 79 C5
La Côte-St. André F 55 C5
La Cotinière F 52 C3
La Courtine F 54 C2
La Crau F 65 C5
La Crèche F 53 B4
La Croix F 53 A5
La Croix-Valmer F 65 C5
La Cumbre E 79 B5
La Douze F 63 A3
La Espina E 72 A4
La Estrella E 80 C1
La Farga de Moles E 77 A4
La Fatarella E 76 B3
La Felipa E 81 C5
La Fère F 45 A4
La Ferrière F 52 B3
La Ferrière-en-Parthenay F 53 B4
La-Ferté-Alais F 44 B3
La Ferté-Bernard F 44 B1
La Ferté-Frênel F 44 B1
La Ferté-Gaucher F 45 B4
La Ferté-Imbault F 54 A1
La Ferté-Macé F 43 B5
La Ferté-Milon F 45 A4
La Ferté-St. Aubin F 44 C2
La Ferté-St.Cyr F 44 C2
La Ferté-sous-Jouarre F 45 B4
La Ferté-Vidame F 44 B1
La Ferté Villeneuil F 44 C2
La Feuillie F 44 A2
La Flèche F 43 C5
La Flotte F 52 B3
La Font de la Figuera E 82 C2
La Fouillade F 63 B5
La Fregeneda E 73 D4
La Fresneda E 76 C3
La Fuencubierta E 86 B1
La Fuente de San Esteban E 73 D4
La Fulioala E 77 B4
La Gacilly F 43 C3
La Galera E 76 C3
La Garde-Freinet F 65 C5
La Garnache F 52 B3
La Garriga E 77 B5
La Garrovilla E 79 C4
La Gaubretière F 52 B3
La Gineta E 81 C4
La Granadella, *Alicante* E 82 C3
La Granadella, *Lleida* E 76 B3
La Grand-Combe F 64 B3
La Grande-Croix F 55 C4
La Grande-Motte F 64 C3
La Granja d'Escarp E 76 B3
La Granjuela E 79 C5
La Grave F 65 A5
La Gravelle F 43 B4
La Guardia E 81 C3
La Guardia de Jaén E 86 B2
La Guerche-de-Bretagne F 43 C4
La Guerche-sur-l'Aubois F 54 B2
La Guérinière F 52 B2
La Haba E 79 C5
La Haye-du-Puits F 43 A4
La Haye-Pesnel F 43 B4
La Herlière F 34 C3
La Hermida E 74 A2
La Herrera E 81 D4
La Higuera E 82 C1
La Hiniesta E 74 C1
La Horcajada E 80 B1
La Horra E 74 C3
La Hulpe B 35 C5
La Hutte F 43 B6
La Iglesuela E 80 B2
La Iglesuela del Cid E 76 C2
La Iruela E 86 B3
La Javie F 65 B5
La Jonchère-St. Maurice F 53 B6
La Jonquera E 77 A5
La Lantejuela E 85 B5
La Línea de la Concepción E 85 C5
La Llacuna E 77 B4
La Londe-les-Maures F 65 C5
La Loupe F 44 B2
La Louvière B 35 C5
La Luisiana E 85 B5
La Machine F 54 B3
la Maddalena I 96 B2
La Mailleraye-sur-Seine F 44 A1
La Malène F 64 B2
La Mamola E 86 C2
La Manresana dels Prats E 77 B4
La Masadera E 76 B2
La Mata E 80 C2
La Mata de Ledesma E 73 C5
La Mata de Monteagudo E 74 B1
La Meilleraye-de-Bretagne F 43 C4
La Ménitré F 53 A4
La Mojonera E 87 C3
La Mole F 65 C5
La Molina E 77 A4
La Monnerie-le-Montel F 54 C3
La Morera E 79 C4
La Mothe-Achard F 52 B3
La Mothe-St. Héray F 53 B4
La Motte-Chalançon F 65 B4
La Motte-du-Caire F 65 B5
La Motte-Servolex F 55 C5
La Mudarra E 74 C2

La Muela E 76 B1
La Mure F 65 B4
La Nava E 85 B4
La Nava de Ricomalillo E 80 C2
La Nava de Santiago E 79 B4
La Neuve-Lyre F 44 B1
La Neuveville CH 56 A2
La Nocle-Maulaix F 54 B3
La Nuez de Arriba E 74 B3
La Paca E 87 B4
La Pacaudière F 54 B3
La Palma d'Ebre E 76 B3
La Palma del Condado E 85 B4
La Palme F 64 D2
La Palmyre F 52 C3
La Parra E 79 C4
La Pedraja de Portillo E 74 C2
La Peraleja E 81 B4
La Petit-Pierre F 46 B3
La Pinilla E 87 B4
La Plagne F 56 C1
La Plaza E 72 A4
La Pobla de Lillet E 77 A4
La Pobla de Vallbona E 82 B2
La Pobla Llarga E 82 B2
La Pola de Gordón E 74 B1
la Porta F 96 A2
La Pouëze F 52 A4
La Póveda de Soria E 75 B4
La Preste F 77 A5
La Primaube F 63 B5
La Puebla de Almoradie E 81 C3
La Puebla de Cazalla E 85 B5
La Puebla de los Infantes E 85 B5
La Puebla de Montalbán E 80 C2
La Puebla de Roda E 76 A3
La Puebla de Valdavia E 74 B2
La Puebla de Valverde E 82 A2
La Puebla del Río E 85 B4
La Pueblanueva E 80 C2
La Puerta de Segura E 87 A3
La Punt CH 57 B4
La Quintana E 86 B1
La Quintera E 85 B5
La Rábita, *Granada* E 86 C2
La Rábita, *Jaén* E 86 B1
La Rambla E 86 B1
La Reale I 96 B1
La Redondela E 84 B3
La Réole F 62 B2
La Riera E 72 A4
La Riera de Gaià E 77 B4
La Rinconada E 85 B4
La Rivière-Thibouville F 44 A1
La Robla E 74 B1
La Roca de la Sierra E 79 B4
La Roche CH 56 B2
La Roche-Bernard F 52 A2
La Roche-Canillac F 54 C1
La Roche-Chalais F 53 C5
La Roche Derrien F 42 B2
La Roche-des-Arnauds F 65 B4
La Roche-en-Ardenne B 35 C6
La Roche-en-Brénil F 55 A4
La Roche-Guyon F 44 A2
La Roche-Posay F 53 B5
La Roche-sur-Foron F 55 B6
La Roche-sur-Yon F 52 B3
La Rochebeaucourt-et-Argentine F 53 C5
La Rochefoucauld F 53 C5
La Rochelle F 52 B3
La Rochette F 65 B4
La Roda, *Albacete* E 81 C4
La Roda, *Oviedo* E 72 A4
La Roda de Andalucía E 86 B1
La Roque-Gageac F 63 B4
La Roque-Ste. Marguerite F 64 B2
La Roquebrussanne F 65 C4
La Rubia E 75 C4
La Sagrada E 73 D4
La Salceda E 80 A3
La Salle F 65 B5
la Salute di Livenza I 58 C2
La Salvetat-Peyralés F 63 B5
La Salvetat-sur-Agout F 64 C1
La Sarraz CH 55 B6
La Seca E 74 C2
La Selva del Camp E 77 B4
La Senia E 76 C3
La Serra E 77 B4
La Seu d'Urgell E 77 A4
La Seyne-sur-Mer F 65 C4
La Solana E 81 D3
La Souterraine F 53 B6
La Spézia I 67 B3
La Storta I 88 B2
La Suze-sur-Sarthe F 43 C6
La Teste F 62 B1
La Thuile I 56 C1
La Toba E 81 B5
La Toledana E 80 C2
La Torre de Cabdella E 76 A3
La Torre de Esteban Hambrán E 80 B2
La Torre del l'Espanyol E 76 B3
La Torresaviñán E 81 B4
La Tour d'Aigues F 65 C4
La Tour de Peilz CH 56 B1
La Tour-du-Pin F 55 C5
La Tranche-sur-Mer F 52 B3
La Tremblade F 52 C3
La Trimouille F 53 B6
La Trinité F 42 C2
La Trinité-Porhoët F 42 B3
La Turballe F 52 A2
La Uña E 74 A1
La Unión E 87 B5
La Vall d'Uixó E 82 B2
La Vecilla de Curueño E 74 B1
La Vega, *Asturias* E 74 A1
La Vega, *Asturias* E 74 A1
La Vega, *Cantabria* E 74 A2
La Velilla E 80 A3
La Velles E 80 A1
La Ventosa E 81 B4
La Victoria E 86 B1
La Vid E 75 C3
La Vilavella E 82 B2
La Vilella Baixa E 76 B3
La Villa de Don Fadrique E 81 C3
La Ville Dieu-du-Temple F 63 B4
La Villedieu F 53 B4
La Voulte-sur-Rhône F 64 B3
La Wantzenau F 46 B3
La Yesa E 82 B2
La Zubia E 86 B2
Laa an der Thaya A 50 B2
Laage D 30 B4
Laatzen D 37 A5
Labastide-Murat F 63 B4
Labastide-Rouairoux F 63 C5
Labastide-St. Pierre F 63 C4
Lábatlan H 51 C4
Labenne F 62 C1
Labin HR 68 A3
Łabiszyn PL 32 C3
Lablachère F 64 B3
Lábod H 60 B3
Laboe D 30 A2
Labouheyre F 62 B2
Łabowa PL 51 A6
Labrit F 62 B2
Labros E 81 A5
Labruguière F 63 C5
Labrujo P 73 C2
L'Absie F 53 B4
Lacalahorra E 86 B2
Lacanau F 62 B1
Lacanau-Océan F 62 A1
Lacanche F 55 A4
Lacapelle-Marival F 63 B4
Laćarak YU 71 A4
Lacaune F 64 C1
Lacedónia I 90 A2
Láces I 57 B5
Lachen CH 56 A3
Lachendorf D 30 C2
Lachowice PL 51 A5
Łąck PL 33 C5
Läckeby S 26 C6
Läckö S 21 C3
Láconi I 96 D2
Lacq F 62 C2
Lacroix-Barrez F 63 B5
Lacroix-St. Ouen F 44 A3
Lacroix-sur-Meuse F 46 C1
Łącznik PL 40 C2
Lad H 60 B2
Ladbergen D 36 A3
Lądek-Zdrój PL 40 C1
Ladelund D 25 E2
Ladendorf A 50 B2
Ladignac-le-Long F 53 C6
Ladíspoli I 88 B2
Ladoeiro P 79 B3
Ladon F 44 C3
Ladushkin RUS 33 A6
Laer D 36 A3
Lærdalsøyri N 2 F10
Lafnitz A 59 A6
Lafrançaise F 63 B4
Lagan S 26 C3
Laganadi I 95 A4
Lagares, *Coimbra* P 78 A3
Lagares, *Porto* P 73 C2
Lagaro I 67 B5
Lagartera E 80 C1
Lage D 37 B4
Lägerdorf D 29 B6
Łagiewniki PL 40 C1
Láglio I 57 C4
Lagnieu F 55 C5
Lagny-sur-Marne F 44 B3
Lago, *Calabria* I 92 B3
Lago, *Veneto* I 58 C2
Lagôa P 84 B2
Lagoaça P 73 C4
Lagonegro I 90 B2
Lagos P 84 B2
Lagosanto I 68 B1
Łagów PL 31 C7
Łagów PL 41 C6
Lagrasse F 63 C5
Laguardia E 75 B4
Laguarres E 76 A3
Laguenne F 54 C1
Laguépie F 63 B4
Laguiole F 64 B1
Laguna de Duera E 74 C2
Laguna de Negrillos E 74 B1
Laguna del Marquesado E 81 B5
Lagundo I 57 B6
Lagunilla E 79 A4
Laharie F 62 B2
Lahden D 29 C4
Laheycourt F 45 B6
Lahnstein D 36 C3
Laholm S 26 C3
Lahr D 46 B3
Lahti FIN 3 F19
Laichingen D 47 B5
L'Aigle F 44 B1
Laignes F 45 C5
Laiguéglia I 66 C2
L'Aiguillon-sur-Mer F 52 B3
Laimbach am Ostrong A 49 B6
Laina E 81 A4
Lairg GB 4 G4
Laissac F 64 B1
Láives I 57 B6
Lajkovac YU 71 B5
Lajoskomárom H 60 B3
Lajosmizse H 61 A4
Lak H 51 B6
Lakitelek H 61 B5
Lakolk DK 25 D1
Łąkorz PL 33 B5
Lakšárska Nová Ves SK 50 B3
Lakselv N 2 A19
Laktaši BIH 70 B2
L'Albagès E 76 B3
Lalbenque F 63 B4
L'Alcudia E 82 B2
L'Aldea E 76 C3
Lalín E 72 B2
Lalinde F 63 B3
Lalley F 65 B4
Lalling D 48 B4
L'Alpe-d'Huez F 65 A5
Lam D 48 A4
Lama dei Peligni I 89 A4
Lama Mocogno I 67 B4
Lamagistére F 63 B3
Lamarche F 46 B1
Lamarche-sur-Saône F 55 A5
Lamarosa P 78 B2
Lamarque F 62 A2
Lamas P 78 A2
Lamas de Moaro P 73 B2
Lamastre F 64 B3
Lambach A 49 B4
Lamballe F 42 B3
Lambesc F 65 C4
Lamego P 73 C3
L'Ametlla de Mar E 76 C3
Lamía GR 15 S18
Lammhult S 26 B4
Lamothe-Cassel F 63 B4
Lamothe-Montravel F 62 B3
Lamotte-Beuvron F 44 C3
Lampaul F 42 B0
Lampertheim D 47 A4
L'Ampolla E 76 C3
Lamprechtshausen A 48 C3
Lamsfeld D 39 B4
Lamspringe D 37 B6
Lamstedt D 29 B6
Lamure-sur-Azergues F 55 B4
Lana I 57 B6
Lanaja E 76 B2
Lanarce F 64 B2
Lancaster GB 4 J5
Lanciano I 89 A4
Lancova Vas SLO 59 B5
Landau, *Bayern* D 48 B3
Landau, *Rheinland-Pfalz* D 47 A4
Landeck A 57 A5
Landen B 35 C6
Landerneau F 42 B1
Landeryd S 26 B3
Landesbergen D 29 C6
Landete E 82 B1
Landévant F 42 C2
Landévennec F 42 B1
Landivisiau F 42 B1
Landivy F 43 B4
Landl A 48 C3
Landos F 64 B2
Landouzy-le-Ville F 45 A5
Landquart CH 57 B4
Landrecies F 35 C4
Landreville F 45 B5
Landriano I 57 C4
Lands-berg D 38 B2
Landsberg D 48 B1
Landsbro S 26 B4
Landscheid D 36 D2
Landshut D 48 B3
Landskrona S 27 D2
Landstuhl D 46 A3
Lanester F 42 C2
Lanestosa E 75 A3
Langå DK 25 C2
Langa de Duero E 75 C3
Langangen N 19 B6
Långaryd S 26 B3
Långås S 26 C2
Långasjö S 26 C5
Langau A 49 B6
Langeac F 64 A2
Langeais F 53 A5
Langedijk NL 28 C1
Langeln D 37 B6
Langelsheim D 37 B6
Langemark-Poelkapelle B 34 C3
Langen, *Hessen* D 37 D4
Langen, *Niedersachsen* D 29 B5
Langenau D 47 B6
Langenberg D 36 B4
Langenbruck CH 56 A2
Langenburg D 47 A5
Längenfeld A 57 A5
Langenfeld D 36 B2
Langenlois A 49 B6
Langenlonsheim D 46 A3
Langennaudorf D 38 B3
Langenneufnach D 48 B1
Langenthal CH 56 A2
Langenzenn D 48 A1
Langeoog D 29 B4
Langeskov DK 25 D3
Langesund N 19 B6
Langewiesen D 37 C6
Langförden D 29 C5
Langhagen D 30 B4
Länghem S 26 B3
Langhirano I 67 B4
Langnau CH 56 B2
Langø DK 25 E4
Langogne F 64 B2
Langon F 62 B3
Langquaid D 48 B3
Langreo E 74 A1
Langres F 45 C6
Långserud S 20 B4
Langset N 20 A3
Långshyttan S 22 A3
Langueux F 42 B3
Languidic F 42 C2
Längvik S 22 B5
Langwarden D 29 B5
Langwedel D 29 C6
Langweid D 48 B1
Langwies CH 57 B4
Lanheses P 73 C2
Lanięta PL 33 C5
Lanildut F 42 B1
Lanjarón E 86 C2
Lanmeur F 42 B2
Lanna, *Jönköping* S 26 B3
Lanna, *Örebro* S 22 B1
Lännaholm S 22 B4
Lannéanou F 42 B2
Lannemezan F 63 C3
Lanneuville-sur-Meuse F 45 A6
Lannilis F 42 B1
Lannion F 42 B2
Lanouaille F 53 C6
Lanškroun CZ 50 A2
Lanslebourg-Mont-Cenis F 56 C1
Lanta F 63 C4
Lantadilla E 74 B2
Lanton F 62 B1
Lantosque F 65 C6
Lanusei I 96 D2
Lanúvio I 88 B2
Lanvollon F 42 B3
Lánycsók H 60 B3
Lanz D 30 B3
Lanza E 72 A2
Lanzada E 72 B2
Lanzahita E 80 B2
Lanžhot CZ 50 B2
Lanzo Torinese I 56 C2
Laole YU 71 B6
Laon F 45 A4
Laons F 44 B2
Lapalisse F 54 B3
Łapczyna Wola PL 41 C4
Lapeyrade F 62 B2
Lapeyrouse F 54 B2
Laplume F 63 B3
Lapoutroie F 46 B3
Lapovo YU 71 B6
Lappeenranta FIN 3 F21
Lapseki TR 16 R20
Lapua FIN 3 E18
L'Áquila I 89 A3
Laracha E 72 A2
Laragne-Montéglin F 65 B4
l'Arboç E 77 B4
L'Arbresle F 55 C4
Lärbro S 23 D5
Larceveau F 62 C1
Larche, *Alpes-de-Haute-Provence* F 65 B5
Larche, *Corrèze* F 63 A4
Lårdal N 19 B5
Lardosa P 78 B3
Laredo E 75 A3
Largentière F 64 B3
L'Argentière-la-Bessée F 65 B5
Lari I 67 C4
Lariño E 72 B1
Larino I 89 B4
Lárisa GR 15 S18
Larkollen N 20 B2
Larmor-Plage F 42 C2
Larne GB 4 J4
Larochette L 46 A2
Laroque d'Olmes F 63 D4
Laroque-Timbaut F 63 B3
Laroquebrou F 63 B5
Larouco E 73 B3
Larraga E 75 B5
Larrau F 62 C2
Larrazet F 63 C4
Laruns F 62 C2
Larva E 86 B2
Larvik N 19 B7
Las Arenas E 74 A2
Las Cabezadas E 81 A3
Las Cabezas de San Juan E 85 C5
Las Correderas E 86 A2
Las Cuevas de Cañart E 76 C2
Las Gabias E 86 B2
Las Herencias E 80 C2
Las Labores E 81 C3
Las Mesas E 81 C4
Las Minas E 87 A4
Las Navas E 86 B1
Las Navas de la Concepción E 85 B5
Las Navas del Marqués E 80 B2
Las Navillas E 80 C2
Las Negras E 87 C4
Las Pajanosas E 85 B4
Las Pedroñas E 81 C4
Las Planes d'Hostoles E 77 A5
Las Rozas, *Cantabria* E 74 B2
Las Rozas, *Madrid* E 80 B3
Las Uces E 73 C4
Las Veguillas E 80 B1
Las Ventas con Peña Aguilera E 80 C2
Las Ventas de San Julián E 80 B1
Las Villes E 82 A3
Lasarte E 75 A4
Łasin PL 33 B5
Lask PL 41 B4
Łaskarzow PL 41 B6
Laško SLO 59 B5
Laskowice PL 33 B4
Laspaules E 76 A3
Laspuña E 76 A3
Lassan D 31 B5
Lassay-les-Châteaux F 43 B5
Lassigny F 44 A3
Lastovo HR 70 D1
Lastras de Cuéllar E 80 A2
Lästringe S 23 C4
Lastrup D 29 C4
Lastva BIH 70 D3
Latasa E 75 B5
Látera I 88 A1
Laterza I 91 B3
Lathen D 29 C4
Latiano I 91 B4
Latina I 88 B2
Latisana I 58 C3
Látky SK 51 B5
Latowicz PL 41 A6
Latrónico I 90 B3
Latronquière F 63 B5
Latterbach CH 56 B2
Laubach D 37 C4
Laubert F 64 B2
Laucha D 38 B1
Lauchhammer D 39 B3
Lauchheim D 47 B6
Lauda-Königshofen D 47 A5
Laudal N 19 C4
Lauenau D 37 A5
Lauenburg D 30 B2
Lauf D 48 A2
Laufach D 37 C5
Laufen CH 56 A2
Laufen D 48 C3
Lauffen D 47 A5
Lauingen D 47 B6
Laujar de Andarax E 86 C3
Laukaa FIN 3 E19
Launceston GB 4 L4
Launois-sur-Vence F 45 A5
Laupheim D 47 B5
Laureana di Borrello I 92 C3
Laurenzana I 90 B2
Lauria I 90 B2
Laurière F 53 B6
Laurino I 90 B2
Lausanne CH 55 B6
Laussonne F 64 B3
Lauta D 39 B4
Lautenthal D 37 B6
Lauterach A 57 A4
Lauterbach D 37 C5
Lauterbrunnen CH 56 B2
Lauterecken D 46 A3
Lauterhofen D 48 A2
Lautrec F 63 C5
Lauvvik N 18 C3
Lauzerte F 63 B4
Lauzès F 63 B4
Lauzun F 63 B3
Lavagna I 66 B3
Laval F 43 B5
Lavamünd A 59 B4
Lavardac F 62 B3
Lavaris P 78 A2
Lavarone I 57 C6
Lavau F 45 C3
Lavaur F 63 C5
Lavelanet F 63 D4
Lavello I 90 A2
Lavelsloh D 29 C5
Laveno I 56 C3
Lavezzola I 67 B5
Laviano I 90 B2
Lavilledieu F 64 B3
Lavinio-Lido di Enea I 88 B2
Lavis I 57 B6
Lavit F 63 C3
Lavoncourt F 46 C1
Lavos P 78 A2
Lavoûter-Chilhac F 54 C3
Lavradio P 78 C1
Lavre P 78 C2
Lávrion GR 16 T19
Ławy PL 31 C6
Laxå S 23 C1
Laxe E 72 A2
Laxhall S 21 C5
Laxvik S 26 C2
Laza E 73 B3
Lazarevac YU 71 B5
Lazarevo YU 61 C5
Lazise I 57 C5
Łaziska Grn. PL 40 C3
Lazkao E 75 A4
Lázně Bělohrad CZ 39 C5
Lázně Bohdaneč CZ 39 C5
Lázně Kynžvart CZ 38 C2
Łazy PL 32 A2
Lazzaro I 95 B4
Le Bar-sur-Loup F 65 C5
Le Barp F 62 B2
Le Béage F 64 B3
Le Beausset F 65 C4
Le Bessat F 55 C4
Le Blanc F 53 B6
Le Bleymard F 64 B2
Le Boullay-Mivoye F 44 B2
Le Boulou F 77 A5
Le Bourg F 63 B4
Le Bourg-d'Oisans F 65 A5
Le Bourget-du-Lac F 55 C5
Le Bourgneuf-la-Forêt F 43 B5
Le Bousquet d'Orb F 64 C2
Le Brassus CH 55 B6
Le Breuil F 54 B3
Le Breuil-en-Auge F 43 A6
Le Brusquet F 65 B5
Le Bry CH 56 B2
Le Bugue F 63 B3
Le Buisson F 63 B3
Le Caloy F 62 C2
Le Cap d'Agde F 64 C2
Le Cateau Cambrésis F 35 C4
Le Caylar F 64 C2
Le Cayrol F 64 B1
Le Chambon-Feugerolles F 55 C4
Le Chambon-sur-Lignon F 64 A3
Le Château d'Oléron F 52 C3
Le Châtelard F 55 C6
Le Châtelet F 54 B2
Le Chatelet-en-Brie F 44 B3
Le Chesne F 45 A5
Le Cheylard F 64 B3
Le Collet-de-Deze F 64 B2
Le Conquet F 42 B1
Le Creusot F 55 B4
Le Croisic F 52 A2
Le Crotoy F 34 C2
Le Deschaux F 55 B5
Le Donjon F 54 B3
Le Dorat F 53 B6
Le Faou F 42 B1
Le Faoüet F 42 B2
Le Folgoet F 42 B1
Le Fossat F 63 C4
Le Fousseret F 63 C4
Le Fugeret F 65 B5
Le Gault-Soigny F 45 B4
Le Grand-Bornand F 55 C6
Le-Grand-Bourg F 53 B6
Le Grand-Lucé F 44 C1
Le Grand-Pressigny F 53 B5
Le Grand-Quevilly F 44 A2
Le Grau-du-Roi F 64 C3
Le Havre F 43 A6
Le Hohwald F 46 B3
Le Houga F 62 C2
Le Lardin-St. Lazare F 53 C6
Le Lauzet-Ubaye F 65 B5
Le Lavandou F 65 C5
Le Lion-d'Angers F 43 C5
Le Locle CH 56 A1
Le Loroux-Bottereau F 52 A3
Le Louroux-Béconnais F 52 A4
Le Luc F 65 C5
Le Lude F 43 C6
Le Malzieu-Ville F 64 B2
Le Mans F 43 B6
Le Mas-d'Azil F 63 C4
Le Massegros F 64 B2
Le May-sur-Evre F 52 A4
Le Mayet-de-Montagne F 54 B3
Le Mêle-sur-Sarthe F 44 B1
Le Ménil F 46 B2
Le Merlerault F 43 B6
Le Mesnil-sur-Oger F 45 B5
Le Miroir F 55 B5
Le Molay-Littry F 43 A5
Le Monastier-sur-Gazeille F 64 B2
Le Monêtier-les-Bains F 65 B5
Le Mont-Dore F 54 C2
Le Mont-St. Michel F 43 B4
Le Montet F 54 B3
Le Muret F 62 B2
Le Muy F 65 C5
Le Neubourg F 44 A1
Le Nouvion-en-Thiérache F 35 C4
Le Palais F 52 A1
Le Parcq F 34 C3
Le Péage-de-Roussillon F 55 C4
Le Pellerin F 52 A3
Le Perthus F 77 A5
Le Pertuis F 64 A3
Le Petit-Bornand F 55 C6
Le Poët F 65 B4
Le Poiré-sur-Vie F 52 B3
Le Pont CH 55 B6
Le Pont-de-Montvert F 64 B2
Le Porge F 62 B1
Le Portel F 34 C2
Le Pouldu F 42 C2
Le Pouliguen F 52 A2
le Prese I 57 B5
Le Puy-en-Velay F 64 A2
Le Puy-Ste. Réparade F 65 C4
Le Quesnoy F 35 C4
Le Rayol F 65 C5
Le Rœulx B 35 C5
Le Rouget F 63 B5
Le Rozier F 64 B2
Le Russey F 56 A1
Le Sel-de-Bretagne F 43 C4
Le Sentier CH 55 B6
Le Souquet F 62 C1
Le Teil F 64 B3
Le Teilleul F 43 B5
Le Temple-de-Bretagne F 52 A3
Le Theil F 44 B1
Le Thillot F 46 C2
Le Touquet-Paris-Plage F 34 C2
Le Touvet F 55 C5
Le Translay F 34 D2
Le Tréport F 34 C2
Le Val F 65 C5
Le Val-André F 42 B3
Le Val-d'Ajol F 46 C2
Le Verdon-sur-Mer F 52 C3
Le Vernet F 65 B5
Le Vigan F 64 C2
le Ville I 68 C1
Le Vivier-sur-Mer F 43 B4
Łeba PL 32 A3
Lebach D 46 A2
Lebedyn UA 7 L24
Lebekke B 35 B5
Lébény H 50 C3
Łebno PL 33 A4
Leboreiro E 73 B3
Lębork PL 32 A3
Lebrija E 85 C4
Lebring A 59 B5
Lebus D 31 C6
Lebusa D 38 B3
Leca da Palmeira P 73 C2
Lecce I 91 B5
Lecco I 57 C4
Lécera E 76 B2
Lećevica HR 69 C5
Lech A 57 A5
Lechbruck D 48 C1
Lechovice CZ 50 B2
Leck D 25 E1
Lectoure F 63 C3
Łęczyca, *Płock* PL 41 A4
Łęczyca, *Szczecin* PL 31 B7
Ledaña E 81 C5
Lede B 35 C4
Ledeč nad Sazavou CZ 49 A6
Ledenice CZ 49 B5
Ledesma E 73 C4
Lédignan F 64 C3
Lédigos E 74 B2
Ledince CZ 50 B2
Lednicke-Rovné SK 50 A4
Lędyczek PL 32 B2
Lędziny PL 41 C4
Leeds GB 4 K6
Leek NL 28 B3
Leens NL 28 B3
Leer D 29 B4
Leerdam NL 35 B6
Leerhafe D 29 B4
Leese D 29 C6
Leeuwarden NL 28 B2
Leezen D 30 B2
Leganés E 80 B3
Legau D 47 C6
Legbąd PL 32 B3
Legé F 52 B3
Lège-Cap-Ferret F 62 B1
Legionowo PL 41 A5
Léglise
Legnago I
Legnano I 56 C3
Legnaro I 58 C1
Legnica PL 39 B6
Łęgowo PL 33 A4
Legrad HR 60 B1
Léguevin F 63 C4
Legutiano E 75 B4
Lehesten D 38 C1
Lehnice SK 50 B3
Lehnin D 38 A2
Lehrberg D 47 A6
Lehre D 30 C2
Lehrte D 30 C1
Lehsen D 30 B3
Leibnitz A 59 B5
Leicester GB 4 K6
Leiden NL 35 A5
Leidschendam NL 35 A5
Leignon B 35 C6
Leimen D 47 A4
Leinefelde D 37 B6
Leipzig D 38 B2
Leiria P 78 B2
Leirvik N 18 B2
Leisach A 58 B2
Leisnig D 38 B2
Leitrim IRL 4 J2
Leitza E 75 A5
Leitzkau D 38 A1
Łękawa PL 41 B4
Łękawica PL 51 A5
Lekeitio E 75 A4
Lekenik HR 59 C6
Lekeryd S 26 B4
Łęknica PL 39 B4
Lekunberri E 75 A5
Lekvattnet S 20 A4
Lelkowo PL 33 A6
Lelów PL 41 C4
Lelystad NL 28 C2
Lem, *Ringkøbing* DK 25 C1
Lem, *Viborg Amt.* DK 24 C1
Lembach F 46 A3
Lemberg F 46 A3
Lembèye F 62 C2
Lemelerveld NL 28 C3
Lemförde D 29 C5
Lemgo D 37 A4
Lemmer NL 28 C2
Lempdes F 54 C3
Lemvig DK 24 C1
Lemwerder D 29 B5
Lenart SLO 59 B5
Lenartovce SK 51 B6
Lenauheim RO 61 C5
Lencloître F 53 B5
Lend A 58 A3
Lendava SLO 59 B6
Lendery RUS 3 E22
Lendinara I 67 A5
Lendorf A 58 B3
Lendum DK 24 B3
Lengefeld D 38 C3
Lengerich, *Niedersachsen* D 29 C4
Lengerich, *Nordrhein-Westfalen* D 36 A3
Lenggries D 48 C2
Lengyeltóti H 60 B2
Lenhovda S 26 C5
Lenk CH 56 B2
Lennartsfors S 20 B3
Lennestadt D 36 B4
Leno I 57 C5
Lénola I 89 B3
Lens B 35 C4
Lens F 34 C3
Lens Lestang F 55 C5
Lensahn D 30 A2
Lentellais E 73 B3
Lentföhrden D 30 B1
Lenti H 60 B1
Lentini I 95 B3
Lenzburg CH 56 A3
Lenzen D 30 B3
Lenzerheide CH 57 B4
Leoben A 59 A5
Leogang A 58 A2
Leominster GB 4 K5
León E 74 B1
Léon F 62 C1
Leonberg D 47 B5
Léoncel F 65 B4
Leonding A 49 B5
Leonessa I 88 A2
Leonforte I 95 B3
Leopoldsburg B 35 B6
Leopoldsdorf im Marchfeld A 50 B2
Leopoldshagen D 31 B5
Leova MD 11 N21
Lepe E 84 B3
Lepenac YU 71 C6
Lepenac YU 71 D4
L'Epine F 65 B4
Lepoglava HR 59 B6
Leppävirta FIN 3 E20
Leppin D 30 C3
Lepsény H 60 B3
Léquile I 91 B5
Lercara Friddi I 94 B2
Lerdal S 21 C3
Leré F 54 A2
Lérici I 67 B3
Lerin E 75 B5
Lerm-et-Musset F 62 B2
Lerma E 74 B3
Lermoos A 57 A5
Lérouville F 46 B1
Lerum S 21 D4
Lervik N 20 B2
Lerwick GB 4 F6
Lés E 63 D3
Les Abrets F 55 C5
Les Aix-d'Angillon F 54 A2
Les Ancizes-Comps F 54 C2
Les Andelys F 44 A2

Les Arcs, *Savoie* F 56 C1
Les Arcs, *Var* F 65 C5
Les-Aubiers F 53 B4
Les Baux-de-Provence F 64 C3
Les Bézards F 44 C3
Les Bois CH 56 A1
Les Bordes F 44 C3
Les Borges Blanques E 76 B3
Les Borges del Camp E 77 B4
Les Brunettes F 54 B3
Les Cabannes F 63 D4
Les Contamines-Montjoie F 56 C1
les Coves de Vinroma E 82 A3
Les Déserts F 55 C5
Les Deux-Alpes F 65 B5
Les Diablerets CH 56 B2
Les Echelles F 55 C5
Les Escaldes AND 77 A4
Les Essarts F 52 B3
Les Estables F 64 B3
Les Eyzies-de-Tayac F 63 B4
Les Gets F 56 B1
Les Grandes-Ventes F 44 A2
Les Haudères CH 56 B2
Les Herbiers F 52 B3
Les Hôpitaux-Neufs F 55 B6
Les Lucs-sur-Boulogne F 52 B3
Les Mages F 64 B3
Les Mazures F 45 A5
Les Mées F 65 B4
Les Mureaux F 44 B2
Les Omergues F 65 B4
Les Ormes-sur-Voulzie F 45 B4
Les Orres F 65 B5
Les Pieux F 43 A4
Les Ponts-de-Cé F 53 A4
Les Ponts-de-Martel CH 56 B1
Les Praz F 56 C1
Les Riceys F 45 C5
Les Roches F 55 C4
Les Rosaires F 42 B3
Les Rosiers F 53 A4
Les Rousses F 55 B6
Les Sables-d'Olonne F 52 B3
Les Settons F 54 A4
Les Ternes F 64 A1
Les Thilliers en-Vexin F 44 A2
Les Touches F 52 A3
Les Trois Moûtiers F 53 A5
Les Vans F 64 B3
Les Verrières CH 55 B6
Les Vignes F 64 B2
Lešak YU 71 C5
Lesaka E 75 A5
L'Escala E 77 A6
Lescar F 62 C2
L'Escarène F 66 C1
Lesce SLO 59 B4
Lescheraines F 55 C6
Lesconil F 42 C1
Lesdins F 45 A4
Lesično SLO 59 B5
Lésina I 89 B5
Lesjaskog N 2 E11
Lesjaverk N 2 E11
Lesjöfors S 20 B6
Leskova Dolina SLO 59 C4
Leskovac YU 15 Q17
Leskovec CZ 50 A3
Leskovec SLO 59 C5
Leskovice CZ 49 A6
Lesmont F 45 B5
Leśna PL 39 B5
Lesneven F 42 B1
Leśnica PL 40 C3
Lešnica YU 71 B4
Leśniów Wielkoplski PL 39 B5
Lesnoye RUS 7 G24
Lesparre-Médoc F 52 C4
Lesponne F 62 C3
L'Espunyola E 77 A4
Lessach A 58 A3
Lessay F 43 A4
Lessebo S 26 C4
Lessines B 35 C4
L'Estany E 77 B5
Lesterps F 53 B5
Leszno PL 40 B1
Leszno PL 41 A5
Leszno Górne PL 39 B5
Letenye H 60 B1
Letino I 89 B4
Letohrad CZ 40 C1
Letovice CZ 50 A2
Letschin D 31 C6
Letterkenny IRL 4 J3
Letur E 87 A3
Letux E 76 B2
Letzlingen D 30 C3
Leucate F 64 D2
Leuglay F 45 C5
Leuk CH 56 B2
Leukerbad CH 56 B2
Leuna D 38 B2
Leusden NL 35 A6
Leutenberg D 38 C1
Leuterschach D 47 C6
Leutershausen D 47 A6
Leutkirch D 47 C6
Leuven B 35 C5
Leuze-en-Hainaut B 35 C4
Levádhia GR 15 S18
Levanger N 2 E12
Levanjska Varoš HR 60 C3
Lévanto I 66 B3
Levata I 57 C5
Leverano I 91 B4
Leverkusen D 36 B2
Levern D 29 C5
Levet F 54 B2
Levice SK 51 B4
Lévico Terme I 57 B6
Levie F 96 B2
Levier F 55 B6
Lévignen F 45 A3
Levinovac HR 60 C2
Levoča SK 51 A6
Levroux F 53 B6
Lewin Brzeski PL 40 C2
Leysin CH 56 B2
Lezajsk PL 11 L18
Lézardrieux F 42 B2
Lézat-sur-Léze F 63 C4
Lezay F 53 B4
Lezhë AL 15 R16
Lézignan-Corbières F 64 C1
Lezignan-la-Cèbe F 64 C2
Ležimir YU 71 A4
Lézinnes F 45 C5
Lezoux F 54 C3
Lezuza E 81 D4
Lgov RUS 7 L24
Lhenice CZ 49 B5
Lherm F 63 C4
Lhommaizé F 53 B5
L'Hospitalet F 77 A4
L'Hospitalet de l'Infant E 76 C3
L'Hospitalet de Llobregat E 77 B5
L'Hospitalet-du-Larzac F 64 C2
Lhuître F 45 B5
Liancourt F 44 A3
Liart F 45 A5
Liatorp S 26 C4
Libáň CZ 39 C5
Libceves CZ 39 C3
Liběchov CZ 39 C4
Liber E 72 B3
Liberec CZ 39 C5
Libiąż PL 41 C4
Libina CZ 50 A3
Libochovice CZ 39 C4
Libourne F 62 B2
Libramont B 46 A1
Librilla E 87 B4
Libros E 82 A1
Licata I 94 B2
Licciana Nardi I 67 B4
Licenza I 88 A2
Liceros E 75 C3
Lich D 37 C4
Lichères-près-Aigremont F 45 C4
Lichfield GB 4 K6
Lichtenau A 49 B6
Lichtenau D 37 B4
Lichtenberg D 38 C1
Lichtenfels D 38 C1
Lichtensteig CH 57 A4
Lichtenstein D 38 C2
Lichtenvoorde NL 36 B2
Lichtervelde B 35 B4
Lička Jesenica HR 69 A4
Lickershamn S 23 D5
Lički Osik HR 69 B4
Ličko Lešće HR 69 B4
Licodia Eubéa I 95 B3
Lida BY 7 K19
Lidečko CZ 50 A4
Lidhult S 26 C3
Lidköping S 21 C5
Lido I 58 C2
Lido Azzurro I 91 B4
Lido degli Estensi I 68 B1
Lido degli Scacchi I 68 B1
Lido della Nazioni I 68 B1
Lido di Camaiore I 67 C4
Lido di Casalbordino I 89 A4
Lido di Castél Fusano I 88 B2
Lido di Cincinnato I 88 B2
Lido di Classe I 68 B1
Lido di Fermo I 68 C2
Lido di Fondi I 89 B3
Lido di Jésolo I 58 C2
Lido di Lícola I 89 C4
Lido di Metaponto I 91 B3
Lido di Óstia I 88 B2
Lido di Policoro I 91 B3
Lido di Pomposa I 68 B1
Lido di Savio I 68 B1
Lido di Scanzano I 91 B3
Lido di Siponto I 90 A2
Lido di Squillace I 92 C3
Lido di Volano I 68 B1
Lido Riccio I 89 A4
Lido Silvana I 91 B4
Lidzbark PL 33 B5
Lidzbark Warmiński PL 33 A6
Liebenau A 49 B5
Liebenau D 29 C6
Liebenwalde D 31 C5
Lieberose D 39 B4
Liebling RO 61 C6
Lieboch A 59 B5
Liège B 35 C6
Lieksa FIN 3 E22
Lienen D 36 A3
Lienz A 58 B2
Liepāja LV 6 H17
Lier B 35 B5
Lierbyen N 20 B2
Liernais F 55 A4
Liesing A 58 B2
Liestal CH 56 A2
Liétor E 87 A4
Lieurey F 44 A1
Liévin F 34 C3
Liezen A 59 A4
Liffol-le-Grand F 46 B1
Lifford IRL 4 J3
Liffré F 43 B4
Ligardes F 63 B3
Lignano Sabbiadoro I 58 C3
Ligne F 52 A3
Lignières F 54 B2
Ligny-en-Barrois F 45 B6
Ligny-le-Châtel F 45 C4
Ligoła Polska PL 40 B2
Ligowo PL 33 C5
Ligueil F 53 A5
Likavka SK 51 A5
Likhoslavl RUS 7 H24
Lild Strand DK 24 B1
L'Île-Bouchard F 53 A5
l'Île-Rousse F 96 A1
Lilienfeld A 49 B6
Lilienthal D 29 B5
Lilla Edet S 21 C4
Lilla Tjärby S 26 C3
Lille B 35 B5
Lille F 35 C4
Lillebonne F 44 A1
Lillehammer N 2 F12
Lillerød DK 27 D2
Lillers F 34 C3
Lillesand N 19 C5
Lillestrøm N 20 B3
Lillkyrka S 22 B4
Lillo E 81 C3
Limanowa PL 51 A6
Limbach-Oberfrohna D 38 C2
Limbaži LV 6 H19
Limbourg B 36 C1
Limburg D 36 C4
Limerick IRL 4 K2
Limes I 57 C5
Limésy F 44 A1
Limmared S 26 B3
Limoges F 53 C6
Limogne-en-Quercy F 63 B4
Limone Piemonte I 66 B1
Limone sul Garda I 57 C5
Limons F 54 C3
Limours F 44 B3
Limoux F 63 C5
Linares E 86 A2
Linares de Mora E 82 A2
Linares de Riofrio E 79 A5
Linas de Broto E 76 A2
Lincoln GB 4 K6
Lind DK 25 C1
Lindau D 57 A4
Lindelse DK 25 E3
Lindenberg D 39 A4
Lindenberg im Allgäu D 47 C5
Lindern D 29 C4
Linderöd S 27 D3
Lindesberg S 22 B2
Lindesnes N 19 D4
Lindholmen S 22 B5
Lindhos GR 16 T21
Lindknud DK 25 D2
Lindlar D 36 B3
Lindö S 23 C3
Lindome S 21 D4
Lindoso P 73 C2
Lindow D 31 C4
Lindsdal S 26 C6
Lindshammar S 26 B5
Lindstedt D 30 C3
Lindved DK 25 D2
Linë CZ 49 A4
Lingen D 29 C4
Linghem S 23 C2
Linguaglossa I 95 B4
Linia PL 32 A3
Linie PL 31 B6
Liniewo PL 33 A4
Linkenheim D 47 A4
Linköping S 23 C2
Linneryd S 26 C5
Linnes Hammarby S 22 B4
Linnich D 36 C2
Linthal CH 56 B4
Linyola E 76 B3
Linz A 49 B5
Linz D 36 C3
Lion-sur-Mer F 43 A5
Lioni I 90 B2
Lipany SK 51 A6
Lipar YU 61 C4
Lípari I 95 A3
Lipcani MD 11 M20
Liperi FIN 3 E21
Lipiany PL 31 B6
Lipik HR 60 C2
Lipka PL 32 B3
Lipki Wielkie PL 32 C1
Lipnica PL 32 B3
Lipnica Murowana PL 51 A6
Lipnik PL 41 C6
Lipník nad Bečvou CZ 50 A3
Lipno PL 33 C5
Lipno PL 40 B3
Liposthey F 62 B2
Lipovac HR 70 A4
Lipovec CZ 50 A2
Lipovets UA 11 M21
Lipovljani HR 60 C1
Lipowina PL 33 A5
Lippborg D 36 B4
Lippó H 60 C3
Lippoldsberg D 37 B5
Lippstadt D 37 B4
Lipsko PL 41 B6
Liptál CZ 50 A3
Liptovská-Lúžna SK 51 B5
Liptovská Osada SK 51 B5
Liptovská-Teplička SK 51 B6
Liptovský Hrádok SK 51 A5
Liptovský Milkuláš SK 51 A5
Lipusz PL 32 A3
Lipůvka CZ 50 A2
Liré F 52 A3
Lisa YU 71 C5
Lisac BIH 70 B2
Lisboa P 78 C1
Lisburn GB 4 J3
Lisewo PL 33 B4
Lisia Góra PL 41 C6
Lisięcice PL 40 C2
Lisieux F 43 A6
L'Isle CH 55 B6
L'Isle-Adam F 44 A3
L'Isle-de-Noé F 63 C3
L'Isle-en-Dodon F 63 C3
L'Isle-Jourdain, *Gers* F 63 C4
L'Isle-Jourdain, *Vienne* F 53 B5
L'Isle-sur-la-Sorgue F 65 C4
L'Isle-sur-le Doubs F 55 A6
L'Isle-sur-Serein F 54 A4
Lisle-sur-Tarn F 63 C4
Lišov CZ 49 A5
Lisów PL 31 C6
Lisów PL 40 C3
Lisse NL 35 A5
List D 25 D1
Listerby S 27 C5
Listowel IRL 4 K2
Listrac-Médoc F 62 A2
Liszki PL 41 C4
Liszkowo PL 32 B3
Lit S 2 E14
Lit-et-Mixe F 62 B1
Litava SK 51 B5
Litija SLO 59 B4
Litke H 51 B5
Litlabø N 18 B2
Litókhoron GR 15 R18
Litoměřice CZ 39 C4
Litomyšl CZ 50 A2
Litovel CZ 50 A3
Litschau A 49 B6
Litvínov CZ 38 C3
Livarot F 43 B6
Livernon F 63 B4
Liverovici YU 70 D4
Liverpool GB 4 K5
Livigno I 57 B5
Livno BIH 70 C1
Livold SLO 59 C4
Livorno I 67 C4
Livorno Ferraris I 56 C3
Livron-sur-Drôme F 64 B3
Livry-Louvercy F 45 A5
Lixheim F 46 B3
Lizy-sur-Ourcq F 45 A4
Lizzano I 91 B4
Lizzano in Belvedere I 67 B4
Ljig YU 71 B5
Ljosland N 19 C4
Ljubija BIH 69 B5
Ljubinje BIH 70 D3
Ljubljana SLO 59 B4
Ljubno ob Savinji SLO 59 B4
Ljubovija YU 71 B4
Ljubuški BIH 70 C2
Ljugarn S 6 H16
Ljung S 21 D5
Ljunga S 23 C3
Ljungby S 26 C3
Ljungbyhed S 27 C3
Ljungbyholm S 26 C6
Ljungsarp S 26 B3
Ljungsbro S 23 C2
Ljungskile S 21 C3
Ljusdal S 2 F15
Ljusfallshammar S 23 C2
Ljusne S 2 F15
Ljusterö S 22 B5
Ljutomer SLO 59 B6
Lladurs E 77 A4
Llafranc E 77 B6
Llagostera E 77 B5
Llançà E 77 A6
Llandeilo GB 4 L5
Llandovery GB 4 L5
Llandrindod Wells GB 4 K5
Llandudec F 42 B1
Llandudno GB 4 K5
Llanelli GB 4 L4
Llanes E 74 A2
Llangollen GB 4 K5
Llanteno E 75 A3
Llavorsi E 77 A4
Lleida E 76 B3
Llera E 79 C4
Llerena E 85 A4
Lles E 77 A4
Llessui E 77 A4
Llinars E 77 A4
Lliria E 82 B2
Llivia E 77 A4
Lljezd u Brna CZ 50 A2
Llodio E 75 A4
Lloret de Mar E 77 B5
Llosa de Ranes E 82 B2
Lloseta, *Mallorca* E 83
Llucena del Cid E 82 A2
Llucmajor, *Mallorca* E 83
Llutxent E 82 C2
Lnáře CZ 49 A4
Lniano PL 33 B4
Lo Pagán E 87 B5
Loano I 66 B2
Loarre E 76 A2
Löbau D 39 B4
Löbejün D 38 B1
Löberöd S 27 D3
Łobez PL 32 B1
Löbnitz D 31 A4
Lobón E 79 C4
Loburg D 38 A2
Łobżenica PL 32 B3
Locana I 56 C2
Locarno CH 56 B3
Loccum D 29 C6
Loče SLO 59 B5
Loch Baghasdail GB 4 H3
Loch nam Madadh GB 4 H3
Lochau A 57 A4
Lochem NL 36 A2
Loches F 53 A5
Lochgilphead GB 4 H4
Lochinver GB 4 G4
Ločika YU 71 C6
Lockenhaus A 59 A6
Lockerbie GB 4 J5
Löcknitz D 31 B6
Locmaria F 52 A1
Locmariaquer F 42 C3
Locminé F 42 C3
Locorotondo I 91 B4
Locquirec F 42 B2
Locri I 92 C3
Locronan F 42 B1
Loctudy F 42 C1
Lodares de Osma E 75 C4
Lodé I 96 C2
Lodève F 64 C2
Lodi I 57 C4
Lødingen N 2 B14
Lodosa E 75 B4
Lödöse S 21 C4
Łódź PL 41 B4
Loeches E 81 B3
Løfallstrand N 18 A3
Lofer A 58 A2
Loftahammar S 23 D3
Lofthus N 18 A3
Loga N 18 C3
Logatec SLO 59 C4
Lograto I 57 C5
Logroño E 75 B4
Logrosán E 79 B5
Løgstør DK 24 C2
Løgumgårde DK 25 D1
Løgumkloster DK 25 D1
Lohals DK 25 D3
Lohja FIN 3 F19
Löhlbach D 37 B4
Lohmen, *Mecklenburg-Vorpommern* D 30 B4
Lohmen, *Sachsen* D 39 C4
Löhnberg D 36 C4
Lohne, *Niedersachsen* D 29 C5
Löhne, *Nordrhein-Westfalen* D 37 A4
Lohr D 37 D5
Lohra D 37 C4
Lohsa D 39 B4
Loiano I 67 B5
Loimaa FIN 3 F18
Lóiri I 96 C2
Loitz D 31 B5
Loivos P 73 C3
Loivos do Monte P 73 C3
Loja E 86 B1
Lojanice YU 71 B4
Løjt Kirkeby DK 25 D2
Lok SK 51 B4
Lokca SK 51 A5
Løken N 20 B3
Lokeren B 35 B4
Loket CZ 38 C2
Lokhvitsa UA 7 L23
Løkken DK 24 B2
Løkken N 2 E11
Loknya RUS 7 H22
Lökösháza H 61 B6
Lokot RUS 7 K24
Lokve YU 71 A6
Lollar D 37 C4
L'Olleria E 82 C2
Lölling-Graben A 59 B4
Lom BG 15 Q18
Lom N 2 F11
Lom SK 51 B5
Lombez F 63 C3
Lomello I 66 A2
Łomianki PL 41 A5
Lomma S 27 D3
Lommaryd S 23 D1
Lommatzsch D 38 B3
Lommel B 35 B6
Lommersum D 36 C2
Lomnice CZ 50 A2
Lomnice nad Lužnici CZ 49 A5
Lomnice-nad Popelkou CZ 39 C5
Łomza PL 6 K18
Lönashult S 26 C4
Lønborg DK 25 D1
Londerzeel B 35 B5
Londinières F 44 A2
London GB 4 L6
Londonderry GB 4 J3
Longare I 58 C1
Longares E 76 B1
Longarone I 58 B2
Longastrino I 67 B6
Longchamp-sur-Aujon F 45 B5
Longchaumois F 55 B5
Longeau F 45 C6
Longecourt-en-Plaine F 55 A5
Longeville-les-St. Avold F 46 A2
Longeville-sur-Mer F 52 B3
Longford IRL 4 K3
Longi I 95 A3
Longny-au-Perche F 44 B1
Longobucco I 92 B3
Longré F 53 B4
Longroiva P 73 D3
Longué-Jumelles F 53 A4
Longueau F 44 A3
Longuyon F 46 A1
Longvic F 55 A5
Longvilly B 36 C1
Longwy F 46 A1
Lonigo I 57 C6
Löningen D 29 C4
Lonja HR 60 C1
Lönneberga S 26 B5
Lons-le-Saunier F 55 B5
Lönsboda S 27 C4
Lønstrup DK 24 B2
Loon op Zand NL 35 B6
Loone-Plage F 34 B3
Loosdorf A 49 B6
Lopar HR 69 B3
Lopare BIH 70 B3
Lopera E 86 B1
Loppersum NL 28 B3
Łopuszna PL 51 A6
Łopuszno PL 41 C5
Lor F 45 A5
Lora de Estepa E 86 B1
Lora del Río E 85 B5
Loranca del Campo E 81 B4
Lörby S 27 C4
Lorca E 87 B4
Lorch D 36 C3
Lørenfallet N 20 A3
Lørenskog N 20 B2
Loreo I 68 A1
Loreto I 68 C2
Lorgues F 65 C5
Lorica I 92 B3
Lorient F 42 C2
Lorignac F 53 C4
Lőrinci H 51 C5
Loriol-sur-Drôme F 64 B3
Lormes F 54 A3
Loro Ciuffenna I 67 C5
Lorqui E 87 A4
Lörrach D 46 C3
Lorrez-le-Bocage F 45 B3
Lorris F 44 C3
Lorup D 29 C4
Łoś PL 41 B5
Los Alcázares E 87 B5
Los Arcos E 75 B4
Los Barios de Luna E 74 B1
Los Barrios E 85 C5
Los Caños de Meca E 85 C4
Los Cerricos E 87 B3
Los Corrales E 86 B1
Los Corrales de Buelna E 74 A2
Los Dolores E 87 B4
Los Gallardos E 87 B4
Los Hinojosos E 81 C4
Los Isidros E 82 B1
Los Molinos E 80 B2
Los Morales E 85 B5
Los Navalmorales E 80 C2
Los Navalucillos E 80 C2
Los Nietos E 87 B5
Los Palacios y Villafranca E 85 B5
Los Pozuelos de Calatrava E 86 A1
Los Rábanos E 75 C4
Los Santos E 79 A5
Los Santos de la Humosa E 81 B3
Los Santos de Maimona E 79 C4
Los Tijos E 74 A2
Los Villares E 86 B2
Los Yébenes E 80 C3
Losacino E 73 C4
Losar de la Vera E 79 A5
Losenstein A 49 C5
Losheim, *Nordrhein-Westfalen* D 36 C2
Losheim, *Saarland* D 46 A2
Losne F 55 A5
Løsning DK 25 D2
Lossburg D 47 B4
Losser NL 36 A3
Lössnitz D 38 C2
Loštice CZ 50 A2
Lotorp S 23 C2
Lotyń PL 32 B2
Lotzorai I 96 D2
Louargat F 42 B2
Loudéac F 42 B3
Loudun F 53 A5
Loué F 43 C5
Loughborough GB 4 K6
Loughrea IRL 4 K2
Louhans F 55 B5
Loukhi RUS 3 C23
Loulay F 53 B4
Loulé P 84 B2
Louny CZ 39 C3
Lourdes F 62 C2
Lourenzá E 72 A3
Loures P 78 C1
Loures-Barousse F 63 C3
Louriçal P 78 A2
Lourinhã P 78 B1
Loury F 44 C3
Lousa, *Bragança* P 73 C3
Lousa, *Castelo Branco* P 78 B3
Lousã, *Coimbra* P 78 A2
Lousa, *Lisboa* P 78 C1
Lousada E 72 B3
Lousada P 73 C2
Louth GB 4 K7
Louverné F 43 B5
Louvie-Juzon F 62 C2
Louviers F 44 A2
Louvigné-du-Désert F 43 B4
Louvois F 45 A5
Lova I 58 C2
Lovasberény H 60 A3
Lovászpatona H 60 A2
Lovech BG 16 Q19
Lövenich D 36 B2
Lóvere I 57 C5
Lövestad S 27 D3
Loviisa FIN 3 F20
Lovinobaňa SK 51 B5
Loviste HR 70 C2
Lovke HR 59 C4
Lövö H 60 A1
Lovosice CZ 39 C4
Lovozero RUS 3 C24
Lovran HR 59 C4
Lovreć HR 70 C1
Lovrenc na Pohorju SLO 59 B5
Lovrin RO 61 C5
Lövstabruk S 22 A4
Löwenberg D 31 C5
Löwenstein D 47 A5
Lowestoft GB 4 K7
Łowicz PL 41 A4
Loxstedt D 29 B5
Loyew BY 11 L22
Lož SLO 59 C4
Loza CZ 49 A4
Loznica YU 71 B4
Lozničko Polje YU 71 B4
Lozorno SK 50 B3
Lozovik YU 71 B6
Lozoya E 80 B3
Lozoyuela E 81 B3
Lozzo di Cadore I 58 B2
Luanco E 74 A1
Luarca E 72 A4
Lubaczów PL 11 L18
Lubań PL 39 B5
Lubanów PL 41 B4
Lubars D 38 A2
Lubasz PL 32 C2
Lubawa PL 33 B5
Lubawka PL 39 C6
Lübbecke D 37 A4
Lübben D 39 B3
Lübbenau D 39 B3
Lubczyna PL 31 B6
Lübeck D 30 B2
Lubenec CZ 38 C3
Lubersac F 53 C6
Lübesse D 30 B3
Lubia E 75 C4
Lubian E 73 B4
Lubiatowo PL 31 B7
Lubichowo PL 33 B4
Lubicz Dolny PL 33 B4
Lubień PL 51 A5
Lubień Kujawski PL 33 C5
Lubienia PL 41 B6
Lubieszewo PL 32 B1
Lubin, *Legnica* PL 39 B6
Lubin, *Szczecin* PL 31 B6
Lublin PL 11 L18
Lubliniec PL 40 C3
Lubmin D 31 A5
Lubniewice PL 32 C1
Lubny UA 11 L23
Lubochnia PL 41 B5
Lubomierz, *Jelenia Góra* PL 39 B5
Lubomierz, *Nowy Secz* PL 51 A6
Lubomino PL 33 A6
Luboń PL 32 C2
L'ubotín SK 51 A6
Lubowidz PL 33 B5
Łubowo PL 32 B2
Łubowo PL 32 C3
Lubraniec PL 33 C4
Lubrin E 87 B3
Lubrza PL 40 C2
Lubsko PL 39 B4
Lübtheen D 30 B3
Lubuczewo PL 32 A3
Luby CZ 38 C2
Lübz D 30 B4
Luc F 64 B2
Luc-en-Diois F 65 B4
Luc-sur-Mer F 43 A5
Lucainena de las Torres E 87 B3
Lučani YU 71 C5
Lúcar E 87 B3
Luçay-le-Mâle F 53 A6
Lucca I 67 C4
Lucciana F 96 A2
Lucé F 44 B2
Luče SLO 59 B4
Lucena, *Córdoba* E 86 B1
Lucena, *Huelva* E 85 B4
Lucenay-les-Aix F 54 B3
Lucenay-l'Evéque F 55 A4
Lučenec SK 51 B5
Luceni E 76 B1
Lucens CH 56 B1
Lucera I 90 A2
Luceram F 66 C1
Lüchow D 30 C3
Luciana E 80 D2
Lucignano I 67 C5
Lucija SLO 58 C3
Lucka D 38 B2
Luckau D 39 B3
Luckenwalde D 38 A3
Lückstedt D 30 C3
Luco dei Marsi I 89 B3
Luçon F 52 B3
Ludanice SK 50 B4
Ludbreg HR 60 B1
Lüdenscheid D 36 B3
Lüderitz D 30 C3
Lüdersdorf D 30 B2
Ludgo S 23 C4
Lüdinghausen D 36 B3
Ludlow GB 4 K5
Ludomy PL 32 C2
Ludvika S 22 A2
Ludweiler Warndt D 46 A2
Ludwigsburg D 47 B5
Ludwigsfelde D 38 A3
Ludwigshafen D 47 A4
Ludwigslust D 30 B3
Ludwigsstadt D 38 C1
Ludza LV 7 H20
Luesia E 76 A1
Luftkurort Arendsee D 30 C3
Lug BIH 70 D3
Lug HR 60 C3
Luga RUS 7 G21
Lugagnano Val d'Arda I 67 B3
Lugano CH 56 B3
Lugau D 38 C2
Lugnas S 21 C5
Lúgnola I 88 A2
Lugny F 55 B4
Lugo E 72 A3
Lugo I 67 B5
Lugoj RO 10 P17
Lugones E 74 A1
Lugros E 86 B2
Luhačovice CZ 50 A3
Luhe D 48 A3
Luino I 56 C3
Luintra E 73 B3
Lújar E 86 C2
Luka nad Jihlavou CZ 49 A6
Lukavac BIH 70 B3
Lukavika BIH 70 B3
Lukovica SLO 59 B4
Lukovit BG 16 Q19
Lukovo HR 69 B3
Lukovo YU 71 C6
Lukovo Šugorje HR 69 B4
Łuków PL 11 L18
Łukowice Brzeskie PL 40 C2
Luksefjell N 19 B6
Łukta PL 33 B6
Lula I 96 C2
Luleå S 3 D18
Lüleburgaz TR 16 R20
Lumbarda HR 70 D2
Lumbier E 76 A1
Lumbrales E 73 D4
Lumbreras E 75 B4
Lumbres F 34 C3
Lummelunda S 23 D5
Lummen B 35 C6
Lumpiaque E 76 B1
Lun HR 69 B3
Luna E 76 A2
Lunamatrona I 96 D1
Lunano I 68 C1
Lunas F 64 C2
Lund S 27 D3
Lunde DK 25 D1
Lunde N 19 B6
Lunden D 29 A6
Lunderseter N 20 A4
Lunderskov DK 25 D2
Lundsberg S 20 B6
Lüneburg D 30 B2
Lunel F 64 C3
Lünen D 36 B3
Lunéville F 46 B2
Lungern CH 56 B3
Lungro I 92 B3
Luninyets BY 7 K20
Lünne D 29 C4
Lunner N 20 A2
Lunteren NL 35 A6
Lunz am See A 49 C6
Luogosanto I 96 B2
Łupawa PL 32 A3
Lupión E 86 A2
Lupoglav HR 59 C4
Luppa D 38 B2
Luque E 86 B1
Lurago d'Erba I 57 C4
Lúras I 96 C2
Lurcy-Lévis F 54 B2
Lure F 46 C2
Lurgan GB 4 J3
Lury-sur-Arnon F 54 A2
Lušci Palanka BIH 69 B5
Lusévera I 58 B3
Lushnjë AL 15 R16
Lusignan F 53 B5
Lusigny-sur-Barse F 45 B5
Lusnić BIH 70 C1
Luso P 78 A2
Lusówko PL 32 C2
Lussac F 62 B2
Lussac-les-Châteaux F 53 B5
Lussac-les-Eglises F 53 B6
Lussan F 64 B3
Lüssow D 30 B4
Lustenau A 57 A4
Luštěnice CZ 39 C4
Lutago I 58 B1
Lutherstadt Wittenberg D 38 B2
Lütjenburg D 30 A2
Lutocin PL 33 C5
Lutomiersk PL 41 B4
Luton GB 4 L6
Lutry CH 56 B1
Lutry PL 33 A6
Lutsk UA 11 L19
Lutter am Barenberge D 37 B6
Lututów PL 40 B3
Lützen D 38 B2
Lutzow D 30 B3

Luxembourg L 46 A2
Luxeuil-les-Bains F 46 C2
Luxey F 62 B2
Luz, *Évora* P 84 A3
Luz, *Faro* P 84 B2
Luz, *Faro* P 84 B3
Luz-St-Sauveur F 62 D2
Luzarches F 44 A3
Luže CZ 50 A2
Luzech F 63 B4
Luzern CH 56 A3
Luzino PL 33 A4
Luzy F 54 B3
Luzzi I 92 B3
L'viv UA 11 M19
Lwówek PL 32 C2
Lwówek Śląski PL 39 B5
Lyakhavichy BY 7 K20
Lychen D 31 B5
Lychkova RUS 7 H23
Lyckeby S 27 C5
Lycksele S 3 D16
Lyepyel BY 7 J21
Lykling N 18 B2
Lyngdal, *Buskerud* N 19 B6
Lyngdal, *Vest-Agder* N 19 C4
Lyngør N 19 C6
Lyngsa DK 24 B3
Lyntupy BY 7 J20
Lyon F 55 C4
Lyons-la-Forêt F 44 A2
Lyozna BY 7 J22
Lyrestad S 21 C6
Lysá nad Labem CZ 39 C4
Lysá pod Makytou SK 50 A4
Lysebotn N 18 B3
Lysekil S 21 C3
Lysice CZ 50 A2
Lysomice PL 33 B4
Lyss CH 56 A2
Lystrup DK 25 C3
Lysvik S 20 A5
Łyszkowice PL 41 B4
Lyuban RUS 7 G22
Lyubertsy RUS 7 J25
Lyuboml' UA 11 L19
Lyubotyn UA 7 M24
Lyubytino RUS 7 G23
Lyudinovo RUS 7 K24

M

Maarheeze NL 35 B6
Maaseik B 36 B1
Maastricht NL 36 C1
Mablethorpe GB 4 K7
Mably F 54 B4
Macael E 87 B3
Maçanet de Cabrenys E 77 A5
Mação P 78 B2
Macau F 62 A2
Maccagno-Agra I 56 B3
Maccarese I 88 B2
Macchiagódena I 89 B4
Macclesfield GB 4 K5
Maceda E 73 B3
Macedo de Cavaleiros P 73 C4
Maceira, *Guarda* P 78 A3
Maceira, *Leiria* P 78 B2
Macelj HR 59 B5
Macerata I 68 C2
Macerata Féltria I 68 C1
Machault F 45 A5
Machecoul F 52 B3
Machynlleth GB 4 K5
Macieira P 73 C2
Maciejowice PL 41 B6
Macinaggio F 66 D3
Mackenrode D 37 B6
Mačkovci SLO 59 B6
Macomer I 96 C1
Macon B 35 C5
Mâcon F 55 B4
Macotera E 80 B1
Macroom IRL 4 L2
Macugnaga I 56 C2
Madängsholm S 21 C5
Madaras H 61 B4
Maddaloni I 89 B4
Made NL 35 B5
Maderuelo E 75 C3
Madocsa H 61 B3
Madona LV 7 H20
Madonna di Campiglio I 57 B5
Madrid E 80 B3
Madridejos E 81 C3
Madrigal de la Vera E 80 B1
Madrigal de las Altas Torres E 80 A1
Madrigalejo E 79 B5
Madrigalejo de Monte E 74 B3
Madriguera E 75 C3
Madrigueras E 81 C5
Madroñera E 79 B5
Maël-Carhaix F 42 B2
Maella E 76 B3
Maello E 80 B2
Mafra P 78 C1
Magacela E 79 C5
Magallon E 75 C5
Magaluf, *Mallorca* E 83
Magán E 80 C3
Magaña E 75 C4
Magasa I 57 C5
Magaz E 74 C2
Magdeburg D 38 A1
Magenta I 56 C3
Magescq F 62 C1
Magione I 68 C1
Maglaj BIH 70 B3
Maglehem S 27 D4
Magliano de'Marsi I 89 A3
Magliano in Toscana I 88 A1
Magliano Sabina I 88 A2
Maglić YU 61 C4
Máglie I 91 B5
Maglód H 61 A4
Magnac-Bourg F 53 C6
Magnac-Laval F 53 B6
Magnieres F 46 B2
Magnor N 20 B4
Magnuszew PL 41 B6
Magny-Cours F 54 B3
Magny-en-Vexin F 44 A2
Mágocs H 60 B3
Magoute P 78 C1
Maguilla E 79 C5
Magyarbóly H 60 C3
Magyarkeszi H 60 B3
Magyarszék H 60 B3
Mahide E 73 C4
Mahilyow BY 7 K22
Mahora E 81 C5
Mahovo HR 59 C6
Mähring D 48 A3
Maia E 62 C1
Maia P 73 C2
Maiaelrayo E 81 A3
Maials E 76 B3
Maîche F 56 A1
Máida I 92 C3
Maidstone GB 4 L7
Maienfeld CH 57 A4
Maignelay Montigny F 44 A3
Maillezais F 53 B4
Mailly-le-Camp F 45 B5
Mailly-le-Château F 45 C4
Mainar E 75 C5
Mainbernheim D 47 A6
Mainburg D 48 B2
Mainhardt D 47 A5
Maintal D 37 C4
Maintenon F 44 B2
Mainvilliers F 44 B2
Mainz D 36 C4
Maiorca P 78 A2
Mairena de Aljarafe E 85 B4
Mairena del Alcor E 85 B5
Maisach D 48 B2
Maishofen A 58 A2
Maison-Rouge F 45 B4
Maissau A 50 B1
Maisse F 44 B3
Maizières-lès-Vic F 46 B2
Maja HR 59 C6
Majadahonda E 80 B3
Majadas E 79 B5
Majs H 60 C3
Majšperk SLO 59 B5
Makarska HR 70 C2
Makkum NL 28 B2
Maklár H 51 C6
Makó H 61 B5
Makoszyce PL 40 C2
Makov SK 51 A4
Makovac YU 71 D6
Maków Podhalański PL 51 A5
Mąkowarsko PL 32 B3
Mala Bosna YU 61 B4
Mala Klacuša BIH 59 C5
Mala Krsna YU 71 B6
Malá Lehota SK 51 B4
Mala Pijace YU 61 B4
Mala Subotica HR 59 B6
Mala Vyska UA 11 M22
Malacky SK 50 B3
Maladzyechna BY 7 J20
Málaga E 86 C1
Malagón E 80 C3
Malaguilla E 81 B3
Malalbergo I 67 B5
Malanów PL 40 B3
Malaucène F 65 B4
Malaunay F 44 A2
Malaya Vishera RUS 7 G23
Malborghetto I 58 B3
Malbork PL 33 A5
Malborn D 46 A2
Malbuisson F 55 B6
Malcésine I 57 C5
Malchin D 31 B4
Malching D 49 B4
Malchow D 30 B4
Malcocinado E 85 A5
Malczyce PL 40 B1
Maldegem B 35 B4
Małdyty PL 33 B5
Malè I 57 B5
Malemort F 53 C6
Malente D 30 A2
Målerås S 26 C5
Malesherbes F 44 B3
Malestroit F 42 C3
Maletto I 95 B3
Malexander S 23 C2
Malfa I 95 A3
Malgrat de Mar E 77 B5
Malhadas P 73 C4
Mali Lošinj HR 69 B3
Malicorne-sur-Sarthe F 43 C5
Malijai F 65 B5
Malildjoš YU 61 C4
Målilla S 26 B5
Málinec SK 51 B5
Malingsbo S 22 B2
Maliniec PL 40 A3
Malinska HR 69 A3
Maljevac HR 59 C5
Malkara TR 16 R20
Małki PL 33 B5
Malko Tŭrnovo BG 16 Q20
Mallaig GB 4 H4
Mallemort F 65 C4
Mallén E 75 C5
Mallersdorf-Pfaffenberg D 48 B3
Málles Venosta I 57 B5
Malling DK 25 C3
Mallnitz A 58 B3
Mallow IRL 4 K2
Malmbäck S 26 B4
Malmberget S 3 C17
Malmédy B 36 C2
Malmköping S 22 B3
Malmö S 27 D3
Malmon S 21 C3
Malmslätt S 23 C2
Malnate I 56 C3
Malo I 57 C6
Maloarkhangelsk RUS 7 K25
Małogoszcz PL 41 C5
Maloja CH 57 B4
Małomice PL 39 B5
Måløy N 2 F9
Maloyaroslovets RUS 7 J25
Malpartida E 79 B4
Malpartida de la Serena E 79 C5
Malpartida de Plasencia E 79 B4
Malpas E 76 A3
Malpica P 78 B3
Malpica de Bergantiños E 72 A2
Malpica de Tajo E 80 C2
Malsch D 47 B4
Malšice CZ 49 A5
Malta A 58 B3
Maltat F 54 B3
Malung S 2 F13
Malungsfors S 2 F13
Maluszów PL 31 C7
Maluszyn PL 41 C4
Malva E 74 C1
Malvaglia CH 56 B3
Malveira P 78 C1
Malyn UA 11 L21
Mamarrosa P 78 A2
Mamer L 46 A2
Mamers F 44 B1
Mamirolle F 55 A6
Mammendorf D 48 B2
Mámmola I 92 C3
Mamoiada I 96 C2
Mamonovo RUS 33 A5
Maňa SK 50 B4
Manacor, *Mallorca* E 83
Manavgat TR 16 T22
Mancera de Abajo E 80 B1
Mancha Real E 86 B2
Manchester GB 4 K5
Manching D 48 B2
Manchita E 79 C4
Manciano I 88 A1
Manciet F 62 C3
Mandal N 19 C4
Mandanici I 95 A4
Mándas I 96 D2
Mandatoríccio I 93 B3
Mandayona E 81 B4
Mandelieu-la-Napoule F 65 C5
Mandello del Lário I 57 C4
Mandelsloh D 29 C6
Manderfeld B 36 C2
Manderscheid D 36 C2
Mandino Selo BIH 70 C2
Mandoúdhion GR 15 S18
Mandúria I 91 B4
Mane, *Alpes-de-Haute-Provence* F 65 C4
Mane, *Haute-Garonne* F 63 C3
Manérbio I 57 C5
Mañeru E 75 B5
Manetin CZ 38 D3
Manfredónia I 90 A2
Mangalia RO 16 Q21
Manganeses de la Lampreana E 74 C1
Manganeses de la Polvorosa E 74 B1
Mangen N 20 B3
Mangiennes F 46 A1
Mangualde P 78 A3
Maniago I 58 B2
Manilva E 85 C5
Manisa TR 16 S20
Manises E 82 B2
Mank A 49 B6
Månkarbo S 22 A4
Manlleu E 77 B5
Männedorf CH 56 A3
Mannersdorf am Leithagebirge A 50 C2
Mannheim D 47 A4
Manoppello I 89 A4
Manosque F 65 C4
Manresa E 77 B4
Månsarp S 26 B4
Manschnow D 31 C6
Mansfeld D 38 B1
Mansfield GB 4 K6
Mansilla de Burgos E 74 B3
Mansilla de las Mulas E 74 B1
Manskog S 20 B4
Mansle F 53 C5
Manso F 96 A1
Manteigas P 78 A3
Mantel D 48 A3
Mantes-la-Jolie F 44 B2
Mantes-la-Ville F 44 B2
Manthelan F 53 A5
Mantorp S 23 C2
Mántova I 57 C5
Mänttä FIN 3 E19
Manuel E 82 B2
Manzanal de Arriba E 73 B4
Manzanares E 81 C3
Manzanares el Real E 80 B3
Manzaneda, *León* E 73 B4
Manzaneda, *Orense* E 73 B3
Manzanedo E 74 B3
Manzaneque E 80 C3
Manzanera E 82 A2
Manzanilla E 85 B4
Manzat F 54 C2
Manziana I 88 A2
Manziat F 55 B4
Maó, *Menorca* E 83
Maoča BIH 70 B3
Maqueda E 80 B2
Mara E 75 C5
Maraña E 74 A1
Maranchón E 81 A4
Maranello I 67 B4
Marano I 89 C4
Marano Lagunare I 58 C3
Marans F 52 B4
Maratea I 90 C2
Marateca P 78 C2
Marbach, *Baden-Württemberg* D 47 B5
Marbach, *Hessen* D 37 C5
Marbach F 46 B2
Marbäck S 26 B3
Mårbacka S 20 B5
Marbella E 86 C1
Marboz F 55 B5
Marburg D 37 C4
Marcali H 60 B2
Marčana HR 68 B2
Marcaria I 67 A4
Marcelová SK 50 C4
Marcenat F 54 C2
Marchamalo E 81 B3
Marchaux F 55 A6
Marche-en-Famenne B 35 C6
Marchegg A 50 B2
Marchena E 85 B5
Marchenoir F 44 C2
Marcheprime F 62 B2
Marciac F 62 C3
Marciana Marina I 67 D4
Marcianise I 89 B4
Marcigny F 54 B4
Marcilla E 75 B5
Marcillac-la-Croisille F 54 C2
Marcillac-Vallon F 63 B5
Marcillat-en-Combraille F 54 B2
Marcille-sur-Seine F 45 B4
Marcilloles F 55 C5
Marcilly-le-Hayer F 45 B4
Marcinkowice PL 32 B2
Marciszów PL 39 C6
Marck F 34 C2
Marckolsheim F 46 B3
Marco de Canevezes P 73 C2
Marek S 23 D2
Marennes F 52 C3
Maresquel F 34 C2
Mareuil F 53 C5
Mareuil-en-Brie F 45 B4
Mareuil-sur-Arnon F 54 B2
Mareuil-sur-Lay F 52 B3
Mareuil-sur-Ourcq F 45 A4
Margate GB 4 L7
Margaux F 62 A2
Margerie-Hancourt F 45 B5
Margès F 55 C5
Margherita di Savóia I 90 A3
Margita YU 61 C6
Margone I 56 C2
Margonin PL 32 C3
Marguerittes F 64 C3
Margut F 45 A6
Maria E 87 B3
Maria Neustift A 49 C5
Maria Saal A 59 B4
Mariager DK 24 C2
Mariana E 81 B4
Mariannelund S 26 B5
Marianópoli I 94 B2
Mariánské Lázně CZ 38 D2
Mariapfarr A 58 A3
Mariazell A 49 C6
Maribo DK 25 E4
Maribor SLO 59 B5
Marieberg S 22 B2
Mariefred S 22 B4
Marieholm S 27 D3
Mariembourg B 35 C5
Marienbaum D 36 B2
Marienberg D 38 C3
Marienheide D 36 B3
Mariental D 37 A6
Mariestad S 21 C5
Marigliano I 89 C4
Marignane F 65 C4
Marigny, *Jura* F 55 B5
Marigny, *Manche* F 43 A4
Marigny-le-Châtel F 45 B4
Marija Bistrica HR 59 B6
Marijampolė LT 6 J18
Marín E 73 B2
Marina HR 69 C5
Marina del Cantone I 89 C4
Marina di Acquappesa I 92 B2
Marina di Alberese I 88 A1
Marina di Amendolara I 91 C3
Marina di Árbus I 96 D1
Marina di Campo I 67 D4
Marina di Carrara I 67 B4
Marina di Castagneto-Donorático I 67 C4
Marina di Cécina I 67 C4
Marina di Gáiro I 96 D2
Marina di Ginosa I 91 B3
Marina di Gioiosa Iónica I 92 C3
Marina di Grosseto I 67 D4
Marina di Léuca I 93 B5
Marina di Massa I 67 B4
Marina di Nováglie I 93 B5
Marina di Pisa I 67 C4
Marina di Ragusa I 95 C3
Marina di Ravenna I 68 B1
Marina di Torre Grande I 96 D1
Marina Romea I 68 B1
Marinaleda E 86 B1
Marine de Sisco F 66 D3
Marinella I 94 B1
Marinella di Sarzana I 67 B4
Marineo I 94 B2
Marines F 44 A2
Maringues F 54 C3
Marinha das Ondas P 78 A2
Marinha Grande P 78 B2
Marinhas P 73 C2
Marino I 88 B2
Marjaliza E 80 C3
Markaryd S 26 C3
Markdorf D 47 C5
Markelo NL 36 A2
Markgröningen D 47 B5
Markhausen D 29 C4
Marki PL 41 A6
Markina-Xemein E 75 A4
Märkische Buchholz D 39 A3
Markkleeberg D 38 B2
Marklohe D 29 C6
Marknesse NL 28 C2
Markneukirchen D 38 C2
Markovac YU 71 B6
Markowice PL 40 C3
Markranstädt D 38 B2
Marksuhl D 37 C6
Markt Allhau A 59 A6
Markt Bibart D 47 A6
Markt Erlbach D 48 A1
Markt-heidenfeld D 47 A5
Markt Indersdorf D 48 B2
Markt Rettenbach D 47 C6
Markt Schwaben D 48 B2
Markt-Übelbach A 59 A5
Marktbreit D 47 A6
Marktleuthen D 38 C1
Marktoberdorf D 48 C1
Marktredwitz D 38 C2
Markusica HR 60 C3
Markušovce SK 51 B6
Marl D 36 B3
Marle F 45 A4
Marlieux F 55 B5
Marlow D 31 A4
Marma S 22 A4
Marmagne F 55 B4
Marmande F 62 B3
Marmaris TR 16 T21
Marmelete P 84 B2
Marmolejo E 86 A1
Marmoutier F 46 B3
Marnay F 55 A5
Marne D 29 B6
Marnheim D 47 A4
Marnitz D 30 B3
Maroldsweisach D 37 C6
Marolles-les-Braults F 44 B1
Maromme F 44 A2
Marone I 57 C5
Maroslele H 61 B5
Maróstica I 58 C1
Marotta I 68 C2
Marquion F 35 C4
Marquise F 34 C2
Marradi I 67 B5
Marratxi, *Mallorca* E 83
Marrehamn FIN 3 F16
Marrúbiu I 96 D1
Marrum NL 28 B2
Marrupe E 80 B2
Mars-la-Tours F 46 A1
Marsac F 63 C5
Marsac-en-Livradois F 54 C3
Marságlia I 66 B3
Marsala I 94 B1
Marsberg D 37 B4
Marsciano I 68 D1
Marseillan F 64 C2
Marseille F 65 C4
Marseille en Beauvaisis F 44 A2
Mársico Nuovo I 90 B2
Marson F 45 B5
Märsta S 22 B4
Marstal DK 25 E3
Marstrand S 21 D3
Marta I 88 A1
Martano I 91 B5
Martel F 63 B4
Martelange B 46 A1
Martfeld D 29 C6
Martfű H 61 A5
Marthon F 53 C5
Martiago E 79 A4
Martigné-Briand F 53 A4
Martigné-Ferchaud F 43 C4
Martigny CH 56 B2
Martigny-les-Bains F 46 B1
Martigues F 65 C4
Martim-Longo P 84 B3
Martin SK 51 A4
Martin de la Jara E 86 B1
Martin Muñoz de las Posadas E 80 A2
Martina CH 57 B5
Martina Franca I 91 B4
Martinamor E 80 B1
Martinengo I 57 C4
Martinsberg A 49 B6
Martinšćica HR 68 B3
Martinshöhe D 46 A3
Martinsicuro I 68 D2
Martinszell D 47 C6
Mártis I 96 C1
Martofte DK 25 D3
Martonvásár H 60 A3
Martorell E 77 B4
Martos E 86 B2
Martres Tolosane F 63 C3
Marugán E 80 B2
Marúggio I 91 B4
Marvão P 78 B3
Marvejols F 64 B2
Marville F 46 A1
Marwałd PL 33 B5
Marzabotto I 67 B5
Marzahna D 38 B2
Marzahne D 31 C4
Marzamemi I 95 C4
Marzocca I 68 C2
Mas de Barberáns E 76 C3
Mas de las Matas E 76 C2
Masa E 74 B3
Máscali I 95 B4
Mascaraque E 80 C3
Mascarenhas P 73 C3
Mascioni I 89 A3
Masegoso E 87 A3
Masegoso de Tajuña E 81 B4
Masera I 56 B3
Masevaux F 46 C2
Maside E 73 B2
Maslacq F 62 C2
Maslinica HR 69 C5
Maslovare BIH 70 B2
Masone I 66 B2
Massa I 67 B4
Massa Fiscáglia I 67 B6
Massa Lombarda I 67 B5
Massa Lubrense I 89 C4
Massa Marittima I 67 C4
Massa Martana I 68 D1
Massafra I 91 B4
Massamagrell E 82 B2
Massanassa E 82 B2
Massarosa I 67 C4
Massat F 63 D4
Massay F 54 A1
Massbach D 37 C6
Masseret F 53 C6
Masseube F 63 C3
Massiac F 54 C3
Massing D 48 B3
Massmechelen B 36 C1
Masty BY 6 K19
Masúa I 96 D1
Masueco E 73 C4
Mašun SLO 59 C4
Maszewo, *Szczecin* PL 31 B7
Maszewo, *Zielona Góra* PL 39 A4
Mata de Alcántara E 79 B4
Matalebreras E 75 C4
Matallana de Torío E 74 B1
Matamala E 75 C4
Mataporquera E 74 B2
Matapozuelos E 74 C2
Mataró E 77 B5
Mataruge YU 71 C4
Mataruška Banja YU 71 C5
Matélica I 68 C2
Matera I 91 B3
Mateševo YU 71 D4
Mátészalka H 11 N18
Matet E 82 B2
Matha F 53 C4
Mathay F 56 A1
Matignon F 43 B3
Matilla de los Caños del Rio E 73 D5
Matosinhos P 73 C2
Matour F 55 B4
Mátrafüred H 51 C5
Mátraterenye H 51 B5
Matre N 18 B2
Matrei am Brenner A 57 A6
Matrei in Osttirol A 58 B2
Matrice I 89 B4
Mattarello I 57 B6
Mattersburg A 50 C2
Mattighofen A 48 B4
Mattinata I 90 A3
Mattos P 78 B2
Mattsee A 48 C4
Matulji HR 59 C4
Maubert-Fontaine F 45 A5
Maubeuge F 35 C4
Maubourguet F 62 C3
Mauer-kirchen A 48 B4
Mauern D 48 B2
Mauguio F 64 C3
Maulbronn D 47 B4
Maule F 44 B2
Mauléon F 53 B4
Mauléon-Barousse F 63 D3
Mauléon-Licharre F 62 C2
Maulévrier F 53 A4
Maurach A 58 A1
Maure-de-Bretagne F 43 C4
Maureilhan F 64 C2
Mauriac F 54 C2
Mauron F 43 B3
Maurs F 63 B5
Maury F 63 D5
Maussane-les-Alpilles F 64 C3
Mautern A 49 B6
Mautern im Steiermark A 59 A4
Mauterndorf A 58 A3
Mauthausen A 49 B5
Mauthen A 58 B2
Mauvezin F 63 C3
Mauzé-sur-le-Mignon F 53 B4
Maxent F 43 C3
Maxey-sur-Vaise F 46 B1
Maxial P 78 B1
Maxieira P 78 B2
Mayalde E 80 A1
Mayen D 36 C3
Mayenne F 43 B5
Mayet F 44 C1
Mayorga E 74 B1
Mayres F 64 B3
Mayrhofen A 58 A1
Mazagón E 85 B4
Mazaleón E 76 B3
Mazamet F 63 C5
Mazan F 65 B4
Mazara del Vallo I 94 B1
Mazarambroz E 80 C2
Mazarete E 81 B4
Mazaricos E 72 B2
Mazarrón E 87 B4
Mažeikiai LT 6 H18
Mazères F 63 C4
Mazères-sur-Salat F 63 C3
Mazières-en-Gâtine F 53 B4
Mazin HR 69 B4
Mazuelo E 74 B3
Mazyr BY 7 K21
Mazzarino I 95 B3
Mazzarrà Sant'Andrea I 95 A4
Mazzo di Valtellina I 57 B5
Mchowo PL 33 B6
Mdzewo PL 33 C6
Mealhada P 78 A2
Meana Sardo I 96 D2
Meaulne F 54 B2
Meaux F 45 B3
Mecerreyes E 75 B3
Mechelen B 35 B5
Mechernich D 36 C2
Mechnica PL 40 C3
Mechterstädt D 37 C6
Mecikal PL 32 B3
Mecina-Bombarón E 86 C2
Meckenbeuren D 47 C5
Meckenheim, *Rheinland-Pfalz* D 36 C3
Meckenheim, *Rheinland-Pfalz* D 47 A4
Meckesheim D 47 A4
Mecseknádasd H 60 B3
Meda I 57 C4
Meda P 73 D3
Medak HR 69 B4
Mede I 66 A2
Medebach D 37 B4
Medelim P 79 A3
Medemblik NL 28 C2
Medena Selista BIH 69 B5
Medesano I 67 B4
Medevi S 23 C1
Medgidia RO 11 P21
Medgyesháza H 61 B6
Medhamn S 20 B5
Mediaș RO 11 N19
Medicina I 67 B5
Medina de las Torres E 85 A4
Medina de Pomar E 75 B3
Medina de Rioseco E 74 C1
Medina del Campo E 74 C2
Medina Sidonia E 85 C5
Medinaceli E 81 A4
Medinilla E 79 A5
Medja YU 61 C5
Medjedja BIH 71 C4
Medulin HR 68 B2
Meduno I 58 B2
Medveda YU 71 C5
Medvedja YU 71 C6
Medvedov SK 50 C3
Medvide HR 69 B4
Medvode SLO 59 B4
Medzev SK 51 B6
Meerane D 38 C2
Meerle B 35 B5
Meersburg D 47 C5
Meeuwen B 35 B6
Mégara GR 15 T18
Mégève F 55 C6
Meggenhofen A 49 B4
Mehedeby S 22 A4
Mehun-sur-Yèvre F 54 A2
Meijel NL 36 B1
Meilen CH 56 A3
Meilhan F 62 C2
Meimôa P 79 A3
Meina I 56 C3
Meine D 30 C2
Meinersen D 30 C2
Meinerzhagen D 36 B3
Meiningen D 37 C6
Meira E 72 A3
Meiringen CH 56 B3
Meisenheim D 46 A3
Meissen D 38 B3
Meitingen D 48 B1
Meix-devant-Virton B 46 A1
Męka PL 40 B3
Meka Gruda BIH 70 C3
Mel I 58 B2
Melč CZ 50 A3
Méldola I 68 B1
Meldorf D 29 A6
Melegnano I 57 C4
Melenci YU 61 C5
Melendugno I 91 B5
Melfi I 90 A2
Melgaço P 73 B2
Melgar de Arriba E 74 B1
Melgar de Fernamental E 74 B2
Melgar de Yuso E 74 B2
Melhus N 2 E12
Meliana E 82 B2
Melide CH 56 C3
Melide E 72 B2
Melides P 84 A2
Melilli I 95 B4
Melinovac HR 69 B4
Melisenda I 96 D2
Melisey F 46 C2
Mélito di Porto Salvo I 95 B4
Melk A 49 B6
Mellansel S 3 E16
Mellbystrand S 26 C2
Melle B 35 B4
Melle D 36 A4
Melle F 53 B4
Mellendorf D 29 C6
Mellerud S 21 C4
Mellösa S 23 B3
Mellrichstadt D 37 C6
Mělnické Vtelno CZ 39 C4
Mělník CZ 39 C4
Melón E 73 B2
Mels CH 57 A4
Melsungen D 37 B5
Melun F 44 B3
Mélykút H 61 B4
Melzo I 57 C4
Membrilla E 81 D3
Membrio E 79 B3
Memer F 63 B4
Memmelsdorf D 48 A1
Memmingen D 47 C6
Memoria P 78 B2
Mena UA 7 L23
Menággio I 57 B4
Menasalbas E 80 C2
Menat F 54 B2
Mendavia E 75 B4
Mendaza E 75 B4
Mende F 64 B2
Menden D 36 B3
Mendig D 36 C3
Mendiga P 78 B2
Mendrisio CH 56 C3
Ménéac F 42 B3
Menemen TR 16 S20
Menen B 35 C4
Menetou-Salon F 54 A2
Menfi I 94 B1
Ménfőcsanak H 50 C3
Mengamuñoz E 80 B2
Mengen D 47 B5
Mengeš SLO 59 B4
Mengibar E 86 B2
Mengkofen D 48 B3
Mens F 65 B4
Menslage D 29 C4
Mentana I 88 A2
Menton F 66 C1
Méntrida E 80 B2
Méounes-les-Montrieux F 65 C4
Meppel NL 28 C3
Meppen D 29 C4
Mequinenza E 76 B3
Mer F 44 C2
Mera, *Coruña* E 72 A2
Mera, *Coruña* E 72 A3
Merano I 57 B6
Merate I 57 C4
Mercadillo E 75 A3
Mercatale I 68 C1
Mercatino Conca I 68 C1
Mercato San Severino I 89 C4
Mercato Saraceno I 68 C1
Merching D 48 B1
Merchtem B 35 C5
Merdrignac F 42 B3
Merdžanići BIH 70 C2
Meré E 74 A2
Meréville F 44 B3
Merfeld D 36 B3
Méribel F 55 C6

Méribel Motraret F 55 C6
Mérida E 79 C4
Mérignac F 62 B2
Měřín CZ 50 A1
Mering D 48 B1
Merkendorf D 48 A1
Merklin CZ 49 A4
Merksplas B 35 B5
Merlimont Plage F 34 C2
Mern DK 25 D5
Mernye H 60 B2
Mers-les-Bains F 34 C2
Mersch L 46 A2
Merseburg D 38 B1
Merthyr Tydfil GB 4 L5
Mertingen D 48 B1
Mértola P 84 B3
Méru F 44 A3
Merufe P 73 B2
Mervans F 55 B5
Merville F 34 C3
Méry-sur-Seine F 45 B4
Merzig D 46 A2
Mesagne I 91 B4
Mesão Frio P 73 C3
Mesas de Ibor E 79 B5
Meschede D 36 B4
Meschers-sur-Gironde F 52 C4
Meshchovsk RUS 7 J24
Meslay-du-Maine F 43 C5
Mesocco CH 57 B4
Mésola I 68 B1
Mesolóngion GR 15 S17
Mesoraca I 93 B3
Messac F 43 C4
Messancy B 46 A1
Messdorf D 30 C3
Messei F 43 B5
Messejana P 84 B2
Messina I 95 A4
Messíni GR 15 T18
Messkirch D 47 C5
Messtetten D 47 B4
Mestanza E 86 A1
Městec Králové CZ 39 C5
Mestlin D 30 B3
Město Albrechtice CZ 40 C2
Město Libavá CZ 50 A3
Město Touškov CZ 49 A4
Mestre I 58 C2
Mesvres F 55 B4
Mesztegnyő H 60 B2
Meta I 89 C4
Metajna HR 69 B4
Metelen D 36 A3
Methóni GR 15 T17
Metković HR 70 C2
Metlika SLO 59 C5
Metnitz A 59 B4
Metslawier NL 28 B3
Metten D 48 B3
Mettendorf D 36 D2
Mettet B 35 C5
Mettingen D 36 A3
Mettlach D 46 A2
Mettlen CH 56 B2
Mettmann D 36 B2
Metz F 46 A2
Metzervisse F 46 A2
Metzingen D 47 B5
Meulan F 44 A2
Meung-sur-Loire F 44 C2
Meuselwitz D 38 B2
Meuzac F 53 C6
Meximieux F 55 C5
Meyenburg D 30 B4
Meyerhöfen D 29 C5
Meylan F 55 C5
Meymac F 54 C2
Meyrargues F 65 C4
Meyrueis F 64 B2
Meyssac F 63 A4
Meysse F 64 B3
Meyzieu F 55 C4
Mèze F 64 C2
Mézériat F 55 B5
Mežica SLO 59 B4
Mézidon-Canon F 43 A5
Mézières-en-Brenne F 53 B6
Mézières-sur-Issoire F 53 B5
Mézilhac F 64 B3
Mézilles F 45 C4
Mézin F 62 B3
Mezőberény H 61 B6
Mezőcsát H 51 C6
Mezőfalva H 60 B3
Mezőhegyes H 61 B5
Mezőkeresztes H 51 C6
Mezőkomárom H 60 B3
Mezőkövácsháza H 61 B5
Mezőkövesd H 51 C6
Mezőörs H 60 A2
Mézos F 62 B1
Mezőszilas H 60 B3
Mezőtúr H 61 A5
Mezquita de Jarque E 76 C2
Mezzano, *Emilia Romagna* I 68 B1
Mezzano, *Trentino Alto Adige* I 58 B1
Mezzojuso I 94 B2
Mezzoldo I 57 B4
Mezzolombardo I 57 B6
Mglin RUS 7 K23
Miajadas E 79 B5
Mianowice PL 32 A3
Miasteczko Krajeńskie PL 32 B3
Miasteczko Śl. PL 40 C3
Miastko PL 32 A2
Michalovce SK 10 M17
Michałowice PL 41 C4
Michelau D 47 A6
Michelbach D 47 A6
Micheldorf A 49 C5
Michelhausen A 50 B1
Michelsneukirchen D 48 A3
Michelstadt D 47 A5
Michendorf D 38 A3
Michurin BG 16 Q20
Middelburg NL 35 B4
Middelfart DK 25 D2
Middelharnis NL 35 B5
Middelkerke B 34 B3
Middelstum NL 28 B3
Middlesbrough GB 4 J6
Midlum D 29 B5
Midwolda NL 29 B4
Miechów PL 41 C5
Miedes de Aragón E 81 A5
Miedes de Atienza E 81 A3
Międzybodzie Bielskie PL 51 A5
Międzybórz PL 40 B2
Międzychód PL 32 C1
Międzylesie PL 40 C1
Międzyrzec Podlaski PL 11 L18
Międzyrzecz PL 32 C1
Międzywodzie PL 31 A6
Międzyzdroje PL 31 B6
Miejska Górka PL 40 B1
Miélan F 62 C3
Mielec PL 41 C6
Mielęcin PL 31 B6
Mielno PL 32 A2
Mielno PL 33 B6
Miengo E 74 A3
Miercurea Ciuc RO 11 N19
Mieres, *Asturias* E 74 A1
Mieres, *Girona* E 77 A5
Mieroszów PL 39 C6
Mierzyn PL 41 B4
Miesau D 46 A3
Miesbach D 48 C2
Mieścisko PL 32 C3
Mieste D 30 C3
Miesterhorst D 30 C3
Mieszków PL 40 A2
Mieszkowice PL 31 C6
Mietków PL 40 C1
Migennes F 45 C4
Miggiano I 93 B5
Migliánico I 89 A4
Migliarino I 67 B5
Migliónico I 91 B3
Mignano Monte Lungo I 89 B3
Migné F 53 B6
Miguel Esteban E 81 C3
Miguelturra E 80 D3
Mihajlovac YU 71 B5
Miháld H 60 B2
Mihaliççik TR 16 S22
Mihályi H 60 A2
Mihla D 37 B6
Mihohnić HR 69 A3
Miholjsko HR 59 C5
Mihovljan HR 59 B5
Mijares E 80 B2
Mijas E 86 C1
Mijoska YU 71 D4
Mike H 60 B2
Mikhnevo RUS 7 J25
Mikkeli FIN 3 F20
Mikleuš HR 60 C2
Mikołajki Pomorskie PL 33 B5
Mikolów PL 40 C3
Mikorzyn PL 40 B3
Mikstat PL 40 B2
Mikulášovice CZ 39 C4
Mikulov CZ 50 B2
Mikulovice CZ 40 C2
Milagro E 75 B5
Miłakowo PL 33 A6
Miland N 19 B5
Milano I 57 C4
Milano Marittima I 68 B1
Milâs TR 16 T20
Milazzo I 95 A4
Milejewo PL 33 A5
Milelín CZ 39 C5
Miletić YU 61 C4
Miletićevo YU 61 C6
Mileto I 92 C3
Milevsko CZ 49 A5
Milford Haven GB 4 L4
Milhão P 73 C4
Milići BIH 70 B4
Miličin CZ 49 A5
Milicz PL 40 B2
Milín CZ 49 A5
Militello in Val di Catánia I 95 B3
Miljevina BIH 70 C3
Milkowice PL 39 B6
Millançay F 54 A1
Millares E 82 B2
Millas F 77 A5
Millau F 64 B1
Millesimo I 66 B2
Millevaches F 54 C2
Millstatt A 58 B3
Milly-la-Forêt F 44 B3
Milmarcos E 81 A5
Milmersdorf D 31 B5
Milna HR 69 C5
Miločaj YU 71 C5
Milogórze PL 33 A6
Miłomłyn PL 33 B5
Miloševo YU 71 B6
Miłosław PL 40 A2
Milówka PL 51 A5
Miltach D 48 A3
Miltenberg D 47 A5
Milton Keynes GB 4 K6
Milutovac YU 71 C6
Milzyn PL 33 C4
Mimice HR 70 C1
Mimizan F 62 B1
Mimizan-Plage F 62 B1
Mimoň CZ 39 C4
Mina de Juliana P 84 B2
Mina de São Domingos P 84 B3
Minas de Riotinto E 85 B4
Minateda E 87 A4
Minaya E 81 C4
Minde P 78 B2
Mindelheim D 47 B6
Mindelstetten D 48 B2
Minden D 37 A4
Mindszent H 61 B5
Minehead GB 4 L5
Mineo I 95 B3
Minerbe I 57 C6
Minérbio I 67 B5
Minervino Murge I 90 A3
Minglanilla E 82 B1
Mingorria E 80 B2
Minnesund N 20 A3
Miño E 72 A2
Miño de San Esteban E 75 C3
Minsen D 29 B4
Minsk BY 7 K20
Mińsk Mazowiecki PL 41 A6
Minturno I 89 B3
Mionica BIH 70 B3
Mionica YU 71 B5
Mios F 62 B2
Mira E 82 B1
Mira I 58 C2
Mira P 78 A2
Mirabel E 79 B4
Mirabel-aux-Baronnies F 65 B4
Mirabella Eclano I 90 A2
Mirabella Imbáccari I 95 B3
Mirabello I 67 B5
Miradoux F 63 B3
Miraflores de la Sierra E 80 B3
Miralrio E 81 B4
Miramar P 73 C2
Miramare I 68 B1
Miramas F 64 C3
Mirambeau F 53 C4
Miramont-de-Guyenne F 63 B3
Miranda de Arga E 75 B5
Miranda de Ebro E 75 B4
Miranda do Corvo P 78 A2
Miranda do Douro P 73 C4
Mirande F 63 C3
Mirandela P 73 C3
Mirandilla E 79 C4
Mirándola I 67 B5
Miranje HR 69 B4
Mirano I 58 C2
Miravet E 76 B3
Miré F 43 C5
Mirebeau F 53 B5
Mirebeau-sur-Bèze F 55 A5
Mirecourt F 46 B2
Mirepoix F 63 C4
Miribel F 55 C4
Miričina BIH 70 B3
Mirna SLO 59 C5
Miroslav CZ 50 B2
Mirosławice PL 40 C1
Mirosławiec PL 32 B2
Mirošov CZ 49 A4
Mirotice CZ 49 A5
Mirovice CZ 49 A5
Mirow D 31 B4
Mirsk PL 39 C5
Mirzec PL 41 B6
Misilmeri I 94 A2
Miske H 61 B4
Miskolc H 51 B6
Mislinja SLO 59 B5
Missanello I 90 B3
Missillac F 52 A2
Mistelbach A 50 B2
Mistelbach D 48 A2
Misterbianco I 95 B4
Misterhult S 23 D3
Mistretta I 95 B3
Misurina I 58 B2
Mitchelstown IRL 4 K2
Mitilíni GR 16 S20
Mittelberg, *Tirol* A 57 B5
Mittelberg, *Vorarlberg* A 57 A5
Mittenwald D 57 A6
Mittenwalde D 38 A3
Mitter-Kleinarl A 58 A3
Mitterback A 49 C6
Mitterdorf im Mürztal A 59 A5
Mittersheim F 46 B2
Mittersill A 58 A2
Mitterskirchen D 48 B3
Mitterteich D 38 D2
Mittweida D 38 C2
Mitwitz D 38 C1
Mizhhir'ya UA 11 M18
Mjällby S 27 C4
Mjöbäck S 26 B2
Mjölby S 23 C2
Mjøndalen N 19 B7
Mladá Boleslav CZ 39 C4
Mladá Vožice CZ 49 A5
Mladé Buky CZ 39 C5
Mladenovac YU 71 B5
Mladenovo YU 61 C4
Mladikovine BIH 70 B3
Mława PL 33 B6
Mlinište BIH 70 B1
Młodzieszyn PL 41 A5
Mlogoszyn PL 41 A5
Mlynary PL 33 A5
Mnichóvice CZ 49 A5
Mnichovo Hradiště CZ 39 C4
Mniów PL 41 B5
Mnisek nad Hnilcom SK 51 B6
Mníšek pod Brdy CZ 49 A5
Mniszek PL 41 B5
Mniszków PL 41 B5
Mo, *Hedmark* N 20 A3
Mo, *Telemark* N 19 B4
Mo S 21 C3
Mo i Rana N 2 C14
Moaña E 73 B2
Mocejón E 80 C3
Močenok SK 50 B3
Mochales E 81 A4
Mochowo PL 33 C5
Mochy PL 39 A6
Mockern D 38 A1
Mockfjärd S 22 A1
Möckmühl D 47 A5
Mockrehna D 38 B2
Moclín E 86 B2
Mocsa H 50 C4
Möcsény H 60 B3
Modane F 56 C1
Módena I 67 B4
Módica I 95 C3
Modigliana I 67 B5
Modlin PL 33 C6
Mödling A 50 B2
Modliszewice PL 41 B5
Modliszewko PL 32 C3
Modogno I 91 A3
Modra SK 50 B3
Modran BIH 70 B2
Modriča BIH 70 B3
Modrý Kamen SK 51 B5
Moëlan-sur-Mer F 42 C2
Moena I 58 B1
Moerbeke B 35 B4
Moers D 36 B2
Mões P 73 D3
Moffat GB 4 J5
Mogadouro P 73 C4
Mogata S 23 C3
Móggio Udinese I 58 B3
Mogielnica PL 41 B5
Mogilany PL 51 A5
Mogilno PL 32 C3
Mogliano I 68 C2
Mogliano Véneto I 58 C2
Mogor E 73 B2
Mógoro I 96 D1
Moguer E 85 B4
Mohács H 60 C3
Moheda S 26 B4
Mohedas E 79 A4
Mohedas de la Jara E 80 C1
Mohelnice CZ 50 A2
Möhlin CH 56 A2
Moholm S 21 C6
Mohorn D 38 B3
Mohyliv-Podil's'kyy UA 11 M20
Moi N 18 C3
Moià E 77 B5
Móie I 68 C2
Moimenta da Beira P 73 D3
Moirans F 55 C5
Moirans-en-Montagne F 55 B5
Moisaküla EST 7 G19
Moisdon-la-Rivière F 43 C4
Moissac F 63 B4
Moita, *Coimbra* P 78 A2
Moita, *Guarda* P 79 A3
Moita, *Santarém* P 78 B2
Moita, *Setúbal* P 78 C1
Moita dos Ferreiros P 78 B1
Moixent E 82 C2
Mojacar E 87 B4
Mojados E 74 C2
Mojkovac YU 71 D4
Mojmírovce SK 50 B4
Mojtin SK 51 B4
Möklinta S 22 A3
Mokošica HR 70 D3
Mokra Gora YU 71 C4
Mokro Polje HR 69 B5
Mokronog SLO 59 C5
Mokrzyska PL 41 C5
Møkster N 18 A2
Mol B 35 B6
Mol YU 61 C5
Mola di Bari I 91 A4
Molare I 66 B2
Molaretto I 56 C2
Molas F 63 C3
Molassano I 66 B2
Molbergen D 29 C4
Moldava nad Bodvou SK 51 B7
Molde N 2 E10
Møldrup DK 24 C2
Moledo do Minho P 73 C2
Molfetta I 91 A3
Molfsee D 30 A2
Molières F 63 B4
Molina de Aragón E 81 B5
Molina de Segura E 87 A4
Molinar E 75 A3
Molinaseca E 72 B4
Molinella I 67 B5
Molinet F 54 B3
Molini di Tures I 58 B1
Molinicos E 87 A3
Molinos de Duero E 75 C4
Molins de Rei E 77 B5
Moliterno I 90 B2
Molkom S 20 B5
Möllbrücke A 58 B3
Mölle S 27 C2
Molledo E 74 A2
Möllenbeck D 31 B5
Mollerussa E 76 B3
Mollet de Perelada E 77 A5
Mollina E 86 B1
Mölln D 30 B2
Molló E 77 A5
Mollösund S 21 C3
Mölltorp S 23 C1
Mölnbo S 23 C3
Mölndal S 21 D4
Mölnlycke S 21 D4
Molompize F 54 C3
Moloy F 55 A4
Molsheim F 46 B3
Moltzow D 31 B4
Molve HR 60 B2
Molveno I 57 B5
Molvizar E 86 C2
Molzbichl A 58 B3
Mombaróccio I 68 C1
Mombeltrán E 80 B1
Mombris D 37 C5
Mombuey E 73 B4
Momchilgrad BG 16 R19
Mommark DK 25 E3
Momo I 56 C3
Monasterace Marina I 92 C3
Monasterio de Rodilla E 75 B3
Monastir I 96 D2
Monbahus F 63 B3
Monbazillac F 63 B3
Moncada E 82 B2
Moncalieri I 66 A1
Moncalvo I 66 A2
Monção P 73 B2
Moncarapacho P 84 B3
Moncel-sur-Seille F 46 B2
Monchegorsk RUS 3 C23
Mönchen-gladbach D 36 B2
Mónchio della Corti I 67 B4
Monchique P 84 B2
Monclar-de-Quercy F 63 C4
Moncofa E 82 B2
Moncontour F 42 B3
Moncoutant F 53 B4
Monda E 86 C1
Mondariz E 73 B2
Mondavio I 68 C1
Mondéjar E 81 B3
Mondello I 94 A2
Mondim de Basto P 73 C3
Mondolfo I 68 C2
Mondoñedo E 72 A3
Mondorf-les-Bains L 46 A2
Mondoubleau F 44 C1
Mondovì I 66 B1
Mondragon F 64 B3
Mondragone I 89 B3
Mondsee A 49 C4
Monéglia I 66 B3
Monegrillo E 76 B2
Monein F 62 C2
Monemvasía GR 15 T18
Mónesi I 66 B1
Monesiglio I 66 B2
Monesterio E 85 A4
Monestier-de-Clermont F 65 B4
Monestiés F 63 B5
Monéteau F 45 C4
Monfalcone I 58 C3
Monfero E 72 A2
Monflanquin F 63 B3
Monflorite E 76 A2
Monforte P 78 B3
Monforte da Beira E 78 B3
Monforte da Beira P 78 B3
Monforte d'Alba I 66 B1
Monforte de Lemos E 72 B3
Monforte de Moyuela E 76 B1
Monforte del Cid E 82 C2
Monghidoro I 67 B5
Mongiana I 92 C3
Monguelfo I 58 B2
Monheim D 48 B1
Monistrol-d'Allier F 64 B2
Monistrol de Montserrat E 77 B4
Monistrol-sur-Loire F 54 C4
Mönkebude D 31 B5
Monmouth GB 4 L5
Monnaie F 53 A5
Monnerville F 44 B3
Monnickendam NL 28 C2
Monópoli I 91 B4
Monor H 61 A4
Monóvar E 82 C2
Monpazier F 63 B3
Monreal D 36 C3
Monreal E 75 B5
Monreal del Campo E 81 B5
Monreale I 94 A2
Monroy E 79 B4
Monroyo E 76 C2
Mons B 35 C4
Monsaraz P 78 C3
Monschau D 36 C2
Monségur F 62 B3
Monsélice I 58 C1
Monster NL 35 A5
Mönsterås S 26 B6
Monsummano Terme I 67 C4
Mont-de-Marsan F 62 C2
Mont-Louis F 77 A5
Mont-roig del Camp E 76 B3
Mont-St. Aignan F 44 A2
Mont-St. Vincent F 55 B4
Mont-sous-Vaudrey F 55 B5
Montabaur D 36 C3
Montafia I 66 B2
Montagnac F 64 C2
Montagnana I 57 C6
Montaigu F 52 B3
Montaigu-de-Quercy F 63 B4
Montaiguët-en-Forez F 54 B3
Montaigut F 54 B2
Montaigut-sur-Save F 63 C4
Montalbán E 76 C2
Montalbán de Córdoba E 86 B1
Montalbano Elicona I 95 A4
Montalbano Iónico I 91 B3
Montalbo E 81 C4
Montalcino I 67 C5
Montaldo di Cósola I 66 B3
Montalegre P 73 C3
Montalieu-Vercieu F 55 C5
Montalivet-les-Bains F 52 C3
Montallegro I 94 B2
Montalto delle Marche I 68 D2
Montalto di Castro I 88 A1
Montalto Pavese I 66 B3
Montalto Uffugo I 92 B3
Montalvão P 78 B3
Montamarta E 74 C1
Montana BG 15 Q18
Montana-Vermala CH 56 B2
Montánchez E 79 B4
Montanejos E 82 A2
Montano Antilia I 90 B2
Montans F 63 C4
Montargil P 78 B2
Montargis F 44 C3
Montastruc-la-Conseillère F 63 C4
Montauban F 63 B4
Montauban-de-Bretagne F 43 B3
Montbard F 45 C5
Montbarrey F 55 A5
Montbazens F 63 B5
Montbazon F 53 A5
Montbéliard F 56 A1
Montbenoit F 55 B6
Montbeugny F 54 B3
Montblanc E 77 B4
Montbozon F 55 A6
Montbrison F 54 C4
Montbron F 53 C5
Montbrun-les-Bains F 65 B4
Montceau-les-Mines F 55 B4
Montcenis F 55 B4
Montchanin F 55 B4
Montcornet F 45 A5
Montcuq F 63 B4
Montdardier F 64 C2
Montdidier F 44 A3
Monte-Carlo MC 66 C1
Monte Clara P 78 B3
Monte Clérigo P 84 B2
Monte da Pedra P 78 B3
Monte de Goula P 78 B3
Monte do Trigo P 78 C3
Monte Gordo P 84 B3
Monte Juntos P 78 C3
Monte Porzio I 68 C2
Monte Real P 78 B2
Monte Redondo P 78 B2
Monte Romano I 88 A1
Monte San Giovanni Campano I 89 B3
Monte San Savino I 67 C5
Monte Sant'Ángelo I 90 A2
Monte Vilar P 78 B1
Monteagudo E 87 A4
Monteagudo de las Vicarias E 75 C4
Montealegre E 74 C2
Montealegre del Castillo E 82 C1
Montebello Iónico I 95 B4
Montebello Vicentino I 57 C6
Montebelluna I 58 C2
Montebourg F 43 A4
Montebruno I 66 B3
Montecarotto I 68 C2
Montecassiano I 68 C2
Montecastrilli I 88 A2
Montecatini Terme I 67 C4
Montécchio I 68 C1
Montécchio Emilia I 67 B4
Montécchio Maggiore I 57 C6
Montech F 63 C4
Montechiaro d'Asti I 66 A2
Montecórice I 90 B1
Montecorvino Rovella I 90 B1
Montederramo E 73 B3
Montedoro I 94 B2
Montefalco I 68 D1
Montefalcone di Val Fortore I 90 A2
Montefalcone nel Sánnio I 89 B4
Montefano I 68 C2
Montefiascone I 88 A2
Montefiorino I 67 B4
Montefortino I 68 D2
Montefranco I 88 A2
Montefrío E 86 B2
Montegiordano Marina I 91 B3
Montegiórgio I 68 C2
Montegranaro I 68 C2
Montehermoso E 79 A4
Montejicar E 86 B2
Montejo de la Sierra E 81 A3
Montejo de Tiermes E 75 C3
Monteleone di Púglia I 90 A2
Monteleone di Spoleto I 88 A2
Monteleone d'Orvieto I 68 D1
Montelepre I 94 A2
Montelibretti I 88 A2
Montelier F 65 B4
Montélimar F 64 B3
Montella E 77 A4
Montella I 90 B2
Montellano E 85 B5
Montelupo Fiorentino I 67 C5
Montemaggiore Belsito I 94 B2
Montemagno I 66 B2
Montemayor E 86 B1
Montemayor de Pinilla E 74 C2
Montemésola I 91 B4
Montemilletto I 90 A1
Montemilone I 90 A2
Montemolín E 85 A4
Montemónaco I 68 D2
Montemor-o-Novo P 78 C2
Montemor-o-Velho P 78 A2
Montemurro I 90 B2
Montendre F 53 C4
Montenegro de Cameros E 75 B4
Montenero di Bisáccia I 89 B4
Monteneuf F 43 C3
Monteparano I 91 B4
Montepescali I 67 D5
Montepiano I 67 B5
Montepulciano I 67 C5
Montereale I 88 A3
Montereale Valcellina I 58 B2
Montereau-Faut-Yonne F 45 B3
Monterénzio I 67 B5
Monteroni d'Arbia I 67 C5
Monteroni di Lecce I 91 B5
Monterosso al Mare I 66 B3
Monterosso Almo I 95 B3
Monterosso Grana I 65 B6
Monterotondo I 88 A2
Monterotondo Maríttimo I 67 C4
Monterrey E 73 C3
Monterroso E 72 B3
Monterrubio de la Serena E 79 C5
Monterubbiano I 68 C2
Montes Velhos P 84 B2
Montesa E 82 C2
Montesalgueiro E 72 A2
Montesano sulla Marcellana I 90 B2
Montesárchio I 89 B4
Montescaglioso I 91 B3
Montesclaros E 80 B2
Montesilvano I 89 A4
Montespértoli I 67 C5
Montesquieu-Volvestre F 63 C4
Montesquiou F 63 C3
Montestruc-sur-Gers F 63 C3
Montevarchi I 67 C5
Montevéglio I 67 B5
Montfaucon F 52 A3
Montfaucon-d'Argonne F 45 A6
Montfaucon-en-Velay F 55 C4
Montferrat, *Isère* F 55 C5
Montferrat, *Var* F 65 C5
Montfort-en-Chalosse F 62 C2
Montfort-l'Amaury F 44 B2
Montfort-le-Gesnois F 44 B1
Montfort-sur-Meu F 43 B4
Montfort-sur-Risle F 44 A1
Montgai E 76 B3
Montgaillard F 62 C3
Montgenèvre F 65 B5
Montgiscard F 63 C4
Montguyon F 53 C4
Monthermé F 45 A5
Monthey CH 56 B1
Monthois F 45 A5
Monthureux-sur-Saône F 46 B1
Monti I 96 C2
Monticelli d'Ongina I 67 A3
Montichiari I 57 C5
Monticiano I 67 C5
Montiel E 86 A3
Montier-en-Der F 45 B5
Montieri I 67 C5
Montiglio I 66 A2
Montignac F 63 A4
Montigny-le-Roi F 46 C1
Montigny-lès-Metz F 46 A2
Montigny-sur-Aube F 45 C5
Montijo E 79 C4
Montijo P 78 C2
Montilla E 86 B1
Montillana E 86 B2
Montilly F 54 B3
Montivilliers F 43 A6
Montjaux F 64 B1
Montjean-sur-Loire F 52 A4
Montlhéry F 44 B3
Montlieu-la-Garde F 53 C4
Montlouis-sur-Loire F 53 A5
Montluçon F 54 B2
Montluel F 55 C5
Montmarault F 54 B2
Montmartin-sur-Mer F 43 B4
Montmédy F 45 A6
Montmélian F 55 C6
Montmeyran F 64 B3
Montmirail, *Marne* F 45 B4
Montmirail, *Sarthe* F 44 B1
Montmirat F 64 C3
Montmirey-le-Château F 55 A5
Montmoreau-St. Cybard F 53 C5
Montmorency F 44 B3
Montmorillon F 53 B5
Montmort-Lucy F 45 B4
Montoir-de-Bretagne F 52 A2
Montoire-sur-le-Loir F 44 C1
Montoito P 78 C3
Montolieu F 63 C5
Montório al Vomano I 89 A3
Montoro E 86 A1
Montpellier F 64 C2
Montpezat-de-Quercy F 63 B4
Montpezat-sous-Bouzon F 64 B3
Montpon-Ménestérol F 62 A3
Montpont-en-Bresse F 55 B5
Montréal, *Aude* F 63 C5
Montréal, *Gers* F 62 C3
Montredon-Labessonnié F 63 C5
Montréjeau F 63 C3
Montrésor F 53 A6
Montresta I 96 C1
Montret F 55 B5
Montreuil, *Pas de Calais* F 34 C2
Montreuil, *Seine St. Denis* F 44 B3
Montreuil-aux-Lions F 45 A4
Montreuil-Bellay F 53 A4
Montreux CH 56 B1
Montrevault F 52 A3
Montrevel-en-Bresse F 55 B5
Montrichard F 53 A6
Montricoux F 63 B4
Montrond-les-Bains F 55 C4
Montrose GB 4 H5
Montroy E 82 B2
Monts-sur-Guesnes F 53 B5
Montsalvy F 63 B5
Montsauche-les-Settons F 54 A4
Montseny E 77 B5
Montsoreau F 53 A5
Montsûrs F 43 B5
Montuenga E 80 A2
Montuïri, *Mallorca* E 83
Monturque E 86 B1
Monza I 57 C4
Monzón E 76 B3
Monzón de Campos E 74 B2
Moorbad Lobenstein D 38 C1
Moordorf D 29 B4
Moorslede B 35 C4
Moosburg D 48 B2
Moosburg im Kärnten A 59 B4
Mór H 60 A3
Mora E 80 C3
Móra P 78 C2
Mora S 2 F14
Mora de Rubielos E 82 A2
Móra d'Ebre E 76 B3
Móra la Nova E 76 B3
Moraby S 22 A2
Moradillo de Roa E 74 C3
Morąg PL 33 B5
Mórahalom H 61 B4
Moraime E 72 A1
Morais P 73 C4

Place	Country	Page	Grid
Moral de Calatrava	E	86	A2
Moraleda de Zafayona	E	86	B2
Moraleja	E	79	A4
Moraleja del Vino	E	74	C1
Morales de Toro	E	74	C1
Morales de Valverde	E	74	C1
Morales del Vino	E	74	C1
Moralina	E	73	C4
Morano Cálabro	I	92	B3
Mörarp	S	27	C2
Morasverdes	E	79	A4
Morata de Jalón	E	75	C5
Morata de Jiloca	E	81	A5
Morata de Tajuña	E	81	B3
Moratalla	E	87	A4
Moravče	SLO	59	B4
Moravec	CZ	50	B2
Moravița	RO	61	C6
Morávka	CZ	51	A4
Moravská Třebová	CZ	50	A2
Moravské Budějovice	CZ	50	A1
Moravské Lieskové	SK	50	B3
Moravske Toplice	SLO	59	B6
Moravský-Beroun	CZ	50	A3
Moravský Krumlov	CZ	50	A2
Moravský Svätý Ján	SK	50	B3
Morawica	PL	41	C5
Morawin	PL	40	B3
Morbach	D	46	B3
Morbegno	I	57	B4
Morbier	F	55	B6
Mörbisch am See	A	50	C2
Mörbylånga	S	26	C5
Morcenx	F	62	B2
Morciano di Romagna	I	68	C1
Morcone	I	89	B4
Morcuera	E	75	C3
Mordelles	F	43	B4
Moréac	F	42	C3
Morecambe	GB	4	J5
Moreda, Granada	E	86	B3
Moreda, Oviedo	E	74	A1
Morée	F	44	C2
Moreles de Rey	E	74	B1
Morella	E	76	C2
Moreruela de los Infanzones	E	74	C1
Morés	E	75	C5
Móres	I	96	C1
Morestel	F	55	C5
Moret-sur-Loing	F	44	B3
Moretta	I	66	B1
Moreuil	F	44	A3
Morez	F	55	B6
Mörfelden	D	37	D4
Morgano	I	58	C2
Morgat	F	42	B1
Morges	CH	55	B6
Morgex	I	56	C2
Morgongåva	S	22	B3
Morhange	F	46	B2
Morhet	B	49	D6
Mori	I	57	C5
Morialmé	B	35	C5
Morianes	I	84	B3
Moriani Plage	F	96	A2
Mórichida	H	60	A2
Moriles	E	86	B1
Morille	D	37	B5
Moringen	D	37	B5
Morjärv	S	3	C18
Morkarla	S	22	B3
Mørke	DK	25	B3
Mørkøv	DK	25	D4
Morkovice-Slížany	CZ	50	A3
Morlaàs	F	62	C3
Morlaix	F	42	B2
Mörlunda	S	26	B5
Mormanno	I	92	B3
Mormant	F	45	B3
Mornant	F	55	C4
Morokovo	YU	71	D4
Morón de Almazán	E	75	C4
Morón de la Frontera	E	85	B5
Morović	YU	71	D4
Morozzo	I	66	B1
Mörrum	S	27	C4
Morsbach	D	36	C3
Mörsch	D	37	B4
Mörsil	S	2	E13
Morsum	D	25	E1
Mortagne-au-Perche	F	44	B1
Mortagne-sur-Gironde	F	52	C4
Mortagne-sur-Sèvre	F	52	B4
Mortágua	P	78	A2
Mortain	F	43	B5
Mortara	I	55	A6
Mortegliano	I	55	A4
Mortelle	I	95	A4
Mortemart	F	53	B5
Mortrée	F	43	B6
Mörtschach	A	58	B2
Mortsel	B	35	B4
Moryń	PL	45	C6
Morzeszczyn	PL	33	B5
Morzewo	PL	33	B5
Morzine	F	56	B1
Mosalsk	RUS	7	J24
Mosbach	D	47	A5
Mosby	N	19	C4
Mosca	P	78	A3
Moscavide	P	78	C1
Moščenica	HR	59	C6
Moščenice	HR	59	C4
Moščenicka Draga	HR	59	C4
Mosciano Sant'Ángelo	I	68	D2
Mościsko	PL	40	C1
Mosina	PL	40	A1
Mosjøen	N	2	D13
Moskorzew	PL	41	C4
Moskva	RUS	7	J24
Moslavina Podravska	HR	60	C3
Mosnița Nouă	RO	61	C6
Moso in Passíria	I	57	B6
Moson-magyaróvár	H	50	C3
Mošorin	YU	58	A3
Mošovce	SK	51	B4
Moss	N	20	B2
Mössingen	D	47	B5
Mosstrand	N	19	B5
Most	CZ	50	A2
Most na Soči	SLO	58	B3
Mostar	BIH	70	C2
Mosterhamn	N	18	B2
Mostki	PL	39	A5
Móstoles	E	80	B3
Mostová	SK	50	B3
Mostowo	PL	32	A2
Mostuéjouls	F	64	B3
Mosty	PL	31	B6
Mostys'ka	UA	11	M18
Mota del Cuervo	E	81	C4
Mota del Marqués	E	74	C1
Motala	S	23	C2
Möthlow	D	31	C4
Motilla del Palancar	E	81	C5
Motnik	SLO	59	B4
Motovun	HR	58	C3
Motril	E	86	C2
Motta	I	57	C6
Motta di Livenza	I	58	C2
Motta Montecorvino	I	90	A2
Móttola	I	91	B4
Mou	DK	24	C3
Mouchard	F	55	B5
Moúdhros	GR	16	S19
Moudon	CH	56	B1
Mougins	F	65	C5
Mouilleron-en-Pareds	F	52	B4
Mouliherne	F	53	A5
Moulinet	F	66	C1
Moulins	F	54	B3
Moulins-Engilbert	F	54	B1
Moulins-la-Marche	F	44	B1
Moulismes	F	53	B5
Moult	F	43	A5
Moura	P	84	A3
Mourenx	F	62	C3
Mouriés	F	64	C2
Mourmelon-le-Grand	F	45	A5
Mouronho	P	78	A2
Mouscron	B	34	C3
Moussac	F	64	C3
Moussey	F	46	B2
Mousteru	F	42	B2
Moustey	F	62	B3
Moustiers-Ste.-Marie	F	65	C5
Mouthe	F	55	B6
Mouthier-Haute-Pierre	F	55	A6
Mouthoumet	F	63	D5
Moutier	CH	56	A2
Moûtiers	F	55	C6
Moutiers-les-Mauxfaits	F	52	B3
Mouy	F	44	B3
Mouzon	F	45	A6
Møvik	N	18	A2
Moyenmoutier	F	46	B2
Moyenvic	F	46	B2
Mózar	E	74	C1
Mozhaysk	RUS	7	J25
Mozirje	SLO	59	B4
Mózs	H	74	B3
Mozzanica	I	57	C4
Mramorak	YU	71	D3
Mrčajevci	YU	71	C5
Mrkonjić Grad	BIH	70	B2
Mrkopalj	HR	59	C4
Mrmoš	YU	71	C5
Mrocza	PL	32	B3
Mroczeń	PL	40	B3
Mroczno	PL	33	B5
Mrozy	PL	41	A5
Mrzezyno	PL	31	A6
Mšec	CZ	39	C3
Mšeno	CZ	39	C4
Mstów	PL	41	C4
Mstislaw	BY	7	J22
Mszana Dolna	PL	41	C5
Mszczonów	PL	41	B5
Mtsensk	RUS	7	K25
Muć	HR	69	C5
Múccia	I	68	C3
Much	D	36	C3
Mücheln	D	38	B1
Muchów	PL	39	B6
Mucientes	E	74	C1
Muda	P	84	B1
Mudanya	TR	16	R21
Mudau	D	47	B5
Müden	D	30	C2
Mudersbach	D	36	C3
Mudurnu	TR	16	R22
Muel	E	76	B1
Muelas del Pan	E	73	C5
Muess	N	30	B3
Mugardos	E	72	A2
Muge	P	78	B2
Mügeln, Sachsen-Anhalt	D	38	B3
Mügeln, Sachsen	D	38	B3
Múggia	I	58	C3
Muğla	TR	16	T21
Mugnano	I	68	C1
Mugron	F	62	C2
Mugueimes	E	73	C3
Muhi	H	51	C6
Mühlacker	D	47	B4
Mühlbach am Hochkönig	A	58	A3
Mühlberg, Brandenburg	D	38	B3
Mühlberg, Thüringen	D	37	C6
Mühldorf	D	48	B3
Mühlen-Eichsen	D	30	B1
Mühlhausen, Bayern	D	48	A1
Mühlhausen, Thüringen	D	37	B6
Mühltroff	D	38	C1
Muhos	FIN	3	D20
Muhr	A	58	B3
Muirteira	P	78	B1
Mukacheve	UA	11	M18
Mula	E	87	A4
Mulegns	CH	57	B4
Mules	I	57	B6
Mülheim	D	36	B2
Mulhouse	F	46	D2
Muljava	SLO	59	C4
Müllheim	D	46	D2
Mullhyttan	S	22	B1
Mullinavat	IRL	4	K3
Mullingar	IRL	4	B3
Mullsjö	S	21	D5
Müllrose	D	39	A4
Mulseryd	S	26	B3
Munana	E	80	B1
Muñás	E	74	A2
Münchberg	D	38	C1
Müncheberg	D	31	C6
München	D	48	C2
Münchhausen	D	37	C4
Mundaka	E	75	A4
Münden	D	37	B5
Munderfing	A	49	B4
Munderkingen	D	47	B5
Munera	E	81	C4
Mungia	E	75	A4
Muñico	E	80	B1
Muniesa	E	65	C5
Munka-Ljungby	S	27	C2
Munkebo	DK	25	D3
Munkedal	S	21	C3
Munkfors	S	20	B5
Munktorp	S	22	B3
Münnerstadt	D	37	C6
Muñopepe	E	80	B1
Muñotello	E	80	B1
Münsingen, CH	CH	56	B2
Münsingen	D	47	B5
Munsö	S	22	B3
Münster, Hessen	D	47	A4
Munster, Niedersachsen	D	30	C2
Munster	F	46	B3
Muntibar	E	75	A4
Münzkirchen	A	49	B4
Muonio	FIN	3	C18
Muotathal	CH	56	B3
Mur-de-Barrez	F	63	B6
Mur-de-Bretagne	F	42	B2
Mur-de-Sologne	F	53	A6
Murakeresztúr	H	60	B1
Murán	SK	51	B6
Murano	I	58	C2
Muras	E	72	A3
Murat	F	64	A1
Murat-sur-Vèbre	F	64	C1
Muratlı	TR	16	R20
Murato	F	96	A2
Murau	A	59	A4
Muravera	I	96	D2
Murazzano	I	66	B2
Murça	P	73	C3
Murchante	E	75	C5
Murcia	E	87	B4
Murczyn	PL	32	C3
Mureck	A	59	B5
Muret	F	63	C4
Murguia	E	75	B4
Muri	CH	56	A3
Murias de Paredes	E	74	B1
Muriedas	E	74	A3
Muriel Viejo	E	75	C4
Murillo de Rio Leza	E	75	B4
Murillo el Fruto	E	75	B5
Murmansk	RUS	3	B23
Murmashi	RUS	3	B23
Murnau	D	48	C2
Muro, Mallorca	E	83	
Muro de Alcoy	E	82	C2
Muro Lucano	I	90	B2
Murol	F	52	C6
Muros	E	72	B1
Muros de Nalón	E	74	A1
Murowana Goślina	PL	32	C3
Mürren	CH	56	B2
Murrhardt	D	47	B5
Murska Sobota	SLO	59	B6
Mursko Središče	HR	59	B6
Murtas	E	86	C3
Murten	CH	56	B2
Murter	HR	69	C4
Murtosa	P	73	D2
Murvica	HR	69	B4
Murviel-lès-Béziers	F	64	C2
Mürzsteg	A	49	C6
Mürzzuschlag	A	49	C6
Musculdy	F	62	C2
Muskö	S	23	B5
Mušov	CZ	50	B2
Musselkanaal	NL	29	C4
Mussidan	F	63	A3
Mussomeli	I	94	B2
Musson	B	46	A1
Mussy-sur-Seine	F	45	C5
Mustafakemalpaşa	TR	16	R21
Muszaki	PL	33	B6
Muszyna	PL	51	A6
Muta	SLO	59	B5
Mutné	SK	51	A5
Mutriku	E	75	A4
Mutterbergalm	A	57	A6
Muxía	E	72	A1
Muxilka-Ugarte	E	75	A4
Muzillac	F	52	A3
Mužla	SK	51	C4
Muzzano del Turgnano	I	58	C3
Myennes	F	54	A2
Myjava	SK	50	B3
Mykland	N	19	C5
Mykolayiv	UA	11	N23
Myra	N	20	B3
Myresjö	S	26	B3
Myrhorod	UA	11	M23
Mysen	N	20	B3
Mysłakowice	PL	39	C5
Myślenice	PL	41	C5
Myślibórz	PL	31	C6
Mysłowice	PL	41	C4
Mysłków	PL	41	C4
Mytishchi	RUS	7	J25
Mýtne Ludany	SK	51	B4

N

Place	Country	Page	Grid
N Unnaryd	S	26	B3
Naaldwijk	NL	35	B5
Naantali	FIN	3	F17
Naas	IRL	4	K3
Nabais	P	78	A3
Načeradec	CZ	49	C6
Náchod	CZ	39	C6
Nacław	PL	32	A2
Nadarzyce	PL	32	B2
Nadarzyn	PL	41	A5
Nádasd	H	60	B1
Nádlac	RO	61	C5
Nádudvar	H	61	A5
Nadvirna	UA	11	M19
Nærbø	N	18	C2
Næstved	DK	25	D4
Näfels	CH	56	A4
Nagel	D	38	D1
Nagele	NL	28	C2
Nagłowice	PL	41	C4
Nagold	D	47	C4
Nagore	E	75	B5
Nagyatád	H	60	B2
Nagybajom	H	60	B2
Nagybaracska	H	60	C3
Nagybátony	H	51	C5
Nagyberény	H	60	B2
Nagybörzsöny	H	51	C4
Nagycenk	H	60	A1
Nagydorog	H	60	B3
Nagyfüged	H	51	C5
Nagyhersány	H	60	C3
Nagyigmánd	H	60	A3
Nagyiván	H	61	A4
Nagykanizsa	H	60	B1
Nagykáta	H	61	A4
Nagykonyi	H	60	B3
Nagykörös	H	61	A4
Nagykörü	H	61	A5
Nagylóc	H	51	C5
Nagymágocs	H	61	B5
Nagymányok	H	60	B3
Nagymaros	H	51	C4
Nagyoroszi	H	51	C4
Nagyrábé	H	61	A5
Nagyréde	H	51	C5
Nagyszékely	H	60	B3
Nagyszénás	H	61	B5
Nagyszokoly	H	60	B3
Nagytöke	H	61	B5
Nagyvázsony	H	60	B2
Nagyvenyim	H	60	B3
Naharros	E	81	B4
Nahe	D	30	B1
Naila	D	38	C1
Nailloux	F	63	C4
Naintré	F	53	B5
Nairn	GB	4	H5
Najac	F	63	B5
Nájera	E	75	B4
Nak	H	60	B3
Nakksjø	N	19	B6
Nakło nad Notecią	PL	32	B3
Nalda	E	75	B4
Nálepkovo	SK	51	B6
Nallihan	TR	16	R22
Nalliers	F	52	B3
Nalzen	F	63	D4
Nalžouské Hory	CZ	49	A4
Náměšť nad Oslavou	CZ	50	A2
Námestovo	SK	51	A5
Namná	RO	11	P19
Namsos	N	2	D12
Namur	B	35	C5
Namysłów	PL	40	B2
Nançay	F	54	A2
Nanclares de la Oca	E	75	B4
Nancy	F	46	B2
Nangis	F	45	C4
Nannestad	N	20	A3
Nant	F	64	B2
Nanterre	F	44	B3
Nantes	F	52	A3
Nanteuil-le-Haudouin	F	44	B3
Nantiat	F	53	B6
Nantua	F	55	B5
Napajedla	CZ	50	B3
Napiwoda	PL	33	B6
Nápoli	I	89	C4
Naraval	E	74	A2
Narberth	GB	4	C2
Narbonne	F	64	C1
Narbonne-Plage	F	64	C2
Narcao	I	96	D1
Nardò	I	91	B5
Narni	I	88	A2
Naro	I	94	B2
Naro Fominsk	RUS	7	J25
Narón	E	72	A2
Narros del Castillo	E	80	B1
Narta	HR	60	C1
Naruszewo	PL	33	C6
Narva	EST	7	G21
Narvik	N	2	B15
Narzole	I	66	B1
Nås	S	20	B5
Näsåud	RO	11	N19
Nasavrky	CZ	50	A1
Nasbinals	F	64	B2
Näshull	S	26	B3
Našice	HR	60	C3
Nasielsk	PL	33	C6
Naso	I	95	A3
Nassandres	F	44	B1
Nassau	D	36	C3
Nassenfels	D	48	B2
Nassenheide	D	31	C5
Nassereith	A	57	A5
Nässjö	S	26	B3
Nastätten	D	36	C3
Näsum	S	27	C4
Natalinci	YU	71	B5
Nater-Stetten	D	48	C2
Naters	CH	56	B3
Nattheim	D	47	B6
Nättraby	S	27	C4
Naturno	I	57	B6
Naucelle	F	63	B6
Nauders	A	57	B5
Nauen	D	31	C4
Naumburg	D	38	B1
Naundorf	D	38	B3
Naunhof	D	38	B2
Naustdal	N	2	F9
Nava	E	74	A1
Nava de Arévalo	E	80	B1
Nava de la Asunción	E	80	A2
Nava del Rey	E	74	C1
Navacerrada	E	80	B3
Navaconcejo	E	79	A5
Navafría	E	80	A3
Navahermosa	E	80	C2
Navahrudak	BY	7	K19
Naval	E	76	B2
Navalacruz	E	80	B1
Navalcán	E	80	B1
Navalcarnero	E	80	B3
Navaleno	E	75	C3
Navalmanzano	E	80	A2
Navalmoral	E	80	B2
Navalmoral de la Mata	E	79	C5
Navalón	E	82	C2
Navalonguilla	E	79	B5
Navalperal de Pinares	E	80	B2
Navalpino	E	80	C1
Navaltalgordo	E	80	B1
Navaltoril	E	80	C1
Navaluenga	E	80	B1
Navalvillar de Pela	E	79	C5
Navan	IRL	4	B3
Navaperal de Tormes	E	80	B1
Navapolatsk	BY	7	J21
Navarclés	E	77	B4
Navarredonda de Gredos	E	80	B1
Navarrenx	F	62	C3
Navarrés	E	82	B2
Navarrete	E	75	B4
Navarrevisca	E	80	B1
Navás	E	77	B4
Navas de Oro	E	80	A2
Navas de San Juan	E	86	A3
Navas del Madroño	E	79	B4
Navas del Rey	E	80	B3
Navas del Sepillar	E	86	B2
Navascués	E	76	B1
Navasfrias	E	79	B4
Nave	I	57	C5
Nave de Haver	P	79	A4
Nävekvarn	S	23	C3
Navelli	I	89	A4
Navenby	GB	4	K6
Näverede	S	21	C4
Navés	E	80	C1
Navezuelas	E	80	C1
Navia	E	74	A2
Navia de Suarna	E	72	B4
Nălępkowo?	P	55	B5
Nálepkovo	SK	51	B6
Nallihan	TR	16	R22
Náprad	RO	16	Q21
Návpaktos	GR	15	S17
Návplion	GR	15	T18
Náxos	GR	16	T19
Nay	F	78	B1
Nazaré	P	78	B1
Nazilli	TR	16	T21
Nazza	D	37	B6
Néa Epídhavros	GR	15	T18
Néa Moudhaniá	GR	15	R18
Neath	GB	4	L5
Nebljusi	HR	69	B4
Neblo	SLO	58	B3
Nebolchy	RUS	7	G23
Nebra	D	38	B1
Nebreda	E	75	C3
Nechanice	CZ	50	A1
Neckargemünd	D	47	A4
Neckarsulm	D	47	A5
Neda	E	72	A2
Nedelišće	HR	59	B6
Nederweert	NL	36	B1
Nedstrand	N	18	B2
Nedvědice	CZ	50	A2
Nędza	PL	40	C3
Neede	NL	36	A2
Neermoor	D	29	B4
Neeroeteren	B	36	B1
Neerpelt	B	35	B6
Neesen	D	30	C2
Neetze	D	30	B2
Negbina	YU	11	J25
Negotin	YU	11	P18
Negrar	I	57	C5
Negredo	E	81	A4
Negreira	E	72	B2
Nègrepelisse	F	63	B5
Negru Vodă	RO	16	Q21
Negueira de Muñiz	E	72	A4
Neheim	D	36	B3
Neila	E	75	B4
Néive	I	66	B2
Nejdek	CZ	38	C2
Nekla	PL	40	A2
Nekső	DK	27	D5
Nelas	P	78	A3
Nelaug	N	19	C5
Nelidovo	RUS	7	H23
Nellingen	D	47	B5
Neman	RUS	6	J18
Nemesgörzsöny	H	60	A2
Nemeskér	H	60	A1
Nemesnádudvar	H	60	A1
Nemesszalók	H	60	A2
Németkér	H	60	B3
Nemešská Lúka	SLO	59	C5
Nemšová	SK	50	B3
Nenagh	IRL	4	K2
Nenince	SK	51	C5
Nenzing	A	57	A4
Nepi	I	88	A3
Nepomuk	CZ	49	B4
Nérac	F	63	B4
Neratovice	CZ	39	C4
Nerchau	D	38	B2
Néré	F	53	B4
Nereresham?			
Neresheim	D	47	B6
Nereto	I	89	A4
Nerezine	HR	68	B3
Nerežišća	HR	68	B2
Neringa	LT	6	J17
Néris-les-Bains	F	54	B2
Nerja	E	86	C2
Néronde	F	55	C4
Nérondes	F	54	B2
Nerpio	E	87	A4
Nersingen	D	47	B6
Nerva	E	85	B3
Nervesa della Battáglia	I	58	C2
Nervi	I	66	B3
Nes	NL	28	B2
Nesbyen	N	2	F11
Nesflaten	N	19	A4
Nesland	N	19	B4
Neslandsvatn	N	19	C6
Nesle	F	45	A4
Nesodden	N	20	B2
Nesoddtangen	N	20	B2
Nesovice	CZ	50	B3
Nesselwang	D	57	A5
Nesslau	CH	57	A4
Nessmersiel	D	29	B4
Nesso	I	57	C4
Nesterov	UA	11	L18
Nestvady?	SK	50	C4
Nesvady	SK	50	C4
Nesvatnstemmen	N	19	C5
Netland	N	19	C5
Netolice	CZ	49	B5
Netphen	D	36	C3
Netstal	CH	56	A4
Nettancourt	F	45	C6
Nettetal	D	36	B1
Nettlingen	D	37	A5
Nettuno	I	88	B3
Neu Darchau	D	30	B2
Neu Kaliss	D	30	B2
Neu-markt am Wallersee	A	49	C4
Neu-Ravensburg	D	47	D5
Neu-Ulm	D	47	B6
Neualbenreuth	D	38	D3
Neubeckum	D	36	B3
Neubrandenburg	D	31	B5
Neubruchhausen	D	29	C5
Neubukow	D	30	A2
Neuburg	D	48	C2
Neuchâtel	CH	56	B1
Neudietendorf	D	37	C6
Neudorf	RO	11	R21
Neuenburg, Baden-Württemberg	D	47	C4
Neuenbürg			
Neuenburg, Niedersachsen	D	29	B4
Neuendorf	D	31	A5
Neuenhagen	D	31	C5
Neuenhaus	D	28	C3
Neuenkirchen, Niedersachsen	D	29	C5
Neuenkirchen, Niedersachsen	D	29	C5
Neuenkirchen, Nordrhein-Westfalen	D	36	A3
Neuenrade	D	36	B3
Neuenwalde	D	29	B5
Neuerburg	D	36	C2
Neuf-Brisach	F	46	D3
Neufahrn, Bayern	D	48	B2
Neufahrn, Bayern	D	48	B3
Neufchâteau	B	46	B1
Neufchâteau	F	46	B1
Neufchâtel-en-Bray	F	44	A2
Neufchâtel-sur-Aisne	F	45	B5
Neuflize	F	45	B5
Neugersdorf	D	39	C4
Neuhardenberg	D	31	C6
Neuhaus, Bayern	D	48	A2
Neuhaus, Bayern	D	49	B4
Neuhaus, Niedersachsen	D	29	B5
Neuhaus, Niedersachsen	D	30	B2
Neuhaus, Niedersachsen	D	37	B5
Neuhaus a Rennweg	D	38	C1
Neuhausen	CH	47	C4
Neuhausen ob Eck	D	47	C5
Neuhof	D	48	A1
Neuhofen an der Krems	A	49	A4
Neuil lé-Pont-Pierre	F	53	A5
Neuilly-en-Thelle	F	44	B3
Neuilly-le-Réal	F	54	B3
Neuilly-St.-Front	F	45	B4
Neukalen	D	31	B4
Neukirch	D	39	B4
Neukirchen	D	48	B4
Neukirchen, Hessen	D	37	C5
Neukirchen, Schleswig-Holstein	D	25	E4
Neukirchen-am Grossvenediger	A	58	A2
Neukirchen bei Heiligen Blut	D	48	A3
Neukloster	D	30	B2
Neulengbach	A	50	A1
Neulise	F	54	C3
Neum	BIH	70	C2
Neumagen	D	46	B2
Neumarkt im Hausruckkreis	A		
Neumarkt im Mühlkreis	A		
Neumarkt im Steiermark	A		
Neumarkt Sankt Veit	D	48	B3
Neumünster	D	30	A1
Neunburg vorm Wald	D	48	A3
Neung-sur-Beuvron	F	54	A1
Neunkirch, Luzern	CH	56	B3
Neunkirch, Schaffhausen	CH	47	C4
Neunkirchen, Nordrhein-Westfalen	D	36	C3
Neunkirchen, Saarland	D	46	B3
Neunkirchen am Brand	D	48	A2
Neuötting	D	48	B3
Neureut	D	47	B4
Neuruppin	D	31	B4
Neusäss	D	48	B1
Neusiedl	D	36	B2
Neuss	D	36	B2
Neussargues-Moissac	F	54	C2
Neustadt, Bayern	D	48	A1
Neustadt, Bayern	D	48	A2
Neustadt, Bayern	D	48	A3
Neustadt, Brandenburg	D	31	C4
Neustadt, Hessen	D	37	C4
Neustadt, Niedersachsen	D	29	C6
Neustadt, Rheinland-Pfalz	D	47	B4
Neustadt, Sachsen	D	39	B4
Néa Epídhavros	GR	15	T18
Neuenhagen	D	31	C5
Neuenhaus	D	28	C3
Neuenkirchen, Schleswig-Holstein	D	30	A1
Neustadt, Thüringen	D	38	C1
Neustadt, Thüringen	D	38	C1
Neustadt-Glewe	D	30	B3
Neustift im Stubaital	A	57	A6
Neustrelitz	D	31	B5
Neutal	A	59	A6
Neutrebbin	D	31	C6
Neuves-Maisons	F	46	B2
Neuvic, Corrèze	F	54	C2
Neuvic, Dordogne	F	63	A3
Neuville-aux-Bois	F	44	B3
Neuville-de-Poitou	F	53	B5
Neuville-les-Dames	F	55	B5
Neuville-sur-Saône	F	55	C4
Neuvy-le-Roi	F	44	C1
Neuvy-St.-Sépulchre	F	54	B1
Neuvy-Santour	F	45	B4
Neuvy-sur-Barangeon	F	54	A2
Neuwied	D	36	C3
Neuzelle	D	39	A4
Névache	F	65	A5
Neveklov	CZ	49	B5
Nevel	RUS	7	H21
Nevers	F	54	B3
Nevesinje	BIH	70	C3
Névez	F	42	C2
Nevlunghavn	N	19	C6
Newark-on-Trent	GB	4	K6
Newbury	GB	4	L6
Newcastle	GB	4	K5
Newcastle-under-Lyme	GB	4	K5
Newcastle-upon-Tyne	GB	4	J6
Newcastle West	IRL	4	K2
Newhaven	GB	4	L7
Newmarket	IRL	4	K2
Newport, Isle of Wight	GB	4	L6
Newport, Newport	GB	4	L5
Newquay	GB	4	L4
Newry	GB	4	K2
Newton Abbot	GB	4	L5
Newton Stewart	GB	4	J4
Newtonmore	GB	4	H4
Newtownards	GB	4	K2
Nexon	F	53	C6
Nibbiano	I	66	B3
Nibe	DK	24	C2
Nicastro	I	92	C3
Niccone	I	68	C1
Nice	F	65	C6
Nickelsdorf	A	50	C3
Nicolosi	I	95	B4
Nicosia	I	95	B3
Nicótera	I	92	C2
Nidda	D	37	C5
Nidzica	PL	33	B6
Niebla	E	85	B4
Nieborów	PL	41	A5
Niebüll	D	25	E1
Niechanowo	PL	32	C3
Niechorze	PL	31	A7
Niedalino	PL	32	A2
Nieder-Olm	D	47	A4
Niederaudorf	D	48	C3
Niederaula	D	37	C5
Niederbipp	CH	56	A2
Niederbronn-les-Bains	F	46	B3
Niederfischbach	D	36	C3
Niedergörsdorf	D	38	B2
Niederkrüchten	D	36	B2
Niederndorf	A	48	C2
Niedersachs-werfen	D	37	B6
Niederstetten	D	47	A5
Niederurnen	D	56	A4
Niederwölz	A	59	A4
Niedoradz	PL	39	B5
Niedzica	PL	51	A6
Niegosławice	PL	39	B6
Nieheim	D	37	B5
Niemcza	PL	40	C1
Niemegk	D	38	A2
Niemodlin	PL	40	C2
Nienburg, Niedersachsen	D	29	C6
Nienburg, Sachsen-Anhalt	D	38	B1
Niepołomice	PL	41	C4
Nierstein	D	47	A4
Niesky	D	39	B4
Niestronno	PL	32	C3
Nieświń	PL	41	B4
Nieszawa	PL	33	C4
Nieul-sur-Mer	F	52	B3
Nieuw-Amsterdam	NL	28	C3
Nieuw-Buinen	NL	28	C3
Nieuw-Weerdinge	NL	28	C3
Nieuwe Niedorp	NL	28	C1
Nieuwe-Pekela	NL	28	B3
Nieuwe-schans	NL	29	B4
Nieuwerkerken	B	35	C5
Nieuwolda	NL	28	B3
Nieuwpoort	B	34	B2
Nigrita	GR	15	R18
Nigüelas	E	86	C3
Níjar	E	87	C4

Osterburken D 47 A5
Österbybruk S 22 A4
Österbyhavn DK 24 B4
Österbymo S 23 D2
Ostercappeln D 29 C5
Österfärnebo S 22 A3
Osterfeld D 38 B1
Osterhofen D 48 B4
Osterholz-Scharmbeck D 29 B5
Østerild DK 24 B1
Österlövsta S 22 A4
Ostermiething A 48 B3
Osterode am Harz D 37 B6
Östersund S 2 E14
Östervåla S 22 A4
Östervallskog S 20 B3
Osterwieck D 37 B6
Osterzell D 48 C1
Ostffyasszonyfa H 60 A2
Östhammar S 22 A5
Ostheim F 46 B3
Ostheim vor der Rhön D 37 C6
Osthofen D 47 A4
Ostiano I 57 C5
Ostíglia I 67 A5
Ostiz E 62 D1
Östmark S 20 A4
Ostojićevo YU 61 C5
Ostra I 68 C2
Östra Amtervik S 20 B5
Östra Husby S 23 C3
Östra Ljungby S 27 C3
Östra Ryd S 23 C3
Östraby S 27 D3
Ostrach D 47 C5
Ostrau D 38 B3
Ostrava CZ 50 A4
Østre Halsen N 21 B2
Ostrhauderfehn D 29 B4
Ostritz D 39 B4
Ostróda PL 33 B5
Ostroh UA 11 L20
Ostrołęka PL 6 K17
Ostropole PL 32 B2
Ostroróg PL 32 C2
Ostrošovac BIH 69 B4
Ostrov CZ 38 C2
Ostrov RUS 7 H21
Ostrov nad Oslavou CZ 50 A1
Ostrów Mazowiecka PL 6 K17
Ostrów Wielkopolski PL 40 B2
Ostrówek PL 40 B3
Ostrowiec PL 32 A2
Ostrowiec-Świętokrzyski PL 41 C6
O[illegible] PL 33 B5
O[illegible] PL 33 C4
O[illegible] BIH 70 C2
Os[illegible] PL 40 B2
[illegible]orn
Ost[illegible] D 30 A3
Osu[illegible] 91 B4
Osv[illegible] 85 B5
Osw[illegible] 50 A3
Ośw[illegible] 4 K5
Oszt[illegible] C4
Oteiž[illegible] B2
Otele[illegible] B5
Oteo[illegible]
Oterb[illegible] C5
Otero [illegible] Herr[illegible]
Otero [illegible] Bod[illegible]
Othem
Otmuch[illegible]
Otočac
Otok
Otok
Otoka
Otranto
Otrić
Otrícoli
Otrokovic[illegible]
Ottana
Ottaviano
Ottenby
Ottendorf-Okrilla
Ottenhöfen
Ottenschlag
Ottensheim
Otterbach
Otterbäcken
Otterberg
Otterndorf
Ottersburg
Ottersweier
Otterup
Ottignies
Ottmarsheim
Ottobeuren
Öttömös
Ottone
Ottweiler
Ötvöskónyi
Otwock
Ouanne
Ouarville
Oucques
Oud-Beijerland N[illegible]
Oud Gastel NL
Ouddorp NL
Oude-Pekela NL
Oude-Tonge NL
Oudemirdum NL
Oudenaarde B
Oudenbosch NL
Oudenburg B
Oudewater NL
Oudon F
Ouguela P
Ouistreham F
Oulainen FIN
Oulchy-le-Château F

Oullins F 55 C4
Oulmes F 53 B4
Oulu FIN 3 D19
Oulx I 65 A5
Ourense E 73 B3
Ourique P 84 B2
Ourol E 72 A3
Ouroux-en-Morvan F 54 A3
Oust F 63 D4
Outeiro P 78 A2
Outeiro de Rei E 72 A3
Outes E 72 B2
Outokumpu FIN 3 E21
Outreau F 34 C2
Ouzouer-le-Marché F 44 C2
Ouzouer-sur-Loire F 44 C3
Ovada I 66 B2
Ovar P 73 D2
Ove DK 24 C2
Ovelgönne D 29 B5
Over-jerstal DK 25 D2
Overath D 36 C3
Overdinkel NL 36 A3
Överenhörna S 22 B4
Overijse B 35 C5
Överkalix S 3 C18
Overlade DK 24 C2
Överlida S 26 B2
Overpelt B 35 B6
Övertorneå S 3 C18
Överum S 23 D3
Ovidiopol UA 11 N22
Oviedo E 74 A1
Oviglio I 66 B2
Ovíndoli I 89 A3
Ovodda I 96 C2
Øvre Årdal N 2 F10
Øvre Sirdal N 18 C3
Övre Ullerud S 20 B5
Øvrebygd N 18 C3
Ovruch UA 11 L21
Ovtrup DK 25 D1
Owińska PL 32 C2
Oxelösund S 23 C4
Oxford GB 4 L6
Oxie S 27 D3
Øyenkilen N 20 B2
Øyfiell N 19 B5
Øygärdslia N 19 C5
Øymark N 20 B3
Oyonnax F 55 B5
Øyslebø N 19 C4
Oyten D 29 B6
Øyuvsbu N 19 B4
Ozaeta E 75 B4
Ozalj HR 59 C5
Ożarów PL 41 C6
Ożarów Maz PL 41 A5
Ožbalt SLO 59 B5
Ózd H 51 B6
Oždany SK 51 B5
Ozieri I 96 C2
Ozimek PL 40 C3
Ozimica BIH 70 B3
Ozora H 60 B3
Ozorków PL 41 B4
Ozzano Monferrato I 66 A2

P

Paal B 35 B6
Pabianice PL 41 B4
Pacanów PL 41 C6
Paceco I 94 B1
Pachino I 95 C4
Pačir YU 61 C4
[illegible]ack A 59 A5
[illegible]os de [illegible]reira P 73 C2
[illegible] CZ 49 A6
[illegible] H 60 B2
[illegible]-Eure F 44 A2
[illegible] PL 40 C2
[illegible] DK 25 E2
[illegible] YU 61 C5
[illegible] HR 69 B5
[illegible] 37 B4
[illegible] 84 B2
[illegible] 71 A5
[illegible] 71 B5
[illegible] C2
[illegible] C1
[illegible]
Privl
Prive
Privl
Priv
Priz
Pri
Pr

Palaciòs de la Valduerna E 74 B1
Palacios de Sanabria E 73 B4
Palacios del Sil E 72 B4
Palaciosrubios E 80 A1
Palafrugell E 77 B6
Palagiano I 91 B4
Palagonía I 95 B3
Paláia I 67 C4
Palaiokhóra GR 16 U18
Palaiseau F 44 B3
Palamòs E 77 B6
Palanga LT 6 J17
Palanzano I 67 B4
Palárikovo SK 50 B4
Palas de Rei E 72 B3
Palata I 89 B4
Palatna YU 71 C6
Palau I 96 B2
Palavas-les-Flots F 64 C2
Palazuelos de la Sierra E 75 B3
Palazzo Adriano I 94 B2
Palazzo del Pero I 67 C5
Palazzo San Gervásio I 90 B2
Palazzolo Acréide I 95 B3
Palazzolo sull Oglio I 57 C4
Palazzuolo sul Senio I 67 B5
Paldiski EST 6 G19
Pale BIH 70 C3
Palena I 89 B4
Palencia E 74 B2
Palenciana E 86 B1
Palermo I 94 A2
Palestrina I 88 B2
Pálfa H 60 B3
Palfau A 49 C5
Palhaça P 78 A2
Palheiros da Tocha P 78 A2
Palheiros de Quiaios P 78 A2
Palić YU 61 B4
Palidoro I 88 B2
Palinuro I 89 B3
Paliseul B 45 A6
Pallanza I 56 C3
Pallares E 85 A4
Pallaruelo de Monegros E 76 B2
Pallerols E 77 A4
Palling D 48 B3
Palluau F 52 B3
Palma P 78 C2
Palma Campània I 89 C4
Palma de Mallorca, Mallorca E 83
Palma del Rio E 85 B5
Palma di Montechiaro I 94 B2
Palma Nova, Mallorca E 83
Palmanova I 58 C3
Palmela P 78 C2
Palmerola E 77 A5
Palmi I 92 C2
Pálmonostora H 61 B4
Palo del Colle I 91 A3
Palomares E 87 B4
Palomares del Campo E 81 C4
Palomas E 79 C4
Palombara Sabina I 88 A2
Palos de la Frontera E 85 B4
Palotaboszok H 60 B3
Palotás H 51 C5
Pals E 77 B6
Pålsboda S 23 B2
Paluzza I 58 B3
Pamhagen A 50 C2
Pamiers F 63 C4
Pamiętowo PL 32 B3
Pampaneira E 86 C2
Pamparato I 66 B1
Pampilhosa, Aveiro P 78 A2
Pampilhosa, Coimbra P 78 A3
Pampliega E 74 B3
Pamplona E 75 B5
Panagyurishte BG 16 Q19
[P]ancalieri I 66 B1
[Pa]nčevo YU 71 B5
[illegible]ey F 45 B6
[illegible]rvo E 75 B3
[illegible]do E 76 C1
[illegible] I 57 C4
[illegible] DK 24 B2
[illegible] CZ 39 C3
[illegible] E 74 A2
[illegible] 6 J19
[illegible] 55 C4
[illegible] 40 C3
[illegible] 44 B3
[illegible] 3 B1
[illegible] A2
[illegible] 4
[illegible] 5
[illegible] B5

Paraćin YU 71 C6
Parád H 51 C6
Parada, Bragança P 73 C4
Parada, Viseu P 78 A2
Paradas E 85 B5
Paradela E 72 B3
Parades de Rubiales E 80 A1
Paradinas de San Juan E 80 B1
Paradiso di Cevadale I 57 B5
Paradyż PL 41 B5
Parainen FIN 3 F18
Parakhino Paddubye RUS 7 G23
Paramé F 43 B4
Páramo E 72 A4
Páramo del Sil E 72 B4
Parandaça P 73 C3
Paravadella E 72 A3
Paray-le-Monial F 54 B4
Parceiros P 78 B2
Parcey F 55 A5
Parchim D 30 B3
Parcice PL 40 B3
Pardilla E 74 C3
Pardubice CZ 39 C5
Paredes E 81 B4
Paredes P 73 C2
Paredes de Coura P 73 C2
Paredes de Nava E 74 B2
Paredes de Siguenza E 81 A4
Pareja E 81 B4
Parennes F 43 B5
Parenti I 92 B3
Parentis-en-Born F 62 B1
Parey D 30 C3
Parfino RUS 7 H22
Parg HR 59 C4
Párga GR 15 S17
Pargny-sur-Saulx F 45 B5
Parigné-l'Évêque F 44 C1
Parikkala FIN 3 F21
Paris F 44 B3
Parisot F 63 B4
Parkano FIN 3 E18
Parla E 80 B3
Parlavá E 77 A6
Parma I 67 B4
Parndorf A 50 C2
Párnica SK 51 A5
Parnu EST 6 G19
Parolis E 87 A3
Parrillas E 80 B1
Parsberg D 48 A2
Parstein D 31 C6
Partakko FIN 3 B20
Partanna I 94 B1
Parthenay F 53 B4
Partinico I 94 A2
Partizani YU 71 B5
Partizánske SK 51 B4
Påryd S 26 C5
Parysów PL 41 B6
Parzymiechy PL 40 B3
Paşcani RO 11 N20
Pasewalk D 31 B5
Pašina Voda YU 71 C4
Påskallavik S 26 B6
Pasłęk PL 33 A5
Pašman HR 69 C4
Passail A 59 A5
Passais F 43 B5
Passau D 49 B4
Passegueiro P 78 B2
Passignano sul Trasimeno I 68 C1
Passo di Trèia I 68 C2
Passopisciaro I 95 B4
Passow D 31 B6
Passy F 56 C1
Pastavy BY 7 J20
Pástena I 89 B4
Pastrana E 81 B4
Pastrengo I 57 C5
Pasym PL 33 B6
Pásztó H 51 C5
Pata SK 50 B3
Patay F 44 C2
Paterek PL 32 B3
Paterna E 82 B2
Paterna de Rivera E 85 C5
Paterna del Campo E 85 B4
Paterna del Madera E 87 A3
Paternion A 58 B3
Paternò I 95 B3
Paternópoli I 90 B2
Patersdorf D 48 A3
Paterswolde NL 28 B3
Pątnow PL 40 A3
Patos AL 15 R16
Pátrai GR 15 S17
Patrimonio F 96 A2
Pattada I 96 C2
Pattensen, Niedersachsen D 30 B2
Pattensen, Niedersachsen D 37 A5
Patti I 95 A3
Páty H 60 A3
[illegible]au F 62 C2
[illegible]illac F 53 C4
[illegible]aro I 58 B3
[illegible]guet F 54 C3
[illegible] F 64 C2
[illegible] I 96 C1
[illegible] S 26 B5
[illegible] I 57 C4
[illegible] D 38 C1
[illegible]via I 57 C4
Pavia P 78 C2
Pavias E 82 B2
Pavilly F 44 A1

Pävilosta LV 6 H17
Pavino Polje YU 71 C4
Pavullo nel Frignano I 67 B4
Pawlowice PL 51 A4
Pawłowice PL 40 B2
Payerne CH 56 B1
Paymogo E 84 B3
Payrac F 63 B4
Pazardzhik BG 16 Q19
Pazin HR 58 C3
Paziols F 64 D1
Pčelić HR 60 C2
Peal de Becerro E 86 B2
Peć YU 71 D5
Péccioli I 67 C4
Pécel H 61 A4
Pechao P 84 B3
Pechenga RUS 3 B22
Pechenizhyn UA 11 M19
Pecica RO 61 B6
Pećinci YU 71 B4
Pecka YU 71 B4
Peckelsheim D 37 B5
Pečory RUS 7 H20
Pécs H 60 B3
Pécsvárad H 60 B3
Peczniew PL 40 B3
Pedaso I 68 C3
Pedavena I 58 B1
Pedérobba I 58 C1
Pedersker DK 27 D4
Pedescala I 57 C6
Pedrafita E 72 B3
Pedrajas de San Esteban E 74 C2
Pedralba E 82 B2
Pedralba de la Praderia E 73 B4
Pedraza E 80 A3
Pedreguer E 82 C3
Pedrera E 86 B1
Pedro Abad E 86 B1
Pedro Bernardo E 80 B2
Pedro-Martinez E 86 B2
Pedro Muñoz E 81 C4
Pedrocho E 86 A1
Pedrógão P 78 B2
Pedrógão, Beja P 84 A3
Pedrogao, Castelo Branco P 79 A3
Pedrógão Grande P 78 B2
Pedrola E 76 B1
Pedrosa de Tobalina E 75 B3
Pedrosa del Rey E 74 C1
Pedrosa del Rio Urbel E 74 B3
Pedrosillo de los Aires E 80 B1
Pedrosillo el Ralo E 80 A1
Pędzewo PL 33 B4
Peebles GB 4 J5
Peenemünde D 31 A5
Peer B 35 B6
Pega P 79 A3
Pegalajar E 86 B2
Pegau D 38 B2
Peggau A 59 A5
Pegli I 66 B2
Pegnitz D 48 A2
Pego E 82 C2
Pegões-Estação P 78 C2
Pegões Velhos P 78 C2
Pęgów PL 40 B1
Peguera, Mallorca E 83
Peine D 37 A6
Peisey-Nancroix F 56 C1
Peissenberg D 48 C2
Peiting D 48 C1
Peitz D 39 B4
Péjo I 57 B5
Pelagićevo BIH 70 B3
Pelahustán E 80 B2
Pełczyce PL 31 B7
Pelhřimov CZ 49 A6
Pélissanne F 65 C4
Pelkosenniemi FIN 3 C20
Pellegrino Parmense I 67 B3
Pellegrue F 62 B3
Pellérd H 60 B3
Pellestrina I 58 C2
Pellevoisin F 53 B6
Pellizzano I 57 B5
Pello FIN 3 C19
Peloche E 80 C1
Pelplin PL 33 B4
Pelussin F 55 C4
Pély H 61 A5
Pembroke GB 4 L4
Peña de Cabra E 79 A5
Peñacerrada E 75 B4
Penacova P 78 A2
Peñafiel E 74 C2
Penafiel P 73 C2
Peñaflor E 85 B5
Peñalba de Santiago E 72 B4
Peñalsordo E 79 C5
Penalva do Castelo P 78 A3
Penamacôr P 79 A3
Peñaparda E 79 A4
Peñaranda de Bracamonte E 80 B1
Peñaranda de Duero E 75 C3
Peñarroya de Tastavins E 76 C3
Peñarroya-Pueblonuevo E 85 A5
Peñarrubla E 72 B3
Peñas de San Pedro E 87 A4
Peñascosa E 87 A3

Peñausende E 74 C1
Penc H 51 C5
Pendueles E 74 A2
Penedono P 73 D3
Penela P 78 A2
Penhas Juntas P 73 C3
Peniche P 78 B1
Penig D 38 C2
Penilhos P 84 B3
Peñíscola E 76 C3
Penkun D 31 B6
Penmarch F 42 C1
Pennabilli I 68 C1
Penne I 89 A3
Penne-d'Agenais F 63 B3
Pennes I 57 B6
Peno RUS 7 H23
Penrith GB 4 J5
Penzance GB 4 L4
Penzberg D 48 C2
Penzlin D 31 B5
Pepeljevac YU 71 C6
Pepinster B 36 C1
Pér H 60 A2
Pera Boa P 78 A3
Perafita P 73 C2
Peraleda de la Mata E 79 B5
Peraleda de San Román E 80 C1
Peraleda del Zaucejo E 79 C5
Perales de Alfambra E 76 C1
Perales de Tajuña E 81 B3
Perales del Puerto E 79 A4
Peralta E 75 B5
Peralta de la Sal E 76 B3
Peralva P 84 B3
Peralveche E 81 B4
Perbál H 51 C4
Perchtoldsdorf A 50 B2
Percy F 43 B4
Perdasdefogu I 96 D2
Perdiguera E 76 B2
Peredo P 73 C4
Peregu Mare RO 61 B5
Pereiro, Faro P 84 B3
Pereiro, Guarda P 73 D3
Pereiro, Santarém P 78 B2
Pereiro de Aguiar E 73 B3
Perelada E 77 A6
Perelejos de las Truchas E 81 B5
Pereña E 73 C4
Pereruela E 74 C1
Pereyaslav-Khmelnytskyy UA 11 L22
Pérfugas I 96 C1
Perg A 49 B5
Pérgine Valsugana I 57 B6
Pérgola I 68 C1
Pergusa I 95 B3
Periam RO 61 B5
Periana E 86 C1
Périers F 43 A4
Périgueux F 53 C5
Perino I 66 B3
Perjasica HR 59 C5
Perkáta H 60 A3
Perković HR 69 C5
Perleberg D 30 B3
Perlez YU 61 C5
Pernarec CZ 48 A4
Pernek SK 50 B3
Pernes P 78 B2
Pernes-les-Fontaines F 65 C4
Pernik BG 15 Q18
Pernink CZ 38 C2
Pernitz A 50 C1
Pero Pinheiro P 78 C1
Peroguarda P 84 A2
Pérols F 64 C2
Péronne F 45 A3
Péronnes B 35 C5
Perorrubio E 80 A3
Perosa Argentina I 65 B6
Perozinho P 73 C2
Perpignan F 77 A5
Perrecy-les-Forges F 55 B4
Perrero I 65 B6
Perrignier F 55 B6
Perros-Guirec F 42 B2
Persan F 44 A3
Persberg S 20 B6
Persenbeug A 49 B6
Perstorp S 27 C3
Perth GB 4 H5
Pertisau A 58 A1
Pertoča SLO 59 B6
Pertuis F 65 C4
Perućac YU 71 C4
Perúgia I 68 C1
Perušić HR 69 B4
Péruwelz B 35 C4
Pervomaysk UA 11 M22
Perwez B 35 C5
Pesadas de Burgos E 75 B3
Pesaguero E 74 A2
Pésaro I 68 C1
Pescantina I 57 C5
Pescara I 89 A4
Pescasséroli I 89 B3
Peschici I 90 A3
Peschiera del Garda I 57 C5
Péscia I 67 C4
Pescina I 89 A3
Pesco Sannita I 89 B4
Pescocostanzo I 89 B4
Pescopagano I 90 B2
Peshkop AL 15 R17
Pesmes F 55 A5

Pesnica SLO 59 B5
Peso da Régua P 73 C3
Pesquera de Duero E 74 C2
Pessac F 62 B2
Pestovo RUS 7 G24
Pétange L 46 A1
Peteranec HR 60 B1
Peterborough GB 4 K6
Peterhead GB 4 H6
Petershagen, Brandenburg D 31 C5
Petershagen, Brandenburg D 31 C6
Petershagen, Nordrhein-Westfalen D 29 C5
Petershausen D 48 B2
Pétervására H 51 B6
Petília Policastro I 93 B3
Petín E 73 B3
Petkus D 38 B3
Petlovac HR 60 C3
Petlovača YU 71 B4
Petöfiszállás H 61 B4
Petra, Mallorca E 83
Petralia Sottana I 95 B3
Petrčane HR 69 B4
Petrella Tifernina I 89 B4
Petrer E 82 C2
Petreto-Bicchisano F 96 B1
Petrich BG 15 R18
Petrijevci HR 60 C3
Petrinja HR 59 C6
Petrodvorets RUS 7 G21
Pétrola E 82 C1
Petronà I 93 B3
Petronell A 50 B2
Petroșani RO 11 P18
Petrovac YU 71 B6
Petrovaradin YU 61 C4
Petrovice BIH 70 B3
Petrovice CZ 39 C3
Pettenbach A 49 C5
Peuerbach A 49 B4
Peuntenansa E 74 A2
Peveragno I 66 B1
Pewsum D 29 B4
Peyrat-le-Château F 54 C1
Peyrehorade F 62 C1
Peyriac-Minervois F 63 C5
Peyrins F 65 A4
Peyrissac F 53 C6
Peyrolles-en-Provence F 65 C4
Peyruis F 65 B4
Pézarches F 45 B3
Pézenas F 64 C2
Pezinok SK 50 B3
Pezuls F 63 B3
Pfaffenhausen D 47 B6
Pfaffenhofen, Bayern D 47 B6
Pfaffenhofen, Bayern D 48 B2
Pfaffenhoffen F 46 B3
Pfäffikon CH 56 A3
Pfarrkirchen D 48 B3
Pfeffenhausen D 48 B2
Pfetterhouse F 56 A2
Pforzheim D 47 B4
Pfreimd D 48 A3
Pfronten D 57 A5
Pfullendorf D 47 C5
Pfullingen D 47 B5
Pfunds A 57 B5
Pfungstadt D 47 A4
Pfyn CH 47 C4
Phalsbourg F 46 B3
Philippeville B 35 C5
Philippsreut D 49 B4
Philippsthal D 37 C5
Pinarhisar TR 16 R20
Piacenza I 67 A3
Piacenza d'Adige I 67 A5
Piádena I 67 A4
Piana F 96 A1
Piana Crixia I 66 B2
Piana degli Albanesi I 94 B2
Piana di Monte Verna I 89 B4
Piancastagnaio I 67 D5
Piandelagotti I 67 B4
Pianella, Abruzzi I 89 A4
Pianella, Toscana I 67 C5
Pianello Val Tidone I 66 B3
Piano I 66 B2
Pianoro I 67 B5
Pians A 57 A5
Pías E 73 B4
Pias P 84 A3
Piaseczno PL 41 A5
Piasek PL 31 C6
Piaski PL 33 A5
Piastów PL 41 A5
Piaszczyna PL 32 A3
Piątek PL 41 A4
Piatra Neamţ RO 11 N20
Piazza al Sérchio I 67 B4
Piazza Armerina I 95 B3
Piazza Brembana I 57 C4
Piazze I 67 D5
Piazzola sul Brenta I 58 C1
Picassent E 82 B2
Piccione I 68 C1
Picerno I 90 B2
Picher D 30 B3
Pico I 89 B3
Picón E 80 C2
Picquigny F 44 A3
Piechowice PL 39 C5
Piecnik PL 32 B2

Piedicavallo I 56 C2
Piedicroce F 96 A2
Piedimonte Etneo I 95 B4
Piedimonte Matese I 89 B4
Piedimulera I 56 B3
Piedipaterno I 68 D1
Piedrabuena E 80 C2
Piedraescrita E 80 C2
Piedrafita E 74 A1
Piedrahita E 80 B1
Piedralaves E 80 B2
Piedras Albas E 79 B4
Piedras Blancas E 74 A1
Piegaro I 68 D1
Piekary Śl. PL 40 C3
Piekoszów PL 41 C5
Pieksämäki FIN 3 E20
Pielenhofen D 48 A2
Pielgrzymka PL 39 B5
Pieniężno PL 33 A6
Pieńsk PL 39 B5
Pienza I 67 C5
Piera E 77 B4
Pieranie PL 33 C4
Pierre-Buffière F 53 C6
Pierre-de-Bresse F 55 B5
Pierrefeu-du-Var F 65 C5
Pierrefitte-Nestalas F 62 D2
Pierrefitte-sur-Aire F 45 B6
Pierrefonds F 45 A3
Pierrefontaine-les-Varans F 55 A6
Pierrefort F 64 B1
Pierrelatte F 64 B3
Pierrepont, Aisne F 45 A4
Pierrepont, Meurthe-et-Moselle F 46 A1
Piesendorf A 58 A2
Piešťany SK 50 B3
Pieszkowo PL 33 A6
Pieszyce PL 40 C1
Pietarsaari FIN 3 E18
Pietra Ligure I 66 B2
Pietragalla I 90 B2
Pietralunga I 68 C1
Pietramelara I 89 B4
Pietraperzia I 95 B3
Pietrasanta I 67 C4
Pietravairano I 89 B4
Pieve del Cáiro I 66 A2
Pieve di Bono I 57 C5
Pieve di Cadore I 58 B2
Pieve di Cento I 67 B5
Pieve di Soligo I 58 C2
Pieve di Teco I 66 B1
Pieve Santo Stefano I 68 C1
Pieve Torina I 68 C2
Pievepélago I 67 B4
Píglio I 88 B3
Pigna I 66 C1
Pignataro Maggiore I 89 B4
Pijnacker NL 35 A5
Pikalevo RUS 7 G24
Piła PL 32 B2
Pilar de la Horadada E 87 B5
Pilas E 85 B4
Pilastri I 67 B5
Piława PL 41 B6
Piława Górna PL 40 C1
Piławki PL 33 B5
Pilchowice PL 40 C3
Pilica PL 41 C4
Pilis H 61 A4
Piliscaba H 51 C4
Pilisszántó H 51 C4
Pilisvörösvár H 51 C4
Pilos GR 15 T17
Pilsting D 48 B3
Pilszcz PL 40 C2
Pilu RO 61 B6
Pilzno PL 41 D6
Pina de Ebro E 76 B2
Piñar E 86 B2
Pinas F 63 C3
Pincehely H 60 B3
Pińczów PL 41 C5
Pineda de la Sierra E 75 B3
Pineda de Mar E 77 B5
Pinerella I 68 B1
Pinerolo I 65 B6
Pineta Grande I 89 C3
Pineto I 89 A4
Piney F 45 B5
Pinggau A 59 A6
Pinhal Novo P 78 C2
Pinhão P 73 C3
Pinheiro, Aveiro P 73 C2
Pinheiro, Aveiro P 73 D2
Pinheiro Grande P 78 B2
Pinhel P 73 D3
Pinilla E 87 A4
Pinilla de Toro E 74 C1
Pinkafeld A 59 A6
Pinneberg D 30 B1
Pinnow D 39 B4
Pino F 66 D3
Pino de Val E 72 B2
Pino del Rio E 74 B2
Pinofranqueado E 79 A4
Pinols F 64 A2
Piñor E 72 B2
Pinos del Valle E 86 C2
Pinos Puente E 86 B2
Pinoso E 82 C1
Pinsk BY 7 K20
Pinto E 80 B3
Pinzano al Tagliamento I 58 B2
Pinzio P 79 A3

Name	Country	Map	Grid
Osterburken	D	47	A5
Österbybruk	S	22	A4
Österbyhavn	DK	24	B4
Österbymo	S	23	D2
Ostercappeln	D	29	C5
Osterfärnebo	S	22	A3
Osterfeld	D	38	B1
Osterhofen	D	48	B4
Osterholz-Scharmbeck	D	29	B5
Østerild	DK	24	B1
Österlövsta	S	22	A4
Ostermiething	A	48	B3
Osterode am Harz	D	37	B6
Östersund	S	2	E14
Östervåla	S	22	A4
Östervallskog	S	20	B3
Osterwieck	D	37	B6
Osterzell	D	48	C1
Ostffyasszonyfa	H	60	A2
Östhammar	S	22	A4
Ostheim	F	46	B3
Ostheim vor der Rhön	D	37	C6
Osthofen	D	47	A4
Ostiano	I	57	C5
Ostíglia	I	57	C5
Ostiz	E	62	D1
Östmark	S	20	A4
Ostojićevo	YU	61	C5
Ostra	I	20	B5
Östra Amtervik	S	20	B5
Östra Husby	S	23	C3
Östra Ljungby	S	27	C3
Östra Ryd	S	23	C3
Östraby	S	27	D2
Ostrach	D	47	C5
Ostrau	D	39	B4
Ostrava	CZ	50	A4
Østre Halsen	N	21	B2
Ostrhauderfehn	D	29	B4
Ostritz	D	39	B4
Ostróda	PL	33	B5
Ostroh	UA	11	L20
Ostrołęka	PL	6	K17
Ostropole	PL	32	B2
Ostrorog	PL	32	C2
Ostrošovac	BIH	69	B4
Ostrov	CZ	52	C2
Ostrov	RUS	7	H21
Ostrov nad Oslavou	CZ	50	A1
Ostrów Mazowiecka	PL	6	K17
Ostrów Wielkopolski	PL	40	B3
Ostrówek	PL	40	B3
Ostrowiec	PL	32	A2
Ostrowiec-Świętokrzyski	PL	41	C6
Ostrowite	PL	33	B5
Ostrowo	PL	33	C4
Ostrožac	BIH	70	C2
Ostrzeszów	PL	40	B2
Ostseebad Kühlungsborn	D	30	A3
Ostuni	I	91	B4
Osuna	E	99	B5
Osvětimany	CZ	50	A3
Oswestry	GB	4	K5
Oświęcim	PL	40	A3
Osztopán	H	60	B2
Oteiza	E	75	B5
Otelec	RO	61	C5
Oteo	E	20	B2
Oterbekk	N	20	B2
Otero de Herreros	E	80	B2
Otero de O Bodas	E	73	C4
Othem	S	30	D5
Otmuchów	PL	40	C3
Otočac	HR	69	B4
Otok	HR	69	C5
Otok	HR	70	A3
Otoka	BIH	70	B5
Otranto	I	93	A5
Otrić	I	88	A2
Otrokovice	CZ	50	A3
Ottana	I	96	C2
Ottaviano	I	89	C4
Ottenby	S	27	C6
Ottendorf-Okrilla	D	39	B3
Ottenhöfen	D	49	B6
Ottenschlag	A	49	A6
Ottensheim	A	49	A5
Otterbach	D	46	A3
Otterbäcken	S	21	D5
Otterberg	D	46	A3
Otterndorf	D	29	B5
Ottersberg	D	29	B6
Otterswier	D	47	B4
Otterup	DK	25	C3
Ottignies	B	35	C5
Ottmarsheim	F	46	B3
Ottobeuren	D	47	C6
Öttömös	H	61	B4
Ottone	I	66	B3
Ottweiler	D	46	B3
Ötvöskónyi	H	60	B2
Otwock	PL	41	B6
Ouanne	F	45	C4
Ouarville	F	44	C2
Oucques	F	44	C2
Oud-Beijerland	NL	35	B5
Oud Gastel	NL	35	B5
Ouddorp	NL	35	B5
Oude-Pekela	NL	28	B4
Oude-Tonge	NL	35	B5
Oudemirdum	NL	28	C2
Oudenaarde	B	35	C4
Oudenbosch	NL	35	B5
Oudenburg	NL	35	B5
Oudewater	NL	35	A5
Oudon	F	52	A4
Ouguela	P	79	B3
Ouistreham	F	43	A5
Oulainen	FIN	3	D19
Oulchy-le-Château	F	45	A4
Oullins	F	55	C4
Oulmes	F	53	B4
Oulu	FIN	3	D19
Oulx	I	65	A5
Ourense	E	73	B3
Ourique	P	84	B2
Ourol	E	72	A3
Ouroux-en-Morvan	F	54	A3
Oust	F	63	D4
Outeiro	E	78	A2
Outeiro de Rei	E	72	A3
Outes	E	72	B2
Outokumpu	FIN	3	E21
Outreau	F	34	C2
Ouzouer-le-Marché	F	44	C2
Ouzouer-sur-Loire	F	44	C3
Ovada	I	66	B2
Ovar	P	73	D2
Ove	DK	24	C2
Ovelgönne	D	29	B5
Over-jerstal	DK	25	D2
Overath	D	36	C3
Overdinkel	NL	36	A3
Överenhörna	S	22	B4
Overijse	B	35	C5
Överkalix	S	3	C18
Overlade	DK	24	C2
Överlida	S	26	B2
Overpelt	B	35	B6
Övertorneå	S	3	C18
Överum	S	23	D3
Ovidiopol	UA	11	N22
Oviedo	E	74	A1
Oviglio	I	66	B2
Övindoli	I	89	A3
Ovodda	I	96	C2
Øvre Årdal	N	2	F10
Øvre Sirdal	N	18	C3
Øvre Ullerud	S	20	B5
Øvrebygd	N	18	C3
Ovruch	UA	11	L10
Ovtrup	DK	25	D1
Owińska	PL	32	C2
Oxelösund	S	23	D3
Oxford	GB	4	L6
Oxie	S	27	D2
Øyenkilen	N	20	B2
Oyfiell	N	19	B5
Øygårdslia	N	19	C4
Øymark	N	20	B3
Oyonnax	F	55	B5
Øyslebø	N	19	C4
Oyten	D	29	B6
Øyuvsbu	N	19	B4
Ozaeta	E	75	B4
Ozalj	HR	59	C5
Ożarów	PL	41	C6
Ożarów Maz	PL	41	B5
Ožbalt	SLO	59	B5
Ozd	H	51	B6
Ozieri	I	96	C2
Ozimek	PL	40	C3
Ozimica	BIH	70	B3
Ozora	H	60	B3
Ozorków	PL	41	B5
Ozzano Monferrato	I	66	A2

P

Name	Country	Map	Grid
Paal	B	35	B6
Pabianice	PL	41	B4
Pacanów	PL	41	C6
Paceco	I	94	B1
Pachino	I	95	C4
Pačir	YU	61	C4
Pack	A	59	A4
Paços de Ferreira	P	73	C2
Pacov	CZ	49	A6
Pacsa	H	60	B2
Pacy-sur-Eure	F	44	C2
Paczków	PL	40	C2
Padborg	DK	25	D2
Padej	YU	61	C5
Padene	HR	69	B5
Paderborn	D	37	B4
Paderne	P	84	B2
Padina	YU	71	A5
Padinska Skela	YU	71	B5
Padornelo	P	73	C2
Pádova	I	58	C1
Padragkút	H	60	A2
Padria	I	96	C2
Padrón	E	72	B2
Padru	I	96	C2
Padul	E	86	B3
Padula	I	90	A3
Paduli	I	90	A1
Paesana	I	65	B6
Paese	I	58	C2
Pag	HR	69	B4
Pagani	I	89	C4
Pagánica	I	89	A3
Paganico	I	81	D5
Paglieta	I	89	A4
Pagny-sur-Moselle	F	46	B1
Páhi	H	61	B4
Pahl	D	48	C2
Paide	EST	7	G19
Paimboeuf	F	52	A2
Paimpol	F	42	B3
Paimpont	F	43	B4
Painten	D	48	B2
Paisley	GB	3	C18
Pajala	S	3	C18
Pajares de los Oteros	E	74	B1
Pajęczno	PL	40	B3
Páka	H	60	B1
Pakość	PL	33	C4
Pakoslawice	PL	40	C2
Pakoštane	HR	69	C4
Pakrac	HR	60	C2
Paks	H	60	B3
Palacios de la Sierra	E	75	C3
Palaciòs de la Valduerna	E	74	B1
Palacios de Sanabria	E	73	B4
Palacios del Sil	E	72	B4
Palaciosrubios	E	80	A1
Palafrugell	E	77	B6
Palagiano	I	91	B4
Palagonía	I	95	B3
Paláia	I	81	C4
Palaiokhóra	GR	16	U18
Palaíseau	F	44	C3
Palamòs	E	77	B6
Palanga	LT	6	J17
Palanzano	I	67	B5
Palárikovo	SK	50	C3
Palas de Rei	E	72	B3
Palata	I	89	B4
Palatna	YU	71	C6
Palau	I	96	B2
Palavas-les-Flots	F	64	C2
Palazuelos de la Sierra	E	75	B3
Palazzo Adriano	I	94	B2
Palazzo del Pero	I	67	C5
Palazzo San Gervásio	I	90	B2
Palazzolo Acréide	I	95	B3
Palazzolo sull Oglio	I	57	C4
Palazzuolo sul Senio	I	67	B5
Paldiski	EST	6	G19
Pale	BIH	70	C3
Palena	I	89	B4
Palencia	E	74	B2
Palenciana	E	86	B1
Palermo	I	94	A2
Palestrina	I	88	B2
Pálfa	H	60	B3
Palfau	A	49	C5
Palhaça	P	78	A2
Palheiros da Tocha	P	78	A2
Palheiros de Quiaios	P	78	A2
Palić	YU	61	B4
Palidoro	I	88	B2
Palinuro	I	90	B2
Paliseul	B	45	A6
Pallanza	I	56	C3
Pallares	E	85	A4
Pallaruelo de Monegros	E	76	B2
Pallerols	E	77	A4
Palling	D	48	B3
Palluau	F	52	B3
Palma	I	78	C2
Palma Campánia	I	89	C4
Palma de Mallorca, Mallorca	E	83	
Palma del Río	E	85	B5
Palma di Montechiaro	I	94	B2
Palma Nova, Mallorca	E	83	
Palmanova	I	58	C3
Palmela	P	78	C2
Palmerola	E	77	A5
Palmi	I	92	C2
Pälmonostora	H	61	B4
Palo del Colle	I	91	A3
Palomares	E	87	B4
Palomares del Campo	E	81	C4
Palomas	E	79	C4
Palombara Sabina	I	88	A2
Palos de la Frontera	E	85	B4
Palotaboszok	H	60	B3
Palotás	H	51	C5
Pals	E	77	B6
Pålsboda	S	23	B2
Paluzza	I	58	B3
Pamhagen	A	51	A6
Pamiers	F	63	C4
Pamiętowo	PL	32	B3
Pampaneira	E	86	C2
Pamparato	I	66	B1
Pampilhosa, Aveiro	P	78	A2
Pampilhosa, Coimbra	P	78	A3
Pamplona	E	75	B5
Panagyurishte	BG	16	Q19
Pancalieri	I	66	B1
Pancey	F	45	B6
Pancorvo	E	75	B3
Pancrudo	E	76	C1
Pandino	I	57	C4
Pandrup	DK	24	A2
Panenský-Týnec	CZ	39	C3
Panes	E	74	A2
Panevėžys	LT	6	J19
Panissières	F	55	C4
Panki	PL	40	C3
Pannes	F	44	C3
Pannonhalma	H	60	A2
Panschwitz-Kuckau	D	39	B4
Pantano de Cijara	E	80	C2
Pantín	E	76	A2
Pantón	E	72	B3
Panxon	E	72	B2
Páola	I	92	B2
Pápa	H	60	A2
Papasídero	I	92	B2
Pápateszér	H	60	A2
Papenburg	D	29	B4
Pappenheim	D	47	A6
Paprotnia	PL	41	A5
Parábita	I	91	B5
Paraćin	YU	71	C6
Parád	H	51	C6
Parada, Bragança	P	73	C4
Parada, Viseu	P	78	A3
Paradas	E	85	B5
Paradela	E	72	B3
Parades de Rubiales	E	80	A1
Paradinas de San Juan	E	80	B1
Paradiso di Cevadale	I	57	B5
Paradyż	PL	41	B5
Parainen	FIN	3	F18
Parakhino Paddubye	RUS	7	G23
Paramé	F	43	B4
Páramo del Sil	E	72	B4
Parandaça	P	73	C3
Paravadella	E	72	A3
Paray-le-Monial	F	54	B4
Parceiros	P	78	B2
Parcey	F	55	A5
Parchim	D	30	B3
Parcice	PL	40	B3
Pardilla	E	74	C3
Pardubice	CZ	39	C5
Paredes	P	73	C2
Paredes de Coura	P	73	C2
Paredes de Nava	E	74	B2
Paredes de Siguenza	E	81	A4
Pareja	E	81	B4
Parennes	F	43	B5
Parenti	I	92	B3
Parentis-en-Born	F	62	B1
Parey	D	30	C3
Parfino	RUS	7	H22
Párga	GR	15	S17
Pargny-sur-Saulx	F	45	C4
Parikkala	FIN	3	F21
Paris	F	44	B3
Parisot	F	63	B4
Parkano	FIN	3	E18
Parla	E	80	B3
Parlavá	E	77	A6
Parma	I	67	B4
Parndorf	A	50	C2
Párnica	SK	51	A4
Pärnu	EST	6	G19
Parolis	E	87	A3
Parrillas	E	80	B1
Parsberg	D	48	B2
Parstein	D	31	C5
Partakko	FIN	3	B20
Partanna	I	94	B1
Parthenay	F	53	B4
Partinico	I	94	A2
Partizani	YU	71	B5
Partizánske	SK	51	B4
Påryd	S	26	C5
Parysow	PL	41	B6
Parzymiechy	PL	40	B3
Paşcani	RO	11	N20
Pasewalk	D	31	B5
Pašina Voda	YU	71	C4
Påskallavik	S	26	B5
Pasłęk	PL	33	A5
Pašman	HR	69	C4
Passail	A	59	A5
Passais	F	43	B5
Passau	D	49	B4
Passegueiro	P	78	A2
Passignano sul Trasimeno	I	68	C1
Passo di Tréia	I	68	C2
Passopisciaro	I	95	B4
Passow	D	31	B5
Passy	F	56	C1
Pastavy	BY	7	J20
Pástena	I	89	B4
Pastrana	E	81	B4
Pastrengo	I	57	C5
Pasym	PL	33	B6
Pászto	H	51	C5
Pata	SK	50	C3
Patay	F	44	C2
Paterek	PL	32	B3
Paterna	E	82	B2
Paterna de Rivera	E	85	C5
Paterna del Campo	E	85	B4
Paterna del Madera	E	87	A3
Paternò	I	95	B3
Paternópoli	I	90	C1
Paterswolde	NL	28	B3
Patos	AL	15	R16
Pátrai	GR	15	S17
Patrimonio	F	96	A2
Pattada	I	96	C2
Pattensen, Niedersachsen	D	30	B2
Pattensen, Niedersachsen	D	29	A6
Patti	I	95	A3
Páty	H	60	A3
Pau	F	62	C2
Pauillac	F	53	B4
Paularo	I	58	B3
Paulhaguet	F	54	C2
Paulhan	F	64	C2
Paulilâtino	I	96	C2
Paullo	I	57	C4
Pausa	D	38	C2
Pavia	I	67	A4
Pavia	P	78	C2
Pavias	E	82	A2
Pavilly	F	44	A1
Pävilosta	LV	6	H17
Pavino Polje	YU	71	C4
Pavullo nel Frignano	I	67	B4
Pawlowice	PL	51	A4
Pawłowice	PL	40	A1
Payerne	CH	56	B1
Paymogo	E	84	B3
Payrac	F	63	B4
Pazardzhik	BG	16	Q19
Pazin	HR	58	C3
Paziols	F	64	D1
Pčelić	HR	60	C2
Peal de Becerro	E	86	B2
Peć	YU	71	D5
Péccioli	I	67	C4
Pécel	H	61	A4
Pechao	P	84	B2
Pechea	RO	11	M19
Pechenga	RUS	3	B22
Pechenizhyn	UA	11	M19
Pecica	RO	61	B5
Pecinci	YU	71	B4
Pecka	YU	71	B4
Peckelsheim	D	37	B5
Pecory	RUS	7	H20
Pécs	H	60	B3
Pécsvárad	H	60	B3
Pér	H	60	A3
Pera Boa	P	78	A3
Perafita	P	73	C2
Peral de la Mata	E	79	B5
Peraleda de San Román	E	80	C1
Peraleda del Zaucejo	E	79	C5
Perales de Alfambra	E	76	C1
Perales de Tajuña	E	81	B3
Perales del Puerto	E	79	A4
Peralta	E	75	B5
Peralta de la Sal	E	76	B3
Peralva	P	84	B2
Peralveche	E	81	B4
Perbál	H	51	C4
Perchtoldsdorf	A	50	B2
Percy	F	43	B4
Perdasdefogu	I	96	C3
Perdiguera	E	76	B2
Peredo	P	73	C3
Pereiro, Guarda	P	73	D3
Pereiro, Faro	P	84	B2
Pereiro, Santarém	P	78	B2
Pereiro de Aguiar	E	73	B3
Perelada	E	77	A6
Perelejos de las Truchas	E	81	B5
Pereña	E	73	C4
Pereruela	E	74	C1
Pereyaslav-Khmelnytskyy	UA	11	L22
Pérfugas	I	96	C2
Perg	A	49	A5
Pérgine Valsugana	I	57	B6
Pérgola	I	68	C2
Pergusa	I	95	B3
Periam	RO	61	B5
Periana	E	86	C2
Périers	F	43	A4
Perino	I	66	B3
Perjasica	HR	59	C5
Perkáta	H	60	B3
Perković	HR	69	C5
Perl	D	46	B2
Perleberg	D	30	B3
Perlez	YU	71	A5
Pernarec	CZ	48	B4
Pernes	P	78	B2
Pernes-les-Fontaines	F	65	C4
Pernik	BG	16	Q18
Pernink	CZ	38	C2
Pero Pinheiro	P	78	C1
Peroguarda	P	84	A2
Pérols	F	64	C2
Péronne	F	35	A3
Péronnes	B	35	C4
Perorrubio	E	80	A3
Perosa Argentina	I	65	B6
Perozinho	P	73	C2
Perpignan	F	77	A5
Perrecy-les-Forges	F	55	B4
Perrero	I	65	B6
Perrignier	F	55	B6
Perros-Guirec	F	42	B3
Persan	F	44	B3
Persenbeug	A	49	A6
Perstorp	S	27	D2
Perth	GB	4	H5
Pertisau	A	58	A1
Pertoča	SLO	60	B1
Pertuis	F	65	C4
Perućac	YU	71	C4
Perúgia	I	68	C1
Péruwelz	B	35	C3
Pervomaysk	UA	11	M22
Perwez	B	35	C5
Pesadas de Burgos	E	75	B3
Pésaro	I	68	C2
Pescara	I	89	A4
Pescasséroli	I	89	B4
Péschici	I	90	A3
Peschiera del Garda	I	57	C5
Péscia	I	67	C5
Pescina	I	89	A4
Pesco Sannita	I	89	B5
Pescocostanzo	I	89	B4
Pescopagano	I	90	A2
Pescopennataro	I	89	B4
Peshkopi	AL	15	R17
Peshtera	BG	16	Q19
Pesmes	F	55	A5
Pesnica	SLO	59	B5
Peso da Régua	P	73	C3
Pesquera de Duero	E	74	C2
Pessac	F	62	B2
Pestovo	RUS	7	G24
Pétange	L	46	A1
Peteranec	HR	60	B1
Peterborough	GB	4	K6
Peterhead	GB	4	H6
Petershagen, Brandenburg	D	31	C5
Petershagen, Brandenburg	D	31	C6
Petershagen, Nordrhein-Westfalen	D	29	C5
Petershausen	D	48	B2
Petília Policastro	I	93	B3
Petín	E	73	B3
Petkus	D	38	B3
Petlovac	HR	60	C3
Petlovača	YU	71	B4
Petöfiszállás	H	61	B4
Petra, Mallorca	E	83	
Petralia	I	95	B3
Petrčane	HR	69	B4
Petrella Tifernina	I	89	B4
Petrer	E	82	C2
Petreto-Bicchisano	F	96	B1
Petrich	BG	15	R18
Petrijevci	HR	60	C3
Petrinja	HR	60	C1
Petrodvorets	RUS	7	G21
Pétrola	E	82	C1
Petronà	I	93	B3
Petronell	A	50	B2
Petroşani	RO	11	P18
Petrovac	YU	71	B6
Petrovaradin	YU	61	C4
Petrovice	BIH	70	B3
Petrovice	CZ	39	C5
Pettenbach	A	49	C5
Pettneu	A	57	A5
Peuerbach	A	49	A4
Peuntenansa	E	74	A2
Peveragno	I	66	B1
Pewsum	D	29	B4
Peyrat-le-Château	F	54	C1
Peyrehorade	F	62	C1
Peyriac-Minervois	F	63	C5
Peyrins	F	65	A4
Peyrissac	F	54	C1
Peyrolles-en-Provence	F	65	C4
Peyruis	F	65	B4
Pézenas	F	64	C2
Pezinok	SK	50	C3
Pezuls	F	63	B4
Pfaffenhausen	D	47	B6
Pfaffenhofen, Bayern	D	47	A6
Pfaffenhofen, Bayern	D	48	B2
Pfaffenhoffen	F	46	B3
Pfaffnau	CH	56	A2
Pfarrkirchen	D	48	B3
Pfeffenhausen	D	48	B2
Pforzheim	D	47	C4
Pfreimd	D	48	B3
Pfronten	D	47	C6
Pfullendorf	D	47	C5
Pfullingen	D	47	C5
Pfunds	A	57	B5
Pfungstadt	D	47	B4
Phalsbourg	F	46	B3
Philippeville	B	35	C4
Philippsreut	D	49	B4
Philippsthal	D	37	C5
Pinarhisar	TR	16	R20
Piacenza	I	67	A4
Piádena	I	67	A5
Piana	F	96	A1
Piana Crixia	I	66	B2
Piana degli Albanesi	I	94	B2
Piana di Monte Verna	I	89	C4
Piancastagnáio	I	81	D5
Piandelagotti	I	67	B5
Pianella, Abruzzi	I	89	A4
Pianella, Toscana	I	68	C1
Pianello Val Tidone	I	66	B3
Piano	I	66	B3
Pianoro	I	67	B6
Pians	A	57	A5
Pías	E	73	B4
Pías	P	84	A2
Piaseczno	PL	41	B6
Piasek	PL	31	C5
Piaski	PL	41	A6
Piastów	PL	41	B5
Piaszczyna	PL	32	A3
Piątek	PL	41	B5
Piatra Neamt	RO	11	N20
Piazza Armerina	I	95	B3
Piazza Brembana	I	57	C4
Piazze	I	81	D5
Piazzola sul Brenta	I	58	C1
Picassent	E	82	B2
Picerno	I	90	A2
Picher	D	30	B2
Pico	I	89	B4
Picón	E	94	A1
Picquigny	F	34	C2
Piechcin	PL	33	C4
Piechowice	PL	39	C5
Piecnik	PL	32	B2
Piedicavallo	I	56	C2
Piedicroce	F	96	A2
Piediluco	I	88	A3
Piedimonte Etneo	I	95	B4
Piedimonte Matese	I	89	B4
Piedimulera	I	56	B3
Piedipaterno	I	68	D3
Piedrabuena	E	80	C2
Piedraescrita	E	80	C2
Piedrafita	E	74	A1
Piedrahita	E	80	B1
Piedralaves	E	80	B1
Piedras Albas	E	79	B4
Piedras Blancas	E	74	A1
Piegaro	I	68	D1
Piekary Śl.	PL	40	C3
Piekoszów	PL	41	C5
Pieksämäki	FIN	3	E20
Pielenhofen	D	48	B2
Pielgrzymka	PL	39	B5
Pieniężno	PL	33	A6
Pień	PL	39	B5
Pienza	I	67	C5
Pieranie	PL	33	C4
Piera	E	77	B4
Pierre-Buffière	F	53	C6
Pierre-de-Bresse	F	55	B5
Pierrefeu-du-Var	F	65	C5
Pierrefitte-Nestalas	F	62	D2
Pierrefitte-sur-Aire	F	45	B6
Pierrefonds	F	45	A3
Pierrefontaine-les-Varans	F	55	A6
Pierrefort	F	64	B1
Pierrelatte	F	64	B3
Pierrepont, Aisne	F	45	A4
Pierrepont, Meurthe-et-Moselle	F	46	B1
Piesendorf	A	58	A2
Pieštany	SK	50	B3
Pieszkowo	PL	33	A6
Pieszyce	PL	40	C1
Pietarsaari	FIN	3	E18
Pietra Ligure	I	66	B2
Pietragalla	I	90	B2
Pietralunga	I	68	C1
Pietramelara	I	89	B4
Pietraperzía	I	95	B3
Pietrasanta	I	67	C5
Pietravairano	I	89	B4
Pieve di Bono	I	57	C5
Pieve di Cadore	I	58	B2
Pieve di Cento	I	67	B5
Pieve di Soligo	I	58	C2
Pieve di Teco	I	66	B1
Pieve Santo Stefano	I	68	C1
Pieve Torina	I	68	C2
Pievepélago	I	67	B5
Píglio	I	88	B3
Pigna	I	66	C1
Pignataro Maggiore	I	89	C4
Pijnacker	NL	35	A5
Pikalevo	RUS	7	G24
Piła	PL	32	B2
Pilar de la Horadada	E	87	B5
Pilas	E	85	B4
Pilastri	I	67	B6
Pilawa	PL	41	B6
Piława Górna	PL	40	C1
Piławki	PL	33	B5
Pilchowice	PL	40	C4
Pilica	PL	41	C4
Pilis	H	35	A5
Piliscaba	H	51	A4
Pilisvörösvár	H	51	A4
Pílos	GR	18	T3
Pilsting	D	48	B3
Pilszcz	PL	47	A4
Pilu	RO	61	B6
Pina de Ebro	E	76	B2
Piñar	E	86	B3
Pinas	F	63	C3
Pincehely	H	60	B3
Pińczów	PL	41	C5
Pineda de la Sierra	E	75	B3
Pineda de Mar	E	77	B5
Pinerella	I	68	B2
Pinerolo	I	65	B6
Pineta Grande	I	89	A4
Pineto	I	89	A4
Pinggau	A	59	A6
Pinhal Novo	P	78	C2
Pinhão	P	73	C3
Pinheiro, Aveiro	P	73	C2
Pinheiro, Aveiro	P	78	A2
Pinheiro Grande	P	78	B2
Pinhel	P	73	D3
Pinilla de Toro	E	74	C1
Pinkafeld	A	59	A6
Pinneberg	D	30	B1
Pinnow	D	31	B5
Pino	F	96	A2
Pino del Río	E	74	B2
Pinofranqueado	E	79	A4
Piñor	E	72	B2
Pinos del Valle	E	86	C3
Pinos Puente	E	86	B3
Pinoso	E	87	A4
Pinsk	BY	7	K20
Pinto	E	80	B3
Pinzano al Tagliamento	I	58	B2
Pinzio	P	79	A3

Pinzolo I 57 B5
Piòbbico I 68 C1
Piombino I 67 D4
Pionki PL 41 B6
Pionsat F 54 B2
Pióraco I 68 C1
Piornal E 79 A5
Piotrków-Kujawski PL 33 C4
Piotrków Trybunalski PL 41 B4
Piotrkowice PL 41 C5
Piotrowice PL 41 A6
Piotrowo PL 32 C2
Piove di Sacco I 58 C2
Piovene I 57 C6
Piperskärr S 23 D3
Pipriac F 43 C4
Piraiévs GR 15 T18
Piran SLO 58 C3
Piré-sur-Seiche F 43 B4
Pírgos GR 15 T17
Piriac-sur-Mer F 52 A2
Piringsdorf A 59 A6
Pirmasens D 46 A3
Pirna D 39 C3
Pirot YU 15 Q18
Pirovac HR 69 C4
Pisa I 67 C4
Pisany F 53 C4
Pisarovina HR 59 C5
Pischelsdorf in der Steiermark A 59 A5
Pişchia RO 61 C6
Pisciotta I 90 B2
Písek CZ 49 A5
Pisogne I 57 C5
Pissos F 62 B2
Pisticci I 91 B3
Pistóia I 67 C4
Piteå S 3 D17
Pitești RO 11 P19
Pithiviers F 44 B3
Pitigliano I 88 A1
Pitkyaranta RUS 3 F22
Pitlochry GB 4 H5
Pitomača HR 60 C2
Pitres E 86 C2
Pitvaros H 61 B5
Pivka SLO 59 C4
Pivnice YU 61 C4
Piwniczna PL 51 A6
Pizarra E 86 C1
Pizzano I 57 B5
Pizzighettone I 57 C4
Pizzo I 92 C3
Pizzoli I 89 A3
Pizzolungo I 94 A1
Plabennec F 42 B1
Placencia E 75 A4
Plaffeien CH 56 B2
Plaisance, *Gers* F 62 C3
Plaisance, *Haute-Garonne* F 63 C4
Plaisance, *Tarn* F 63 C5
Plan E 76 A3
Plan-de-Baix F 65 B4
Plan-d'Orgon F 64 C3
Planá CZ 48 A3
Planá nad Lužnici CZ 49 A5
Plaňany CZ 39 C5
Planchez F 54 A3
Plancoët F 43 B3
Plancy-l'Abbaye F 45 B4
Plandište YU 61 C6
Plánice CZ 49 A4
Planina SLO 59 B5
Planina SLO 59 C4
Plankenfels D 48 A2
Plasencia E 79 A4
Plasenzuela E 79 B4
Plaški HR 69 A4
Plášťovce SK 51 B5
Plasy CZ 49 A4
Platamona Lido I 96 C1
Platania I 92 B3
Plátanos GR 16 U18
Platí I 92 C3
Platičevo YU 71 B4
Platja d'Aro E 77 B6
Plattling D 48 B3
Plau D 30 B4
Plaue, *Brandenburg* D 30 C4
Plaue, *Thüringen* D 37 C6
Plauen D 38 C2
Plavecký Mikuláš SK 50 B3
Plavinas LV 7 H19
Plavna YU 61 C4
Plavnica SK 51 A6
Plavno HR 69 B5
Plavsk RUS 7 K25
Playben F 42 B2
Pléaux F 54 C2
Pleine-Fougères F 43 B4
Pleinfeld D 48 A1
Pleinting D 48 B4
Plélan-le-Grand F 43 B3
Plémet F 42 B3
Pléneuf-Val-André F 42 B3
Plentzia E 75 A4
Plérin F 42 B3
Plešivec SK 51 B6
Plessa D 38 B3
Plessé F 52 A3
Plestin-les-Grèves F 42 B2
Pleszew PL 40 B2
Pleternica HR 60 C2
Plettenberg D 36 B3
Pleubian F 42 B2
Pleumartin F 53 B5
Pleumeur-Bodou F 42 B2
Pleurs F 45 B4
Pleven BG 16 Q19
Plevlja YU 71 C4
Plevnik-Drienové SK 51 A4
Pleyber-Christ F 42 B2
Pliego E 87 B4
Pliešovce SK 51 B5
Plitvička Jezera HR 69 B4
Plitvički Ljeskovac HR 69 B4
Ploaghe I 96 C1
Ploče HR 70 C2
Plochingen D 47 B5
Płock PL 33 C5
Ploemeur F 42 C2
Ploërmel F 42 C3
Plœuc-sur-Lie F 42 B3
Plogastel St. Germain F 42 C1
Plogoff F 42 B1
Ploiești RO 11 P20
Plombières-les-Bains F 46 C2
Plomin HR 68 A3
Plön D 30 A2
Plonéour-Lanvern F 42 C1
Płonia PL 31 B6
Płońsk PL 33 C6
Plössberg D 48 A3
Płoty PL 31 B7
Plouagat F 42 B2
Plouaret F 42 B2
Plouay F 42 C2
Ploubalay F 43 B3
Ploubazlanec F 42 B2
Ploudalmézeau F 42 B1
Ploudiry F 42 B1
Plouescat F 42 B1
Plouézec F 42 B3
Plougasnou F 42 B2
Plougastel-Daoulas F 42 B1
Plougonven F 42 B2
Plougonver F 42 B2
Plougrescant F 42 B2
Plouguenast F 42 B3
Plouguerneau F 42 B1
Plouha F 42 B3
Plouhinec F 42 B1
Plouigneau F 42 B2
Ploumanach F 42 B2
Plounévez-Quintin F 42 B2
Plouray F 42 B2
Plouzévédé F 42 B1
Plovdiv BG 16 Q19
Plozévet F 42 C1
Pluméliau F 42 C3
Plumlov CZ 50 A3
Plungė LT 6 J17
Pluty PL 33 A6
Pluvigner F 42 C2
Plužine BIH 70 C3
Plužine YU 70 C3
Płużnica PL 33 B4
Plymouth GB 4 L4
Płytnica PL 32 B2
Plyusa RUS 7 G21
Plzeň CZ 49 A4
Pniewy PL 32 C2
Pobes E 75 B4
Poběžovice CZ 48 A3
Pobiedziska PL 32 C3
Pobierowo PL 31 A6
Pobla de Segur E 76 A3
Pobla-Tornesa E 82 A3
Pobladura del Valle E 74 B1
Pobra de Trives E 73 B3
Pobra do Brollón E 72 B3
Pobra do Caramiñal E 72 B2
Pobudje BIH 71 B4
Počátky CZ 49 A6
Poceirão P 78 C2
Pochep RUS 7 K23
Pochinok RUS 7 J23
Pöchlarn A 49 B6
Pociecha PL 41 B5
Pockau D 38 C3
Pocking D 49 B4
Poda YU 71 D4
Podbořany CZ 38 C3
Podbrdo SLO 58 B3
Podbrezová SK 51 B5
Podčetrtek SLO 59 B5
Poddębice PL 40 B3
Poděbrady CZ 39 C5
Podence P 73 C4
Podensac F 62 B2
Podenzano I 66 B3
Podersdorf am See A 50 C2
Podgaje PL 32 B2
Podgora HR 70 C2
Podgóra PL 41 B6
Podgorač HR 60 C3
Podgorica YU 15 Q16
Podgrad SLO 59 C4
Podhájska SK 51 B4
Podlapača HR 69 B4
Podlejki PL 33 B6
Podlužany SK 51 B4
Podnovlje BIH 70 B3
Podolie SK 50 B3
Podolínec SK 51 A6
Podolsk RUS 7 J25
Podromanija BIH 70 C3
Podturen HR 60 B1
Podujevo YU 71 D6
Podvín CZ 50 B2
Podwilk PL 51 A5
Poetto I 96 D2
Poggendorf D 31 A5
Poggiardo I 93 A5
Poggibonsi I 67 C5
Póggio a Caiano I 67 C5
Poggio Imperiale I 90 A2
Póggio Mirteto I 88 A2
Póggio Moiano I 88 A2
Póggio Renatico I 67 B5
Póggio Rusco I 67 B5
Pöggstall A 49 B6
Pogny F 45 B5
Pogorzela PL 40 B2
Pogorzelice PL 32 A3
Pogrodzie PL 33 A5
Pohorelá SK 51 B6
Pohořelice CZ 50 B2
Pohronská Polhora SK 51 B5
Poiares P 78 A2
Poio E 72 B2
Poirino I 66 B1
Poisson F 54 B4
Poissons F 45 B6
Poissy F 44 B3
Poitiers F 53 B5
Poix-de-Picardie F 44 A2
Poix-Terron F 45 A5
Pokój PL 40 C2
Pokupsko HR 59 C5
Pol E 72 A3
Pola RUS 7 H22
Pola de Allande E 72 A4
Pola de Laviana E 74 A1
Pola de Lena E 74 A1
Pola de Siero E 74 A1
Pola de Somiedo E 72 A4
Polaincourt-et-Clairefontaine F 46 C2
Połajewo PL 32 C2
Polán E 80 C2
Polanica-Zdrój PL 40 C1
Połaniec PL 41 C6
Polanów PL 32 A2
Polatsk BY 7 J21
Polch D 36 C3
Pólczno PL 32 A3
Połczyn-Zdrój PL 32 B2
Poleñino E 76 B2
Polesella I 67 B5
Polessk RUS 6 J17
Polgárdi H 60 A3
Polhov Gradec SLO 59 B4
Police PL 31 B6
Police nad Metují CZ 39 C6
Polička CZ 50 A2
Poličnik HR 69 B4
Policoro I 91 B3
Policzna PL 41 B6
Polignano a Mare I 91 B4
Poligny F 55 B5
Polistena I 92 C3
Políyiros GR 15 R18
Polizzi Generosa I 95 B3
Poljana YU 71 B6
Poljanák HR 69 B4
Poljčane SLO 59 B5
Polje BIH 70 B2
Poljice BIH 69 B5
Poljice BIH 70 B3
Poljna YU 71 C6
Polkowice PL 39 B6
Polla I 90 B2
Pollas E 74 C1
Pöllau A 59 A5
Polleben D 38 B1
Pollença, *Mallorca* E 83
Pollenfeld D 48 B2
Póllica I 90 B2
Polminhac F 63 B5
Polná CZ 49 A6
Polna RUS 7 G21
Polne PL 32 B2
Polomka SK 51 B5
Polonne UA 11 L20
Pöls A 59 A4
Polska Cerekiew PL 40 C3
Poltár SK 51 B5
Põltsamaa EST 7 G19
Polyarny RUS 3 B23
Polyarnyye Zori RUS 3 C23
Polzela SLO 59 B5
Pomarance I 67 C4
Pomarez F 62 C2
Pomárico I 91 B3
Pomáz H 51 C5
Pombal P 78 B2
Pomézia I 88 B2
Pomichna UA 11 M22
Pommard F 55 A4
Pommelsbrunn D 48 A2
Pomonte I 67 D4
Pomorie BG 16 Q20
Pompei I 89 C4
Pompey F 46 B2
Pomposa I 68 B1
Poncin F 55 B5
Pondorf D 48 B2
Ponferrada E 72 B4
Poniec PL 40 B1
Ponikva SLO 59 B5
Poniky SK 51 B5
Pons F 53 C4
Ponsacco I 67 C4
Pont-a-Celles B 35 C5
Pont-a-Marcq F 35 C4
Pont-à-Mousson F 46 B2
Pont-Audemer F 44 A1
Pont-Aven F 42 C2
Pont Canavese I 56 C2
Pont-Croix F 42 B1
Pont-d'Ain F 55 B5
Pont-de-Beauvoisin F 55 C5
Pont-de-Buis-lès-Quimerch F 42 B1
Pont-de-Chéruy F 55 C5
Pont de Dore F 54 C3
Pont-de-Labeaume F 64 B3
Pont-de-l'Arche F 44 A2
Pont de Molins E 77 A5
Pont-de-Roide F 56 A1
Pont-de-Salars F 64 B1
Pont de Suert E 76 A3
Pont-de-Vaux F 55 B4
Pont-de-Veyle F 55 B4
Pont-d'Espagne F 62 D2
Pont d'Ouilly F 43 B5
Pont-du-Château F 54 C3
Pont-du-Navoy F 55 B5
Pont-en-Royans F 65 A4
Pont Farcy F 43 B4
Pont-l'Abbé F 42 C1
Pont-l'Évêque F 43 A6
Pont-Remy F 34 C2
Pont-St. Esprit F 64 B3
Pont-St. Mamet F 63 B3
Pont-St. Martin F 52 A3
Pont-St. Martin I 56 C2
Pont-St. Vincent F 46 B2
Pont-Ste-Maxence F 44 A3
Pont Scorff F 42 C2
Pont-sur-Yonne F 45 B4
Pontacq F 62 C2
Pontailler-sur-Saône F 55 A5
Pontão P 78 B2
Pontarion F 54 C1
Pontarlier F 55 B6
Pontassieve I 67 C5
Pontaubault F 43 B4
Pontaumur F 54 C2
Pontcharra F 55 C6
Pontcharra-sur-Turdine F 55 C4
Pontchâteau F 52 A2
Ponte a Moriano I 67 C4
Ponte Arche I 57 B5
Ponte Cáffaro I 57 C5
Ponte-Caldelas E 73 B2
Ponte da Barca P 73 C2
Ponte de Sor P 78 B2
Ponte dell'Ólio I 66 B3
Ponte di Barbarano I 58 C1
Ponte di Legno I 57 B5
Ponte di Nava I 66 B1
Ponte di Piave I 58 C2
Ponte do Lima P 73 C2
Ponte Felcino I 68 C1
Ponte Gardena I 57 B6
Ponte-Leccia F 96 A2
Ponte nelle Alpi I 58 B2
Ponte San Giovanni I 68 C1
Ponte San Pietro I 57 C4
Ponteareas E 73 B2
Pontebba I 58 B3
Pontecagnano I 90 B1
Ponteceso E 72 A2
Pontecesures E 72 B2
Pontecorvo I 89 B3
Pontedássio I 66 C2
Pontedécimo I 66 B2
Pontedera I 67 C4
Pontedeume E 72 A2
Ponteginori I 67 C4
Pontelagoscuro I 67 B5
Pontelandolfo I 89 B4
Pontelongo I 58 C2
Pontenure I 67 B3
Pontenx-les-Forges F 62 B1
Pontevedra E 72 B2
Pontevico I 57 C5
Pontfaverger-Moronvillers F 45 A5
Pontgibaud F 54 C2
Ponticino I 67 C5
Pontigny F 45 C4
Pontijou F 44 C2
Pontínia I 88 B3
Pontinvrea I 66 B2
Pontivy F 42 B3
Pontlevoy F 53 A6
Pontoise F 44 A3
Pontones E 87 A3
Pontonx-sur-l'Abour F 62 C2
Pontorson F 43 B4
Pontrémoli I 67 B3
Pontresina CH 57 B4
Pontrieux F 42 B2
Ponts E 77 B4
Ponts-aux-Dames F 45 B3
Pontvallain F 43 C6
Ponza I 88 C2
Poo E 74 A2
Poole GB 4 L6
Poperinge B 34 C3
Pópoli I 89 A3
Popovača HR 60 C1
Popow PL 40 C3
Poppel B 35 B6
Poppenhausen, *Bayern* D 37 C6
Poppenhausen, *Hessen* D 37 C5
Poppi I 67 C5
Poprad SK 51 A6
Popučke YU 71 B4
Pópulo P 73 C3
Populónia I 67 D4
Pörböly H 60 B3
Porcuna E 86 B1
Pordenone I 58 C2
Pordic F 42 B3
Poręba PL 41 C4
Poreč HR 58 C3
Pori FIN 3 F17
Porjus S 3 C16
Porkhov RUS 7 H21
Porlezza I 57 B4
Pörnbach D 48 B2
Pornic F 52 A2
Pornichet F 52 A2
Porodin YU 71 B6
Poronin PL 51 A5
Poroszló H 51 C6
Porozina HR 68 A3
Porquerolles F 65 D5
Porrentruy CH 56 A2
Porreres, *Mallorca* E 83
Porretta Terme I 67 B4
Porsgrunn N 19 B6
Porspoder F 42 B1
Port-a-Binson F 45 A4
Port Askaig GB 4 J3
Port-Barcarès F 64 D2
Port-Camargue F 64 C3
Port d'Andratx, *Mallorca* E 83
Port-de-Bouc F 64 C3
Port-de-Lanne F 62 C1
Port de Pollença, *Mallorca* E 83
Port de Sóller, *Mallorca* E 83
Port-des-Barques F 52 C3
Port Ellen GB 4 J3
Port-en-Bessin F 43 A5
Port-Joinville F 52 B2
Port-la-Nouvelle F 64 C2
Port Laoise IRL 4 K3
Port Louis F 42 C2
Port Manech F 42 C2
Port-Navalo F 52 A2
Port-St.-Louis-du-Rhône F 64 C3
Port-Ste. Marie F 63 B3
Port-sur-Saône F 46 C2
Port Talbot GB 4 L5
Port-Vendres F 77 A6
Portadown GB 4 J3
Portaje E 79 B4
Portalegre P 78 B3
Portbail F 43 A4
Portbou E 77 A6
Portegrandi I 58 C2
Portel P 84 A3
Portela P 78 A2
Portelo P 73 C4
Portemouro E 72 B2
Port'Ercole I 88 A1
Portes-lès-Valence F 64 B3
Portets F 62 B2
Portezuelo E 79 B4
Porthmadog GB 4 K4
Porticcio F 96 B1
Portici I 89 C4
Portico di Romagna I 67 B5
Portilla de la Reina E 74 A2
Portillo E 74 C2
Portimao P 84 B2
Portinatx E 83 B4
Portinho da Arrabida P 78 C1
Portman E 87 B5
Porto F 96 A1
Porto P 73 C2
Porto-Alto P 78 C2
Porto Azzurro I 67 D4
Porto Cerésio I 56 C3
Porto Cervo I 96 B2
Porto Cesáreo I 91 B4
Porto Colom, *Mallorca* E 83
Porto Covo P 84 B2
Porto Cristo, *Mallorca* E 83
Porto d'Áscoli I 68 D2
Porto de Lagos P 84 B2
Porto de Mos P 78 B2
Porto de Rei P 84 A2
Porto do Son E 72 B2
Porto Empédocle I 94 B2
Porto Garibaldi I 68 B1
Porto Petro, *Mallorca* E 83
Porto Pino I 96 E1
Porto Potenza Picena I 68 C2
Porto Recanati I 68 C2
Porto San Giórgio I 68 C2
Porto Sant'Elpídio I 68 C2
Porto Santo Stéfano I 88 A1
Porto Tolle I 68 B1
Porto Tórres I 96 C1
Porto-Vecchio F 96 B2
Portocannone I 89 B5
Portoferráio I 67 D4
Portofino I 66 B3
Portogruaro I 58 C2
Portomaggiore I 67 B5
Portomarin E 72 B3
Portonovo E 73 B2
Portopalo di Capo Passero I 95 C4
Portør N 19 C6
Portoscuso I 96 D1
Portovénere I 67 B3
Portree GB 4 H3
Portsall F 42 B1
Portsmouth GB 4 L6
Portugalete E 75 A4
Portumna IRL 4 K2
Porvoo FIN 3 F19
Porzuna E 80 C2
Posada, *Oviedo* E 74 A1
Posada, *Oviedo* E 74 A2
Posada, *Sardegna* I 96 C2
Posada de Valdeón E 74 A2
Posadas E 85 B5
Poschiavo CH 57 B5
Posedarje HR 69 B4
Positano I 89 C4
Possagno I 58 C1
Posseck D 38 C2
Possesse F 45 B5
Pössneck D 38 C1
Posta I 88 A3
Posta Piana I 90 A2
Postal I 57 B6
Postbauer-Heng D 48 A2
Posterholt NL 36 B2
Postioma I 58 C2
Postira HR 69 C5
Postojna SLO 59 C4
Postoloprty CZ 39 C3
Postomino PL 32 A2
Posušje BIH 70 C2
Potenza I 90 B2
Potenza Picena I 68 C2
Potes E 74 A2
Potigny F 43 B5
Potkrajci YU 71 C4
Potočari BIH 71 B4
Potoci BIH 69 B5
Potoci BIH 70 C2
Potony H 60 C2
Potries E 82 C2
Potsdam D 31 C5
Potštát CZ 50 A3
Pottenbrunn A 49 B6
Pottendorf A 50 C2
Pottenstein A 50 C2
Pottenstein D 48 A2
Pöttmes D 48 B2
Pöttsching A 50 C2
Potworów PL 41 B5
Pouancé F 43 C4
Pougues-les-Eaux F 54 A3
Pouilly-en-Auxois F 55 A4
Pouilly-sous Charlieu F 54 B4
Pouilly-sur-Loire F 54 A2
Poujol-sur-Orb F 64 C2
Poullaouen F 42 B2
Pourcy F 45 A4
Pourrain F 45 C4
Pouy-de-Touges F 63 C4
Pouyastruc F 62 C3
Pouzauges F 52 B4
Pova de Santa Iria P 78 C1
Považská Bystrica SK 51 A4
Povedilla E 87 A3
Povlja HR 70 C1
Povljana HR 69 B4
Póvoa, *Beja* P 84 A3
Póvoa, *Santarém* P 78 B2
Póvoa de Lanhosa P 73 C2
Póvoa de Varzim P 73 C2
Póvoa e Meadas P 78 B3
Powidz PL 32 C3
Poyales del Hoyo E 80 B1
Poysdorf A 50 B2
Poza de la Sal E 75 B3
Pozaldez E 74 C2
Pozán de Vero E 76 A3
Požarevac YU 71 B6
Požega HR 60 C2
Požega YU 71 C5
Poznań PL 32 C2
Pozo Alcón E 86 B3
Pozo Cañada E 87 A4
Pozo de Guadalajara E 81 B3
Pozo de la Serna E 86 A2
Pozoantiguo E 74 C1
Pozoblanco E 86 A1
Pozohondo E 87 A4
Pozondón E 81 B5
Poźrzadło Wielkie PL 32 B1
Pozuel del Campo E 81 B5
Pozuelo de Alarcón E 80 B3
Pozuelo de Calatrava E 86 A2
Pozuelo de Zarzón E 79 A4
Pozuelo del Páramo E 74 B1
Pozzallo I 95 C3
Pozzomaggiore I 96 C1
Pozzuoli I 89 C4
Pozzuolo I 67 C5
Prabuty PL 33 B5
Prača BIH 70 C3
Prachatice CZ 49 A4
Prada E 73 B3
Pradelle F 65 B4
Pradelles F 64 B2
Prades E 76 B3
Prades F 77 A5
Pradła PL 41 C4
Prado E 74 A1
Prado P 73 C2
Prado del Rey E 85 C5
Pradoluengo E 75 B3
Præstø DK 25 D5
Pragelato I 65 A5
Pragersko SLO 59 B5
Prägraten A 58 A2
Praha CZ 39 C4
Prahecq F 53 B4
Praia P 78 B1
Práia a Mare I 92 B2
Praia da Rocha P 84 B2
Praia da Viera P 78 B2
Praia de Mira P 78 A2
Praiano I 89 C4
Pralboino I 57 C5
Pralognan-la-Vanoise F 56 C1
Pranjani YU 71 B5
Prapatnica HR 69 C5
Praszka PL 40 B3
Prat de Compte E 76 C3
Prata I 67 C4
Prata di Pordenone I 58 C2
Pratau D 38 B2
Pratdip E 76 B3
Pratella I 89 B4
Prato I 67 C5
Prátola Peligna I 89 A3
Prátola Serra I 89 C4
Prats-de-Mollo-la-Preste F 77 A5
Prauthoy F 45 C6
Pravia E 72 A4
Praxmar A 57 A6
Prayssac F 63 B4
Prazzo I 65 B6
Pré-en-Pail F 43 B5
Prebold SLO 59 B5
Précy-sur-Thil F 55 A4
Predáppio I 67 B5
Predazzo I 58 B1
Předin CZ 49 A6
Preding A 59 B5
Predjame SLO 59 C4
Predlitz A 58 A3
Predmeja SLO 58 C3
Predoi I 58 A2
Preetz D 30 A2
Préfailles F 52 A2
Pregarten A 49 B5
Pregrada HR 59 B5
Preili LV 7 H20
Preitenegg A 59 B4
Prekaja BIH 69 B5
Preko HR 69 B4
Preljina YU 71 C5
Prelog HR 60 B1
Prelošćica HR 60 C1
Přelouč CZ 39 C5
Prem SLO 59 C4
Premantura HR 68 B2
Prémery F 54 A3
Prémia I 56 B3
Premià de Mar E 77 B5
Premnitz D 30 C4
Prémont F 35 C4
Prenzlau D 31 B5
Preodac BIH 69 B5
Přerov CZ 50 A3
Prerow D 30 A4
Presencio E 74 B3
Presicce I 93 B5
Presly F 54 A2
Prešov SK 10 M17
Pressac F 53 B5
Pressath D 48 A2
Pressbaum A 50 B2
Prestebakke N 21 C3
Přeštice CZ 49 A4
Preston GB 4 K5
Prettin D 38 B2
Preturo I 89 A3
Pretzchendorf D 38 C3
Pretzier D 30 C3
Pretzsch D 38 B2
Preuilly-sur-Claise F 53 B5
Prevalje SLO 59 B4
Prevenchères F 64 B2
Préveranges F 54 B2
Préveza GR 15 S17
Prevršac HR 59 C6
Prezid HR 59 C4
Priaranza del Bierzo E 72 B4
Priay F 55 B5
Pribeta SK 50 C4
Priboj BIH 70 B3
Priboj YU 71 C4
Příbor CZ 50 A4
Příbram CZ 49 A5
Pribylina SK 51 A5
Přibyslav CZ 49 A6
Pričević YU 71 B4
Pridjel BIH 70 B3
Priego E 81 B4
Priego de Córdoba E 86 B1
Priekule LV 6 H17
Prien D 48 C3
Prienai LT 6 J18
Prievidza SK 51 B4
Prigradica HR 70 D1
Prigrevica YU 61 C4
Prijeboj HR 69 B4
Prijedor BIH 69 B5
Prijepolje YU 71 C4
Prilep MK 15 R17
Priluka BIH 70 C1
Primda CZ 48 A3
Primel-Trégastel F 42 B2
Primišje HR 59 C5
Primorsk RUS 3 F21
Primorsk RUS 33 A6
Primošten HR 69 C4
Primstal D 46 A2
Principina a Mare I 88 A1
Priolo Gargallo I 95 B4
Prioro E 74 B2
Priozersk RUS 3 F22
Prisoje BIH 70 C2
Pristen RUS 7 L25
Priština YU 71 D6
Pritzerbe D 30 C4
Pritzier D 30 B3
Pritzwalk D 30 B4
Privas F 64 B3
Priverno I 88 B3
Privlaka HR 60 C3
Privlaka HR 69 B4
Prizna HR 69 B3
Prizren YU 15 Q17
Prizzi I 94 B2
Prnjavor BIH 70 B2
Prnjavor HR 59 C5
Prnjavor YU 71 B4
Proaza E 72 A4
Probstzella D 38 C1
Prócchio I 67 D4
Prochowice PL 39 B6
Prócida I 89 C4
Prodo I 68 D1
Proença-a-Nova P 78 B3
Proença-a-Velha P 79 A3
Profondeville B 35 C5
Prokuplje YU 15 Q17
Propriano F 96 B1
Prosec CZ 50 A2
Prösen D 38 B3
Prosenjakovci SLO 59 B6
Prostějov CZ 50 A3
Prószków PL 40 C2
Proszowice PL 41 C5
Protić BIH 70 B1
Protivanov CZ 50 A2
Protivín CZ 49 A5
Prötzel D 31 C5
Provins F 45 B4
Prozor BIH 70 C2
Prudnik PL 40 C2
Pruggern A 58 A3
Prüm D 36 C2
Pruna E 85 C5
Prunelli-di-Fiumorbo F 96 A2
Prunetta I 67 B4
Pruniers F 54 B2
Prusice PL 40 B1
Pruské SK 50 A4
Pruszce PL 33 B4
Pruszcz Gdański PL 33 A4
Pruszków PL 41 A5
Prutz A 57 A5
Prüzen D 30 B4
Pruzhany BY 6 K19
Pružina SK 51 A4
Pryluky UA 7 L23
Pryzlęg PL 31 C7
Przechlewo PL 32 B3
Przecław PL 41 C6
Przedbórz PL 41 B4
Przedecz PL 33 C4
Przejęslav PL 39 B5
Przemków PL 39 B5
Przemocze PL 31 B6
Przemyśl PL 11 M18
Przerąb PL 41 B4
Przewodnik PL 33 B4
Przewóz PL 39 B4
Przezmark PL 33 B5
Przodkowo PL 33 A4
Przybiernów PL 31 B6
Przyborowice PL 33 C6
Przybyszew PL 41 B5
Przybyszów PL 41 B4
Przylęg PL 32 C1
Przysucha PL 41 B5
Przytóczna PL 32 C1
Przytyk PL 41 B5
Przywidz PL 33 A4
Psary PL 40 B3
Pskov RUS 7 H21
Pszczew PL 32 C1
Pszczółki PL 33 A4
Pszczyna PL 51 A4
Pszów PL 40 C3
Ptolemaís GR 15 R17
Ptuj SLO 59 B5
Puch A 48 C4
Puchberg am Schneeberg A 50 C1
Puchheim D 48 B2
Púchov SK 50 A4
Pučišća HR 69 C5
Puck PL 33 A4
Puçol E 82 B2
Puconci SLO 59 B6
Pudasjärvi FIN 3 D20
Puderbach D 36 C3
Puebla de Albortón E 76 B2
Puebla de Alcocer E 79 C5
Puebla de Beleña E 81 B3
Puebla de Don Fadrique E 87 B3
Puebla de Don Rodrigo E 80 C2
Puebla de Guzmán E 84 B3
Puebla de la Calzada E 79 C4
Puebla de la Reina E 79 C4
Puebla de Lillo E 74 A1
Puebla de Obando E 79 B4
Puebla de Sanabria E 73 B4
Puebla de Sancho Pérez E 79 C4
Puebla del Maestre E 85 A4
Puebla del Principe E 86 A3
Puente Almuhey E 74 B2
Puente de Domingo Flórez E 72 B4
Puente de Génave E 87 A3
Puente de Montañana E 76 A3
Puente del Congosto E 80 B1
Puente Duero E 74 C2
Puente-Genil E 86 B1
Puente la Reina E 75 B5
Puente la Reina de Jaca E 76 A2
Puente Mayorga E 85 C5

Puente Viesgo E 74 A3
Puentelarra E 75 B3
Puertas, *Asturias* E 74 A2
Puertas, *Salamanca* E 73 C4
Puerto de Mazarrón E 87 B4
Puerto de San Vicente E 80 C1
Puerto de Santa Cruz E 79 B5
Puerto-Lápice E 81 C3
Puerto Lumbreras E 87 B4
Puerto Moral E 85 B4
Puerto Real E 85 C4
Puerto Rey E 80 C1
Puerto Seguro E 73 D4
Puerto Serrano E 85 C5
Puertollano E 86 A1
Puget-Sur-Argens F 65 C5
Puget-Théniers F 65 C5
Puget-ville F 65 C5
Pugnochiuso I 90 A3
Puig Reig E 77 B4
Puigcerdà E 77 A4
Puigpunyent, *Mallorca* E 83
Puillon F 62 C2
Puimichel F 65 C5
Puimoisson F 65 C5
Puiseaux F 44 B3
Puisieux F 34 C3
Puisserguier F 64 C2
Puivert F 63 D5
Pujols F 62 B2
Pukanec SK 51 B4
Pukavik S 27 C4
Pukë AL 15 Q16
Pula HR 68 B2
Pula I 96 D1
Puławy PL 10 L17
Pulfero I 58 B3
Pulgar E 80 C2
Pulheim D 36 B2
Pulkau A 50 B1
Pulpi E 87 B4
Pulsano I 91 B4
Pulsnitz D 39 B4
Pułtusk PL 6 K17
Punat HR 69 A3
Punta Marina I 68 B1
Punta Prima, *Menorca* E 83
Punta Sabbioni I 58 C2
Punta Umbria E 85 B4
Puntas de Calnegre E 87 B4
Puolanka FIN 3 D20
Puračić BIH 70 B3
Purbach am Neusiedler See A 50 C2
Purchena E 87 B3
Purgstall A 49 B6
Purkersdorf A 50 B2
Purmerend NL 28 C1
Purullena E 86 B2
Pushkin RUS 7 G22
Pushkino RUS 7 H25
Püspökladány H 61 A6
Pusté Ulany SK 50 B3
Pustelnik PL 41 A6
Pustoshka RUS 7 H21
Puszcza Mariańska PL 41 B5
Puszczykowo PL 40 A1
Pusztamagyaród H 60 B1
Pusztamonostor H 61 A4
Pusztaszabolcs H 60 A3
Pusztavám H 60 A3
Putanges-Pont-Ecrepin F 43 B5
Putbus D 31 A5
Putignano I 91 B4
Putlitz D 30 B4
Putnok H 51 B6
Putte B 35 B5
Puttelange-aux-Lacs F 46 A2
Putten NL 35 A6
Puttgarden D 30 A3
Püttlingen D 46 A2
Putzu Idu I 96 C1
Puy-Guillaume F 54 C3
Puy-l'Évêque F 63 B4
Puylaroque F 63 B4
Puylaurens F 63 C5
Puymirol F 63 B3
Puyôo F 62 C2
Puyrolland F 53 B4
Pwllheli GB 4 K4
Pyetrikaw BY 7 K21
Pyhäjärvi FIN 3 E19
Pyla-sur-Mer F 62 B1
Pyryatyn UA 7 L23
Pyrzyce PL 31 B6
Pysely CZ 49 A5
Pyskowice PL 40 C3
Pytalovo RUS 7 H20
Pyzdry PL 40 A2

Q

Quakenbrück D 29 C4
Quargnento I 66 B2
Quarré-les-Tombes F 54 A3
Quarteira P 84 B2
Quartu Sant'Élena I 96 D2
Quatre-Champs F 45 A5
Quedlinburg D 38 B1
Queige F 55 C6
Queipo E 85 B4
Queixans E 77 A4
Quel E 75 B4
Queljada P 73 C2
Quemada E 75 C3
Queralbs E 77 A5
Quercianella I 67 C4
Querfurt D 38 B1
Quérigut F 77 A5
Quero E 81 C3
Quero I 58 C1
Querqueville F 43 A4
Quesada E 86 B2
Questembert F 42 C3
Quettehou F 43 A4
Quevauvillers F 44 A3
Quevy B 35 C5
Quiaois P 78 A2
Quiberon F 52 A1
Quiberville F 44 A1
Quickborn D 30 B1
Quiévrain B 35 C4
Quillan F 63 D5
Quillebeuf F 44 A1
Quimper F 42 B1
Quimperlé F 42 C2
Quincampoix F 44 A2
Quincoces de Yuso E 75 B3
Quincy F 54 A2
Quinéville F 43 A4
Quingey F 55 A5
Quinson F 65 C5
Quinssaines F 54 B2
Quinta-Grande P 78 C2
Quintana de la Serena E 79 C5
Quintana del Castillo E 72 B4
Quintana del Marco E 74 B1
Quintana del Puenta E 74 B2
Quintana-Martin Galindez E 75 B3
Quintanaortuño E 74 B3
Quintanapalla E 75 B3
Quintanar de la Orden E 81 C3
Quintanar de la Sierra E 75 C3
Quintanar del Rey E 81 C5
Quintanilla de la Mata E 74 C3
Quintanilla de Onésimo E 74 C2
Quintanilla de Somoza E 73 B4
Quintanilla del Coco E 75 C3
Quintas de Valdelucio E 74 B2
Quintela P 73 D3
Quintin F 42 B3
Quinto E 76 B2
Quinzano d'Oglio I 57 C5
Quiroga E 72 B3
Quismondo E 80 B2
Quissac F 64 C2
Quistello I 67 A4

R

Raab A 49 B4
Raabs an der Thaya A 49 B6
Raahe FIN 3 D19
Raalte NL 28 C3
Raamsdonksveer NL 35 B5
Rab HR 69 B3
Rabac HR 68 A3
Rábade E 72 A3
Rábafüzes H 59 B6
Rábahidvég H 60 A1
Rabanales E 73 C4
Rábapatona H 50 C3
Rabapordány H 50 C3
Rabastens F 63 C4
Rabastens-de-Bigorre F 62 C3
Rabat M 14 U14
Rabča SK 51 A5
Rabe YU 61 B5
Rabi CZ 49 A4
Rabino PL 32 B1
Rabka PL 51 A5
Rača YU 71 B6
Rača YU 71 C6
Rácale I 91 C5
Racalmás H 61 A3
Racalmuto I 94 B2
Racconigi I 66 B1
Rače SLO 59 B5
Rachecourt-sur-Marne F 45 B6
Raciąż PL 33 C6
Racibórz PL 40 C3
Račinovci HR 70 B3
Ráckeve H 61 A3
Racławice PL 41 C5
Racławice Sląskie PL 40 C2
Racot PL 40 A1
Råda, *Skaraborg* S 21 C5
Råda, *Värmland* S 20 A5
Radalj YU 71 B4
Rădăuţi RO 11 N19
Radda in Chianti I 67 C5
Raddusa I 95 B3
Radeberg D 39 B3
Radebeul D 38 B3
Radeburg D 39 B3
Radeče SLO 59 B5
Radekhiv UA 11 L19
Radenci SLO 59 B6
Radenthein A 58 B3
Radevormwald D 36 B3
Radicófani I 67 D5
Radicóndoli I 67 C5
Radišići BIH 70 C2
Radizel SLO 59 B5
Radków PL 40 C1
Radlje ob Dravi SLO 59 B5
Radlów PL 41 C5
Radmer an der Stube A 59 A4
Radnice CZ 49 A4
Radohova BIH 70 B2
Radolfzell D 47 C4
Radom PL 41 B6
Radomice PL 33 C5
Radomin PL 33 B5
Radomsko PL 41 B4
Radomyshl UA 11 L21
Radomyśl Wielki PL 41 C6
Radošina SK 50 B3
Radošovce SK 50 B3
Radostowo PL 33 B6
Radoszewice PL 40 B3
Radoszyce PL 39 B6
Radoszyce PL 41 B5
Radotin CZ 39 D4
Radovljica SLO 59 B4
Radowo Wielkie PL 32 B1
Radstadt A 58 A3
Raduc HR 69 B4
Radviliškis LT 6 J18
Radzanów, *Mazowieckie* PL 33 C6
Radzanów, *Mazowieckie* PL 41 B5
Radziejów PL 33 C4
Radziejowice PL 41 A5
Radzovce SK 51 B5
Radzyń Chełmiński PL 33 B4
Raeren B 36 C2
Raesfeld D 36 B2
Raffadali I 94 B2
Ragachow BY 7 K22
Ragály H 51 B6
Ragnitz A 59 B5
Ragusa I 95 C3
Rahden D 29 C5
Råholt N 20 A3
Raiano I 89 A3
Raigada E 73 B3
Rain D 48 B1
Rainbach im Mühlkreis A 49 B5
Rairiz de Veiga E 73 B3
Raisdorf D 30 A2
Raisio FIN 3 F18
Raiva, *Aveiro* P 73 C2
Raiva, *Coimbra* P 78 A2
Raja Jooseppi RUS 3 B21
Rajcza PL 51 A5
Rajec SK 51 A4
Rájec-Jestřebi CZ 50 A2
Rajecké Teplice SK 51 A4
Rajevo Selo HR 70 B3
Rajhrad CZ 50 A2
Rajić HR 60 C2
Rajka H 50 C3
Rakaca H 51 B6
Rakek SLO 59 C4
Rakhiv UA 11 M19
Rakitna SLO 59 C4
Rakkestad N 20 B3
Rákóczifalva H 61 A5
Rakoniewice PL 39 A6
Rakoszyce PL 40 B1
Raková SK 51 A4
Rakovac BIH 70 A2
Rakovica HR 69 B4
Rakovník CZ 39 C3
Rakow D 31 A5
Raków PL 41 C6
Rakvere EST 7 G20
Ralja YU 71 B5
Ramacastañas E 80 B1
Ramacca I 95 B3
Ramales de la Victoria E 75 A3
Rambervillers F 46 B2
Rambouillet F 44 B2
Rambucourt F 46 B1
Ramdala S 27 C5
Ramerupt F 45 B5
Ramingstein A 58 A3
Ramirás E 73 B2
Ramiswil CH 56 A2
Ramkvilla S 26 B4
Ramme DK 24 C1
Rämmen S 20 A6
Ramnäs S 22 B3
Ramnes N 20 B2
Râmnicu Vâlcea RO 11 P19
Ramonville-St. Agne F 63 C4
Ramsau D 48 C3
Ramsbeck D 37 B4
Ramsberg S 22 B2
Ramsey GB 4 J4
Ramsgate GB 4 L7
Ramstein-Meisenbach D 46 A3
Ranalt A 57 A6
Rånåsfoss N 20 A3
Rance B 35 C5
Ránchio I 68 C1
Randaberg N 18 B2
Randan F 54 B3
Randazzo I 95 B3
Randegg A 49 B5
Randers DK 24 C3
Randin E 73 C3
Rånes F 43 B5
Rångedala S 21 D5
Ranis D 38 C1
Rankweil A 57 A4
Rånnaväg S 26 B3
Ränneslöv S 26 C3
Ransäter S 20 B5
Ransbach-Baumbach D 36 C3
Ransta S 22 B3
Ranua FIN 3 D20
Ranum DK 24 C2
Ranvalhal P 78 B1
Raon-l'Étape F 46 B2
Ráossi I 57 C6
Rapallo I 66 B3
Rapla EST 6 G19
Rapolano Terme I 67 C5
Rapolla I 90 B2
Raposa P 78 B2
Rapperswil CH 56 A3
Raša HR 68 A3
Rasal E 76 A2
Rascafria E 80 B3
Rasdorf D 37 C5
Raseiniai LT 6 J18
Rašica SLO 59 C4
Rasines E 75 A3
Raška YU 71 C5
Rasquera E 76 B3
Rássina I 67 C5
Rastatt D 47 B4
Rastede D 29 B5
Rastenberg D 38 B1
Rastošnica BIH 70 B3
Rastovac YU 70 D3
Rasueros E 80 A1
Rasy PL 41 B4
Raszków PL 40 B2
Rataje YU 71 C6
Rätansbyn S 2 E14
Rateče SLO 58 B3
Ratekau D 30 B2
Ratež SLO 59 C5
Rathebur D 31 B5
Rathenow D 30 C4
Ratibořské Hory CZ 49 A5
Ratingen D 36 B2
Ratková SK 51 B6
Ratkovo YU 61 C4
Ratne UA 11 L19
Rattelsdorf D 37 C6
Ratten A 59 A5
Rättvik S 2 F14
Ratzeburg D 30 B2
Rätzlingen D 30 C3
Raucourt-et-Flaba F 45 A5
Raufoss N 2 F12
Rauland N 19 B5
Raulhac F 63 B5
Rauma FIN 3 F17
Rauris A 58 A3
Rautavaara FIN 3 E21
Rauzan F 62 B2
Rava-Rus'ka UA 11 L18
Ravanusa I 94 B2
Ravča HR 70 C2
Ravels B 35 B5
Rävemåla S 26 C5
Ravenna I 68 B1
Ravensburg D 47 C5
Rävlanda S 26 B2
Ravna Gora HR 59 C4
Ravne na Koroškem SLO 59 B4
Ravnište YU 71 C6
Ravnje YU 71 B4
Ravno BIH 70 D2
Ravno Selo YU 61 C4
Rawa Mazowiecka PL 41 B5
Rawicz PL 40 B1
Ražana YU 71 B4
Ražanac HR 69 B4
Razboj BIH 70 A2
Razbojna YU 71 C6
Razes F 53 B6
Razgrad BG 16 Q20
Razkrižie SLO 59 B6
Razo E 72 A2
Reading GB 4 L6
Réalmont F 63 C5
Rebais F 45 B4
Reboly RUS 3 E22
Rebordelo P 73 C3
Recanati I 68 C2
Recas E 80 B3
Recaş RO 10 P17
Recco I 66 B3
Recey-sur-Ource F 45 C5
Recezinhos P 73 C2
Rechnitz A 59 A6
Rechytsa BY 7 K22
Recke D 29 C4
Recklinghausen D 36 B3
Recoaro Terme I 57 C6
Recogne B 45 A6
Recoules-Prévinquières F 64 B1
Recsk H 51 C6
Recz PL 32 B1
Reda PL 33 A4
Redange L 46 A1
Redcar GB 4 J6
Redditch GB 4 K6
Redefin D 30 B3
Redics H 59 B6
Redkino RUS 7 H25
Redlin D 30 B4
Redon F 43 C3
Redondela E 73 B2
Redondo P 78 C3
Redruth GB 4 L4
Redzikowo PL 32 A3
Rees D 36 B2
Reetz D 30 B3
Reftele S 26 B3
Regalbuto I 95 B3
Regen D 48 B4
Regensburg D 48 A3
Regenstauf D 48 A3
Reggello I 67 C5
Réggio di Calábria I 95 A4
Réggio nell'Emília I 67 B4
Reggiolo I 67 B4
Reghin RO 11 N19
Régil E 75 A4
Regna S 23 C2
Regniéville F 46 B1
Regny F 55 C4
Rego da Leirosa P 78 A2
Regöly H 60 B3
Regueiro E 72 B2
Reguengo, *Portalegre* P 78 B3
Reguengo, *Santarém* P 78 B2
Reguengos de Monsaraz P 78 C3
Rehau D 38 C2
Rehburg D 29 C6
Rehden D 29 C5
Rehna D 30 B3
Reichelsheim D 47 A4
Reichelshofen D 47 A6
Reichenau A 50 C1
Reichenbach, *Sachsen* D 38 C2
Reichenbach, *Sachsen* D 39 B4
Reichenfels A 59 A4
Reichensachsen D 37 B6
Reichertshofen D 48 B2
Reichshoffen F 46 B3
Reiden CH 56 A2
Reigada E 72 A4
Reigada P 73 D4
Reigate GB 4 L6
Reillanne F 65 C4
Reillo E 81 C5
Reims F 45 A5
Reinach CH 56 A3
Reinbek D 30 B2
Reinberg D 31 A5
Reinfeld D 30 B2
Reinheim D 47 A4
Reinosa E 74 A2
Reinstorf D 30 B3
Reisach A 58 B3
Rejmyre S 23 C2
Rekavice BIH 70 B2
Rekovac YU 71 C6
Relleu E 82 C2
Rém H 61 B4
Remagen D 36 C3
Rémalard F 44 B1
Rembercourt-aux-Pots F 45 B6
Remedios P 78 B1
Remels D 29 B4
Remich L 46 A2
Rémilly F 46 A2
Remiremont F 46 C2
Remolinos E 76 B1
Remoulins F 64 C3
Remscheid D 36 B3
Rémuzat F 65 B4
Renaison F 54 B3
Renazé F 43 C4
Renchen D 47 B4
Rencurel F 65 A4
Rende I 92 B3
Rendsburg D 29 A6
Renedo E 74 C2
Renens CH 55 B6
Reni UA 11 P21
Rennerod D 36 C4
Rennertshofen D 48 B2
Rennes F 43 B4
Rennes-les-Bains F 63 D5
Rennweg A 58 A3
Rens DK 25 D2
Rentería E 75 A5
Répcelak H 60 A2
Requena E 82 B1
Réquista F 63 B5
Rerik D 30 A3
Resana I 58 C1
Resarö S 22 B5
Resende P 73 C3
Résia (Reschen) I 57 B5
Reşiţa RO 10 P17
Resko PL 32 B1
Resnik YU 71 B5
Ressons-sur-Matz F 44 A3
Restábal E 86 C2
Resuttano I 95 B3
Retamal E 79 C4
Rethel F 45 A5
Rethem D 29 C6
Réthimnon GR 16 U19
Retie B 35 B6
Retiers F 43 C4
Retkow PL 39 B6
Retortillo E 73 D4
Retortillo de Soria E 75 C3
Retournac F 54 C4
Rétság H 51 C5
Rettenegg A 59 A5
Retuerta del Bullaque E 80 C2
Retz A 50 B1
Retzbach D 47 A5
Reuden D 38 A2
Reuilly F 54 A2
Reus E 77 B4
Reusel NL 35 B6
Reuterstadt Stavenhagen D 31 B4
Reuth D 48 A3
Reutlingen D 47 B5
Reutte A 57 A5
Reuver NL 36 B2
Revel F 63 C4
Revello I 66 B1
Revenga E 80 B2
Revest-du-Bion F 65 B4
Révfülöp H 60 B2
Revigny-sur-Ornain F 45 B5
Revin F 45 A5
Řevnice CZ 49 A5
Řevničov CZ 39 C3
Revo I 57 B6
Revúca SK 51 B6
Rewa PL 33 A4
Rewal PL 31 A7
Reyero E 74 B1
Rezé F 52 A3
Rēzekne LV 7 H20
Rezovo BG 16 R21
Rezzato I 57 C5
Rezzoáglio I 66 B3
Rhaunen D 46 A3
Rhayader GB 4 K5
Rheda-Wiedenbrück D 36 B4
Rhede, *Niedersachsen* D 29 B4
Rhede, *Nordrhein-Westfalen* D 36 B2
Rheinau D 46 B3
Rheinbach D 36 C2
Rheinberg D 36 B2
Rheine D 36 A3
Rheinfelden D 56 A2
Rheinsberg D 31 B4
Rhêmes-Notre-Dame I 56 C2
Rhenen NL 35 B6
Rhens D 36 C3
Rheydt D 36 B2
Rhinow D 30 C4
Rho I 56 C4
Rhoden D 37 B5
Rhondda GB 4 L5
Rhyl GB 4 K5
Riala S 22 B5
Riallé F 52 A3
Riaño E 74 B1
Riano I 88 A2
Rians F 65 C4
Rianxo E 72 B2
Riaza E 81 A3
Riba E 75 A3
Riba de Saelices E 81 B4
Riba-Roja de Turia E 82 B2
Riba-roja d'Ebre E 76 B3
Ribadavia E 73 B2
Ribadeo E 72 A3
Ribadesella E 74 A1
Ribaflecha E 75 B4
Ribaforada E 75 C5
Ribare YU 71 B6
Ribariće YU 71 D5
Ribe DK 25 D1
Ribeauvillé F 46 B3
Ribécourt-Dreslincourt F 45 A3
Ribeira da Pena P 73 C3
Ribeira de Piquín E 72 A3
Ribemont F 45 A4
Ribera I 94 B2
Ribera de Cardós E 77 A4
Ribera del Fresno E 79 C4
Ribérac F 53 C5
Ribes de Freser E 77 A5
Ribesalbes E 82 A2
Ribiers F 65 B4
Ribnica BIH 70 B3
Ribnica SLO 59 C4
Ribnica YU 71 C5
Ribnica na Potorju SLO 59 B5
Ribnik HR 59 C5
Rîbniţa MD 11 N21
Ribnitz-Damgarten D 30 A4
Ribolla I 67 D5
Říčany, *Jihomoravský* CZ 50 A2
Říčany, *Středočeský* CZ 39 D4
Riccia I 89 B4
Riccione I 68 B1
Ricco Del Golfo I 67 B3
Richebourg F 45 B6
Richelieu F 53 A5
Richisau CH 56 A3
Richtenberg D 31 A4
Richterswil CH 56 A3
Rickling D 30 A2
Ricla E 75 C5
Riddarhyttan S 22 B2
Ridderkerk NL 35 B5
Riddes CH 56 B2
Ridjica YU 61 C4
Riec-sur-Bélon F 42 C2
Ried A 49 B4
Ried im Oberinntal A 57 A5
Riedenburg D 48 B2
Riedlingen D 47 B5
Riedstadt D 47 A4
Riegersburg A 59 B5
Riego de la Vega E 74 B1
Riego del Camino E 74 C1
Riello E 74 B1
Riemst B 35 C6
Rienne B 35 D5
Riénsena E 74 A2
Riesa D 38 B3
Riese Pio X I 58 C1
Riesi I 95 B3
Riestedt D 38 B1
Rietberg D 37 B4
Rieti I 88 A2
Rietschen D 39 B4
Rieumes F 63 C4
Rieupeyroux F 63 B5
Rieux F 63 C4
Riez F 65 C5
Riga LV 6 H19
Riggisberg CH 56 B2
Rignac F 63 B5
Rignano Gargánico I 90 A2
Rigolato I 58 B2
Rigutino I 67 C5
Riihimäki FIN 3 F19
Rijeka HR 59 C4
Rijen NL 35 B5
Rijkevorsel B 35 B5
Rijssen NL 36 A2
Rilić BIH 70 C2
Rilievo I 94 B1
Rillo de Gallo E 81 B5
Rimavská Baňa SK 51 B5
Rimavská Seč SK 51 B6
Rimavská Sobota SK 51 B6
Rimbo S 22 B5
Rimforsa S 23 C2
Rímini I 68 B1
Rîmnicu Sărat RO 11 P20
Rimogne F 45 A5
Rimpar D 47 A5
Rimske Toplice SLO 59 B5
Rincón de la Victoria E 86 C1
Rincón de Soto E 75 B5
Ringarum S 23 C3
Ringe DK 25 D3
Ringkøbing DK 25 C1
Ringsted DK 25 D4
Rinkaby S 27 D4
Rinkabyholm S 26 C6
Rinlo E 72 A3
Rinn A 57 A6
Rinteln D 37 A5
Rio E 72 B3
Rio do Coures P 78 B2
Rio Douro P 73 C3
Rio Frio P 78 C2
Rio frio de Riaza E 81 A3
Rio Maior P 78 B2
Rio Marina I 67 D4
Rio Tinto P 73 C2
Riobo E 72 B2
Riodeva E 82 A1
Riofrio E 80 B2
Riofrio de Aliste E 73 C4
Riogordo E 86 C1
Rioja E 87 C3
Riola I 67 B5
Riola Sardo I 96 D1
Riolobos E 79 B4
Riom F 54 C3
Riom-ès-Montagnes F 54 C2
Riomaggiore I 67 B3
Rion-des-Landes F 62 C2
Rionegro del Puente E 73 B4
Rionero in Vúlture I 90 B2
Riopar E 87 A3
Riós E 73 C3
Rioseco E 74 A1
Rioseco de Tapia E 74 B1
Riotord F 55 C4
Riotorto E 72 A3
Rioz F 55 A6
Ripač BIH 69 B4
Ripacándida I 90 B2
Ripanj YU 71 B5
Ripatransone I 68 D2
Ripoll E 77 A5
Ripon GB 4 J6
Riposto I 95 B4
Risan YU 15 Q16
Rischenau D 37 B5
Riscle F 62 C2
Rišňovce SK 50 B3
Risør N 19 C6
Risøyhamn N 2 B14
Ritterhude D 29 B5
Riva del Garda I 57 C5
Riva Lígure I 66 C1
Rivanazzano I 66 B3
Rivarolo Canavese I 56 C2
Rivarolo Mantovano I 67 A4
Rive-de-Gier F 55 C4
Rivedoux-Plage F 52 B3
Rivello I 90 B2
Rivergaro I 66 B3
Rives F 55 C5
Rivesaltes F 64 D1
Rivignano I 58 C3
Rivne UA 11 L20
Rívoli I 66 A1
Rivolta d'Adda I 57 C4
Rixheim F 46 C3
Rixo S 21 C3
Rjukan N 19 B5
Rø DK 27 D4
Rö S 22 B5
Roa E 74 C3
Roa N 20 A2
Roager DK 25 D1
Roaldkvam N 18 B3
Roanne F 54 B4
Robakowo PL 33 B4
Róbbio I 56 C3
Röbel D 31 B4
Robertville B 36 C2
Robleda E 79 A4
Robledillo de Trujillo E 79 B5
Robledo, *Albacete* E 87 A3
Robledo, *Orense* E 72 B4
Robledo de Chavela E 80 B2
Robledo del Buey E 80 C2
Robledo del Mazo E 80 C2
Robledollano E 79 B5
Robles de la Valcueva E 74 B1
Robliza de Cojos E 73 D5
Robres E 76 B2
Robres del Castillo E 75 B4
Rocafort de Queralt E 77 B4
Rocamadour F 63 B4
Rocca di Mezzo I 89 A3
Rocca di Papa I 88 B2
Rocca Imperiale I 91 B3
Rocca Priora I 68 C2
Rocca San Casciano I 67 B5
Rocca Sinibalda I 88 A2
Roccabernarda I 93 B3
Roccabianca I 67 A4
Roccadáspide I 90 B2
Roccagorga I 88 B3
Roccalbegna I 67 D5
Roccalumera I 95 B4
Roccamena I 94 B2
Roccamonfina I 89 B3
Roccanova I 90 B3
Roccapalumba I 94 B2
Roccapassa I 88 A3
Roccaraso I 89 B4
Roccasecca I 89 B3
Roccastrada I 67 C5
Roccatederighi I 67 C5
Roccella Iónica I 92 C3
Rocchetta Sant'António I 90 A2
Roche-lez-Beaupré F 55 A6
Rochechouart F 53 C5
Rochefort B 35 C6
Rochefort F 52 C4
Rochefort-en-Terre F 43 C3
Rochefort-Montagne F 54 C2
Rochefort-sur-Nenon F 55 A5
Rochemaure F 64 B3
Rocheservière F 52 B3
Rochlitz D 38 B2
Rociana del Condado E 85 B4
Rockenhausen D 46 A3
Rockhammar S 22 B2
Rockneby S 26 C6
Ročko Polje HR 59 C4
Rocroi F 45 A5
Roda de Bara E 77 B4
Roda de Ter E 77 B5
Rodach D 37 C6
Rodalben D 46 A3
Rødberg N 19 A5
Rødby DK 30 A3
Rødbyhavn DK 30 A3
Rødding, *Sonderjyllands Amt.* DK 25 D2
Rødding, *Viborg Amt.* DK 24 C1
Rödeby S 27 C5
Rodeiro E 72 B3
Rødekro DK 25 D2
Roden NL 28 B3
Ródenas E 81 B5
Rodenkirchen D 29 B5
Rödental D 38 C1
Rödermark D 37 D4
Rodewisch D 38 C2
Rodez F 63 B5
Ródhos GR 16 T21
Rodi Gargánico I 90 A2
Roding D 48 A3
Rødkærsbro DK 25 C2
Rodoñá E 77 B4
Rødvig DK 27 D2
Roermond NL 36 B1
Roesbrugge B 34 C3
Roeschwoog F 47 B4
Roeselare B 35 C4
Roetgen D 36 C2
Roffiac F 64 A2
Röfors S 23 C1
Rofrano I 90 B2
Rogač HR 69 C5
Rogačica YU 71 B4
Rogalinek PL 40 A1
Rogaška Slatina SLO 59 B5
Rogatec SLO 59 B5
Rogatica BIH 70 C4
Rogatyn UA 11 M19
Rogätz D 38 A1
Roggendorf D 30 B3
Roggiano Gravina I 92 B3
Rogliano F 66 D3
Rogliano I 92 B3
Rognes F 65 C4
Rogny-les-7-Ecluses F 45 C3
Rogowo PL 32 C3
Rogóz PL 33 A6
Rogoznica HR 69 C4
Rogoźnica PL 39 B6
Rogoźno PL 32 C2
Rohan F 42 B3
Röhlingen D 47 B6
Rohožník SK 50 B3
Rohr D 37 C6
Rohr im Gebirge A 49 C6
Rohrbach A 49 B4
Rohrbach-lès-Bitche F 46 A3
Rohrberg D 30 C3
Röhrnbach D 49 B4
Roisel F 45 A4
Roja LV 6 H18
Rojales E 82 C2
Rokiciny PL 41 B4
Rokietnica PL 32 C2
Rokiškis LT 7 J19
Rokitki PL 39 B5
Rokitno RUS 7 L24
Rokycany CZ 49 A4
Rolampont F 45 C6
Rold DK 24 C2
Røldal N 18 B3
Rolde NL 28 C3
Rollag N 19 A6
Rollán E 80 B1
Rolle CH 55 B6
Roma I 88 B2
Roma S 23 D5
Romagnano Sésia I 56 C3

Romagné F 43 B4
Romakloster S 23 D5
Roman RO 11 N20
Romana I 96 C1
Romanèche-Thorins F 55 B4
Romano di Lombardia I 57 C4
Romans-sur-Isère F 65 A4
Romanshorn CH 57 A4
Rombas F 46 A2
Romeán E 72 B3
Romenay F 55 B5
Romeral E 81 C3
Römerstein D 47 B5
Rometta I 95 A4
Romhány H 51 C5
Römhild D 37 C6
Romilly-sur-Seine F 45 B4
Romny UA 7 L23
Romodan UA 11 M23
Romont CH 56 B1
Romorantin-Lanthenay F 54 A1
Romrod D 37 C5
Rømskog N 20 B3
Rønbjerg DK 24 C1
Roncal E 62 D2
Ronce-les-Bains F 52 C3
Ronchamp F 46 C2
Ronchi dei Legionari I 58 C3
Ronciglione I 88 A2
Ronco Canavese I 56 C2
Ronco Scrivia I 66 B2
Ronda E 85 C5
Rønde DK 25 C3
Rönnäng S 21 D3
Rønne DK 27 D4
Ronneburg D 38 C2
Ronneby S 27 C5
Rönneshytta S 23 C2
Rönninge S 22 B4
Rönö S 23 C3
Ronov nad Doubravou CZ 49 A6
Ronse B 35 C4
Roosendaal NL 35 B5
Ropczyce PL 41 C6
Ropeid N 18 B3
Ropuerelos del Páramo E 74 B1
Roquebillière F 65 B6
Roquebrun F 64 C2
Roquecourbe F 63 C5
Roquefort F 62 B2
Roquemaure F 64 B3
Roquesteron F 65 C6
Roquetas de Mar E 87 C3
Roquetes E 76 C3
Roquevaire F 65 C4
Rørbæk DK 24 C2
Rore BIH 69 B5
Röro S 21 D3
Røros N 2 E12
Rorschach CH 57 A4
Rørvig DK 25 D4
Rørvik N 2 D12
Rörvik S 26 B4
Rosà I 58 C1
Rosa Marina I 91 B4
Rosal de la Frontera E 84 B3
Rosalina Mare I 58 C2
Rosans F 65 B4
Rosário P 84 B2
Rosarno I 92 C3
Rosbach D 36 C3
Rosche D 30 C2
Rościszewo PL 33 C5
Roscoff F 42 B2
Roscommon IRL 4 K2
Rosdorf D 37 B5
Rose I 92 B3
Rosegg A 59 B4
Rosel GB 43 A3
Rosell E 76 C3
Roselló E 76 B3
Rosendal N 18 B3
Rosenfeld D 47 B4
Rosenfors S 26 B5
Rosenheim D 48 C3
Rosenow D 31 B5
Rosenthal D 37 B4
Rosersberg S 22 B4
Roses E 77 A6
Roseto degli Abruzzi I 89 A4
Roseto Valfortore I 90 A2
Rosheim F 46 B3
Rosia I 67 C5
Rosice CZ 50 A2
Rosières-en-Santerre F 44 A3
Rosignano Maríttimo I 67 C4
Rosignano Solvay I 67 C4
Roşiori-de-Vede RO 11 P19
Roskilde DK 25 D5
Röslau D 38 C1
Roslavl RUS 7 K23
Roslev DK 24 C1
Rosmaninhal P 79 B3
Rosnowo PL 32 A2
Rosolini I 95 C3
Rosova YU 71 C4
Rosoy F 45 B4
Rosporden F 42 C2
Rosquete P 78 B2
Rosrath D 36 C3
Rossa CH 57 B4
Rossano I 92 B3
Rossas, *Aveiro* P 73 D2
Rossas, *Braga* P 73 C2
Rossdorf D 37 C6
Rosshaupten D 48 C1
Rossiglione I 66 B2
Rossignol B 46 A1
Rossla D 38 B1
Rosslare IRL 4 K3
Rosslau D 38 B2
Rossleben D 38 B1
Rossoszyca PL 40 B3
Rosswein D 38 B3
Röstånga S 27 C3
Roštár SK 51 B6
Rostock D 30 A4
Rostrenen F 42 B2
Röszke H 61 B5
Rot am See D 47 A6
Rota E 85 C4
Rota Greca I 92 B3
Rotella I 68 D2
Rotenburg, *Hessen* D 37 C5
Rotenburg, *Niedersachsen* D 29 B6
Roth, *Bayern* D 48 A2
Roth, *Rheinland-Pfalz* D 36 C3
Rothemühl D 31 B5
Rothenkempenow D 31 B6
Röthenbach D 48 A2
Rothenburg D 39 B4
Rothenburg ob der Tauber D 47 A6
Rothéneuf F 43 B4
Rothenstein D 48 B2
Rotherham GB 4 K6
Rothesay GB 4 J4
Rotnes N 20 A2
Rotonda I 90 C3
Rotondella I 91 B3
Rotova E 82 C2
Rott, *Bayern* D 48 C1
Rott, *Bayern* D 48 C3
Rottach-Egern D 48 C2
Röttenbach D 48 A2
Rottenbuch D 48 C1
Rottenburg, *Baden-Württemberg* D 47 B4
Rottenburg, *Bayern* D 48 B3
Rottenmann A 59 A4
Rotterdam NL 35 B5
Rotthalmünster D 49 B4
Röttingen D 47 A5
Rottleberode D 37 B6
Rottne S 26 B4
Rottneros S 20 B5
Rottofreno I 66 A3
Rottweil D 47 B4
Rötz D 48 A3
Roubaix F 35 C4
Roudnice nad Labem CZ 39 C4
Roudouallec F 42 B2
Rouen F 44 A2
Rouffach F 46 C3
Rougé F 43 C4
Rougemont F 55 A6
Rougemont le-Château F 46 C2
Rouillac F 53 C4
Rouillé F 53 B5
Roujan F 64 C2
Roulans F 55 A6
Rousínov CZ 50 A2
Roussac F 53 B6
Rousses F 64 B2
Roussillon F 55 C4
Rouvroy-sur-Audry F 45 A5
Rouy F 54 A3
Rovaniemi FIN 3 C19
Rovato I 57 C4
Rovensko pod Troskami CZ 39 C5
Roverbella I 57 C5
Rovereto I 57 C6
Rövershagen D 30 A4
Roverud N 20 A4
Rovigo I 67 A5
Rovinj HR 68 A2
Rovišce HR 60 C1
Rów PL 31 C6
Rowy PL 32 A3
Royal Tunbridge Wells GB 4 L7
Royan F 52 C3
Royat F 54 C3
Roybon F 55 C5
Roye F 44 A3
Røykenvik N 20 A2
Royos E 87 B3
Rozadas E 72 A4
Rožaj YU 71 D5
Rozalén del Monte E 81 C4
Różańsko PL 31 C6
Rožanstvo YU 71 C4
Rozay-en-Brie F 45 B3
Roždalovice CZ 39 C5
Rozdilna UA 11 N22
Rozental PL 33 B5
Rozhyshche UA 11 L19
Rožmitál pod Třemšínem CZ 49 A4
Rožňava SK 51 B6
Rožnov pod Radhoštěm CZ 50 A4
Rozoy-sur-Serre F 45 A5
Rozprza PL 41 B4
Roztoky CZ 39 C4
Rozvadov CZ 48 A3
Rozzano I 57 C4
Ruanes E 79 B5
Rubbestadneset N 18 B2
Rubi E 77 B5
Rubiá E 72 B4
Rubiacedo de Abajo E 75 B3
Rubielos Bajos E 81 C4
Rubielos de Mora E 82 A2
Rubiera I 67 B4
Rucandio E 75 B3
Rud, *Akershus* N 20 A3
Rud, *Buskerud* N 19 A7
Ruda PL 40 B3
Ruda S 26 B6
Ruda Maleniecka PL 41 B5
Ruda Pilczycka PL 41 B5
Ruda Śl. PL 40 C3
Rudabánya H 51 B6
Ruden A 59 B4
Rudersberg D 47 B5
Rudersdorf A 59 A6
Rüdersdorf D 31 C5
Ruderting D 49 B4
Rüdesheim D 36 D3
Rudkøbing DK 25 E3
Rudmanns A 49 B6
Rudna CZ 39 C4
Rudna PL 39 B6
Rudnik YU 71 B5
Rudnik YU 71 D5
Rudniki PL 40 B3
Rudniki PL 41 C4
Rudno PL 33 B4
Rudno PL 40 B1
Rudnya RUS 7 J22
Rudo BIH 71 C4
Rudolstadt D 38 C1
Rudowica PL 39 B5
Rudozem BG 16 R19
Ruds Vedby DK 25 D4
Rudskoga S 21 B6
Rudy PL 40 C3
Rue F 34 C2
Rueda E 74 C2
Rueda de Jalón E 76 B1
Ruelle-sur-Touvre F 53 C5
Ruerrero E 74 B3
Ruffano I 93 B5
Ruffec F 53 B5
Rufina I 67 C5
Rugby GB 4 K6
Rugles F 44 B1
Rugozero RUS 3 D23
Rühen D 30 C2
Ruhla D 37 C6
Ruhland D 39 B3
Ruhle D 29 C4
Ruhpolding D 48 C3
Ruhstorf D 49 B4
Ruidera E 81 D4
Ruillé-sur-le-Loir F 44 C1
Ruinen NL 28 C3
Ruiselede B 35 B4
Rulles B 46 A1
Rülzheim D 47 A4
Rum H 60 A1
Ruma YU 71 A4
Rumboci BIH 70 C2
Rumburk CZ 39 C4
Rumenka YU 61 C4
Rumia PL 33 A4
Rumigny F 45 A5
Rumilly F 55 C5
Rumont F 45 B6
Rumy PL 33 B6
Runa P 78 B1
Rungsted DK 27 D2
Runhällen S 22 A3
Runowo PL 33 A6
Ruokolahti FIN 3 F21
Ruoms F 64 B3
Ruoti I 90 B2
Rupa HR 59 C4
Ruppichteroth D 36 C3
Rupt-sur-Moselle F 46 C2
Rus E 86 A2
Ruse BG 16 Q20
Ruše SLO 59 B5
Ruševo HR 60 C3
Rusiec PL 40 B3
Rusinowo PL 32 B1
Rusinowo PL 32 B2
Ruski Krstur YU 61 C4
Rusovce SK 50 B3
Rüsselsheim D 37 D4
Russi I 67 B6
Rust A 50 C2
Rustrel F 65 C4
Ruszki PL 41 A5
Ruszów PL 39 B5
Rute E 86 B1
Rüthen D 37 B4
Rüti CH 56 A3
Rutigliano I 91 A4
Rutoši YU 71 C4
Rutuna S 23 C4
Ruurlo NL 36 A2
Ruvo del Monte I 90 B2
Ruvo di Púglia I 91 A3
Ružic HR 69 C5
Ružomberok SK 51 A5
Ruzsa H 61 B4
Ry DK 25 C2
Rybany SK 50 B4
Rybina PL 33 A5
Rybinsk RUS 7 G26
Rybnik PL 40 C3
Rybno PL 33 B5
Rychliki PL 33 B5
Rychlocice PL 40 B3
Rychnov nad Kněžnou CZ 40 C1
Rychnowo PL 33 B6
Rychtal PL 40 B2
Rychwał PL 40 A3
Ryczywól PL 32 C2
Ryczywół PL 41 B6
Ryd S 26 C4
Rydaholm S 26 C4
Rydal S 21 D3
Rydbo S 22 B5
Rydboholm S 26 B2
Rydöbruk S 26 C3
Rydsgård S 27 D3
Rydsnäs S 23 D2
Rydultowy PL 40 C3
Rydzyna PL 40 B1
Rygge N 20 B2
Ryjewo PL 33 B4
Rykene N 19 C5
Rylsk RUS 7 L24
Rymań PL 32 B1
Rýmařov CZ 50 A3
Rynarzewo PL 32 B3
Ryomgård DK 25 C3
Rypin PL 33 B5
Ryssby S 26 C4
Rytel PL 32 B3
Rytro PL 51 A6
Rywociny PL 33 B6
Rzeczenica PL 32 B3
Rzeczniów PL 41 B6
Rzeczyca PL 41 B5
Rzęgnowo PL 33 B6
Rzejowice PL 41 B4
Rzemień PL 41 C6
Rzepin PL 31 C6
Rzesznikowo PL 32 B1
Rzeszów PL 10 L17
Rzgów PL 41 B4
Rzhev RUS 7 H24

S

Sa Pobla, *Mallorca* E 83
Sa Savina E 83 C4
Saal, *Bayern* D 37 C6
Saal, *Bayern* D 48 B2
Saalbach A 58 A2
Saalburg D 38 C1
Saales F 46 B3
Saalfeld D 38 C1
Saalfelden am Steinernen Meer A 58 A2
Saanen CH 56 B2
Saarbrücken D 46 A2
Saarburg D 46 A2
Saarijärvi FIN 3 E19
Saarlouis D 46 A2
Saas-Fee CH 56 B2
Šabac YU 71 B4
Sabadell E 77 B5
Sabáudia I 88 B3
Sabbioneta I 67 B4
Sabero E 74 B1
Sabiñánigo E 76 A2
Sabiote E 86 A2
Sablé-sur-Sarthe F 43 C5
Sables-d'Or-les-Pins F 42 B3
Sabóia P 84 B2
Saborsko HR 69 A4
Sabres F 62 B2
Sabrosa P 73 C3
Sabugal P 79 A3
Săcălaz RO 61 C6
Sacecorbo E 81 B4
Saceda del Rio E 81 B4
Sacedón E 81 B4
Săcele RO 11 P19
Saceruela E 80 D2
Sachsenburg A 58 B3
Sachsenhagen D 29 C6
Sacile I 58 C2
Sacramenia E 74 C3
Sada E 72 A2
Sádaba E 76 A1
Sadernes E 77 A5
Sadki PL 32 B3
Sadkowice PL 41 B5
Sadów PL 39 A4
Sadská CZ 39 C4
Sæbøvik N 18 B2
Sæby DK 24 B3
Saelices E 81 C4
Saelices de Mayorga E 74 B1
Saerbeck D 36 A3
Særslev DK 25 D3
Sætre N 20 B2
Saeul L 46 A1
Sævareid N 18 A2
Safara P 84 A3
Säffle S 20 B4
Safonovo RUS 7 J23
Säfsnäs S 22 A1
Şag RO 61 C6
Sagard D 31 A5
S'Agaro E 77 B6
Sagone F 96 A1
Sagres P 84 C2
Ságújfalu H 51 B5
Sagunt E 82 B2
Sagvåg N 18 B2
Ságvár H 60 B3
Sagy F 55 B5
Sahagún E 74 B1
Šahy SK 51 B4
Saignelégier CH 56 A1
Saignes F 54 C2
Saillagouse F 77 A5
Saillans F 65 B4
Sains F 45 A4
St. Affrique F 64 C1
St.-Agnan F 54 B3
St. Agnant F 52 C4
St. Agrève F 64 A3
St. Aignan F 53 A6
St. Aignan-sur-Roë F 43 C4
St. Alban-sur-Limagnole F 64 B2
St. Albans GB 4 L6
St. Amand-en-Puisaye F 54 A3
St. Amand-les-Eaux F 35 C4
St. Amand-Longpré F 44 C2
St. Amand-Montrond F 54 B2
St. Amans F 64 B2
St. Amans-Soult F 63 C5
St. Amant-Roche-Savine F 54 C3
St. Amarin F 46 C2
St.-Ambroix F 64 B3
St. Amé F 46 B2
St. Amour F 55 B5
St.-André-de-Corcy F 55 C4
St. André-de-Cubzac F 62 B2
St. André-de-l'Eure F 44 B2
St. André-de-Sangonis F 64 C2
St. Andre-de-Valborgne F 64 B2
St. André-les-Alpes F 65 C5
St. Andrews GB 4 H5
St. Angel F 54 C2
St. Anthème F 54 C3
St. Antoine-de-Ficalba F 63 B3
St. Antönien CH 57 B4
St. Antonin-Noble-Val F 63 B4
St. Août F 54 B1
St. Armant-Tallende F 54 C3
St. Arnoult F 44 B2
St. Astier F 63 A3
St. Auban F 65 C5
St.-Aubin CH 56 B1
St. Aubin F 55 A5
St. Aubin GB 43 A3
St. Aubin-d'Aubigné F 43 B4
St. Aubin-du-Cormier F 43 B4
St. Aubin-sur-Aire F 45 B6
St. Aubin-sur-Mer F 43 A5
St. Aulaye F 53 C5
St. Austell GB 4 L4
St. Avit F 54 C2
St. Avold F 46 A2
St. Aygulf F 65 C5
St. Bauzille-de-Putois F 64 C2
St-Béat F 63 D3
St. Benim-d'Azy F 54 B3
St. Benoît-du-Sault F 53 B6
St. Benoit-en-Woëvre F 46 B1
St. Berthevin F 43 B5
St. Blaise-la-Roche F 46 B3
St. Blin F 45 B6
St. Bonnet F 65 B5
St. Bonnet-de-Joux F 55 B4
St. Bonnet-le-Château F 54 C4
St. Bonnet-le-Froid F 55 C4
St. Brévin-les-Pins F 52 A2
St. Briac-sur-Mer F 43 B3
St. Brice-en-Coglès F 43 B4
St. Brieuc F 42 B3
St. Bris-le-Vineux F 45 C4
St. Broladre F 43 B4
St. Calais F 44 C1
St. Cannat F 65 C4
St. Cast-le-Guildo F 43 B3
St. Céré F 63 B4
St. Cergue CH 55 B6
St. Cergues F 55 B6
St. Cernin F 63 A5
St. Chamant F 63 A4
St. Chamas F 65 C4
St. Chamond F 55 C4
St. Chély-d'Apcher F 64 B2
St. Chély-d'Aubrac F 64 B1
St. Chinian F 64 C1
St. Christol-lès-Alès F 64 B3
St. Christoly-Médoc F 52 C4
St. Christophe-du-Ligneron F 52 B3
St. Christophe-en-Brionnais F 55 B4
St. Ciers-sur-Gironde F 53 C4
St. Clair-sur-Epte F 44 A2
St. Clar F 63 C3
St. Claud F 53 C5
St. Claude F 55 B5
St. Come-d'Olt F 64 B1
St. Cosme-en-Vairais F 44 B1
St. Cyprien, *Dordogne* F 63 B4
St-Cyprien, *Pyrénées-Orientales* F 77 A6
St. Cyr-sur-Loire F 53 A5
St. Cyr-sur-Mer F 65 C4
St. Cyr-sur-Methon F 55 B4
St. Denis F 44 B3
St. Denis-d'Oléron F 52 B3
St. Denis d'Orques F 43 B5
St. Didier F 55 B4
St. Didier-en-Velay F 55 C4
St. Dié F 46 B2
St. Dizier F 45 B5
St. Dizier-Leyrenne F 53 B6
St. Efflam F 42 B2
St. Égrève F 55 C5
St. Eloy-les-Mines F 54 B2
St. Émilion F 62 B2
St. Esteben F 62 C1
St. Estèphe F 53 C4
St. Étienne F 55 C4
St. Etienne-de-Baigorry F 62 C1
St. Étienne-de-Cuines F 55 C6
St. Etienne-de-Fursac F 53 B6
St. Etienne-de-Montluc F 52 A3
St. Etienne-de-St. Geoirs F 55 C5
St. Étienne-de-Tinée F 65 B5
St. Étienne-du-Bois F 55 B5
St. Étienne-du-Rouvray F 44 A2
St. Etienne-les-Orgues F 65 B4
St. Fargeau F 45 C4
St. Félicien F 64 A3
St. Felix-de-Sorgues F 64 C1
St. Félix-Lauragais F 63 C4
St. Firmin F 65 B5
St. Florent F 96 A2
St. Florent-le-Vieil F 52 A3
St. Florent-sur-Cher F 54 B2
St. Florentin F 45 C4
St. Flour F 64 A2
St. Flovier F 53 B6
St. Fort-sur-le-Né F 53 C4
St. Fulgent F 52 B3
St. Galmier F 55 C4
St-Gaudens F 63 C3
St. Gaultier F 53 B6
St. Gély-du-Fesc F 64 C2
St. Genest-Malifaux F 55 C4
St. Gengoux-le-National F 55 B4
St. Geniez F 65 B5
St. Geniez-d'Olt F 64 B1
St. Genis-de-Saintonge F 53 C4
St.-Genis-Pouilly F 55 B6
St. Genix-sur-Guiers F 55 C5
St. Georges Buttavent F 43 B5
St. Georges-d'Aurac F 54 C3
St. Georges-de-Commiers F 65 A4
St. Georges-de-Didonne F 52 C4
St. Georges-de-Luzençon F 64 B1
St. Georges-de Mons F 54 C2
St. Georges-de-Reneins F 55 B4
St. Georges d'Oléron F 52 C3
St. Georges-en-Couzan F 54 C3
St. Georges-lès-Baillargeaux F 53 B5
St. Georges-sur-Loire F 53 A4
St. Georges-sur-Meuse B 35 C6
St. Geours-de-Maremne F 62 C1
St. Gérand-de-Vaux F 54 B3
St. Gérand-le-Puy F 54 B3
St. Germain F 46 C2
St. Germain-Chassenay F 54 B3
St. Germain-de-Calberte F 64 B2
St. Germain-de-Confolens F 53 B5
St. Germain-de-Joux F 55 B5
St. Germain-des-Fossés F 54 B3
St. Germain-du-Bois F 55 B5
St. Germain-du-Plain F 55 B4
St. Germain-du Puy F 54 A2
St. Germain-en-Laye F 44 B3
St. Germain-Laval F 54 C4
St. Germain-Lembron F 54 C3
St. Germain-les-Belles F 53 C6
St.-Germain-Lespinasse F 54 B3
St. Germain-l'Herm F 54 C3
St. Gervais-d'Auvergne F 54 B2
St. Gervais-les-Bains F 56 C1
St. Gervais-sur-Mare F 64 C2
St. Gildas-de-Rhuys F 52 A2
St. Gildas-des-Bois F 52 A2
St. Gilles, *Gard* F 64 C3
St. Gilles, *Ille-et-Vilaine* F 43 B4
St. Gilles-Croix-de-Vie F 52 B3
St. Gingolph F 56 B1
St-Girons, *Ariège* F 63 D4
St. Girons, *Landes* F 62 C1
St. Girons-Plage F 62 C1
St. Gobain F 45 A4
St. Guénolé F 42 C1
St. Helier GB 43 A3
St. Herblain F 52 A3
St. Hilaire, *Allier* F 54 B3
St. Hilaire, *Aude* F 63 C5
St. Hilaire-de-Riez F 52 B3
St. Hilaire-de-Villefranche F 53 C4
St. Hilaire-des-Loges F 53 B4
St. Hilaire-du-Harcouët F 43 B4
St. Hilaire-du-Rosier F 65 A4
St. Hippolyte, *Aveyron* F 63 B5
St. Hippolyte, *Doubs* F 56 A1
St. Hippolyte-du-Fort F 64 C2
St. Honoré-les-Bains F 54 B3
St. Hubert B 35 C6
St. Imier CH 56 A2
St. Izaire F 64 C1
St. Jacques-de-la-Lande F 43 B4
St. Jacut-de-la-Mer F 43 B3
St. James F 43 B4
Saint Jaume d'Enveja E 76 C3
St. Jean-Brévelay F 42 C3
St. Jean-d'Angély F 53 C4
St. Jean-de-Belleville F 55 C6
St. Jean-de-Bournay F 55 C5
St. Jean-de-Braye F 44 C2
St. Jean-de-Côle F 53 C5
St. Jean-de-Daye F 43 A4
St. Jean de Losne F 55 A5
St. Jean-de-Luz F 62 C1
St. Jean-de-Maurienne F 55 C6
St. Jean-de-Monts F 52 B2
St. Jean-d'Illac F 62 B2
St. Jean-du-Bruel F 64 B2
St. Jean-du-Gard F 64 B2
St. Jean-en-Royans F 65 A4
St. Jean-la-Riviere F 65 C6
St. Jean-Pied-de-Port F 62 C1
St. Jean-Poutge F 63 C3
St. Jeoire F 55 B6
St. Joachim F 52 A2
St. Jorioz F 55 C6
St. Joris Winge B 35 C5
St. Jouin-de-Marnes F 53 B4
St. Juéry F 63 C5
St. Julien-Chapteuil F 64 A3
St. Julien-de-Vouvantes F 43 C4
St. Julien-du-Sault F 45 B4
St. Julien-du-Verdon F 65 C5
St. Julien-en-Born F 62 B1
St. Julien-en-Genevois F 55 B6
St. Julien la-Vêtre F 54 C3
St. Julien-l'Ars F 53 B5
St. Julien-Mont-Denis F 55 C6
St. Julien-sur-Reyssouze F 55 B5
St. Junien F 53 C5
St. Just F 64 B3
St. Just-en-Chaussée F 44 A3
St. Just-en-Chevalet F 54 C3
St. Just-St. Rambert F 55 C4
St. Justin F 62 C2
St. Lary-Soulan F 63 D3
St. Laurent-d'Aigouze F 64 C3
St. Laurent-de-Chamousset F 55 C4
St. Laurent-de-Condel F 43 A5
St. Laurent-de-la-Cabrerisse F 64 C1
St-Laurent-de-la-Salanque F 64 D1
St. Laurent-des-Autels F 52 A3
St. Laurent-du-Pont F 55 C5
St. Laurent-en-Caux F 44 A1
St. Laurent-en-Grandvaux F 55 B5
St. Laurent-Médoc F 62 A2
St. Laurent-sur-Gorre F 53 C5
St. Laurent-sur-Mer F 43 A5
St. Laurent-sur-Sèvre F 52 B4
St. Leger B 46 A1
St. Léger-de-Vignes F 54 B3
St. Léger-sous-Beuvray F 54 B4
St. Léger-sur-Dheune F 55 B4
St. Léonard-de-Noblat F 53 C6
St. Lô F 43 A4
St. Lon-les-Mines F 62 C1
St. Louis F 46 C3
St. Loup F 54 B3
St. Loup-de-la-Salle F 55 B4
St. Loup-sur-Semouse F 46 C2
St. Lunaire F 43 B3
St. Lupicin F 55 B5
St. Lyphard F 52 A2
St. Lys F 63 C4
St. Macaire F 62 B2
St. Maclou F 44 A1
St. Maixent-l'École F 53 B4
St. Malo F 43 B3
St. Mamet-la-Salvetat F 63 B5
St. Mandrier-sur-Mer F 65 C4
St. Marcel, *Drôme* F 64 B3
St. Marcel, *Saône-et-Loire* F 55 B4
St. Marcellin F 55 C5
St. Marcellin sur Loire F 54 C4
St. Marcet F 63 C3
St. Mards-en-Othe F 45 B4
St. Mars-la-Jaille F 52 A3
St. Martin-d'Ablois F 45 B4
St. Martin-d'Auxigny F 54 A2
St. Martin-de-Belleville F 55 C6
St. Martin-de-Bossenay F 45 B4
St. Martin-de-Crau F 64 C3
St. Martin-de-Londres F 64 C2
St. Martin-de-Queyrières F 65 B5
St. Martin-de-Ré F 52 B3
St.-Martin-de-Valamas F 64 B3
St. Martin-d'Entraunes F 65 B5
St. Martin des Besaces F 43 A5
St. Martin-d'Estreaux F 54 B3
St. Martin-d'Hères F 55 C5
St. Martin-du-Frêne F 55 B5
St. Martin-en-Bresse F 55 B5
St.-Martin-en-Haut F 55 C4
St. Martin-la-Méanne F 54 C1
St. Martin-sur-Ouanne F 45 C4
St. Martin-Valmeroux F 63 A5
St. Martin-Vésubie F 65 B6
St-Martory F 63 C3
St. Mathieu F 53 C5
St. Mathieu-de-Tréviers F 64 C2
St. Maurice CH 56 B1
St. Maurice-Navacelles F 64 C2
St. Maurice-sur-Moselle F 46 C2
St. Maximin-la-Ste. Baume F 65 C4
St. Méard-de-Gurçon F 62 B3
St. Médard-de-Guizières F 62 A2
St. Médard-en-Jalles F 62 B2
St. Méen-le-Grand F 43 B3
St. Menges F 45 A5
St. Město CZ 40 C1
St. M'Hervé F 43 B4
St. Michel, *Aisne* F 45 A5
St. Michel, *Gers* F 63 C3
St. Michel-Chef-Chef F 52 A2
St. Michel-de-Maurienne F 55 C6
St. Michel-en-Grève F 42 B2
St. Michel-en-l'Herm F 52 B3
St. Michel-Mont-Mercure F 52 B4
St. Mihiel F 46 B1
St. Montant F 64 B3
St. Moritz CH 57 B4
St. Nazaire F 52 A2
St. Nazaire-en-Royans F 65 A4
St. Nazaire-le-Désert F 65 B4
St. Nectaire F 54 C2
St. Nicolas-de-Port F 46 B2
St. Nicolas-de-Redon F 43 C3
St. Nicolas-du-Pélem F 42 B2
St. Niklaas B 35 B5
St. Omer F 34 C3

Sant Josep E 83 C4
Sant Julià de Lòria AND 77 A4
Sant Llorenç de Morunys E 77 A4
Sant Llorenç des Carctassar, *Mallorca* E 83
Sant Llorenç Savall E 77 B5
Sant Luis, *Menorca* E 83
Sant Marti de Llemaná E 77 A5
Sant Marti de Maldá E 77 B4
Sant Marti Sarroca E 77 B4
Sant Mateu E 76 C3
Sant Miquel E 83 B4
Sant Pau de Seguries E 77 A5
Sant Pere de Riudebitlles E 77 B4
Sant Pere Pescador E 77 A6
Sant Pere Sallavinera E 77 B4
Sant Quirze de Besora E 77 A5
Sant Rafel E 83 C4
Sant Ramon E 77 B4
Sant Vincenç de Castellet E 77 B4
Santa Agnès E 83 B4
Santa Amalia E 79 B4
Santa Ana, *Cáceres* E 79 B5
Santa Ana, *Jaén* E 86 B2
Santa Ana de Pusa E 80 C2
Santa Barbara E 76 C3
Santa Barbara de Casa E 84 B3
Santa Bárbara de Padrões P 84 B3
Santa Catarina P 84 B3
Santa Caterina di Pittinuri I 96 C1
Santa Caterina Villarmosa I 95 B3
Santa Cesárea Terme I 93 A5
Santa Clara-a-Nova P 84 B2
Santa Clara-a-Velha P 84 B2
Santa Clara de Louredo P 84 B3
Santa Coloma de Farners E 77 B5
Santa Coloma de Gramenet E 77 B5
Santa Coloma de Queralt E 77 B4
Santa Colomba de Curueño E 74 B1
Santa Colomba de Somoza E 72 B4
Santa Comba E 72 A2
Santa Comba Dáo P 78 A2
Santa Comba de Rossas P 73 C4
Santa Cristina I 57 C4
Santa Cristina de la Polvorosa E 74 B1
Santa Croce Camerina I 95 C3
Santa Croce di Magliano I 89 B4
Santa Cruz E 72 A2
Santa Cruz P 78 B1
Santa Cruz de Alhama E 86 B2
Santa Cruz de Campezo E 75 B4
Santa Cruz de Grio E 75 C5
Santa Cruz de la Salceda E 75 C3
Santa Cruz de la Sierra E 79 B5
Santa Cruz de la Zarza E 81 C3
Santa Cruz de Moya E 82 B1
Santa Cruz de Mudela E 86 A2
Santa Cruz de Paniagua E 79 A4
Santa Cruz del Retamar E 80 B2
Santa Cruz del Valle E 80 B1
Santa Doménica Talao I 92 B2
Santa Doménica Vittória I 95 B3
Santa Elena E 86 A2
Santa Elena de Jamuz E 74 B1
Santa Eufemia E 86 A1
Santa Eufémia d'Aspromonte I 92 C2
Santa Eulalia E 81 B5
Santa Eulália P 79 C3
Santa Eulalia de Oscos E 72 A3
Santa Eulàlia des Riu E 83 C4
Santa Fe E 86 B2
Santa Fiora I 67 D5
Santa Gertrude I 57 B5
Santa Giustina I 58 B2
Santa Iria P 84 B3
Santa Leocadia P 73 C2
Santa Lucia-de-Porto-Vecchio F 96 B2
Santa Lucia del Mela I 95 A4
Santa Luzia P 84 B2
Santa Maddalena Vallalta I 58 B2
Santa Magdalena de Polpis E 76 C3
Santa Margalida, *Mallorca* E 83
Santa Margarida P 78 B2
Santa Margarida do Sado P 84 A2
Santa Margaridao de Montbui E 77 B4
Santa Margherita I 96 E1
Santa Margherita di Belice I 94 B2
Santa Margherita Ligure I 66 B3
Santa Maria CH 57 B5
Santa Maria E 76 A2
Santa Maria al Bagno I 91 B4
Santa Maria Cápua Vétere I 89 B4
Santa Maria da Feira P 73 D2
Santa Maria de Cayón E 74 A3
Santa Maria de Corco E 77 A5
Santa Maria de Huerta E 81 A4
Santa Maria de la Alameda E 80 B2
Santa Maria de las Hoyas E 75 C3
Santa Maria de Mercadillo E 75 C3
Santa Maria de Nieva E 87 B4
Santa Maria de Trassierra E 86 B1
Santa Maria del Camí, *Mallorca* E 83
Santa Maria del Campo E 74 B3
Santa Maria del Campo Rus E 81 C4
Santa Maria del Páramo E 74 B1
Santa Maria del Taro I 66 B3
Santa Maria della Versa I 66 B3
Santa Maria di Licodia I 95 B3
Santa Maria-di-Rispéscia I 67 D5
Santa Maria la Real de Nieva E 80 A2
Santa Maria Maggiore I 56 B3
Santa Maria Ribarredonda E 75 B3
Santa Marina del Rey E 74 B1
Santa Marinella I 88 A1
Santa Marta, *Albacete* E 81 C4
Santa Marta, *Badajoz* E 79 C4
Santa Marta de Magasca E 79 B4
Santa Marta de Penaguião P 73 C3
Santa Marta de Tormes E 80 B1
Santa Ninfa I 94 B1
Santa Olalla, *Huelva* E 85 B4
Santa Olalla, *Toledo* E 80 B2
Santa Pau E 77 A5
Santa Pola E 82 C2
Santa Ponça, *Mallorca* E 83
Santa Severa F 66 D3
Santa Severa I 88 A1
Santa Severina I 93 B3
Santa Sofia I 67 C5
Santa Suzana, *Évora* P 78 C3
Santa Suzana, *Setúbal* P 78 C2
Santa Teresa di Riva I 95 B4
Santa Teresa Gallura I 96 B2
Santa Uxía E 72 B2
Santa Valburga I 57 B5
Santa Vittória in Matenano I 68 C2
Santacara E 75 B5
Santadi I 96 D1
Santaella E 86 B1
Sant'Àgata dei Goti I 89 B4
Sant'Àgata di Ésaro I 92 B2
Sant'Àgata di Puglia I 90 A2
Sant'Agata Feltria I 68 C1
Sant'Àgata Militello I 95 A3
Santana, *Évora* P 78 C2
Santana, *Setúbal* P 78 C1
Santana da Serra P 84 B2
Sant'Ana de Cambas P 84 B3
Santana do Mato P 78 C2
Sant'Anastasia I 89 C4
Santander E 74 A3
Sant'Andrea Frius I 96 D2
Sant'Àngelo dei Lombardi I 90 B2
Sant'Angelo in Vado I 68 C1
Sant'Angelo Lodigiano I 57 C4
Sant'Antíoco I 96 D1
Sant'Antonio-di-Gallura I 96 C2
Santanyí, *Mallorca* E 83
Santarcángelo di Romagna I 68 B1
Santarém P 78 B2
Santas Martas E 74 B1
Sant'Caterina I 67 D5
Santed E 81 A5
Sant'Egídio alla Vibrata I 68 D2
Sant'Elia a Pianisi I 89 B4
Sant'Elia Fiumerapido I 89 B3
Santelices E 74 A3
Sant'Elpídio a Mare I 68 C2
Santéramo in Colle I 91 B3
Santervas de la Vega E 74 B2
Santhià I 56 C3
Santiago de Alcántara E 79 B3
Santiago de Calatrava E 86 B1
Santiago de Compostela E 72 B2
Santiago de la Espade E 87 A3
Santiago de la Puebla E 80 B1
Santiago de la Ribera E 87 B5
Santiago de Litem P 78 B2
Santiago del Campo E 79 B4
Santiago do Cacém P 84 B2
Santiago do Escoural P 78 C2
Santiago Maior P 78 C3
Santibáñez de Béjar E 79 A5
Santibáñez de la Peña E 74 B2
Santibáñez de Murias E 74 A1
Santibáñez de Vidriales E 73 B4
Santibáñez el Alto E 79 A4
Santibáñez el Bajo E 79 A4
Santillana E 74 A2
Santiponce E 85 B4
Santisteban del Puerto E 86 A2
Santiuste de San Juan Bautiste E 80 A2
Santiz E 80 A1
Sant'Ilario d'Enza I 67 B4
Santo Aleixo P 84 A3
Santo Amado P 84 A3
Santo Amaro P 78 C3
Santo André P 84 A2
Santo Domingo E 79 C3
Santo Domingo de la Calzada E 75 B4
Santo Domingo de Silos E 75 C3
Santo Estêvão, *Faro* P 84 B3
Santo Estêvão, *Santarém* P 78 C2
Santo-Pietro-di Tenda F 96 A2
Santo Spirito I 91 A3
Santo Stefano d'Aveto I 66 B3
Santo Stéfano di Camastra I 95 A3
Santo Stefano di Magra I 67 B3
Santo Stéfano Quisquina I 94 B2
Santo Tirso P 73 C2
Santo Tomé E 86 A2
Santok PL 32 C1
Santomera E 87 A4
Santoña E 75 A3
Sant'Oreste I 88 A2
Santotis E 74 A2
Santovenia, *Burgos* E 75 B3
Santovenia, *Zamora* E 74 C1
Santpedor E 77 B4
Santu Lussurgiu I 96 C1
Santutzi E 75 A3
Sanxenxo E 72 B2
Sanza I 92 A2
São Aleixo P 78 C3
São Barnabé P 84 B2
São Bartolomé da Serra P 84 A2
São Bartolomeu de Messines P 84 B2
São Bento P 73 C2
São Brás P 84 B3
São Brás de Alportel P 84 B3
São Braz do Reguedoura P 78 C2
São Cristóvão P 78 C2
São Domingos P 84 B2
São Geraldo P 78 C2
São Jacinto P 78 A2
São João da Madeira P 73 D2
São João da Pesqueira P 73 C3
São João da Ribeira P 78 B2
São João da Serra P 73 D2
São João da Venda P 84 B3
São João dos Caldeireiros P 84 B3
São Julião P 78 B3
São Leonardo P 78 C3
São Luis P 84 B2
São Manços P 78 C3
São Marcos da Ataboeira P 84 B3
Saõ Marcos da Serra P 84 B2
São Marcos de Campo P 78 C3
São Martinho da Cortiça P 78 A2
São Martinho das Amoreiras P 84 B2
São Martinho do Porto P 78 B1
São Matias, *Beja* P 84 A3
São Matias, *Évora* P 78 C2
São Miguel d'Acha P 78 A3
São Miguel de Machede P 78 C3
São Pedro da Torre P 73 C2
São Pedro de Muel P 78 B1
São Pedro de Solis P 84 B3
São Pedro do Sul P 73 D2
São Romão P 78 C2
São Sebastião dos Carros P 84 B3
São Teotónio P 84 B2
São Torcato P 73 C2
Saorge F 66 C1
Sapanca TR 16 R22
Sapataria P 78 C1
Sápes GR 16 R19
Sapiãos P 73 C3
Sappada I 58 B2
Sapri I 90 B2
Sarajevo BIH 70 C3
Saramon F 63 C3
Sarandës AL 15 S17
Saranovo YU 71 B5
Saraorci YU 71 B6
Saray TR 16 R20
Sarayköy TR 16 T21
Sarbia PL 32 C2
Sarbinowo PL 31 C6
Sarbinowo PL 32 A1
Sárbogárd H 60 B3
Sarcelles F 44 A3
Sarche I 57 B5
Sardoal P 78 B2
Sardón de Duero E 74 C2
Sare F 62 C1
S'Arenal, *Mallorca* E 83
Šarengrad HR 61 C4
Sarentino I 57 B6
Sarezzo I 57 C5
Sargans CH 57 A4
Sári H 61 A4
Sari-d'Orcino F 96 A1
Sarıgöl TR 16 S21
Sarilhos Grandes P 78 C2
Sariñena E 76 B2
Sárisáp H 51 C4
Sarıyer TR 16 R21
Sarkad H 61 B6
Sárkeresztes H 60 A3
Sárkeresztúr H 60 A3
Şarköy TR 16 R20
Sarlat-la-Canéda F 63 B4
Sarliac-sur-l'Isle F 53 C5
Sármellék H 60 B2
Särna S 2 F13
Sarnadas P 78 B3
Sarnano I 68 C2
Sarnen CH 56 B3
Sárnico I 57 C4
Sarno I 89 C4
Sarnonico I 57 B6
Sarnow D 31 B5
Sarny UA 11 L20
Särö S 24 B4
Saronno I 56 C4
Sárosd H 60 A3
Šarovce SK 51 B4
Sarpsborg N 20 B3
Sarracín E 74 B3
Sarral E 77 B4
Sarralbe F 46 A3
Sarrancolin F 63 D4
Sarras F 55 C4
Sarre I 56 C2
Sarre-Union F 46 B3
Sarreaus E 73 B3
Sarrebourg F 46 B3
Sarreguemines F 46 A3
Sárrétudvari H 61 A6
Sarria E 72 B3
Sarrià de Ter E 77 A5
Sarrión E 82 A2
Sarroca de Lleida E 76 B3
Sarroch I 96 D2
Sarron F 62 C2
Sársina I 68 C1
Sarstedt D 37 A5
Sárszentlõrinc H 60 B3
Sárszentmihaly H 60 A3
Sárszentmiklós H 60 B3
Sarteano I 67 D5
Sartène F 96 B1
Sartilly F 43 B4
Sartirana Lomellina I 66 A2
Sárvár H 60 A1
Sarzana I 67 B3
Sarzeau F 52 A2
Sarzedas P 78 B3
Sas van Gent NL 35 B4
Sasamón E 74 B2
Sásd H 60 B3
Sasino PL 32 A3
Sássari I 96 C1
Sassello I 66 B2
Sassenberg D 36 B4
Sassetta I 67 C4
Sassnitz D 31 A5
Sasso d'Ombrone I 67 D5
Sasso Marconi I 67 B5
Sassocorvaro I 68 C1
Sassoferrato I 68 C1
Sassoleone I 67 B5
Sassuolo I 67 B4
Sástago E 76 B2
Šaštinske Stráže SK 50 B3
Satão P 73 D3
Såtenäs S 21 C4
Säter S 22 A2
Sätila S 26 B2
Satillieu F 55 C4
Satnica Đakovačka HR 60 C3
Sátoraljaújhely H 10 M17
Satow D 30 B3
Sätra-brunn S 22 B3
Satrup D 29 A6
Satteins A 57 A4
Satu Mare RO 11 N18
Saturnia I 88 A1
Saucats F 62 B2
Saucelle E 73 C4
Sauda N 18 B3
Saudasjøen N 18 B3
Sauerlach D 48 C2
Saugues F 64 B2
Sauherad N 19 B6
Saujon F 52 C4
Sauland N 19 B5
Saulces Monclin F 45 A5
Saulgau D 47 B5
Saulgrub D 48 C2
Saulieu F 55 A4
Sault F 65 B4
Sault-Brénaz F 55 C5
Sault-de-Navailles F 62 C2
Saulx F 46 C2
Saulxures-sur-Moselotte F 46 C2
Saulzais-le-Potier F 54 B2
Saumos F 62 B1
Saumur F 53 A4
Saurat F 63 D4
Sáuris I 58 B2
Sausset-les-Pins F 65 C4
Sauteyrargues F 64 C2
Sauvagnat F 54 C2
Sauve F 64 C2
Sauveterre-de-Béarn F 62 C2
Sauveterre-de-Guyenne F 62 B2
Sauviat-sur-Vige F 53 C6
Sauxillanges F 54 C3
Sauzé-Vaussais F 53 B5
Sauzet, *Drôme* F 64 B3
Sauzet, *Lot* F 63 B4
Sauzon F 52 A1
Sava I 91 B4
Savarsin RO 11 N18
Savci SLO 59 B6
Säve S 21 D3
Savelletri I 91 B4
Savelli I 93 B3
Savenay F 52 A3
Saverdun F 63 C4
Saverne F 46 B3
Savières F 45 B4
Savigliano I 66 B1
Savignac-les-Eglises F 53 C5
Savignano Irpino I 90 A2
Savignano sul Rubicone I 68 B1
Savigny-sur-Braye F 44 C1
Saviñán E 75 C5
Savines-le-lac F 65 B5
Savino Selo YU 61 C4
Savio I 68 B1
Sävja S 22 B4
Šavnik YU 71 D4
Savognin CH 57 B4
Savona I 66 B2
Savonlinna FIN 3 F21
Sävsjö S 26 B4
Sävsjöström S 26 B5
Savudrija HR 58 C3
Sax E 82 C2
Saxdalen S 22 A1
Saxmundham GB 4 K7
Sayalonga E 86 C1
Sayatón E 81 B4
Sayda D 38 C3
Sázava, *Jihomoravský* CZ 50 A1
Sázava, *Středočeský* CZ 49 A5
Scaër F 42 B2
Scafa I 89 A4
Scalea I 92 B2
Scaletta Zanclea I 95 A4
Scandale I 93 B3
Scandiano I 67 B4
Scandicci I 67 C5
Scandolara Ravara I 67 A4
Scanno I 89 B3
Scansano I 88 A1
Scanzano Jónico I 91 B3
Scarborough GB 4 J6
Scardovari I 68 B1
Scarperia I 67 C5
Scey-sur-Saône et St. Albin F 46 C1
Sch-en-feld D 48 A3
Schachendorf A 59 A6
Schaffhausen CH 47 C4
Schafstädt D 38 B1
Schafstedt D 29 A6
Schäftlarn D 48 C2
Schagen NL 28 C1
Schalkau D 37 C7
Schangnau CH 56 B2
Schapbach D 47 B4
Scharbeutz D 30 A2
Schärding A 49 B4
Scharnitz A 57 A6
Scharrel D 29 B4
Schattendorf A 50 C2
Scheemda NL 28 B3
Scheessel D 29 B6
Schéggia I 68 C1
Scheibbs A 49 B6
Scheibenberg D 38 C2
Scheidegg D 47 C5
Scheifling A 59 A4
Scheinfeld D 47 A6
Schelklingen D 47 B5
Schenefeld, *Schleswig-Holstein* D 29 A6
Schenefeld, *Schleswig-Holstein* D 30 B1
Schenklengsfeld D 37 C5
Scherfede D 37 B5
Schermbeck D 36 B2
Scherpenzeel NL 35 A6
Schesslitz D 38 D1
Scheveningen NL 35 A5
Schiedam NL 35 B5
Schieder-Schwalenberg D 37 B5
Schierling D 48 B3
Schiers CH 57 B4
Schildau D 38 B2
Schillingen D 46 A2
Schillingsfürst D 47 A6
Schilpário I 57 B5
Schiltach D 47 B4
Schiltigheim F 46 B3
Schio I 57 C6
Schirmeck F 46 B3
Schirnding D 38 C2
Schkeuditz D 38 B2
Schkölen D 38 B1
Schlabendorf D 39 B3
Schladen D 37 A6
Schladming A 58 A3
Schlangen D 37 B4
Schleiden D 36 C2
Schleiz D 38 C1
Schleswig D 29 A6
Schleusingen D 37 C6
Schlieben D 38 B3
Schliengen D 46 C3
Schliersee D 48 C2
Schlitz D 37 C5
Schloss Neuhans D 37 B4
Schlossvippach D 38 B1
Schlotheim D 37 B6
Schluchsee D 47 C4
Schlüchtern D 37 C5
Schmallenberg D 36 B4
Schmelz D 46 A2
Schmidmühlen D 48 A2
Schmiedeberg D 39 C3
Schmiedefeld D 37 C6
Schmirn A 58 A1
Schmölln, *Brandenburg* D 31 B6
Schmölln, *Sachsen* D 38 C2
Schnaittach D 48 A2
Schneeberg D 38 C2
Schneizlreuth D 48 C3
Schneverdingen D 30 B1
Schöder A 59 A4
Schoenburg B 36 C2
Schollene D 30 C4
Schöllkrippen D 37 C5
Schomberg D 47 B4
Schönach D 48 B3
Schönau, *Baden-Württemberg* D 46 C3
Schönau, *Bayern* D 48 B3
Schönbeck D 31 B5
Schönberg, *Bayern* D 49 B4
Schönberg, *Mecklenburg-Vorpommern* D 30 B2
Schönberg, *Schleswig-Holstein* D 30 A2
Schönebeck D 38 A1
Schöneck D 38 C2
Schönecken- D 36 C2
Schönermark D 31 B5
Schönewalde D 38 B3
Schongau D 48 C1
Schöngrabern A 50 B2
Schönhagen D 37 B5
Schönhausen D 30 C4
Schöningen D 37 A6
Schönkirchen D 30 A2
Schönsee D 48 A3
Schönthal D 48 A3
Schonungen D 37 C6
Schönwalde D 30 A2
Schoondijke NL 35 B4
Schoonebeek NL 28 C3
Schoonhoven NL 35 B5
Schopfheim D 46 C3
Schöppenstedt D 37 A6
Schörfling A 49 C4
Schorndorf D 47 B5
Schortens D 29 B4
Schotten D 37 C5
Schramberg D 47 B4
Schraplau D 38 B1
Schrattenberg A 50 B2
Schrecksbach D 37 C5
Schrems A 49 B6
Schrobenhausen D 48 B2
Schröcken A 57 A5
Schrozberg D 47 A5
Schruns A 57 A4
Schüpfheim CH 56 B3
Schüttorf D 36 A3
Schwaan D 30 B4
Schwabach D 48 A2
Schwäbisch Gmünd D 47 B5
Schwäbisch Hall D 47 A5
Schwabmünchen D 48 B1
Schwadorf A 50 B2
Schwagstorf D 29 C4
Schwaigern D 47 A5
Schwalmstadt D 37 C5
Schwanberg A 59 B5
Schwanden CH 56 B4
Schwandorf D 48 A3
Schwanebeck D 38 B1
Schwanenstadt A 49 B4
Schwanewede D 29 B5
Schwanfeld D 47 A6
Schwangau D 48 C1
Schwarmstedt D 29 C6
Schwarz-heide D 39 B3
Schwarza D 37 C6
Schwarzach im Pongau A 58 A3
Schwarzau im Gebirge A 49 C6
Schwarzenau A 49 B6
Schwarzenbach Markt D 38 C1
Schwarzenbach am Wald D 38 C1
Schwarzenbek D 30 B2
Schwarzenberg D 38 C2
Schwarzenburg CH 56 B2
Schwaz A 58 A1
Schwechat A 50 B2
Schwedt D 31 B6
Schwei D 29 B5
Schweich D 46 A2
Schweighausen D 46 B3
Schweinfurt D 37 C6
Schweinitz D 38 B3
Schweinrich D 31 B4
Schwelm D 36 B3
Schwemsal D 38 B2
Schwendt A 48 C3
Schwenningen D 47 B4
Schwepnitz D 39 B3
Schwerin D 30 B3
Schwerte D 36 B3
Schwetzingen D 47 A4
Schwyz CH 56 A3
Sciacca I 94 B2
Scicli I 95 C3
Ściechów PL 31 C6
Scigliano I 92 B3
Scilla I 92 C2
Ścinawa PL 39 B6
Scionzier F 55 B6
Scoglitti I 95 C3
Scopello, *Piemonte* I 56 C3
Scopello, *Sicilia* I 94 A1
Scordia I 95 B3
Scorzè I 58 C2
Scritto I 68 C1
Scunthorpe GB 4 K6
Scuol CH 57 B5
Scúrcola Marsicana I 89 A3
Sebazac-Concourès F 63 B5
Sebečevo YU 71 C5
Seben TR 16 R22
Sebersdorf A 59 A5
Sebezh RUS 7 H21
Sebnitz D 39 C4
Seborga I 66 C1
Seč, *Vychodočeský* CZ 49 A6
Seč, *Západočeský* CZ 49 A4
Sečanj YU 61 C5
Secemin PL 41 C4
Seckau A 59 A4
Seclin F 35 C4
Secondigny F 53 B4
Seda P 78 B3
Sedan F 45 A5
Sedano E 74 B3
Sedella E 86 C1
Séderon F 65 B4
Sedico I 58 B2
Sédilo I 96 C1
Sédini I 96 C1
Sedlarica HR 60 C2
Sedlčany CZ 49 A5
Sedlec-Prčice CZ 49 A5
Sedlice CZ 49 A4
Sędziejowice PL 41 B4
Sędziszów PL 41 C5
Sędziszów Małapolski PL 41 C6
Seebach F 46 B3
Seeboden A 58 B3
Seefeld, *Brandenburg* D 31 C5
Seefeld, *Niedersachsen* D 29 B5
Seefeld in Tirol A 57 A6
Seehausen, *Sachsen-Anhalt* D 30 C3
Seehausen, *Sachsen-Anhalt* D 38 A1
Seeheim-Jugenheim D 47 A4
Seelbach D 46 B3
Seelow D 31 C6
Seelze D 29 C6
Seerhausen D 38 B3
Sées F 43 B6
Seesen D 37 B6
Seeshaupt D 48 C2
Seewalchen A 49 C4
Seferihisar TR 16 S20
Sefkerin YU 71 A5
Segerstad S 20 B5
Segesd H 60 B2
Segmon S 20 B5
Segonzac F 53 C4
Segorbe E 82 B2
Segovia E 80 B2
Segré F 43 C5
Ségur-les-Villas F 54 C2
Segura E 75 B4
Segura P 79 B3
Segura de León E 85 A4
Segura de los Baños E 76 C2
Segurrilla E 80 B2
Sehnde D 30 C1
Seia P 78 A3
Seiches-sur-le-Loir F 43 C5
Seifhennersdorf D 39 C4
Seignelay F 45 C4
Seijo E 73 C2
Seilhac F 53 C6
Seilles B 35 C6
Seinäjoki FIN 3 E18
Seissan F 63 C3
Seitenstetten Markt A 49 B5
Seixal P 78 C1
Seiz A 59 A4
Seizthal A 59 A4
Sejerslev DK 24 C1
Seksna RUS 7 G26
Selárgius I 96 D2
Selb D 38 C2
Selby GB 4 K6
Selca HR 70 C1
Selce HR 59 C4
Selçuk TR 16 T20
Selde DK 24 C2
Selenča YU 61 C4
Sélestat F 46 B3
Seleuš YU 71 A5
Selevac YU 71 B5
Selgua E 76 B3
Selice SK 50 B3
Seligenstadt D 37 C4
Seligenthal D 37 C6
Selizharovo RUS 7 H23
Seljord N 19 B5
Sellano I 68 D1
Selles-St. Denis F 54 A1
Selles-sur-Cher F 53 A6
Sellières F 55 B5
Sellin D 31 A5
Sellye H 60 C2
Selm D 36 B3
Selnica ob Dravi SLO 59 B5
Selongey F 45 C6
Selonnet F 65 B5
Selow D 30 B3
Selsingen D 29 B6
Selters D 36 C3
Seltso RUS 7 K24
Seltz F 47 B4
Selva, *Mallorca* E 83
Selva di Cadore I 58 B2
Selva di Val Gardena I 58 B1
Selvik N 20 B2
Selvino I 57 C4
Selyatyn UA 11 N19
Sem N 20 B2
Semeljci HR 60 C3
Semenovka, *Chernihiv* UA 7 K23
Semenovka, *Kremenchuk* UA 11 M23
Semič SLO 59 C5
Semide F 45 A5
Semide P 78 A2
Semily CZ 39 C5
Seminara I 92 C2
Semlac RO 61 B5
Semmen-stedt D 37 A6
Šempeter SLO 59 B5
Semriach A 59 A5
Semur-en-Auxois F 55 A4
Sena E 76 B2
Sena de Luna E 74 B1
Senarpont F 44 A2
Sénas F 65 C4
Senčanski Trešnjevac YU 61 C4
Sencelles, *Mallorca* E 83
Senčur SLO 59 B4
Senden, *Bayern* D 47 B6

Tyringe S 27 C3
Tyrislöt S 23 C3
Tyristrand N 20 A2
Tysnes N 18 A2
Tyssedal N 18 A3
Tystberga S 23 C4
Tysvær N 18 B2
Tzummarum NL 28 B2

U

Ub YU 71 B5
Ubby DK 25 D4
Úbeda E 86 A2
Überlingen D 47 C5
Ubidea E 75 A4
Ubli HR 70 D1
Ubrique E 85 C5
Ucero E 75 C3
Uchaud F 64 C3
Uchte D 29 C5
Uckerath D 36 C3
Uclés E 81 C4
Ucria I 95 A3
Udbina HR 69 B4
Uddebo S 26 B3
Uddeholm S 20 A5
Uddevalla S 21 C3
Uddheden S 20 B4
Uden NL 35 B6
Uder D 37 B6
Udiča SK 51 A4
Údine I 58 B3
Udvar H 60 C3
Ueckermünde D 31 B6
Uelsen D 28 C3
Uelzen D 30 C2
Uetendorf CH 56 B2
Uetersen D 29 B6
Uetze D 30 C2
Uffenheim D 47 A6
Ugarana E 75 A4
Ugento I 93 B5
Ugerldse DK 25 D4
Uggerslev DK 25 D3
Uggiano la Chiesa I 93 A5
Ugijar E 86 C2
Ugine F 55 C6
Uglejevik BIH 70 B4
Uglenes N 18 A2
Uglich RUS 7 H26
Ugljane HR 69 C5
Ugod H 60 A2
Uherské Hradiště CZ 50 A3
Uherský Brod CZ 50 A3
Uherský Ostroh CZ 50 B3
Uhingen D 47 B5
Uhlířské-Janovice CZ 49 A6
Uhřiněves CZ 39 C4
Uhyst D 39 B4
Uig GB 4 H3
Uitgeest NL 28 C1
Uithoorn NL 35 A5
Uithuizen NL 28 B3
Uithuizermeeden NL 28 B3
Uivar RO 61 C5
Ujazd PL 40 C3
Ujazd PL 41 B4
Ujhartyán H 61 A4
Újkígyós H 61 B6
Ujpetre H 60 C3
Ujście PL 32 B2
Ujsolt H 61 B4
Újszász H 61 A5
Ujué E 75 B5
Ukanc SLO 58 B3
Ukmergė LT 6 J19
Ukna S 23 C3
Ul'anka SK 51 B5
Ulàssai I 96 D2
Ulcinj YU 15 R16
Uldum DK 25 D2
Ulefoss N 19 B6
Uleila del Campo E 87 B3
Ulfborg DK 25 C1
Uljma YU 71 A6
Ullapool GB 4 H4
Ullared S 26 B2
Ullatun N 18 B3
Ulldecona E 76 C3
Ulldemolins E 76 B3
Ullerslev DK 25 D3
Ullervad S 21 C5
Üllés H 61 B4
Üllö H 61 A4
Ullvi S 22 B3
Ulm D 47 B5
Ulme P 78 B2
Ulmen D 36 C2
Ulog BIH 70 C3
Ulricehamn S 21 D5
Ulrichstein D 37 C5
Ulrika S 23 C2
Ulrum NL 28 B3
Ulsberg N 2 E12
Ulsted DK 24 B3
Ulstrup, *Vestsjællands Amt.* DK 25 D3
Ulstrup, *Viborg Amt.* DK 25 C2
Ulubey TR 16 S21
Uluborlu TR 16 S22
Umag HR 58 C3
Uman UA 11 M22
Umba RUS 3 C24
Umbértide I 68 C1
Umbriático I 93 B3
Umčari YU 71 B5
Umeå S 3 E17
Umhausen A 57 A5
Umka YU 71 B5
Umljanovic HR 69 C5
Uncastillo E 76 A1
Undenäs S 23 C1
Unecha RUS 7 K23
Unešić HR 69 C5
Úněšov CZ 48 A4
Ungheni MD 11 N20
Unhais da Serra P 78 A3
Unhošt CZ 39 C4
Unichowo PL 32 A3
Uničov CZ 50 A3
Uniejów PL 40 B3
Unisław PL 33 B4
Unkel D 36 C3
Unken A 48 C3
Unna D 36 B3
Unnaryd S 26 C3
Unquera E 74 A2
Unter Langkampfen A 58 A2
Unter-steinbach D 47 A6
Unterach A 49 C4
Unterägeri CH 56 A3
Unterammergau D 48 C2
Unterhaching D 48 B2
Unteriberg CH 56 A3
Unterkochen D 47 B6
Unterlaussa A 49 C5
Unterlüss D 30 C2
Untermünkheim D 47 A5
Unterschächen CH 56 B3
Unterschleissheim D 48 B2
Unterschwaningen D 48 A1
Untersiemau D 37 C6
Unterweissenbach A 49 B5
Unterzell D 48 A3
Úpice CZ 39 C6
Upphärad S 21 C4
Upplands-Väsby S 22 B4
Uppsala S 22 B4
Ur F 77 A4
Uras I 96 D1
Uraz PL 40 B1
Urbánia I 68 C1
Urbino I 68 C1
Urçay F 54 B2
Urda E 80 C3
Urdax E 62 C1
Urdilde E 72 B2
Urdos F 62 D2
Urk NL 28 C2
Úrkút H 60 A2
Urla TR 16 S20
Urnäsch CH 57 A4
Uroševac YU 15 Q17
Urracal E 87 B3
Urries E 76 A1
Urroz E 75 B5
Ursensollen D 48 A2
Urshult S 26 C4
Uršna Sela SLO 59 C5
Urszulewo PL 33 C5
Ury F 44 B3
Urziceni RO 11 P20
Urzulei I 96 C2
Usagre E 79 C4
Uşak TR 16 S21
Ušće YU 71 C5
Usedom D 31 B5
Useldange L 46 A1
Usellus I 96 D1
Ushakovo RUS 33 A6
Usingen D 37 C4
Usini I 96 C1
Uskedal N 18 B2
Uslar D 37 B5
Úsov CZ 50 A3
Usquert NL 28 B3
Ussássai I 96 D2
Ussé F 53 A5
Usséglio I 56 C2
Ussel, *Cantal* F 64 A1
Ussel, *Corrèze* F 54 C2
Usson-du-Poitou F 53 B5
Usson-en-Forez F 54 C3
Usson-les-Bains F 63 D5
Ust Luga RUS 7 G21
Ustaritz F 62 C1
Uštěk CZ 39 C4
Uster CH 56 A3
Ústi CZ 50 A3
Ústí nad Labem CZ 39 C4
Ústí nad Orlicí CZ 39 D6
Ustibar BIH 71 C4
Ustikolina BIH 70 C3
Ustipračà BIH 70 C4
Ustka PL 32 A2
Ustroń PL 51 A4
Ustronie Morskie PL 32 A1
Ustyuzhna RUS 7 G25
Uszód H 60 B3
Utåker N 18 B2
Utebo E 76 B2
Utena LT 7 J19
Utery CZ 48 A4
Utiel E 82 B1
Utö S 23 C5
Utrecht NL 35 A6
Utrera E 85 B5
Utrillas E 76 C2
Utsjoki FIN 3 B20
Utstein kloster N 18 B2
Uttendorf A 58 A2
Uttenweiler D 47 B5
Utterslev DK 25 E4
Utvälinge S 27 C2
Uusikaarlepyy FIN 3 E18
Uusikaupunki FIN 3 F17
Uvac BIH 71 C4
Uvaly CZ 39 C4
Uvdal N 19 A5
Uzdin YU 61 C5
Uzdowo PL 33 B6
Uzel F 42 B3
Uzerche F 53 C6
Uzès F 64 B3
Uzhhorod UA 11 M18
Uzhok UA 11 M18
Užice YU 71 C4
Uznach CH 56 A3
Uzunköprü TR 16 R20

V

Vaas F 44 C1
Vaasa FIN 3 E17
Vaassen NL 36 A1
Vabre F 63 C5
Vác H 51 C5
Vacha D 37 C6
Váchartyán H 51 C5
Väckelsång S 26 C4
Vacqueyras F 64 B3
Vad S 22 A2
Vada I 67 C4
Väddö S 22 B5
Väderstad S 23 C1
Vadheim N 2 F9
Vadillo de la Sierra E 80 B1
Vadillos E 81 B4
Vadla N 18 B3
Vado I 67 B5
Vado Ligure I 66 B2
Vadsø N 2 A21
Vadstena S 23 C1
Vadum DK 24 B2
Vaduz FL 57 A4
Væggerløse DK 30 A3
Vafos N 19 C6
Vág H 60 A2
Vaggeryd S 26 B4
Vaglia I 67 C5
Váglio Basilicata I 90 B2
Vagney F 46 B2
Vagnhärad S 23 C4
Vagnsunda S 22 B5
Vagos P 78 A2
Vaiano I 67 C5
Vaiges F 43 B5
Vaihingen D 47 B4
Vaillant F 45 C6
Vailly-sur-Aisne F 45 A4
Vailly-sur-Sauldre F 54 A2
Vairano Scalo I 89 B4
Vaison-la-Romaine F 65 B4
Vaite F 46 C1
Väjern S 21 C3
Vajszló H 60 C2
Vál H 60 A3
Val de San Lorenzo E 72 B4
Val de Santo Domingo E 80 B2
Val d'Esquières F 65 C5
Val-d'Isère F 56 C1
Val-Suzon F 55 A4
Val Thorens F 55 C6
Valaam RUS 3 F22
Valada P 78 B2
Valadares P 73 C2
Valado P 78 B1
Valandovo MK 15 R18
Valaská SK 51 B5
Valaská Belá SK 51 B4
Valaská Dubová SK 51 A5
Valašská Polanka CZ 50 A3
Valašské Klobouky CZ 50 A4
Valašské Meziříčí CZ 50 A3
Valberg F 65 B5
Vålberg S 20 B5
Valbo S 22 A4
Valbom P 73 C2
Valbondione I 57 B5
Valbonnais F 65 B4
Valbuena de Duero E 74 C2
Vâlcani RO 61 C5
Valdagno I 57 C6
Valdahon F 55 A6
Valdaracete E 81 B3
Valday RUS 7 H23
Valdealgorfa E 76 C2
Valdecaballeros E 80 C1
Valdecabras E 81 B4
Valdecarros E 80 B1
Valdeconcha E 81 B4
Valdeflores E 85 B4
Valdefresno E 74 B1
Valdeganga E 81 C5
Valdelacasa E 79 A5
Valdelacasa de Tajo E 80 C1
Valdelarco E 85 B4
Valdelosa E 80 A1
Valdeltormo E 76 C3
Valdelugeros E 74 B1
Valdemanco de Esteras E 86 A1
Valdemarsvik S 23 C3
Valdemorillo E 80 B2
Valdemoro E 80 B3
Valdemoro Sierra E 81 B5
Valdenoceda E 75 B3
Valdeobispo E 79 A4
Valdeolivas E 81 B4
Valdepeñas E 86 A2
Valdepeñas de Jaén E 86 B2
Valdepiélago E 74 B1
Valdepolo E 74 B1
Valderas E 74 B1
Valdérice I 94 A1
Valderrobres E 76 C3
Valderrueda E 74 B2
Valdestillas E 74 C2
Valdetorres E 79 C4
Valdetorres de Jarama E 81 B3
Valdeverdeja E 80 C1
Valdevimbre E 74 B1
Valdieri I 66 B1
Valdilecha E 81 B3
Valdobbiádene I 58 C1
Valdocondes E 75 C3
Valdoviño E 72 A2
Vale de Açor, *Beja* P 84 B3
Vale de Açor, *Portalegre* P 78 B3
Vale de Agua P 84 B2
Vale de Cambra P 73 D2
Vale de Lobo P 84 B2
Vale de Prazeres P 78 A3
Vale de Reis P 78 C2
Vale de Rosa P 84 B3
Vale de Santarém P 78 B2
Vale de Vargo P 84 B3
Vale do Peso P 78 B3
Valea lui Mihai RO 11 N18
Valega P 73 D2
Valéggio sul Mincio I 57 C5
Valeiro P 78 C2
Valença P 73 B2
Valençay F 53 A6
Valence, *Charente* F 53 C5
Valence, *Drôme* F 64 B3
Valence d'Agen F 63 B3
Valence-d'Albigeois F 63 B5
Valence-sur-Baise F 63 C3
Valencia E 82 B2
Valencia de Alcántara E 79 B3
Valencia de Don Juan E 74 B1
Valencia de las Torres E 79 C4
Valencia de Mombuey E 85 A3
Valencia del Ventoso E 85 A4
Valenciennes F 35 C4
Valensole F 65 C4
Valentano I 88 A1
Valentigney F 56 A1
Valentine F 63 C3
Valenza I 66 A2
Valenzuela E 86 B1
Valenzuela de Calatrava E 86 A2
Våler N 20 B2
Valera de Abajo E 81 C4
Valeria E 81 C4
Valestrand N 18 B2
Valevåg N 18 B2
Valfabbrica I 68 C1
Valflaunes F 64 C2
Valga EST 7 H20
Valgorge F 64 B3
Valgrisenche I 56 C2
Valguarnera Caropepe I 95 B3
Valhelhas P 78 A3
Valjevo YU 71 B4
Valka LV 7 H19
Valkeakoski FIN 3 F19
Valkenburg NL 36 C1
Valkenswaard NL 35 B6
Valkó H 51 C5
Vall d'Alba E 82 A2
Valla S 23 B3
Vallada E 82 C2
Vallado E 72 A4
Valladolid E 74 C2
Vallåkra S 27 D2
Vallata I 90 A2
Vallberga S 26 C3
Valldemossa, *Mallorca* E 83
Valle N 19 B4
Valle Castellana I 68 D2
Valle de Abdalajís E 86 C1
Valle de Cabuérniga E 74 A2
Valle de la Serena E 79 C5
Valle de Matamoros E 79 C4
Valle de Santa Ana E 79 C4
Valle Mosso I 56 C3
Valledolmo I 94 B2
Vallelado E 74 C2
Vallelunga Pratameno I 94 B2
Vallendar D 36 C3
Vallentuna S 22 B5
Valleraugue F 64 B2
Vallermosa I 96 D1
Vallet F 52 A3
Valletta M 14 U14
Vallfogona de Riucorb E 77 B4
Valli del Pasúbio I 57 C6
Vallo della Lucánia I 90 B2
Valloire F 55 C6
Vallombrosa I 67 C5
Vallon-Pont-d'Arc F 64 B3
Vallorbe CH 55 B6
Vallouise F 65 B5
Valls E 77 B4
Vallstena S 23 D5
Valmadrid E 76 B2
Valmiera LV 7 H19
Valmojado E 80 B2
Valmont F 44 A1
Valmontone I 88 B2
Valö S 22 A5
Valognes F 43 A4
Valonga P 78 A2
Valongo P 73 C2
Válor E 86 C2
Valoria la Buena E 74 C2
Valozhyn BY 7 J20
Valpaços P 73 C3
Valpelline I 56 C2
Valpiana I 67 C4
Valpovo HR 60 C3
Valras-Plage F 64 C2
Valréas F 64 B3
Vals CH 57 B4
Vals-les-Bains F 64 B3
Valsavarenche I 56 C2
Vålse DK 25 E4
Valsequillo E 79 C5
Valsonne F 55 C4
Valstagna I 58 C1
Valtablado del Rio E 81 B4
Valtice CZ 50 B2
Valtiendas E 74 C3
Valtierra E 75 B5
Valtopina I 68 C1
Valtorta I 57 C4
Valtournenche I 56 C2
Valverde E 75 C5
Valverde de Burguillos E 79 C4
Valverde de Júcar E 81 C4
Valverde de la Vera E 79 A5
Valverde de la Virgen E 74 B1
Valverde de Llerena E 85 A5
Valverde de Mérida E 79 C4
Valverde del Camino E 85 B4
Valverde del Fresno E 79 A4
Vamberk CZ 40 C1
Vamdrup DK 25 D2
Vammala FIN 3 F18
Vámosmikola H 51 C4
Vámosszabadi H 50 C3
Vanault-les-Dames F 45 B5
Vandel DK 25 D2
Vandenesse F 54 B3
Vandenesse-en-Auxois F 55 A4
Vandóies I 58 B1
Väne-Åsaka S 21 C4
Vänersborg S 21 C4
Vänersnäs S 21 C4
Vänge S 22 B4
Vangsnes N 2 F10
Vännäs S 3 E16
Vannes F 42 C3
Vansbro S 20 A6
Vanse N 18 C3
Vantaa FIN 3 F19
Vanyarc H 51 C5
Vaour F 63 B4
Vapnyarka UA 11 M21
Vaprio d'Adda I 57 C4
Vaqueiros P 84 B3
Vara S 21 C4
Varacieux F 55 C5
Varades F 52 A3
Varages F 65 C4
Varaldsøy N 18 A2
Varallo I 56 C3
Varano de'Melegari I 67 B4
Varaždin HR 59 B6
Varaždinske Toplice HR 59 B6
Varazze I 66 B2
Varberg S 26 B2
Varde DK 25 D1
Vardø N 2 A22
Vardomb H 60 B3
Varel D 29 B5
Varėna LT 6 J19
Vårenes N 18 B2
Varengeville-sur-Mer F 44 A1
Varenna I 57 B4
Varennes-en-Argonne F 45 A6
Varennes-le-Grand F 55 B4
Varennes-St. Sauveur F 55 B5
Varennes-sur-Allier F 54 B3
Varennes-sur-Amance F 46 C1
Vareš BIH 70 B3
Varese I 56 C3
Varese Ligure I 66 B3
Vârfurile RO 11 N18
Vårgårda S 21 C4
Vargas E 74 A3
Vargas P 78 B2
Vargön S 21 C4
Varhaug N 18 C2
Variaş RO 61 B5
Variaşu Mic RO 61 B6
Varilhes F 63 C4
Varin SK 51 A4
Väring S 21 C5
Váriz P 73 C4
Varkaus FIN 3 E20
Värmlands Bro S 20 B5
Värmskog S 20 B4
Varna BG 16 Q20
Varna YU 71 B4
Värnamo S 26 B4
Varnhem S 21 C5
Varnsdorf CZ 39 C4
Värö S 26 B2
Varoška Rijeka BIH 69 A5
Városlöd H 60 A2
Várpalota H 60 A3
Varreddes F 45 B3
Vars F 65 B5
Varsi I 67 B3
Varsseveld NL 36 B2
Vårsta S 22 B4
Vartofta S 21 C5
Varvarin YU 71 C6
Vårvik S 20 B4
Várvölgy H 60 B2
Varzi I 66 B3
Varzjelas P 78 A2
Varzo I 56 B3
Varzy F 54 A3
Vasad H 61 A4
Väse S 20 B5
Vašica YU 71 A4
Vasilevichi BY 7 K21
Väskinde S 23 D5
Vaskút H 61 B3
Vaslui RO 11 N20
Vassieux-en-Vercors F 65 B4
Vassmolösa S 26 C6
Vassy F 43 B5
Västerås S 22 B3
Västerby S 22 A2
Västerfärnebo S 22 B3
Västerhaninge S 22 B5
Västervik S 23 D3
Vasto I 89 A4
Västra Ämtervik S 20 B5
Västra-Bodarne S 21 D4
Västra Karup S 27 C2
Vasvár H 60 A1
Vasylkiv UA 11 L22
Vát H 60 A1
Vatan F 54 A1
Vatin YU 61 C6
Vatnås N 19 B6
Vätö S 22 B5
Vatra-Dornei RO 11 N19
Vatry F 45 B5
Vättholma S 22 B4
Vättis CH 57 B4
Vauchamps F 45 B4
Vauchassis F 45 B4
Vaucouleurs F 46 B1
Vaudoy-en-Brie F 45 B4
Vaulen N 18 C2
Vaulruz CH 56 B1
Vaulx Vraucourt F 34 C3
Vaumas F 54 B3
Vausseroux F 53 B4
Vauvenargues F 65 C4
Vauvert F 64 C3
Vauvillers F 46 C2
Vaux-sur-Sure B 46 A1
Vawkavysk BY 6 K19
Vaxholm S 22 B5
Växjö S 26 C4
Våxtorp S 27 C3
Vayrac F 63 B4
Važec SK 51 A5
Veberöd S 27 D3
Vechelde D 37 A6
Vechta D 29 C5
Vecinos E 80 B1
Vecsés H 61 A4
Vedavågen N 18 B2
Veddige S 26 B2
Vedersø DK 25 C1
Vedeseta I 57 C4
Vedevåg S 22 B2
Vedra E 72 B2
Vedum S 21 C4
Veendam NL 28 B3
Veenendaal NL 35 A6
Vega, *Asturias* E 74 A1
Vega, *Asturias* E 74 A1
Vega de Espinareda E 72 B4
Vega de Infanzones E 74 B1
Vega de Pas E 74 A3
Vega de Valcarce E 72 B4
Vega de Valdetronco E 74 C1
Vegadeo E 72 A3
Vegårshei N 19 C5
Vegas de Coria E 79 A4
Vegas del Condado E 74 B1
Vegby S 26 B3
Veggli N 19 A6
Veghel NL 35 B6
Véglie I 91 B4
Veguillas E 81 B3
Vegusdal N 19 C5
Veikåker N 19 A6
Veinge S 26 C3
Vejbystrand S 27 C2
Vejen DK 25 D2
Vejer de la Frontera E 85 C5
Vejle DK 25 D2
Vejprty CZ 38 C3
Vela Luka HR 69 D5
Velada E 80 B2
Velayos E 80 B2
Velbert D 36 B3
Velburg D 48 A2
Velden, *Bayern* D 48 A2
Velden, *Bayern* D 48 B3
Velden am Worther See A 59 B4
Velefique E 87 B3
Velen D 36 B2
Velenje SLO 59 B5
Veles MK 15 R17
Velesevec HR 59 C6
Velešin CZ 49 B5
Velestínon GR 15 S18
Velez Blanco E 87 B3
Vélez de Benaudalla E 86 C2
Vélez-Málaga E 86 C1
Vélez Rubio E 87 B3
Veli Lošinj HR 69 B3
Veliiki Radinci YU 71 A4
Velika HR 60 C2
Velika Drenova YU 71 C6
Velika Gorica HR 59 C6
Velika Grdevac HR 60 C2
Velika Greda YU 61 C6
Velika Ilova BIH 70 B2
Velika Kladuša BIH 59 C5
Velika Kopanica HR 60 C3
Velika Krsna YU 71 B5
Velika Obarska BIH 71 B4
Velika Pisanica HR 60 C2
Velika Plana YU 71 B5
Velika Zdenci HR 60 C2
Velike Lašče SLO 59 C4
Veliki Gaj YU 61 C6
Veliki Popović YU 71 B6
Velikiye Luki RUS 7 H22
Veliko Orašje YU 71 B6
Veliko Selo YU 71 B6
Veliko Tŭrnovo BG 16 Q19
Velilla de San Antonio E 81 B3
Velilla del Rio Carrió E 74 B2
Velizh RUS 7 J22
Veljun HR 59 C5
Velká Biteš CZ 50 A2
Velka Hled'scbe CZ 38 D2
Velká Lomnica SK 51 A6
Velká nad Veličkou CZ 50 B3
Velké Bystřice CZ 50 A3
Velké Heraltice CZ 50 A3
Velké Karlovice CZ 50 A4
Vel'ké Leváre SK 50 B3
Velké Losiny CZ 40 C2
Velké Meziříčí CZ 50 A2
Velké Pavlovice CZ 50 B2
Vel'ké Rovné SK 51 A4
Vel'ké Uherce SK 51 B4
Vel'ké Zálužie SK 50 B3
Vel'ke'Kostol'any SK 50 B3
Vel'ký Blahovo SK 51 B6
Velky Bor CZ 49 A4
Vel'ký Cetin SK 50 B4
Vel'ký Krtíš SK 51 B5
Vel'ký Meder SK 50 C3
Velky Ujezd CZ 50 A3
Vellahn D 30 B2
Vellberg D 47 A5
Velles F 53 B6
Velletri I 88 B2
Vellinge S 27 D3
Vellisca E 81 B4
Velliza E 74 C2
Vellmar D 37 B5
Velp NL 36 A1
Velten D 31 C5
Velvary CZ 39 C4
Vemb DK 25 C1
Veme N 20 A2
Véménd H 60 B3
Vemmedrup DK 25 D5
Vena S 26 B5
Venaco F 96 A2
Venafro I 89 B4
Venarey-les-Laumes F 55 A4
Venaría I 56 C2
Venasca I 66 B1
Venčane YU 71 B5
Vence F 65 C6
Venda Nova, *Coimbra* P 78 A2
Venda Nova, *Leiria* P 78 B2
Vendas Novas P 78 C2
Vendays-Montalivet F 52 C3
Vendel S 22 B4
Vendelso S 22 B5
Vendeuil F 45 A4
Vendeuvre-sur-Barse F 45 B5
Vendœuvres F 53 B6
Vendôme F 44 C2
Venelles F 65 C4
Venézia I 58 C2
Venialbo E 74 C1
Vénissieux F 55 C4
Venlo NL 36 B2
Vennesla N 19 C4
Vennesund N 2 D13
Venosa I 90 B2
Venray NL 36 B1
Vent A 57 B5
Venta de Baños E 74 C2
Venta de los Santos E 86 A2
Venta del Moro E 82 B1
Venta las Ranas E 74 A1
Ventanueva E 72 A4
Ventas de Huelma E 86 B2
Ventas de Zafarraya E 86 C1
Ventavon F 65 B4
Ventimíglia I 66 C1
Ventosa de la Sierra E 75 C4
Ventosilla E 75 C4
Ventspils LV 6 H17
Venturina I 67 C4
Venzolasca F 96 A2
Venzone I 58 B3
Vép H 60 A1
Vera E 87 B4
Vera Cruz P 84 A3
Vera de Bidasoa E 62 C1
Vera de Moncayo E 75 C5
Verbánia I 56 C3
Verberie F 44 A3
Verbicaro I 92 B2
Verbier CH 56 B2
Vercel-Villedieu-le-Camp F 55 A6
Vercelli I 56 C3
Verchen D 31 B4
Vercheny F 65 B4
Verclause F 65 B4
Verdalsøra N 2 E12
Verden D 29 C6
Verdens Ende N 21 B2
Verdille F 53 C4
Verdú E 77 B4
Verdun F 45 A6
Verdun-sur-Garonne F 63 C4
Verdun-sur-le-Doubs F 55 B5
Veresegyház H 51 C5
Verfeil F 63 C4
Vergato I 67 B5
Vergel E 82 C3
Vergeletto CH 56 B3
Verges E 77 A6
Vergiate I 56 C3
Vergt F 63 A3
Verín E 73 C3
Veringenstadt D 47 B5
Verkhovye RUS 7 K25
Verl D 37 B4
Vermand F 45 A4
Vermelha P 78 B1
Vermenton F 45 C4
Vern-d'Anjou F 43 C5
Vernago I 57 B5
Vernante I 66 B1
Vernantes F 53 A5
Vernár SK 51 B6
Vernasca I 67 B3
Vernayaz CH 56 B2
Vernazza I 67 B3
Verneřice CZ 39 C4
Vernet F 63 C4
Vernet-les-Bains F 77 A5
Verneuil F 45 A4
Verneuil-sur-Avre F 44 B1
Vernier CH 55 B6
Vérnio I 67 B5
Vérnole I 91 B5
Vernon F 44 A2
Vernoux-en-Vivarais F 64 B3
Veróce H 51 C5
Véroia GR 15 R18
Verolanuova I 57 C5
Véroli I 89 B3
Verona I 57 C6
Verpelét H 51 C6
Verrès I 56 C2
Verrey-sous-Salmaise F 55 A4
Verrières F 53 B5
Versailles F 44 B3
Versam CH 57 B4
Verseg H 51 C5
Versmold D 36 A4
Versoix CH 55 B6
Verteillac F 53 C5
Vértesacsa H 60 A3
Vertou F 52 A3
Vertus F 45 B4
Verviers B 36 C1
Vervins F 45 A4
Veržej SLO 59 B6
Verzuolo I 66 B1
Verzy F 45 A5
Vescovato F 96 A2
Vése H 60 B2
Veselí nad Lužnicí CZ 49 A5
Veselí nad Moravou CZ 50 B3
Veseliy BG 16 Q20
Vésime I 66 B2
Vesoul F 46 C2
Vespolate I 56 C3
Vessigebro S 26 C2
Vestbygd N 18 C3
Vestenanova I 57 C6
Vester Husby S 23 C3
Vester Nebel DK 25 D2
Vester Torup DK 24 B2
Vester Vedsted DK 25 D1
Vesterøhavn DK 24 B3
Vestervig DK 24 C1
Vestfossen N 19 B6
Vestmarka N 20 B3
Vestone I 57 C5
Vesyegonsk RUS 7 G25
Veszprém H 60 A2
Veszprémvarsány H 60 A2
Vésztő H 61 B6
Vetlanda S 26 B5
Vetovo HR 60 C2
Vetralla I 88 A2
Větrný Jeníkov CZ 49 A6
Vétroz CH 56 B2
Vetschau D 39 B4
Vetto I 67 B4
Vetulónia I 67 D4
Veules-les-Roses F 44 A1
Veulettes-sur-Mer F 44 A1
Veum N 19 B5
Veurne B 34 B3
Veverská Bitýška CZ 50 A2
Vevey CH 56 B1
Vex CH 56 B2
Veynes F 65 B4
Veyre-Monton F 54 C3
Veyrier F 55 C6
Vézelay F 54 A3
Vézelise F 46 B2
Vézenobres F 64 B3
Vezins F 53 A4
Vézins-de-Lévézou F 64 B1
Vezza di Óglio I 57 B5
Vezzani F 96 A2
Vezzano I 57 B6
Vezzano sul Cróstolo I 67 B4
Via Gloria P 84 B3
Viadana I 67 B4
Viana E 75 B4
Viana do Alentejo P 84 A2
Viana do Bolo E 73 B3
Viana do Castelo P 73 C2
Vianden L 46 A2
Viaréggio I 67 C4
Viator E 87 C3
Vibble S 23 D5
Vibo Valéntia I 92 C3
Viborg DK 24 C2
Vibraye F 44 B1
Vic E 77 B5
Vic-en-Bigorre F 62 C3
Vic-Fézensac F 62 C3
Vic-le-Comte F 54 C3
Vic-sur-Aisne F 45 A4
Vic-sur-Cère F 63 B5
Vicar E 87 C3
Vicarello I 67 C4
Vicari I 94 B2
Vicchio I 67 C5

Vicdesses F 63 D4
Vicenza I 57 C6
Vichy F 54 B3
Vickan S 24 B5
Vico F 96 A1
Vico del Gargano I 90 A2
Vico Equense I 89 C4
Vicopisano I 67 C4
Vicosoprano CH 57 B4
Vicovaro I 88 A2
Vidago P 73 C3
Vidauban F 65 C5
Vide P 78 A3
Videbæk DK 25 C1
Videm SLO 59 C4
Videseter N 2 F10
Vidigueira P 84 A3
Vidin BG 15 Q18
Vidzy BY 7 J20
Viechtach D 48 A3
Vieille-Brioude F 54 C3
Vieira P 78 B2
Vieira do Minho P 73 C2
Vieiros P 78 C3
Vielha E 76 A3
Vielle-Aure F 63 D3
Viellevigne F 52 B3
Vielmur-sur-Agout F 63 C5
Viels Maison F 45 B4
Vielsalm B 36 C1
Vienenburg D 37 B6
Vienne F 55 C4
Vieritz D 30 C4
Viernheim D 47 A4
Vierraden D 31 B6
Viersen D 36 B2
Vierville-sur-Mer F 43 A5
Vierzon F 54 A2
Vieselbach D 38 C1
Vieste I 90 A3
Vieteren B 34 C3
Vietri di Potenza I 90 B2
Vietri sul Mare I 90 B1
Vieux-Boucau-les-Bains F 62 C1
Vif F 65 A4
Vig DK 25 D4
Vigásio I 57 C5
Vigaun A 49 C4
Vigeland N 19 C4
Vigeois F 53 C6
Vigévano I 56 C3
Viggianello I 90 C3
Viggiano I 90 B2
Vigliano I 88 A3
Vigmostad N 19 C4
Vignale I 66 A2
Vignanello I 88 A2
Vigneulles-lès-Hattonchâtel F 46 B1
Vignola I 67 B5
Vignory F 45 B6
Vignoux-sur Barangeon F 54 A2
Vigo E 73 B2
Vigo di Fassa I 58 B1
Vigone I 66 B1
Vigrestad N 18 C2
Vihiers F 53 A4
Viitasaari FIN 3 E19
Vik, *Rogaland* N 18 C2
Vik S 27 D4
Vika S 22 A2
Vikajärvi FIN 3 C20
Vikane N 20 B2
Vikedal N 18 B2
Vikeland N 19 C4
Viken S 27 C2
Viker N 20 A2
Vikersund N 19 B6
Vikeså N 18 C3
Vikevåg N 18 B2
Vikingstad S 23 C2
Vikja, *Sogn og Fjordane* N 2 F10
Vikmanshyttan S 22 A2
Vikøy N 18 A3
Viksta S 22 A4
Vila Boim P 78 C3
Vila Chã de Ourique P 78 B2
Vila de Cruces E 72 B2
Vila de Rei P 78 B2
Vila do Bispo P 84 B2
Vila do Conde P 73 C2
Vila Flor P 73 C3
Vila Franca das Navas P 78 A3
Vila Franca de Xira P 78 C1
Vila Fresca P 78 C1
Vila Nogueira P 78 C1
Vila Nova da Baronia P 84 A2
Vila Nova de Cerveira P 73 C2
Vila Nova de Famalicão P 73 C2
Vila Nova de Foz Côa P 73 C3
Vila Nova de Gaia P 73 C2
Vila Nova de Milfontes P 84 B2
Vila Nova de Ourém P 78 B2
Vila Nova de Paiva P 73 D3
Vila Nova de São Bento P 84 B3
Vila Pouca de Aguiar P 73 C3
Vila Praja de Ancora P 73 C2
Vila Real P 73 C3
Vila-real de los Infantes E 82 B2
Vila Real de Santo António P 84 B3
Vila-Rodona E 77 B4
Vila Ruiva P 84 A3
Vila Seca P 78 A2
Vila Velha de Ródão P 78 B3
Vila Verde, *Braga* P 73 C2
Vila Verde, *Lisboa* P 78 B1
Vila Verde de Filcalho P 84 B3
Vila Viçosa P 78 C3
Viladamat E 77 A6
Viladrau E 77 B5
Vilafranca del Maestrat E 76 C2
Vilafranca del Penedès E 77 B4
Vilagarcía de Arousa E 72 B2
Vilajuiga E 77 A6
Vilamarin E 72 B3
Vilamartín de Valdeorras E 72 B3
Vilanova de Castelló E 82 B2
Vilanova de Sau E 77 B5
Vilanova i la Geltrú E 77 B4
Vilapedre E 72 A3
Vilar de Santos E 73 B3
Vilar Formosa P 79 A4
Vilarandelo P 73 C3
Vilardevós E 73 C3
Vilasantar E 72 A2
Vilaseca E 77 B4
Vilassar de Mar E 77 B5
Vilches E 86 A2
Vildbjerg DK 25 C1
Vilémov CZ 49 A6
Vileyka BY 7 J20
Vilhelmina S 2 D15
Viljandi EST 7 G19
Villa Castelli I 91 B4
Villa Cova de Lixa P 73 C2
Villa de Peralonso E 73 C4
Villa del Prado E 80 B2
Villa del Rio E 86 B1
Villa di Chiavenna I 57 B4
Villa Minozzo I 67 B4
Villa San Giovanni I 95 A4
Villa Santa Maria I 89 B4
Villa Santina I 58 B2
Villabáñez E 74 C2
Villablanca E 84 B3
Villablino E 72 B4
Villabona E 75 A4
Villabragima E 74 C1
Villabuena del Puente E 74 C1
Villacadima E 81 A3
Villacañas E 81 C3
Villacarriedo E 74 A3
Villacarrillo E 86 A2
Villacastín E 80 B2
Villach A 58 B3
Villacidro I 96 D1
Villaconejos E 81 B3
Villaconejos de Trabaque E 81 B4
Villada E 74 B2
Villadangos del Páramo E 74 B1
Villadecanes E 72 B4
Villadepera E 73 C4
Villadiego E 74 B2
Villadompardo E 86 B1
Villadóssola I 56 B3
Villaeles de Valdavia E 74 B2
Villaescusa de Haro E 81 C4
Villafáfila E 74 C1
Villafeliche E 81 A5
Villaflores E 80 A1
Villafrades de Campos E 74 B2
Villafranca, *Avila* E 80 B1
Villafranca, *Navarra* E 75 B5
Villafranca de Córdoba E 86 B1
Villafranca de los Barros E 79 C4
Villafranca de los Caballeros E 81 C3
Villafranca del Bierzo E 72 B4
Villafranca di Verona I 57 C5
Villafranca in Lunigiana I 67 B3
Villafranca-Montes de Oca E 75 B3
Villafranca Tirrena I 95 A4
Villafranco del Campo E 81 B5
Villafranco del Guadalquivir E 85 B4
Villafrati I 94 B2
Villafrechós E 74 C1
Villafruela E 74 C3
Villagarcia de las Torres E 85 A4
Villaggio Mancuso I 92 B3
Villagonzalo E 79 C4
Villagotón E 72 B4
Villagrains F 62 B2
Villaharta E 86 A1
Villahermosa E 86 A3
Villaherreros E 74 B2
Villahoz E 74 B3
Villaines-la-Juhel F 43 B5
Villajoyosa E 82 C2
Villalago I 89 B3
Villalba E 72 A3
Villalba I 94 B2
Villalba de Calatrava E 86 A2
Villalba de Guardo E 74 B2
Villalba de la Sierra E 81 B4
Villalba de los Alcores E 74 C2
Villalba de los Barros E 79 C4
Villalba del Alcor E 85 B4
Villalba del Rey E 81 B4
Villalcampo E 73 C4
Villalcázar de Sirga E 74 B2
Villalengua E 75 C5
Villalgordo del Júcar E 81 C4
Villalgordo del Marquesado E 81 C4
Villalmóndar E 75 B3
Villalón de Campos E 74 B1
Villalonga E 82 C2
Villalonso E 74 C1
Villalpando E 74 C1
Villaluenga E 80 B3
Villalumbroso E 74 B2
Villálvaro E 75 C3
Villamalea E 82 B1
Villamanán E 74 B1
Villamanín E 74 B1
Villamanrique E 86 A3
Villamanrique de la Condesa E 85 B4
Villamanta E 80 B2
Villamantilla E 80 B2
Villamar I 96 D1
Villamartín E 85 C5
Villamartín de Campos E 74 B2
Villamartín de Don Sancho E 74 B1
Villamassárgia I 96 D1
Villamayor E 74 A1
Villamayor de Calatrava E 86 A1
Villamayor de Campos E 74 C1
Villamayor de Santiago E 81 C4
Villamblard F 63 A3
Villamejil E 72 B4
Villamesias E 79 B5
Villaminaya E 80 C3
Villamor de los Escuderos E 80 A1
Villamoronta E 74 B2
Villamuelas E 80 C3
Villamuriel de Cerrato E 74 C2
Villandraut F 62 B2
Villanova I 91 B4
Villanova d'Asti I 66 B1
Villanova del Battista I 90 A2
Villanova Mondovi I 66 B1
Villanova Monteleone I 96 C1
Villante E 74 B3
Villantério I 57 C4
Villanubla E 74 C2
Villanueva de Alcardete E 81 C3
Villanueva de Alcorón E 81 B4
Villanueva de Algaidas E 86 B1
Villanueva de Argaña E 74 B3
Villanueva de Bogas E 80 C3
Villanueva de Córdoba E 86 A1
Villanueva de Gállego E 76 B2
Villanueva de la Concepcion E 86 C1
Villanueva de la Fuente E 87 A3
Villanueva de la Jara E 81 C5
Villanueva de la Reina E 86 A2
Villanueva de la Serena E 79 C5
Villanueva de la Sierra E 79 A4
Villanueva de la Vera E 80 B1
Villanueva de las Manzanas E 74 B1
Villanueva de las Peras E 74 C1
Villanueva de las Torres E 86 B2
Villanueva de los Castillejos E 84 B3
Villanueva de los Infantes E 86 A3
Villanueva de Mesia E 86 B2
Villanueva de Nía E 74 B2
Villanueva de Oscos E 72 A4
Villanueva de San Carlos E 86 A2
Villanueva de San Juan E 85 B5
Villanueva de Tapia E 86 B1
Villanueva de Valdegovia E 75 B3
Villanueva del Aceral E 80 A2
Villanueva del Arzobispo E 86 A3
Villanueva del Campo E 74 C1
Villanueva del Duque E 86 A1
Villanueva del Fresno E 79 C3
Villanueva del Huerva E 76 B1
Villanueva del Rey E 85 A5
Villanueva del Rio E 85 B5
Villanueva del Río y Minas E 85 B5
Villanueva del Rosario E 86 C1
Villanueva del Trabuco E 86 B1
Villány H 60 C3
Villaputzu I 96 D2
Villaquejida E 74 B1
Villaquilambre E 74 B1
Villaquiran de los Infantes E 74 B2
Villar de Barrio E 73 B3
Villar de Cañas E 81 C4
Villar de Chinchilla E 82 C1
Villar de Ciervo E 73 D4
Villar de Domingo Garcia E 81 B4
Villar de los Navarros E 76 B1
Villar de Rena E 79 B5
Villar del Arzobispo E 82 B2
Villar del Buey E 73 C4
Villar del Cobo E 81 B5
Villar del Humo E 81 C5
Villar del Pedroso E 80 C1
Villar del Rey E 79 B4
Villar del Rio E 75 B4
Villar del Saz de Navalón E 81 B4
Villar Perosa I 65 B6
Villaralto E 86 A1
Villarcayo E 75 B3
Villard-de-Lans F 65 A4
Villardeciervos E 73 C4
Villardefrades E 74 C1
Villarejo E 81 A3
Villarejo de Fuentes E 81 C4
Villarejo de Orbigo E 74 B1
Villarejo de Salvanes E 81 B3
Villarejo-Periesteban E 81 C4
Villares del Saz E 81 C4
Villaretto I 65 A6
Villargordo del Cabriel E 82 B1
Villarino E 73 C4
Villarino de Conso E 73 B3
Villarluengo E 76 C2
Villarobe E 75 B3
Villarosa I 95 B3
Villaramiel E 74 B2
Villarrasa E 85 B4
Villarreal de San Carlos E 79 B4
Villarrin de Campos E 74 C1
Villarrobledo E 81 C4
Villarroya de la Sierra E 75 C5
Villarroya de los Pinares E 76 C2
Villarrubia de los Ojos E 81 C3
Villarrubia de Santiago E 81 C3
Villarrubio E 81 C4
Villars-les-Dombes F 55 B5
Villarta E 81 C5
Villarta de los Montes E 80 C2
Villarta de San Juan E 81 C3
Villasana de Mena E 75 A3
Villasandino E 74 B2
Villasante E 75 A3
Villasarracino E 74 B2
Villasayas E 75 C4
Villasdardo E 73 C4
Villaseca de Henares E 81 B4
Villaseca de la Sagra E 80 C3
Villaseca de Laciana E 72 B4
Villaseco de los Gamitos E 73 C4
Villaseco de los Reyes E 73 C4
Villasequilla de Yepes E 80 C3
Villasimíus I 96 D2
Villasmundo I 95 B4
Villasor I 96 D1
Villastar E 82 A1
Villastellone I 66 B1
Villatobas E 81 B3
Villatorp E 80 B1
Villatoya E 82 B1
Villavaliente E 82 B1
Villavelayo E 75 B4
Villavella E 73 B3
Villaver de de Guadalimar E 87 A3
Villaverde del Rio E 85 B5
Villaviciosa E 74 A1
Villaviciosa de Córdoba E 86 A1
Villaviciosa de Odón E 80 B3
Villavieja de Yeltes E 73 D4
Villayón E 72 A4
Villé F 46 B3
Ville-di-Pietrabugno F 96 A2
Ville-sous-la-Ferté F 45 B5
Ville-sur-Illon F 46 B2
Ville-sur-Tourbe F 45 A5
Villebois-Lavalette F 53 C5
Villecerf F 45 B3
Villecomtal F 63 B5
Villedieu-les-Poêles F 43 B4
Villedieu-sur-Indre F 53 B6
Villefagnan F 53 B5
Villefontaine F 55 C5
Villefort F 64 B2
Villefranche-d'Albigeois F 63 C5
Villefranche-d'Allier F 54 B2
Villefranche-de-Lauragais F 63 C4
Villefranche-de-Lonchat F 62 B3
Villefranche-de-Panat F 64 B1
Villefranche-de-Rouergue F 63 B5
Villefranche-du-Périgord F 63 B4
Villefranche-sur-Cher F 54 A1
Villefranche-sur-Mer F 65 C6
Villefranche-sur-Saône F 55 B4
Villegenon F 54 A2
Villel E 82 A1
Villemaur-sur-Vanne F 45 B4
Villemur-sur-Tarn F 63 C4
Villena E 82 C2
Villenauxe-la-Grande F 45 B4
Villenave-d'Ornon F 62 B2
Villeneuve CH 56 B1
Villeneuve F 63 B5
Villeneuve-d'Ascq F 35 C4
Villeneuve-de-Berg F 64 B3
Villeneuve-de-Marsan F 62 C2
Villeneuve-de-Rivière F 63 C3
Villeneuve-la-Guyard F 45 B4
Villeneuve-l'Archevêque F 45 B4
Villeneuve-le-Comte F 44 B3
Villeneuve-lès-Avignon F 64 C3
Villeneuve-les-Corbières F 64 D1
Villeneuve-St. Georges F 44 B3
Villeneuve-sur-Allier F 54 B3
Villeneuve-sur-Lot F 63 B3
Villeneuve-sur-Yonne F 45 B4
Villeréal F 63 B3
Villerias E 74 C2
Villeromain F 44 C2
Villers-Bocage, *Calvados* F 43 A5
Villers-Bocage, *Somme* F 34 D3
Villers-Bretonneux F 44 A3
Villers-Carbonnel F 45 A3
Villers-Cotterêts F 45 A4
Villers-Farlay F 55 B5
Villers-le-Gambon B 35 C5
Villers-le-Lac F 56 A1
Villers-sur-Mer F 43 A6
Villersexel F 55 A6
Villerupt F 46 A1
Villerville F 43 A6
Villeseneux F 45 B5
Villetrun F 44 C2
Villetta Barrea I 89 B3
Villeurbanne F 55 C4
Villeveyrac F 64 C2
Villevocance F 55 C4
Villiers-St. Benoit F 45 C4
Villiers-St. Georges F 45 B4
Villingen D 47 B4
Villmar D 36 C4
Villoldo E 74 B2
Villoria E 80 B1
Vilnius LT 7 J19
Vils A 57 A5
Vils DK 24 C1
Vilsbiburg D 48 B3
Vilseck D 48 A2
Vilshofen D 49 B4
Vilshult S 27 C4
Vilusi YU 70 D3
Vilvestre E 73 C4
Vilvoorde B 35 C5
Vimeiro P 78 B1
Vimercate I 57 C4
Vimianzo E 72 A1
Vimieiro P 78 C3
Vimioso P 73 C4
Vimmerby S 26 B5
Vimoutiers F 43 B6
Vimperk CZ 49 A4
Vimy F 34 C3
Vinadi CH 57 B5
Vinadio I 65 B6
Vinaixa E 76 B3
Vinarós E 76 C3
Vinay F 55 C5
Vinberg S 26 C2
Vinca F 77 A5
Vinča YU 71 B5
Vinchiaturo I 89 B4
Vinci I 67 C4
Vindeby DK 25 D3
Vindeln S 3 D16
Vinderup DK 24 C1
Vindsvik N 18 B3
Vinets F 45 B5
Vineuil F 53 A6
Vinga RO 61 B6
Vingåker S 23 B2
Vingrau F 64 D1
Vinhais P 73 C4
Vinica HR 59 B6
Vinica SK 51 B5
Vinica SLO 59 C5
Vinicka YU 71 D4
Viniegra de Arriba E 75 B4
Vinje, *Sør-Trøndelag* N 2 E11
Vinje, *Telemark* N 19 B4
Vinkovci HR 60 C3
Vinninga S 21 C5
Vinnytsya UA 11 M21
Vinon-sur-Verdon F 65 C4
Vinslöv S 27 C3
Vintrosa S 22 B1
Viñuela de Sayago E 74 C1
Viñuelas E 81 B3
Vinuesa E 75 C4
Vinzelberg D 30 C3
Viöl D 29 A6
Viola I 66 B1
Violay F 55 C4
Vipava SLO 58 C3
Vipiteno I 57 B6
Vipperow D 31 B4
Vir BIH 70 C2
Vir HR 69 B4
Vira CH 56 B3
Vire F 43 B5
Vireux F 35 C5
Virgen A 58 A2
Virgen de la Cabeza E 86 A1
Virieu F 55 C5
Virieu-le-Grand F 55 C5
Virje HR 60 B1
Virklund DK 25 C2
Virovitica HR 60 C2
Virsbo S 22 B3
Virserum S 26 B5
Virton B 46 A1
Virtsu EST 6 G18
Viry F 55 B6
Vis HR 69 C5
Visbek D 29 C5
Visby DK 25 D1
Visby S 23 D5
Visé B 36 C1
Višegrad BIH 71 C4
Viserba I 68 B1
Viseu P 78 A3
Visiedo E 76 C1
Viskafors S 26 B2
Visland N 18 C3
Vislanda S 26 C4
Visnes N 18 B2
Višnja Gora SLO 59 C4
Višnjan HR 58 C3
Višnové CZ 50 B2
Visnums-Kil S 20 B6
Viso del Marqués E 86 A2
Visoko BIH 70 C3
Visoko SLO 59 B4
Visone I 66 B2
Visp CH 56 B2
Vissefjärda S 26 C5
Visselhövede D 29 C6
Vissenbjerg DK 25 D3
Visso I 68 D2
Vistabella del Maestrat E 82 A2
Vita I 94 B1
Vitanje SLO 59 B5
Vitanovac YU 71 C5
Viterbo I 88 A2
Vitez BIH 70 B2
Vitigudino E 73 C4
Vitina BIH 70 C2
Vitis A 49 B6
Vitkov CZ 50 A3
Vitkovac YU 71 C5
Vitomirica YU 71 D5
Vitoria-Gasteiz E 75 B4
Vitré F 43 B4
Vitrey-sur-Mance F 46 C1
Vitry-en-Artois F 34 C3
Vitry-le-François F 45 B5
Vitry-sur-Seine F 44 B3
Vitsand S 20 A4
Vitsyebsk BY 7 J22
Vittangi S 3 C17
Vittaryd S 26 C3
Vitteaux F 55 A4
Vittel F 46 B1
Vittinge S 22 B4
Vittória I 95 C3
Vittório Véneto I 58 C2
Vittsjö S 27 C3
Viù I 56 C2
Viul N 20 A2
Vivario F 96 A2
Viveiro E 72 A3
Vivel del Rio Martin E 76 C2
Viver E 82 B2
Viverols F 54 C3
Viveros E 87 A3
Viviers F 64 B3
Vivonne F 53 B5
Vivy F 53 A4
Vize TR 16 R20
Vizille F 65 A4
Viziñada HR 58 C3
Viziru RO 11 P20
Vizovice CZ 50 A3
Vizvár H 60 B2
Vizzavona F 96 A2
Vizzini I 95 B3
Vlachovice CZ 50 A3
Vlachovo SK 51 B6
Vláchovo Březi CZ 49 A4
Vladimirci YU 71 B4
Vladimirovac YU 71 A5
Vladislav CZ 50 A1
Vlagtwedde NL 29 B4
Vlajkovac YU 71 A6
Vlasenica BIH 70 B3
Vlašim CZ 49 A5
Vlatkovići BIH 70 B2
Vledder NL 28 C3
Vlissingen NL 35 B4
Vlorë AL 15 R16
Vlotho D 37 A4
Vnanje Gorice SLO 59 C4
Vobarno I 57 C5
Voćin HR 60 C2
Vöcklabruck A 49 B4
Vöcklamarkt A 49 C4
Vodanj YU 71 B5
Voderady SK 50 B3
Vodice, *Istarska* HR 59 C4
Vodice, *Šibenska* HR 69 C4
Vodice SLO 59 B4
Vodňany CZ 49 A5
Vodnjan HR 68 B2
Vodskov DK 24 B3
Voerså DK 24 B3
Voghera I 66 B3
Vogogna I 56 B3
Vogošća BIH 70 C3
Vogué F 64 B3
Vohburg D 48 B2
Vohenstrauss D 48 A3
Vöhl D 37 B4
Vöhrenbach D 47 B4
Vöhringen D 47 B6
Void-Vacon F 46 B1
Voiron F 55 C5
Voise F 44 B2
Voisey F 46 C1
Voiteg RO 61 C6
Voiteur F 55 B5
Voitsberg A 59 A5
Vojens DK 25 D2
Vojka YU 71 B5
Vojlovica YU 71 B5
Vojnić HR 59 C5
Vojnice SK 51 C4
Vojnik SLO 59 B5
Vojvoda Stepa YU 61 C5
Volargne I 57 C5
Volary CZ 49 B4
Volče SLO 58 B3
Volda N 2 E10
Volendam NL 28 C2
Volga RUS 7 G26
Volkach D 47 A6
Völkermarkt A 59 B4
Volkhov RUS 7 G23
Völklingen D 46 A2
Volkmarsen D 37 B5
Vollenhove NL 28 C2
Vollore-Montagne F 54 C3
Vollsjö S 27 D3
Volodymyr-Volyns'kyy UA 11 L19
Volokolamsk RUS 7 H24
Vólos GR 15 S18
Volosovo RUS 7 G21
Volovets UA 11 M18
Volta Mantovana I 57 C5
Voltággio I 66 B2
Volterra I 67 C4
Voltri I 66 B2
Volturara Áppula I 90 A2
Volturara Irpina I 90 B1
Volvic F 54 C3
Volyně CZ 49 A4
Vónitsa GR 15 S17
Vönöck H 60 A2
Vonsild DK 25 D2
Voorschoten NL 35 A5
Vorau A 59 A5
Vorbasse DK 25 D2
Vorchdorf A 49 C4
Vorden NL 36 A2
Vordernberg A 59 A4
Vordingborg DK 25 D4
Voreppe F 55 C5
Vorey F 54 C3
Vorgod DK 25 C1
Vormsund N 20 A3
Voronezh RUS 7 L23
Võru EST 7 H20
Voss N 2 F10
Votice CZ 49 A5
Voué F 45 B5
Vouillé F 53 B5
Voulx F 45 B3
Voussac F 54 B3
Vouvray F 53 A5
Vouvry CH 56 B1
Vouzela P 73 D2
Vouziers F 45 A5
Voves F 44 B2
Voynitsa RUS 3 D22
Voznesensk UA 11 N22
Vrå DK 24 B2
Vrå S 26 C3
Vráble SK 50 B4
Vračenovići YU 70 D3
Vračev Gaj YU 71 B6
Vraćevsnica YU 71 B5
Vrådal N 19 B5
Vrana HR 69 B3
Vranduk BIH 70 B2
Vrångö S 24 B4
Vrani RO 71 A6
Vranić YU 71 B5
Vraniči BIH 70 C3
Vranja HR 59 C4
Vranjak BIH 70 B3
Vranje YU 15 Q17
Vranov nad Dyje CZ 50 B1
Vranovice CZ 50 B2
Vransko SLO 59 B4
Vrapčići BIH 70 C2
Vratimov CZ 50 A4
Vratsa BG 15 Q18
Vrbanja HR 70 B3
Vrbanjci BIH 70 B2
Vrbas YU 61 C4
Vrbaška BIH 60 C2
Vrbnik, *Primorsko-Goranska* HR 69 A3
Vrbnik, *Zadarsko-Kninska* HR 69 B5
Vrbno p. Pradědem CZ 40 C2
Vrboska HR 69 C5
Vrbov SK 51 A6
Vrbovce SK 50 B3
Vrbové SK 50 B3
Vrbovec HR 59 C6
Vrbovski YU 71 B5
Vrbovsko HR 59 C5
Vrchlabí CZ 39 C5
Vrčin YU 71 B5
Vrdy CZ 49 A6
Vrebac HR 69 B4
Vreden D 36 A2
Vrela YU 71 D5
Vreoci YU 71 B5
Vretstorp S 23 B1
Vrginmost HR 59 C5
Vrgorac HR 70 C2
Vrhnika SLO 59 C4
Vrhovine HR 69 B4
Vrhpolje YU 71 B4
Vriezenveen NL 28 C3
Vrigne-aux-Bois F 45 A5
Vrigstad S 26 B4
Vrlika HR 69 C5
Vrmbaje YU 71 C5
Vrnjačka Banja YU 71 C5
Vrnograč BIH 59 C5
Vron F 34 C2
Vroomshoop NL 28 C3
Vroutek CZ 38 C3
Vrpolje HR 60 C3
Vršac YU 71 A6
Vrsar HR 68 A2
Vrsi HR 69 B4
Vrtoče BIH 69 B5
Vrútky SK 51 A4
Všeruby CZ 48 A3
Všestary CZ 39 C5
Vsetín CZ 50 A3
Vuča YU 71 D5
Vučitrn YU 71 D5
Vučkovica YU 71 C5
Vught NL 35 B6
Vuillafans F 55 A6
Vukovar HR 61 C4
Vulcan RO 11 P18
Vulcanești MD 11 P21
Vuolijoki FIN 3 D20
Vuzenica SLO 59 B5
Vy-lès Lure F 46 C2
Vyartsilya RUS 3 E22
Vyazma RUS 7 J24
Vyborg RUS 3 F21
Výčapy CZ 50 A1
Výčapy-Opatovce SK 50 B4
Východna SK 51 A5
Vydrany SK 50 B3
Vyerkhnyadzvinsk BY 7 J20
Vyhne SK 51 B4
Vylkove UA 11 P21
Vynohradiv UA 11 M18
Vyshniy Volochek RUS 7 H24
Vyškov CZ 50 A3
Vysoká nad Kysucou SK 51 A4
Vysoké Mýto CZ 39 D6
Vysokovsk RUS 7 H25
Vyšší Brod CZ 49 B5

W

Waabs D 30 A1
Waalwijk NL 35 B6
Waarschoot B 35 B4
Wabern D 37 B5
Wąbrzeźno PL 33 B4
Wąchock PL 41 B6
Wachow D 31 C4
Wachów PL 40 C4
Wächtersbach D 37 C5
Wackersdorf D 48 A3
Wadelsdorf D 39 B4
Wädenswil CH 56 A3
Wadern D 46 A2
Wadersloh D 36 B4
Wadlew PL 41 B4
Wadowice PL 51 A5
Wagenfeld D 29 C5
Wageningen NL 35 B6
Waghäusel D 47 A4
Waging D 48 C3
Wagrain A 58 A3
Wągrowiec PL 32 C3
Wahlsdorf D 38 B3
Wahlstedt D 30 B2
Wahrenholz D 30 C2
Waiblingen D 47 B5
Waidhaus D 48 A3
Waidhofen an der Thaya A 49 B6
Waidhofen an der Ybbs A 49 C5
Waimes B 36 C2
Waizenkirchen A 49 B4
Wałbrzych PL 39 C6
Walchensee D 48 C2
Walchsee A 48 C3
Wałcz PL 32 B2
Wald CH 56 A3
Wald-Michelbach D 47 A4
Waldaschaff D 37 D5
Waldbach A 59 A5
Waldböckelheim D 46 A3
Waldbröl D 36 C3
Waldeck D 37 B5
Waldenburg D 38 C2

Place	Country	Map	Grid
Waldfischbach-Burgalben	D	46	A3
Waldheim	D	38	B3
Waldkappel	D	37	B5
Waldkirch	D	46	B3
Waldkirchen	D	49	B4
Waldkirchen am Wesen	A	49	B4
Waldkraiburg	D	48	B3
Waldmohr	D	46	A3
Waldmünchen	D	48	A3
Waldring	A	48	C3
Waldsassen	D	38	C2
Waldshut	CH	47	C4
Waldstatt	CH	57	A4
Waldwisse	F	46	A2
Walenstadt	CH	57	A4
Walentynów	PL	41	B6
Walichnowy	PL	41	B4
Walincourt	F	35	C4
Walkenried	D	37	B6
Walldürn	D	47	A5
Wallenfells	D	38	C1
Wallenhorst	D	29	C5
Wallers	F	35	C4
Wallersdorf	D	48	B3
Wallerstein	D	47	B6
Wallitz	D	31	B4
Wallsbüll	D	25	E2
Walsall	GB	4	K6
Walshoutem	B	35	C6
Walsrode	D	29	C6
Waltenhofen	D	47	C6
Waltershausen	D	37	C6
Wamba	E	74	C2
Wanderup	D	29	A6
Wandlitz	D	31	C5
Wanfried	D	37	B6
Wangen im Allgäu	D	47	C5
Wangerooge	D	29	B4
Wangersen	D	29	B6
Wängi	CH	56	A3
Wanna	D	29	B5
Wanzleben	D	38	A1
Waplewo	PL	38	B5
Wapnica	PL	32	B1
Wapno	PL	32	C3
Warburg	D	37	B5
Wardenburg	D	29	B5
Waregem	B	35	C4
Waremme	B	35	C6
Waren	D	31	B4
Warendorf	D	36	B3
Warga	NL	28	B2
Warin	D	30	B3
Warka	PL	41	B6
Warlubie	PL	33	B4
Warnemünde	D	30	A4
Warnow	D	30	B3
Warnsveld	NL	36	B2
Warrington	GB	4	K5
Warsingsfehn	D	29	B4
Warsow	D	30	B3
Warstein	D	37	B4
Warszawa	PL	41	A6
Warta	PL	40	B3
Wartberg	A	49	C5
Warth	A	57	A5
Warwick	GB	4	K6
Warza	D	37	C6
Wąsosz	PL	40	B1
Wasselonne	F	46	B3
Wassen	CH	56	B3
Wassenaar	NL	35	A5
Wasserauen	CH	57	A4
Wasserburg	D	48	B3
Wassertrüdingen	D	47	A6
Wassy	F	45	B5
Wasungen	D	37	C6
Waterford	IRL	4	K3
Waterloo	B	35	C5
Watford	GB	4	L6
Wathlingen	D	30	C2
Watten	F	34	C3
Wattens	A	58	A1
Wattwil	CH	57	A4
Wavignies	F	44	A3
Wavre	B	35	C5
Wąchadlow	PL	41	C5
Wedel	D	29	B6
Wedemark	D	29	C6
Weener	D	29	B4
Weert	NL	36	C1
Weesp	NL	35	A6
Weeze	D	36	B2
Weferlingen	D	38	A1
Wegeleben	D	38	B1
Weggis	CH	56	A3
Węgierska-Górka	PL	51	B5
Węgliniec	PL	39	B5
Węgorzyno	PL	32	B1
Węgrzynice	PL	39	A5
Wegscheid	D	49	B4
Wehdel	D	29	B5
Wehr	D	46	C3
Weibersbrunn	D	47	A5
Weichering	D	48	C2
Weida	D	38	C2
Weiden	D	48	A3
Weidenberg	D	38	D1
Weidenhain	D	38	B2
Weidenstetten	D	47	B5
Weierbach	D	46	B3
Weikersheim	D	47	A5
Weil	D	48	B1
Weil am Rhein	D	46	C2
Weil der Stadt	D	47	C5
Weilburg	D	36	C4
Weilerswist	D	36	C2
Weilheim, Baden-Württemberg	D	47	B5
Weilheim, Bayern	D	48	C2
Weilmünster	D	47	B4
Weiltensfeld	A	59	B4
Weimar	D	38	C1
Weinberg	D	47	A6
Weinfelden	CH	47	C5
Weingarten, Baden-Württemberg	D	47	C5
Weinheim	D	47	A4
Weinstadt	D	47	B5
Weismain	D	38	C1
Weissbriach	A	58	B3
Weissbach	D	57	A5
Weissenberg	D	39	B4
Weissenbrunn	D	38	C1
Weissenburg	D	48	A1
Weissenfels	D	38	B1
Weissenhorn	D	47	B6
Weissenkirchen	A	49	B6
Weissensee	D	38	B1
Weissenstadt	D	38	C1
Weisskirchen im Steiermark	A	59	A4
Weisstannen	CH	57	B4
Weisswasser	D	39	B4
Weitendorf	D	30	B3
Weitersfeld	A	50	B1
Weitersfelden	A	49	B5
Weitnau	D	47	C6
Wéitra	A	49	B5
Weiz	A	59	A5
Wejherowo	PL	33	A4
Welkenraedt	B	36	C1
Wellaune	D	38	B2
Wellin	B	35	C6
Wells-next-the-Sea	GB	4	K7
Wels	A	49	B5
Welschenrohr	CH	56	A2
Welshpool	GB	4	K5
Welver	D	36	B3
Welzheim	D	47	B5
Welzow	D	39	B4
Wemding	D	48	B1
Wenden	D	36	C3
Wendisch Rietz	D	39	A4
Wendlingen	D	47	B5
Weng	A	49	B4
Weng bei Admont	A	49	C5
Wengen	CH	56	B2
Wenigzell	A	59	A5
Wennigsen	D	37	A5
Wenns	A	57	A6
Wenzenbach	D	48	A3
Weppersdorf	A	50	C2
Werben	D	30	C2
Werbig	D	38	B3
Werdau	D	38	C2
Werder	D	31	C4
Werdohl	D	36	B3
Werfen	A	58	A3
Werkendam	NL	35	B5
Werl	D	36	B3
Werlte	D	29	C4
Wermelskirchen	D	36	B3
Wermsdorf	D	38	B2
Wernberg Köblitz	D	48	A3
Werne	D	36	B3
Werneck	D	37	D6
Werneuchen	D	31	C5
Wernigerode	D	37	B6
Wertach	D	48	C1
Wertheim	D	47	A5
Wertingen	D	48	B1
Weseke	D	36	B2
Wesel	D	36	B2
Wesenberg	D	31	B4
Wesendorf	D	30	C2
Wesołowo	PL	33	B6
Wesselburen	D	29	A5
Wesseling	D	36	C2
West-Terschelling	NL	28	B2
Westendorf	A	58	A2
Westensee	D	30	A1
Westerbork	NL	28	B3
Westerburg	D	36	C3
Westerhaar	NL	28	B3
Westerholt	D	29	B4
Westerkappeln	D	36	A3
Westerland	D	25	E1
Westerlo	B	35	B5
Westerstede	D	29	B4
Westheim	D	48	A1
Westkapelle	B	35	B4
Westkapelle	NL	35	B4
Weston-super-Mare	GB	4	L5
Westport	IRL	4	K2
Wetter, Hessen	D	37	C4
Wetter, Nordrhein-Westfalen	D	36	B3
Wetteren	B	35	B4
Wettin	D	38	B1
Wettringen	D	36	A3
Wetzikon	CH	47	C4
Wetzlar	D	37	C4
Wewelsfleth	D	29	B6
Wexford	IRL	4	K3
Weyer Markt	A	49	C5
Weyerbusch	D	36	C3
Weyersheim	F	46	B3
Weyhe	D	29	C5
Weymouth	GB	4	L5
Weyregg	A	49	C4
Wężyska	PL	39	A4
Whitehaven	GB	4	J5
Wichów	PL	40	C1
Wick	GB	4	G5
Wickede	D	36	B3
Wicklow	IRL	4	K3
Wicko	PL	32	A3
Widawa	PL	40	B3
Widdern	D	47	B5
Widnes	GB	4	K5
Widuchowa	PL	31	B6
Więcbork	PL	32	B3
Wiefelstede	D	29	B5
Wiehe	D	38	B1
Wiehl	D	36	C3
Wiek	D	31	A5
Więk	PL	32	B3
Większyce	PL	40	C2
Wiele	PL	33	B4
Wieleń	PL	32	C1
Wielenbach	D	48	C2
Wielgie	PL	47	A4
Wielgie	PL	40	B3
Wielgie	PL	41	B6
Wielgomłyny	PL	41	A5
Wielichowo	PL	39	A6
Wieliczka	PL	51	B5
Wielka Łąka	PL	33	B4
Wielowies	PL	40	C3
Wieluń	PL	40	B3
Wien	A	50	B2
Wiener Neustadt	A	50	C2
Wiepke	D	30	C3
Wierden	NL	28	C3
Wieren	D	30	C2
Wieruszów	PL	40	B3
Wierzbica	PL	41	B6
Wierzbie	PL	40	B3
Wierzbięcin	PL	31	B7
Wierzchowo	PL	32	B2
Wierzchucino	PL	33	A4
Wierzchy	PL	40	B3
Wies	A	59	B5
Wiesau	D	48	A3
Wiesbaden	D	36	C4
Wieselburg	A	49	B6
Wiesen	CH	57	B4
Wiesenburg	D	38	A2
Wiesensteig	D	47	C5
Wiesentheid	D	48	A1
Wiesloch	D	47	A4
Wiesmath	A	50	C2
Wiesmoor	D	29	B4
Wietmarschen	D	29	C4
Wietze	D	30	C1
Wiggen	CH	56	B2
Wijchen	NL	36	B1
Wijhe	NL	28	C3
Wijk bij Duurstede	NL	35	B5
Wil	CH	56	A4
Wilamowice	PL	51	B5
Wilczęta	PL	33	A5
Wilczkowice	PL	41	A4
Wilczna	PL	40	A3
Wilczyn	PL	33	C4
Wildalpen	A	49	C5
Wildbad	D	47	B4
Wildberg, Baden-Württemberg	D	47	B4
Wildberg, Brandenburg	D	31	C4
Wildegg	CH	56	A3
Wildendürnbach	A	50	B2
Wildeshausen	D	29	C5
Wildon	A	59	B5
Wilfersdorf	A	50	B2
Wilga	PL	41	B6
Wilhelmsburg	A	49	A6
Wilhelmsburg	D	31	B5
Wilhelmsdorf	D	47	C5
Wilhelmshaven	D	29	B5
Willebadessen	D	37	B5
Willebroek	B	35	B5
Willhermsdorf	D	48	A1
Willich	D	36	B2
Willingen	D	37	B4
Willisau	CH	56	A3
Wilsdruff	D	38	B3
Wilster	D	29	B6
Wilsum	D	28	C3
Wiltz	L	36	D1
Wimereux	F	34	C2
Wimmenau	F	46	B3
Wimmis	CH	56	B2
Winchester	GB	4	L6
Windischeschenbach	D	48	A3
Windischgarsten	A	49	C5
Windorf	D	49	B4
Windsbach	D	48	A1
Wingene	B	35	B4
Winklern	A	58	B2
Winnenden	D	47	B5
Winnigstedt	D	37	A6
Winnweiler	D	46	B3
Winschoten	NL	29	B4
Winsen, Niedersachsen	D	29	B6
Winsen, Niedersachsen	D	30	B2
Wińsko	PL	40	B1
Winsum, Friesland	NL	28	B2
Winsum, Groningen	NL	28	B3
Winterberg	D	37	B4
Winterfeld	D	30	C2
Winterswijk	NL	36	B2
Winterthur	CH	47	C4
Wintzenheim	F	46	B3
Winzer	D	48	B3
Wipperdorf	D	37	B6
Wipperfürth	D	36	B3
Wisbech	GB	4	K7
Wischhafen	D	29	B6
Witney	GB	4	L6
Witnica	PL	31	C6
Witonia	PL	41	A4
Wittislingen	D	47	B6
Wittlich	D	36	D2
Wittmannsdorf	A	59	B5
Wittmund	D	29	B4
Wittorf	D	29	B6
Wittstock	D	30	B4
Witzenhausen	D	37	B5
Władysławowo	PL	33	A4
Wleń	PL	39	B5
Włocławek	PL	33	C5
Włodawa	PL	11	L18
Włodzimierzów	PL	41	B4
Włoszakowice	PL	39	B5
Włostów	PL	41	C6
Włoszczowa	PL	41	C4
Wöbbelin	D	30	B3
Wodzisław	PL	41	C4
Wodzisław Śląski	PL	51	A4
Woerden	NL	35	A5
Wœrth	F	46	B3
Wohlen	CH	56	A3
Woippy	F	46	A2
Wojciechy	PL	33	A6
Wojcieszów	PL	39	C5
Wojkowice Kościelne	PL	41	C4
Wojnicz	PL	51	A6
Woking	GB	4	L6
Wola Jachowa	PL	41	C5
Wola Niechcicka	PL	41	B4
Wolbórz	PL	41	B4
Wolbrom	PL	41	C4
Wołczyn	PL	40	B3
Woldegk	D	31	B5
Wolfach	D	47	C4
Wolfegg	D	47	C5
Wolfen	D	38	B2
Wolfenbüttel	D	37	A6
Wolfersheim	D	37	C4
Wolfhagen	D	37	B4
Wolfratshausen	D	48	C2
Wolfsberg	A	59	B4
Wolfsburg	D	30	C2
Wolfshagen	D	31	B5
Wolfstein	D	46	A3
Wolfurt	A	57	A4
Wolgast	D	31	A5
Wolhusen	CH	56	A3
Wolin	PL	31	B6
Wolka	PL	41	B6
Wolkenstein	D	38	C3
Wolkersdorf	A	50	B2
Wöllersdorf	A	50	C2
Wollin	D	38	A2
Wöllstadt	D	37	C4
Wolmirstedt	D	38	A1
Wolnzach	D	48	B2
Wołów	PL	40	B1
Wolsztyn	PL	39	A6
Wolvega	NL	28	C2
Wolverhampton	GB	4	K5
Worb	CH	56	B2
Worcester	GB	4	K5
Wördern	A	50	B2
Wörgl	A	58	A2
Workington	GB	4	J5
Workum	NL	28	B2
Wörlitz	D	38	B2
Wormer	NL	28	C1
Wormhout	F	34	C3
Worms	D	47	A4
Worpswede	D	29	B5
Wörrstadt	D	47	A4
Wörschach	A	49	C5
Wörth, Bayern	D	47	A5
Wörth, Bayern	D	48	B3
Wörth, Rheinland-Pfalz	D	47	A4
Worthing	GB	4	L6
Woudsend	NL	28	C2
Woumen	B	34	C3
Woźniki	PL	41	C4
Wręczyca Wlk.	PL	40	C3
Wredenhagen	D	30	B3
Wremen	D	29	B5
Wrexham	GB	4	K5
Wriedel	D	30	B2
Wriezen	D	31	C6
Wrist	D	29	B6
Wróblew	PL	32	C2
Wróblewo	PL	40	B1
Wrocki	PL	33	B5
Wrocław	PL	40	B3
Wronki	PL	32	C2
Września	PL	40	A2
Wrzosowo	PL	32	A1
Wschowa	PL	39	B6
Wulfen, Nordrhein-Westfalen	D	36	B2
Wulfen, Sachsen-Anhalt	D	38	B1
Wulkau	D	30	C3
Wünnenberg	D	37	B4
Wünsdorf	D	38	B3
Wunsiedel	D	38	C2
Wunstorf	D	29	C6
Wuppertal	D	36	B3
Wurmannsquick	D	48	B3
Würselen	D	36	C2
Würzbach	D	47	B4
Würzburg	D	37	C4
Wurzen	D	38	B2
Wust	D	30	C3
Wusterhausen	D	30	C3
Wustrau-Altfriesack	D	31	C4
Wustrow	D	30	A4
Wustrow	D	31	B4
Wusterwitz	D	30	C3
Wyględów	PL	41	B6
Wyk	D	29	A5
Wykroty	PL	39	B5
Wymiarki	PL	39	B5
Wyrzysk	PL	32	B3
Wyśmierzyce	PL	41	B4
Wysoka	PL	32	B3
Wysoka	PL	40	B1
Wyszanów	PL	40	B3
Wyszków	PL	41	A6
Wyszogród	PL	33	C6
X			
Xanten	D	36	B2
Xánthi	GR	16	R19
Xàtiva	E	82	C2
Xeraco	E	82	B2
Xert	E	76	C3
Xerta	E	76	C3
Xertigny	F	46	B2
Xinzo de Limia	E	73	B3
Xove	E	72	A3
Xubia	E	72	A2
Xunqueira de Ambia	E	73	B3
Xunqueira de Espadañedo	E	73	B3
Y			
Yablanitsa	BG	16	Q19
Yahotyn	UA	11	L22
Yalova	TR	16	R21
Yalvaç	TR	16	S22
Yambol	BG	16	Q20
Yampil	UA	11	M21
Yaremcha	UA	11	M19
Yasinya	UA	11	M19
Yatağan	TR	16	T21
Yavoriv	UA	11	M18
Ybbs	A	49	B6
Ybbsitz	A	49	C5
Ydby	DK	24	C1
Yddal	N	18	A2
Yebra de Basa	E	76	A2
Yecla	E	82	C1
Yecla de Yeltes	E	73	D4
Yelnya	RUS	7	J23
Yelsk	BY	11	L21
Yenice	TR	16	S20
Yenice	TR	16	S20
Yenihisar	TR	16	T20
Yenişehir	TR	16	R21
Yenne	F	55	C5
Yeovil	GB	4	L5
Yepes	E	81	C3
Yerseke	NL	35	B5
Yerville	F	44	A1
Yeşildağ	TR	16	T21
Yesnogorsk	RUS	7	J25
Yeste	E	87	A3
Yezerishche	BY	7	J21
Ygos-St.Saturnin	F	62	C2
Ygrande	F	54	B2
Yiannitsa	GR	15	R18
Yiñuela	E	86	C1
Yíthion	GR	15	T18
Ylitornio	FIN	3	C18
Ylivieska	FIN	3	D19
Ymonville	F	44	B2
Yngsjö	S	27	D4
York	GB	4	K6
Youghal	IRL	4	L3
Yport	F	44	A1
Yssingeaux	F	54	C4
Ystad	S	27	D3
Ystebrød	N	18	C2
Ytre Arna	N	20	F9
Ytre Enebakk	N	20	B3
Yukhnov	RUS	7	J24
Yunak	TR	16	S22
Yuncos	E	80	B3
Yunquera	E	86	C1
Yunquera de Henares	E	81	B3
Yushkozero	RUS	3	D23
Yverdon-les-Bains	CH	56	B1
Yvetot	F	44	A1
Yvignac	F	43	B3
Yvoir	B	35	C5
Yvonand	CH	56	B1
Yxnerum	S	23	D2
Yzeure	F	54	B3
Z			
Zaamslag	NL	35	B4
Zaanstad	NL	28	C1
Žabalj	YU	61	C5
Žabari	YU	61	B6
Zabiče	SLO	59	C4
Zabierzów	PL	41	C4
Ząbki	PL	41	A6
Ząbkowice Śląskie	PL	40	C1
Zablaće	HR	70	C2
Žabljak	YU	71	C5
Žabno	PL	41	C5
Zabok	HR	59	B5
Žabokreky	SK	50	B4
Zabor	PL	39	B5
Zábřeh	CZ	50	A2
Zabrdje	BIH	70	B3
Zabrze	PL	40	C3
Zabrzeź	PL	51	B5
Zadar	HR	69	B4
Zadzim	PL	40	B3
Zafarraya	E	86	C1
Zafferana Etnea	I	95	B4
Zafra	E	79	C4
Żagań	PL	39	B5
Zaglav	HR	69	C4
Zaglavak	YU	71	C6
Zagnansk	PL	41	C5
Zagorc	SLO	59	B5
Zagorje	SLO	59	B5
Zagórów	PL	40	A2
Zagradje	YU	71	B5
Zagreb	HR	59	C5
Zagrilla	E	86	B1
Zagvozd	HR	70	C2
Zagyvarekas	H	61	A5
Zagyvaróna	H	51	B5
Zahara	E	85	C5
Zahara de los Atunes	E	85	C5
Zahinos	E	79	C4
Zahna	D	38	B2
Záhoří	CZ	49	A5
Zahrádka	CZ	50	B1
Zahrensdorf	D	30	B2
Zaidin	E	76	B3
Zaječar	YU	15	Q18
Zákamenné	SK	50	B3
Zákány	H	60	B1
Zákányszék	H	61	B4
Zákinthos	GR	15	T17
Zakliczyn	PL	51	A6
Zakopane	PL	51	B5
Zakroczym	PL	33	C6
Zakrzew	PL	41	B6
Zakrzewo	PL	33	C4
Zakupy	CZ	39	C4
Zalaapáti	H	60	B2
Zalabaksa	H	60	B1
Zalaegerszeg	H	60	B1
Zalakomár	H	60	B2
Zalakoppány	H	60	B2
Zalalövő	H	60	B1
Zalamea de la Serena	E	79	C5
Zalamea la Real	E	85	B4
Zalaszentgrót	H	60	B2
Zalaszentiván	H	60	B1
Zalău	RO	11	N18
Zalavár	H	60	B2
Zaldibar	E	75	A4
Zalesie	PL	33	B6
Zalewo	PL	33	B5
Zalishchyky	UA	11	M19
Zaltbommel	NL	35	B6
Zamárdi	H	60	B2
Zamarte	PL	32	B3
Zámberk	CZ	40	C1
Zambra	E	86	B1
Zambugueira do Mar	P	84	B2
Zámoly	H	60	A3
Zamora	E	74	C1
Zamość	PL	11	L18
Zams	A	57	A5
Zandhoven	B	35	B5
Zandvoort	NL	28	C1
Žandov	CZ	39	C4
Zánka	H	60	B2
Zaorejas	E	81	B4
Zaovine	YU	71	C4
Zapadnaya Dvina	RUS	7	H23
Zapfend	D	37	C6
Zapole	PL	40	B3
Zapolyarnyy	RUS	3	B22
Zapponeta	I	90	A2
Zaprešić	HR	59	C5
Zaragoza	E	76	B2
Zarasai	LT	7	J20
Zarautz	E	75	A4
Zarcilla de Ramos	E	87	B4
Żarki	PL	41	C4
Žarnovica	SK	51	B4
Żarnów	PL	41	B4
Zarnowiec	PL	41	C4
Zarošice	CZ	50	B2
Żarów	PL	40	B1
Zarren	B	34	C3
Zarrentin	D	30	B2
Żary	PL	39	B5
Zarza Capilla	E	79	C5
Zarza de Alange	E	79	C4
Zarza de Granadilla	E	79	A4
Zarza de Tajo	E	81	B3
Zarza la Mayor	E	79	B4
Zarzadilla de Totana	E	87	B4
Zarzuela del Monte	E	80	B2
Zarzuela del Pinar	E	80	A2
Zas	E	72	A2
Zasavica	YU	71	B4
Zasieki	PL	39	B4
Zásmuky	CZ	39	D5
Zatec	CZ	38	C3
Zaton	HR	70	D3
Zatonie	PL	39	B5
Zator	PL	41	D4
Zauchwitz	D	38	A3
Zavala	BIH	70	D2
Zavalje	YU	71	C5
Zavattarello	I	66	B3
Zavidovići	BIH	70	B3
Zavlaka	YU	71	B4
Zawady	PL	41	A5
Zawadzkie	PL	40	C3
Zawdy	PL	40	B3
Zawidów	PL	39	B5
Zawiercie	PL	41	C4
Zawoja	PL	51	B5
Zawonia	PL	40	B1
Žažina	HR	59	C5
Zázrivá	SK	51	A5
Zbarazh	UA	11	M19
Zbąszyń	PL	39	A6
Zbehy	SK	50	B3
Zblewo	PL	33	B4
Zbiroh	CZ	49	A4
Zblewo	PL	33	B5
Zbójno	PL	33	B5
Zbrachlin	PL	33	B4
Zbraslav	CZ	49	A4
Zbraslavice	CZ	49	A6
Žďala	HR	60	B2
Ždánice	CZ	50	B2
Žďár	CZ	50	A3
Žďár nad Sázavou	CZ	50	A1
Zdenci	HR	60	C2
Ždiar	SK	51	A6
Zdice	CZ	49	A5
Zdirec nad Doubravou	CZ	50	A1
Zdolbuniv	UA	11	L20
Zdounky	CZ	50	B3
Zdravinje	YU	71	C6
Zduńska Wola	PL	40	B3
Zduny	PL	40	B2
Zduny	PL	41	A4
Żdżary	PL	41	B5
Zdziechowice	PL	40	B2
Zdziechowice	PL	40	A2
Zdzieszowice	PL	40	C3
Zeberio	E	75	A4
Žebrák	CZ	49	A4
Zebreira	P	79	B3
Zebrzydowa	PL	39	B5
Žednik	YU	61	C4
Zeebrugge	B	35	B4
Zehdenick	D	31	C5
Zeil	D	37	B6
Zeist	NL	35	A5
Zeithain	D	38	B3
Zeitz	D	38	B2
Želatava	CZ	49	A6
Železná Ruda	CZ	49	A4
Železnice	CZ	39	C5
Železnik	YU	71	B5
Železniki	SLO	59	B4
Železný Brod	CZ	39	C5
Zelhem	NL	36	A2
Želiezovce	SK	51	B4
Želkowo	PL	32	A3
Zell, Baden-Württemberg	D	46	C3
Zell, Baden-Württemberg	D	47	B4
Zell, Rheinland-Pfalz	D	36	C3
Zell am See	A	58	A2
Zell am Ziller	A	58	A1
Zell an der Pram	A	49	B4
Zell bei Zellhof	A	49	B5
Zella-Mehlis	D	37	C6
Zellerndorf	A	50	B2
Zellingen	D	47	A5
Zelów	PL	41	B4
Zeltweg	A	59	A4
Zelzate	B	35	B4
Zemberovce	SK	51	B4
Zembrzyce	PL	51	B5
Zemianske-Kostol'any	SK	51	B4
Zemitz	D	31	B5
Zemné	SK	50	C3
Zemst	B	35	C5
Zemun	YU	71	B5
Zemunik Donji	HR	69	B4
Zenica	BIH	70	B3
Žepče	BIH	70	B3
Zepponami	I	88	A2
Zerbst	D	38	B2
Zerf	D	46	B2
Zerków	PL	40	A2
Zermatt	CH	56	B2
Zernez	CH	57	B5
Zerpenschleuse	D	31	C5
Zestoa	E	75	A4
Zetel	D	29	B4
Zeulenroda	D	38	C1
Zeven	D	29	B6
Zevenaar	NL	36	B2
Zevenbergen	NL	35	B4
Zévio	I	57	C6
Zgierz	PL	41	B4
Zgorzelec	PL	39	B5
Zgošća	BIH	70	B3
Zhabinka	BY	6	K19
Zharkovskiy	RUS	7	J23
Zhashkiv	UA	11	M22
Zheleznogorsk	RUS	7	K24
Zhizdra	RUS	7	K23
Zhlobin	BY	7	K22
Zhmerynka	UA	11	M21
Zhodzina	BY	7	J21
Zhovtneve	UA	11	N23
Zhukovka	RUS	7	K23
Zhytomyr	UA	11	L21
Žiar nad Hronom	SK	51	B4
Zicavo	F	96	B2
Zickhusen	D	30	B3
Zidani Most	SLO	59	B5
Ziddorf	D	31	B4
Zidlochovice	CZ	50	B2
Ziębice	PL	40	C1
Ziegenrück	D	38	C1
Zieleniec	PL	40	C1
Zielona	PL	33	B6
Zielona Góra	PL	39	B5
Zieluń-Osada	PL	33	B5
Ziemetshausen	D	37	B6
Zierbena	E	75	A3
Zierenberg	D	37	B5
Zierikzee	NL	35	B4
Zierzow	D	30	B3
Ziersdorf	A	50	B2
Ziesar	D	38	A2
Ziesendorf	D	30	B1
Ziethen	D	31	B4
Ziltendorf	D	39	A4
Zimandu Nou	RO	11	M22
Zimna Woda	PL	33	B6
Zimnicea	RO	16	Q19
Zinasco	I	66	A3
Zingst	D	31	A4
Zinkgruvan	S	23	C2
Žinkovy	CZ	49	A4
Zinnowitz	D	31	A5
Zirc	H	60	A2
Žiri	SLO	59	B4
Zirl	A	57	A6
Zirndorf	D	48	A1
Žirovnica	YU	71	B6
Žirovnice	CZ	49	A6
Zisterdorf	A	50	B2
Žitište	YU	61	C5
Zittau	D	39	C4
Živaja	HR	60	C1
Živinice	BIH	70	B3
Zlatar	HR	59	B6
Zlatar Bistrica	HR	59	B6
Zlate Hory	CZ	40	B2
Zlaté Klasy	SK	50	B3
Zlaté Moravce	SK	51	B4
Zlatná na Ostrove	SK	50	C3
Zlatniky	SK	50	B3
Zlatograd	BG	16	R19
Žlebič	SLO	59	B4
Zlín	CZ	50	A3
Złocieniec	PL	32	B2
Złoczew	PL	40	B3
Zlonice	CZ	39	C4
Złotniki Kujawskie	PL	33	C4
Złotoryja	PL	39	B5
Złotów	PL	32	B3
Złoty Stok	PL	40	C1
Zlutice	CZ	38	C3
Zmajevac	BIH	69	B5
Zmajevo	YU	61	C4
Żmigród	PL	40	B1
Zmijavci	HR	70	C2
Žminj	HR	68	A2
Znamyanka	UA	11	M23
Žnin	PL	32	C3
Znojmo	CZ	50	B2
Zöblitz	D	38	C3
Zocca	I	67	B4
Zoetermeer	NL	35	A5
Zofingen	CH	56	A2
Zogno	I	57	C4
Zohor	SK	50	B2
Zolling	D	48	B2
Zolochiv	UA	11	M19
Zolotonosha	UA	11	M23
Zomba	H	60	B3
Zomergem	B	35	B4
Zoñán	E	72	A3
Zonguldak	TR	16	R22
Zonhoven	B	35	C5
Zonza	F	96	B2
Zörbig	D	38	B2
Zorita	E	79	B5
Żory	PL	40	C3
Zossen	D	38	A3
Zottegem	B	35	C4
Zoutkamp	NL	28	B3
Zovi Do	BIH	70	C3
Zreče	SLO	59	B5
Zrenjanin	YU	61	C5
Žrnovica	HR	69	C5
Zruč nad Sázavou	CZ	49	A6
Zsámbék	H	60	A3
Zsámbok	H	61	A4
Zsana	H	61	B4
Zschopau	D	38	C3
Zuberec	SK	51	A5
Zubieta	E	75	A5
Zubin Potok	YU	71	D5
Zubiri	E	62	D1
Zubtsov	RUS	7	H24
Zucaina	E	82	A2
Zudar	D	31	A5
Zuera	E	76	B2
Zufre	E	85	B4
Zug	CH	56	A3
Zuheros	E	86	B1
Zuidhorn	NL	28	B3
Zuidlaren	NL	28	B3
Zuidwolde	NL	28	C3
Zújar	E	87	B3
Żukowo	PL	33	A4
Zülpich	D	36	C2
Zundert	NL	35	B4
Županja	HR	71	A4
Zurgena	E	87	B3
Zürich	CH	56	A3
Żuromin	PL	33	B5
Zurzach	CH	47	C4
Zusmarshausen	D	47	B6
Zusow	D	30	B3
Züssow	D	31	B5
Žuta Lovka	HR	69	B4
Zutphen	NL	36	A2
Žužemberk	SLO	59	C4
Zvečan	YU	71	D5
Zvenyhorodka	UA	11	M22
Zvíkovské Podhradí	CZ	49	A5
Zvolen	SK	51	B5
Zvolenská Slatina	SK	51	B5
Zvornik	BIH	71	B4
Zwartsluis	NL	28	C3
Zweibrücken	D	46	B3
Zweisimmen	CH	56	B2
Zwettl	A	49	B6
Zwettl an der Rodl	A	49	B5
Zwickau	D	38	C2
Zwiefalten	D	47	C5
Zwierzno	PL	33	A5
Zwierzyniec	PL	11	L18
Zwiesel	D	49	B4
Zwieselstein	A	57	B6
Zwoleń	PL	41	B6
Zwolle	NL	28	C3
Zwönitz	D	38	C2
Zychlin	PL	41	A4
Żydowo	PL	32	A2
Żydowo	PL	32	C3
Żyrardów	PL	41	A4
Żytno	PL	41	C4
Żywiec	PL	51	A5